Deviant Behavior

SEVENTH EDITION

Deviant Behavior

Crime, Conflict, and Interest Groups

Charles H. McCaghy
Bowling Green State University

Timothy A. Capron
California State University

J. D. Jamieson
Texas State University

Sandra Harley Carey
Texas State University

PEARSON

Boston   New York   San Francisco
Mexico City   Montreal   Toronto   London   Madrid   Munich   Paris
Hong Kong   Singapore   Tokyo   Cape Town   Sydney

Series Editor: Jennifer Jacobson
Series Editorial Assistant: Emma Christensen
Senior Marketing Manager: Kelly May
Production Editor: Patrick Cash-Peterson
Editorial Production Service: Walsh & Associates, Inc.
Composition Buyer: Linda Cox
Manufacturing Buyer: Megan Cochran
Electronic Composition: Omegatype Typography, Inc.
Cover Administrator: Linda Knowles

For related titles and support materials, visit our online catalog at ww.ablongman.com.

Between the time website information is gathered and then published, it is not unusual for some sites to have closed. Also, the transcription of URLs can result in typographical errors. The publisher would appreciate notification where these occur so that they may be corrected in subsequent editions.

Library of Congress Cataloging-in-Publication Data

Deviant behavior : crime, conflict, and interest groups / Charles H. McCaghy ... [et al.].—
    7th ed.
        p.   cm.
    Rev. ed. of: Deviant behavior / Charles H. McCaghy. 6th ed. c2003.
    Includes bibliographical references and index.
    ISBN 0-205-44728-7
    1. Criminology. 2. Deviant behavior. I. McCaghy, Charles H. II. McCaghy, Charles H.
    Deviant behavior.

HV6025.M375 2006
364—dc22

                                                                2005045861

Printed in the United States of America

10   9   8   7   6   5   4   3   2   1   08   07   06   05

CONTENTS

PREFACE

The first edition of this text was published in 1976, before many of today's student readers were born. The years have brought dramatic changes to the field of deviant behavior. There has been a continuing diffusion of traditional deviant behavior subject matter into other disciplines inside and outside sociology. The most notable examples include family studies and gender studies, both of which now provide new approaches to such issues as violence against women and children, and the changing social, legal, and political status of homosexuals. Researchers in these areas come from a wide range of disciplines and have produced a wealth of imaginative and controversial studies. Their research agendas are not incursions onto the hallowed ground of deviant behavior; instead, they complement the field and reveal the importance of interdisciplinary study for providing fresh insights. Indeed, criminology is a discipline whose subject matter has consistently overlapped with deviant behavior, and the latter field continues to profit from the theoretical and methodological breakthroughs of criminologists.

Despite the valuable contributions of these new approaches to deviance, one traditional premise of the field remains unchanged: the definition of deviance—that is, what is "deviant"—is fluid and depends upon the vagaries of time, place, and the influence of those who attempt to impose the label. In this edition we continue the theoretical theme of earlier editions by discussing specific behaviors in the context of *interest group conflict.* This approach recognizes that American society consists of groups with diverse notions of what should be defined as "immoral," "illegal," and "pathological." Whether behaviors are so defined depends upon the groups' dedication to their causes, to the efficiency of their organizations, and ultimately, to their adeptness in molding public opinion and the political process.

The United States continues to experience interest group conflicts that constantly redefine the contents of deviance texts. One example is the heated clash over abortion on demand. Which side will prevail—pro-choice or pro-life? Depending upon the outcome, future textbooks may well include a section or even a chapter on abortion as "deviant" behavior. Along these same lines we may anticipate a raging debate on the issue of human cloning. Is the concept moral? Is it safe? Is it wise? Will it be legal? Are the cloners and the cloned to be labeled *deviant?*

In another arena, widespread dissatisfaction with the progress of the "war on drugs" has created calls for legalization of some currently prohibited drugs. For decades vocal but essentially powerless groups advocated legalization of drugs, especially marijuana. Now their position is supported by influential judiciaries, law enforcement officials, and legislators. Perhaps in the future marijuana and even heroin use will be regarded in the same light as alcohol use. And what of the prospect of homosexuality continuing to be labeled as deviant? Not too long ago social reaction made homosexuality "the love that dares not speak its name." A shorter time ago an analyst of the burgeoning "gay pride" movement referred to it as "the love that won't shut up." The growth of gay political power is readily evident in the current discussions over gays' status in the military, legal recognition of same-sex families and marriages, and laws banning discrimination based on sexual orientation. These issues simply would have been unthinkable as matters of public debate just a few decades ago. Clearly, the status of homosexuality has changed dramatically in recent years. The goals of gay interest groups still meet considerable resistance, however. It remains to be seen whether they will continue to make legal gains and whether the public will ultimately accept homosexuality as a mainstream alternative, rather than a deviant, lifestyle.

A textbook can play only a limited role in dealing with rapidly changing contemporary issues. We have done our best to offer recent statistics, research reviews, and theories. It is incumbent upon the instructor to make the most of ongoing developments in the politics of abortion, cloning, drugs, homosexuality, and other issues. This is a field in which being up to date is especially important. And this is the stuff that makes it all so interesting. The wild expansion of the Internet provides not only the potential for new forms of research and learning but also a vehicle for new forms of deviance, and a worldwide arena for traditional deviant behavior. Our chapter on "Cyberdeviance," treats the Internet-based computer underground as an emerging subculture. The various types of actors, along with their unique methods, motivations, and communication, are examined. New dimensions in sexual deviance, facilitated by the Internet, are also discussed. Sandy Carey has done an excellent, thoughtful presentation of the issues in our new chapter on suicide. Sociological theories regarding suicide in a worldwide context are discussed, along with current attitudes, incidence rates, important risk factors, and correlates of suicide.

We wish once again to thank the reviewers of earlier editions and of this text: Gary L. Faulkner, University of North Carolina at Wilmington; James E. Gallagher, University of Maine; Mathew T. Lee, University of Akron; Xiaoru Liu, San Diego State University; and Nathan W. Pino, Georgia Southern University. Please be assured that your efforts are greatly appreciated and your criticisms taken to heart and addressed. We wish also to thank Jennifer Jacobson and Emma Christensen, our editors at Allyn and Bacon for keeping us on target and occasionally guiding us back to earth. Thanks also to our colleagues and graduate assistants for their generous investments in wisdom, support, and time and, finally, to our families for patience and the widest array of other forms of support.

Deviant Behavior

PART ONE

The Concept
of Deviant Behavior

Deviant behavior remains a fluid concept. This text attempts to examine the fact that *deviance* as a concept is subject to many changes that are dependent on time, place, and the influence of those who may impose a label of deviance. The first three chapters provide theoretical perspectives on deviance. We ask the question, "Who is deviant?" and answer it by discussing perspectives that attempt to explain deviant behavior.

Chapter 1 discusses the classical school of criminology theory and the observation that deviance is a choice, made by a rational individual. This is in marked contrast to the positivist school, which is presented next. Positivists place an emphasis on determinism, on factors beyond the control of the individual. Chapter 2 then expands on this determinism by stressing explanations such as economic determinism, social structural theories, subcultural explanations, and control theory. Chapter 3 revisits the production of deviance and examines labels and interest group conflicts. By the end of this section, students will recognize that deviance is not a fixed concept. They will also recognize that life in the United States is characterized by conflicts of interest, that interest groups exert varying influences on legislation and law enforcement, and that the more powerful interest groups use this application of law to contain those less powerful. *Deviant behavior* is thus a rational, learned response to social, economic, and political conditions. These deviant responses are in turn supported by learned traditions, rewards, and motives.

1 Perspectives on Deviants

The Early Development
of Criminal Deviance Theory

If any single factor makes human social life possible and bearable, it is the ability of individuals to predict the behavior of others. One often hears that "human behavior cannot be predicted," but some reflection will reveal that the adage is not really true. In your daily activities you constantly behave on the basis of predictions; they provide sets of assumptions or expectations upon which to act. For example, you come to class assuming that the instructor will be there to lecture; you take notes assuming that they will be of some use in furthering your intellectual development or at least your grade average; and you answer test questions assuming that the instructor reads the responses and grades according to the degree to which your answers reflect the "truths" he or she communicated and expected you to learn.

Should the instructor fail to meet your predictions by consistently missing classes, by posing trivial or unrelated examination questions, and by assigning grades on the basis of students' looks, you would feel cheated, put on, and generally ripped off—all because your predictions did not materialize.

Not that all unpredictability is bad. Surprises and departures from routine are certainly welcome at times. We are concerned here with people who behave in both unexpected and unacceptable ways. What constitutes unexpected and unacceptable behavior may seem to be rather personal and individual judgments. To some extent they are, yet group life would obviously be difficult without considerable agreement among members concerning the ground rules regulating behavior. Regardless of how dedicated they may be to personal gratification, group members must operate under some constraints if the group is to survive. It is difficult to imagine any viable group in which members did whatever they wished regardless of the feelings and well-being of others. If, for example, a group of free spirits formed a ruleless community in which everyone could follow any impulse, how long would it last if a member decided to enjoy some sadism followed by cannibalistic snacks or, worse yet, refused to help with the dishes? Unless the others were extremely pliant masochists, one can safely assume that some restrictions would shortly be forthcoming.

If any group is to continue as an operating entity, there must be some agreement among members about how they shall act toward one another; obversely, there must be at least tacit consensus about what constitutes unacceptable behavior. We aren't necessarily consistent or logical about it, however, and our lack of consistency can have serious consequences. It is easy to envision an attractive, outgoing person making suggestive remarks at a party. The individual might acquire the social label of "flirt," and the behavior might be categorized as playful or fun-loving. However, an ugly, unpopular person who made *exactly the same remarks* might be perceived entirely differently and earn the individual the label of "creep," "pervert," or even "stalker" or "sexual harasser."

Even so, your ventures into the world of human relations depend on these complicated rules and the immediate consensus about them. You reasonably assume, generally on the basis of experience, that such relations will be conducted according to the rules as you understand them. In everyday life you are usually secure from unpleasant surprises. Although those about you are seeking to satisfy their own interests and appetites, their behavior is usually predictable and within acceptable limits. These rules governing human relations within social groups are what sociologists call *norms*. Specifically, a norm is defined as "an ideal standard of behavior to which people conform to a greater or lesser extent."[1]

But, as we know, human relations do have their unsettling moments. Some people ignore or defy the norms. They do not conform to your expectations and therefore are the source of an entire range of negative emotions such as irritation, disgust, suspicion, and even fear. They are people who are not on time, who deceive, who renege on promises, who take things that do not belong to them, who are inconsiderate, who cannot be trusted, and so on. In short, they are deviant.

Who Is Deviant?

In July 2001, *Newsweek* magazine carried an article by George Will[2] regarding a book entitled *Neighbors,* written by Professor Jan Gross.[3] In the book Gross describes an event that occurred sixty years ago in the Polish town of Jedwabne as the invading German army occupied the area. With the consent of the German officials, the Polish residents of Jedwabne murdered almost all of the town's 3,600 Jewish residents. Although the Germans suggested sparing some Jewish craftsmen and professional families, the Polish residents decided, in a democratic forum held by the town's leaders, to kill all of the Jews. The mayor supervised the slaughter, which took on a "carnival" atmosphere and was attended by Poles from nearby villages along with the local residents. Of the town's 3,600 Jews, only about a dozen escaped death. The rest were burned alive, impaled with pitchforks, killed slowly with clubs and metal hooks, or hacked to pieces.

How could people inflict such homicidal atrocities on their neighbors? These were people they had known all their lives in the small community. Although Professor Gross doesn't answer this question directly, George Will contends that the Poles massacred the Jewish members of their community simply because they were given permission to do so. Unfortunately, what happened at Jedwabne was not an isolated incident. Deadly persecution between neighbors on a grand scale happens fairly frequently. More recently, Chinese neighbors killed each other off during Mao's Cultural Revolution in the 1960s. In the late 1970s, young, impressionable soldiers recruited from poor rural areas by the Khmer Rouge exterminated 1.5 million of their compatriots in the "killing fields" of Cambodia. The

Rwandan genocide of 1994, described in chilling detail by Alan Kuperman[4] and others, involved several hundred thousand Hutu extremists systematically hacking their Tutsi neighbors to death in churches, in public buildings, and at road barricades. Over a half million perished. The list continues on to include Central and South Americans; Arabs and Israelis in the Middle East; and the complex, ethnicity-driven neighborhood battles between Serbs, Croats, Muslims, Bosnians, Montenegrins, Macedonians, and Albanians in the former Yugoslavia, and the continuing conflicts Iran, Afghanistan, and Sudan.

In our own backyard we can observe equally disturbing events almost every day. On June 20, 2001, Andrea Yates killed her five children by drowning them one by one in the bathtub of their suburban Texas home. The victims were four boys, aged 2 to 7 years, and a 6-month-old baby girl. Autopsy reports[5] indicated that the boys all struggled violently as they were held under water. Yates subsequently called the police and apparently told them that she thought the children were developing too slowly and so she had decided to "send them back to God." Although Yates was charged with capital murder, many experts, including Michelle Oberman,[6] who has written extensively on the subject of post-childbirth depression, believe that Yates was in the desperate throes of postpartum psychosis. While a majority of women experience the "baby blues" form of mild depression following childbirth, around one in five suffer significant depression. In rare cases involving psychosis the mother loses touch with reality and may become dangerous to herself, the child, and others.[7] The psychosis and desperation deepen if the woman believes she cannot meet society's demands for proper parenting. Yates was perceived generally as a devoted parent, although she had a history of hospitalization and medication for depression and suicide attempts following previous births and stressful events. Clearly, her behavior was deviant and rare, but it may have been a strong manifestation of a symptom common to many mothers.

What about nonlethal forms of behavior that have traditionally been categorized as deviant? On the same day that the Yates children lost their lives, law enforcement agencies were cooperating to break up the largest commercial child pornography ring ever discovered in the United States. Hundreds of people were implicated and many arrested. On that day, millions of people around the world woke up in prison or jail for criminal behavior (or perhaps political behavior), millions viewed explicit images on pornography Web sites, millions ingested illegal drugs, and uncounted numbers were mentally ill in some way, were involved in prostitution, or were homosexual. Traditional deviant behavior, then, is quite common, and we are all probably susceptible to some of the influences associated with the different types. What could possibly make someone start murdering neighbors? Perhaps a chemical imbalance is all it takes, or a mesmerizing leader, or permission.

It is rather disturbing to think that beneath a thin, fragile veneer of civilization lurks a strong tendency to torture and kill other people when an opportunity pops up and we can get away with it. It might help to conceptualize an intricate competition for behavior. On one side are the positive influence of social learning and expectation, genetic strength, balanced chemicals in our bodies, law and leadership, and opportunity for all manner of legitimate success; on the other are genetic liabilities, ineffective socialization, abuse and neglect, stress and chemical confusion, and unlawful opportunity—all complicated by Sigmund Freud's churning maelstrom of impulsive drives for gratification. Deviant behavior really should not surprise us. It is common. The real surprise would be finding people who had never done anything wrong.

How may we decide, academically, what and whom to classify as deviant? This seems to be a simple question. A simple answer is: The deviant is the person involved in deviance. Clearly, the Unabomber, an individual linked to 16 mail-bomb attacks that killed 3 and injured 23, is an example of what many would consider a deviant. But when the Unabomber declared that he would cease his bombing if the *Washington Post* and the *New York Times* published his manifesto, which they did, the editors of both newspapers were regarded as "deviant" and criticized by many for abetting terrorism.[8] *Deviance,* according to one dictionary, means "differing from a norm or from accepted standards of society."[9] An introductory sociology text defines *deviance* as "any behavior or physical appearance that is socially challenged and condemned because it departs from the norms and expectations of a group."[10] But the question is not as simple as it sounds. We must ask, "What are the *accepted* standards and social expectations?" You personally know what is accepted and expected within your circle of family and friends, but what about within other social circumstances? To what degree do your notions of proper conduct match those of strangers out there in "society"? Is it possible that some of your behaviors are unacceptable to some people and that in their eyes *you* are a deviant?

Some years ago, the sociologist Jerry L. Simmons conducted a study involving 180 people of various characteristics and backgrounds. He asked them to list "things or types of persons" they regarded as deviant. Concerning his results, he writes:

> The sheer range of responses predictably included homosexuals, prostitutes, drug addicts, radicals, and criminals. But it also included liars, career women, Democrats, reckless drivers, atheists, Christians, suburbanites, the retired, young folks, card players, bearded men, artists, pacifists, priests, prudes, hippies, straights, girls who wear makeup, the President, conservatives, integrationists, executives, divorcees, perverts, motorcycle gangs, smart-alec students, know-it-all professors, modern people, and Americans.[11]

Undoubtedly, if Simmons's study were replicated today, there would be several changes from the list formulated over two decades ago. The conclusion drawn from the study probably would not change, however. Although there is wide agreement that some behaviors are deviant, many other behaviors are considered deviant by smaller numbers of people. Thus, standards and expectations concerning behavior depend less upon either universal norms or consensus about norms than upon a particular, and perhaps temporary, point of view.

To complicate matters, a given individual's standards may fluctuate significantly with the events and stresses of daily life. As our moods and our concerns change, so does our capacity for tolerance. Yet it is scarcely enlightening simply to say that deviance is relative and let the matter rest. Some types of deviance are definitely more relative than others. For example, the members of a society are likely to express greater agreement over banning murder than over banning spitting on the sidewalk. Even granting that under some circumstances a majority of the population might condemn expectorations before they would executions, in any society guidelines concerning the taking of human life are deemed important ones. In the United States there is disagreement over the acceptability of some killings, such as the slaying of civilians in the time of war, capital punishment, abortion, and euthanasia (mercy killing). But evidence indicates considerable agreement over the unacceptability of more conventional murder and an assortment of other behaviors.

John E. Conklin interviewed a sample of 266 people in a suburb and in one area of a large eastern metropolitan center.[12] In seeking to measure the degree of support for certain laws, Conklin posed specific examples such as the following:

An unarmed man breaks into an unoccupied house at night and steals $100 in cash. (burglary)

A man enters a bar, says he is going to kill another man, and attacks this man with a knife. He doesn't kill him, but he injures him seriously. (aggravated assault)

A man forcibly rapes a woman. (rape)

For these and other examples Conklin asked, "In your opinion, should there be a law to punish this person?" He found that several behaviors elicited a practically unanimous response: over 95 percent of the sample said yes for burglary, aggravated assault, rape, robbery, auto theft, murder, and larceny. There was considerably less agreement concerning other acts, such as marijuana use and gambling.

It would appear from Conklin's findings that even within the highly heterogeneous environment of a metropolitan area there is nearly perfect consensus that certain actions are unacceptable. This seems especially true since a more recent national survey, conducted by Marvin E. Wolfgang and other researchers, found similar results after sampling more than 60,000 individuals.[13] But such a conclusion is misleading without some qualification. Imagine if Conklin's examples had read as follows:

An American soldier breaks into a citizen's home in enemy territory and steals $100 cash.

A man stabs and seriously injures a homosexual who made a pass at him.

A man rapes a woman he knows to be a prostitute.

We can be reasonably certain that the consensus of responses to these examples would be less than that for the original versions. It must be understood that *agreement concerning the deviant character of actions applies primarily when those actions are directed against the interests of one's own group.* Similar acts against the interests of those who are defined as "enemies," "strangers," or "not our kind" do not readily qualify for the same interpretation. Thus, it is not enough to say that people are "against" stealing. It depends upon who is being robbed. For example, businesspeople are unalterably against stealing if it involves shoplifting. But they will differ in their opinions about whether clerks should persuade gullible customers to buy needless and overpriced items. They may feel that anyone so dumb as to listen to a fast-talking clerk deserves what he or she gets. After all, business is business. Apparently, however, stealing is not stealing.

Definitions of who and what are deviant revolve around the protections of interests. Obviously, the larger and more diverse a society, the more fragmented the interests of its members. But if deviance tends to be relative, how does one study it? Most theorists have sidestepped the issue by assuming that the agreed-upon norms of a society can be found in its criminal law. The theorists' position is that the criminal law concerns the well-being of all and reflects the conscience of the total society, regardless of the diverse interests of various individuals or groups. Thus, the deviant is a criminal—a person whose behaviors are formally forbidden by legislation and punishable by the state. But this interpretation of criminal law is subject to criticism. The making and application of law are essentially political activities. Legislation is not made by all in a society but by those with the power to do so, and such power is not equally distributed. Stuart L. Hills describes the process this way:

> The unequal distribution of power and authority means that some interest groups will have greater access to the decision-making process and will use their power and influence to have legislation enacted to protect and maintain their interest at the expense of the less powerful groups. . . .
>
> Criminal laws (including legislative statutes, administrative rulings, and judicial decisions) will change with modification in the interest-power structure of society. As social conditions change—altering the distribution of power and the relative fortunes of various interest groups, threatening the economic, political, religious, and status interests of dominant groups, or modifying the values and interests at stake—criminal-law definitions will change, adapting to these shifting conditions.[14]

We will elaborate later on the relationship between interest groups and law. But first, we will present a review of theorists who assume that there is social consensus about what constitutes deviance. They ask why "criminals" behave in ways that most others concur are bad, disgusting, antisocial, and so on. These theorists seek the explanation of such behavior *within the deviants;* thus, they assume that deviant behavior is symptomatic of personal characteristics distinguishing criminal from normal actors. According to these writers, to understand deviance is to understand the forces motivating some individuals to act in ways that most others avoid.

The Rational Deviant—The Classical School

The first generally recognized school of criminology, the *classical school,* did not emerge until the middle of the eighteenth century. Its principal author was the Italian mathematician and economist Cesare Beccaria (1738–1794), who was strongly influenced by the French writers Montesquieu, Rousseau, and Voltaire and other enlightened thinkers of the time.

A single work by Beccaria constitutes the manifesto of the classical school of criminology. Entitled *On Crimes and Punishments* (published as *Dei delitti e delle pene* in 1764), the book is essentially a plea for the reform of the judicial and penal systems of the time, which were characterized by secret accusations, extensive use of torture, harsh penalties for trivial offenses, the application of law to implement political policy, and extreme arbitrariness by judges in levying punishments.

Because Beccaria's work was aimed at reforming a cruel and ineffective justice system, it did not deal directly with the question of why deviants develop. Nevertheless, some underlying assumptions about the nature of humanity are made, and from these a kind of theory of deviant behavior emerges.

Perhaps in reaction to the extreme inconsistency of his government's response to criminal behavior, Beccaria favored the application of law to all persons in an absolutely equal manner, with no variations for the circumstances of convicted criminals. According to him, the law should assume that all humans are fundamentally rational and hedonistic; they possess free will and make deliberate decisions to behave based upon a calculation of the pain and pleasure involved. It is from these characteristics that society emerges. To avoid continual chaos resulting from total individual freedom, humans essentially enter a contract in which they submit to a civil authority in exchange for security under the laws of a state. Humans are basically self-serving, however. Given the opportunity, they will enhance their own positions at the expense of other humans. Thus, the role of the state is to prevent crime. Beccaria wrote that

> it is better to prevent crimes than to punish them. This is the ultimate end of every good legislation, which, to use the general terms for assessing the good and evils of life, is the art of leading men to the greatest possible happiness or to the least possible unhappiness.[15]

To this end Beccaria argued that the law should be clear and simple and directed against only those behaviors that obviously endanger society and individuals in it. Compliance with the law should be rewarded, and it is necessary to convince individuals that punishment for violations will be unavoidable, prompt, and only in slight excess of the pleasure derived from the illegal act. Unlike the criminological theorists who were to dominate the field for the next 200 years, Beccaria believed it necessary to treat humans as equal, self-determining individuals whose freedom and responsibility were preeminent and unaffected by personal characteristics, extenuating circumstances, and experiences.

Beccaria's work was the basis of many judicial and penal reforms. Or was it? An article by Graeme Newman and Pietro Marongiu[16] questions the lofty stature of Beccaria. They suggest that he was not a great reformer, was obtuse in his writing, possibly plagiarized (or at least did not document his sources), and may have been lazy, timid, and reclusive.

Beccaria's ideas were promulgated widely, nonetheless. Whether he deserves accolades or only happened to be stating the obvious at just the right time remains a matter of debate. It may be said that the conceptualized code of strict adherence to proscribed punishments for specific crimes has never been truly tested, for societies have not been willing to ignore the mitigating and aggravating circumstances surrounding criminal events, accused persons, and victims.

However, when the actual legal changes were made, the strict interpretation of human rationality underwent modification by those of the so-called *neoclassical school.* As a practical matter the neoclassicists recognized that not all persons are equally rational, particularly the young, the mentally disturbed, and those confronted with other unusual circumstances that decrease responsibility. As a result, judges were allowed some discretion in sentencing to account for extenuating circumstances.

Despite their considerable influence on Western legal systems, the classical and neoclassical schools failed to produce a viable theory of deviance for many years. Classical criminology serves as the basis for some recent efforts. However, for too long their preoccupation with the rationality of humans resulted in overlooking how society can adversely affect behavior. Society rarely treats its members impartially. There are inequities in the distribution of wealth and power, and some classes of people face greater hardships and disadvantages than do other classes. This means that even if people are equal in their rationality, they are decidedly unequal in so many other respects, including their abilities to determine the content of the laws governing them. Even if the law punishes with equity— which it often does not—the theft of a hamburger, what does that mean to one who can barely afford the bun?[17]

The Deviant as Determined—Positivist Criminology

The nineteenth century produced several revolutionary landmarks in various branches of the physical sciences. To name but a few, consider the rediscovery of the atomic constitution of matter, the establishment of stratigraphic geology for dating geological formations, the founding of the science of oceanography, and the formulation of the fundamental laws of genetics. Developments in biology were particularly rapid with the publication of works by Charles Darwin (1809–1882). In 1859 his *Origin of Species* set forth the idea of natural selection among living things, and in 1871 his *Descent of Man* linked *Homo sapiens* with early, nonhuman animal life. The simultaneous growth and development of the scientific method and revelation that humans had evolved from apelike ancestors brought about a revolution in thinking about the nature of human beings and how their behavior might be interpreted. One result was what has come to be known as the positive school of criminology.

To understand the changes in criminological perspective occurring in the nineteenth century, it is important to become acquainted with two terms. The first, *positivism,* is a philosophical approach founded by Auguste Comte (1798–1857), which replaced speculation with scientific inquiry as the source of knowledge about social life. More specifically, positivism is defined as

> the doctrine formulated by Comte which asserts that the only true knowledge is scientific knowledge, i.e., knowledge which describes and explains the coexistence and succession of observable phenomena, including both physical and social phenomena.[18]

Positivism does not concern itself with the abstract and unprovable but rather with the tangible and quantifiable. It involves investigating the world by objective data that can be counted or measured. In short, if you cannot feel it, hear it, see it, or smell it—forget it.

The second term, *determinism,* refers to the principle that all events, including human behavior, have sufficient causes. Specifically,

> the term *determinism* denotes a doctrine which claims that all objects or events of some kind . . . are determined, that is to say must be as they are and as they will be [by] virtue of some laws or forces which necessitate their being so.[19]

The term becomes the name of a specific doctrine when the *kind* of determinism is indicated. For instance, *economic determinism* tends to mean the doctrine that economic factors determine others, whereas *sociological determinism* is likely to mean the assertion that social facts are determined, *and* that they are determined by social factors.

In dealing with deviance scientifically, the positivist approach shifts attention away from the rational deviant seeking happiness to one whose behavior is determined by forces beyond her or his control. Following this logic, positivists do not advise punishment as a remedy because deviant behavior is not a matter of choice. Obviously, the recommended procedure for halting deviant behavior depends upon the brand of determinism favored. Thus if the presumed cause is located in the body, the body must be "treated"; if it is located in social factors, anything from the family, the neighborhood, or the entire economic system may need renovation. Of course, it is difficult to reconcile some deterministic perspectives to law and justice, since culpability and perhaps the remedy for the behavior can be external to the offender.

In this chapter we concentrate on positivists who believe that the source of deviance is *within* the individual. Thus it is the individual who is the target of scientific investigation and scientific cure.[20] The differences between this type of positivism and the classical school are shown in Table 1.1.

Although the use of scientific methods appears to be superior to mere conjecture, methodology alone carries no assurance that truth is around the corner. Inaccurate assumptions, the misinterpretation and misapplication of findings, and intellectual arrogance can all conspire to make a positivist approach not only misleading but also dangerous. Because determinism is involved, the scientist must make some assumptions about what is doing the determining. Specific factors to be investigated as possible causes must be selected out of a great universe of factors that might differentiate the deviant from others. The selection ultimately depends upon how the scientist theorizes the nature of human behavior; is it biologically, economically, or socially oriented? If the theory of human behavior is inappropriate for the scientist's purposes, the resulting findings will be of little value.

Since there are many possible theories concerning the fundamental nature of humans, it should not be surprising that since the advent of positivism every human appendage has been measured, every emotion plumbed, every social influence probed, and every bodily fluid scrutinized. As a further result of such theories, social environments have been engineered, parts of the brain removed, families counseled, organs lopped off, and many sorts of chemicals injected into the human system (legally, of course). All this has been done in the apparently unlimited search for answers to the question of why some ignore or disobey others' concepts of righteous behavior.

TABLE 1.1 Comparison of the Classical and Positivist Schools of Criminology

Characteristic	Classical	Positivist
Date developed	Eighteenth century	Nineteenth century
Purpose	Reform of the judicial and penal systems	Application of scientific methods to study of the criminal as an individual
Definition of criminal behavior	Definition by the legal code: *nullum crimen sine lege* (no crime without law)	Rejection of legal definitions in favor of definitions such as "natural crime," "antisocial behavior," and "offends the sentiments of the community"
Explanation of criminal behavior	Free will, rationality; deviants and nondeviants are essentially similar	Determinism: biological, psychological, economic, genetic, etc.; deviants and nondeviants are different
Method of behavior change	Fear of punishment as a deterrent	Scientific treatment, alteration, or elimination

Source: Adapted in part from Clarence Ray Jeffrey, "Historical Development of Criminology," in *Pioneers in Criminology,* 2nd ed., ed. Hermann Mannheim (Montclair, NJ: Patterson Smith Publishing Corporation, 1972), pp. 458–498.

The positivist approach has often been responsible for another, although less explicit, assumption—that the source of deviant behavior invariably can be traced to a *pathology*. Deviation in behavior can be interpreted as a departure from normality, and the positivists' research consistently indicates a presupposition that a "normal" organism in a "normal" environment would not so act. The logic here is certainly comforting. If we regard deviance as unnatural, incomprehensible, weird, and so on, everything attains an orderliness if we can conclude that the behavior is a result of imperfections or inferiorities. How often do we say, when confronted with unexpected and unacceptable behavior, "She must be sick" or "What's wrong with him?" Even our prison systems, despite repeated failures at rehabilitation, continue to operate in this manner. Upon conviction the first stop for the offender is a "diagnostic center" where he or she will be "diagnosed" and then subjected to a "treatment plan" to speed the person on the way to becoming a productive member of society.

Thus positivism can be viewed as a combination of scientific method, a search for pathology, and the application of treatment based upon scientific findings. This is a corrosive blend, however. The presumption of pathology results in the abandonment of rationality as a causal factor. This means, in turn, that because humans are viewed as not being completely responsible for their behavior, there is justification for taking control of deviating individuals and for applying treatment to mend them. No one is better equipped than the state for doing just that—all for the good of the individual and the society, of course.

George B. Vold and Thomas J. Bernard point out that the implications of positivism easily fit into the patterns of totalitarian government:

> It is centered on the core idea of the superior knowledge and wisdom of the scientific expert who, on the basis of scientific knowledge, decides what kind of human beings commit crimes, and prescribes treatment without concern for public opinion and without consent from the person so diagnosed (i.e., the criminal). There is an obvious similarity between the control of power in society advocated in positivism and the political reality of centralized control of the life of the citizen by a government bureaucracy indifferent to public opinion.[21]

The potential abuses inherent in positivism are often masked by the good will and good intentions of the scientific researchers and the staffs of institutions where citizens are committed. But the facts are unavoidable. Untold numbers of people have been incarcerated on the basis of erroneous or at best tentative theories of deviance. They have had their minds and bodies tampered with by "treatments" of no proven benefit (if they have been dignified by such attention at all). For examples, one can reach into the past; during the eugenics movement (to be discussed later) a 4-year-old girl was committed to an Ohio institution as part of an effort to rid the community of the feeble-minded, who were presumed to pose a great number of potential evils. In 1974 officials had no explanation of why she remained incarcerated until she died at age 103.

If we could be assured that the positivists had contributed mightily to our understanding of human behavior, some acceptance of the approach could be mustered even while keeping a careful eye on its potential dangers. In fact, however, nearly all positivist attempts to explain deviance have been disappointing. The expected differences between deviants and nondeviants rarely materialize when the evidence is carefully examined. Nevertheless, positivism remains the dominant approach among students of deviance and shows only slight indication of giving way to other approaches.[22]

Despite its weakness in explanatory power, positivism continues to have appeal for several reasons:

1. It avoids the issue of possible fundamental normative conflicts within society. Normality is the status quo, and in the positivist approach, it is assumed that there is a high degree of consensus concerning what behavior is improper. Questions concerning social conflicts are unnecessary because the deviant is simply someone who needs to be brought back into line with everyone else.
2. It avoids the issue of choice. The normal person and the deviant are both seen as compelled to conform and deviate, respectively. Put another way, the normal person could not possibly choose to deviate. Thus deviation is seen as a symptom of abnormality requiring treatment. This has an added feature of being humanitarian because punishment is considered inappropriate.
3. It is scientific. The prestige of the scientific approach and technology promises that truth shall be found and remedies are forthcoming.[23]

The following sections deal with a variety of positivist approaches ranging from the constitutional to the social-psychological and the sociocultural. The purpose is to acquaint the student with the major theoretical positions and schools of thought and to indicate that practically every conceivable variable that might distinguish the deviant from anyone else has been investigated with less than definitive results. The theories are presented in the approximate chronological order of their periods of greatest popularity. The reader should bear in mind, however, that criminologists' adoptions of theories often overlapped and that limited research interest in some theories may continue well after their general acceptance has declined.

Physical Characteristics of Deviants— Early Approaches

Of all the positivist approaches to the explanation of deviance, the investigation of a possible relationship between anatomical attributes and behavior is not only the oldest but also the most persistent. Today, scarcely a month goes by without some revelation concerning the possible connection between a biological characteristic and human behavior. In fairness to the scientists of today, they are generally far less sweeping in their claims than were researchers of a few decades ago, but the probing of every nook and cranny of the human system goes on. One can only sense the public's anticipation that someday a DNA patch or a swipe of a scalpel will put an end to all sorts of deviant behavior.

Such faith is understandable in view of the fact that it is a biological organism doing the acting and that such an organism is far easier to measure and examine than other possible variables. Furthermore, despite admonitions that "Beauty is only skin deep" and "You can't judge a book by its cover," we constantly make decisions about people solely on the basis of their appearance. We also know that the way we feel affects the way we act. If a friend behaves strangely, his or her explanation, "I feel lousy," is usually sufficient.

The influence of biology on human behavior may be easily overestimated and over-simplified, however. In 1966, for example, Charles Whitman, after killing his mother and wife, climbed with six guns and provisions to the top of a tower on the University of Texas campus. From there he shot 46 people, killing 16. His behavior was especially puzzling because he was an architectural engineering honor student and a former Eagle Scout leader, scarcely the popular notion of a homicidal maniac. In a final note complaining about tremendous headaches, Whitman requested an autopsy to determine whether he had a mental disorder. The autopsy revealed a brain tumor. Some medical experts doubted the explanatory value of the tumor, but others, the press, and evidently Whitman himself thought that his physical condition could somehow account for his behavior.

There is no pretense here of offering an explanation of why Whitman acted as he did; our purpose is simply to use his case as an illustration. Whatever pressures or sensations his tumor might have caused do not satisfactorily explain his complex action of carefully arming himself, going to a practically impregnable position, and sniping at passersby. Why did he not take a nap, or commit suicide, or go duck hunting? Physical conditions may well contribute to the spontaneity of behavior, but the behavior's content is far more complex than can be explained by a particular physical condition. Sheer bursts of aggressive behavior, regardless of content, may be curbed by disposing of part of the brain; but the reason for the direction of hostilities, be they against others, animals, property, or oneself, must be sought elsewhere.

We shall return to this issue of contemporary biological explanations after reviewing the historical highlights of similar efforts.

Phrenology—The Beginning of the Scientific Study of the Deviant

All of us make judgments about people based solely upon their appearances. Faces in particular provide evidence for making quick decisions about everything from strangers' honesty ("He looks shifty to me") to their mental stability ("She doesn't seem too tightly wrapped").[24] From the middle of the eighteenth century to the middle of the nineteenth, scholars formulated several classifications of human character on the assumption that body features were indicators of behavior. The most systematic and logically constructed approach was *phrenology*—the determination of mental facilities and character traits from the shape of the skull.[25] Readers may see a vestige of this approach hanging on the walls of fortune tellers and in shops dealing in occult products: a chart depicting a profile of a human head divided into segments, each representing particular "powers" or "propensities."

The fundamental logic of phrenology may be illustrated with an analogy comparing muscle and brain tissue. With strenuous exercise, a particular muscle changes size and shape, and the change is observable via the outer skin. Phrenologists believed that brain tissue also expanded with vigorous use and that the skull would form accordingly.

The first scholar to investigate the validity of phrenology scientifically was Franz Gall (1758–1828), a famed Austrian anatomist who spent twenty years touring insane asylums and prisons to measure head shapes. According to Leonard Savitz, Stanley H. Turner, and Toby Dickman, Gall believed that

1. The brain was the center of thought.
2. Specific brain areas controlled behavioral activities.

3. Brain areas . . . of greater importance were greater in size and area.
4. The skull precisely and accurately covered the cranial cortex, so that [areas] of disproportionate importance (and disproportionate growth and size) produce concomitant protuberances on the skull.[26]

Thus Gall measured skulls as a practical means of measuring the brains they held. On the basis of his findings and his comparisons of the heads of institutionalized and noninstitutionalized individuals, he concluded that a biological theory of criminal nature could be developed. The notion that there may be a link between protuberances on the head and criminal behavior was widely circulated throughout Europe and the United States. The principal promoter in the United States was Charles Caldwell (1772–1853), who divided the brain into thirty-four areas, three of which were related to criminal behavior—"philoprogenitiveness [love for offspring], destructiveness, and covetiveness [*sic*]":

Concerning philoprogenitiveness it was noted that of twenty-nine females who had been guilty of infanticide the development of this organ was defective in twenty-seven. Of destructiveness it was said that when not properly balanced and regulated by superior faculties it led to murder, while of covetiveness. . . . Caldwell remarked that unless restrained and properly directed it led to great selfishness and even to theft.[27]

Up to the end of the nineteenth century, phrenology provided the basis for a moderate amount of theory and research on the nature of criminal beings, but in the final analysis it made no contribution to the understanding of deviant behavior. Knowing what we do today, we can see that the approach's failure was inevitable because its assumptions were wrong. One cannot detect the subtle shape of the brain by examining the exterior of the skull, and no single sections of the brain are completely responsible for the complex behaviors attributed to them by the phrenologists.

But phrenology did not decline because it was scientifically disproven. It first lost its respectability as it became popular:

While American phrenology was comparatively diffused throughout the population by the 1840s, it had lost its scientific quality; . . . the already present element of popularization gained preeminence. In the end phrenology was driven to telling people how to be happy, how to select a wife, and how to raise children. It became something akin to a contemporary course in Marriage and the Family, and with about the same level of accuracy, we would judge.[28]

A more serious obstacle to the development of phrenology was that the intellectual community was unwilling to accept the fatalism that a biologically based theory implied. The major works by Gall and Caldwell were done when humans were seen by most social thinkers as directing their own lives, not being manipulated by accidents of biology. This philosophical viewpoint was to change, but too late for the advocates of phrenology. (Ironically, these advocates—especially Gall—vehemently asserted that their approach was not fatalistic and that bodily drives were secondary to will and spirit.)[29]

Although phrenology was relegated to the status of quackery—through no fault of Gall's—the approach marked the beginning of the scientific investigation of deviants. The notion of biology as a fundamental cause of deviant behavior was to reemerge permanently toward the end of the nineteenth century.

The Positivist School

The notion that biology plays a significant, if not paramount, role in causing deviant behavior is usually associated with the writings of Cesare Lombroso (1838–1909). He has been described as "one of the best known and possibly one of the least well understood figures in criminology."[30] Typically, he has been called the founder of the positivist school of criminology because he sought the explanation of criminal behavior by using scientific methods. This is unfair to Gall, however, whose research preceded Lombroso's by several decades. Nevertheless, Lombroso's writings made a considerable impact, and their importance in spurring research on criminals is undeniable.

Lombroso's reputation has been treated unfairly as well. It is customary to attack Lombroso solely on the basis of his biological orientation, especially his concept of the "born criminal." This concept represents only a portion of his voluminous work and does not take into account modifications in his thinking.[31] But as we shall see, the idea that criminals are born and not made has a remarkable longevity. Perhaps it is not surprising that critics hammer away at the idea's creator, whether he changed his mind or not.

Lombroso's most important book was *L'Uomo Delinquente* (*The Criminal Man*), first published in Italy in 1876. Here, he presented his doctrine of evolutionary *atavism*. Criminals were seen as distinct types of humans who could be distinguished from noncriminals by certain physical traits. These observable "stigmata" did not cause criminal behavior but rather served to identify persons who were out of step with the evolutionary scheme. Such persons were considered to be closer to apes or to early primitive humans than were most modern individuals; they were throwbacks (atavists) to an earlier stage in human development.

Lombroso was a physician trained in psychiatry and biology, and he was aware of the then-dying phrenology movement and the recent works of Charles Darwin, who connected modern humans with a nonhuman past through his theory of evolution. Lombroso had been involved for some time in the study of physical differences among criminals, the insane, and normals, but his notion of atavism as a cause of crime emerged as a bolt from the blue during his autopsy of an infamous robber, whom Lombroso found to have skull depressions characteristic of lower primates:

> This was not merely an idea, but a revelation. At the sight of that skull, I seemed to see all of a sudden, lighted up as a vast plain under a flaming sky, the problem of the nature of the criminal—an atavistic being who reproduces in his person the ferocious instincts of primitive humanity and the inferior animals. Thus were explained anatomically the enormous jaws, high cheek bones, prominent superciliary arches, solitary lines in the palms, extreme size of the orbits, handle-shaped or sessile ears found in criminals, savages, and apes, insensibility to pain, extremely acute sight, tattooing, excessive idleness, love of orgies, and the irresistible craving for evil for its own sake, the desire not only to extinguish life in the victim, but to mutilate the corpse, tear its flesh, and drink its blood.[32]

This was decidedly someone to avoid meeting in a dark alley. (Together, Gall and Lombroso might be said to have founded the "Bumps and Grunts School of Criminology.")

In the face of extreme criticism and contradictory scientific evidence, Lombroso later deemphasized the importance of atavism in explaining the total range of criminality. In his last publications he conceded that the born criminal probably constituted only a third of all criminals. By this time he had supplemented his approach with the idea that epilepsy might form an underlying basis for predisposing individuals to crime. His final classification of criminals included (1) the born criminal, (2) the insane criminal, (3) the epileptic criminal, and (4) the occasional criminal.

The last group represented those who were apparently unaffected by atavism or epilepsy and whose criminal behavior was a result of any of a multitude of environmental or situational factors: climate, structure of government, corruption of police, poverty, and so on. However, even for this group, Lombroso never totally abandoned his ideas that criminal individuals were different from others and that they were abnormal to some degree. In short, he never allowed for the possible existence of "normal" criminals. Many criminologists after Lombroso were less sweeping in their application of biological determinism, but the idea that at least *some* criminal behavior might be explained by abnormal biological factors never disappeared and receives significant attention today.

Lombroso's most famous students, Enrico Ferri (1856–1929) and Raffaele Garofalo (1852–1934), broke away decisively from an exclusive concentration on physical factors in classifying criminals. Ferri suggested five types:

1. Insane criminals who act from epilepsy, imbecility, paranoia (delusions of being persecuted), and other forms of mental infirmity
2. Born criminals "whose anti-human conduct is the inevitable effect of an indefinite series of hereditary influences which accumulate in the course of generations"
3. Habitual criminals who show in an indistinct way the marks of the born criminal and act through moral weakness as influenced by a corrupt environment
4. Criminals of passion who act under the impulse of uncontrolled emotion on occasion during otherwise moral lives
5. Occasional criminals who "have not received from nature an active tendency towards crime but have fallen into it, goaded by the temptation incident to their personal condition or physical and social environment"[33]

These last individuals are characterized by a lack of foresight and are stimulated by factors such as age, sexuality, poverty, and the weather.

From this admittedly brief description the reader might see that Ferri was advocating a theory of multiple causation involving not only individual factors but social ones as well. Furthermore, he was substituting *heredity* for atavism in the born criminal; that is, he believed there existed a criminal type whose behavior was congenital but stemmed from more immediate generations than implied in the notion of atavism.

Garofalo disagreed with Ferri on many counts but not on the hereditary basis of crime derived from recent generations. Garofalo suggested a theory of moral degeneracy. This degeneracy resulted from "retrogressive selection" and caused the individual

> to lose the better qualities which he had acquired by secular evolution, and has led him back to the same degree of inferiority whence he had slowly risen. This retrogressive selection is due to the mating of the weakest and most unfit, of those who have become brutalized by alcohol or abased by extreme misery against which their apathy has prevented them from struggling. Thus are formed demoralized and outcast families whose interbreeding in time produces a true race of inferior quality.[34]

Even among writers far less sympathetic to Lombroso than were Ferri and Garofalo, heredity loomed as the major explanation of criminal behavior. Lombroso's principal critic was Charles Goring (1870–1919), who in 1902 set out to discover whether any physical attributes distinguished the criminal from the noncriminal. From a sample of 3,000 English male convicts he gathered a large number of physical measurements, items of personal history, and measures of "mental qualities."[35] For comparative purposes he obtained similar measurements from college undergraduates, hospital patients, and soldiers. Goring concluded that after allowing for variations in dimensions for all the groups, there was no evidence confirming the existence of a physical criminal type as described by Lombroso and his disciples. However, he did find that the criminal sample was differentiated from the noncriminal samples by shorter height and lesser weight. Goring speculated that in and of itself this finding did not indicate that criminals were inferior; instead, it reflected an inbreeding of the "criminal class." Goring's logic on this point is far from convincing but went something like this: Shorter individuals have more difficulty in obtaining honest work and are more likely to be apprehended and convicted should they commit crimes. Thus, by a process of selection the slight-of-stature criminals are separated from the general community. They have sons who inherit their fathers' small size and who also become convicted. In the course of generations this process leads to an inbred physical differentiation of the "criminal class."

Goring also found that mental defectiveness characterized his convict sample. After comparing various traits of fathers and sons, he concluded that not only small stature but also a proclivity for criminality must be inherited:

> A comparison of the results that have emerged from the present investigation, . . . wherein the relations of mental defectiveness, and of environmental conditions upon the genesis of crime, are presented . . . leads to two very general conclusions. The one is that the criminal diathesis [constitutional predisposition], revealed by the tendency to be convicted and imprisoned by crime, is inherited at much the same rate as are other physical and mental qualities and pathological conditions in man. The second is that the influence of parental contagion [example] . . . is, on the whole, inconsiderable, relative to the influence of inheritance, and of mental defectiveness: which are by far the most significant factors we have been able to discover in the etiology of crime.[36]

The early positivist theories were good scientific efforts for their time. The simple notions of criminal physical type and of physical traits by which the criminal could be identified were eventually laid to rest. They were resurrected, as it turns out, but the efforts of many criminologists at the turn of the century were directed toward the roles of heredity and intellect in deviant behavior.

CRITICAL THINKING EXERCISES

1. In your own opinion, is the consumption of alcohol a form of deviant behavior? Describe a person whom you would classify as deviant due to alcohol consumption.

2. If a person gets one speeding ticket in a year's time, is that person deviant? How about 100 tickets in a year? How about 1,000? How many speeding tickets would it take for you to classify someone as deviant?

3. If there were scientific proof that childbirth always results in changes in women's body chemistry and that significant imbalances can cause psychosis and loss of the ability to perceive reality consistently, how would you personally judge Andrea Yates? What are your verdict and sentence?

CHECK IT OUT ON THE WEB

The Internet addresses listed below are intended to provide the reader with understanding of a wide range of perspectives regarding the subject matter discussed in this chapter. Some sites may contain objectionable material. The list is not intended to reflect the viewpoints or opinions of the authors or the publisher.

http://www.forensicexaminers.com
    forensic evaluation and treatment of deviant behavior
http://www.harlingen.tstc.edu
    major varieties of deviant behavior from a sociological perspective
http://www.ags.uci.edu/~dkieso/crimth.htm
    deviant behavior from the legal perspective
http://www.asanet.org/sections/crime.html
    sociology of law and deviant behavior
http://www.gruterinstitute.org/news/vls.html
    biology, behavior, and criminal law
http://www.uplink.com.au/lawlibrary/Documents/Docs/Doc18.html
    explanations of aggressive behavior

ENDNOTES

1. Michael Mann, ed., *The International Encyclopedia of Sociology* (New York: The Continuum Publishing Company, 1984), p. 266. For a detailed discussion of norms and their various aspects, see Jack P. Gibbs, *Norms, Deviance, and Social Control: Conceptual Matters* (New York: Elsevier, 1981), pp. 7–21.

2. George F. Will, "July 10, 1941, In Jedwabne: Why Did Half of a Polish Town Murder the Other Half? The Answer May Be Terribly Simple," *Newsweek,* July 9, 2001, pp. 2–5.

3. Jan Gross, *Neighbors* (Princeton, NJ: Princeton University Press, 2001).

4. Alan J. Kuperman, "Rwanda in Retrospect: Could the Genocide Have Been Stopped?," *Foreign Affairs, 79* (January/February 2000), pp. 94–116.

5. Pam Easton, "Drowned Children Were Struggling," Associated Press news article published in the *Austin American Statesman,* June 22, 2001, Section A, p. 1.

6. Michelle Oberman, "Mothers Who Kill: Coming to Terms with Modern American Infanticide," *American Criminal Law Review, 34* (Fall 1996), pp. 1–90.

7. Cheryl L. Meyer and Michelle Oberman, *Mothers Who Kill Their Children* (New York: New York University Press, 2001).

8. Patrick M. Reilly and Joann S. Lublin, "Should Businesses Negotiate with Terrorists?" *The Wall Street Journal,* September 20, 1995, pp. B1–B4.

9. *The American Heritage Dictionary,* 2nd college ed. (Boston: Houghton Mifflin, 1982), p. 389.

10. Joan Ferrante, *Sociology: A Global Perspective* (Belmont, CA: Wadsworth Publishing Company, 1992), p. 230.

11. Jerry L. Simmons, *Deviants* (Berkeley, CA: Glendessary Press, 1969), p. 3. See also Jerry L. Simmons and Hazel Chambers, "Public Stereotypes of Deviants," *Social Problems, 13* (Fall 1965), pp. 223–232.

12. John E. Conklin, "Criminal Environment and Support for the Law," *Law and Society Review, 6* (November 1971), pp. 247–265.

13. Marvin E. Wolfgang, Robert M. Figlio, Paul E. Tracy, and Simon I. Singer, *The National Survey of Crime Severity* (Washington, DC: U.S. Department of Justice, 1985). For a more detailed discussion on the issue of

measuring the perceived seriousness of crime, see Mark Warr, "What Is the Perceived Seriousness of Crimes?" *Criminology, 27* (November 1989), pp. 795–829.

14. Stuart L. Hills, *Crime, Power, and Morality: The Criminal Law Process in the United States* (Scranton, PA: Chandler Publishing, 1971), pp. 4–5. See also a recent effort dealing with the complex nature of deviance and politics: Nachman Ben-Yehuda, *The Politics and Morality of Deviance: Moral Panics, Drug Abuse, Deviant Science, and Reversed Stigmatization* (Albany: State University of New York Press, 1990), esp. pp. 4–14, 35–63.

15. Cesare Beccaria, *On Crimes and Punishments,* trans. Henry Paolucci (Indianapolis, IN: Bobbs-Merrill, 1963), p. 93.

16. Graeme Newman and Pietro Marongiu, "Penological Reform and the Myth of Beccaria," *Criminology, 28* (May 1990), pp. 325–346.

17. For more detailed discussions of the classical and neoclassical schools, see George B. Vold and Thomas J. Bernard, *Theoretical Criminology,* 3rd ed. (New York: Oxford University Press, 1986), pp. 18–35; and Ysabel Rennie, *The Search for Criminal Man* (Lexington, MA: D. C. Heath, 1978), pp. 11–25.

18. David Jary and Julia Jary, *Collins Dictionary of Sociology* (Glasgow: HarperCollins Publishing, 1991), p. 484.

19. Julius Gould and William L. Kolb, *A Dictionary of the Social Sciences* (New York: The Free Press, 1964), pp. 194–195.

20. For more detailed discussions of the assumptions of the positivist school, see David Matza, *Delinquency and Drift* (New York: John Wiley, 1964), pp. 1–27; and Ian Taylor, Paul Walton, and Jock Young, *The New Criminology* (London: Routledge & Kegan Paul, 1973), pp. 10–40.

21. Vold and Bernard, *Theoretical Criminology,* p. 42.

22. A survey of research published in major sociological journals between 1940 and 1970 indicates that this is definitely the case regarding delinquency studies. See John F. Galliher and James L. McCartney, "The Influence of Funding Agencies on Juvenile Delinquency Research," *Social Problems, 21* (Summer 1973), pp. 77–90. See also Vold and Bernard, *Theoretical Criminology,* pp. 340–361.

23. Paraphrased from Taylor, Walton, and Young, *The New Criminology,* pp. 31–33.

24. Of course, people still have notions of what criminals look like. For research on these notions, see Donald J. Shoemaker, Donald L. Smith, and Jay Lowe, "Facial Stereotypes of Deviants and Judgements of Guilt or Innocence," *Social Forces, 51* (June 1973), pp. 427–433.

25. For a more detailed discussion of phrenology as it applied to criminology, see Arthur E. Fink, *Causes of Crime: Biological Theories in the United States, 1800–1915* (New York: A. S. Barnes & Co., 1962).

26. Leonard Savitz, Stanley H. Turner, and Toby Dickman, "The Origin of Scientific Criminology: Franz Joseph Gall as the First Criminologist," in *Theory in Criminology: Contemporary Views,* ed. Robert F. Meier (Beverly Hills, CA: Sage Publications, 1977), p. 43.

27. Fink, *Causes of Crime,* p. 5.

28. Savitz, Turner, and Dickman, "The Origin of Scientific Criminology," p. 49.

29. This discussion is based on *ibid.,* pp. 41–56; and Vold and Bernard, *Theoretical Criminology,* pp. 47–50.

30. Sawyer F. Sylvester, Jr., ed., *The Heritage of Modern Criminology* (Cambridge, MA: Schenkman Publishing, 1972), p. 63.

31. For a review and generally sympathetic evaluation of Lombroso, see Marvin E. Wolfgang, "Cesare Lombroso," in *Pioneers in Criminology,* 2nd ed., ed. Hermann Mannheim (Montclair, NJ: Patterson Smith Publishing Corporation, 1972), pp. 232–291.

32. Cesare Lombroso, "Introduction," in *Criminal Man According to the Classification of Cesare Lombroso,* ed. Gina Lombroso-Ferrero (New York: Putnam, 1911), p. xiv; quoted in *ibid.,* p. 184.

33. Enrico Ferri, *Criminal Sociology,* trans. Joseph I. Kelly and John Lisle (Boston: Little, Brown, 1917), pp. 138–157.

34. Baron Raffaele Garofalo, *Criminology,* trans. Robert W. Millar (Boston: Little, Brown, 1914), p. 110.

35. Charles Goring, *The English Convict: A Statistical Study,* abridged ed. (London: His Majesty's Stationery Office, 1919), p. 21. For a recent review of Goring, see Piers Beirne, "Heredity Versus Environment: A Reconsideration of Charles Goring's English Convict (1913)," *The British Journal of Criminology, 28* (Summer 1988), pp. 315–339.

36. *Ibid.,* pp. 267–268.

2 Theories of Criminal Deviance

The concept of crime, like the concept of deviant behavior, has always been a fluid notion, changing dramatically from place to place, from time to time, and from culture to culture. In our world today, there exist wide differences in the ways in which criminal behavior is defined. Extramarital sexual relations, for example, may be ignored or lightly regarded by the legal system in some cultures but punished by the death penalty in others. There are general trends, of course, regarding harmful, predatory behavior, but there are always exceptions to be found somewhere.

Generally speaking, crime is behavior perceived to be threatening to the degree that it cannot be left unchecked. It is behavior that is believed to be dangerous, one way or another, to individuals, to groups, and ultimately perhaps, to the existence of the society as a whole. Because it is dangerous, we have always wanted to get rid of it, and through our history we have tried to figure out why it happens.

In the last few centuries the scientific tools and methods at our disposal have become remarkably sophisticated and accurate. Sound scientific theories explain and predict behavior, and in some areas our scientists are quite effective. The development of scientific law and theory in chemistry, biology, and physics, for example, has enabled us to understand our world from those perspectives in exquisite detail. We haven't arrived at that level of understanding in the social sciences yet because we aren't scientifically sophisticated enough to identify the constants associated with human behavior. As a scientific subject, human behavior is still too complex for our scientific tools. We can count on chemicals, plants, or falling objects to behave the same way every time under constant conditions. We can thus understand the behavior of hydrogen or wheat more effectively than, say, the behavior of New Yorkers or Texans. If your scientific endeavor involves the behavior of a metal ball dropping from a tower in Italy, you can expect the ball to behave the same way every time, and you have the tools to explain any variance that you might observe. The ball will never cry, or curse, or grab you by the throat and drop *you* from the tower, as a New Yorker or a Texan might.

So, in the social sciences we try to explain and predict human behavior in terms of probabilities and trends. We will arrive eventually at a level of detailed scientific understanding of human behavior and be able to explain and predict deviance and crime accurately at all levels. In this chapter we will examine our progress thus far in the area of criminal deviance.

Heredity and Mental Deficiencies—
Early Approaches

In most detailed histories of the attempts to explain deviant behavior, theories based upon heredity and upon mental deficiencies would not be casually thrown together. Heredity concerns the process of passing characteristics from one generation to another; mental deficiencies are specific characteristics that may or may not be seen by the theorists as inherited. One of these explanations does not, therefore, imply the other, but in practice the reader would find it difficult to separate most theorists into one or the other category. For example, Goring believed that something he called "criminal diathesis" was inherited, but in addition he believed that mental defectiveness, also believed to be inherited, played an important role in criminal behavior. Other theorists who considered deviance stemming primarily from defectiveness relied heavily upon heredity as a supplementary explanation.

Part of the impetus for stressing heredity as an important factor came from a book written in 1877, *The Jukes*. Juke was a fictitious name given by the author, Robert L. Dugdale, to a rural New York family whose ancestry reached back to the early colonists—truly an American family. They had lived in relative isolation in the same locality for generations. With few exceptions the group was propagated through intermarriage. Their deviance spanned the generations and extended beyond incest to all forms of assault and theft as well as prostitution and cruelty to animals. They were so despised by others in the area that "Juke" was used locally as a common term of censure. Dugdale described their colony:

> [Their ancestors] lived in log or stone houses similar to slave-hovels, all ages, sexes, relations and strangers "bunking" indiscriminately. . . . To this day some of the "Jukes" occupy the self-same shanties built nearly a century ago. The essential features of the habitat have remained stationary, and the social habits seem to survive in conformity to the persistence of the domiciliary environment. I have seen rude shelters made of boughs covered with sod. . . . Others of the habitations have two rooms, but so firmly has habit established modes of living that, nevertheless, they often use but one congregate dormitory.[1]

In his investigation of the family tree and criminal careers of the Jukes, Dugdale intended to suggest an explanation of the relative influence of heredity and environment on the production of crime. In his conclusions he expressed his belief that criminal behavior might be transmitted intergenerationally, although he was also convinced that environment was ultimately the controlling factor that could modify even inherited behavior patterns. But his work came at a time when evolution and genetics had caught the attention of the scientific world. Furthermore, the book appeared just a year after Lombroso's *L'Uomo Delinquente* was published in Italy. With these facts in mind, it is perhaps not surprising that *The Jukes* was commonly used as proof of hereditary criminality and served to encourage other studies of similar families.

Perhaps even more popular than *The Jukes* was *The Kallikak Family* by Henry H. Goddard. The Kallikak saga began during the Revolutionary War, when a young militiaman from a "respectable" family became involved with a feeble-minded bargirl. Their liaison resulted in a feeble-minded son and the beginning of what Goddard called a "line of mental defectives that is truly appalling." Of the son's 480 descendants, 143 were feeble-minded, 46 normal, and the remainder in doubt. Also, 36 were illegitimate, 33 "sexually immoral," 24 alcoholic, 3 epileptic, and 3 criminal, and 8 ran houses of prostitution.[2] In the meantime, the militiaman married well, and from this line came 496 descendants, none of whom were feeble-minded or criminal.

From these findings Goddard concluded that feeble-mindedness was hereditary and related to deviant behavior and poverty. He also suggested that Lombroso's types might have been derived from varieties of feeble-mindedness that were influenced by environment to produce deviant types.[3] Between 1911 and 1914 Goddard and others tried to substantiate further the relationship between deviance and mental deficiency by conducting tests of intelligence on juvenile and adult inmates of reformatories and prisons. In a lecture delivered in 1919 Goddard left no doubt as to the cause of crime:

> Are the persons who commit offenses really of low mental quality? The answer is no longer in doubt. . . . Every investigation of the mentality of criminals, misdemeanants, delinquents, and other anti-social groups has proven beyond the possibility of contradiction that nearly all persons in these classes and in some cases all are of low mentality. Moreover, a large percentage of all of the groups are of such low mentality as to be properly denominated feeble-minded.[4]

But the evidence contradicted Goddard's claim about the role of low mentality as a cause of criminality. During World War I the first large-scale intelligence testing program was performed on the U.S. draft army. Using the generally accepted criteria of what constituted feeble-mindedness, 34 percent of the cream of U.S. youth would have had to be characterized as feeble-minded. Considering only nonwhites and whites from southern states, that percentage would have been nearly doubled. Obviously, something was very wrong. Once the criteria had been modified and the test scores of prisoners carefully compared with those of males among the general population, it appeared that the proportion of feeble-minded among inmates was less than 5 percent instead of the 50 percent once suggested by Goddard. Furthermore, intelligence tests generally showed little significant difference between inmates and the general population. Thus low mental ability could no longer be maintained as an explanation of deviance.[5]

A Short Note on Eugenics

We briefly interrupt here the outline of deviance theories to acquaint the reader with one side effect of positivism, which occurred around the turn of the century. You will recall an earlier discussion that pointed out that the determinism inherent in positivism carried a fatalistic assumption that certain human beings could not escape their predestined fates. Their genetic makeup effectively locked them into a life of crime, intemperance, and perverseness. Although environment might have a minimal influence on behavior, the fundamental cause of the behavior lay within the individual. Thus, to call someone a "born criminal" or "feeble-minded" was to make a firm prediction about that person's future, regardless of his or her actions up to that point.

The logic of determinism was fertile ground for the growth of eugenics, a science concerned with improving the quality of human offspring, especially through the manipulation of heredity by such means as selection of parents. A eugenics movement attained some importance in the United States during the first two decades of the twentieth century. Today, much of its literature seems naive and highly moralistic.

A representative example is a 1916 handbook entitled *Eugenics,* whose title page claims that within its covers lie "important hints on social purity, heredity, physical manhood and womanhood." The contents include chapters on etiquette, hygienic bathing, ethics of the unmarried, childbearing, the dangers of "self-pollution" (masturbation, which among other things is said to make the eyes become glassy and permanently fall back into their sockets), and cures for a wide range of diseases. One of the hints is that

> over-indulgence in the sexual act . . . lowers the whole moral and physical tone of the race. Men and women lose their vitality; the children are puny, scrawny beings, many of whom in early life pass to untimely graves.[6]

The accompanying photograph shows a puny, scrawny being, confined to a wheelchair. The caption reads, "Results of conception when the father was intoxicated."

Most eugenics literature was a mixture of common sense and essentially harmless hokum. But the movement had a far grimmer side. As long as the deviance was believed to be inherited, either as a form of mental deficiency or as a tendency in its own right, eugenics was a logical source of a solution. What was "scientifically" found as a cause could be "scientifically" eliminated. In their extreme forms the elimination plans anticipated the mass execution methods employed by Nazi Germany during World War II. In 1901 a textbook on social problems reported on a proposal whereby "defective and confirmed criminals" would be placed in airtight chambers and put to death by "poisonous, but not unpleasant, gas."[7]

Most suggestions involved less drastic, but nevertheless serious, measures such as sterilization or castration. The latter was advocated by those who felt that mere sterilization would not curtail lustful behavior or the spread of venereal diseases. Between 1907 and 1937 a total of 31 states enacted laws permitting the sterilization of certain individuals without their consent. (Even before 1907 secret sterilizations had been performed on inmates in state institutions for many years.)[8] These laws were applicable to three classes of individuals: the mentally ill, the mentally deficient, and epileptics. The legacy of the eugenics movement is with us today in the form of the legal codes of several states that still permit involuntary sterilization. The majority of the sterilization statutes include in their scope the mentally ill or developmentally disabled (or retarded). Many old statutes regarding sterilization included epileptics among persons targeted, but today only three states extend coverage to this group.[9]

The fruits of positivism in the United States were not a series of purifying executions, but close to 70,000 individuals were involuntarily sterilized, and many more were confined because their behavior, intellects, or backgrounds were judged by state bureaucrats to be below standards. If any one place deserved the title "Sterilization City, USA," it was Lynchburg, Virginia. There, in the state hospital, approximately 8,000 individuals were sterilized between 1924 and 1972. Everything was very routine: men on Tuesdays, women on Thursdays. Such practices were given the legal blessing of the Supreme Court when, in a 1927 test case, Justice Oliver Wendell Holmes said of the plaintiff, "Three generations of imbeciles are enough."[10]

Is this all ancient history? Perhaps. But the spirit of eugenics displays a remarkable stamina. As recently as 1980, we found the head of welfare in Texas suggesting compulsory sterilization for welfare recipients. This is the same year we heard about a group of male

Nobel Prize winners donating to a sperm bank, the hope being that intelligent women will bring forth offspring transcending the common herd. Public debate regarding genetic engineering with DNA replacement, cloning technology, mandatory contraception for some types of female offenders, and voluntary castration for male sex offenders is continually in the news. These are sobering reminders of how a "scientific" theory of human behavior, whether correct or erroneous, proven or unproven, can justify the degradation of whole classes of people. Covered with the mantle of objectivity and science, this approach is, of course, exercised only for the "good" of everyone concerned. But however benevolent programs of "scientific treatment" or "scientific prevention" may appear, they may be not only ineffectual but also threatening to human freedom.

The eugenics discussion and speculation about future ethics questions become quite complex with the scientific capability to genetically change an individual's susceptibility to disease or behavior problems, or to clone genetic duplicates of animals and humans. The image of a genetically engineered society is certainly no longer science fiction but has become a rapidly advancing scientific possibility. Again, we must hope that such wondrous capabilities are used in the future with wisdom and careful attention to freedom and human dignity.

Twin Studies

Although the tracing of family backgrounds had reached its limit of usefulness after Goddard's study of the Kallikaks, the notion of hereditary criminality was far from abandoned. One study offered in support of hereditary determinism was that of Johannes Lange, a German physiologist, who published his results in 1929 in *Verbrechen als Schicksal* (*Crime as Destiny*). The title is certainly not ambiguous. Lange compared criminal records of the two types of twins: *identical* twins, those produced from a single egg, who therefore have identical genetic makeups, and *fraternal* twins, those produced from two eggs, who therefore have dissimilar makeups. Lange reasoned that a pair of twins would experience similar environments and that any behavioral differences between them would therefore necessarily be biologically caused. If environment were the cause of criminality, then there should be no differences between a pair of twins, regardless of whether they were identical or fraternal.

Lange then examined male inmates of a prison and a psychiatric institute to determine which were twins. The other twin was then traced to determine whether he also had been imprisoned. Lange found a group of 13 identical twins; 10 of these pairs (77 percent) had both been imprisoned. For a group of 17 fraternal twins, both had been imprisoned in only 2 instances (12 percent).

The implications of these findings were clear to Lange, and his suggestions were consistent with the determinist philosophy:

> We should make every attempt to discover as early as possible those who must be permanently segregated if society is to be protected from grave damage. The detailed examination of all law-breakers and the thorough training of real experts in this subject are essential toward this end.
>
> Finally, and this is our most important task, we must take preventive measures. We must try to make it impossible for human beings with positive criminal tendencies to be born.[11]

Lange's work has been followed by many other studies designed to test *concordance rates* (percentage of cases in which both twins were labeled as criminal) of identical (monozygotic) and fraternal (dizygotic) twins. Generally speaking, concordance rates for monozygotic twins were observed to be higher in alcoholism risk,[12] suicidal behavior,[13] bipolar and other mood disorders,[14] impulsive-compulsive disorders,[15] and intelligence.[16]

In studies that are perhaps characterized by better samples, the link between heredity and crime is far from obvious. For example, a Norwegian study published in 1976 found a concordance rate of 22 percent for identical twins and 18 percent for fraternal twins. Not only are the differences between rates trivial, but the *discordance rate* (cases in which one twin was criminal and the other was not) is more remarkable than the concordance: among identical twins, only one twin was criminal in 78 percent of the cases. The researchers go on to point out that

> since [identical] twins experience a more similar upbringing and an identity with each other than that of [fraternal] twins, we have compared [identical twins with fraternal twins] who by and large have experienced this same close twin relationship and report the same type of upbringing with regard to dressing and treatment by parents. In such a comparison the difference in concordance . . . practically disappears altogether. These findings lead us to conclude that *the significance of hereditary factors in registered crime is nonexistent.*[17]

In 1997 Christiane Charlemaine challenged the utility of twin studies by using new methods to examine the zygotic identity of identical twins. She concluded that there were *major* differences within monozygotic twins and therefore many reasons why they may be genetically discordant.[18] Thus there is serious concern regarding the traditional logic surrounding scientific twin studies.

Without a doubt, a person's genetic background sets limits upon his or her behavior and potential. But the extent to which such limits translate into a predisposition or a vulnerability is an issue of great complexity. Glenn D. Walters and Thomas W. White, in an article entitled "Heredity and Crime: Bad Genes or Bad Research?" tackled the heredity and crime issue by conducting a review of research that focused on four research methodologies: family studies, twin studies, adoption studies, and gene-environment studies. They concluded that

> genetic factors are undoubtedly correlated with various measures of criminality, but the large number of methodological flaws and limitations in research should make one cautious in drawing any causal inferences at this point in time. Our review leads us to the inevitable conclusion that current genetic research on crime has been poorly designed, ambiguously reported, and exceedingly inadequate in addressing the relevant issues.[19]

Their review sparked a controversy. One of the researchers criticized in their article (who was also a colleague) replied that Walters and White's conclusion was "questionable due to the flawed nature of the critical comments on which it is based."[20] Walters later replied to this by stating that the conclusions stand.[21] At present the relationship between heredity and deviance remains unproven. The reader probably recognizes, however, that such proof, should it ever emerge, can have consequences well beyond simply "explaining" crime. For example, will new eugenic procedures emerge? If so, who will be the targets of such programs? Will corrupt lawmakers and corporation leaders undergo the same treatment as robbers and burglars to prevent their "bad seed" from proliferating? Don't hold your breath.

The Bell Curve

Perhaps no one book has sparked more fury and debate recently than *The Bell Curve: Intelligence and Class Structure in American Life,* by Richard J. Herrnstein and Charles Murray. Published in 1994, it purported to demonstrate the following:

1. IQ or cognitive ability exists and can be measured. Standardized tests measure this ability.
2. IQ or cognitive ability is generally stable over much of a person's life.
3. IQ tests are not biased against social, economic, ethnic, or racial groups.
4. Cognitive ability is substantially heritable.[22]

Although supporters and critics argue over whether the book accomplished its goal, it clearly did raise the issue of race and intelligence. It did not resolve any issues but provided a forum for discussion. Too, the text suggests that a "cognitive elite" exists in the United States and that these individuals are the ones who will shape the society. Herrnstein and Murray's book is lengthy and deserves more attention than we can provide here. However, they do address crime and offer some interesting comments. For example, using self-report data, they note that individuals with higher IQ scores reported fewer problems with police and the criminal justice system. They also declare that "among the most firmly established facts about criminal offenders is that their distribution of IQ scores differs from that of the population at large. . . . Criminal offenders have average IQs of about 92, eight points below the mean."[23] And they recognize that critics will argue that offenders whose IQs are unrepresentative of the criminal population—that is, the "smart ones"—did not get caught. The authors admit that this may be true but question whether it really introduces a bias into the data.[24] Recent publications generally reflect moral outrage at Herrnstein and Murray's conclusions and refute their methods and assumptions. Descriptions of the weaknesses in the work range from "misleading"[25] to "fraudulent."[26] Reactions to this book will continue to be forthcoming.

Physical Characteristics Revisited

Biological Inferiority

As was mentioned, attempting to explain deviance by reference to anatomical features is a venerable and long-lived goal of positivist methodology. Goring's findings did not lay the matter to rest, and the hand of Lombroso continued to be felt for many years. Probably Lombroso's greatest latter-day champion was Earnest Albert Hooton, a Harvard anthropologist who was highly critical of Goring's research and was convinced that criminals were an "inferior" physical type. In 1926 Hooton launched a 12-year survey of nearly 14,000 inmates of jails and prisons and, for comparison, 3,200 college students, firemen, and so on.

On these samples 22 measurements were taken of the head and body. From this incredible mass of data Hooton concluded that

> criminal behavior is capable of considerable diversification in the manner and kind of overt act, but . . . whatever the crime may be, it ordinarily arises from a deteriorated organism which so far as we know, manifests its inferiority in comparatively few and uniform ways. . . . The primary cause of crime is biological inferiority. . . . The penitentiaries of our society are built upon the shifting sands and quaking bogs of inferior human organisms.[27]

This is not radically different from Lombroso's vision of the criminal organism emerging from the primeval slime, and it appropriately drew a barrage of criticism. Four principal reasons for rejecting Hooton's work are of interest because they—especially the first two—can often be applied to any research that attempts to distinguish between the characteristics of the "criminal" and the "noncriminal."[28]

   1. Inmates of institutions do not accurately represent the population of people who have been involved in criminal behavior. For various reasons many who steal, kill, rape, fail to pay alimony, and so on do not get caught. Both the highly skilled professional criminal and the one-time offender may have that much in common (not getting caught) because they are smart and lucky. Furthermore, only a portion of those caught will be found in institutions; others are spared that fate because they have a good lawyer, are "too respectable" to go to prison, or are good probation risks. This is especially the case for white-collar criminals whose social positions protect them regardless of how much economic damage they have caused. Thus, researchers seeking a sample of criminals, deviants, or whatever in an institution must face the fact they are dealing with an extremely select group: those who, for a variety of reasons, were apprehended, tried, convicted, and sentenced to an institution. To complicate the issue further, many of these persons may in fact be innocent of the accused behavior.

   2. The other side of the coin is that a sample of noninstitutionalized persons does not necessarily represent the population of noncriminals or nondeviants. If you sampled a number of convents and monasteries, you could be reasonably assured of a "holy" but hardly representative group of noncriminals. The problem is that within practically any sample you select from the *general* population, you will include people who have committed acts identical to those committed by people who are imprisoned. Although this may be an exaggeration for some acts—such as murder, kidnapping, and bank robbery—for other acts, such as drug abuse, shoplifting, assaults, and traffic offenses, the distinctions between institutionalized and noninstitutionalized samples would be less than clear-cut.

Somatology

Somatology is the science of classifying human physical characteristics. The application of this science to the study of deviance represents the heritage of Lombroso and Hooton in its most sophisticated form. The principal proponent in the United States was William H. Sheldon (1899–1963), who attempted to explain juvenile delinquency by examining the relationship between body type or physique and particular patterns of mental and behavioral characteristics or temperaments.

Somatotyping individuals according to Sheldon's scheme is a complex procedure that involves assigning scores to the physique on the basis of three components. Although it is possible for someone to be described solely by a single component, most persons would be scored as a combination. Each physique component in its purest form can be characterized by a component of temperament. For any specific individual the components of temperament vary with components of physique, according to Sheldon. The components, with their brief descriptions, are described in Table 2.1.[29]

To complicate matters, there are also "psychiatric components," but they do not coincide directly with the others. Between endomorphy and mesomorphy occurs the manic component (exuberance, expressiveness); between mesomorphy and ectomorphy is the paranoid component (vigilance, alertness); and between ectomorphy and endomorphy falls the hebephrenic component (withdrawal).

Sheldon's study involved the somatotyping of 200 boys who from 1939 to 1942 were connected with a center for "problem" children referred by social agencies and courts in Boston. In comparison to a sample of 4,000 college males, the center's children were found to be more mesomorphic—"a little on the hefty and meaty side."[30] They also tended toward the manic and paranoid components. After presenting 200 biographies and a mass of data, Sheldon concluded that few of the youths in the center were normal. The "varieties of delinquent youth" were generally characterized by one of the following: mental insufficiency, medical insufficiency, or psychopathy.

Sheldon's research and his interpretations fell prey to most of the problems of such studies. In particular the delinquency of the boys was frequently ambiguous, often involving merely "troublesome" or "disappointing" behavior. Furthermore, a reanalysis of his data failed to support his conclusions about the relationship between delinquency and any of the components.[31] Thus the role of physical characteristics in differentiating deviants from nondeviants remained unproven.

The ineffectiveness of somatology does not mean that attempts to establish a relationship between physical characteristics and deviant behavior have abated. The most recent efforts have been less ambitious than those of the past, however, because they concentrate on narrower ranges of behavior such as violence or homosexuality. We will briefly discuss two such approaches to the explanation of violence: the XYY chromosome syndrome and the brain malfunction theory.

TABLE 2.1 Physique and Temperament Components of Somatotyping

Components of Physique	Components of Temperament
Endomorphy—floats easily, is soft, round, roly-poly	Viscerotonia—is relaxed, loves to eat, needs company and affection
Mesomorphy—is muscular, strong, hard	Somatotonia—is assertive and vigorous, loves action and power
Ectomorphy—is flat, fragile, lean	Cerebrotonia—restrains emotions, loves privacy, is apprehensive

XYY Chromosome Syndrome

Human cells have 46 chromosomes arranged in 23 pairs, each parent having donated one member of each pair. Two of the 46 chromosomes, labeled either X or Y because of their shape, determine sexual characteristics. Every normal cell in a woman's body contains two X chromosomes, and each cell in a male has one X and one Y. The existence of the Y chromosome is the basic distinction between men and women. However, exceptions to this genetic pattern do occur. Of interest here are the estimated 0.1 percent (1 in 1,000) of the males who possess an extra Y chromosome, a condition first reported in 1961.

This genetic anomaly received no public attention until 1968, when a defense attorney in a French murder trial claimed that his client possessed an extra Y chromosome and therefore was not responsible for his offense. This claim was based on very limited research indicating that some chromosomally abnormal men had histories of antisocial behavior. Shortly thereafter, the XYY syndrome was introduced into the trial publicity of murderers in Australia and West Germany as well as in three cases in the United States. The most publicized case was that of Richard Speck, who murdered eight Chicago student nurses. In 1968 Speck's attorney claimed to the press that Speck had XYY chromosomes, a contention that made front-page headlines. As it developed, Speck was simply XY, but *that* finding received very little publicity.

The stage was set for a flurry of research and claims concerning the syndrome's influence on behavior.[32] Agreement among the researchers is difficult to pinpoint, but the best evidence indicates the following:

1. The syndrome occurs in a greater proportion among institutionalized males than among the general population. Since the most obvious feature of XYYs is their greater than average height, critics of the studies suggest that such height might bias authorities toward incarcerating XYYs rather than releasing them back on the streets.[33] This is an intriguing notion, but it is unproven. Instead, recent research indicates that the overrepresentation of XYYs in prison populations is not explained by tallness alone.[34]

2. It is becoming clear that early claims linking the XYY syndrome with aggression are false. Now it appears that the crimes of XYYs are *less violent* than those of XYs.[35]

Despite these clarifications, the disproportionate number of XYYs in prison remains a nagging issue. But even if it is resolved by the discovery of an accompanying individual problem—such as slow intellectual development—it is obvious that only a minute portion of crime will be thus explained. Or will it? What about the majority of XYYs who lead law-abiding lives? It is unlikely that a chromosomal arrangement can ever clearly distinguish any group, however small, that will inevitably be involved in deviance.

Brain Malfunction

Looking to the brain for an explanation of behavior is scarcely a recent innovation. We have already discussed the phrenologists who believed that the contours of the brain provided clues to the personality. However, the systematic manipulation of the brain for purposes of *altering* behavior was not initiated until 1935, when prefrontal lobotomy was introduced by the Portuguese physician Antonio Moniz. In this operation Moniz destroyed large sections of the frontal lobes of the brain. His subjects were 20 mental patients who had been unaffected by other treatments; according to Moniz, 15 showed some degree of improvement as a result of the operation. One lobotomized patient was later to pump five bullets into Moniz, but the operation and variations of it were widely hailed as the answer to many behavioral problems.

Moniz's lobotomies were the beginning of what is known today as *psychosurgery:* the surgical removal, destruction, or cutting of brain tissue to disconnect one part of the brain from another with the intent of altering behavior.[36] Between 1936 and the mid-1950s approximately 50,000 psychosurgical operations, mostly lobotomies, were performed in the United States alone. Many of the patients were World War II veterans with severe emotional problems.

Such operations were not performed without a growing controversy. Although the notion that lobotomies produced placid "vegetables" was a popular one, it did overstate the case. Side effects did occur: Many patients lost the ability to fantasize, to think abstractly, or to be creative. And other abuses arose:

> Some doctors performed lobotomies for mental patients that did not require such radical treatment. Horror tales proliferated: Walter Freeman of George Washington University, who brought lobotomy to the United States from Lisbon, performed some 4,000 of the operations with an ice pick. Critics told of a Freeman lobotomy on a Peeping Tom. After the operation, the patient no longer slunk through back alleys to take his visual pleasures—he walked right up to the front windows. The operation had apparently freed him of any sense of shame, but not his abnormal tendencies.[37]

Defenders of the operation claimed that such abuses were in the distinct minority and that lobotomies were usually performed only as a last resort. They claimed that the alternatives were leaving patients raving or depressed in back wards of hospitals for the rest of their lives or taking a chance on improving their condition even though their mentality might be lower as a consequence.

The controversy over lobotomies diminished as their use was eventually replaced by drugs and shock treatment.[38] These, too, have their limitations and side effects, including the likelihood of the patient's relapse to his or her previous condition. In recent years new and more sophisticated surgical techniques have been developed to penetrate more deeply and precisely into various areas of the brain. The new methods include the use of ultrasonic beams and tiny electrodes to destroy brain cells electrically. Along with the improved techniques have come recommendations and theories about how various forms of deviant behavior might be eliminated by psychosurgery. Seen as likely candidates for new surgical methods are various forms of mental disorder, homosexuality, childhood behavior disorders, some narcotics addictions, and criminal behavior. We will focus our attention on the use of psychosurgery to control aggressive behavior, selecting this area because it is within the context of a plausible theoretical framework and because the research results have occasionally been dramatic.

The major proponents of psychosurgery as a remedy for aggression are Vernon H. Mark and Frank R. Ervin, co-authors of *Violence and the Brain.* They claim that an appreciable percentage of persons who get involved in repeated personal violence do so because their brains do not function in a normal manner. In particular, they refer to individuals characterized by a set of symptoms labeled the *dyscontrol syndrome*. These symptoms, which are not always present at the same time, may include the following:

> 1) A history of physical assault, especially wife and child beating; 2) the symptom of pathological intoxication—that is, drinking even a small amount of alcohol triggers acts of senseless brutality; 3) a history of impulsive sexual behavior, at times including sexual assaults; and 4) a history (in those who [drive] cars) of many traffic violations and serious automobile accidents.[39]

Mark and Ervin's theory of aggression is primarily concerned with persons who exhibit this dyscontrol syndrome, but they also believe that their theory will have wider application once better diagnostic techniques are developed. The theory is based on the following evidence: (1) Animal research indicates that surgery and electrical stimulation of the limbic brain (a central portion of the brain) significantly alter the amount of aggressive or attack behavior, and (2) individuals with histories of violent rages who show abnormal electrical activity in the limbic brain have had their aggression curbed by psychosurgery. Mark and Ervin concede that environment, culture, and social experiences in general do play a role in structuring aggressive behavior. But they believe that such learning principally serves a programming function; it defines the degree to which particular situations will be perceived as threatening. The retrieval of learned experiences is a memory process, hence a brain process. As such, it is subject to distortion if the brain is malfunctioning:

> The kind of violent behavior related to brain malfunction may have its origins in the environment, but once the brain structure has been permanently affected, the violent behavior can no longer be modified by manipulating psychological or social influences. . . .
>
> Our past environment, once it is past, is no longer a sociological phenomenon. It is embedded in our brain and its use is dependent on the function or malfunction of the cerebral tissue.[40]

Thus Mark and Ervin do confront one of the objections leveled at most biological theories, such as the XYY syndrome: that the suggested relationship between a defect and behavior is overly simplistic in view of the complexity of the behavior involved. Nevertheless, there still exists considerable controversy over whether the stimulation or destruction of certain areas of the human brain results in predictable changes in behavior.[41] It is argued, in a manner reminiscent of the critiques of phrenology, that no specific and consistent human behavior results from psychosurgery and that the practice thus leaves the results as much to chance as to scientific predictability.

Assuming that psychosurgery can become a method of obtaining predictably controlled behavior, another serious issue remains: What and whose behavior should be controlled? Mark and Ervin believe the targets should be those engaging in "unacceptable violence" (a term they admit is plagued with problems), and they urge the development of "early-warning tests for violence." The Antisocial and Violent Behavior Branch of the National Institutes of Health (it really exists!) funded a research project that asked, "How Early Can We Tell? Predictors of Childhood Conduct Disorder and Adolescent Delinquency." The study concludes that it appears that some preschool predictors can be strong statistical predictors of later antisocial outcome. Due to the high rate of false positives among those children predicted to have antisocial outcomes, the usefulness of preschool behavioral predictors for selecting children for intensive early intervention efforts may be limited at present.[42]

Aside from the point that such predictive devices would truly set precedents in regard to human behavior, this approach sounds very much like a kind of neo-eugenics. As with any deterministic approach to deviance, there is a potential for the more powerful in a society to define who is "unacceptable" or "dangerous" on the basis of what they *might* do. Just as lobotomies and drugs were used to neutralize troublesome individuals in institutions, dissidents could be subdued through psychosurgery because their brains were "malfunctioning."

Psychosurgery should not be totally abandoned, however, especially in light of its successes in treating epilepsy and other neurological disorders. Brain-imaging technology may prove successful in reducing the suffering associated with depression and obsessive-compulsive disorders.[43] But its potential for misuse should not be ignored; it could be a powerful means for changing behavior. Under serious consideration not long ago were plans for implanting electrical relays in people's brains to provide continuous monitoring of their activities and to alter behavior:

> Dr. Barton L. Ingraham of the School of Criminology at the University of California at Berkeley [in 1974 suggested] that bugging the brain could provide not only continuous surveillance of those with "criminal tendencies" but also "automatic deterrence or 'blocking' of the criminal activity by electronic stimulation of the brain prior to the commission of the act." Dr. Ingraham concedes that the use of [electronic stimulation of the brain] would "require a Government with virtually total powers" but sees a number of things in its favor, including the fact that it would be "completely effective" and "relatively cheap." As for the economy of the matter, an electrical engineer named Curtiss Schafer agrees: "The once-human being thus controlled would be the cheapest of machines to create and operate."[44]

Emerging Biology-Based Theories

As our scientific tools improve rapidly, so does our understanding of relationships between behavior and the biological environment in the human body. Recent success in decoding human DNA has been extremely exciting scientifically, as is the developing ability to recombine DNA molecules. It is possible that DNA links to unacceptable levels of aggression, addiction tendency, or other criminogenic influences may be forthcoming. Recent studies, sometimes appearing under the nomenclature of *biochemical* or *psychobiological* theory, have investigated the possible relationships between delinquent behavior and vitamin deficiency, hormone productivity, diet and nutrition, pollution in the environment, and physical injury and trauma.

Abram Hoffer reported as early as 1976[45] that B vitamin deficiencies were associated with disruptive behavior in children. Subsequent studies in this area have not been scientifically conclusive, although the possibility of links between vitamins and delinquency are very interesting.

Testosterone, the hormone associated with the development of male characteristics, has been the subject of extensive behavioral research in recent years. In 1976 Rada, Laws, and Kellner[46] found a strong correlation between testosterone levels and the level of violence present in forcible rape events. Reiss and Roth,[47] in their 1993 work entitled *Understanding and Preventing Violence,* implied that there were hereditary links to testosterone productivity and maintenance levels in the body and that abnormally high levels were significantly common to violent male sex offenders. Their conclusions were tempered somewhat by the covariance observed with alcohol abuse, which is, of course, also associated with violent crime.

Serotonin, a chemical that has an important presence in the human brain, is thought to inhibit impulsive, aggressive responses to irritating stimuli.[48] Although we certainly have a lot to learn about the whole *neurotransmission* network in the brain, research has shown that low serotonin levels reduce the ability to resist violent impulses.

Ongoing research involving relationships between behavior and allergies, thyroid imbalances, and blood sugar irregularities had shown interesting, although inconclusive linkages. Biological approaches in criminology perhaps hold the greatest promise for the future.

Personality Defects and Attributes

We turn now from approaches based primarily on biological determinism to approaches based upon mental processes and characteristics; the most appropriate term embracing these approaches is *psychogenic determinism.* As with the theories discussed previously, the causes of deviant behavior are considered as being *in* the mind or personality and, as such, are not measurable through any physical characteristic such as body type, brain waves, or genetic structure. These conditions might be personality factors that directly result in deviant behavior or simply factors that contribute to deviance whenever individuals possessing them are in particular situations or environments. Some psychogenic theories define deviant individuals as "sick," "emotionally disturbed," or "psychopathic." In any case the deviants are considered unlike nondeviants and are distinguishable from them.

The beginnings of psychogenic determinism can be found in the writings of the English physician James Cowles Prichard (1786–1848). Prichard believed that a major portion of crime could be explained by a disorder he called *moral insanity.* This differed from ordinary insanity, which involved disorders in intellectual faculties. Moral insanity was madness consisting in a morbid perversion of the natural feelings, affections, inclinations, temper, habits, moral dispositions, and natural impulses, without any remarkable disorder or defect of the intellect or knowing and reasoning faculties, and particularly without any insane illusion or hallucination.[49]

The concept of moral insanity had a long and stormy history, but of greatest interest to us here is an offshoot that, unlike moral insanity, is still very much alive.

Psychopathy

The term *psychopathy,* which was first applied to deviants in 1896, referred to the behavior of a group of individuals who apparently committed crimes upon impulse with no motive except perhaps some satisfaction from the act itself.[50] Over time, the concept has undergone considerable elaboration, including a new name, *sociopathy*. The introduction of the latter term is not meant to confuse the reader. We mention it because the term is frequently used as a synonym for *psychopathy*. Sometimes it is considered akin to but different from psychopathy, and other times one or the other term is ignored. To compound the confusion, the second and third editions of the American Psychiatric Association's *Diagnostic and Statistical Manual of Mental Disorders* mention neither, although a later edition contains an entry for *antisocial personality,* which is reminiscent of both terms:

> The essential feature of this disorder is a pattern of irresponsible and antisocial behavior beginning in childhood or early adolescence and continuing into adulthood. . . . Lying, stealing, truancy, vandalism, initiating fights, running away from home, and physical cruelty to animals are typical childhood signs. In adulthood, the antisocial pattern continues, and may include failure to honor financial obligations, to function as a responsible parent or to plan ahead, and an inability to sustain consistent work behavior. These people fail to conform to social norms and repeatedly perform antisocial acts that are grounds for arrest, such as destroying property, harassing others, stealing, and having an illegal occupation. . . . Finally, they generally have no remorse about the effects of their behavior on others; they may even feel justified in having hurt and mistreated others.[51]

The traits attributed to the psychopath have been many; one author counted 55.[52] The most careful compilation is that of Hervey M. Cleckley, who lists 16, including superficial charm, unreliability, insincerity, lack of remorse or shame, inability to learn by experience, incapacity for love, impersonal sex life, and a lack of any life plan.[53] In practice, few concepts have proven to be so vague, so confusing, and so useless as that of psychopathy. According to Michael Hakeem, "Without exception, on every point regarding psychopathic personality, psychiatrists present varying or contradictory views." The following are questions that Hakeem asks about the psychopathic personality and the range of answers he finds in the psychiatric literature:

1. Is psychopathic personality a clinical entity?—Yes and No.
2. Is psychopathy a serious condition?—Yes and No.
3. In what proportion is psychopathy found among criminals?—Anywhere from 0 to 100 percent.
4. What types of crimes do psychopaths commit?—Serious violent offenses are "typical"; usually the offenses are "relatively minor."
5. What causes psychopathy?—Endocrine dysfunction to cerebral trauma to blood sugar to poverty to broken homes to inadequate child training.
6. Can the psychopath be diagnosed?—Yes and No.
7. Can the psychopath be treated?—Yes and No.[54]

In general, psychopathy has served as a "garbage can" diagnosis. Individuals are so labeled as a matter of convenience when they do not readily fit other diagnostic categories, and a diagnosis of psychopathy more likely reflects the particular orientation of the psychiatrist than any peculiarity of the patient.

The whole concept of psychopathy might be lightly dismissed if it were simply a footnote in the history of attempts to explain criminality. Unfortunately, it was taken very seriously. Despite the fact that there was no agreement upon a definition of a psychopath, no consensus on what proportion of the criminal population was psychopathic, and a continuing debate over whether the concept was even a valid one, between 1937 and 1949, 29 states and the District of Columbia passed special legislation directed at the psychopathic offenders involved in sex crimes. The laws provided for indeterminate confinement and psychiatric treatment until the offenders were "cured" according to psychiatric judgment. The basis of such judgment remains a mystery since treatment was directed at a condition whose very existence was questionable.

We shall return to the issue of sex psychopath laws and their relatives in subsequent chapters. For now, the reader may consider them as yet another example of the dangers when scientists claim they can distinguish the bad folks from the good.[55] Scientists have not yet successfully located any attribute—whether a "defective" gene or a measure of psychopathy—that positively predicts the deviant behavior of any individual, although they continue to try.[56]

Traits and Thinking

All of us recognize and understand the phrase "It takes a particular kind of person to do that," whatever "that" might be: entering an occupation, leaving a religion, quitting school at midsemester, or building birdhouses. And we have all experienced the blind date described to us as "not real good-looking, but someone with a good personality whom everybody in the dorm likes." "Kind of person" and "personality" are terms we use in acknowledging the fact that people are seldom alike in their reactions to certain situations, in their moods, in their self-assurance, in their concern over the feelings of others, and in their readiness to display their emotions.

It seems logical that if personality plays an important role in everyday living, it should at least be a factor in being deviant. Some formidable problems stand in the way of ascertaining the exact nature of that role, however. Personality cannot be encompassed in a single phrase. You would not be satisfied to describe yourself or your friends in that fashion, preferring instead to list a number of attributes or traits. So too, researchers in the area of personality must deal with an often bewildering number of traits, only some of which may prove to be key variables in explaining certain kinds of behavior. Furthermore, these same researchers must find ways in which to measure those traits, a difficult problem in itself. In practice, no researcher would claim to have an instrument for measuring personality in all possible facets. Instead, the researcher relies upon tests to measure a limited number of traits considered to be relevant for the purpose at hand.

In 1950 Karl F. Schuessler and Donald R. Cressey published a survey of research that had attempted to distinguish, by means of personality tests, between persons found guilty of delinquencies or crimes and persons who were noncriminal and nondelinquent. As we have pointed out, this type of comparison is based on the questionable assumption that deviants and nondeviants really differ in their behavior. The survey covered the period from 1925 to 1948 and examined 113 studies using 30 different tests. The latter figure will give you some idea of the variety of ways to approach personality traits.

The authors found that only 42 percent of the studies showed any difference between the two groups. They concluded that the evidence favored the view that personality traits are distributed in the criminal population in about the same way as in the general population. . . . This overlap makes it impossible to predict individual behavior from an individual test score.

One other conclusion is worthy of mention because of its applicability to any studies attempting to interpret personality differences as causes of behavior:

> The results of this method do not indicate whether criminal behavior is the result of a certain personality trait or whether the trait is the result of criminal experiences. In other words, whether a given trait was present at the onset of a delinquent career or whether the trait developed during that career is not shown.[57]

Thus with any deviant or group of deviants, their personality traits, attitudes, and beliefs may not have contributed to their behavior but rather may have resulted from their experiences as deviants. This would seem to be particularly pertinent to those involved in the behavior over a long time who have undergone reactions to their behavior from family, friends, police, treatment practitioners, and so on. This is not to say that such traits, attitudes, or beliefs necessarily do not exist prior to involvement in a particular form of behavior, but that the reader should view with caution any claims about their predisposing individuals to deviance.[58]

A similar survey of research between 1950 and 1965 was conducted by Gordon P. Waldo and Simon Dinitz.[59] This consisted of 94 studies using 29 different tests, only 4 of which had been represented in the Schuessler-Cressey survey. Eighty-one percent of the studies reported finding differences between groups, compared with the previous 42 percent. Although this result appears to be an improvement, the authors expressed considerable caution, particularly regarding the instrument that most consistently finds differences between delinquents and nondelinquents: the Minnesota Multiphasic Personality Inventory (MMPI). Originally designed to aid diagnosis in psychiatric clinics, the MMPI does not provide an adequate theoretical explanation of delinquency, nor is it clear what it measures. These problems, plus the continuing use of samples inappropriate to locating predisposing factors, led Waldo and Dinitz to conclude that

> although the results appear more positive than they did a few years ago, in terms of the number of studies showing differences between criminals and noncriminals, the findings are far from conclusive. The conflict over the role of personality in criminality has not been resolved.[60]

In 1976 a study was published that many believe does specify the role of personality in criminality. Unambiguously entitled *The Criminal Personality,* it reports the results of 14 years of research on 240 "hard-core" criminals who were psychiatric patients at a hospital in Washington, DC. The authors, Samuel Yochelson and Stanton E. Samenow, dismiss environmental and social factors as trivial influences; they assert that criminals mold their environments and are characterized by 52 "thinking errors." These constitute "criminal thinking patterns," which begin as early as age 3 when the child displays several disagreeable habits, including showing "inordinate curiosity about sexual matters": "he peeps through cracks in doors and peers through keyholes to catch glimpses of mother, sister, or a friend's mother or sister as she dresses, bathes, or uses the toilet."[61]

Besides growing up to be "irresponsible" in their sex lives (indiscriminately selecting sexual partners, emphasizing conquest and gratification, and so on), criminals are characterized as being

1. Inordinately fearful of put-downs and injury
2. Chronically angry
3. Inflexibly proud of themselves
4. Habitually lying
5. Lacking in trust
6. Deferring responsible activities such as writing letters, paying bills, filing tax returns, and so on

The Criminal Personality was enthusiastically received by the media with headlines such as "You Can Stop Feeling Sorry for Criminals," "Criminals Are Born, Not Made," and "Sam Yochelson Says: Criminals Are Not Crazy or Otherwise Deprived. They Simply Prefer to Be Criminals."[62] But the study is not the major breakthrough proclaimed by the press. It suffers the same defects plaguing attempts to isolate a deviant "type." The following criticisms can be applied to personality studies generally:

1. **Sampling problems.** As was mentioned in connection with research on physical characteristics, there is no reason to assume that people who are officially designated as deviant are representative of others who deviate but escape the label. Yochelson and Samenow's research is especially vulnerable on this point. Their sample of patients in a hospital for mentally disordered criminals could be expected to contain individuals with problems in "thinking." Do the results mean that most criminals—whether murderers, tax cheaters, shoplifters, or bookies—are bad thinkers? Or do they simply mean that among criminals, there are some bad thinkers who are referred to psychiatric institutions? And what do we know about the proportion of bad thinkers among "noncriminals"? Without a control group for comparison, there is no way of knowing whether bad thinking is unique to criminals.

2. **Relativity of deviance.** Studies attempting to link aspects of personality to specific forms of deviance must confront the problem of the relativity of deviance. A specific form of behavior is deviant only in terms of its context. Being violent, for example, is not inherently deviant. The child abuser is jailed for being violent; the football player is paid for it. In one context dishonesty may be "cheating"; in another it may be "good business."

Two psychological researchers, Starke R. Hathaway and Elio D. Monachesi, who pioneered use of the MMPI as a predictor of delinquent behavior, were well aware of this problem of relative definition. They point out the fallacy of attempting to explain such behavior by personality alone:

> What is and what is not called delinquent behavior varies with social values—even killing and pillage have been condoned in some cultures. Men in our culture have been called heroes for killing other men and for destruction of property when such acts were committed

in conduct of war. Acts like these are endemic in all cultures and even though we may deplore them, the fact remains that in our society, policemen carry guns and shoot to kill, ardent proponents of causes may destroy property, and organized crime, if not officially accepted, at least gives a subcultural sanction to violence. Our teen-agers live with conflict and contrasts. . . . There are many adults whose antisocial behavior provides examples for uncritical emulation by young people. . . . Often the family itself approves of behavior among its members that the surrounding society considers to be objectionable. . . . The delinquent behavior for many of the youngsters studied probably occurred so naturally that no specifically characteristic personality pattern existed as a precursor.[63]

3. The cause-and-effect problem. Personality characteristics found to be associated with deviance may be an *effect,* not a cause. That is, certain personality traits may develop as a consequence of long-term involvement with behaving or being identified and treated as a deviant. An alcoholic may lack self-assurance, but the relationship between such lack and alcoholism could be explained in contradictory ways. Does a lack of self-assurance lead to a reliance on the sense of well-being that alcohol provides? Or do the problems stemming from excessive alcohol use produce feelings of uncertainty and dependence? That is not to say that specific emotional difficulties or personality characteristics do not contribute to specific behavioral patterns. But being deviant involves a whole tangle of contributory factors such as opportunity, encouragement by others, and a variety of experiences that may either override or accentuate the effects of personality variables.

Unconscious Motivation

Anyone reading the psychiatric literature concerning deviant behavior will quickly discover that there are many approaches and theories, some of which seem to have little in common. Our purpose in this section is to acquaint the reader with one general theoretical approach associated with the work of Sigmund Freud (1856–1939) and a branch of psychiatry known as *psychoanalysis*. Although few unreservedly adhere to Freud's teachings today, his work provides a basis to which much of today's psychiatric writing can be ultimately traced.

The psychiatric approach is based upon the following propositions:

1. The human personality consists of three parts: the id, the ego, and the superego. The *id,* which is the source of all instinctual demands and drives, such as the sexual drive, forms the basis of all behavior. The id is present at birth and operates primarily below the level of awareness, that is, it is *unconscious*. The drives are unrestrained at birth and, in their primitive state, are not compatible with living in society. But as children grow and become more aware of their environment, they develop a means to control the id in the form of an *ego.* The ego is a decision-maker that is not present in infancy but develops with awareness of one's surroundings. The ego considers both the realities of environment and the demands of the id in order to seek the greatest possible gratification without encountering painful reaction from the environment. The ego may be thought of as the conscious aspect of the personality. The *superego* develops as children begin adolescence and is the result of all the learning processes concerning morality and ethics. It acts as a restraint upon the id by calling forth the ideals and standards that the person has learned. The superego may be thought of as one's *conscience* and is partially conscious.

2. All behavior has a purpose. Much behavior is a direct result of the operation of the ego, but other behavior stems from less conscious sources. Conflicts may develop between the id and superego at the unconscious level and result in behavior that is *symbolic* of the ongoing unconscious conflicts. The most famous example of such a conflict is the Oedipus complex, which, according to Freudian theory, occurs in all males. This complex concerns the boy's id urging him to have sexual intercourse with his mother and to murder his father. The superego will have none of this, of course, and the ego feels guilty over the whole mess. If this conflict is not adequately resolved but repressed, the individual may engage in substitute behavior in an attempt to resolve the conflict. Examples here are assaulting somebody as a substitute for doing away with one's father and committing political crimes as a means of venting hatred against a father figure (the state) without feeling guilt. Generally, guilt is involved somewhat differently in the psychoanalytic explanation of crime: suffering from a sense of guilt, a person commits a crime while unconsciously wanting to be apprehended and punished for both the crime and the desires coming from the id. In any event, criminal behavior is interpreted in terms of unconscious motivation.

3. All behavior can ultimately be explained in terms of early life experiences. Since the heart of the psychoanalytic approach lies in the development of the ego and superego and their ability to restrain the id, the cause of deviant behavior is presumed to stem from conflicts initiated during that development. To ascertain the nature of these events, psychoanalysts ask patients to relate very early experiences; the psychoanalysts then, in turn, document the cause of the behavior by interpreting those experiences.

Of the three propositions just outlined, only the specific references to the id, the ego, and the superego may not be immediately evident in contemporary psychoanalytic literature concerning deviance. The assumption concerning unconscious motivations stemming from guilt over mental conflicts is very much in evidence. It is on this very issue that psychoanalysis is most vulnerable to criticism. Although its practitioners claim that psychoanalysis is a science, the fact that it depends upon unconscious factors, symbolic behavior, and the interpretation of someone else's recalled events places the approach beyond the boundaries of scientific demonstration. It is a tenet of good science that a theory can be proven wrong. In this instance there is no way to disprove a psychoanalyst's interpretation of a life story, because that story is unheard by anyone else. As long as the interpretations are subjective, psychoanalysis remains unscientific.[64]

Aside from the foregoing criticism, the concentration on conflict-producing experiences, especially early occurring in the family context, to the exclusion of other learning, further weakens the psychoanalytic case. Although psychiatrists vary in the weight they assign to social factors, the emphasis remains on experiences resulting in psychic conflict. The following hypotheses dealing with sex offenders illustrate this emphasis in the psychiatric approach:

1. There is a specific kind of psychosexual trauma, occurring at some point in the early developmental experience of the individual, that makes a satisfactory, adequately pleasurable, adult heterosexual adjustment impossible. As a result, these individuals turn to other, less mature, or variant sexual patterns of behavior in their attempts to seek sexual gratification.

2. There is a failure or distortion of the mechanisms of conscience formation that permits these individuals to act out their aberrant sexual patterns, rather than use some other method of handling the sexual conflicts, such as fantasy or sublimation [diverting the energy of impulse to acceptable behavior].[65]

What is ignored here is that all behavior, whether it involves engaging in homosexual activity or singing an operatic aria, requires learning experiences, including the acquiring of rationales justifying the behavior. *How* to behave and *why* to behave are often far too complicated to be attributed solely to some subconscious proddings.

Sociobiology—Trailblazing or Backtracking?

It should be apparent by now that practically every aspect of the human physiological and mental being has been proposed as a link to deviant behavior. It is difficult to imagine how genes can doom one to deviancy unless appropriate opportunities and social situations are likewise predestined. For example, a person presumably could be loaded with "predispositions" to violence. But we cannot predict or explain the violent behavior without predicting or explaining the circumstances triggering the violence. To complicate matters, the social *context* of an act determines its deviance. If a person is violent in a bar brawl, he is a criminal; if he is violent on a battlefield, he is heroic. Thus even if one could predict violence, one would not necessarily be predicting deviance.

Despite past failures, attention to associating biological factors with deviant behavior underwent vigorous recasting and revival in the 1970s. During that period, there was a renewed interest concerning the influence of biology on human behavior generally, not just deviant behavior. This interest is exemplified by the popular success of two books by Edward O. Wilson: *Sociobiology: The New Synthesis* (1975) and *On Human Nature* (1978).[66]

Wilson defines *sociobiology* as

the systematic study of the biological basis of all forms of social behavior, in all kinds of organisms, including man. . . . [It is a] hybrid discipline that incorporates knowledge from ethology (the naturalistic study of whole patterns of behavior), ecology (the study of the relationships of organisms to their environment), and genetics in order to derive general principles concerning the biological properties of entire societies.[67]

As you can see, Wilson conceives of sociobiology as a science with a broad scope: entire societies. Nevertheless, his general assumptions underlie the work of those attempting to apply biology to explaining deviant behavior. Wilson assumes that human social behavior is genetically determined to the extent that biology defines human learning potential. The human mind is not a blank that simply records and assimilates experiences; instead it is biologically programmed to accept certain experiences while rejecting others.

Consider Wilson's discussion of the incest taboo, the one instance in which he deals directly with a form of deviant behavior. Wilson asks, "Why do instances of sexual intercourse between parents and their offspring and between brothers and sisters result in sanctions within every society?" The sociobiological explanation is based on consequences resulting from inbreeding, such as higher infant mortality and the greater likelihood of mental and physical defects. But, says Wilson, the cultural aversion to incest is not a rational decision based on experience and observation of these consequences; the aversion is innate:

> The ultimate cause [of the incest taboo] is the loss of genetic fitness that results from incest. It is a fact that incestuously produced children leave fewer descendants. The biological hypothesis states that individuals with a genetic predisposition for bond exclusion and incest avoidance contribute more genes to the next generation. Natural selection has probably ground away along these lines for thousands of generations, and for that reason human beings intuitively avoid incest.[68]

Wilson conceives of social learning as a process influenced by genetic adaptation. This adaptation—the product of evolution—controls learning to the extent that people are genetically prepared to learn some things and genetically restrained from learning other things. Wilson's concern with social learning underlines the major difference between the new and the old biological theories on deviance. Gone is the simple equation A → Deviant behavior, where A = some biological factor such as the XYY chromosome syndrome or a particular body type. In its place is a yet unformulated equation in which biological, psychological, and social factors combine. Heredity and the social environment (or genetics and learning, if you wish) are not regarded as competing perspectives but as interacting components.

More specifically, how is sociobiology used in studying deviant behavior? Researchers are going in many directions, but let us consider the approach of Sarnoff A. Mednick. Consistent with the sociobiological perspective, Mednick argues that law-abiding behavior must be learned; it is not inherent that people will conform. Mednick feels that in most instances of deviant behavior—perhaps as high as 99 percent of criminal offenses—the sporadic deviance is due to socioeconomic and situational factors that briefly interfere with or neutralize learning. Of primary interest to Mednick is the small minority of individuals whose nonconformity is highly repetitive and appears to have no social cause. For these individuals, says Mednick, something is defective in the way in which they learn to inhibit antisocial behavior.

Mednick bases his theory on the assumption that people learn to conform because they are afraid not to. This type of learning is known as *passive avoidance*. One avoids punishment or fear by *not* doing something for which he or she was previously punished. The sequence goes like this:

1. A person contemplates a deviant act.
2. He or she experiences fear because of previous punishment for such an act.
3. He or she does not carry out the act.
4. The fear dissipates. As it does, the dissipation *reinforces* step 3.

According to Mednick:

> The speed and size of reinforcement determine its effectiveness. An effective reinforcement is one that is delivered *immediately* after the relevant response. . . . The faster the reduction of fear, the faster the delivery of reinforcement. The fear response is, to a large extent, controlled by the autonomic nervous system (ANS). . . . If [a person] has an ANS that charac-

teristically recovers very quickly from fear, then he will receive a quick and large reinforcement and learn inhibition quickly. If he has an ANS that recovers very slowly, he will receive a slow, small reinforcement and learn to inhibit the [response] very slowly, if at all. This orientation would predict that (holding constant critical extraindividual variables such as social status, crime training, and poverty level) those who commit asocial acts would be characterized by slow autonomic recovery. The slower the recovery, the more serious and repetitive the asocial behavior predicted.[69]

As Mednick points out, his is a learning theory. It is a *social* learning theory to the extent that people's behavior is influenced by previous reactions of others. It is a *biological* theory to the extent that biological factors (in this case, the ANS) regulate the efficiency of the learning process.

There are many other sociobiological approaches; although they differ in which biological factor is emphasized, the approaches themselves generally fall into one of three categories:

1. Evolutionary processes. These theories are concerned with the long-term development of specific behaviors over the course of many generations. Wilson's thesis on how the incest taboo evolved is an example. It is doubtful that such theories will have much impact on the study of deviant behavior; they are too broad in scope and too speculative to provide researchable questions. At most, the theories sensitize us to the manner in which biological factors may affect behavior.

2. Genetic differences. These theories are concerned with how behavior is influenced by hereditary factors that are more immediate than those formed during evolution. Contemporary proponents of this approach are unlikely to claim the Jukes and Kallikaks as evidence. But they rely heavily on family and twin studies to demonstrate that some traits and behaviors may be inherited. Of particular interest is the hypothesis that certain mental disorders often recur among generations of the same family. Is there a genetic predisposition to mental disorder, or is it caused by something else?

3. Neurophysiological differences. These theories concern a wide range of physiological factors that might influence human behavior. They include hormone imbalance, vitamin deficiency, brain malfunction (e.g., Mark and Ervin's theory of aggression discussed earlier), or any organic aspect that might interfere with learning or behaving. Of course, Mednick's thesis about the impact of the ANS on the speed of reinforcement is an example.[70]

In fairness to sociobiology, it may be too early for it to prove its point. But even before research results begin pouring in, sociobiology must face some nagging questions if today's biology is to be more successful than yesterday's in understanding deviance.

First, can sociobiological explanations accommodate the relativity of deviant behavior? Whether a behavior is "deviant" depends upon the context in which it occurs. Earlier, we mentioned violence. By itself it is not deviant; that is a matter of time and situation. Thus, to be of help, sociobiology must go beyond explaining individuals' violence; it must assist in distinguishing socially *disapproved* from socially approved violence.

Second, because deviant behavior is so diverse and so variable in its complexity, can sociobiology help in explaining more than a minute portion? It is one thing to seek biological factors related to seemingly uncontrolled outbursts of aggression. But should the same factors be investigated to explain the calculated murdering of competitors in a narcotics war? Or an engineer's decision to dispose of the company's poisonous wastes in a lake used for a city's drinking water? Or a woman's murdering her husband who had been brutally mistreating her for years? These are all instances of violence in one way or another, but they are also extremely different. How many types of brain malfunctions or variations in the ANS need to be found to make sense of it all? As Albert K. Cohen so aptly writes:

> When we remind ourselves of what we mean by deviant behavior, or more narrowly by crime and delinquency—e.g., check forging, street fighting, income tax evasion, highway speeding, drug use, rent law violation, police corruption—we must realize that we are dealing with an enormous variety of behaviors as different from one another as filling prescriptions, selling used cars, and teaching algebra. The most reasonable expectation, it seems to us, is that the linkages of biology to the various forms of deviance will be as various, indirect, and remote as its linkages to the varieties of conforming behavior.[71]

Third, to what use will the findings of sociobiology be put? Despite claims that sociobiology is an integration of biology with the social sciences, the area's research predominantly consists of attempts to distinguish deviants from nondeviants. Are sociobiologists embarking on another futile search reminiscent of Lombroso's, Hooton's, and countless others' efforts to find uniqueness among wrongdoers? Perhaps. But suppose that some distinguishing neurophysiological quirk is found. (One early assumption can be made: This quirk will *not* be found among those holding law degrees, MBAs, or large blocks of stock from among the top thousand companies.) Will the quirk be the basis of just another facile explanation that justifies the use of inexpensive control measures while ignoring social conditions of poverty and inequalities?

Sociobiologists vehemently deny that they seek simplistic biological explanations, but the policies for handling deviants do not depend upon the good intentions of scientists. Policies depend upon the interests of politicians. Imagine a congressional hearing in which a scientist testifies that he or she has discovered in some persons a "quirk" that is related to violent outbursts. But these outbursts usually occur only when the persons are exposed to conditions from poor nutrition and economic frustrations found among the poor. Not wishing to tamper with the rights of individuals, the scientist recommends a program to upgrade nutritional and economic conditions for the poor. But a budget-minded member of Congress asks, "If we can identify those with this quirk, why not have a program to find them and deal with the matter more directly?" I will let the reader speculate on which alternative is more likely to be adopted. While it is important that scientists pursue whatever avenues they believe might add to our understanding of human behavior, there are potential dangers and social costs too important to be ignored. Whether sociobiology can add to knowledge and avoid biology's earlier pitfalls remains to be seen.[72]

The Rise of Social Determinism

At this point, we will retreat in time again to gain an historic understanding of a sociology-based perspective on criminology theory that would ultimately be dominated by scholars from leading universities in the United States.

With the decline in academic acceptance of the free will position of Cesare Beccaria and the classical school, the determinist position emerged in the form of two fundamental approaches to the study of deviance. One sought the causes *within the deviant;* the goal was to discover individual characteristics contributing to becoming involved in deviant behavior. The other approach stressed the importance of *social factors* as causes of deviance; the goal was to explain both the existence of deviant behavior and its distribution in society. In short, the first approach was concerned with explaining the deviant by means of biological and psychological positivism; the second was concerned with explaining the varying amounts of deviance between groups by means of *social determinism.*

As was mentioned earlier, the first biological positivist was Franz Gall, who began publishing in 1807. The earliest social determinists were a French lawyer, André-Michel Guerry, whose initial publication appeared in 1833, and a Belgian mathematician and astronomer, Lambert A. J. Quetelet. Today, Guerry and Quetelet usually are classified under such varied headings as "moral statisticians," "cartographic school," and "human ecology." As these terms indicate, they conducted their research by analyzing official statistics on variables such as suicides, educational levels, illegitimate births, crimes committed, and age and sex of criminal offenders within given geographic areas for specific time periods.[73] From such analyses both Guerry and Quetelet noted two phenomena: first, that types and amount of deviance vary according to geographic region and, second, that annual recorded deviance within a specific area varies little from one year to another.[74] These findings led Quetelet to speculate that an "annual budget of crime" exists:

> This remarkable constancy with which the same crimes appear annually in the same order, drawing down on their perpetrators the same punishments, in the same proportions, is a singular fact. . . . I have never failed annually to repeat that there is a *budget* which we pay with frightful regularity—it is that of prison, dungeons, and scaffolds. . . . We might even predict annually how many individuals will stain their hands with the blood of their fellow-men, how many will be forgers, how many will deal in poison pretty nearly in the same way as we may foretell the annual births and deaths.[75]

Quetelet denied that a particular individual's future conduct could be so predicted, just as you could not predict his or her death from a table of mortality rates for age groups. But mortality tables do provide accurate estimations of the number of persons annually who will die within a group. The regularity and predictability of group rates of crime, suicide, and so on presumably place such behavior beyond the realm of purely individual conduct. Although better known for his claims concerning the effects of climate and seasons on crime, Quetelet also found that age, sex, occupation, alcohol use, and heterogeneity of population were related to a "propensity" toward crime.

But Quetelet believed that the blame for crime lay ultimately with society. Although humans may have free will, that will becomes neutralized in society, and behavior emerges as a product of that society. Quetelet argued that fluctuations in rates of deviance will occur as a result of substantial changes in basic social, economic, and political conditions:

> Society includes within itself the germs of all the crimes committed, and at the same time the necessary facilities for their development. It is the social state, in some measure, which prepares these crimes, and the criminal is merely the instrument to execute them. Every social

state supposes, then, a certain number and a certain order of crimes, these being merely the necessary consequences of its organization.[76]

Thus arrived social determinism as an explanation of deviance. Throughout the nineteenth century, however, enthusiasm for this approach was never overwhelming; eventually it was to be the biological determinism of Cesare Lombroso that provided the greater impact upon the intellectual climate. Social determinism's lack of popularity lay in its implication that those in power within society might play no small role in creating the conditions that cause deviance. Nevertheless, the nineteenth century spawned two social interpretations of deviance that were to have a profound influence upon twentieth-century thought. The first concerned *economic influences,* the second *anomie.*

Economic Influences

An economic interpretation of deviance was an aspect of the work of Quetelet when he, for example, considered the price of grain to be a crucial variable in the operation of society. Similar conjectures provided impetus for several studies in Europe and the United States that attempted to find relationships between crime and a variety of economic factors such as the prices of various grains, business cycles, and income levels of convicted persons. Just how economic conditions are related to deviance has been the subject of a multitude of interpretations.[77] For our purposes, we will consider two: the effect of economic structure as seen by Karl Marx and Willem Bonger, and the effect of pauperism as seen by Frank W. Blackmar.

Karl Marx

Karl Marx's (1818–1883) best-known works are the *Communist Manifesto* (1848), co-authored with Friedrich Engels, and *Capital: A Critique of Political Economy* (1867). In these and other works Marx developed an economic interpretation of societies. He claimed that all social phenomena—legal codes, political institutions, religion, ethics, the arts, the family—are products of a society's economy in the form of its *means of production.* In a capitalistic economy there is private ownership of the means of production, distribution, and exchange of wealth; as a consequence, there exists intense competition, resulting in the exploitation of the *proletariat* (working class) by the *bourgeoisie* (owners and controllers of the means of production).

According to Marx, the continual competition requires that minimal wages be paid for labor; the bourgeoisie becomes richer and richer, and the proletariat becomes poorer and more miserable. The conditions of poverty and continued exploitation produce all forms of social problems. A classless society, free of economic exploitation and its attendant evils, will emerge only when the economic system is ultimately destroyed by the proletariat in violent revolution.

Marx was proposing a grand theory of the evolutionary process of contemporary industrial society. He never actually spelled out a theory of deviance, but inferences can be made, and his writings have influenced students of deviance in at least two respects.

First, Marx's writings provide a basis for viewing deviance as a product of social conflict. According to Marxist thought, deviance cannot be eliminated by adjustments within capitalist societies; deviance is inherent in capitalism, and only the total destruction of the economic substructure will provide a remedy. Marx saw capitalist society as comprising a one-sided conflict between groups. From his perspective deviance was an expression of a struggle in which the economically powerless attempt to cope with the exploitation and poverty imposed upon them. Marx's interpreters claim that he portrayed the deviant as "demoralized and brutalized by the day-to-day experience of employment (and unemployment) under industrial capitalism . . . but still able to grasp at the necessities of life through theft and graft."[78]

So far, the economic class struggle has not resulted in the proletarian revolution predicted by Marx. Nevertheless, his conception of society as consisting of conflicting economic groups remains an important contribution to social theory. Political, military, economic, and legislative actions are not the products of harmonious decision making by concerned and affected parties. Often such actions are at best matters of compromise; at worst they represent only the opinions of the powerful and may be detrimental to, or against the wishes of, a sizable segment of the population.

Second, Marx points to the interrelationship of the deviant and nondeviant aspects of society. With a touch of sarcasm he shows how deviance serves many purposes in support of the existing society. Without deviance, police, judges, juries, and law professors would have no jobs; the mechanical inventions derived from innovations in torture would be undiscovered; and the fields of locksmithing, engraving of monetary instruments, and chemical detection of illegal adulterations of products would all remain unadvanced. Furthermore,

> the criminal breaks the monotony and everyday security of bourgeois life. In this way he keeps it from stagnation, and gives rise to that uneasy tension and agility without which even the spur of competition would get blunted. Thus he gives a stimulus to the productive forces. While crime takes a part of the superfluous population off the labor market and thus reduces competition among the laborers—up to a certain point preventing wages from falling below the minimum—the struggle against crime absorbs another part of this population. Thus the criminal comes in as one of those natural "counterweights" which bring about a correct balance and open up a whole perspective of "useful" occupations.[79]

It should be noted that some writers object to classifying Marx as an economic determinist. They claim that he conceived of humans as both "determining" (i.e., having free will) and "determined."[80] We are deliberately going to sidestep this debate by emphasizing that Marx did focus on economics as the determinant of all aspects of social life and that he proposed that society be reformed by reforming its economics. To this extent, he appropriately can be regarded as an economic determinist. In the next chapter we shall see that contemporary Marxists deal more with economic causation than with human rationality in trying to explain deviant behavior. In short, the enduring legacy of Marx lies in his thesis that society's foundation is its economic structure.

Willem Bonger

The first author to suggest a grand-scale Marxist theory of crime was the Dutch scholar Willem Bonger (1876–1940). The thrust of his argument is outlined by the following propositions:

1. Notions of what constitutes immoral behavior and crime change with changes in the social structure.
2. Behaviors prohibited by the criminal law are those harmful to the interests of the powerful. Although some law may protect both the upper and lower classes, rarely will an act be punished if it does not injure the interest of the upper class.
3. The capitalist system is held together by force, not by the consensus of all groups. Thus relationships are based on exploitation and force, not on cooperation and trust.
4. Humans are basically pleasure-seeking, but pleasures in capitalist societies require lots of money. Consequently, *egoism* (selfishness) is stimulated. In their pursuit of pleasure, both the bourgeoisie and the proletariat become prone to crime as they lose compassion and a sense of responsibility toward others.
5. Poverty resulting from capitalism prompts crime to the extent that (a) it creates a desperate need for food and other life necessities and (b) economic advantage is equated with a person's intrinsic superiority.
6. Crime also results when there is a perceived opportunity to gain an advantage through illegal means and/or when opportunities to achieve pleasure are closed off by a biased legal system.
7. Capitalism is characterized by the conditions described. Such conditions will ultimately be eliminated by socialism.[81]

Thus, according to Bonger, capitalism with its competition and its subordinate class struggling for the necessities of life weakens "social feelings" and encourages unrestrained egoism:

> This state of things especially stifles men's social instincts; it develops, on the part of those with power, the spirit of domination, and of insensibility to the ill of others, while it awakens jealousy and servility on the part of those who depend upon them.[82]

Bonger's theory brings to our attention the importance of conflicts of interest within society as they affect both the formulation and the enforcement of law. Unrecognized by his theory, however, is the fact that conflicts of interest are neither limited to economic matters nor restricted to a two-party struggle between those who do and those who do not control the wealth. The owners of economic power in the United States, for example, do not exercise total control over the justice system. The system is subject to varying influences by interest groups whose power does not necessarily derive from control over means of production but over votes. Furthermore, Bonger's theory oversimplifies the sources of deviant behavior. The link proposed between egoism and deviance ignores many motivations that may not be selfish from some other standpoint. If someone commits a "deviant" act to further the interest of her or his group, it is a matter of judgment whether the act stems from egoism or altruism.

Although Bonger's theory possesses several weaknesses as an explanation of deviance, its focus on social conflict remains an important contribution. Nevertheless, the conflict perspective was not influential in American criminology during the first sixty years of the twentieth century. Although economic factors were considered important, they were seen merely as isolated problems in an otherwise healthy, congenial society. The poor were considered victims not of economic conflict, but of themselves or their station in society.

Poverty and deviance, as products of the social environment, were studied by Emile Durkeim, who pioneered the direction that would be taken by many twentieth-century sociologists, who argued that the causes of deviance could be found in the conditions of the lower economic classes. The presumptions behind this approach are that deviance is confined primarily to such classes and that a general consensus rather than a conflict of interests exists within society. It was evident that poverty alone has little explanatory power, but the principal thrust of American sociology has been to find factors related to economic class that would explain deviance. One of the most important factors was *anomie*.

Anomie

Emile Durkheim (1858–1917), a French sociologist, wrote his major works when the study of deviant behavior was dominated by those who viewed deviants as the products of defective biology. As such, deviants could not be the products of society. Carried to its logical conclusion, the argument of the biological positivists was that deviance could be eliminated merely by eliminating deviants. Society could be faulted only to the extent of its failure to locate and neutralize the potential troublemakers.

Durkheim argues, however, that a society without deviance is impossible:

> In a society in which criminal acts are no longer committed, the sentiments they offend would have to be found without exception in all individual consciousnesses, and they must be found to exist with the same degree as sentiments contrary to them. Assuming that this condition could actually be realized, crime would thereby disappear; it would only change its form, for the very cause which would thus dry up the sources of criminality would immediately open up new ones. . . .
>
> Imagine a society of saints, a perfect cloister of exemplary individuals. Crimes, properly so called, will there be unknown; but faults which appear venial to the layman will create there the same scandal that the ordinary offense does in ordinary consciousnesses. If, then, this society has the power to judge and punish, it will define these acts as criminal and will treat them as such.[83]

Thus short of a society of robots, it is impossible to have a collection of humans so inflexible in their behavior that none will diverge to some degree from the ideal. In a society of apparently minor divergences there will be reactions even against these infractions based on the society's consensus concerning norms—what Durkheim called the "collective conscience." An important corollary drawn from this view will be crucial for our later discussion of recent sociological theorists. The corollary states that deviance is not inherent in any given act but is defined by the reaction to that act:

> Thus, since there cannot be a society in which the individuals do not differ more or less from the collective type, it is also inevitable that, among these divergences, there are some with a criminal character. *What confers this character upon them is not the intrinsic quality of a given act but that definition which the collective conscience lends them.*[84]

Durkheim further claims that deviance is not only inevitable but also necessary for the health and progress of society. Without deviance society would be static. New ideas and approaches to problem solving would not be tolerated, since the status quo would be considered beyond improvement. Thus deviance is actually useful to society:

> Nothing is good indefinitely and to an unlimited extent. The authority which the moral conscience enjoys must be excessive; otherwise no one would dare criticize it, and it would too easily congeal into an immutable form. To make progress, individual originality must be able to express itself. In order that the originality of the idealist whose dreams transcend his century may find expression, it is necessary that the originality of the criminal, who is below the level of his time, shall also be possible. One does not occur without the other.[85]

The inevitability and desirability of deviance led Durkheim to conclude that deviance is "normal" in society. This did not mean that Durkheim necessarily regarded the individual deviant as normal. Instead, he was careful to distinguish between deviance as a sociological fact and deviance as the result of psychological factors within a given individual. The one does not necessarily imply the other. Because a person suffers from some abnormality does not imply that he or she will focus behavior in a deviant direction, nor does deviant behavior imply that an actor is suffering from an abnormality. From the standpoint of society, deviance is an expression of individual freedom and one of the prices to be paid for social change.

Durkheim's conception of deviance as normal was unique for his time and did not gain wide acceptance even among sociologists until quite recently. Instead, one other of his major contributions was elaborated upon to fit more closely the then predominant conception of deviance as a symptom of disorder in an otherwise organized society.

Durkheim's Anomie

Durkheim first used the concept of anomie in *The Division of Labor in Society* (1893).[86] Here it played a minor role; its purpose was to signify a lack of integration and adjustment that threatens the cohesiveness of contemporary industrial societies, which, unlike hunting and agricultural societies, are characterized by a complex variety of occupations and interests.

Four years later, in his work *Suicide,* the concept was to play a larger role by designating a particular type of suicide. Durkheim was influenced by Quetelet and others who believed that the regularity of suicide rates in given geographic areas must be caused by properties of the society, not of the individuals. Durkheim noted that different social variables were related to suicide rates in different ways. He suggested therefore that there are different forms of suicide.[87] Anomic suicide was one of four types and was considered to stem from a state of "normlessness" or "deregulation" in society. Such suicides occur because society allows its members to have unlimited aspirations and imposes no discipline on notions of what may be realistically achieved. These suicides arise particularly during periods of sudden economic prosperity:

> From top to bottom of the ladder, greed is aroused without knowing where to find ultimate foothold. Nothing can calm it, since its goal is far beyond all it can attain. Reality seems valueless by comparison with the dreams of fevered imaginations; reality is therefore abandoned, but so too is possibility abandoned when it in turn becomes reality. A thirst arises for novelties, unfamiliar pleasures, nameless sensations, all of which lose their savor once known. Henceforth one has no strength to endure the least reverse. The whole fever subsides and the sterility of all the tumult is apparent, and it is seen that all these new sensations in

their infinite quantity cannot form a solid foundation of happiness to support one during days of trial.[88]

Thus Durkheim was convinced that humans are susceptible to limitless ambition. Unless society imposes regulations upon aspirations, unless there is some check upon the passions aroused by perceived undiminishing prosperity, personal crises will develop and result in suicide. Durkheim in turn had a profound effect upon the thinking of the sociologists who succeeded him. His influence is particularly noticeable in the theories developed by American scholars who applied his principles to social experience in the United States.

Merton's Anomie

In 1938 Robert K. Merton elaborated upon the theme of unobtainable aspirations and extended it beyond suicide to all forms of deviance. His theoretical perspective is often called *strain theory* because of its emphasis on the idea that crime is caused by the disjunction between the goals for success that people set for themselves and the available means by which those goals might be achieved.[89] Merton's version of anomie differs from Durkheim's in two important respects. First, Durkheim felt that human aspirations are essentially limitless and that in times of rapid social change they can exceed reasonable expectations; Merton argues that aspirations are products of society and limited but that they can exceed what is obtainable through acceptable means. Second, Durkheim claimed that anomie results from a disruption of regulation, a failure to maintain limits over the aspirations of society's members; in contrast Merton suggests that anomie results from strains in the social structure that exert pressures on individuals, pushing them toward unrealistic aspirations.

Merton's theory involves the interaction of two social components: (1) culture goals—the aspirations and aims that define success in society—and (2) institutionalized means—the socially acceptable methods and ways available for achieving goals.[90]

According to Merton, there is an overemphasis in the United States on success as a goal. It is the American dream that everyone, regardless of class origin, religion, or ethnic characteristics, can acquire material wealth. This seems fine as an egalitarian ideal, but the realities of American society do not match it. The acceptable means to attain success are often in short supply, and what means exist are not uniformly distributed to all groups. It is not the mere lack of opportunity *or* the excessive emphasis on the accumulation of wealth that creates anomie; it is when both exist in a situation in which all or most members of a society believe the opportunities are available to them that anomie results. In Merton's words,

> it is only when a system of cultural values extols, virtually above all else, certain *common* success-goals *for the population at large* while the social structure rigorously restricts or completely closes access to approved modes of reaching these goals *for a considerable part of the same population,* that deviant behavior ensues on a large scale.[91]

Anomie thus constitutes

> a breakdown in the cultural structure, occurring particularly when there is an acute disjunction between cultural norms and goals and the socially structured capacities of members of the group to act in accord with them.[92]

The premium placed on financial success in the absence of opportunities creates a disjunction between the goal and the capacities or means of individuals to attain it. In American society the competition for wealth is not satisfactory in itself; one must be a *winner.* The means used to compete become secondary to the victory. Attempting to stay within the bounds of the norms while faced with sure failure can create frustration and unrelieved tension. As Bonger claimed some thirty years earlier, deviance can result if economic success is seen as an indication of intrinsic superiority when one's image as a person is on the line. The alternatives are to continue playing by the rules, to undertake other means toward the goal, or to seek avenues of escape from the anomic situation.

Undoubtedly, one of the most important contributions of Merton's theory is the provision of alternative behaviors that may result from the disjunction between goals and means. What Merton calls "modes of individual adaptation" (Figure 2.1) are essentially the logically possible behavioral alternatives expressed in terms of the acceptance and rejection of goals and means.

From this scheme the reader can see that there are four adaptations apart from conformity that can be defined as deviant: innovation, ritualism, retreatism, and rebellion. *Innovation* is the adaptation in which most property crimes would be found. It occurs when people accept without qualification the importance of attaining the goals and will use any means, regardless of their propriety, morality, or legality, to achieve them. In short, their philosophy can be described in the words of football coach Vince Lombardi when he said, "Winning isn't everything; it's the only thing."

To continue in the sports vein, perhaps the most all-American example of innovation occurred at the 1973 National Soap Box Derby. After the race it was discovered that the winner's car had been equipped with an electromagnetic device that gave it extra velocity at the starting point. The innovator was not the 14-year-old driver but his uncle, who was subsequently charged with contributing to the delinquency of a minor. There was evidence that at least 34 cars in the race, including six of the top ten finishers, had been doctored. Furthermore, it turned out that the uncle's son had won the Derby the previous year. That car mysteriously disappeared before it could be checked, however.[93] All this flies in the face of the conformist adage: It's not whether you win or lose but how you play the game.

Merton acknowledges the existence of innovation in high places and mentions it as a route to white-collar crime, but he is primarily interested in explaining the official statistics that attribute higher rates of crime to lower economic groups. These groups, according to Merton, have accepted American success goals yet are especially lacking in opportunities

FIGURE 12.1   Merton's Modes of Individual Adaptation

for their fulfillment. It is not poverty itself but its combination with expectations and limited opportunity that predisposes these classes toward higher rates of robbery, burglary, auto theft, and other property crimes.

Ritualism is a behavioral alternative in which great aspirations are abandoned in favor of careful adherence to the available means. Early morning classes contain ritualists—failing students who faithfully attend lectures and just as faithfully fall asleep. Attendance is not a means for them to attain success; they are there simply because they should be. Merton uses the example of people in factories and other bureaucracies who staunchly perform their duties but who have neither the intention nor the inclination to advance themselves. They carefully avoid rocking the boat and prefer to play it safe. There may be some argument as to whether such behavior is really deviant, but the lack of ambition certainly is not in keeping with the idealized American way.

Retreatism is the category containing the mentally disordered, drug addicts, alcoholics, and any other group that has apparently withdrawn from the competitive struggle. These people do not strive toward the goals that society encourages, nor do they obey the rules of how to act. They seek their own private rewards and live by rules peculiar to their style of living. Rather than coping with the frustrations of the larger society, they have simply abandoned that society.

Rebellion involves not only a rejection of the goals and means, but also the intention of replacing those goals and means by altering the social structure. In his more recent publications, Merton substituted the term "nonconforming behavior" for "rebellion," while using "aberrant behavior" to include innovation, ritualism, and retreatism. Merton characterizes the nonconformer and the aberrant as follows:

1. The nonconformer publicly expresses his or her dissent with the norms, while the aberrant hides his or her conduct.
2. The nonconformer challenges the legitimacy of the norms while the aberrant acknowledges their legitimacy in a general way, although they may not apply to his or her specific conduct in specific instances.
3. The nonconformer tries to change the norms; the aberrant at most only tries to justify his or her particular conduct.
4. The nonconformer is often recognized by conventional society to be acting for nonpersonal reasons, while the aberrant is acting only in his or her personal interests.
5. The nonconformer claims to act in terms of ultimate values such as justice, freedom of speech, equality, [and] liberty; the aberrant makes no such claims and seeks only to satisfy private interests.[94]

Few theories in sociology have sparked the imagination and controversy that Merton's has. His work has especially influenced writers attempting to explain *lower-class gang delinquency.* The first of these writers, Albert K. Cohen, emphasizes the strain that lower-class boys face in school, where they are evaluated by middle-class teachers using middle-class standards. According to him, lower-class boys are usually not socialized by their families into believing that it is important to

1. Be ambitious, determined to "get ahead," and become "someone."
2. Take responsibility and minimize reliance on others.

3. Become skillful in those things that have economic value.
4. Postpone immediate gratification in the interest of achieving long-term goals.
5. Be rational, plan, and budget available time, not leaving things to chance.
6. Cultivate manners and courtesy in order to get along with people.
7. Keep physical aggression under control.
8. Play constructively and wholesomely, not destructively and wastefully.
9. Respect the property rights of others.[95]

Lower-class boys who find it difficult to meet these "middle-class measuring rod" criteria are disadvantaged in school and in nearly any situation where they must compete with middle-class boys for the approval of middle-class adults. Faced with constant threats to their self-esteem, many lower-class boys retreat to the one group where they can find status: the delinquent gang. According to Cohen,

> the delinquent subculture . . . is a way of dealing with the problems of adjustment. . . . These problems are chiefly status problems: certain children are denied status in the respectable society because they cannot meet the criteria of the respectable status system. The delinquent subculture deals with these problems by providing criteria of status which these children *can* meet.[96]

For example, in the gang context play does not have to be constructive but can be destructive: the boys can either play ball or terrorize smaller children. There is no emphasis on delaying gratification: You do what you want, when you want. And the gang does not inhibit the use of force; indeed, it legitimizes aggression, especially against middle-class people "with their airs of superiority, disdain or condescension."[97] In short, argues Cohen, the gang relieves status frustration by allowing gang members to reverse the standards upheld by the middle-class schools.

However, Richard A. Cloward and Lloyd E. Ohlin believe that Cohen overemphasizes the impact of school standards in creating frustration. They argue that alienation from school is more likely to stem from the nature of some boys' success goals. Some youths have no interest in meeting middle-class standards because they have no interest in a middle-class lifestyle or in middle-class goals. Instead, they want the "crass" signs of economic success: big cars, flashy clothes, and so on.[98] These boys seek higher status within a lower-class context, and they face the acute problem of finding means to reach their goals. According to Cloward and Ohlin, most delinquents come from this group of boys.

Faced with a disjunction between their economic goals and the legitimate means for achieving them, what determines the boys' choice of behavioral alternatives—conformity, innovation, ritualism, retreatism, or rebellion? It is at this point that Cloward and Ohlin elaborate upon Merton's theory by introducing the concept of *differential opportunity*. Simply stated, this means that access to *any* opportunity, whether legitimate or illegitimate, varies according to time and place. In neighborhoods where an adult criminal subculture is strong, youths will have both the role models (such as pimps, bookies, and organized criminals) and the means for becoming successful innovators. But such opportunities are not available in all lower-class neighborhoods. Faced with the frustration of having neither legitimate nor illegitimate means, some boys turn to violence or "retreat" into alcohol and other drugs.

Despite the insights of Cohen, Cloward, and Ohlin, Merton's means-ends schema falls short of its ambitious mark. Criticisms of the theory are many and complex. However, two are critical.

First, Merton relies too heavily upon the assumption that people who are officially treated as deviant accurately represent the population of those involved in similar behavior. Official statistics clearly point to the lower economic class as the primary source of delinquency, crime, alcoholism, illegal drug use, and serious mental disorder. Like Merton, most sociologists have directed their research and theoretical efforts accordingly. A favorite target is urban, lower-class, slum gangs. The reader compiling a bibliography of delinquency studies in the United States might conclude that such gangs constitute practically the sole origin of delinquent behavior. Many sociologists are now recognizing that official records considerably inflate the relationship between class and delinquency. Furthermore, it appears that earlier enthusiasm over explaining the lower-class gang has led to premature and highly selective conclusions concerning the general nature of delinquency.

Maynard L. Erickson, for example, finds that his data do not support the impression left by official statistics:

> Scant evidence is found that would support the contention that group delinquency is more characteristic of the lower-status levels than other socioeconomic status levels. With few exceptions, the evidence shows that the tendency to violate in groups is evenly distributed across social status levels. . . . Only arrests seem to be more characteristic of the low-status category than the other categories. . . . In short, the findings not only fail to support the contention of the group nature of delinquency: they seriously put in question the importance of [socioeconomic status] and delinquency unless, of course, one is willing to define delinquency solely on the basis of aggregate official reaction—arrests, juvenile court referrals, and the like.[99]

Other studies reveal that the lower class has no monopoly on crime, alcoholism, illegal drug use, and so on. Indeed, many acts are monopolized by the upper classes but never reach the statistics: illegal corporation practices, influence peddling by politicians, and medical malpractice, for example. In addition, nonconforming behavior is more likely to come from the middle rather than the lower class, as evidenced by campus disruptions during the Vietnam War.

A second criticism of Merton's theory concerns his assumptions of common cultural goals and institutionalized means. The ethnic, religious, and cultural heterogeneity of the United States and the rapidly changing concepts of morality in many of its segments cast doubt on whether any single set of goals-means can be said to characterize the society. Although there may be a success theme in the United States, it is scarcely limited to financial or material achievement. Accomplishment is defined in many ways by many individuals, and the paths to it are equally diverse. Depending upon the audience, who is more "successful": the president of IBM, the hard-driving reporter who exposes business crime and political corruption, the religious leader who draws tens of thousands to rallies, the high school athlete whose last-second score wins the "big game," the star whose fame rests on a series of pornographic films, or the jazz musician who is highly esteemed but who lives in near poverty? Each succeeds in his or her own fashion by appealing to a specific audience, and each would probably have it no other way.[100]

States of conflict, whether reduced by accommodation or not, undermine the premises of anomie theory. American society is characterized as much by disagreement as by consensus over moral conditions, success goals, and the means toward those goals. Furthermore, the apparent preponderance of deviance among the lower class as reflected by official statistics may be as indicative of that group's powerlessness as of its behavior.

Researchers attempting to demonstrate that there truly is a relationship between social class and delinquency, a key issue in Merton's concept, have a very difficult time even measuring social class. Researchers today refer to social class as *socioeconomic status,* or *SES.* Charles R. Tittle and Robert F. Meier comment:

> Research published since 1978, using both official and self-reported data, suggests . . . that there is no pervasive relationship between individual SES and delinquency. . . . The evidence provides little confidence that using particular indicators of social rank will specify the SES/delinquency relationship.[101]

Their work reviews many studies that have attempted to measure social class or SES and link it to delinquency. Some of the SES measures include the following:

Whether family utilizes welfare, employment status of father
Whether family receives free meals
Occupation of breadwinner
Total periods of unemployment
Education
Income of family
Social class
Social structure relative to the means of production

Tittle and Meier clearly state that more work is needed to establish whether there is a link between social class and delinquency.[102]

Robert Agnew developed a new twist on Merton's anomie by criticizing the latter's theory for being unable to explain why only *some* strained individuals resort to delinquency. Agnew also contended that Merton's model cannot account for the broad range of delinquency in America's middle class. In his general strain theory Agnew goes beyond monetary success as the only important measure of goal achievement and views negative relationships, which are *not* goal-related, as important causes of strain and delinquency.[103] Negative treatment or abuse by others, along with circumstances in which people "remove or threaten to remove" valued stimuli from others or apply or threaten to apply "negatively valued" stimuli to others, causes strain and influences delinquent tendencies. Agnew considers a wide range of possible negative experience and concludes that *adaptations,* or the coping mechanisms developed in social learning, determine whether a given individual's strain experience will result in delinquency. Empirical evaluations of Agnew's perspective have shown that it is a valuable extension of Merton's model and fits well with other sociological crime theories. Paul Mazerolle,[104] for example, found that negative relationships with adults and losing family members increase criminal tendencies in young males. Agnew has recently attempted to apply general strain principles to group behavior at the community level as well.[105]

Steven Messner and Richard Rosenfeld[106] make a good case for the concept that Americans emphasize the accumulation of money and property as the most important measure of success at all levels of society. As a result, the billionaire CEO, the accountant, the small business entrepreneur, the factory worker, and the street tough are never satisfied with the level of wealth they have achieved and may resort to innovative crime. Changing the intense focus on monetary success would be a way to reduce crime.

Subcultures of Deviance

Merton's theory of anomie locates the specific cause of deviance within the general social structure. In this section we shall consider theories based upon the assumption that deviance arises from membership in a group whose beliefs and attitudes support such behavior. Although interpreted by outsiders as deviant, the behavior in question conforms to the expectations of a particular group. Such theories are usually labeled *subcultural theories,* although they may also be described as *cultural transmission theories*[107] or *cultural deviance theories.*[108]

Exactly what constitutes a subculture has not been completely resolved in the sociological literature, but the following are generally considered distinguishing characteristics:

1. A special vocabulary, or argot, usually concerning the activities that differentiate the group from those around it. For example, urban lower-class heroin users possess a jargon that is practically incomprehensible to those unfamiliar with the activities involved.
2. A set of shared beliefs and norms, which contrast in direction or emphasis with the norms of other groups, such as the larger society.
3. Contacts between members through which behavior is learned and membership in the group is confirmed.
4. Sometimes a specialized way of dressing and acting that, like argot, serves to distinguish the members from those of other groups and to assist in identifying members to one another.

Obviously, not all subcultures are necessarily deviant in a narrow, negative sense. The Amish, for example, can be described as a subculture as a result of their religious beliefs that isolate members from the general community, require the wearing of plain clothing, and forbid the use of motorized vehicles. Although characterized as a deviant subculture, the Amish rarely break the criminal code and are highly respected for their industriousness and honest dealing.

In a pluralistic society, many groups—ethnic, religious, and political—could be characterized as subcultures by one or more such criteria. Therein lies the problem in comparing any group with the larger culture. Sociologists, when suggesting the existence of deviant subcultures, usually begin with a particular form of behavior and then attempt to ascertain whether the individuals involved receive support for the behavior and/or instruction from others.

The contribution of a subculture to deviance can be twofold. First, it can be viewed as the *source* of the behavior; the individual enters the group, usually although not necessarily by birth, and there acquires the knowledge and values that prompt him or her to behave in ways defined by outsiders as deviant. In short, the subculture teaches the individual to be deviant. This is usually the sequence suggested by the subcultural theories of delinquency, which we will consider briefly in a moment.

The second way in which a subculture can contribute to deviance is by providing *support* for deviant behavior. The individual is already defined by others (or by herself or himself) as a deviant and as a consequence gravitates toward groups that share common interests. Admission to such groups provides the individual with a more positive image and, in all likelihood, with greater opportunity to engage in deviance. At the same time that the group provides support and opportunities for deviance, it also insulates the individual from influences that might alter the deviant career path. This sequence is often associated with the homosexual subculture—the web of acquaintances, cliques, bars, argot, and lifestyle that frequently accompanies a commitment to the gay life. The individual is not likely to become first oriented toward homosexuality in the subculture; rather, involvement in the subculture probably comes only after experience with homosexuality.

Unquestionably, subcultures as sources of deviance and as supports for deviance are interrelated notions. If a subculture has been instrumental in introducing someone to the rationales and techniques of a behavior, that person must continue to rely upon the reinforcement that only the subculture can provide; once a person has entered the subculture, the deviance becomes necessary to adhere to the norms of the subculture. In this case the subculture serves as both a support for and a source of behavior.

Social Disorganization and Learning

We have already mentioned Quetelet, who in the nineteenth century utilized census statistics in an attempt to explain group influence upon rates of deviance. However, after a few years such studies were overshadowed by the influence of Charles Darwin:

> The importance of Darwinism in the late nineteenth century can hardly be overestimated. Evolution and natural selection [survival of the fittest] were concepts adopted and adapted wholesale in almost every field of intellectual inquiry from biology to sociology. . . . Studies of motivation were more attractive partly because they came nearer to the vitality of human behavior, and partly because by existing at a lower level of abstraction they required less intellectual effort, a fact which led to the vulgarisations of popular pseudo-science, the notion of the "born criminal" being a case in point.[109]

Ironically, although Darwin influenced the development of Lombrosianism, his work also was later to advance the study of the ecology of deviance pioneered by Quetelet. According to Amos H. Hawley, human ecology is indebted to Darwin for his conceptions of "1) the web of life in which organisms are adjusted or are seeking adjustment to one another, 2) the adjustment process as a struggle for existence, and 3) the environment comprising a highly complex set of conditions of adjustment."[110]

It was the application of such ideas to human relationships within cities that sparked the studies of Clifford R. Shaw (1896–1957), who attempted to explain the geographic distribution of crime and delinquency. Basing his approach upon ecological theories of the time, Shaw viewed the "adjustment process" of city growth as involving a segregation into "natural areas" in which the inhabitants possess similar qualities, interests, and cultures. In time these areas take on the character and quality of the people living there; characteristics of the community thus reflect social processes occurring among its members.

Another aspect of city growth treated by Shaw was the threat of encroachment by industry upon residential areas, which creates a "zone of transition." This zone, immediately adjacent to the central business district, is characterized by deteriorating buildings, falling rental costs but rising land values resulting from speculation, and decreasing population. The social characteristics of this zone are a large number of recent immigrant groups; poverty; high crime and delinquency rates; and a highly heterogeneous mixture of the young, the aged, the down-and-outers, the aspiring, students, freethinkers, professional criminals, and so on. The growth of the city thus affects and is affected by both physical and social conditions.

Utilizing the records of juvenile probation agencies, courts, and the Cook County, Illinois, jail, Shaw reached the following conclusions:

1. There is great variation between areas (square-mile units) as to the proportions of residents having records of truancy, delinquency, and crime. Some areas show very high rates and others very low rates.
2. Generally, the closer the areas are to the city center, the higher the rates of truancy, delinquency, crime, and repeated delinquency (recidivism).
3. Areas with high rates of delinquency also show high rates of truancy and crime.
4. The highest rates of truancy and the like occur in areas of physical deterioration and declining population.
5. Areas with these high rates have been characterized by such rates for at least 30 years, regardless of which ethnic or racial groups lived there.[111]

The concentration of deviance in areas undergoing the process of transition from residential to industrial use is indicative of a process of social disorganization, according to Shaw. When industry invades the community, the standards of the "conventional" society weaken. Resistance to deviance is lower, and the deviant behavior is progressively more tolerated. Furthermore, the influx of recent immigrants or rural blacks with different values also helps to break down whatever community forces act to control behavior:

> In this state of social disorganization, community resistance is low. *Delinquency and criminal patterns arise and are transmitted socially just as any other cultural and social pattern is transmitted.* In time these delinquent patterns become dominant and shape the attitudes and behavior of persons living in the area. Thus the section becomes an area of delinquency.[112]

Shaw's concept of social disorganization had limited utility (although it is now being reconsidered)[113] and in his 1942 work with Henry D. McKay, *Juvenile Delinquency and Urban Areas,* the concept was replaced by "differences in social values." In this later work the authors implicitly reject the notion of consensus within society by arguing that high-delinquency areas contain competing economic value systems: legitimate business and illegitimate business, as represented by criminal gangs and the rackets. These areas provide the opportunity and incentive for deviance. Although people in the community may be aware that wealth and prestige can be obtained legally, illegal means can often appear more relevant and tangible:

> A boy may be found guilty of delinquency in the court, which represents the values of the larger society, for an act which has had at least tacit approval in the community in which he lives. It is perhaps common knowledge in the neighborhood that public funds are embezzled and that favors and special considerations can be received from some public officials through the payment of stipulated sums; the boys assume that all officials can be influenced in this way. They are familiar with the location of illegal institutions in the community and with the procedures through which such institutions are opened and kept in operation; they know where stolen goods can be sold and the kinds of merchandise for which there is a ready market; they know what the rackets are; and they see in fine clothes, expensive cars, and other lavish expenditures the evidences of wealth among those who openly engage in illegal activities.[114]

From Shaw's earlier work a more provocative concept than social disorganization emerges: the notion that certain areas contain values supportive of deviance and that these values, like any other cultural values, are then transmitted. This is not to imply that Shaw was the first social thinker to suggest that deviant behavior results from learning, but his work heralded the emerging sociological emphasis upon the importance of the learning process in explaining deviance.

It should be noted here that a major sequel to Shaw's studies was a series of works concerning the subculture as an explanation of the existence and activities of urban, lower-class male gang delinquency. The literature on the subcultures of gang delinquency represents some of the most imaginative, insightful work to be found in sociology. It is worthy of the reader's attention.[115]

Differential Association Theory

In 1890 a French magistrate, Gabriel Tarde, published an attack upon Lombroso and his followers. In *Philosophie Penale* (*Penal Philosophy*), Tarde argued that the explanation of crime lay not in biology but in the social world and that crime is transmitted through intimate personal groups:

> The true seminary of crime must be sought for upon each public square or each crossroad of our towns, whether they be small or large, in those flocks of pillaging street urchins who, like bands of sparrows, associate together, at first for marauding, and then for theft, because of a lack of education and food in their homes. Without any natural predisposition on their part, their fate is often decided by the influence of their comrades. . . . The child who was the most normally constituted [could] be more influenced by half a score of perverse friends by whom he is surrounded than by millions of unknown fellow-citizens.[116]

Tarde went on to insist that people learn crime just as they learn a trade—regardless of what characteristics one has at birth, one must learn to become a criminal by association with and imitation of others.

A far more systematic and carefully formulated theory concerning the learning of crime was presented in 1939 by the U.S. criminologist Edwin H. Sutherland (1883–1950).[117] Sutherland agreed with both Tarde and Shaw that criminal behavior patterns are transmitted within a cultural setting. But he believed that crime involved more complex learning processes than the mere imitation of others and that social disorganization was not responsible for high rates of deviance within sections of the population. He argued that the United States comprises diverse cultures and that conflict between such cultures is an essential aspect of crime causation. Crime rates result, therefore, not from disorganization but from *differential group organization:* some groups are organized for criminal activities, and some are organized against these activities.

Consistent with the concept of differential group organization is Sutherland's theory of *differential association,* which he expressed in the form of nine propositions concerning the process by which individuals come to engage in criminal behavior:

1. Criminal behavior is learned. [It is not inherited, nor is it the result of low intelligence, brain damage, and so on.]
2. Criminal behavior is learned in interaction with other persons in a process of communication.
3. The principal part of the learning of criminal behavior occurs within intimate personal groups. [At most, impersonal communications such as television, magazines, and newspapers play only a secondary role in the learning of crime.]
4. When criminal behavior is learned, the learning includes (a) techniques of committing crime, which are sometimes very complicated, sometimes very simple; [and] (b) the specific direction of motives, drives, rationalizations, and attitudes.
5. The specific direction of motives and drives is learned from definitions of the legal codes as favorable or unfavorable. [This acknowledges the existence of conflicting norms. An individual may learn reasons for both adhering to and violating a given rule. For example, stealing is wrong—that is, unless the goods are insured, in which case, of course, nobody really gets hurt.]
6. A person becomes delinquent because of an excess of definitions favorable to violation of law over definitions unfavorable to violation of law. [This is the key proposition of the theory. An individual's behavior is affected by contradictory learning experiences, but the predominance of pro-criminal definitions leads to criminal behavior. It is important to note that the associations are not necessarily only criminal *persons* but also definitions, norms, and patterns of behavior. Furthermore, in keeping with the notion of a learning theory, the proposition can be rephrased: A person becomes non-delinquent because of an excess of definitions unfavorable to violation of law.]
7. Differential associations may vary in frequency, duration, priority, and intensity. [*Frequency* and *duration* are self-explanatory. *Priority* refers to the time in one's life when one is exposed to the association. *Intensity* concerns the prestige of the source of the behavior pattern.]
8. The process of learning criminal behavior by association with criminal and anticriminal patterns involves all of the mechanisms that are involved in any other learning. [Again, there is no unique learning process involved in acquiring deviant ways of behaving.]

9. While criminal behavior is an expression of general needs and values, it is not explained by those general needs and values, since noncriminal behavior is an expression of the same needs and values. [A "need for recognition" can be used to explain mass murder, running for president, or a .320 batting average, but it really explains nothing since it apparently accounts for both deviant and nondeviant actions.][118]

Sutherland's theory has been subject to much research and controversy. Its most ardent defenders concede that it is too imprecise and oversimplified to explain satisfactorily how normative conflicts within society become translated into individual behavior. Furthermore, there is the seemingly insurmountable problem of testing such concepts as an excess of definitions, priority, and intensity.[119] Despite these difficulties, however, no other theory has proven so consistent with the findings of research concerning the prediction of deviant behavior, and attempts to find relationships between deviant behavior, and associations with deviant behavior patterns have met with moderate success.[120] Thus, extensive attempts have been made to modify the theory and make it more suitable for testing.

Among the more recent of such attempts is that of Melvin L. DeFleur and Richard Quinney, who used set theory to reformulate the propositions. Sutherland's sixth proposition, "A person becomes delinquent because of an excess of definitions," thus becomes

> overt criminal behavior has as its necessary and sufficient conditions a set of criminal motivations, attitudes, and techniques, the learning of which takes place when there is exposure to criminal norms in excess of exposure to corresponding anticriminal norms during symbolic interaction in primary groups.[121]

This formulation clarifies the point that the associations are not simply with persons in primary groups (face-to-face relationships in small groups that are relatively permanent, such as families, gangs, and play groups), but also with the motives, attitudes, and techniques transmitted by those groups. It also makes clear that the learning of these motives precedes the commission of the first criminal act. Thus excluded from the theory are behaviors that might be the products of opportunity and social-psychological pressures; in these cases, the attitudes and motivations might develop to justify continuation of the behavior. As DeFleur and Quinney point out,

> in the Sutherland theory, opportunity is assumed; motives, attitudes, and techniques must be developed as prerequisites; and overt action results when these have been sufficiently developed through the differential association process. In an alternative theory, opportunity would be a necessary condition for crime, but some psychological or social pressure would be required to trigger the first overt action, and *attitudes and motivations* would follow as means for handling resulting anxieties, guilt, or other disturbances of the personality system. . . . Sutherland's theory, then, may not fit all crime.[122]

In another reformulation, Ronald L. Akers rephrases the propositions in terms of reinforcement theory, stating that "deviant behavior . . . that has been differentially reinforced over alternative behavior . . . is defined as desirable or justified when the individual is in a situation discriminative for the behavior."[123]

We have no intention of delving into the complexities of reinforcement theory here. Risking misinterpretation through oversimplification, we suggest that the Akers proposition can be interpreted as an increased probability that a person will commit a deviant act if she or he has learned that participating in the behavior will be more rewarding than will be abstaining from it.[124] More important for our purposes are the other implications of Akers's approach. First, the primary group emphasized by Sutherland is not the sole source of influence on behavior; instead, the "normative statements, definitions, and verbalizations" may also come from imaginary groups of persons portrayed in the mass media or from formal organizations such as a corporation, school, government, and so on. Second, Akers emphasizes more than Sutherland the importance of verbal justifications for behavior. These are excuses by which individuals can counteract the accusations and disapproval of others. Such excuses are important for dealing not only with past behavior but also, and even especially, with future behavior. They allow the individual to overcome obstacles in advance. As Akers summarizes it, deviant behavior can be expected if it has been reinforced or rewarded over alternative positive behavior.[125]

Control Theory

This is a good time to review in a brief and general way the theories we have covered so far. The reader will recall that in the first chapter we began with the *classical school,* which regarded humans as rational creatures whose behavior is based on calculating the resulting pain and pleasure. Most of the remaining chapter concerned a variety of *positivist* theories, which replaced the classical. Beginning with phrenology and concluding with sociobiology, these theories focused on several determinants of behavior, including heredity, mental deficiency, brain malfunction, and unconscious motivations. Despite their apparent differences, such theories are similar in one respect: Humans are regarded as determined creatures whose behavior is based on some trait or set of traits buried within the individuals.

So far in this chapter we have dealt with a slightly different breed of positivist theories, which sees the causes of behavior as buried not in the individual's physiology or mind but rather in the individual's social environment. For example, Bonger, using a Marxist approach, claims that conflict over economic power within capitalist society is the basis of crime. Other theorists argue that deviance is caused by poverty (Blackmar), by society's overemphasis on success goals (Merton), and by subcultures that teach and support deviant behavior (Shaw, Sutherland, and others). Again, despite their obvious differences, these theories are similar not only among themselves but with biological and psychological theories: Human behavior is determined by factors over which individuals have no choice. According to the social determinists, individuals in "unfavorable" environments ("bad" home, neighborhood, or economic conditions) seem as predestined to deviance as was Lombroso's born criminal.

Some writers criticize the assumption that the individual lacks a choice in how to behave. Although they do not advocate returning to the classical school of thought, they reject the notion that deviants are different from nondeviants because they are pushed or coerced into socially unacceptable behavior.[126] Control theory is an example of this perspective.

The importance of nurturing relationships to the development of self-control and strong social influences is a prominent feature in the work of some theorists. An individual's strength of conscience and personal moral values regarding deviant behavior are explained as forms of internal control, while shame and rejection resulting from others' perception of an individual's deviance are important external controls.

Durkheim is sometimes classified as an early, and influential, control theorist for his explanation of the social dynamics in different types of societies.[127] His "mechanical" society, with its consistent values and close interpersonal knowledge, was effective in controlling behavior because people generally knew each other and scrutinized each other's actions. Nonconforming behavior was therefore easily noticed and quickly became the object of censure. Durkheim's views certainly influenced subsequent theorists, including Walter Reckless, who developed his *containment theory* in his work entitled *The Crime Problem.*[128] A product of the Chicago school of sociological theorists in the 1950s, Reckless believed that the contemporary theoretical approaches did not pay sufficient attention to the individual's personal ability to resist the impulses, pressures, and temptations that result in criminal behavior. He used an interesting analogy to disease to explain *inner containment,* or the combination of positive self-concept, tolerance for frustration, and realistic goals that gives a person self-direction and the ability to follow social norms. Just as exposure to disease does not result in sickness if a person's immune system is able to fight it off, exposure to deviant behavior may be resisted successfully if a person has healthy inner containment. Reckless explained *external containment* as the power of groups to make sure members comply with expected behavior by providing censure for misbehavior as well as meaningful social roles and rewards for correct behavior. To him, inner controls were significantly more important in determining the final direction of an individual's behavior, especially in diverse, highly mobile environments that limit the time spent with family and other groups that might also provide external control.

From this perspective the social environment does not push one toward deviant behavior; rather, it fails to restrain one from so behaving. Deviance is caused not by the *presence* of deviant values, beliefs, or other motivating factors, but by the *absence* of values and beliefs that normally forbid delinquency. In short, the individual is *allowed* to be deviant.

Control theory, however, comes in several forms.[129] While social control writers subscribe to one basic assumption—that individuals are "freed," not compelled, to deviate—they disagree over the important relevant factors within the social environment. Let us briefly consider the most widely known control theory to illustrate. Travis Hirschi, whose work has attracted a great deal of attention in delinquency research, assumes that it is human nature to be predisposed toward deviance. He insists that deviance can be taken for granted; thus, it does not need explanation. Instead, it is *conformity* that requires explanation, and he believes that conformity depends primarily upon the strength of the individual's bond to society.

In what is called his *bonding theory,*[130] Hirschi argues that the bond to society consists of four interrelated elements:

1. **Attachment.** The closer one's ties to others in society, especially one's parents and peers, the more likely that one will conform to society's expectations.
2. **Commitment.** The more one aspires to invest in legitimate activities, especially in terms of success aspirations and long-range goals, the more likely that one will conform.

3. **Involvement.** The more time and energy one spends on legitimate activities, the more likely that one will conform.
4. **Belief.** The more one attaches moral validity to society's norms, the more likely that one will conform.

Individuals deviate from the expected normative behaviors when these bonds are weak. People with weak attachments to others or those with no commitments have little incentive to comply with the norms. Hirschi's theory is receiving growing support from research on delinquents.[131] However, Michael R. Gottfredson and Hirschi later enlarged on his early effort and developed a general theory of crime. The "self-control" version of the theory presents the following:

1. **Definition of crime.** Acts of force or fraud undertaken in the pursuit of self-interest.
2. **Applicability of theory.** To all crime, including white-collar crime.
3. **Cause of crime.** Weak self-control, the result of poor child-rearing practices. Since crime is committed as the result of impulsive behavior and is unplanned by those seeking quick gratification, much crime results in little real gain[132]

Hirschi and Gottfredson suggest that some people simply pursue pleasure and commit crime in the short term because they have weak self-control. Crimes and deviant acts occur when opportunities present themselves to these individuals. The notion of weak self-control coupled with opportunities for deviance seems to present a simplistic explanation for the complex problem of crime and deviance in all instances. The lack of social bond or weak self-control seems an appropriate explanation for the members of a Hell's Angels motorcycle club who war, deal in drugs, vandalize, and seem quite detached from legality in general. But most people are selective in their deviance. The lack of social bond or self-control may be an incongruent explanation for the bribe-taking police officer and the embezzling accountant who are otherwise solid, family-oriented, church-going citizens. The true value of this effort remains to be seen. Nevertheless, Hirschi and Gottfredson have definitely awakened criminologists.

Classical Theory Revisited

While control theories suggest that individuals are "free" to deviate from norms as a result of poor socialization, other theorists are returning to a much more classical orientation. These theorists emphasize free will, opportunity, and deterrence. What brought back this emphasis in classical theory? Three issues raised the level of interest. First, there was a convincing lack of evidence that any type of rehabilitation worked.[133] Second, there was a realization that a very few serious, chronic offenders were busily committing a great number of crimes.[134] Third, there was a seminal study that suggested that we identify these individuals and deter them from continuing in crime by incapacitating them for very long periods.[135]

Examples of these perspectives can be seen in the work of economists who examine the costs and benefits of crime and of deterrence theorists who ask, "What deters?" Rational choice theorists have a similar view. They assume that offenders examine their situation (need for money, personal values, learning experiences, and so on) and situational factors (how well the target is protected, whether people are at home, how wealthy the neighborhood is, and so on), and then make a reasoned decision to commit a crime.[136] Routine activity theorists explain increases in crime in a given area by suggesting that suitable targets, capable guardians, and motivated offenders interact.[137]

We will briefly examine types of each. Examples of economists who study crime are many. They view the decision to commit crime as a rational one, whereby a potential offender examines the costs and benefits.[138] An example of this is provided by Isaac Ehrlich in his article "Participation in Illegitimate Activities."[139] Samuel Walker summarizes Ehrlich's study by stating that

> if the risks of punishment are slim and the relative monetary gains are high, people will be more inclined to commit crimes. . . . The costs and benefits will differ with a person's circumstances. The unemployed person has more to gain by a successful robbery than the employed person and less to lose in social status by apprehension and conviction.[140]

Hiroya Akiba, another economist examining similar issues, believes that Ehrlich's earlier efforts may have been too simplistic. In a cross-cultural study, he analyzes Japanese data on larceny and considers the cost/benefit question raised by Ehrlich. He concludes by stating that although there is some support for Ehrlich's perspective, making the cost of crime more severe and increasing the probability of apprehension may simply "encourage criminals to devote more of their time to illegal activities."[141] In other words, if you make it increasingly difficult to burglarize your home by using alarms and so on, and if you make punishment more severe and certain, you may make the burglar work harder and simply devote more planning and time to the attempt.

Other studies have focused exclusively on the question of deterrence. An excellent example is Kenneth D. Tunnel's article "Choosing Crime: Close Your Eyes and Take Your Chances." Recognizing that a small number of criminals are responsible for the majority of thefts, he assumed that interviews with incarcerated, repetitive property criminals might prove enlightening. After requiring them to complete a self-report crime survey, which confirmed that they were very busy criminals indeed, he conducted extensive interviews. Tunnel reports on their views on the deterrent effect of legal sanctions:

> All 60 respondents reported that they (and nearly every thief they knew) simply do not think about the possible legal consequences of their criminal actions before committing crimes. This is especially true for criminals of grave concern to deterrence-minded policy makers—those who commit crimes at a very high rate. Rather than thinking of the possible negative consequences of their actions, those offenders reported thinking primarily of the anticipated positive consequences. . . .
>
> The respondents' perceptions of the severity of legal sanctions were unrealistic. . . . The offenders typically believed that the prison sentence for their actions would be less than the actual prescriptive punishment. . . .
>
> During their first incarceration, however, they reached the conclusion that the state's punishment for committing property crimes was not as severe as they had feared. The worst punishment that the state could impose on them could be endured relatively easily; from that time on they viewed it as no great threat.[142]

This is an interesting perspective and one that will give policymakers pause.

Next, consider an example of a rational choice perspective. In this ambitious study Harold G. Grasmick and Robert J. Bursik, Jr., view crime as a function of opportunities presented to potential offenders and study how they might be deterred from crime by certain factors. After reviewing the literature of the "deterrent effect," which emphasizes the cost of legal sanctions, they proposed that threats of shame and embarrassment might prevent some people from engaging in criminal acts, and found some support for this by conducting a survey.[143] As they state,

> at least three kinds of potential costs, emanating from three different sources and linked to different theoretical emphases in criminology, might be taken into account by individuals in their "rational" decision of whether to comply with a law: (1) state-imposed physical and material deprivation, (2) self-imposed shame, and (3) socially imposed embarrassment. The rational choice model need not be restricted to a consideration of legal sanctions.[144]

The final example of the recent classical theories of deviance is known as routine activities theory. Developed by Lawrence Cohen and Marcus Felson, it assumes that

> the motivation to commit crime and the supply of offenders are constant. Consequently, . . . the volume and distribution of *predatory crime* (violent crimes against the person and crimes in which an offender attempts to steal an object directly) are closely related to the interaction of three variables which reflect the routine activities found in everyday American life: the availability of *suitable targets* (such as homes containing easily saleable goods); the absence of *capable guardians* (such as homeowners and their neighbors, friends and relatives); and the presence of *motivated offenders* (such as unemployed teenagers).[145]

An example of routine activities research is a study by Dennis W. Roncek and Pamela A. Maier that links this theory to the concept of "hot spots." Bars or taverns in some crime-ridden areas of cities known as "hot spots" may provide the perfect environment for a coming together of targets and victims. Using frequencies of crimes that occurred in certain areas of a city, they determined that "the amount of crime of every type was significantly higher on residential blocks with taverns or lounges than on others."[146]

These studies raise serious questions. If legal sanctions as currently administered are not effective, what do we do? And do you want to live on a block with several bars? Probably not.

Women and Deviance Theories

Up to this point we have examined the classical perspective, the positivist determinist view (biological, economic, and social), and revisited the classical theory. You may have wondered if any of the research mentioned applies to women. The answer to that, honestly, is that we don't know yet.

Very few of the early theories of crime or the research on crime, deviance, delinquency, or criminology dealt with women. No doubt the major reason for ignoring women has been that they have never been viewed as a serious crime problem. Early attempts at explaining women's involvement in crime are seriously deficient, and most works examined only male behavior. Indeed, Jeanne Flavin[147] used the term *androcentric* to describe the

"male-centered" development of the field of criminology. Until fairly recently, most criminologists were male, and their primary focus was male involvement in crime. Flavin's excellent discussion of the social realities that fostered the male dominated academic arena
surrounding the criminology field included the low offending rates for women, the prosecutorial deference shown toward female lawbreakers historically, differential victimization
rates for women, and discrimination against women in criminal justice system roles. These
crime and justice-related factors, when taken in the larger contexts of gender inequality in
business, politics, and status, and the gender role socialization process that pressures girls to
be "feminine," are logical reasons for the lack of specific attention to women's roles in
deviance and crime. As Sally S. Simpson has noted, "not all criminological research has
ignored women, but too often pre-1970's research on female offenders and victims of crime
fell prey to unreflecting sexism, and in its more extreme form, misogyny."[148] Some of the
research has been similar to that employed for men. Lombroso, the most enthusiastic biological determinist of all time, attempted to use research methods on women similar to those
used on men. He concluded that women were not as evolved as males.[149] Other early efforts
at explaining crime concerning women are downright silly. Meda Chesney-Lind and Randall
G. Shelden outline some of these attempts in a chapter on "Theories of Female Delinquency
and Crime." After reviewing the likes of Lombroso, they continue by discussing others, such
as W. I. Thomas, who in 1928 determined that all female delinquency was an expression of
sexual problems. Sheldon and Eleanor Glueck in 1938 studied incarcerated women and
stated that they saw them, half of whom had been prostitutes and four-fifths of whom had
venereal infections, as "a sorry lot"; they also believed that extensive work with these women,
including lengthy sentences in reformatories and even voluntary sterilization, were remedies.
Writing in 1950 and 1969, Otto Pollack speculated that precocious biological maturity
played an important role in female sexual delinquency. In 1966, Gisela Konopka likewise
assumed that girls and women were largely controlled by their biology and their sexuality.[150]

Although these examples provide a glimpse of the simplistic research on women and
crime, Chesney-Lind and Shelden also review other more accepted theories, such as differential association, and conclude that "key sociological theories of delinquency (ecological, strain, differential association, control, labeling) . . . ignored, for all practical purposes,
the delinquency of girls. . . . Often girls were dismissed in cavalier terms or relegated to
footnotes."[151]

Specific attention to women as an affected group materialized in 1986, in James
Messerschmidt's work on gender class theory.[152] In Messerschmidt's discussion of our
"patriarchal capitalist society," women, like the whole of the working class, are described
as a powerless group that suffers exploitation by the capitalist class. Women, from this perspective, are pressured toward criminal behavior as the working class is, though women
lack the power and opportunity to become involved in traditional crime at the same rates as
males. Messerschmidt developed these ideas further with his explanation of structured
action theory,[153] which suggests that delinquency, especially in violent form, is often an
expression, or *presentation,* of masculinity in response to a challenge for males. The social
process that results in delinquent response to a masculinity challenge does not include girls
and women, usually, and thus explains lower offense rates.[154] John Hagan, Bill McCarthy,
and Todd Woodward developed a theory of Power-Control based on similar principles. The

gender role expectations in *patriarchal* families, in which girls are regulated more than boys and are encouraged to adopt feminine roles rather than the aggressive, masculine roles supported for boys, contrast in an interesting way with those in *egalitarian* families, in which control and gender roles are minimized. Women from the egalitarian environment would emerge less restrained, more likely to take risks, and thus more likely to be involved in delinquent behavior.[155]

The feminist perspective on life and society generally encompasses a much broader system of responsibility for behavior than does the male-dominated perspective that tends to assign responsibility to the individual offender. Indeed, it is easy to imagine Charles Darwin describing early human clans with the men lashing out violently at perceived threats and the women picking up the pieces, following the carnage, and patching everything back together in some kind of working order. The feminist point of view shares responsibility for misbehavior, and restoration, among the various elements of the community. The needs of the offender and consequent attention to the offender are often greater than the victim's needs or society's needs in the continuing process of keeping the community whole and functional. The current trend toward restorative justice in communities is a manifestation of the feminist philosophy.

Regarding of whether the feminist perspective will find a substantial niche in the field of criminology, Kathleen Daly and Meda Chesney-Lind insisted in 1988[156] that "women should be at the center of intellectual inquiry, not peripheral, invisible or appendages to men." They discussed the profound consequences that male dominated social institutions have on the economic, political, and status quality of women's lives in considerable detail and largely set the stage for subsequent research. Lisa Maher[157] explored motivation for women involved in violent crime, and concluded that, at least to some degree, women were influenced to target male victims because of past abuse by males. Maher observed that women may use violent crime to defend themselves, and as a reaction to economic exploitation. Jody Miller[158] did not find motivational differences for robbery between male and female perpetrators but did note that female robbers sometimes used men's tendency to disregard women as a threat as a *modus operandi* to accomplish robbery of male victims. Miller also studied the victimization of female gang members and found gender bias to be an important element in the social process.[159] Her recent book-length treatment of the social processes in female gangs has received much attention in the field.[160]

It is safe to say that the field of criminology will treat women's issues with increasing specificity. New works by Maher and Daly[161] and by Katherine van Wormer and Clemens Bartollas[162] focus on feminist criminology and women generally in the criminal justice system.

There is hope that research and theory will now treat the issue of women and deviance more fairly. Research on gender roles and gender role socialization may be promising.[163] Current efforts are, for example, exploring such subjects as gender and the family, why women murder more men in this country compared to other countries, and gender as a factor in school and delinquency.[164] However, the question remains: how much of the extensive research on crime, deviance, and delinquency, carefully produced over the years with male subjects, applies to women? This is only now being studied in depth and perhaps will soon be understood.

Integration of Theories

Many criminologists have surveyed the bewildering number of theories attempting to interpret deviance and crime. There have been multitudinous efforts at considering an integration of these various explanations.[165] In 1985 James Q. Wilson and Richard J. Herrnstein published *Crime and Human Nature,* in which they boldly attempt just such an integration. They argue that an explanation of crime and criminal behavior must integrate biological factors—such as gender, age, intelligence—and environmental factors like socialization, child-rearing practices, and even opportunity to commit crime.[166] Wilson and Herrnstein suggest that

> if one asks whether criminals are born or made, the answer, in one sense, is that they are both and in a more important sense, that the question is badly phrased. The words "born or made" imply that some part of criminality may be assigned, categorically and permanently, to constitutional (including genetic) factors and the other part, categorically and permanently, to social factors. Such an effort at partitioning variations in criminality between the two types of causes neglects, obviously, the complex interactions that exist between those causes.[167]

The above factors are only a part of the explanation of crime, according to Wilson and Herrnstein. Other variables also play a large role, as they explain:

> We do not assume that a person chooses between crime and noncrime; he may choose both, depending on the way in which opportunities present themselves (while riding home in the subway, an employed delivery boy may grab a woman's purse if he thinks he can get away with it, and a skilled burglar may take a daytime job as a taxi driver if it doesn't interfere with his criminal business).[168]

Why does someone commit crime? Wilson and Herrnstein explain it by suggesting that all these factors play a role:

1. The larger the ratio of the rewards (material and nonmaterial) of noncrime to the rewards (material and nonmaterial) of crime, the weaker the tendency to commit crimes.
2. The approval of peers and any sense of inequity will increase or decrease the total value of crime.
3. The opinions of family, friends, and employers are important benefits of noncrime, as is the desire to avoid the penalties that can be imposed by the criminal justice system.
4. The strength of any reward declines with time, but people differ in the rate at which they discount the future.
5. The strength of a given reward is also affected by the total supply of reinforcers.[169]

The Wilson and Herrnstein model contains elements of both the classical and positivist orientation. Choosing crime over noncrime is a complex process that involves rewards of crime over noncrime, socialization factors, conditioning, reinforcement, and consequences. Their attempt to integrate these various factors is ambitious, and it remains to be seen how successful it will be.

CRITICAL THINKING EXERCISES

1. What are the characteristics of a *good* theory? What theory in this chapter could you use to explain why you are attending college?

2. Think about someone you know who has been in trouble. Try to explain that person's behavior in terms of sociobiology theory.

3. If sociobiology theory turned out to be true, how could we use it today to control or eliminate crime? *Should* we use it?

4. Explain the basics of strain theory. Are college exams a form of strain that might trigger deviant behavior? What characteristics of U.S. society cause potentially harmful strain?

5. Explain the concept of gender role socialization. How are women and men *socialized* into different gender roles?

CHECK IT OUT ON THE WEB

The Internet addresses listed below are intended to provide the reader with understanding of a wide range of perspectives regarding the subject matter discussed in this chapter. Some sites may contain objectionable material. The list is not intended to reflect the viewpoints or opinions of the authors or the publisher.

http://www.talkjustice.con/cybrary.asp
    comprehensive on-line criminal justice library
http://www.acs.appstate.edu/dept/ps-cj/cj-sour.html
    deviance and conformity theory
http://www.crime-times.org
    links between aberrant behavior and brain dysfunction
http://www.ojp.usdoj.gov/nij/pubs-sum/cj2000.htm
    National Institute of Justice library of expert commentary on crime and criminological topics
http://www.crimetheory.com
    general criminology theory

ENDNOTES

1. Robert L. Dugdale, *The Jukes: A Study in Crime, Pauperism, Disease, and Heredity,* 4th ed. (New York: Putnam, 1910), pp. 13–14. For an interesting critique of Dugdale's data-gathering methods, see Samuel Hopkins Adams, "The Juke Myth," *Saturday Review, 14* (April 2, 1955), pp. 13, 48–49.

2. Henry H. Goddard, *The Kallikak Family: A Study in the Heredity of Feeble-Mindedness* (New York: Macmillan, 1927), pp. 18–19.

3. Ibid., p. 59.

4. Henry H. Goddard, *Human Efficiency and Levels of Intelligence* (Princeton, NJ: Princeton University Press, 1920), pp. 71–72.

5. For detailed reviews of research on the intelligence of criminals, see Fink, *Causes of Crime,* pp. 211–239; and Vold and Bernard, *Theoretical Criminology,* pp. 67–83. For a discussion of how "bad" women are characterized in family studies by Dugdale, Goddard, and others of that period, see Nicolas F. Hahn, "Too Dumb to Know Better: Cacogenic Family Studies and the Criminology of Women,"

Criminology, 18 (May 1980), pp. 3–25. This article contains references to 15 major family studies published between 1874 and 1926.

6. T. W. Shannon, *Eugenics* (Marietta, OH: S. A. Mullikin, 1916), p. 160.

7. Charles R. Henderson, *Dependent, Defective, and Delinquent Classes, and Their Social Treatment* (Boston: D. C. Heath, 1901), p. 317.

8. Fink, *Causes of Crime*, p. 209; and Nicholas N. Kittrie, *The Right to Be Different: Deviance and Enforced Therapy* (Baltimore: Penguin Books, 1973), pp. 312–313.

9. Samuel Jan Brakel, John Parry, and Barbara A. Weiner, *The Mentally Disabled and the Law*, 3rd ed. (Chicago: American Bar Foundation, 1985), pp. 523–524.

10. *Buck v. Bell*, 274 U.S. 200, 207 (1927). This discussion draws upon the following articles by Robert Reinhold: "Virginia Sterilized the 'Retarded,'" *The New York Times*, February 23, 1980, p. 6; and "Some Unfortunate Verdicts on Writing Science into the Law," *The New York Times*, March 9, 1980, p. 8E. See also Nicole Hahn Rafter, "White Trash: Eugenics as Social Ideology," *Society, 26* (November–December 1988), pp. 43–49.

11. Johannes Lange, *Crime as Destiny: A Study of Criminal Twins*, trans. Charlotte Haldane (London: George Allen & Unwin, 1931), p. 198.

12. Andrew C. Heath, "Genetic Influences on Alcoholism Risk: A Review of Adoption and Twin Studies," *Alcohol Health and Research World, 19* (Summer 1995), p. 166.

13. Alec Roy, Gunnar Rylander, and Marco Sarchiapone, "Genetic Studies of Suicidal Behavior," *Psychiatric Clinics of North America, 20* (September 1997), pp. 595–611.

14. Leena Vehmanen, Jaakko Kaprio, and Jouko Loennqvist, "Twin Studies on Concordance for Bipolar Disorder," *Psychiatria-Fennica, 26* (1995), pp. 107–116.

15. Robert Cloninger, "Assessment of the Impulsive-Compulsive Spectrum of Behavior by the Seven-Factor Model of Temperament and Character," in *Impulsivity and Compulsivity*, ed. John Oldham (Washington, DC: American Psychiatric Press, 1996), pp. 59–95.

16. Thomas Bouchard, "IQ Similarity in Twins Reared Apart: Findings and Responses to Critics," in *Intelligence, Heredity, and Environment*, ed. Robert Sternberg (New York: Cambridge University Press, 1997), pp. 126–160.

17. Odd Stefen Dalgard and Einar Kringlen, "A Norwegian Twin Study of Criminality," *British Journal of Criminology, 16* (July 1976), p. 226 (emphasis added). See ibid., pp. 213–216 for a review of other twin studies.

18. Christiane Charlemaine, "Twins and Intelligence: Myths and Scientific Approach," in INSERM U155 Genetics Epidemiology VII (Paris: University of Paris/American Sociological Association, 1997).

19. Glenn D. Walters and Thomas W. White, "Heredity and Crime: Bad Genes or Bad Research?" *Criminology, 27* (August 1989), p. 478.

20. Patricia A. Brennan and Sarnoff A. Mednick, "A Reply to Walters and White: Heredity and Crime," *Criminology, 28* (November 1990), p. 657.

21. Glenn D. Walters, "Heredity and Crime, and the Killing-the-Bearer-of-Bad-News Syndrome: A Reply to Brennan and Mednick," *Criminology, 28* (November 1990), pp. 663–667.

22. Paraphrased from Richard J. Herrnstein and Charles Murray, *The Bell Curve: Intelligence and Class Structure in American Life* (New York: The Free Press, 1994), pp. 22, 24.

23. Ibid., pp. 235–247.

24. Ibid., p. 243.

25. Francis Cullen, Paul Gendreau, Roger Jarjoura, and John Paul Wright, "Crime and the Bell Curve: Lessons from Intelligent Criminology," *Crime and Delinquency, 43* (October 1997), p. 387.

26. Michael Nunley, "The Bell Curve: Too Smooth to Be True," *American Behavioral Scientist, 39* (September–October 1995), p. 74.

27. Earnest Albert Hooton, *Crime and the Man* (Cambridge, MA: Harvard University Press, 1939), p. 130.

28. For specific critical evaluations of Hooton's work, see Edwin H. Sutherland, "The American Criminal" and "Crime and the Man," in *The Sutherland Papers*, ed. Albert K. Cohen, Alfred Lindesmith, and Karl Schuessler (Bloomington: Indiana University Press, 1956), pp. 273–278; and Vold and Bernard, *Theoretical Criminology*, pp. 55–57.

29. William H. Sheldon, *Varieties of Delinquent Youth: An Introduction to Constitutional Psychiatry* (New York: Harper, 1949), pp. 14–16, 25–28.

30. Ibid., pp. 726–730. For a more recent study linking delinquency with mesomorphic physique, see Juan B. Cortes and Florence M. Gatti, *Delinquency and Crime: A Biopsychosocial Approach* (New York: Seminar Press, 1972), pp. 44–104.

31. Edwin H. Sutherland, "Varieties of Delinquent Youth," in *The Sutherland Papers*, ed. Cohen, Lindesmith, and Schuessler, pp. 287–288.

32. For reviews of research and discussions of the legal implications, see Brian C. Baker, "XYY Chromosome Syndrome and the Law," *Criminologica, 7* (February 1970), pp. 2–35; Theodore R. Sarbin and Jeffrey Miller, "Demonism Revisited: The XYY Chromosomal Anomaly," *Issues in Criminology, 5* (Summer 1970), pp. 195–207; National Institute of Mental Health, *Report on the XYY Chromosomal Abnormality* (Washington, DC: Government Printing Office, 1970); Richard G. Fox, "The XYY Offender: A Modern Myth?" *Journal of Criminal Law, Criminology, and Police Science, 62* (March 1971),

pp. 59–73; Menachim Amir and Yitzchak Berman, "Chromosomal Deviation and Crime," *Federal Probation, 34* (June 1970), pp. 55–62; Lissy F. Jarvik, Victor Klodin, and Steven S. Matsuyama, "Human Aggression and the Extra Y Chromosome," *American Psychologist, 28* (August 1973), pp. 674–682; Herman A. Witkin et al., "Criminality in XYY and XXY Men," *Science, 193* (August 13, 1976), pp. 547–555; and Lee Ellis, "Genetics and Criminal Behavior," *Criminology, 20* (February 1982), pp. 43–66.

33. H. Hunter, "YY Chromosomes and Klinefelter's Syndrome," *Lancet, 1* (April 1966), p. 984; Sarbin and Miller, "Demonism Revisited," pp. 202–204; and Fox, "The XYY Offender," pp. 69–70.

34. Witkin et al., "Criminality in XYY and XXY Men."

35. Ibid.

36. Bertram S. Brown, Louis A. Wienckowski, and Lyle W. Bivens, *Psychosurgery: Perspectives on a Current Problem* (Washington, DC: U.S. Government Printing Office, 1973), p. 1.

37. Lee Edson, "The Psyche and the Surgeon," *The New York Times Magazine,* September 30, 1973, p. 79; see also Kittrie, *The Right to Be Different,* pp. 305–306.

38. For a discussion of drugs used as "medication" in prison, see Ira Sommers and Deborah R. Baskin, "The Prescription of Psychiatric Medications in Prison: Psychiatric Versus Labelling Perspectives," *Justice Quarterly, 4* (December 1990), pp. 739–755.

39. Vernon H. Mark and Frank R. Ervin, *Violence and the Brain* (New York: Harper & Row, 1970), p. 126.

40. Ibid., pp. 7, 31–33, 141.

41. For a review of research indicating inconsistent results, see Russell R. Monroe, *Brain Dysfunction in Aggressive Criminals* (Lexington, MA: Lexington Books, 1978), pp. 37–42.

42. Jennifer L. White, Terrie E. Moffit, Felton Earls, Lee Robins, and Phil A. Silva, "How Early Can We Tell? Predictors of Childhood Conduct Disorder and Adolescent Delinquency," *Criminology, 28* (November 1990), pp. 507–528.

43. Wray Herbert, "Psychosurgery Redux," *U.S. News & World Report, 123* (November 3, 1997), p. 63.

44. David M. Rorvik, "Bringing the War Home," *Playboy, 21* (September 1974), p. 114.

45. Abram Hoffer, "Children with Learning and Behavioral Disorders," *Journal of Orthomolecular Psychiatry, 5* (1976).

46. R. Rada, D. Laws, and R. Kellner, "Plasma Testosterone Levels in the Rapist," *Psychomatic Medicine, 38* (1976).

47. Reiss and J. Ross, *Understanding and Preventing Violence* (Washington, DC: National Academy Press, 1993).

48. Serotonin research is summarized expertly by Brown, Botsis, and Van Praag in their article "Serotonin and Aggression," which appears in Marc Hillbrand and Nathaniel Pallone's edited publication *The Psychology of Aggression* (New York: Hawthorn Press, 1994), pp. 28–40.

49. James Cowles Prichard, *A Treatise on Insanity and Other Disorders Affecting the Mind* (London: Sherwood, Gilbert, and Piper, 1835); quoted in Fink, *Causes of Crime,* p. 48.

50. Fink, *Causes of Crime,* p. 33.

51. American Psychiatric Association, *Diagnostic and Statistical Manual of Mental Disorders,* 3rd ed., rev. (Washington, DC: American Psychiatric Association, 1987), p. 342.

52. Hulsey Cason, "The Psychopath and the Psychopathic," *Journal of Criminal Psychopathology, 4* (January 1943), pp. 522–527.

53. Hervey M. Cleckley, *The Mask of Sanity,* 2nd ed. (St. Louis: C. V. Mosby, 1950), pp. 355–356.

54. Michael Hakeem, "A Critique of the Psychiatric Approach to Crime and Correction," *Law and Contemporary Problems, 23* (Autumn 1958), pp. 668–676.

55. For a more sympathetic view of attempts to delineate psychopathy, see Rennie, *The Search for Criminal Man,* pp. 251–264.

56. Lee Ellis, "Monoamine Oxidase and Criminality: Identifying an Apparent Biological Marker for Antisocial Behavior," *Journal of Research in Crime and Delinquency, 28* (May 1991), pp. 227–251; and "Identifying Psychopaths (Test Based on the Missouri Descriptive Index: Work of James M. A. Weiss)," *USA Today,* August 12, 1989, p. 12.

57. Karl F. Schuessler and Donald R. Cressey, "Personality Characteristics of Criminals," *American Journal of Sociology, 55* (March 1950), pp. 483–484.

58. For a detailed consideration of problems of causal order in research, see Travis Hirschi and Hanan C. Selvin, *Delinquency Research: An Appraisal of Analytic Methods* (New York: The Free Press, 1967).

59. Gordon P. Waldo and Simon Dinitz, "Personality Attributes of the Criminal: An Analysis of Research Studies, 1950–1965," *Journal of Research in Crime and Delinquency, 4* (July 1967), p. 202.

60. Ibid.

61. Samuel Yochelson and Stanton E. Samenow, *The Criminal Personality,* vol. 1, *A Profile for Change* (New York: Jason Aronson, 1976), p. 178.

62. O. J. Keller, "The Criminal Personality or Lombroso Revisited," *Federal Probation, 44* (March 1980), p. 37.

63. Starke R. Hathaway and Elio D. Monachesi, *Adolescent Personality and Behavior: MMPI Patterns of Normal, Delinquent, Dropout, and Other Outcomes* (Minneapolis: University of Minnesota Press, 1963), pp. 99–100.

64. For articles debating the pros and cons of psychoanalysis as a science, see Sidney Hook, ed., *Psychoanalysis, Scientific Method, and Philosophy* (New York: New York University Press, 1964).

65. Bernard C. Glueck, *Final Report: Research Project for the Study and Treatment of Persons Convicted of Crimes Involving Sexual Aberrations, June 1952 to June 1955* (New York: 1957), pp. 23–24.

66. Edward O. Wilson, *Sociobiology: The New Synthesis* (Cambridge, MA: Harvard University Press, 1975); and *On Human Nature* (Cambridge, MA: Harvard University Press, 1978).

67. Wilson, *On Human Nature,* p. 16.

68. Ibid., p. 38.

69. Sarnoff A. Mednick, "A Biosocial Theory of the Learning of Law-Abiding Behavior," in *Biosocial Bases of Criminal Behavior,* ed. Sarnoff A. Mednick and Karl O. Christiansen (New York: Gardner Press, 1977), p. 5.

70. These categories are based on Allan Mazur, "Biological Explanation in Sociology," *Sociological Quarterly, 19* (Autumn 1978), pp. 604–613.

71. Albert K. Cohen, *Deviance and Control* (Englewood Cliffs, NJ: Prentice-Hall, 1966), p. 54.

72. This discussion of necessity grossly oversimplifies the complex issue of the limits and responsibilities of scientific inquiry. The reader is recommended to begin with the following: Rennie, *The Search for Criminal Man,* pp. 92–96, 223–228; Tony Platt and Paul Takagi, "Biosocial Criminology: A Critique," *Crime and Social Justice, 11* (Spring–Summer 1979), pp. 5–13; and Edward Sagarin, ed., *Taboos in Criminology* (Beverly Hills, CA: Sage Publications, 1980).

73. For discussions of early ecologists, see Harwin L. Voss and David M. Petersen, eds., *Ecology, Crime, and Delinquency* (New York: Appleton-Century-Crofts, 1971), pp. 1–4; Leon Radzinowicz, *Ideology and Crime* (New York: Columbia University Press, 1966), pp. 29–38; Terence Morris, *The Criminal Area: A Study in Social Ecology* (London: Routledge & Kegan Paul, 1957), pp. 44–52; and Hermann Mannheim, *Comparative Criminology* (Boston: Houghton Mifflin, 1965), pp. 95–98.

74. P. Bierne, "Adolph Quetelet and the Origins of Positivist Criminology," *American Journal of Sociology, 92:* 5 (1987), pp. 1140–1169.

75. Lambert A. J. Quetelet, *A Treatise on Man and the Development of His Faculties* (1842; facsimile reprint, Gainesville, FL: Scholars' Facsimiles & Reprints, 1969), p. 6.

76. Ibid., p. 108.

77. George B. Vold and Thomas J. Bernard, *Theoretical Criminology,* 3rd ed. (New York: Oxford University Press, 1986), pp. 130–142; Stephen Schafer, *Theories in Criminology: Past and Present Philosophies of the Crime Problem* (New York: Random House, 1969), pp. 255–290; and Leon Radzinowicz, "Economic Pressures," in *Crime and Justice: The Criminal in Society,* ed. Leon Radzinow-

icz and Marvin E. Wolfgang (New York: Basic Books, 1971), vol. 1, pp. 420–442.

78. Ian Taylor, Paul Walton, and Jock Young, *The New Criminology: For a Social Theory of Deviance* (London: Routledge & Kegan Paul, 1973), p. 218. For a detailed discussion of Marxist thought on deviance, see ibid., pp. 209–221.

79. Karl Marx, *Theories of Surplus Value* (Moscow: Foreign Languages Publishing House, n.d.), p. 375; reprinted in *Monthly Review, 22* (December 1970), p. 38.

80. Taylor, Walton, and Young, *The New Criminology,* pp. 216–218.

81. See Austin T. Turk, "Introduction," in *Criminality and Economic Conditions* by Willem Bonger, abridged by Austin T. Turk (Bloomington: Indiana University Press, 1969), pp. 7–12.

82. Bonger, *Criminality and Economic Conditions,* pp. 194–195.

83. Emile Durkheim, *The Rules of Sociological Method,* 8th ed., trans. Sarah A. Solovay and John H. Mueller (Glencoe, IL: The Free Press, 1938), pp. 67–69.

84. Ibid., p. 70 (emphasis added).

85. Ibid., p. 71.

86. For a detailed history of the development of the concept of anomie, see Marshall B. Clinard, "The Theoretical Implications of Anomie and Deviant Behavior," in *Anomie and Deviant Behavior: A Discussion and Critique,* ed. Marshall B. Clinard (New York: The Free Press, 1964), pp. 1–56. See also Vold and Bernard, *Theoretical Criminology,* pp. 143–159.

87. For a critique of Durkheim's work, see Jack D. Douglas, *The Social Meanings of Suicide* (Princeton: Princeton University Press, 1967), pp. 3–76.

88. Emile Durkheim, *Suicide: A Study in Sociology,* trans. John A. Spaulding and George Simpson (Glencoe, IL: The Free Press, 1951), p. 256.

89. As discussed, for example, by Frank Schmalleger in *Criminology Today,* 2nd ed. (Upper Saddle River, NJ: Prentice-Hall, 1999), p. 290.

90. Robert K. Merton, "Social Structure and Anomie," *American Sociological Review, 3* (October 1938), pp. 672–682. For a revised discussion, see Merton, *Social Theory and Social Structure,* rev. and enl. ed. (Glencoe, IL: The Free Press, 1957), pp. 131–194.

91. Merton, *Social Theory and Social Structure,* p. 146 (emphasis added).

92. Ibid., p. 162.

93. *The New York Times,* August 25, 1973, p. 25; October 6, 1973, p. 21; and October 24, 1973, p. 15.

94. Robert K. Merton, "Introduction," in *Contemporary Social Problems,* 4th ed., ed. Robert K. Merton and Robert Nisbet (New York: Harcourt Brace Jovanovich, 1976), pp. 29–30.

95. Paraphrased from Albert K. Cohen, *Delinquent Boys: The Culture of the Gang* (New York: The Free Press, 1955), pp. 88–92.

96. Ibid., p. 121.

97. Ibid., p. 131.

98. Richard A. Cloward and Lloyd E. Ohlin, *Delinquency and Opportunity: A Theory of Delinquent Gangs* (New York: The Free Press, 1960), p. 96. The following discussion is based on this work. For a review of criticisms of Cohen, Cloward, and Ohlin, see LaMar T. Empey, *American Delinquency* (Homewood, IL: Dorsey Press, 1978), pp. 300–306.

99. Maynard L. Erickson, "Group Violations, Socioeconomic Status, and Official Delinquency," *Social Forces, 52* (September 1973), p. 51. See also Paul Lerman, "Gangs, Networks, and Subcultural Delinquency," *American Journal of Sociology, 73* (July 1967), pp. 63–72; and LaMar T. Empey and Steven G. Lubeck, *The Silverlake Experiment: Testing Delinquency Theory and Community Intervention* (Chicago: Aldine, 1971), pp. 119–133. For a recent explanation of the phenomena, see Charles R. Tittle and Robert F. Meier, "Specifying the SES/Delinquency Relationship," *Criminology, 28* (May 1990), pp. 271–299.

100. For detailed critiques, see Clinard, ed., *Anomie and Deviant Behavior;* Taylor, Walton, and Young, *The New Criminology,* pp. 92–110; Edwin M. Lemert, *Human Deviance, Social Problems, and Social Control,* 2nd ed. (Englewood Cliffs, NJ: Prentice-Hall, 1972), pp. 26–61; and Vold and Bernard, *Theoretical Criminology,* pp. 197–201.

101. Tittle and Meier, "Specifying the SES/Delinquency Relationship," p. 292.

102. Ibid., pp. 273–278, 294–295.

103. Robert Agnew, "Foundation for a General Strain Theory of Crime and Delinquency," *Criminology* (February 1992), pp. 47–87.

104. Paul Mazerolle, "Gender, General Strain, and Delinquency: Empirical Examination," *Justice Quarterly, 15* (March 1998) pp. 65–91.

105. Robert Agnew, "A General Strain Theory of Community Differences in Crime Rates," *The Journal of Research in Crime and Delinquency, 36* (May 1999), pp. 123–155.

106. Steven Messner and Richard Rosenfeld, *Crime and the American Dream,* 2nd ed. (Belmont, CA: Wadsworth, 2000).

107. Albert K. Cohen, *Deviance and Control* (Englewood Cliffs, NJ: Prentice-Hall, 1966), pp. 93–97.

108. Travis Hirschi, *Causes of Delinquency* (Berkeley: University of California Press, 1969), pp. 11–15.

109. Morris, *The Criminal Area,* p. 41.

110. Amos H. Hawley, *Human Ecology: A Theory of Community Structure* (New York: Ronald Press, 1950), pp. 5–6; quoted in Voss and Petersen, eds., *Ecology, Crime, and Delinquency,* p. 9.

111. Clifford R. Shaw, *Delinquency Areas: A Study of the Geographic Distribution of School Truants, Juvenile Delinquents, and Adult Offenders in Chicago* (Chicago: University of Chicago Press, 1929), pp. 198–204.

112. Ibid., pp. 205–206 (emphasis added).

113. For a critique of social disorganization as a concept, see Marshall B. Clinard and Robert F. Meier, *Sociology of Deviant Behavior,* 5th ed. (New York: Holt, Rinehart and Winston, 1979), pp. 63–67. Also see Robert J. Bursik, Jr., "Social Disorganization and Theories of Crime and Delinquency: Problems and Prospects," *Criminology, 26* (November 1988), pp. 519–551.

114. Clifford R. Shaw and Henry D. McKay, *Juvenile Delinquency and Urban Areas* (Chicago: University of Chicago Press, 1942), pp. 166–167.

115. Some of the milestones in theories of gang delinquency are Frederic M. Thrasher, *The Gang* (Chicago: University of Chicago Press, 1927); Solomon Kobrin, "The Conflict of Values in Delinquency Areas," *American Sociological Review, 16* (October 1951), pp. 653–661; Cohen, *Delinquent Boys;* Cloward and Ohlin, *Delinquency and Opportunity;* Lewis Yablonsky, *The Violent Gang* (New York: Macmillan, 1962); and James F. Short, Jr., and Fred L. Strodtbeck, *Group Process and Gang Delinquency* (Chicago: University of Chicago Press, 1965). See also David J. Bordua, "Delinquent Subcultures: Sociological Interpretations of Gang Delinquency," *The Annals of the American Academy of Political and Social Science, 338* (November 1961), pp. 120–136; and Paul Lerman, "Individual Values, Peer Values, and Subcultural Delinquency," *American Sociological Review, 33* (April 1968), pp. 219–235. More recently see Jeffrey Fagan, "The Social Organization of Drug Use and Drug Dealing Among Urban Gangs," *Criminology, 27* (November 1989), pp. 633–669; Malcolm W. Klein, Cheryl L. Maxson, and Lea C. Cunningham, "Crack: Street Gangs and Violence," *Criminology, 29* (November 1991), pp. 623–650; and Pamela Irving Jackson, "Crime, Youth Gangs, and Urban Transition: The Social Dislocations of Postindustrial Economic Development," *Justice Quarterly, 8* (September 1991), pp. 379–397.

116. Gabriel Tarde, *Penal Philosophy,* trans. Rapelje Howell (Boston: Little, Brown, 1912), pp. 252–253.

117. Edwin H. Sutherland, *Principles of Criminology,* 3rd ed. (Philadelphia: J. B. Lippincott, 1939), pp. 4–9. For a discussion of the evolution of the theory, see *The Sutherland Papers,* ed. Albert K. Cohen, Alfred Lindesmith, and Karl Schuessler (Bloomington: Indiana University Press, 1956), pp. 5–43.

118. Edwin H. Sutherland and Donald R. Cressey, *Criminology,* 10th ed. (Philadelphia: J. B. Lippincott, 1978), pp. 80–82.

119. A thorough review of the theory and problems associated with research will be found in Donald R. Cressey, "Epidemiology and Individual Conduct: A Case from Criminology," *Pacific Sociological Review, 3* (Fall 1960), pp. 47–58.

120. Daniel Glaser, "Differential Association and Criminological Prediction," *Social Problems, 8* (Summer 1960), pp. 6–14.

121. Melvin L. DeFleur and Richard Quinney, "A Reformulation of Sutherland's Differential Association Theory and a Strategy for Empirical Verification," *Journal of Research in Crime and Delinquency, 3* (January 1966), p. 7.

122. Ibid., p. 21.

123. Ronald L. Akers, *Deviant Behavior: A Social Learning Approach,* 3rd ed. (Belmont, CA: Wadsworth, 1985), p. 58.

124. For discussions of reinforcement theory as applied to differential association, see ibid., pp. 39–47; Robert K. Burgess and Ronald L. Akers, "A Differential Association–Reinforcement Theory of Criminal Behavior," *Social Problems, 14* (Fall 1966), pp. 128–147; and Reed Adams, "Differential Association and Learning Principles Revisited," *Social Problems, 20* (Spring 1973), pp. 458–470.

125. Akers, *Deviant Behavior,* pp. 57–58.

126. For discussions on the assumptions of various theories, see Diana H. Fishbein, "Biological Perspectives in Criminology," *Criminology, 28* (February 1990), pp. 30–31; and Travis Hirschi, "Exploring Alternatives to Integrated Theory," in *Theoretical Integration in the Study of Deviance and Crime: Problems and Perspectives,* ed. Steven F. Messner, Marvin D. Krohn, and Allen E. Liska (Albany: State University of New York Press, 1989), pp. 37–49.

127. Emile Durkheim, *The Division of Labor in Society* (New York: The Free Press, 1933).

128. Walter Reckless, *The Crime Problem* (New York: Appleton-Century-Crofts, 1967).

129. For a general discussion of a variety of control theories, see Gwynn Nettler, *Explaining Crime,* 3rd ed. (New York: McGraw-Hill, 1984), pp. 288–314.

130. Travis Hirschi, *Causes of Delinquency* (Berkeley: University of California Press, 1969).

131. For example, see Stephen Cernkovich, "Evaluating Two Models of Delinquency Causation: Structural Theory and Control Theory," *Criminology, 16* (November 1978), pp. 335–352; Marvin D. Krohn and James L. Massey, "Social Control and Delinquent Behavior: An Examination of the Elements of the Social Bond," *Sociological Quarterly, 21* (Autumn 1980), pp. 529–543; Michael D. Wiatrowski, David B. Griswold, and Mary K. Roberts, "Social Control Theory and Delinquency," *American Sociological Review, 46* (October 1981), pp. 525–541; and Robert Lyerly and James K. Skipper, Jr., "Differential Rates of Rural-Urban Delinquency: A Social Control Approach," *Criminology, 19* (February 1982), pp. 385–394.

132. See Michael R. Gottfredson and Travis Hirschi, *A General Theory of Crime* (Stanford: Stanford University Press, 1990), pp. 15–20, 153. Also see Travis Hirschi and Michael R. Gottfredson, "The Significance of White-Collar Crime for a General Theory of Crime," *Criminology, 27* (May 1989), pp. 359–371.

133. For a review of the issue, see Walker, *Sense and Nonsense About Crime,* pp. 201–234.

134. Donna Hamparian, Joseph Davis, Judith Jacobson, and Robert McGraw, *The Young Criminal Years of the Violent Few* (Washington, D.C.: U.S. Department of Justice, 1985); see also Alfred Blumstein, *Criminal Careers and Career Criminals* (Washington, DC: National Academy Press, 1986).

135. Peter Greenwood, *Selective Incapacitation* (Santa Monica, CA: Rand Corporation, 1982).

136. Larry J. Siegel and Joseph J. Senna, *Juvenile Delinquency: Theory, Practice, and Law,* 3rd ed. (St. Paul: West Publishing Co., 1988), p. 88.

137. Ibid., p. 87.

138. See Vold and Bernard, *Theoretical Criminology,* pp. 30–35.

139. Isaac Ehrlich, "Participation in Illegitimate Activities: A Theoretical and Empirical Investigation," *Journal of Political Economy* (May–June 1973), pp. 521–565.

140. Walker, *Sense and Nonsense About Crime* (Monterey, CA: Brooks Cole, 1985), p. 257.

141. Hiroya Akiba, "The Deterrent Effect Reconsidered: The Minimum Time Approach," *The Journal of Socio-Economics, 20:* 2 (1990), pp. 181–192.

142. Kenneth D. Tunnel, "Choosing Crime: Close Your Eyes and Take Your Chances," *Justice Quarterly, 7* (December 1990), pp. 673–690.

143. Harold G. Grasmick and Robert J. Bursik, Jr., "Conscience, Significant Others, and Rational Choice: Extending the Deterrence Model," *Law and Society Review, 24:* 3 (1990), pp. 837–861.

144. Ibid., p. 841.

145. Lawrence Cohen and Marcus Felson, "Social Change and Crime Rate Trends: A Routine Activities Approach," *American Sociological Review, 44* (1979), pp. 588–608. This theory is explained in detail in Siegel and Senna, *Juvenile Delinquency,* p. 87.

146. Dennis W. Roncek and Pamela A. Maier, "Bars, Blocks, and Crimes Revisited: Linking the Theory of Routine Activities to the Empiricism of 'Hot Spots,'" *Criminology, 29* (November 1991), pp. 725–753.

147. Jeanne Flavin, "Razing the Wall: A Feminist Critique of Sentencing Theory, Research, and Policy," in *The Cutting Edge in Radical/Critical Criminology and Criminal Justice,* ed. Jeffrey Ross (Westport, CT: Praeger Publishers, 1998), pp. 145–164.

148. Sally S. Simpson, "Feminist Theory, Crime, and Justice," *Criminology, 27* (November 1989), p. 605.

149. Cesare Lombroso and William Ferrero, *The Female Offender* (London: Unwin and Fisher, 1895).

150. Paraphrased from Meda Chesney-Lind and Randall G. Shelden, *Girls: Delinquency and Juvenile Justice*

(Pacific Grove, CA: Brooks/Cole Publishing Company, 1992), pp. 56–62.

151. Ibid., p. 78.

152. James Messerschmidt, *Capitalism, Patriarchy, and Crime* (Totowa, NJ: Rowman and Littlefield, 1986).

153. James Messerschmidt, "From Patriarchy to Gender: Feminist Theory, Criminology, and the Challenge of Diversity," in *International Feminist Perspectives in Criminology: Engendering a Discipline,* ed. Rafter and Heidensohn (Buckingham, UK: Open University Press, 1997), pp. 176–188.

154. James Messerschmidt, *Nine Lives: Adolescent Masculinities, the Body, and Violence* (Boulder, CO: Westview Publishing, 2000).

155. Bill McCarthy, John Hagan, and Todd Woodward, "In the Company of Women: Structure and Agency in a Revised Power-Control Theory of Gender and Delinquency," *Criminology, 37* (November 1999), pp. 761–788.

156. Kathleen Daly and Meda Chesney-Lind, "Feminism and Criminology," *Justice Quarterly, 5* (December 1988), pp. 497–535.

157. Lisa Maher, *Sexed Work: Gender, Race, and Resistance in a Brooklyn Drug Market* (Oxford, UK: Clarendon Press, 1997).

158. Jody Miller, "Up It Up: Gender and the Accomplishment of Street Robbery," *Criminology, 36* (February 1998), pp. 37–65.

159. Jody Miller, "Gender and Victimization Risk Among Young Women in Gangs," *The Journal of Research in Crime and Delinquency, 35* (November 1998), pp. 429–453.

160. Jody Miller, *One of the Guys: Girls, Gangs, and Gender* (New York: Oxford University Press, 2001).

161. Lisa Maher and Kathleen Daly, *Criminology at the Crossroads: Feminist Readings in Crime and Justice* (New York: Oxford University Press, 1998).

162. Katherine van Wormer and Clemens Bartollas, *Women and the Criminal Justice System* (Boston: Allyn and Bacon, 2000).

163. Chesney-Lind and Sheldon, p. 78.

164. Ibid.; see ibid., pp. 79–100, for examples.

165. See Gary D. Hill and Maxine P. Atkinson, "Gender, Familial Control, and Delinquency," *Criminology, 26* (February 1988), pp. 127–149; Robert M. O'Brien, "Exploring the Intersexual Nature of Violent Crimes," *Criminology, 26* (February 1988), pp. 151–170; and Jill Leslie Rosenbaum and James R. Lasley, "School, Community Context, and Delinquency: Rethinking the Gender Gap," *Justice Quarterly, 7* (September 1990), pp. 493–513.

166. James Q. Wilson and Richard J. Herrnstein, *Crime and Human Nature* (New York: Simon & Schuster, 1985).

167. Ibid., pp. 509–510.

168. Ibid., pp. 41–45, 314.

169. Ibid., pp. 61–62.

3 Why Is Certain Behavior Deviant?

Although it may seem logical to probe the reasons why people do not always act the way we would prefer, we must realize that our preferences spring from a particular perspective, namely, our personal view of what the world should be. Whether we call something deviant out of fear, loathing, envy, or disgust, we are making a judgment that the behavior is disagreeable. But even when behavior does not meet our personal notions of social expectations, this does not mean that we are interested in actively seeking either its cause or suppression. Priorities and time limitations dictate the degree of our concern over others' behavior.

We ourselves behave in a world filled with expectations that others have of our behavior. For example, a sign telling us that the speed limit is 35 miles per hour is a tangible indication of a rule made by others and imposed upon us. The rule may not reflect our cautious nature and driving skills, but the rule is there—like it or not. We also know that we technically break the law by exceeding 35 by even a single mile. But we know, of course, that we are good drivers; it would be a source of considerable aggravation to be stopped by police for going anything less than 40 miles per hour. We are aware of the law, but we also know our capabilities.

None of this alters the fact that the police officer is perfectly within his or her authority either to warn us or to issue a ticket for traveling 36 miles per hour. Ticket or no, however, we are simply unwilling to accept that we are speeders in the same sense as those going 55 or more. If we are not "speeders" at 36 miles per hour, when are we—at 37, 40, 43? At what speed do we become "serious" violators, "reckless," "irresponsible," and a "menace to the community"?

This simple example points out that expectations concerning our behavior are not always of our making and that violations of expectations may result in a variety of reactions. Decisions are constantly being made by others about the appropriateness of our behavior. But everyone makes similar decisions about everyone else. We pass judgment on the morality, normalcy, and legality of other people's behavior every day. Furthermore, we respond toward people according to those judgments by hollering at them, ignoring them, calling the cops, and so forth.

But our individual judgments about others and how they should be dealt with usually have little impact beyond our families and circle of friends. There are those, however, who say, "There ought to be a law"—and there is a law. Or they say, "He should be committed" or "She should go to prison"—and it is done. These decisions have wide social consequences and have been practically ignored in the perspectives discussed so far. Decision making about what the rules shall be, who has broken them, and what should be done about the violators is the crux of the approaches to deviance considered in this chapter.

The Labeling Perspective

The nature and consequences of rule-making and rule enforcement are the bases of a sociological approach variously known as the *labeling, societal reaction,* or *interactionist perspective.*[1] This approach, which we shall call the *labeling perspective,* deals with two fundamental problems: the social production of deviance and the effect of labeling on behavior. Unlike traditional approaches that assume deviance is simply a violation of commonly accepted norms and that offenders must be different in ways that cause deviance, the labeling perspective shifts the focus to the audience—those who define persons and their behavior.

The Production of Deviance

The reaction toward deviance is a matter of decision making. This raises a serious question: Does it make sense to call all rule-breaking behavior deviant? From the labeling perspective, the answer is emphatically no. A principal advocate for this view, Howard S. Becker, points out that the enforcement of a rule is highly variable and problematic. Whether others will respond to rule breaking and the degree of that response once it comes depend upon many circumstances, including who is violating the rule, who feels they are being harmed, and the context (time, place, and so on) in which the rule-breaking behavior occurs. Consequently, argues Becker, a distinction must be made between rule breaking and deviance:

> Deviance is not a simple quality, present in some kinds of behavior and absent in others. Rather, it is the product of a process which involves responses of other people to the behavior. . . . Whether a given act is deviant or not depends in part on the nature of the act (that is, whether or not it violates some rule) and in part on what other people do about it.
>
> Some people may object that this is merely a terminological quibble, that one can, after all, define terms any way he wants to and that if some people want to speak of rule-breaking behavior as deviant without reference to the reactions of others they are free to do so. This, of course, is true, yet it might be worthwhile to refer to such behavior as *rule-breaking behavior* and reserve the term *deviant* for those labeled as deviant by some segment of society. . . . Deviance is not a quality that lies in behavior itself, but in the interaction between the person who commits an act and those who respond to it.[2]

This distinction between rule-breaking behavior and deviant behavior lies at the heart of the labeling perspective; it serves to shift attention away from the characteristics of people who break rules toward people who make and apply those rules. Thus, when Becker says that deviance is "created" by society, he is saying not that behavior is caused by social factors such as disjunction between goals and means but that

> *social groups create deviance by making the rules whose infraction constitutes deviance,* and by applying those rules to particular people and labeling them outsiders. From this point

of view, deviance is *not* a quality of the act the person commits, but rather a consequence of the application by others of rules and sanctions to an "offender." The deviant is one to whom that label has successfully been applied; deviant behavior is behavior that people so label.[3]

To claim that social groups create deviance in this sense is to abandon the traditional positivist concern with explaining rule-breaking behavior. The reader will recall that one criticism of positivist research is focused on the assumption that people who are designated as criminals accurately represent the population of those who break the criminal law. A related assumption made by the social determinists is that official rates of deviance reflect the distribution of the behavior within society. The labeling perspective recognizes that sanctions against rule-breaking are not meted out on an indiscriminate basis regardless of race, color, class, sex, intelligence, or any other characteristic. Instead of dealing with questions of why people break rules, the labeling perspective examines the reasons and circumstances under which rules are made and certain rule-breakers become the target of official action. In the words of Kai T. Erikson,

> deviance is not a property *inherent in* certain forms of behavior; it is a property *conferred upon* these forms by the audiences which directly or indirectly witness them. The critical variable in the study of deviance, then, is the social audience which eventually determines whether or not any episode of behavior or any class of episodes is labeled deviant.[4]

The labeling perspective leans heavily upon a relativistic concept of deviance, since it is assumed that the making and enforcing of rules are both inconsistent and problematic. Deviance, according to Becker, is a product of "enterprise." It is the result of efforts by people who, perceiving a threat, act as "moral entrepreneurs" to obtain appropriate legislation and enforcement to bring the behavior under control. One example is the paradox of gambling. In certain states, the governments themselves openly encourage citizens to wager on lotteries and sports to support state programs. In other states, practically any form of gambling is forbidden.

Because deviance is the product of "rate-producing processes," it logically follows in the labeling perspective that the amount of deviance recorded is limited by the capacity of the apparatus to handle deviants. Erikson argues that there will be only as many criminals as the efficiency of the law enforcement system will allow; there will be only as many mentally disordered as the available psychiatric diagnostic system will permit. However, these processes will not underproduce either. The definition of what is to be called deviant will expand and contract to maintain a more or less constant flow:

> The community develops its definition of deviance so that it encompasses a range of behavior roughly equivalent to the available space in its control apparatus—a kind of inverted Parkinson's law. That is, when the community calibrates its control machinery to handle a certain volume of deviant behavior, it tends to adjust its legal and psychiatric definitions of the problem in such a way that this volume is in fact realized. . . . If the police should somehow learn to contain most of the crimes it now contends with, and if at the same time medical science should discover a cure for most of the mental disorders it now treats, it is still improbable that the existing control machinery would go unused. More likely, the agencies of control would turn their attention to other forms of behavior, even to the point of defining as deviant certain styles of conduct which were not regarded so earlier.[5]

Unquestionably, the labeling perspective emphasizes an easily overlooked fact: Rules are the products of social definitions. What is criminal or deviant depends upon what certain powerful groups decide is threatening, disgusting, and so on, and upon the ability of those groups to persuade legislators to agree with them. Who will be criminal or deviant is likewise a matter of decision making by persons and agencies responsible for enforcing rules. Power relationships, rule-making processes, and labeling patterns by police, courts, and other agencies are all aspects of the production of deviance.

However, the reader should be alert to recognize that the explanation of the "production of deviance" should not be confused with an explanation of the occurrence of rule-breaking behavior.[6] Emile Durkheim argued over a half-century ago that the criminal character of acts was not due to "the intrinsic quality of a given act but that definition which the collective conscience lends them."[7] And Willem Bonger emphasized that the criminal law prohibited behaviors that the powerful regarded as most dangerous to their interests. The labeling perspective, then, scarcely tells us anything new but does serve to reacquaint us with the fact that groups deem what shall or shall not be approved behavior.

The Effect of Labeling on Behavior

At the heart of the labeling perspective lies the assumption that *labeling not only involves the defining of persons and their behavior, but may also heighten the likelihood that the behavior will continue.* Note that this differs from the traditional positivist approach, which sought the cause of the original behavior. The labeling approach ignores this problem in favor of explaining *how individuals become committed to deviance* and how their deviant behavior becomes stabilized. Or, to put it another way, why do people undertake *deviant careers*?

The scholar who has most thoroughly explored this aspect of labeling is Edwin M. Lemert. In 1951 he introduced a distinction between *primary* and *secondary deviance.* Primary deviance is violation of norms stemming from original causes, which may be any of several social, situational, physiological, and psychological factors. Lemert suggested the example of heavy drinking. Initially, it may be undertaken for one or more of a variety of personal reasons: death of a loved one, feelings of failure, group pressures, and so on. As long as such deviance can be tolerated and incorporated into an otherwise nondeviant image, the deviant behavior will remain primary and of little consequence for either the individual or those viewing her or his behavior. However, should the drinking precipitate an adverse reaction from others and nevertheless continue unabated, it is possible that it could eventually be attributed not to the original causes but to new problems created by the unfavorable reactions.[8] At this point the deviance becomes secondary. In Lemert's words, "when a person begins to employ his deviant behavior or role based upon it as a means of defense, attack, or adjustment to the overt and covert problems created by the consequent societal reaction to him, his deviation is secondary."[9]

The sequence of events leading to secondary deviance is roughly as follows:

(1) primary deviation; (2) social penalties; (3) further primary deviation; (4) stronger penalties and rejections; (5) further deviation, perhaps with hostilities and resentment beginning to focus upon those doing the penalizing; (6) crisis reached in the tolerance quotient, expressed in formal action by the community stigmatizing of the deviant; (7) strengthening

of the deviant conduct as a reaction to the stigmatizing and penalties; (8) ultimate acceptance of deviant social status and efforts at adjustment on the basis of the associated role.[10]

Becker expands upon this theme by introducing the notion of a deviant career sequence, each step of which involves "career contingencies" or factors that are necessary to ensure that the individual moves to the next stage in that career.[11] According to Becker, an important contingency is the experience of being publicly accused of being deviant. This has serious consequences, not the least of which is a new public identity. Jake the plumber becomes Jake the homosexual. Sally the treasurer becomes Sally the thief.

Along with this new identity come revised expectations and treatment from the public. There is the possibility that both Jake and Sally will end up in prison with all its consequences. But even without this extreme outcome, both will experience diminished participation in activities that had been natural before. Jake will no longer be involved in the Boy Scouts, even though his sexual behavior may have had nothing to do with minors. Sally will find herself uninvited to parties and dates, although her misuse of funds may not have harmed any of her acquaintances. Both will now be seen as persons who cannot be trusted, as persons with whom others do not wish to be involved.

The results of this treatment are twofold: First, it effectively limits the deviants' contacts with the legitimate world, thus making contacts with the illegitimate appear as more acceptable alternatives; second, the images projected upon deviants may later become the self-concepts of the deviants. Jake decides he is a homosexual, and Sally comes to see herself as a thief, thus accepting many of the public's views of what those terms imply.

The final step in the deviant career sequence is to move into an organized deviant group, an alternative that is more relevant for Jake than for Sally. Forced out of the mainstream of society into the gay subculture with its organizations, bars, argot, and lifestyle, Jake finds both justifications for his homosexuality and other individuals sympathetic with him. As was mentioned in Chapter 2, subcultures provide support for deviant behavior by giving it a positive evaluation. In the gay subculture Jake can engage in homosexuality with far less difficulty and guilt than he experienced when first entering the career sequence.

Admittedly, we have oversimplified the nature of Lemert's and Becker's discussions. Nevertheless, the reader can see that a major proposition of the labeling perspective is that "rule-breakers become entrenched in deviant roles because they are labeled 'deviant' by others and are consequently excluded from resuming normal roles in the community."[12] Or, put another way, "societal reaction in the form of labeling or official typing, and consequent stigmatizing, leads to an altered identity in the actor, necessitating a reconstitution of the self."[13]

In neither Lemert's process of secondary deviance nor Becker's deviant career sequence is there an implication that the processes invariably result from labeling or that eventual commitment to deviance necessarily requires such processes. At most, these authors are indicating how societal reaction *can* contribute to future deviant conduct. For example, Lemert referred to secondary deviance when discussing the diversion of juveniles out of the justice system:

> Secondary deviance was never intended to be a general theory of delinquency causation; rather, it is an explanation of how casual, random, or adventitious deviance becomes redefined and stabilized through status change and self-conscious adaptation to secondary problems generated by social control. The number of youths who become secondary, career-type

delinquents is not great, although the damage they do to society may be substantial. For this reason, there is still considerable justification for diversion from official control at critical points where transition to secondary deviance may otherwise occur.[14]

But just how important is societal reaction in explaining the extent or likelihood of career deviance? Most evidence is not supportive of the labeling perspective. It appears that careers in alcoholism, mental disorder, mental retardation, physical handicaps, crime, delinquency, and heroin addiction develop more or less independently of experiences with *official* reactions.[15] On the other hand, it is obvious that many deviants must adjust their self-concepts and lifestyles to cope with actual or potential social reactions. There probably is a core of deviants whose careers have been directly affected by such reactions, but the size of that core remains uncertain. Indeed, the process by which the commitment to deviance develops might be unique to each individual, and is perhaps best conceptualized as a multidimensional framework.[16]

Part of the uncertainty surrounding the importance of societal reactions stems from the variety of types of reactions. Official reaction is relatively easy to understand and measure. A person is arrested, is incarcerated, and spends so many months "being reacted against." But the nature of the audience doing the reacting is not always the police, courts, and prison officials. Other audiences are informal: friends and family who, in subtle or not-so-subtle ways, indicate what they think of a person's behavior. Perhaps a real audience is not even necessary. The labeling could take place just as effectively if the audience is a representation in the actor's mind: He or she witnesses, labels, and may even punish himself or herself without reference to what others actually do. Thus people respond to potential social reaction by taking into account what others might do should the rule-breaking activity become known.

There are other issues under debate concerning the labeling perspective of which the reader should be aware:

1. By minimizing the importance of explaining initial (primary) deviance, whatever meaning the behavior originally had for the deviant is ignored as a contributor to subsequent behavior. Although societal reaction may become a crucial factor in behavior, it is questionable that whatever purpose or reward the behavior first held is invariably replaced. For example, if a person first steals for thrills, do thrills fail to be a factor once societal reaction has taken its toll?

2. As Allen E. Liska points out,

> the emphasis on secondary deviance unobtrusively directs research away from the deviance of the powerful who possess the resources to resist societal reaction actively. As they frequently commit norm and law violations without prosecution and frequently even without detection, their violations tend to be ignored by labeling theorists. The powerless, lacking the resources to avoid labeling, become the object of social labeling, and thus the objects of study.[17]

3. The labeling perspective ignores the actor as being capable of either choice or resistance in the labeling process. The impression emerges that labeled individuals are pushed into further deviance and alliances with deviant subcultures that only compound the problem. At its extreme, the perspective presents an image that Kitsuse calls the passive "man on his back,"

> seemingly incapable of resisting or opposing the inexorable process of attributions of abnormality and inadequacy, stigmatized as morally defective, progressively excluded and subordinated as deviant, and driven to seek comfort and support in the shelter of deviant subcultures.[18]

What this image disregards are those deviants who refuse to be embarrassed and silenced about who they are. Instead, they publicly proclaim their identities and demand that they share the same rights as the so-called normals. These are what Kitsuse calls the "new deviants"; these are the gays, the handicapped, the little, the fat, the old, and others who "do not shrink from the hostile responses of those they confront, and they do not ask tolerance, . . . but demand recognition of the moral and legal bases of their claims."[19] He suggests the concept of "tertiary deviation" might be appropriate to describe "the deviant's confrontation, assessment, and rejection of the negative identity imbedded in secondary deviation, and the transformation of that identity into a positive and viable self-conception."[20]

Although it is true that deviants may be pawns of the powerful, this does not mean that deviants are powerless to resist, to alter their behavior, or to acquire power themselves. Jack P. Gibbs states the case well:

> A theorist can argue that even when a deviance rate is based on reactive data, the rate's primary determinant is the incidence or prevalence of some designated type of behavior, and that when an individual is somehow labeled as deviant by social unit members that action commonly has something to do with that individual's actual behavior.[21]

Conflict Perspectives

In Chapter 2 the reader was introduced to the works of Karl Marx and Willem Bonger, who first viewed deviance as the product of *economic conflict*. Marxist theory is concerned with how the economic organization of capitalistic societies places power in the hands of a single class, namely, the owners of the means of production. Although Marx did not deal directly with the issue, it is inferred from his writings that deviance stems from attempts by the powerless to cope with their exploitation and poverty. It was Bonger who applied Marxist theory specifically to explaining deviance. He argued that economic conflicts destroy human beings' feeling for one another. This egoism consequently causes crime among both the proletariat and bourgeoisie. The criminal law, however, is made and enforced primarily for the benefit of the bourgeoisie to protect its interests.

Thus conflict perspectives come in several variations. Basic to all of them, however, are three assumptions:

1. Laws are enacted as a result of conflict among groups promoting their own interests. Put another way, laws are based not upon the consensus of society, but upon the interests of the groups most able to influence the legal system.

2. As a consequence of assumption 1, the more powerful a group's position, the less likely that the behavior of its members acting in the group's interests will violate the law.

3. As a further consequence of assumption 1, the less powerful a group's position, the more likely that the behavior of its members endangering the interests of a more powerful group will violate the law.

Aside from these assumptions—which essentially say that there is continuing conflict to influence legislative and enforcement processes—conflict theorists are divided over precisely *who* is in conflict. There are the Marxists, who interpret deviance principally from an economic perspective; to them the major conflict is between the ruling class and the working class. Other conflict theorists regard the groups as more numerous and diverse; depending upon the time and the issue, there are several groups maneuvering to protect their interests and having various degrees of influence over the government in general and the legal system in particular. An example of this condition is the case of immigrants from one culture who find themselves under the control of those from the host culture.

Culture Conflict

During the 1930s there was considerable interest among social scientists in the problems of immigrants in the United States. In 1938 Thorsten Sellin published a pamphlet, *Culture Conflict and Crime,* concerning the relationship between immigration and crime.[22] Early in this work, which was to become a milestone in the American conflict perspective, he discusses the nature of criminal law. He sees the law as representing the values treasured by dominant interest groups in society, groups that may not, however, be in the majority.

He continues by pointing out that human beings are born into cultures that provide meanings to behavior, including the norms governing that behavior. As society becomes more complex, an individual cannot possibly identify with or adhere to all norms, because the norms themselves will not be consistent with one another. Thus, according to Sellin, it makes little sense to speak of "antisocial" behavior because it is the group and its norms that determine whether a behavior is "normal."

He next deals with the question of how conflicts of norms come about. He believes that they result from two processes:

1. **Cultural growth.** Society becomes diverse because of population growth, intermingling of cultures, competitive interest, increased technology, and so on. As a result, people living in such a society find themselves in situations governed by conflicting norms; no matter which course they take, they will violate the norms of some concerned group. This process described by Sellin is consistent with the notion of moral pluralism discussed earlier. But Sellin spends little time in developing this theme. The major thrust of his discussion concerns migration of norms.

2. **Migration of norms.** Sellin argues that conflicts of cultures are inevitable when the norms of one come into contact with those of another. These clashes may occur in any one of the following circumstances: (a) when cultural groups are in close proximity to one

another, (b) when the laws of one group are imposed upon another, and (c) when the members of one group migrate into another group. These processes, according to Sellin, account for much of the crime by the foreign-born in the United States. In many instances the crime may simply be the result of a misunderstanding or ignorance of the law. It is in this context that Sellin provides an often quoted example of the Sicilian male who murdered the 16-year-old seducer of his daughter. Because the immigrant had merely defended the family honor in the traditional Sicilian way, he was quite surprised to be arrested. The migration of norms as an explanation of crime had decreasing usefulness with the decline of migration into the United States. It was not until the late 1950s that another conflict perspective emerged in American sociology—group conflict.

Group Conflict

The next American to expand substantially upon the relationship between conflict and deviance was George B. Vold.[23] Although Vold does not mention Sellin's contribution, his group conflict theory of crime is a logical next step from Sellin.

Vold describes conflict as a "principal and essential" social process. Society, he says, consists of many groups of differing interests and power who are constantly jockeying for positions of defense and advantage. Some groups gain political power and seek the aid of the government to protect or further their interest. Law is the outcome of the greatest influence and largest number of votes.

Some crime, says Vold, can be described as "minority group behavior." For example, crime arises from groups such as delinquent gangs that neither achieve their objectives through legitimate channels nor rely upon the protection of the state. For Vold the gang represents a unified group in conflict with an adult world whose values and power advantage threaten the gang members.

Many other criminal acts represent more direct power confrontations—what Vold calls "acts of good soldiers fighting for a cause and against the threat of enemy encroachment."[24] These good soldiers are the company police, the strikers, and the political terrorists—none believe in murder, property destruction, and torture except as applied to accomplishing "higher" goals. Vold cites the following examples of attempts to control the very political and cultural destinies of all society or, at least, substantial portions of that society:

1. **Political reform conflicts.** The ultimate form here is rebellion or revolution, wherein the outcome determines who shall be the criminal. But short of this, there are murders, acts of sabotage, destruction of property, burglary, bribery, and general dishonesty all committed for the sake of winning or retaining power. In short, acts that are normally condemned are condoned when a political purpose is attached to them.

2. **Management-union conflicts.** Strikes and strike-breaking often result in clashes between workers and between workers and police. Vandalism, assault, murder, and theft under such conditions are not uncommon occurrences but again are seen as necessary to obtain a satisfactory settlement.

3. **Union jurisdictional disputes.** Struggles between unions often involve entanglement with organized crime and favoritism from industry. Intimidation and assaults as well

as confrontations with police over trespassing, for example, frequently result from instances in which all parties feel that justice is on their side.

4. Conflicts over racial segregation. To upset patterns of racial segregation, illegal behavior often results. Vold's discussion is sketchy on this issue, but one can assume that he would include here acts of violence and property destruction that accompany attempts by blacks, Latinos, American Indians, and whites to assert their "rights" over each other.

In closing his discussion of group conflict theory, Vold is careful to point out its limitations:

> Group conflict theory is strictly limited to those kinds of situations in which the individual criminal acts flow from the collision of groups whose members are loyally upholding the in-group position. Such theory does not serve to explain many kinds of impulsive, irrational acts of a criminal nature that are quite unrelated to any battle between different interest groups in organized society.[25]

Vold's choice of "impulsive, irrational acts" to be the exceptions to group conflict theory seems to be an understatement. Also unexplained by the theory are "deliberate, rational acts" that occur for primarily, if not purely, personal reasons. Although the conflict theory has value for understanding why an employee might destroy company property during a strike, it may fall short of suggesting why that same individual systematically steals company materials for the house he is building.

Nevertheless, Vold's approach draws attention to the political motivations behind both behavior and laws. And he emphasizes that crime is a matter of definition as well as of behavior:

> Crime always involves both human behavior (acts) and the judgment or definitions (laws, customs, mores) of fellow human beings as to whether specific behavior is appropriate and permissible, or is improper and forbidden. Crime and criminality lie in the area of behavior that is considered improper and forbidden. There is, therefore, always a dual problem of explanation—that of accounting for the behavior, as *behavior,* and equally important, accounting *for the definitions* by which specific behavior comes to be considered as crime or non-crime.[26]

Conflict and Authority

Austin T. Turk rejects Vold's contention that the study of crime involves a dual problem of explaining both behavior and definitions.[27] Turk argues that attempts to explain criminal behavior have always been fruitless and will continue to be so because *criminality is not behavior, but a status conferred upon that behavior.*

Turk presents a series of propositions in which he claims that there are no universal norms prohibiting any behavior. The behavior involved in acting illegally does not differ essentially from acting legally, and the application of law is inaccurate, subjective, and inconsistent. Thus criminality is a state of being officially defined as punishable, and it bears only a slender relationship to actual behavior.

After disposing of behavior as an issue, Turk presents a theory of *criminalization* (the process of being labeled a criminal) based upon the concept of *authority:*

> The study of criminality [is] the study of relations between the statuses and roles of legal *authorities*—creators, interpreters, and enforcers of right-wrong standards for individuals in the political collectivity—and those of *subjects*—acceptors or resisters but not makers of such law creating, interpreting, and enforcing decisions.[28]

However, Turk cannot completely avoid suggesting how behavior might be explained:

> *Lawbreaking* is taken to be an indicator of the failure or lack of authority; it is a measure of the extent to which rules and ruled, decision-makers and decision-acceptors, are not bound together in a perfectly stable authority relationship. Because an authority relationship can never be finally perfected, both accidental and deliberate resistance to legal norms, and therefore challenges to authority, will occur in any political-legal structure.[29]

Turk's theory specifies the factors contributing to the probabilities of conflict between authorities and subjects and the probabilities that those conflicts will result in the assigning of criminal status or criminalization. Central to the theory is a distinction between *cultural norms* (announced or publicized norms) and *social norms* (actual behavior). The *congruence* of these (the degree to which what is said corresponds to what is done) is an important factor in determining the likelihood of conflict. When congruence is high for both authorities and subjects over an issue on which they take opposite views, conflict is most likely. For example, if authorities say that extramarital sex is wrong and do abstain themselves, conflict would probably result if a group of subjects proclaimed in both word and deed their favoring extramarital sex. If congruence is low for both parties, the issue is primarily a symbolic one and is unlikely to provoke conflict.

Other factors crucial to Turk's theory are the degree of *organization* of the subjects—the extent to which there is a system of group support for behavior—and the subjects' *sophistication*—their capacity to assess their own strengths and weaknesses relative to those of the authorities. Turk argues that conflict between authorities and subjects is most probable when there is a high congruence between cultural and social norms and when the subjects involved in the behavior are highly organized but relatively unsophisticated. The likelihood that conflict will result in criminalization depends upon the *power differences* between subjects and authorities and the *realism of moves* by both sides (this refers to the tactical skills at gaining favorable positions of strength against the opposition).

Turk thus alerts us to the political nature of legal authority. Since groups differ in both interests and degrees of power, one can easily imagine how the interests of the more powerful become "right," whereas those of the less powerful become "illegal." In a later work, Turk elaborates on the linkage between power and law when he asserts that law *is* power. He describes law as "a set of resources for which people contend and with which they are better able to promote their own ideas and interests against others."[30] These resources include the following:

1. **Control of violence.** This refers to those who, for example, may "rightfully" depend upon the police to support their claims.

2. **Control of the production, allocation, and use of material resources.** This refers to economic power, which would include such things as determining whose incomes will be taxed and at what rate.
3. **Control of decision-making processes.** This refers to political power, or the ability to interpret and implement law.
4. **Control of definitions of and access to knowledge, beliefs, and values.** This refers to ideological power, which would include the ability to censor the "bad" and "dangerous," while promoting the "good" and "beneficial."[31]

But Turk leaves open the question of precisely *who* the powerful are. Implicit in his scheme is the notion that society is composed of diverse segments that conflict intermittently over one or more of a wide range of issues: abortion, income taxes, conservation of wilderness areas, and mass transit, just to name a few. The groups involved in each of these disputes are not similarly constituted. For example, many people who take opposing sides on abortion may be allies on something else. So those who emerge as powerful in one context may not do so in another. Turk's is a *pluralistic* perspective, one that concerns many groups and many issues, but it is not a perspective universally agreed upon by conflict theorists. Those of the Marxist persuasion in particular believe that only one struggle is important: the economic conflict between those who own the means of production (the ruling class) and those who are employed in the production (the working class). Crime and the legal system are regarded as manifestations of the ruling class's attempt to protect its interests and to defeat those of the working class. In short, the crucial conflict is *class conflict.*

Radical Theory

Those who base their theories on class conflict are generally referred to as *radical criminologists* because they support drastic, fundamental social changes consistent with Marxist principles.[32] They believe that the cause of crime lies at the core of capitalist society and its legal system. Until the capitalist structure fails or is destroyed and is replaced by socialism, the problem of crime will persist.

Perhaps the best way to distinguish the features of radical criminology is to compare it with more traditional sociological theories—such as anomie and differential association—that assume normative consensus in society. As shown in Table 3.1, William J. Chambliss provides this contrast by outlining important areas of disagreement concerning the content of the criminal law, the consequences of crime for society, and the source or etiology of criminal behavior.

As Chambliss's comparisons indicate, radical criminologists stress the importance of the *ruling class* in defining what is deviant and the importance of class position in determining whether one's behavior will be defined as deviant. For an example of the radical approach we will turn to the work of the most widely known U.S. radical criminologist, Richard Quinney. In the early 1970s he was among the first to describe crime in terms of two competing economic classes, the more powerful of which defines the social meanings or "reality" of crime to the rest of society. Quinney characterizes this reality in six propositions:

TABLE 3.1   Comparison of Traditional and Radical Theories

I. Content and Operation of the Criminal Law

Traditional	Radical
1. Acts are defined as criminal because they offend the moral beliefs of the members of the society.	Acts are defined as criminal because it is in the interests of the ruling class to so define them.
2. Those who violate the criminal law will be punished according to the prevailing customs of the society.	Members of the ruling class will be able to violate the laws with impunity while members of the subject classes will be punished.
3. People are labeled criminal because their behavior goes beyond the tolerance limits of the community.	Persons are labeled criminal because it is in the interests of the ruling class to so label them, whether or not the behavior would be tolerated by "the society" at large.
4. The lower classes are more likely to be arrested for and convicted of crime because they commit more crimes.	The lower classes are more likely to be labeled criminal because the bourgeoisie's control of the state protects themselves from such stigmatization.
5. As societies become more specialized in the division of labor, more and more laws will become restitutive rather than repressive (penal).	As capitalist societies industrialize and the gap between the bourgeoisie and the proletariat widens, penal law will expand in an effort to coerce the proletariat into submission.

II. Consequences of Crime for Society

1. Crime establishes the limits of the community's tolerance of deviant behavior and increases moral solidarity among the members of the community.	Crime enables the ruling class to create false consciousness among the ruled by making them think their own interests and those of the ruling class are identical.
2. Crime necessitates the expenditure of energy and resources to eradicate it and is thus an economic drain on the society.	Crime reduces surplus labor by creating employment not only for the criminals but also for law enforcers, locksmiths, welfare workers, professors of criminology, and other people who benefit from the existence of crime.
3. Crime offends the conscience of everyone in the community, thus creating a tighter bond among them.	Crime diverts the lower classes' attention from the exploitation they experience toward other members of their own class rather than toward the capitalist or economic system.
4. Crime makes people aware of the interests they have in common.	Defining people as criminal permits greater control of the proletariat.
5. Crime is a real problem that all communities must cope with to survive.	Crime is a reality which exists only as it is created by those in the society whose interests are served by its presence.

TABLE 3.1   Continued

III. Etiology of Criminal Behavior

Traditional	Radical
1. Every society has a set of agreed-upon customs (rules, norms, values) that most members internalize. Criminal behavior results from the fact that some members get socialized into criminal behavior.	Criminal and noncriminal behavior stem from people acting in ways that are compatible with their class position. Crime is a reaction to the life conditions of a person's social class.
2. Criminal acts are more frequent among lower classes because the agencies of socialization (especially the family, but also the neighborhood, schools, other adult and peer groups) are less likely to work effectively, that is, in ways that lead to the internalization of noncriminal norms and behaviors.	Criminal acts are concentrated in the lower classes because the ruling class can see that only acts that grow out of lower-class life are defined as criminal.
3. The lower classes are more likely to be arrested because they commit more crimes.	The lower classes are more likely to be arrested and will then be labeled criminals because the bourgeoisie controls those who manage the law enforcement agencies.
4. Crime is a constant in societies. All societies need and produce crime.	Crime varies from society to society depending upon the political and economic structures of society.
5. Socialist and capitalist societies should have the same amounts of crime if they have comparable rates of industrialization and bureaucratization.	Socialist societies should have much lower rates of crime because the less intense class struggle should reduce the forces leading to and the functions of crime.

Source: William J. Chambliss, ''Functional and Conflict Theories of Crime: The Heritage of Emile Durkheim and Karl Marx,'' in *Whose Law? What Order? A Conflict Approach to Criminology,* ed. William J. Chambliss and Milton Mankoff (New York: John Wiley & Sons, Inc., 1976), pp. 7–9. Copyright © 1976 John Wiley & Sons, Inc. Reprinted with permission of John Wiley & Sons, Inc. Headings have been changed to be consistent with discussion in the text.

1. **Official Definition of Crime:** Crime is a legal definition of human conduct that is created by agents of the dominant class in a capitalist society. [Crime is not inherent in behavior but is a matter of judgment and definition.]
2. **Formulation of Definitions of Crime:** Definitions of crime are composed of behaviors that conflict with the class interests of the dominant economic class. [It follows that the greater the conflict between class interests, the greater the likelihood that the dominant economic class will *formulate* laws to control others.]
3. **Application of Definitions of Crime:** Definitions of crime are applied by the class that has the power to shape the enforcement and administration of criminal law. [The greater the conflict between class interests, the greater the likelihood that the dominant economic class will influence legal agents to *apply* the criminal law.]

4. **Development of Behavior Patterns in Relation to Definitions of Crime:** Behavior patterns are structured in relation to definitions of crime, and within this context persons engage in actions that have relative probabilities of being defined as criminal. [The behavior of the less powerful is more likely to be defined as criminal; the expectations and experiences of being labeled criminal in turn influence future behavior.]

5. **Construction of Conceptions of Crime:** Conceptions of crime are constructed and diffused in the course of communication. [What and who are criminal are constructed and disseminated by the powerful; the more the powerful are concerned about crime, the greater the likelihood that both the definitions of behavior and the behavior itself will increase.]

6. **Construction of the Social Reality of Crime:** The social reality of crime is constructed by the formulation and application of definitions of crime, the development of behavior patterns in relation to these definitions, and the construction of conceptions of crime. [This is a composite of the previous five propositions.][33]

Quinney also deals directly with the question of *who* possesses the power to manipulate the criminal justice system in the United States. He argues that interest groups are grossly unequal in their influence. Public policy is actually determined by a very few, very powerful economic interests. There is, according to Quinney, a U.S. ruling class consisting of the owners and controllers of the means of production, plus those who benefit directly from the system.

Quinney claims that the "official reality" that presents the legal system as beneficial for all is a myth. That system serves only the ruling class by furnishing it protection and by maintaining the existing social and economic conditions. Agencies and programs set up in recent years for the purposes of the "war on crime" and of legal "reform" are in fact devices to repress "class antagonisms" or potential rebellions that threaten established economic arrangements. "Crime control" under capitalism is actually "class control," according to Quinney.

The police, courts, prisons, and even criminologists are part of this system of repression. Whenever criminologists have sought the sources of crime within the individual, including how the individual was criminally socialized, they have ignored the political nature of the authority defining behavior as criminal. Research grants, university training programs in law enforcement, and government-supported scholarships are all means by which the ruling class secures both the allegiance of criminologists and the strategic information from what Quinney calls "counterinsurgency research." The end product of current research on criminals and crime is the control and manipulation of humans by those who rule.[34]

The reader will recall from Chambliss's comparison that the etiology of criminal behavior is viewed differently by the traditional and radical theories. Whereas the traditionalists stress the learning of the behavior, the radicals see the behavior as a *reaction* to the capitalist system. In Quinney's discussion of this matter, he divides criminal behavior into two major types. Crimes of domination, the first type, are committed by members of the ruling class or by their agents for the purpose of safeguarding capitalism. These include a wide range of acts whereby corporations, the government, and law enforcement agencies violate public trust and interests. For example, corporations often will disregard their workers' safety to increase profit. Or law enforcement personnel will violate civil rights of individuals to defend the "national security" or to ensure that "justice is done." According to Quinney, such crimes of domination are an integral aspect of capitalism.[35]

But what of the other, more "ordinary" crimes? For the most part these too are reactions to capitalism. Specifically, they are the acts of *survival* and *rebellion* by the lower class that faces chronic unemployment and repression.

> Yet, understanding crime as a reaction to capitalist conditions, whether as acts of frustration or means of survival, is only one side of the picture. The other side involves the problematics of the consciousness of *criminality* in capitalist society. The history of the working class is in large part one of rebellion against the conditions of capitalist production, as well as against the conditions of life resulting from work under capitalism. Class struggle involves, after all, a continuous war between two dialectically opposed interests: on one hand, capital accumulation for the benefit of a nonworking minority class that owns and controls the means of production and, on the other hand, control and ownership of production by those who actually labor.[36]

As one might suspect, radical criminology has not lacked critics.[37] The criticisms are in fact numerous and often highly abstract, but the following three are significant for our limited discussion:

1. Radical criminology fails to account for a high degree of public consensus over behaviors that should be illegal. Research consistently shows that overwhelming majorities in all social classes believe that the so-called ordinary crimes involving assaults and theft of personal property should be punished by law.[38] In addition, there is considerable consensus among classes over the relative seriousness of these offenses. More disagreement exists over such acts as abortion, homosexuality, and drug use, but the extent to which these disagreements are class oriented is unclear. The radicals' claims that definitions of crime are based primarily upon class interests is questionable at best.

2. The United States appears to be more pluralistic than the radical criminologists claim. There is no disputing that the upper class controls much of industry and wealth in general. But it is also evident that other interest groups exhibit power as well. Groups other than the upper class have been responsible for the strengthening of labor unions, civil rights legislation, consumer protection legislation, and other laws challenging the position of the upper class: regulations concerning industrial safety, product purity, and environmental standards, to name a few.[39] Also, it is difficult to see any undue influence of the upper class in current interest group struggles over pornography, homosexual rights, drug use, and abortion. The upper class may have paramount influence in economic matters, but radical criminologists exaggerate the impact of that influence on crime and law.

3. Radical criminologists are utopian. They regard capitalist repression as the ultimate cause of crime and therefore believe that crime will disappear with the disappearance of capitalism. But among existing noncapitalist societies this outcome has not occurred. Indeed, in some so-called socialist states, such as Cuba and China, repression far exceeds that found in the United States. Reliable crime statistics are impossible to obtain from these countries. But no one seriously suggests that these nations are crime-free, especially in light of the various "crimes against the state" that pervade their criminal codes. Ronald L. Akers summarizes a basic shortcoming of radical criminology when he writes:

> Quinney does not compare existing Marxist societies to gauge how crime-free and nonrepressive some future socialist society might be. If Quinney were to make this kind of comparison, I believe he would have to conclude that neither the criminal justice system nor the criminologists in communist societies represent a future for which it is worth struggling. It would mean transforming an imperfect but still basically free, open, democratic society into an even more imperfect, closed, repressive, and totalitarian society. Quinney's faith is misplaced. As a blueprint for the good society, the Marxist ideal to which he holds has not proven to be reliable. Socialist societies have been unable to deliver on the promise of classlessness and economic equality. Instead, they have been characterized by self-serving, privileged party elites and ruling cabals or dictatorships which very closely resemble the tightknit, self-perpetuating ruling class controlling the criminal justice system and using criminology to its own end which Quinney says is true for "capitalist" society.[40]

In summary, radical criminologists suggested that patterns of crime are the immediate result of capitalistic economic and social structures. Some have softened the assertion that the solution to the crime problem of capitalism is socialism. They have continued to modify their positions over the years, addressing criticisms such as those cited above. And, as discussed by Michael J. Lynch and W. Byron Groves, they have recognized that measures and reforms can be implemented in the existing criminal justice system:

> If substantial social change involves macrostructural changes, how can criminologists intervene to reduce crime? . . . The fact is that neither traditional nor radical criminologists occupy pivotal positions in the political-economic sphere. . . . Given their commitment to "praxis," how can radicals agitate for meaningful change given their own resources and abilities? . . . In order to build a popular platform, radicals must become involved in policies which affect our current administration of justice.[41]

Some examples they cite are ensuring that the bail system is equitable, increasing employment opportunities, and even attempting to redefine crime in terms of the amount of harm done to society. However, they note that

> in the end, the criminal justice system has failed as an agent of social change because its efforts are directed at an *individual* as opposed to *social* remedies. In fact, as labeling theories point out, the criminal justice system actually contributes to the crime problem through the manner in which it processes and labels individuals as criminals.[42]

Quinney, Harold Pepinsky,[43] and others have subsequently attempted to develop a more compassionate, or *peace-making,* approach to crime control and conflict criminology. This perspective involves solving crime problems and other social suffering through mutual understanding between government control agencies, victims, and individuals or groups that inflict suffering upon others.[44] Community forums would ideally serve to mediate conflict between interest groups. Ultimately, the competition for hegemony, or dominance, to protect resources and interests would diminish, as would the criminogenic intergroup conflict.[45] The philosophy tends toward a Confucian appreciation of virtue and replaces aggressive crime control with proactive peace initiatives.

The idea that justice may be well served by a collaborative interaction involving the offender, the victim, and decision makers in the community may be found in ancient (and contemporary) tribal justice systems, and also in the *Restorative Justice* correctional approach that has developed out of more recent feminist thinking in criminology theory.

Postmodern Criminology

In spite of our long history of theorizing and searching for causes of crime and criminal behavior, we have never had any resounding success in the practical matter of reducing crime levels by adapting and utilizing theoretical principles. Since World War II, a number of interesting theoretical perspectives have been launched with the charge that traditional academic criminology has failed to meet the challenge of practical utility. Indeed, such noted perspectives as constitutive theory, discourse analysis, anarchic criminology, and realist criminology have been mentioned under the *postmodern* title. Most describe traditional perspectives as essentially useless in the real world and thus are sometimes called *deconstructionist* theories.

Dragan Milovanovic and Stuart Henry, as foremost postmodern criminologists, describe "crime" as an active, dynamic product of continuous reinterpretation and social definition.[46] Emile Durkheim might have perceived the concept of crime the same way if he were writing in the twenty-first century.

Once Again: What Is Deviant?

As we have discussed, constructing a single theory of deviance would be a very intricate procedure. Minimally, it would have to explain the existence of both the rules and the behavior. We have outlined attempts at a general theory of crime and an integrated theory of crime that consider behavior. But examining rules alone would involve many questions. Why do particular norms exist? Are they supported generally in society or only by select power groups? Under what conditions do behaviors and individuals become subject to being labeled and reacted against as deviant? Why do particular behaviors defined as deviant arise and persist in society? Why do rates of behavior defined as deviant vary from one group to another, from one time to another, and so on? What is the process by which persons first engage in deviant behavior? Why do they continue in the behavior? Why do they quit?

All of this is much more than any current single theory can deliver. Because the existence of deviance is the result of both rules and behavior, it is unlikely that an explanation of one will explain the other. But even reducing our expectations of any one perspective is not sufficient. Consider the following stories—all true:

1. The board chairman of the American Medical Association is charged with bank fraud in a conspiracy involving nearly $1.8 million.
2. An 11-year-old boy is absent because of illness when a coal slag avalanche kills all 33 of his classmates in a school in Wales. He is shunned, and his life is threatened by others in town who resent his survival.

3. A high school teacher with outstanding references and academic credentials is dismissed from her job for refusing to join her classes in reciting the Pledge of Allegiance.
4. A school board member is forced to resign following his arrest for displaying his naked buttocks from an automobile on an interstate highway.
5. An 8-year-old girl stabs a playmate to death and is sentenced to 18 months in a detention home.
6. A 40-year-old man persists in publicly picking his nose and is constantly admonished by his wife and friends.

Judging by reactions alone, each of these individuals is deviant by someone's standards. Yet some situations seem too trivial or unique to study in detail. Although there are common features among the reactions to all the situations, most readers probably give low priority to the nose-picking. But by what measure do we know that an act is serious enough to warrant scholarly attention? Or, put another way, how shall we define deviance for purposes of formulating a perspective?

As we have seen, defining deviance strictly in terms of official rules—such as the criminal law—is troublesome because such rules reflect the interests of the rule-makers or those with the power to influence the rule-makers. What is officially designated as deviant is often a political decision,[47] and labeling theorists have dismayed of defining deviance in terms of rules. Lemert claims that it is best to leave the term *deviance* undefined and instead to concentrate on the process by which people become "differentiated":

> The center of concern is moral ideas, their rise and fall, their invocation and application either as informal social designations or as administrative categories by agencies of social control. While moral evaluations and judgments may do no more than express "moral indignation," they are part and parcel of informal and formal social control that make up the societal reaction to deviance. Whenever persons and their actions mutually differentiate through processes of stigmatization, rejection, isolation, segregation, punishment, treatment or rehabilitation, the persons, their actions and the processes are data for study of deviance.[48]

Lemert's argument that deviance should be studied in terms of differentiation processes such as stigmatization, rejection, and so on is persuasive. Nevertheless, we should not lose sight of the importance of rules such as law for differentiating who and what are deviant. It is tempting to regard the law as merely a tool of the powerful. But it is more than that. It reflects norms that transcend those of a few influential interest groups. Some laws enjoy a high degree of consensus—neither the rich nor the poor want to be murdered in their beds. Still others are specifically directed toward controlling the actions of the powerful—police, courts, corporations, and so on. This is not to say that such laws, including those having wide public support, are enforced consistently and without bias. Nor is this to claim that sanctions leveled against violators are always dispensed in relationship to the public's loss in lives and dollars. The law is nevertheless an indicator, however distorted, of both the societal norms and the norms of powerful interest groups. Often these overlap, and it is a matter of some conjecture as to which belongs to which, but legal norms do provide us with a means of defining deviance without resorting to definitions based solely upon feelings of moral outrage.

For our purposes, *deviant behavior is behavior subject to legal procedures aimed at curtailing the behavior. Such procedures may involve punishment, restoration of losses to victims, or involuntary hospitalization.*

Certain aspects of this definition require clarification and elaboration. Part of it involves the potential for legal action to stop the behavior. This means that although authorities have the legal capacity to act, they may do anything, from ignoring the behavior to suppressing it actively. In addition, whereas the definition is based upon legal codes, it is not limited to crime.[49] Crime is conduct in violation of the criminal law: "[C]riminal law is a body of specialized rules of a politically organized society which contain provisions for punishment to be administered in the name of society upon substantiation of their violation."[50]

Note that punishment is part of criminal law and usually involves a sentence of a specific time in jail and/or a fine. But crime, with its potential for punishment, is only part of the definition of deviant behavior. Authorities have other means of controlling behavior. Some behaviors may be treated as *torts* or *civil wrongs,* whereby the offenders are ordered to pay victims for their loss. This process of *restitution* is, as we shall see, most likely to be used against respectable offenders such as corporations. The respectable may be deviant, but they are not criminals in the precise sense of that term.

In still other cases the behavior may bring about the offender's commitment to a hospital or some other treatment setting for help. The instances that will concern us are those in which the offenders have had little or nothing to say about this procedure: those defined as mentally ill, potential suicides, and sexual psychopaths.

Given the state of the field, to arrive at a definition of deviant behavior satisfactory to everyone is an impossible task. The reader may well complain that the legal emphasis of our definition is especially misplaced because it excludes the behavior of people who experience social rejection without legality even being at issue. For example, homosexual behavior and prostitution are not illegal in some states. The same is true of nudism and stripteasing, and being an alcoholic is legal anywhere. It can be argued, however, that traditionally people involved in such behaviors have directly confronted the law and that currently their legal status remains precarious at best. There is more than one way to deal legally with deviants: if they don't violate one law, they can be charged with another. If all else fails, they can be hospitalized for "treatment."

But the reader's complaint is legitimate. Deviance and violation of law are not necessarily the same thing. However, our definition will be used in this book for one compelling reason: The existence of legal means to cope with individuals' behavior is tangible evidence of a collective reaction defining the behavior as deviant.

Interest Group Conflict and Deviance

We have indicated that no single perspective adequately explains the existence of both rule-making and rule-breaking behavior. The interest group conflict approach to be employed in the remainder of this book is no exception. The following chapters contain discussions of a wide variety of behaviors, many of which may be more convincingly explained by other perspectives. A conflict approach, however, has two important virtues: (1) It acknowledges that a relationship exists between deviant behavior and the processes of making and enforcing rules, and (2) it recognizes that many acts of rule-breaking are committed in the name of a group or cause, and for purposes other than immediate personal gain or satisfaction. By blending the conflict perspective with other assumptions about the nature of U.S. society, many of the more personal, individual behaviors and authorities' reactions to them become understandable, even if they are not satisfactorily explained.

The following propositions summarize the perspective of this book:

1. Life in U.S. society is characterized by conflicts of interest. Our society contains many diverse groups whose interests are antagonistic to one another. Conflicts of interest are especially evident where access to unequally distributed scarce resources (wealth, status, and power) is concerned. Conflict arises and continues over these resources—which include the power to define what is "moral." The conflict situation in many instances is a one-sided battle, since many groups lack the organization, sophistication, and power to enhance or even protect their interests.

2. Interest groups exert varying degrees of influence upon legislation and enforcement of law. Law and its administration are not the works of gods but of humans; they are responsive to the wishes of those who can provide campaign funds, votes, prestige, and other favors. Consequently, the law is not neutral in monitoring and controlling the activities of various interest groups.

3. The application of law is a method by which more powerful interest groups can exert control over the less powerful. Once power and its benefits have been attained, they are not readily relinquished. The powerful resist any change that might undermine their position, and the law is a powerful weapon that can be used to thwart groups with competing interests. As Turk has indicated, the likelihood of conflicts resulting in the application of law is dependent upon several factors. Nevertheless, existing laws and their enforcement generally favor either (a) both the more and the less powerful or (b) the more powerful alone. Occasionally, laws favor less powerful groups at the expense of the more powerful, but the application of such laws is far less systematic.

4. Deviant behavior is, with few exceptions, a rational, learned response to social, economic, and political conditions. Unlike the more powerful, the less powerful do not have legitimate access to scarce resources. Thus the structure of society contributes to the occurrence of deviance because some groups cannot easily enhance or protect their interest without breaking the legal code. On the other hand, the powerful as well respond to social, economic, and political conditions. In their efforts to maintain the dominance of their interests against incursions by the less powerful *and* by those within their own group, the powerful often violate their own rules. Thus not only does the public cheat corporations, but corporations cheat the public and each other.

5. Deviant responses are supported by the learning of traditions, rewards, and motives. In most instances the law prohibiting a behavior exists prior to the behavior itself; furthermore, most people who violate a law do not do so out of ignorance. Most lawbreakers are aware of the law but break it anyway. The assumption of this book is that people are rarely compelled or driven into a specific behavior, but rather make decisions among various alternative behaviors. The selection of one behavior over another involves a calculation of risk and a justification based upon learning experiences.

These learning experiences are based upon broadly defined traditions of American society: independence, freedom of the individual, progress, and so on. One tradition that plays a predominant role in deviance is our heritage of violence.[51] Although some acts of violence are deplored, the nation has a long history of favoring violence for the purposes of protesting, resisting change, and righting wrongs. The man of the frontier with his six-shooter influences contemporary society more than many would care to believe.

Other learning experiences involve rewards for breaking the law. Despite the admonition "Crime doesn't pay," some crimes do pay exceedingly well. The high profits from organized crime and corporate law-breaking are cases in point. Economic or material gain is but one potential reward. Others might be (1) status and esteem in the eyes of one's friends and family; (2) political advantage by reducing opponents' capacity or desire to resist; (3) escape from the pressures of one's personal misfortunes or from the demands made by family, friends, job, or society; and (4) the sheer joy of fun and adventure—a facet of being "immoral and illegal" that serious-minded social scientists often overlook.[52]

Of course, there are risks in any law-breaking behavior, and the potential rewards must be perceived as compensating for those risks. In reality the risks for minor acts of deviance may be greater than those for major ones; the misuse of millions of dollars may incur a lesser punishment than a filling station robbery of $75. Only the powerful have the opportunity to engage in large-scale deviance with minimal risks. Even among the powerless, however, the risks of deviance are relatively minor in comparison to the possible rewards from illegitimate behavior:

> The "legitimate" jobs open to many ghetto residents, especially to young black males, typically pay low wages, offer relatively demeaning assignments, and carry the constant risk of layoff. In contrast, many kinds of crime "available" in the ghetto often bring higher monetary return, offer even higher social status, and—at least in some cases like numbers running— sometimes carry relatively low risk of arrest and punishment. Given those alternative opportunities, the choice between "legitimate" and "illegitimate" activities is often quite simple.[53]

Finally, learning experiences supporting deviant behavior involve verbalized motives explaining why a law may or should be violated in certain instances. Gresham M. Sykes and David Matza suggest delinquents, for example, may break rules with which they fundamentally agree. According to these authors, delinquents recognize that rules need not be rigidly adhered to if the situation presents unique characteristics. The difference between legal and delinquent positions is that delinquents stretch the number of law-breaking situations beyond those excused by law. When these situations arise, acts of delinquency have been learned as justifiable options. The drift into delinquency can occur because the bind of law can be neutralized.[54] This neutralization is nicely defined by Joseph F. Sheley as *the process by which individuals extend or distort socially accepted conditions for norm violation in order to deviate without forfeiting allegiance to the norm.*[55] Traditional statements and folklore enable the individual to defend her or his actions to others: "Meet force with force," "If somebody's too drunk . . . ," and so on. Such verbalizations allow one to maintain a favorable self-image while attempting to persuade others that there is a reasonable explanation for rule-breaking behavior.

The remaining chapters specifically describe forms of deviance ranging from homicide to the sale of adulterated meat to heroin addiction. You will see that deviant behaviors vary from one social group to another and that interest group conflict serves to define and to sustain those behaviors.

CRITICAL THINKING EXERCISES

1. Do you believe that "rule-breakers become entrenched in deviant roles because they are labeled deviant by others" and kept out of normal roles? Why or why not?

2. Have you ever known anyone who had a reputation that he or she did not deserve? What would it take to change that person's reputation to an honest, reality-based reputation?

3. Is Karl Marx's communist philosophy consistent with human nature? Why does his philosophy appeal to perpetually impoverished people?

4. Do powerful people in the United States try to influence the development of new laws to better protect themselves and their social and economic positions?

CHECK IT OUT ON THE WEB

The Internet addresses listed below are intended to provide the reader with understanding of a wide range of perspectives regarding the subject matter discussed in this chapter. Some sites may contain objectionable material. The list is not intended to reflect the viewpoints or opinions of the authors or the publisher.

http://www.critcrim.org
    information and links for critical and postmodern criminology
http://www.sun.soci.niu.edu/~critcrim/sites/sites.html
    criminology links, postmodern criminology
http://www.stopviolence.com/restjust.htm
    critical perspectives, peacemaking criminology, and restorative justice
http://www.faculty.ncwc.edc/toconnor/301/301links.htm
    lectures, resource links for criminology theory
http://www.westga.edu/~jfuller/peace.html
    ancient peacemaking traditions, peacemaking criminology, and restorative justice

ENDNOTES

1. Some writers have a strong preference for one term over others; see, for example, John I. Kitsuse, "Deviance, Deviant Behavior, and Deviants: Some Conceptual Problems," in *An Introduction to Deviance: Readings in the Process of Making Deviants*, ed. William J. Filstead (Chicago: Markham, 1972), pp. 233, 235. A sampling of articles reveals *labeling* to be the term most often used.

2. Howard S. Becker, *Outsiders: Studies in the Sociology of Deviance* (New York: The Free Press, 1963), p. 14.

3. Ibid., p. 9 (emphasis added).

4. Kai T. Erikson, "Notes on the Sociology of Deviance," in *The Other Side: Perspectives on Deviance,* ed. Howard S. Becker (New York: The Free Press, 1964), p. 11.

5. Kai T. Erikson, *Wayward Puritans: A Study in the Sociology of Deviance* (New York: John Wiley, 1966), pp. 25–26. This claim of constant rates of deviance has been challenged by Walter D. Connor, "The Manufacture of Deviance: The Case of the Soviet Purge, 1936–1938," *American Sociological Review, 37* (August 1972), pp. 403–413; and Daniel Glaser, *Social Deviance* (Chicago: Markham, 1971), pp. 97–100.

6. The critics of the labeling approach are many. The most thorough critique is Walter R. Gove, ed., *The Labelling of Deviance,* 2nd ed. (Beverly Hills: Sage Publications, 1980); for a review of this and related concerns, see Erich Goode, "Positive Deviance: A Viable Concept," *Deviant Behavior, 12* (1992) pp. 289–309.

7. Emile Durkheim, *The Rules of Sociological Method,* 8th ed., trans. Sarah A. Solovay and John H. Mueller (Glencoe, IL: The Free Press, 1938), p. 70.

8. Edwin M. Lemert, *Social Pathology: A Systematic Approach to the Theory of Sociopathic Behavior* (New York: McGraw-Hill, 1951), pp. 75–76. The discussion also incorporates Lemert's more recent work, *Human Deviance,* pp. 62–92.

9. Lemert, *Social Pathology,* p. 76.

10. Ibid., p. 77.

11. The discussion is based upon Becker, *Outsiders,* pp. 25–39.

12. Milton Mankoff, "Societal Reaction and Career Deviance: A Critical Analysis," *Sociological Quarterly, 12* (Spring 1971), p. 204.

13. Nanette J. Davis, "Labeling Theory in Deviance Research: A Critique and Reconsideration," *Sociological Quarterly, 13* (Autumn 1972), p. 460.

14. Edwin M. Lemert, "Diversion in Juvenile Justice: What Hath Been Wrought," *Journal of Research in Crime and Delinquency, 18* (January 1981), p. 38.

15. Gove, ed., *The Labelling of Deviance,* passim. For evidence consistent with the labeling perspective, see Allan Horwitz and Michael Wasserman, "The Effect of Social Control on Delinquent Behavior: A Longitudinal Test," *Sociological Focus, 12* (January 1979), pp. 53–70; and Gary F. Jensen, "Labeling and Identity: Toward a Reconciliation of Divergent Findings," *Criminology, 18* (May 1980), pp. 121–129.

16. As discussed by Jeffrey Ulmer in "Revisiting Stebbins: Labeling and Commitment to Deviance," *Sociological Quarterly, 35* (February 1994), pp. 135–157.

17. Allen E. Liska, *Perspectives on Deviance* (Englewood Cliffs, NJ: Prentice-Hall, 1981), pp. 489–508.

18. John I. Kitsuse, "Coming Out All Over: Deviants and the Politics of Social Problems," *Social Problems, 28* (October 1980), p. 7.

19. Ibid., p. 8.

20. Ibid., p. 9. For a critique similar to Kitsuse's, see Frances Fox Piven, "Deviant Behavior and the Remaking of the World," *Social Problems, 28* (June 1981), pp. 489–508; and Rose Weitz, "From Accommodation to Rebellion: Tertiary Deviance and the Radical Redefinitions of Lesbianism," in *Studies in the Sociology of Social Problems,* ed. Joseph W. Schneider and John I. Kitsuse (Norwood, NJ: Ablex, 1984), pp. 140–161.

21. Jack P. Gibbs, "Three Perennial Issues in the Sociology of Deviance," in *Theoretical Integration in the Study of Deviance and Crime: Problems and Prospects,* ed. Steven F. Messner, Marvin D. Krohn, and Allen E. Liska (Albany: State University of New York Press, 1989), p. 186.

22. Thorsten Sellin, *Culture Conflict and Crime,* Report of the Subcommittee on Delinquency of the Committee on Personality and Culture, Bulletin 41 (New York: Social Science Research Council, 1938). For a discussion of this report, see Donald R. Cressey, "Culture Conflict, Differential Association, and Normative Conflict," in *Crime and Culture: Essays in Honor of Thorsten Sellin,* ed. Marvin E. Wolfgang (New York: John Wiley, 1968), pp. 43–54.

23. George B. Vold, *Theoretical Criminology* (New York: Oxford University Press, 1958), pp. 203–219. See also George B. Vold and Thomas J. Bernard, *Theoretical Criminology,* 3rd ed. (New York: Oxford University Press, 1986), pp. 270–277.

24. Vold, *Theoretical Criminology,* p. 214; and Vold and Bernard, *Theoretical Criminology,* p. 275.

25. Vold, *Theoretical Criminology,* p. 219; and Vold and Bernard, *Theoretical Criminology,* pp. 276–277.

26. Vold and Bernard, *Theoretical Criminolgy,* pp. v–vi.

27. Austin T. Turk, *Criminality and Legal Order* (Chicago: Rand McNally, 1969), pp. 1–78.

28. Ibid., p. 35.

29. Ibid., p. 49.

30. Austin T. Turk, "Law as a Weapon in Social Conflict," *Social Problems, 23* (February 1976), pp. 279–280.

31. Derived from ibid., pp. 280–281. Omitted from the discussion is Turk's concept of "diversionary power."

32. "Radical criminology" is variously named by terms such as "new," "Marxist," and "critical." For a discussion of terminology and related issues, see Robert M. Bohm, "Radical Criminology: An Explication," *Criminology, 19* (February 1982), pp. 565–589.

33. Richard Quinney, "The Social Reality of Crime," in *Current Perspectives on Criminal Behavior,* ed. Abraham S. Blumberg (New York: Alfred A. Knopf, 1974), pp. 38–43. Quinney has provided other versions of these

propositions; this one is presented because it most obviously reflects a Marxist orientation. Cf. Richard Quinney, *Criminology: Analysis and Critique of Crime in America* (Boston: Little, Brown, 1975), pp. 36–41.

34. An excellent example of research with an orientation that Quinney would probably approve of is Martha A. Myers, "Economic Threat and Racial Disparities in Incarceration: The Case of Postbellum Georgia," *Criminology, 28* (November 1990), pp. 627–656.

35. Richard Quinney, *Class, State, and Crime,* 2nd ed. (New York: Longman, 1980), pp. 57–59.

36. Ibid., pp. 64–65.

37. For examples, see Gwynn Nettler, *Explaining Crime,* 2nd ed. (New York: McGraw-Hill, 1978), pp. 213–223; Carl B. Klockars, "The Contemporary Crises of Marxist Criminology," *Criminology, 16* (February 1979), pp. 477–515; and James Inverarity, "Theories of the Political Creation of Deviance: Legacies of Conflict Theory, Marx, and Durkheim," in *A Political Analysis of Deviance,* ed. Pat Lauderdale (Minneapolis: University of Minnesota Press, 1980), pp. 175–217. For a specific critique of Quinney's use of Marxist theory, see R. Serge Denisoff and Donald McQuarie, "Crime Control in Capitalist Society: A Reply to Quinney," *Issues in Criminology, 10* (Spring 1975), pp. 109–119.

38. Graeme Newman, *Comparative Deviance: Perception and Law in Six Cultures* (New York: Elsevier, 1976); and Charles W. Thomas, Robin Cage, and S. Foster, "Public Opinion on Criminal Law and Legal Sanctions: An Examination of Two Conceptual Models," *Journal of Criminal Law and Criminology, 67* (March 1976), pp. 110–116. See also John Hagan, Edward T. Silva, and John H. Simpson, "Conflict and Consensus in the Designation of Deviance," *Social Forces, 56* (December 1977), pp. 320–340.

39. For a discussion of this matter by a radical criminologist, see Robert Lefcourt, "Law Against the People," in *Criminal Justice in America: A Critical Understanding,* ed. Richard Quinney (Boston: Little, Brown, 1974), pp. 261–263.

40. Ronald L. Akers, "Theory and Ideology in Marxist Criminology: Comments on Turk, Quinney, Toby, and Klockars," *Criminology, 16* (February 1979), pp. 542–543. For a response, see David F. Greenberg, ed., *Crime and Capitalism: Readings in Marxist Criminology* (Palo Alto, CA: Mayfield, 1981), pp. 22–25. For works on the Marxist perspective that happen to be interesting and fun (two professors bash each other), see Jeffrey S. Adler, "A Historical Analysis of the Law of Vagrancy," *Criminology, 27* (May 1990), pp. 209–229; William J. Chambliss, "On Trashing Marxist Criminology," *Criminology, 27* (May 1990), pp. 231–238; and Jeffrey S. Adler, "Rejoinder to Chambliss," *Criminology, 27* (May 1990), pp. 239–250. For

advances in critical criminological thinking, see also Stuart Henry and Dragan Milovanovic, "Constitutive Criminology: The Maturation of Critical Theory,"*Criminology, 29* (May 1991), pp. 293–316.

41. Michael J. Lynch and W. Byron Groves, *A Primer in Radical Criminology,* 2nd ed. (New York: Harrow and Heston, 1989), pp. 127–128.

42. Ibid., p. 130.

43. Harold Pepinsky, "Violence as Unresponsiveness: Toward a New Conception of Crime," *Justice Quarterly, 5* (December, 1988), pp. 539–566.

44. Richard Quinney and John Wildeman, *The Problem of Crime: A Peace and Social Justice Perspective,* 3rd ed. (Mayfield, CA: Mountain View Press, 1991).

45. Richard Quinney, "Life of Crime: Criminology and Public Policy as Peacemaking," *Journal of Crime and Justice, 16:* 2 (1993), pp. 3–10.

46. Dragan Milovanovic, *Postmodern Criminology* (Hamden, CT: Garland Press, 1997). The subject matter is also discussed in Stuart Henry and Dragan Milovanovic, *Constitutive Criminology: Beyond Postmodernism* (London: Sage Publications, 1996).

47. For recent works by labeling theorists who emphasize the role of politics, see Lauderdale, ed., *A Political Analysis of Deviance;* and Edwin M. Schur, *The Politics of Deviance* (Englewood Cliffs, NJ: Prentice-Hall, 1980). See also Nachman Ben-Yehuda, *The Politics and Morality of Deviance: Moral Panics, Drug Abuse, Deviant Science, and Reversed Stigmatization* (Albany: State University of New York Press, 1990).

48. Edwin M. Lemert, "Issues in the Study of Deviance," *Sociological Quarterly, 22* (Spring 1981), p. 289. See also Goode, "Positive Deviance," for discussions about defining deviance and discussions concerning whether there is "positive" deviance.

49. The subject matter of criminology and, by implication, the field of deviant behavior have been subject to perennial controversy since the early 1930s. For detailed discussions of the controversy, see two articles by Herman Schwendinger and Julia Schwendinger: "Defenders of Order or Guardians of Human Rights?" *Issues in Criminology, 5* (Summer 1970), pp. 123–157; and "The Continuing Debate on the Legalistic Approach to the Definition of Crime," *Issues in Criminology, 7* (Winter 1972), pp. 71–81. See also Clayton A. Hartjen, "Legalism and Humanism: A Reply to the Schwendingers," *Issues in Criminology, 7* (Winter 1972), pp. 59–69; Gene Grabiner, "The Limits of Three Perspectives on Crime: 'Value-Free Science,' 'Objective Law,' and State 'Morality,'" *Issues in Criminology, 8* (Spring 1973), pp. 35–48; and Ben-Yehuda, *The Politics and Morality of Deviance,* esp. pp. 3–94.

50. Richard Quinney, *The Problem of Crime* (New York: Dodd, Mead & Co., 1970), p. 16.

51. Edwin M. Schur, *Our Criminal Society: The Social and Legal Sources of Crime in America* (Englewood Cliffs, NJ: Prentice-Hall, 1969), pp. 125–131.

52. Some of these and other rewards for juvenile delinquency are discussed by John DeLamater, "On the Nature of Deviance," *Social Forces, 46* (June 1968), pp. 452–454.

53. David M. Gordon, "Capitalism, Class, and Crime in America," *Crime and Delinquency, 19* (April 1973), p. 175.

54. This discussion is based on Gresham M. Sykes and David Matza, "Techniques of Neutralization: A Theory of Delinquency," *American Sociological Review, 22* (December 1957), pp. 664–670; and David Matza, *Delinquency and Drift* (New York: John Wiley, 1964), pp. 69–100.

55. Joseph F. Sheley, "Is Neutralization Necessary for Criminal Behavior?" *Deviant Behavior, 2* (October/December 1980), p. 50.

PART TWO

Crime as Deviant Behavior

At the end of the preceding chapter we determined that *deviant behavior is behavior subject to legal procedures aimed at curtailing that behavior. Such procedures may involve punishment, restoration of losses to victims, or involuntary hospitalization.* Chapters 4 through 7 examine specific instances of deviant behavior. Chapter 4, after an explanation of the difficulty in formally measuring crime or deviant behavior, explores crimes against the person—specifically murder, aggravated assault, and forcible rape—and reviews the violence in our culture. Facts detailing what we know in each case along with explanations of the behaviors are presented. Chapter 5 focuses on property crime, including robbery, burglary, motor vehicle theft, larceny-theft, and arson, and explains the larceny that exists in the United States. Chapter 6 examines assaults against spouses and children. This chapter describes the difficulty in determining the extent of the problem and examines explanations for this abuse. Chapter 7 discusses deviance in organizations, including police corruption, employee theft, corporate deviance, and organized crime. All of this section builds on Part I, describing deviant behaviors that are of concern.

4 Crime in the Streets— Against the Person

One unhappy fact about the urban condition in the United States is citizens' fear of crime. When polled recently about fear of crime, 42 percent of Americans were "very fearful" or "somewhat fearful."[1] For these people the sound of footsteps behind them on a deserted street, the sudden meeting with a stranger in a darkened hallway, and the unexpected knock at their apartment door are occasions of great anxiety. Whether the basis for such fear is real or exaggerated, there are serious consequences. The people concerned make an effort to acquire "street smarts" by taking self-defense courses and learning how to act in the face of danger.[2] The CBS News television show *48 Hours* aired a segment entitled "Fighting Back," which detailed some of these efforts.[3] Women were filmed attending classes on how to foil rape attempts physically and verbally and on how not to look vulnerable on the street. Viewed in the same segment was a Washington, DC, physician who, after delivering babies, attends classes held at the "Ultimate Self-Defense Academy," where he learns a combination of karate and street-fighting techniques that guarantee survival in the urban jungle.

The subject of this chapter is crime in the streets—a term designating the acts that cause this widespread fear. The term used by police and the FBI to discuss and measure crime in the streets is *violent crime*. Violent crimes include murder and nonnegligent manslaughter, forcible rape, robbery, and aggravated assault.[4] While other crimes, such as industrial pollution and the marketing of dangerous products, may be more hazardous to more people, these street crimes have an immediacy, since they directly threaten lives and property. Homicide, assaults, rape, and any loss of valuables are tangible causes for alarm. The multibillion-dollar activities of organized crime, the Enron debacle, and the corruption that taints government are of little concern when some creep is forcing open your window at two in the morning.

The desire for personal safety and security of property is understandable. And that desire lies behind most people's conception of crime: the victimization of good citizens by bad strangers. Most citizens believe that all that stands between themselves and harm is a thin blue line of police officers. Even when the atrocity of the videotaped beating of Rodney King by Los Angeles police officers shakes their faith in police, many people are so "fed up with violent street crime, they are often content to send in the police force and demand that it do whatever is necessary while they look the other way."[5] "Real" crime is the stuff against which police skirmish every day. When we read headlines about a "war on crime," the subject is street crime. How is the war going?

Measuring Crime

In the fall of each year, newspapers and television broadcasts report that crime rates are rising, falling, or staying the same. These reports also include elements of information such as the following: A violent crime occurs every 22.1 seconds; one murder occurs every 32.4 minutes, and the total number of murders in the United States for 2002 was 16,204, or 1.1 percent of the violent crimes reported; and robberies decreased 0.7 percent in 2002 from the previous year. The source of this information is an FBI publication, *Crime in the United States,* usually referred to in the criminological literature as the *Uniform Crime Reports (UCR).*[6] This publication presents crime statistics collected from law enforcement agencies nationwide that represent 260 million persons, or 95 percent of the total population.

The heart of the UCR is "crimes known to police." These statistics are based upon police department counts of citizen complaints about being victimized and, to a lesser extent, upon the number of crimes witnessed by police themselves. Because of the publicity given the UCR, most Americans probably assume that its statistics accurately measure the amount of criminal activity. Unfortunately, the UCR has some glaring shortcomings. One is that not all criminal acts are reported to the police. There are several reasons for this, but the most obvious is that in certain situations there is no victim: No one complains because no one feels that he or she has been coerced or harmed. Examples are illegal drug sales, prostitution, and illegal gambling. Since these behaviors are matters of choice, only uninvolved third parties are likely to report them. The UCR does not even have a category for these types of crimes. The revised UCR, the National Incident-Based Reporting System (NIBRS), will have a new scoring category called "crimes against society" to correct this.[7]

NIBRS will be phased in over the next ten years to replace the UCR, but it will still only address crime reported to police. And much is simply not reported. Research indicates that victims often feel that police are unable to do anything about the matter, that the offense is not serious enough to report, or that the incident is a private or personal matter in which outsiders should not be involved. How many times in the last two years have you been victimized and failed to report the crime to police? For these and other reasons we find, when using victim surveys, that just 39 percent of crime is ever reported to police; only 53 percent of burglaries, 31 percent of rapes, and 57 percent of robberies are reported. The offense most frequently reported to police is auto theft (81 percent).[8] Although it is tempting to say that Americans must care more for their cars than for themselves, the reason for the high reporting rate probably lies with insurance company requirements.

What then does the UCR tell us? It indicates the annual number of known crimes officially considered serious. We mentioned earlier that one of the pronouncements from the UCR is whether crime is rising. This figure does not refer to all types of crime, but to eight offenses that constitute the *Crime Index:* murder, aggravated assault, forcible rape, robbery, burglary, larceny-theft, motor vehicle theft, and arson. Essentially, then, the UCR gauges the amount of activity and time that police departments spend on specific crimes. But since the police can record and act on only the crimes they know about, the UCR figures are of doubtful value as a measure of total criminal activity. The UCR shortcomings, such as failing to audit police reporting and recording only the most serious crime in a case where an offender commits many crimes at once, will be corrected by the NIBRS. But the NIBRS still will deal only with crime reported to police and thus indicate police level of activity.

In 1973 there began a more accurate measure of annual criminal activity—the National Crime Survey (NCS), now called the National Crime Victimization Survey (NCVS). Rather than using police records to determine the amount of crime, the U.S. Bureau of Justice Statistics conducts the NCVS, which is based on households. Using a scientifically selected sample, every six months for three years 100,000 persons aged 12 or older in 50,000 households are interviewed regarding their experience as crime victims.[9] Obviously, there are differences between the UCR and the NCVS. Murder is not one of the NCVS categories, as it is not possible to interview murder victims. Commercial crimes are also excluded, as are consumer fraud, illicit drug use, and vandalism.[10] Too, the UCR and the NCVS data are not strictly comparable.[11] The NCVS surveys households, conducts interviews in person and by telephone, and then estimates the amount of criminal victimization nationally. It also includes crime that is both reported and not reported to the police.

What information concerning crime can be obtained from the NCVS? It estimates (on the basis of a 93 percent response rate) the personal victimizations of rape, robbery, assault, and theft and the household crimes of theft, burglary, and motor vehicle theft.[12] For example, in 2002, 14.6 percent experienced any NCVS crime. This represents a 10 percent decrease from the 25 percent in 1994.[13] Contrast that with the figures from the FBI and the alarmist reports we frequently hear, even when reported crime decreases. For example, the FBI reports that "five- and ten-year percent changes showed the 1993 national experience was 1 percent lower than the 1989 level but 19 percent higher than the 1984 volume."[14]

Crime may be down, but incarceration is up. Since 1995 the nation's prison population has grown at an annual rate of 3.7 percent, with 1 in 32 adults of the United States and territories incarcerated, bringing the total to over 2 million at the end of 2002.[15] What gives? Anyone can tell you there is more crime annually and probably be correct. There are more people annually and therefore more crime. But the *rate* of crime may be less. Whom do you trust? Two bureaus in the same federal department may reach differing conclusions. Or do they? They both report the facts; they just observe different facts.

The NCVS does provide a more accurate picture about the prevalence and distribution of crime than the UCR does. Since this is the case, why do we constantly read about the UCR instead? The NCVS lacks a strong media image, probably because the UCR is older—it was developed in 1930—and more familiar.

Does it really make any difference which data source we use? If both the UCR and the NCVS told us the same thing, we could probably answer, "No." One of the unfortunate aspects of crime statistics is that one can locate practically any "proof" to suit one's purposes. If you want to argue that crime has generally risen over the past decade, check the UCR and you will likely find the evidence you need. If you want to argue that crime is decreasing or stable, consult the NCVS. These inconsistencies can be unnerving for the criminologist until he or she recognizes that while the *NCVS measures changes in reported victimization,* the *UCR measures changes in police recording efficiency.* It *does* make a difference which report is used. As Samuel Walker has stated:

> This is not simply an academic dispute. When crime control policy is formulated, it makes all the difference in the world whether crime is increasing or decreasing. Are we in the midst of a crime wave or are we witnessing a long-term decline in criminality? Perceptions of the crime problem have a major influence on the political debate.[16]

In addition to the UCR or the NCVS, is there any other measure that we can use to determine the amount of crime? Self-reports by offenders have been widely used in studies of juvenile delinquency.[17] Perhaps when we manage to compile and analyze UCR data, NCVS data, and data from a self-report survey, all from the same geographic area for the same time period, we will get a true picture of the crime problem. Whatever crime measure we use, there is little argument that index crimes and NCVS crimes are felt to be serious matters by most citizens. The remainder of this chapter and the next chapter will examine the prevalence and causes of these crimes.

Murder and Aggravated Assault

Murder and aggravated assault will be discussed together because the difference between them is frequently only a matter of degree. In fact, improved emergency medicine is no doubt responsible for many lifesaving procedures that, had they not been used, would have meant that a murder had occurred. The UCR defines murder simply as "the willful (non-negligent) killing of one human being by another." This definition excludes deaths caused by negligence, suicide, accident, or justifiable homicide.

Aggravated assault is defined as "an unlawful attack by one person upon another for the purpose of inflicting severe or aggravated bodily injury. This type of assault is usually accompanied by the use of a weapon or by means likely to produce death or great bodily harm." Murder *attempts* are also included in this category. Admittedly, the distinction between murder and aggravated assault may be simply a matter of circumstances: the potency of the weapon used, the ability of the victim to defend himself or herself, the immediacy and effectiveness of medical care, or luck. This writer recalls the not-too-bright youth who was bewildered by his act of murder, claiming, "I stabbed him in the stomach because I heard it wasn't so dangerous to do that." We will assume for the purposes of discussion that there are enough parallels between homicide and aggravated assault that the motivations for the behavior in both cases should be roughly similar.[18]

Only the UCR provides annual statistical data on homicide. These are considered quite accurate for the obvious reason that dead bodies are evidence not easily disposed of. UCR data are even supported by coroner reports.[19] The flaw in this logic is that an unknown number of bodies *are,* no doubt, effectively disposed of each year. As we shall see, some mass murderers escape discovery for years. We probably can add to this figure the victims of professional killings who disappear underwater or beneath concrete interstate highways. Furthermore, the reader should not be deceived by the image of coroners portrayed on television. A coroner may be an appointed or elected official whose qualifications might depend on his or her ability to remove a body, for example, the local funeral home director or tow truck driver. In fact, the state of Kentucky is one of the few states that mandates extensive training for coroners.[20]

A coroner may receive assistance from the local hospital pathologist, but he or she probably has no training in forensic pathology.[21] Trudy Knicely Henson found that real-life coroners are not always competent. Although medical experts may be available for assistance, they may not be used for a variety of reasons, including expense. One result is that many homicides are ruled as accidents, suicides, or even deaths from natural causes:

A case in point involved one Carl Lyons of Moncks Corner, South Carolina, who died . . . at the age of 27. His death was recorded as a natural death due to cardiac arrest. . . . New evidence led to an exhumation and autopsy of the body. The autopsy revealed that Mr. Lyons' stomach contained "enough strychnine to kill a mule." Verdict? Homicide.[22]

Thus because of offenders' cleverness and officials' lack of same, some murderers get away with murder. But most homicides are not disguised. The offenders, as we shall see, do not even try to conceal them.

Dimensions of Homicide

There is no surer way to fill a courtroom or the front page of a newspaper than with a "spectacular" murder trial. *Spectacular* here means that the offender is either "respectable," had several victims, or both. In such instances a blend of revulsion and fascination attracts us because the killing is "out of character." The respectable should not kill, and the not-so-respectable should not kill so many.

The 1990s were bloody; we saw the "Milwaukee Murders," in which Jeffrey Dahmer confessed to killing 17 people. He would pick victims up at bars or shopping malls, lure them to his apartment, drug them, kill them, and then dismember the bodies. Police even returned one of his future victims to him. A 14-year-old boy, Konerak Sinthasomphone, was found wandering, dazed and naked, on the street. Dahmer convinced police that the boy was his homosexual lover and that they had been quarreling.[23] Dahmer was finally apprehended when his latest catch managed to escape and alert police that someone was trying to kill him.[24]

Donald Leroy Evans, a drifter from Texas, may be attempting to establish a record. Arrested for raping and murdering a 10-year-old homeless girl, he reportedly has confessed to skeptical police that he killed 60 people between 1977 and 1986.[25] The popular press even reports that we may have a rarity: a female serial killer. A Florida prostitute, Aileen Wuornos, allegedly killed customers if they gave her trouble. But her victim count is only seven.[26]

Murder has proven reliable in grabbing headlines and is not unique to any one state. A New Hampshire teacher, Pamela Smart, seduced a 15-year-old student and then convinced him and two friends to kill her husband; Wanda Webb Holloway, of Texas, was accused of plotting the murder of the mother of a girl competing with her daughter for a spot on the cheerleading squad; and George James Trepal, a Florida man, poisoned the family next door because they made too much noise.[27] O. J. Simpson, accused of murdering his ex-wife and her friend Ronald Goldman, was on trial for a year before his acquittal, an event that riveted the nation.[28]

The great majority of homicides, however, are not spectacular and do not involve multiple victims. They usually occur spontaneously and under quite simple circumstances. Our task here is to present the facts of "ordinary" murder that can be ascertained from the UCR and from sociological research.

Fact 1. The murder rate is declining. The lowest national murder rate since 1966—5.6 murders per 100,000 inhabitants—was recorded in 2002, representing a 10 percent drop from the 1998 figure. This rate was 40 percent lower than the 1993 rate.[29] After 1933 rates generally declined, with some fluctuations, until the lowest rate of 4.5 occurred in both

1962 and 1963. It climbed steadily after that. The 1933 rate was surpassed in 1970, rose to the 1980 high, and has fluctuated since then.

The homicide picture may not be good news, but the probability of being murdered if you are a member of certain groups is downright depressing. The probability of being murdered is not evenly distributed throughout the American population. Some groups are far more at risk than others. This leads us to our second fact about murder and to an explanation of the murder rates.

Fact 2. Murder is disproportionately high among young, lower-status, nonwhite males. As we proceed through this and the next chapter, we shall see that violence in the United States spreads across all socioeconomic levels. However, there is no doubt that death by violent means is concentrated in the lower-status levels. In one national analysis of homicide the authors concluded that

> in spite of reporting problems, the true rates of major violence appear to be much greater for those of the lower socioeconomic status than for those of higher status. The poor, uneducated individual with minimal or no employment skills is more likely to commit serious violence than the person higher up on the socioeconomic ladder.[30]

In addition to being concentrated in the lower socioeconomic class, murder is related to sexual and racial characteristics. The FBI produced, as part of a recent UCR, a section called *The Chances of Lifetime Murder Victimization.* They calculated statistics according to sex and race, using the categories of male and female, white, black, and other (defined as Asian, Pacific Islander, and American Indian or Alaskan Native). If you are a white male or female, age 20, your chances of becoming a murder victim are 1 in 488. A black male or female, age 20, faces a 1 in 81 chance. These are dramatically different odds indeed. The odds of being murdered in the remainder of your lifetime if you are a white male, age 20, are 1 in 330. What about a black male, age 20? The odds are positively frightening: 1 in 48.[31] The conclusion is clear: Despite decreases in the murder rate, homicide is still an epidemic, particularly among young black males. Blacks were six times more likely than whites to be murdered in 2000.[32]

Homicide *offenders* have the same characteristics as their victims: they are primarily young and male, and young black males are disproportionately involved in homicide compared to their share of the population. According to the UCR, males made up 90 percent of the offenders for whom gender was reported. Blacks made up 50 percent of the total arrestees for murder in 2002, whites made up 48 percent, and the remainder were of other races.[33] Blacks were seven times more likely than whites to commit homicide in 2000.[34] The UCR also shows that murders are primarily *intraracial.* According to the 2002 data on murder cases in which the race of both offender and victim were known, 92 percent of the black murder victims were slain by black offenders, and 84 percent of the white victims were killed by white offenders. Data on sex composition show that murder is also an *intrasexual* offense; males were most often slain by males (88 percent in single victim/single offender situations). These same data showed that nine out of every ten female victims were murdered by males. However, homicide is clearly a young, male offense in most respects.

Now we are in a position to answer a question raised in connection with the first fact of murder: Why are murder rates falling? Murder rates fell dramatically, and explanations for this are many. One can make a good case for a strong economy and the waning crack cocaine epidemic, as noted in a recent presentation by Elliot Currie, who stated, "the economic boom as explanation . . . fits, for example, with the otherwise perplexing fact that homicide has fallen faster than some property crimes."[35] However, two researchers, John J. Donohoe III and Steven D. Levitt, have presented a case for legalized abortion as an explanation for the reduction in homicide rates as well as "for as much as 50 percent of the recent drop in crime." They acknowledge that others have offered other explanations, including the increasing use of incarceration, growth in the number of police, improved policing strategies, the strong economy, and increased expenditures on victim precautions such as security guards and alarms. They further state:

> Seven years after *Roe* v. *Wade,* over 1.6 million abortions were being performed annually— almost one abortion for every two live births. Moreover, the legalization of abortion in five states in 1970 and then for the nation as a whole in 1973, were abrupt legal developments that might plausibly have a similarly abrupt influence 15–20 years later when cohorts born in the wake of liberalized abortion would start reaching their high crime years. . . . The smaller cohort that results from abortion legalization means that when that cohort reaches the late teens and twenties, there will be fewer young males in their highest-crime years, and thus less crime.[36]

This is not to suggest that there is no longer a significant problem, particularly among the young. According to the Centers for Disease Control in Atlanta, firearm-related homicide is the second leading cause of death among young Americans 15 to 19 years of age. Among African Americans in the same age group it is the leading cause of death.

Fact 3. Most murders are committed by persons acquainted with their victims. One of the greatest fears expressed about crime in the streets is the possibility that the victim will be assaulted by a stranger. As it turns out, however, strangers are less dangerous than your family or friends. In 2002, 12 percent of the homicides were committed by immediate family members, and another 31 percent were committed by other relatives or acquaintances.

Fact 4. A significant proportion of murders occur over trivial matters. It makes interesting literature to plumb the depths of a Macbeth, who murders because he is driven by the urgings of his wife and a lust for power. The ordinary murderer is no Macbeth; the non-Shakespearean dialogue ending in a death is more likely to go something like this:

> "You got a cigarette?"
> "Naw, I ain't got any."

Or:

> "Hey, you're lookin' at me."
> "No, I ain't."
> "Yes, you are. Why you lookin' at me?"

The following newspaper headlines are not unusual:

> "Boy, 15, Shot to Death After Frisbee Hits Car"
> "Poker Player Shot to Death over Fifth Ace"
> "Toothless Man Kills Wife and Daughter for Pork Chop Meal"

"Pals' Fight Ends in Death" (In this case a 32-year-old man pitchforked an old friend in an argument over who discovered America.)

Police data on the immediate events leading up to a homicide are imprecise, but they do indicate that *many murders are spontaneous events occurring as the result of minor disagreements,* not as the result of a long-considered desire to kill.[37] The UCR indicates that arguments account for 28 percent of all murders. No other reason accounts for such a large proportion: 17 percent occurred as a result of felonious activities such as robbery, arson, and the like, while another 1 percent were suspected to have been the result of some felonious activity. Nearly 29 percent of the murders have unknown motives, and the remainder are thinly spread through other categories.[38]

Fact 5. A significant proportion of murder victims contributed substantially to their own deaths. The usual assumption about murder victims is that they were caught up in circumstances over which they had no control. In truth, a great number of homicides are victim-precipitated; that is, the victim was the first to use force in the homicide incident. Data from one study indicate that as many as 63 percent of all murders committed in a California jurisdiction were "started" by the victims. This research used a broad definition of "precipitation."[39] An earlier survey indicated that in at least 22 percent of the murders, the victims themselves precipitated the behavior leading to death. Examples include the following:

> During a lover's quarrel, the man hit his mistress and threw a can of kerosene at her. She retaliated by throwing the liquid on him, and then tossed a lighted match in his direction.

> A drunken husband who was beating his wife in their kitchen gave her a butcher knife and dared her to use it on him. She said if he struck her one more time she would use it. He did, and so did she.[40]

Fact 6. Alcohol and other drugs are associated with a large proportion of homicides. It is important to point out at the onset that no drug, whether alcohol or any narcotic, can compel someone to engage in homicide, rape, petunia pruning, or any other complex form of behavior. In short, drugs do not *cause* murder. But drugs can modify behavior: They may cause a person to become more readily excited to impatience or anger; they may hamper a person's ability to evaluate a situation accurately, leading to aggression and danger; or they may reduce a person's inhibitions that would otherwise restrict the expression of insulting and provocative remarks. A sober man would probably think twice before loudly telling a gathering of bikers that they are "a bunch of Nazi bastards." But a drunken one just might blurt it out. A little whiskey can go a long way toward spilling much blood.

There are no national data on the extent to which alcohol is related to acts of aggression. However, one report by the National Institute on Alcohol Abuse and Alcoholism states that half of all murders each year are alcohol related.[41] In one 1998 report, victims of crime (not homicide) across the country reported that in 35 percent of the cases, the offenders were under the influence of alcohol.[42] In the same report, convicted murderers in state prisons reported that alcohol was a factor in about half the murders they had committed.[43]

The exact nature of the relationship between alcohol use and aggression remains a mystery. There are many studies, but their sampling and methodological shortcomings make it impossible to draw definite conclusions. For example, the studies rarely even distinguish between subjects who were actually intoxicated and those who had merely been drinking. Furthermore, most researchers have structured their studies on the assumption that there is a direct link between alcohol use and crime. But this assumption ignores other possible relationships. Perhaps some third condition causes *both* the alcohol use and the aggressive behavior, or perhaps alcohol use combines with a third factor to produce the violent act. In short, variables such as situational factors need to be explored to understand alcohol's role in homicide.[44] Also, alcohol use by victims needs further investigation. A recent article suggests that alcohol intoxication by the victim may change an aggravated assault into a homicide simply because the presence of a central nervous system depressant may hamper recovery.[45] Furthermore, an analysis of British Crime Survey data indicates "that the young may increase their odds of becoming predatory crime victims by engaging in public drinking routines—which include going to bars and nightclubs, and other alcohol-serving establishments—where exposure to potential offenders and dangerous situations is high."[46]

A related issue is the extent to which drugs other than alcohol contribute to violent crime. We will present more detail in Chapter 8 on how narcotics affect behavior, but for now it is sufficient to say that drugs such as cocaine or heroin do not directly cause an individual to be violent. However, among those inmates incarcerated for violent crimes, a third of state prisoners and more than a third of the incarcerated youth said they had been under the influence of an illegal drug at the time of their offense.[47]

A survey of convicted jail inmates revealed that nearly one in three robbers and burglars reported that they had committed their crimes to obtain money for drugs.[48] Also, there is an overlap between drug use and homicide because of the risks associated with illegality and profitability. The Bureau of Justice Statistics recently tabulated the circumstances surrounding homicides in the United States from 1976 to 1999. For the 18 to 34 age group of victims, 72.4 percent of the homicides were drug related; for the same group of offenders, 75.9 percent of the homicides were drug related.[49] Obviously, any market for highly profitable illegal goods involves violence because business differences cannot be resolved by conventional procedures. The marijuana user who discovers that his latest purchase of "Colombia Gold" is primarily oregano will get little sympathy from officials. And what can be done with untrustworthy people who "know too much," purchasers who do not pay their bills, and competitors who are getting too competitive? In short, the world of illegal drugs enhances the risk of violent death, but the drugs themselves do not cause it.[50]

Violence: A U.S. Value

Attempts to explain homicide are hardly rare; they range from Cesare Lombroso's specifications of the murderer's atavistic characteristics to more recent claims that homicide rates are linked with phases of the moon.[51] Any theory, to have wide application, must deal with the facts of murder as discussed. It must explain why a major proportion of murders are spontaneous affairs between acquaintances who are lower-class males. It is tempting to say that frustration and socioeconomic deprivation are the causes and leave it at that. But social class alone does not account for differences in rates. Sizable segments of any large industrial society occupy disadvantaged positions without producing high homicide rates. The United States is incredibly violent, much more so than other industrialized nations. In fact, Great Britain has a very small homicide rate when compared to the United States.[52] When it comes to murder, we truly are number one (South Africa, Colombia, and Russia excepted).

To understand U.S. homicide, we must first recognize the traditional role that violence has played in this country. Contrary to what many would prefer to believe, U.S. history is filled with violence of great variety. For example,

> the United States has had the bloodiest and most violent labor history of any industrial nation in the world. Labor violence was not confined to certain industries, geographic areas or specific groups in the labor force, although it has been more frequent in some industries than in others. There have been few sections and scarcely any industries in which violence has not erupted at some time, and even more serious confrontations have on occasion followed.[53]

Labor violence is but one example of the many types of violence characterizing American history. We also have a long tradition of racial conflict; the first slave uprising, which was brutally crushed, dates back to 1712. The modern era of racial conflict produced 33 major urban riots between 1900 and 1949. The bloodiest of these occurred in East St. Louis in 1917, when 9 whites and at least 39 blacks lost their lives. From 1964 to 1970 nearly 500 riots resulted in very high property damage and the deaths of almost 250 people, most of them shot by police and National Guardsmen.

Yet another example in our history of violence is the lynch mob, an American invention that originated in the backcountry of South Carolina in 1767 and was later named after Colonel Charles Lynch of Virginia. *The lynch mob is a group formed spontaneously for the purpose of punishing individuals, usually by hanging, for their alleged crimes.* Lynchings are conducted without legal authority, although historically the authorities often chose to look the other way. Lynch mobs were common in the South as a post–Civil War method of maintaining white supremacy. It is estimated that from 1882 to 1903 southern lynch mobs killed a total of 1,985 blacks, often with no proof that an offense had even occurred.[54]

Our violence-drenched history is further exemplified by (1) the great family feuds in the mountains of Kentucky, West Virginia, Virginia, and central Texas during the final half of the nineteenth century; (2) the Indian wars that raged almost continuously from 1607 to 1890—a year that saw the massacre of 300 Sioux men, women, and children by U.S. troops at Wounded Knee, South Dakota; and (3) the activities of organized crime, which between 1919 and 1967 resulted in nearly 1,000 gang murders in Chicago alone.[55]

Whether we refer to the violence at the Boston Tea Party or to organized crime's elimination of informers and competitors, we are speaking of a time-honored American way of dealing with conflict. The U.S. government itself has often used deadly force to control segments of the population. Examples range from the armed skirmishes between strikers and the National Guard in Ludlow, Colorado, in 1914—resulting in over 50 deaths, including those of a dozen strikers' children—to the National Guard's killing of four unarmed students protesting the Vietnam War at Kent State University in 1970.

What is known as the *frontier tradition* exemplifies the American approval of violence to resolve conflicts.[56] Life on the frontier required that individuals rely on their own initiative and resources for nearly everything necessary to exploit what the land had to offer. The same was true of justice. Decisions about lawbreakers often had to be made on the spot. The lack of nearby jails or courts and the lack of funds to hire law enforcement officials often left little choice in handling offenders: either do them in immediately or release them, risking their return on another day. Taking the law into one's own hands was the only practical alternative in many cases.

To establish order and to maintain security in the absence of official law enforcement, men frequently formed *vigilante groups* whose purpose was to implement the law as the occasion demanded. The difference between the lynch mob and the vigilante group was a matter of degree: Vigilantes were more organized and lasted longer—in some cases years. Up to 1910 at least 326 such groups existed in the United States; in many areas, especially west of the Mississippi, they represented the only form of law. Like lynch mobs, the vigilantes depended upon rapid judgment and execution by hanging. Their targets generally included murderers, robbers, horse thieves, and counterfeiters of money and bank notes. But frequently, politics, skin color, or religion was reason enough for being judged. Some vigilante groups persisted despite the eventual presence of legal authorities, and in administering their own brand of justice, these groups became outlaws themselves.[57]

The American frontier's isolation from formal law is best illustrated in contrast to the Canadian experience:

> In the United States, the West was settled by hardy pioneers; in Canada, the advance was led and controlled by the Northwest Mounted Police . . . a national organization enforcing a national criminal code. We had Kit Carson, the Alamo, elected sheriffs and marshals, posses, outlaws, showdowns and shoot-outs, and they had Renfrew of the Mounties. Our heroes, in fact and in legend, were grimy, hard-driving, dusty gunmen; theirs were groomed, shaven, disciplined troops with shiny brass buttons. *We had people before there was law, while they had law before there were people.*[58]

On-the-spot justice was often necessary on the frontier. But the end of the frontier did not completely erase the values to which it had given birth. These values are legacies contributing to contemporary violence. First, in the United States there is an *idealized version of manhood.* Manhood means having confidence in one's physical prowess, being ready to fight for what one believes is right, and standing tall against affronts and danger. The heroes of the frontier were not sissies—they were firm of jaw and purpose against adversity. Second, there is a tradition of *gun ownership.* Guns were once an absolute necessity for food and for defense; today, they are symbols of independence and masculinity. Third, there is a feeling of *independence from authority.* Vigilante groups were democratic organizations— products of the people. Americans still believe that they have the right to avenge wrongs, to take up arms, and to enforce the law themselves if authorities do not perform satisfactorily. The following passage expresses the purpose of one vigilante group formed in 1858; except for the quaint language, the message is applicable to the contemporary United States:

> Whereas, We are believers in the *doctrine of popular sovereignty;* that the people of the country are the real sovereigns, and that whenever the laws, made by those to whom they have delegated their authority, are found inadequate to their protection, it is the right of the people to take the protection of their property into their own hands, and deal with these villains according to their just desserts [*sic*].[59]

Fourth, there is a belief in *violence as a solution to problems.* Violence is a way of directly dealing with a problem. Be it a punch in the nose or a bullet in the brain, violence is a way of sidestepping accommodation; it can quickly eliminate sources of fear, competition, and anger; and it can change people's minds whether they want to change or not.

Violence has done much to make the United States what it is. The frontier was opened by the near elimination of the Indians; the agricultural accomplishments of the South were realized through the subjugation of the blacks; and the labor movement emerged in a crucible of workers' violent conflict with management and government. This history of violence forms the background of contemporary murder and mayhem in the United States. This is not to say that violence as a value is solely the result of tradition. Social and economic inequities undoubtedly play a part in producing violence, but historical precedents cannot be ignored as shapers of contemporary attitude.

What are these attitudes? A survey of U.S. males clearly indicates that a large proportion approve of extreme violence in relatively trivial situations, specifically the political protests of the period. In their conclusions the researchers voiced their concern:

> The fact that almost 50 percent of the American men felt that shooting was a good way of handling campus disturbances "almost always" or at least "sometimes" is particularly disturbing. Most campus disturbances have not involved violence to persons or major damage to property. That 20 percent . . . considered it appropriate to kill in these circumstances indicates the ease with which many people will accept violence to maintain order even when force so used is entirely out of proportion to the precipitating incidents.[60]

The researchers also found that 24 percent of the men agreed that " 'an eye for an eye and a tooth for a tooth' is a good rule for living" and that 44 percent agreed that violence deserves violence.[61]

> Where do Americans learn such values? Are we teaching such values in the early school years when we urge boys to "hit back"? Do we teach such values in the typical courses in American history, with their uncritical justification of the slaughter of the Indians, the fight for independence, the frontier wars and all the other domestic and international conflict in which this country has engaged? Or is the violent retribution served daily by television and the movies as damaging as some critics allege?[62]

More recent research conducted at an eastern university found that males were significantly more likely than females to resort to physical violence or direct coercion to persuade both other males and females.[63] A national survey found that over two-thirds of the respondents believed it was "all right" for one man to "punch a stranger" under some circumstances.[64] One fact is thus inescapable—values justifying violence, whatever their source, are part of the American heritage.

The Subculture of Interpersonal Violence

Recognizing the existence of violence-justifying values in U.S. society brings us only partway toward understanding why physical assaults occur as they do. The problem is that there are different types of violence designed to solve different kinds of problems. For example, a citizen may feel that burglars should be shot on sight, but he or she would never consider using violence to solve personal problems involving spouses, friends, or children. A striking trucker may drop a concrete block from an overpass onto a "scab" driver, but that may be his only violent act. In contrast, there are men who are peaceable in all respects except at home, where they believe that striking wives is an inherent right of husbands. Although the theme of violence has many variations, we will limit ourselves to the major portion of criminal homicides—those involving lower-class acquaintances over personal matters.

The first attempt to explain this type of homicide was made by Marvin E. Wolfgang, who wrote that

> quick resort to physical combat as a measure of daring, courage, or defense of status appears to be cultural expectation, especially for lower socioeconomic class males of both races. When such a culture norm response is elicited from an individual engaged in social interplay with others who harbor the same response mechanism, physical assaults, altercations and violent domestic quarrels that result in homicide are likely to be relatively common.[65]

There is, then, a subculture of violence—groups in which overt physical violence is an acceptable, if not expected, reaction to threats against one's masculinity, reputation, and independence. While such threats may seem "trivial" to some, to others they are not. For example, a male who confronts a professor in a crowded faculty club by calling the professor's mother a practicing whore is likely to receive a reaction quite different from that in a similar confrontation with a stevedore in a crowded dockside tavern. (Any reader doubting that the reactions will be different may wish to experiment. Be sure to ask your instructor for extra credit and medical coverage.) This is not to say that violence is approved in any circumstance but, rather, that there are specific situations in which violence is called for without feelings of guilt:

> It is not farfetched to suggest that a whole culture may accept the violence value, demand or encourage adherence to it, and penalize deviation. During periods of war the whole nation accepts the principle of violence against the enemy. The non-violent citizen turned soldier adopts the value as an intimately internalized re-enforcement for his rationalization to kill. This is, of course, selective killing of an enemy, and in this respect is different from most homicide. But criminal homicide is also "selective," not [in]discriminate slaying. . . . And as in combat on the front lines where the "it-was-either-him-or-me" situation arises, there are similar attitudes and reactions among participants in homicide.[66]

By itself the subculture of personal violence does not account for physical assaults; specific situational factors must also be present. For example, the stevedore in our example would probably have passed his time serenely in a bar had not a student come in and made an inexcusable comment. David F. Luckenbill points out that homicides—which we are calling "ordinary"—do not just "happen" to the victims; there are stages through which victims and offenders progress:

1. The victim and offender enter into a conflict situation in which the victim insults or refuses to obey the offender.
2. The offender interprets the victim's behavior as a personal offense rather than as a joke, as the result of drunkenness, or the like.
3. Rather than withdrawing from the situation the offender attempts to stand his or her ground by retaliating verbally, physically, or both.
4. Rather than complying with the offender's demands, the victim retaliates verbally, physically, or both.
5. Unless one or the other backs down, offender and victim "become committed to battle."
6. The victim falls.[67]

As we can see, had either party decided to alter his or her behavior at any stage, murder probably would have been avoided. So certain situational dynamics must be adhered to: individuals must enter into a conflict situation and refuse to retreat even in the face of impending violence. These individuals may be angry and hostile, having suffered inequality and deprivation. They cannot retreat. A summary of theories is delineated by Luckenbill and Daniel P. Doyle:

> Sociologists propose two models to explain criminal violence. First, the cultural model maintains that crime is a product of conformity to a distinct culture. These theories propose that certain structural positions are characterized by high rates of violence because a significant proportion of their occupants subscribe to and act in terms of a culture that sanctions violence. This may be regarded as the core of a cultural explanation of the relationship between structural position and violence. The second maintains that crime stems from inequality, or the uneven distribution of resources. Inequality entails the deprivation of some relative to others; the perception of relative deprivation engenders feelings of resentment and hostility; and resentment and hostility stimulate impulses that are ultimately expressed as crimes.[68]

We can now illustrate the components of the ordinary homicide in Figure 4.1.

In short, murders comprise several components, even though the results seem to be simple, spontaneous acts of passion. Our general culture provides values that support violence as a means of solving problems. These values, in turn, support subcultural values that permit or even encourage physical aggression to solve interpersonal conflicts. Inequality and resulting hostility exacerbate this, and violence results.[69] When individuals become locked into the sequence of stages described above and a gun is present, the outcome is likely to be fatal to someone.

The Conflict over Guns

Any government wants to maintain a monopoly on violence, if only to prevent its own violent overthrow. Whenever unauthorized violence occurs, the power of the state to manage its members is called into question. In extreme situations the people themselves may usurp the state's power, as they obviously did in the cases of vigilante and lynch groups. One way in

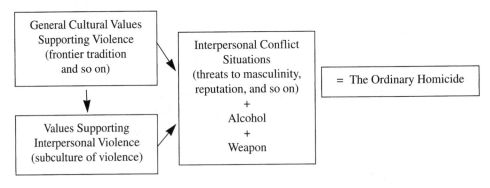

FIGURE 4.1   Components of Ordinary Homicide

which a government might exert control over illegal violence is to disarm the population, thus restricting the most potent means of violence to police and the armed forces. In the United States the citizen's right to bear arms is the focus of vehement interest group conflict.

Before we discuss the nature of this conflict, it will be helpful to examine briefly what guns mean for murder in the United States. Their importance is clear from the UCR statistics presented in Table 4.1: Over 71 percent of homicide victims were shot to death. Handguns alone account for three-fourths of the firearm homicides.

Guns are a tradition of American life: "for many years the armed citizen-soldier was the country's first line of defense; the 'Kentucky' long rifle opened the frontier; the Winchester repeater 'won the West,' and the Colt revolver 'made men equal.'"[70]

The frontier has long since disappeared, but interest in guns has not. Over half of Americans own no firearms, but 40 percent do, and 58 percent of them own handguns.[71] A call to the headquarters of the National Rifle Association (NRA), confirmed by a call to the Bureau of Alcohol, Tobacco, and Firearms, provides their *most recent estimate* of gun ownership—there are 250 million weapons in civilian hands nationwide. About three-quarters of these weapons are owned principally for sport and recreation; the other quarter are mainly for protection and self-defense.[72]

We have seen that over 70 percent of murders are accomplished by guns, over three-fourths by handguns. There is little doubt that when a gun is present in a violent confrontation, the risk of death increases. Add to the numbers of murders involving firearms the fact that recently, according to the *CDC Fact Book 2000/2001,*[73] 30,535 people committed suicide and over half of these suicides were committed with a firearm, and one can begin to understand the strident calls for gun control. However, a recent article in the *Wall Street Journal* by Gary Fields points out that despite more guns than ever, gun-related deaths and woundings dropped 33 percent in the most recent period.[74] As others note, 31 states allow private citizens to carry concealed weapons and have, on average, a 24 percent lower violent crime rate, a 19 percent lower murder rate, and a 39 percent lower robbery rate than states that forbid concealed weapons.[75] In one particularly sad case, a 7-year-old Flint, Michigan, boy found a .32 caliber handgun at home and shot Kayla Rolland, age 6, to death at the Buell Elementary School.[76] Regular media reports on youth gang killings, coupled

TABLE 4.1 Murder by Type of Firearm Used, 2002

Type of Weapon	Distribution (% of Total)
Handguns	76.6
Shotguns	5.1
Rifles	5.1
Unknown Firearm	13.2

Source: Adapted from FBI, *Crime in the United States, 2002: Uniform Crime Reports* (Washington, DC: U.S. Government Printing Office, 2002), p. 22.

with the extraordinary homicides at schools in Paducah, Kentucky; Pearl, Mississippi; Springfield, Oregon; Jonesboro, Arkansas; and Littleton, Colorado, lead to the conclusion that there is an increasing tendency for young people to respond to problems with deadly violence. When guns are readily available, conflict of any sort in our society can easily escalate to a deadly level. Perhaps some or all folks do not need to be armed. If by some magic all guns in the United States would vanish, the number of violent confrontations might not be affected, but homicide rates would decline. Such magic will not occur, so we are left with a basic question: In light of the relationship between homicide and guns, what, if anything, should be done? The usual responses fall into two categories: (1) Something must be done about restricting the availability of firearms and (2) nothing should be done. There is little middle ground between people holding these positions. Indeed, the controversy over what is called "gun control" is one of the most emotional interest group conflicts in our society.

In part, this emotion stems from the murders by guns of prominent individuals, beginning with the assassination of President John F. Kennedy in 1963. There followed the homicides of black leader Martin Luther King, Jr., Senator Robert F. Kennedy, and ex-Beatle John Lennon. In addition, attempts were made on the lives of Alabama Governor George Wallace, President Gerald Ford, and President Ronald Reagan. Following each incident, there were public outcries for more restrictions on gun ownership. But even without these instances, surveys conducted since 1959 have consistently shown that three-quarters of the U.S. public favors "a law which would require a person [to] obtain a police permit before he or she could buy a gun."[77] One survey, asking specifically about registration of handguns, found that 77 percent favored this.[78] While a majority clearly believe there should be controls on the ownership of guns, the same poll asked about a ban on handguns and discovered that only 11 percent oppose banning their possession. We already have an estimated 20,000 state and local laws dealing with gun registration. The problem is that with our decentralized government, none work. If your state or city has restrictive legislation or ordinances, simply cross the state line. A number of federal laws have been enacted to deal with firearms, but none has been very restrictive or significant. Recent federal legislation was supposed to remedy this. The Brady Handgun Prevention Act (known as the Brady Bill) may or may not be effective, depending on which report one reads. A recent report compared states (treatment states) that had to comply with the act with other states (control states) that already had similar legislation, finding no significant differences in rates of homicide and suicide for the most part.[79]

The Brady Bill requires dealers to do a background check on buyers and to keep a record of gun sales. States and local jurisdictions have their own laws, which vary considerably. And while gun control advocates seek to restrict firearms, Thomas Sowell, John R. Lott, Jr., and William M. Landes have all pointed out that perhaps we should consider arming everyone, since crime rates drop.[80]

The year 1981 marked the beginning of strong municipal legislative efforts toward gun control when Morton Grove, Illinois, passed an ordinance banning the possession of handguns; private citizens were given 90 days to place their weapons in a gun club, store them, or sell them outside the city limits. Gun dealers were given the same time to dispose of their inventories. The following year Evanston, Illinois, and San Francisco passed similar legislation.

Do these local ordinances represent a national anti-gun sentiment? Consider the reactions of residents of Kennesaw, Georgia. In 1982 this city enacted a law requiring each household to possess a gun. People scoffed at the idea, but that changed when burglaries dropped 66 percent the next year and the overall crime rate dropped 22 percent. In the years since the law was passed, only one of the three murders involved a gun, there have been no accidental shootings, no firearms have been used in a domestic dispute, and the crime rate remains down even though the city has tripled in size.

The pro-gun argument is embodied in the National Rifle Association, an organization of 2.5 million members that spends several million dollars a year in lobbying efforts. Although only a small fraction of gun owners belong to the NRA, its political clout is considerable. According to one senator,

> I'd rather be a deer in hunting season than a politician who has run afoul of the NRA crowd. Most of us are scared to death of them. They range from bus drivers to bank presidents, from Minutemen [a right-wing organization] to four-star generals, and from morons to geniuses, but they have one thing in common: they don't want *any*one to tell them *any*thing about what to do with their guns, and they *mean* it.[81]

NRA arguments opposing gun control bills generally stress three points:

1. "Gun control is unconstitutional." The Second Amendment to the U.S. Constitution reads, "A well-regulated militia, being necessary to the security of a free State, the right of the people to keep and bear arms shall not be infringed." From this the NRA argues, derives Americans' constitutional right to own and legally use firearms. Opponents of this stand claim that no such guarantee is made for individual citizens and that all that the Second Amendment ensures is the right of the states to maintain armed citizen militias.

2. "Guns don't kill people—people kill people." The logic here is that people, not guns, need regulation. (A couple of decades ago, there was a similar slogan: "Register communists, not guns.") The analogy is occasionally carried to its logical extreme by gun supporters: automobiles, ropes, hammers, and poison kill thousands every year; therefore they should be banned. The NRA supports harsh penalties for people who commit crimes with guns rather than restrictions on the sales of guns themselves. Opponents respond that because guns have a high potential for being lethal, they should be subject to control:

> Homicide is seldom the result of a single-minded intent to kill. Most often it is an attack growing out of an altercation and committed in a rage that leads to fatal injuries. . . . When a gun is used, the chances of death are about five times as great as when a knife is used.[82]

3. "When guns are outlawed, only outlaws will have guns." There are two issues included in this claim. One concerns the likelihood that criminals' possession of guns will be unaffected by legislation. Opponents of the NRA position generally concede that is true because so many guns are already in the hands of persons using them for illegal purposes. However, these opponents argue that laws can limit the transfer of guns to people who might use them in crimes and that the law could drastically reduce the output of new weapons. The second issue focuses on the word *outlawed*. The NRA position is that any control legislation, however limited, opens the door to eventual seizure of private guns, whatever their purpose. Opponents respond that they are not interested in denying weapons to those using them in sports; they simply wish to place some restraints on the availability of a lethal device.

As the reader can see, the two sides of the gun issue are miles apart. On one side is an organization of gun owners with efficient lobbying powers, determined to sidetrack any legislation that threatens the ability to buy and possess weapons. Aligned with the NRA is an array of financial interests such as gun manufacturers, gun dealers, gun magazine publishers, and other related organizations that might suffer from control legislation.[83] On the other side is the larger public, whose attitudes favor more control over guns, and organizations such as Handgun Control, Inc., National Gun Control Center, and National Council for a Responsible Firearms Policy, which support legislation to restrict or eliminate handgun ownership. These groups continue to experience some progress, as the Brady Bill demonstrates. There is a great deal of popular support for gun control. The reason? We are continually bombarded with sad scenes and endless coverage of the latest school shooting. As Gary Kleck, a professor of criminology and criminal justice at Florida State University, observed in a recent article after two school shootings in California:

> One would scarcely guess from the recent heated public discussion that violence, gun violence, mass murder, and school violence have all dramatically declined in recent years, or that the juvenile homicide rate has dropped by 58% since 1991.[84]

Who will win? Despite recent local efforts to control weapons and the Brady Bill, efficient gun control can be achieved only by comprehensive, national legislation. Three factors will continue to hamper such congressional action:

1. Although the NRA is facing stronger lobbying competition, it maintains an effective hold on Congress.
2. The homicide rate is high, but it has been higher.
3. There is evidence that the availability of guns is directly related to higher homicide rates, if only because guns are more lethal than other weapons. But research has failed to find a clear-cut relationship between the availability of guns and the extent of the nonhomicidal violence such as aggravated assault or robbery or between strict gun control legislation and a reduction in violence.[85]

Until there is definite evidence of gun control's effectiveness, strict federal legislation is unlikely. It is clear that there are two camps that are unlikely to ever agree. Gun control advocates will not be content until all guns and gun owners are under some sort of governmental control, arguing that fewer guns mean fewer homicides. On the other hand, as opponents of gun control point out, 31 states have "shall issue" laws that allow private citizens to carry concealed handguns and have lower violent crime rates, murder rates, and robbery rates as a result. Even with the high level of violence in the United States, real gun control is not immediately a possibility.

Forcible Rape

The UCR defines forcible rape as "carnal knowledge of a female forcibly and against her will." The National Crime Victimization Survey's definition is similar but not identical: "carnal knowledge through the use of force or threat of force." Both definitions exclude "statutory rape," a legal term applied to intercourse, with consent, between an adult and a child. The distinction between "adult" and "child" is "age of consent"—usually either 16 or 18—as determined by individual state legislature. Although a few states make no distinctions about the gender of the participants, most states specify that the adult is male and the child female. The major difference between the UCR and the NCVS definitions is in the *sex of the victim.* The UCR definition is consistent with the criminal codes of most states, which legally recognize only females as rape victims. The NCVS definition acknowledges the reality that males also are victimized, especially by other males. The revised UCR, the National Incident-Based Reporting System, defines forcible rape as "the carnal knowledge of a person, forcibly and/or against that person's will; or, not forcibly against that person's will where the victim is incapable of giving consent because of his/her temporary or permanent mental or physical capacity."[86]

Despite the shock and injury that are likely to result from rape/sexual assault, half of victims report the incident to police. According to the NCVS, 54 percent of the female victims do so.[87] About 15 percent of all reported rape cases involving females are listed as "unfounded" by police, and nothing further is done.[88] Being unfounded does not necessarily mean that the report is false, but it does mean that the police have decided for a variety of reasons not to pursue prosecution. A case may be ruled as unfounded under any of the following conditions:

> (1) Evidence that the victim was intoxicated; (2) delay in reporting by the victim; (3) lack of physical condition supporting the allegation; (4) refusal to submit to a medical examination; (5) the previous relationship of the victim and the offender; and (6) the use of a weapon without accompanying battery. Police also "unfound" complaints because the victims fail to preserve the necessary physical evidence (for instance, they may douche before reporting the crime) or because victims are too emotionally upset, too young, too afraid, or too embarrassed to cooperate with the ordeal of the police investigation. Most of these factors are not relevant to whether or not a rape has been committed. They are, however, relevant to the chances of obtaining a conviction in court.[89]

Much of the problem of obtaining accurate information on the occurrence and characteristics of rape stems from the nature of the act itself. Because the offender is usually physically stronger and thus threatening to the victim, the victim may display no signs of being forced into the act: torn clothes, bruises, and so on. In these instances the authorities question whether the claim of rape is false. Police become especially skeptical when the offender was an acquaintance of the victim. Thus under some circumstances the victim faces the problem of convincing the authorities that she was forced, not seduced. The woman who chooses not to risk serious injury by resisting the rapist becomes suspect because of her fear or caution. Add to these problems those that a woman must face as a rape victim, and there is little incentive to report the incident:

> Public exposure of rape will subject the victim to the risk of stigmatization on three levels: negative status is conferred because she is known as a victim and loser, because an actual act of intercourse with an illegal partner has become common knowledge, and because a most intimate experience can be discussed openly. Sexual behavior of women is especially cloaked in secrecy. . . . Public identification as a rape victim contributes to the self-conception and social identity of being "the kind of woman who gets raped."[90]

Despite the above, 54 percent of women who were rape/sexual assault victims reported the rape to authorities. In 60 percent of the cases they did so to prevent the incident from happening again, while 47 percent said they wanted to punish the offender. When police were not informed of a completed rape, the reasons were that they considered the rape to be a private or personal matter that they wanted to resolve themselves; that they feared reprisal by the offender, his family, or friends; and that the police would be inefficient, ineffective, or insensitive.[91]

Dimensions of Rape

When discussing homicide, we had few alternative sources of national data—it was the UCR or nothing. For forcible rape we also have the NCVS data concerning victimizations. Although two data sources should inspire greater confidence in asserting the "facts" about rape, we occasionally find disagreements between them. Also, the NCVS has been criticized for the survey methodology used to collect victimization data concerning rape. Helen M. Eigenberg points out that the NCVS asked respondents screening questions concerning whether someone tried to rob them, beat them, attack them with a weapon, or steal from them. It never directly asked about rape. This was corrected in 1993. Respondents are queried more specifically about sexual attacks. However, NCVS still largely leaves the defining of rape to the individual respondent.[92] Failure to query respondents pointedly about rape may lead to underreporting and raises some concerns, as noted by Eigenberg:

> Low estimates of rape reinforce the myth that rape is a rare occurrence. The NCS reports much more rape than does the UCR, but its estimates are still relatively low. . . . The very agency responsible for gathering seriously deficient data legitimizes the subsequent findings by assuring us that rape is an infrequent crime.[93]

The reader must now be warned that two sets of official statistics may only make things twice as confusing:

Fact 1. The rape rate is generally declining. According to the UCR, the rape rate per 100,000 inhabitants was 33.0 in 2002, an increase of 3.6 percent from the previous year. Keep in mind that the UCR reports rates for total inhabitants, male and female; however, its definition of the crime covers only females. Thus, by definition, the victims of rape are always female, which means they then estimate that for 1999, 64 of every 100,000 females in the country were reported victims of forcible rape. The 2002 rate declined 10.3 percent compared to the rate in 1993.[94] The FBI also points out that a rape occurs every 5.5 minutes.[95] According to the NCVS, while there were significant declines in rates of sexual assault/rape (down 60 percent from 1993), with a rate for 2002 of 1.1 per 1,000 persons, the 2002 rate was actually the same rate as the previous year.[96] And again, remember that with the NCVS, both males and females are asked to report sexual assault/rape. Females were victims of rape and sexual assault at a much greater rate than males. In 2002, 1.8 females per 1,000 were raped or sexually assaulted, compared to 0.3 males per 1,000.[97]

Fact 2. Rape is disproportionately high among young, lower-status nonwhites. Although the UCR may be excellent as a source of information on *reported offenses,* the data are inadequate insofar as descriptions of offenders and victims are concerned. In a typical year the UCR tells us that approximately 57 percent of those arrested for rape were white, 41 percent were black, and the remainder were other races. Does this mean that nearly half of all rapes are committed by nonwhites, or that nonwhites are more likely to be arrested, or both? The UCR also tells us that 44 percent of those arrested were under the age of 25, with 29 percent of the total being under 21. Again, we might wonder whether age is related to the likelihood of arrest. Some of these uncertainties about the characteristics of offenders and victims are cleared up by the NCVS data. Offenders and victims were more likely to be of the same race, when the offender was known to the victim. Of "nonstranger" rapes, 83 percent of the white victims and 91 percent of the black victims were raped by men of the same race as the victim. In rapes committed by strangers, offenders were of the same race as the victim in 60 percent of the rapes of white women and in 77 percent of the rapes of black women.[98]

A major virtue of the NCVS data is what they tell us about the victims of rape. Lower-income individuals, especially nonwhites, face the greatest risk of being raped. About half of all rape victims and almost three-quarters of all black rape victims were in the lowest third of the income distribution. If you are a central city resident, rent, live alone, and are unemployed or a student, you are more likely to be the victim of rape. The NCVS also indicates that women ages 16 through 24 are three times more likely to be raped than other women.[99]

Fact 3. The majority of rapes and attempted rapes are committed by nonstrangers. There are a great many conflicting claims about this aspect of rape. Some point to campus "date rapes" and to rapes by spouses (discussed in Chapter 6) as evidence that the risk of being assaulted by nonstrangers is especially high. But results from the latest NCVS for the year 2000 indicate that 62 percent of all rape or sexual assault victims were victimized by an intimate, other relative or friend/acquaintance, compared to 34 percent committed by a stranger.[100] In a recent study dealing strictly with college females, for both completed and attempted rape, about nine out of ten offenders were known to the women. College professors, at least according to this study, were not identified as committing any rapes, the usual suspects being boyfriend, ex-boyfriend, classmate, friend, acquaintance, or coworker.[101] It is interesting that nonstranger rape usually occurred (48 percent) in the victim's home.

Fact 4. Most rapes are planned, not spontaneous, offenses. Rape may even become addicting to the offender. Forced sex is usually not something that "just happens." Whereas ordinary murders often result from sudden flare-ups of temper, ordinary rapes are preceded by the offender's anticipation that an offense will occur. In an interview study of 75 convicted rapists, the researchers found that the majority had considered the possibility of rape on the day of their offenses:

> 79.5% (58) said *that they were watching their victims before they approached them.* Significantly too, 20.5% (15) reported they had seen their victims twice on the day of the rape incident; they committed their attacks the second time. Although this number is relatively small, its implications should be considered: in *certain instances* the rapist may assess and plan a rape attack after locating a potential victim, returning later to execute the rape. *A considerable amount of forethought about rape* was indicated by the offenders' responses to a question about what they were thinking of when they approached their victims that day. 68.5% (50)—*over two-thirds—of the men said they were thinking of rape* [when they approached their victims].
>
> The [subjects] were asked what factors influenced their selection of a particular victim. Close to two-thirds (61.7%) . . . stated they chose a particular victim because she was available ("she was there") and/or defenseless.[102]

An in-depth study was conducted by Diana Scully and Joseph Marolla. They inter-viewed 114 convicted rapists incarcerated in a Virginia prison. Using an 89-page instrument that included background data; psychological, criminal, and sexual history; attitude scales; and 30 pages of open-ended questions to explore rapists' own perceptions of their crime and themselves, they found that

> revenge, punishment and the collective liability of women . . . can be used to explain a num-ber of rapes in our research. . . . An upsetting event, involving a woman, preceded a number of rapes. . . .
>
> Burglary and robbery commonly accompany rape. . . . In some cases the original intent was rape and robbery an after-thought. However, a number of the men indicated that the reverse was true in their situation. That is, the decision to rape was made subsequent to their original intent which was burglary or robbery. . . .
>
> Many writers emphasize the violent and aggressive character of rape . . . to discount the part that sex plays in the crime. The data clearly indicate that from the rapists' point of view rape is in part sexually motivated. When a woman is unwilling or seems unavailable for sex, the rapist can seize what isn't volunteered. . . . If a woman is picked up at a party or in a bar or while hitchhiking (behavior which a number of rapists saw as a signal of sexual avail-ability), and the woman later resists sexual advances, rape is presumed to be justified. . . .
>
> The idea that rape is an impersonal rather than an intimate or mutual experience appealed to a number of rapists, some of whom suggested it was their preferred form of sex. . . . Rape allowed them to control rather than care. . . . During his interview, another rapist confided that he had been fantasizing about rape for several weeks. . . . Most appeal-ing to him was the idea that he could make the victim "do it all for him" and that he would be in control. . . .
>
> Among gang rapists . . . part of rape's appeal was the sense of male camaraderie. . . . To prove one's self capable of "performing" under these circumstances was a substantial challenge and also a source of reward. . . .
>
> The immediate emotional impact on the rapist is slight. . . . Only eight percent indi-cated that guilt or feeling bad was part of their emotional response. . . . Another offender characterized rape as habit forming: "Rape is like smoking. You can't stop once you start." Finally one man expressed the sentiments of many rapists when he stated, "After the rape, I always felt like I had just conquered something, like I had just ridden the bull at Gilley's."[103]

Fact 5. Alcohol is associated with a large proportion of reported rapes. When it comes to sexual activity, alcohol can provide mixed results. On the one hand, alcohol seem-ingly lowers inhibitions and enables some people to say and do things that they might not do while sober; on the other hand, too much drink reduces the male's sexual capacity—enough alcohol can render him impotent. Nevertheless, evidence from assorted studies indicates that drinking is a factor in one-third to one-half of the reported rape cases.[104] An editorial in a popular magazine asked, "Can a woman who drinks be raped?" The editorial appeared after William Smith, the nephew of Senator Edward Kennedy, allegedly raped a woman he had met in a Palm Beach bar. It makes interesting reading:

> No one knows the truth of the woman's allegations; that after drinking in a bar with William Smith, Patrick Kennedy and Senator Edward Kennedy (whose drink of choice was reported to be a double Chivas), she returned to the Kennedy compound where she says the rape occurred. Though Smith has been charged with second-degree sexual battery, neither a court

nor the public has had an opportunity to judge the evidence. Yet many people seem convinced that the rape could not have occurred. "Come on, she knew what she was getting into" was the overwhelming reaction of the man on the street, a sentiment articulated by syndicated columnist William Safire who wrote, "Apparently neither of these women was taught that drinking all night and going home to a man's home at 3:30 A.M. places one in what used to be called an occasion of sin." . . . Clearly a lot of men feel nostalgic for the old days when women used to know their place. One of them is, perhaps, Cris Roosenraad, Dean of Students at Minnesota's Carleton College. Carleton is now being sued by four women for its handling of their sexual assault cases. One of the women alleges that, after she admitted to drinking before the attack, the dean actually scolded her in front of her attacker. . . . The fact remains: Foolishness is no crime, rape is. . . . A man who falls asleep, drunk, on a park bench, and is rolled for his wallet, isn't dismissed by prosecutors because he was "asking for it."[105]

The actual contribution that alcohol makes to the rape situation is as unclear as it is for the homicide situation. It is unlikely that alcohol can be regarded as the sole determinant of rape. And the entire issue of alcohol and its association with rape has been complicated further by the use of "date rape drugs," which include rohypnol among others, that are used to enhance an experience or drug an unsuspecting victim. Following indictments of members of its lacrosse team on charges of sodomy and sexual abuse, St. John's University in New York City is now mandating classes on sexual ethics. It has also published a brochure entitled *No Means No: A Man's Guide to Sexual Behavior,* that reads in part,

> If the person you are with appears to be incapacitated in any way, that person may not be capable of consent. If you proceed without consent, you are breaking the law of New York State and the St. John's Student Code of Rights and Responsibilities.[106]

After surviving the physical and emotional pain of rape, women now have a new, fatal concern. As a *Newsweek* article discusses, the growing epidemic of heterosexual cases of the AIDS virus raises some very serious questions.[107] If a rapist attacks a female and is apprehended, should he or she be tested for the virus? What if the rapist is HIV positive? In addition to the AIDS virus, there remains the potential for an unwanted pregnancy and a multitude of sexually transmitted diseases. This issue may now be broader, with news reports of homosexual rapes resulting in transmission of the HIV virus. Too, we have seen a decrease in defense attorney attempts to bring up the sexual history of the victim of a sexual attack. If a woman claims she contracted AIDS from a rapist, it opens the door to examining her entire sexual history. The defense will attempt to prove that she got it from someone else in the past and at the same time point out that she was a "loose" woman. The victim may again be victimized by the system of justice.

Violence and Sex

A quick review of the "facts" of forcible rape indicates at least one parallel with homicide and aggravated assault: The incidence is disproportionately high among lower-class nonwhites. Thus it is tempting simply to classify sexual assault as another instance of a subculture of interpersonal violence.[108] But it is important to remember that the values supporting interpersonal violence have their roots in more general cultural values that espouse violence as a means of solving problems. Despite the statistics, the case for assigning responsibility for sexual violence primarily to lower-class nonwhites is not convincing. David J. Maume, Jr., conducted a study of this and concludes that

> rape rates rise with racial composition because blacks live lifestyles that increase their exposure to criminal activity. Minorities make up a large share of the unemployed, are more likely to suffer marital disruption, and live in poor housing. Thus they make up a disproportionate share of persons motivated to rape and of the pool of suitable targets. Blacks also live in areas where "guardianship" against crime is reduced because those areas are transient or are plagued with unstable family structure. . . . Prior research . . . showed that the racial composition of a community determines significantly the amount of violent criminal activity, including rape. A popular explanation for this finding is that blacks are members of a distinctive violent subculture . . . [and that] blacks are more likely to live risk-prone lifestyles. When a measure of racial differences in lifestyles is controlled, the effect of percent black on rape in the community is insignificant.[109]

Still, aggressiveness, if not open violence, by males toward females is a pervasive theme and practice in U.S. society. Indeed, it may be argued that male sexual aggression in the United States is the norm, not the exception.

It is traditional that men, whatever their social class, initiate sexual activity. The problem is that the give-and-take situations between males and females are not at all clearly defined, especially since males often misinterpret situations as having sexual meanings. *She* may be wearing abbreviated shorts to keep cool or simply because she likes the style, but *he* thinks she is trying to get him hot. When she says, "NO!" he still assumes she means, "Yes." As song lyrics of early vintage go, "Your lips tell me, 'No! No!' But there's 'Yes! Yes!' in your eyes." Consequently, males often expect resistance to their advances as a matter of routine. But they expect eventual surrender, too. What remains undetermined is the degree of resistance to be overcome and when it is appropriate to expect surrender. When is it seduction, and when is it rape?

While studies of sexual aggressiveness in the middle class are scarce, they indicate that sexual violence is not limited to the lower classes. The available studies deal with what is labeled *date rape*—assaults that occur during the course of dating behavior. One early study of male students at a large midwestern university in the mid-1960s found that one-fourth had made forceful attempts at intercourse to the point where the females had responded by fighting, crying, screaming, or pleading.[110] Without stretching the data too far, it can be claimed that one-fourth of the males at that university were guilty of at least attempted rape. A more recent study by Mary P. Koss and associates surveyed some 3,187 female university students nationally. The research found that 27.5 percent of those responding reported they had been victims of a rape or attempted rape.[111]

Why do so many women face instances of unwanted sexual aggressiveness from men? Three social factors seem relevant: *the image of men,* the *image of women,* and the *dating game.*

The image of the American male is one we alluded to in our discussion of homicide. It calls to mind strength, activity, and independence. Man is the initiator of sexual behavior, and his degree of success indicates how much of a man he is. In its most extreme form, this image of maleness embodies contempt for women:

> There is the . . . principle, widely shared by most males, that women are to be exploited if possible. Part of the code of *Machismo,* the intense glorification of specifically male char-

acteristics, such as courage in battle, recklessness, independence of family ties, etc., is a contempt for female characteristics, and a philosophy that urges the use of women as a mere instrument of pleasure. To be dependent on a woman and especially to show her tenderness and consideration because she deserves it as a human being rather than because it is a useful device for overcoming her resistance, is thought to be foolish.[112]

Included in this image of maleness is the notion of a masculine sexual force that, once put in motion, is beyond mere rationality. Being confronted by someone whom men believe to be a "tease"—someone who suggests or promises but does not deliver—is a serious matter. Not only does the tease offend the masculine sense of fairness, but she can be held responsible for initiating an irreversible passionate process leading to violence. Even social researchers are influenced by this notion. One researcher attempted to find in rape offenses a counterpart of victim-precipitated homicides. But things are rather muddled when "victim precipitation" is defined as "rape situations in which the victim actually, or so it was deemed, agreed to sexual relations but retracted before the actual act or did not react strongly enough when the suggestion was made by the offender(s)."[113] Another researcher has used the term "victim contribution" to describe forms of intimacy that preceded a violent advance.[114]

It is as though a woman's provocation puts a man out of control so that he requires extraordinary persuasion to divert his efforts. When it comes to sex, a woman changes her mind at her peril.

Complementing the role of the male as the sexual aggressor is the traditional image of women as weak, passive, and dependent. But more to the point in our discussion of rape is the image of women as legitimate victims.[115] As we discussed in Chapter 2, part of learning deviant behavior involves learning *reasons for behavior.* In rape, such justifications rely heavily on stereotyped conceptions of women that make some of them seem legitimate targets of sexual violence. Some common male justifications are as follows:

1. Some women *need* to be raped. These verbalized motives refer to the necessity of keeping women in their place:

> These dumb broads don't know what they want. They get you worked up and then they chicken out. You let 'em get away with stuff like that and the next thing you know they'll be walking all over you. . . .
> Women like a strong man who will knock them around once in a while—that way they know the man is in charge.[116]

2. Some women *deserve* to be raped. This attitude refers to the reputation of the woman. In the study of middle-class college males, the researcher found that

> the definition of a female as being sexually experienced is sufficient in some male groups . . . to render her a legitimate target for any type of sexual approach. Her prior experience qualifies her as public property for all interested males and cancels her prerogative to accept or reject sexual partners.[117]

3. Some women *want* to be raped. As we indicated, the woman is supposed to say no; but there is a male notion that despite what she says, she really wants sexual intimacy. She may seem to be angrily resisting, but that is part of the game. After all, the male reasons, rape allows a woman to enjoy sex without feeling guilty about it. In one study of 85 rape victims, the researcher found two women who received marriage proposals from the offenders. In two other cases, "after being raped by two men, another informant . . . was asked by her rapist which of the two she enjoyed the most. And yet another informant reported that her rapist was 'furious because I wasn't getting turned on.' "[118]

The third factor contributing to the role of the male as a sexual aggressor is the nature of the dating game. This factor is especially relevant for nonstranger rapes. Dating is an integral part of the interaction process for young U.S. males and females; for many it eventually leads to more or less permanent arrangements. However, it also frequently leads to rape because the expectations of the partners are unclear and unmet.[119] The expectations of the male stem from the attention, time, and money he expends on the female. As a reward for his expenditures, he often expects more than pleasant and witty conversation. One television comedian said that when his date told him he could look but not touch, he told her she could order dinner but could not eat it. At the least he anticipates a progression of sexual intimacies with each date. But somewhere in this progression a point of contention can arise over how much he is "buying" and how much she is willing to "sell." This is particularly likely to occur when there is no emotional commitment to the relationship by either party or when the parties do not see themselves as equals in the dating process. For many such couples, confrontations over rewards end dramatically with the demand, "Put out or get out!"

To sum up our discussion so far, it appears that the components contributing to rape align themselves as shown in Figure 4.2.

Violent Sex and Conflict

Forcible sexual intercourse is not restricted to men violating women. Attacks also occur between members of the same sex—both men and women. Little is known about the causes and dynamics of attacks by women on women that occur principally in jails and prisons. And although some of the mass murders we mentioned earlier in this chapter involved sexual attacks of males by males, our knowledge is still scant on this subject as well. The

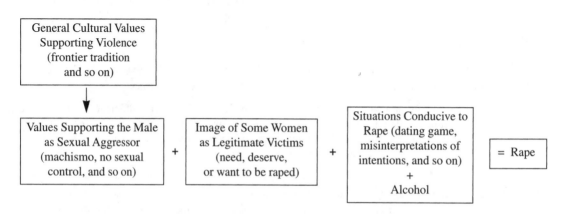

FIGURE 4.2   Components Contributing to Rape

NCVS does contain some data on rape of males and reports that 0.3 of 1,000 males are victimized annually.[120] A recent study on rape did analyze this small sample and found that male victims of rape were less likely than females to resist aggressively.[121] What we do know about male victims comes from studies of prison inmates. It is instructive because it tells us something about rape generally, regardless of the participants' sexes. Estimates of rape in prison are high; perhaps one in five inmates has been raped.[122]

Some of the best evidence on male-male sexual attacks comes from a two-year study of sexual attacks in the Philadelphia prison system. The author, Alan J. Davis, concluded that the City of Brotherly Love had an epidemic of homosexual attacks in its penal institutions. Practically every slightly built young man was sexually approached within a few days of his admission. Many were either repeatedly raped by gangs or had to enter into a homosexual relationship with an individual for protection. Only the strong or the very lucky escaped both situations.[123]

In the three institutions he studied, Davis estimated that 2,000 assaults occurred in the 26-month period. In analyzing the nature of these assaults, he found that they were not motivated by a desire to release long pent-up sexual urges. One of the study's most striking findings is summarized in Table 4.2. As you can see, the majority of assaults—56 percent—involve blacks attacking whites. To Davis this suggests that rape is an expression of contempt and revenge. In short, it is a symptom of conflict:

> A primary goal of the sexual aggressor, it is clear, is the conquest and degradation of his victim. We repeatedly found that aggressors used such language as "Fight or fuck," "We're gonna take your manhood," "You'll have to give up some face," and "We're gonna make a girl out of you." Some of the assaults were reminiscent of the custom in some ancient societies of castrating or buggering a defeated enemy. . . .
>
> Sexual assaults . . . are not primarily caused by sexual deprivation. They are expressions of anger and aggression prompted by the same basic frustrations . . . [that] can be summarized as an inability to achieve masculine identity and pride through avenues other than sex. When these frustrations are intensified by imprisonment, and superimposed upon hostility between the races and a simplistic view of all sex as an act of aggression and subjugation, then the result is assaults on members of the same sex.[124]

TABLE 4.2 Offenders and Victims of Philadelphia Prison Assaults by Race (by Percent of All Assaults)

Victims	Offenders		
	Black	*White*	*Total*
Black	29%	0%	29%
White	56%	15%	71%
Total	85%	15%	100%

Source: Adapted from Alan J. Davis, "Sexual Assaults in the Philadelphia Prison System," in *The Sexual Scene,* ed. John H. Gagnon and William Simon (Chicago: Aldine, 1970), p. 122.

"All sex as an act of aggression and subjugation" is a key phrase here. If we assume that this is an accurate appraisal of the motivation behind homosexual rape, may it not also be pertinent to male-female sexual assaults? By some admissions it is. Perhaps the best description of rape as dominance was expressed by the black revolutionary Eldridge Cleaver:

> I became a rapist. To refine my technique and *modus operandi,* I started out by practicing on black girls in the ghetto—in the black ghetto where dark and vicious deeds appear not as aberrations or deviations from the norm, but as part of the sufficiency of the Evil of a day—and when I considered myself smooth enough, I crossed the tracks and sought out white prey. . . .
> Rape was an insurrectionary act. It delighted me that I was defying the white man's law, upon his system of values, and that I was defiling his women—and this point, I believe, was the most satisfying to me because I was very resentful over the historical fact of how the white man has used the black woman. I felt I was getting revenge.[125]

The extent to which political motivations, such as Cleaver's, explain interracial rape is only now being researched.[126] But the conflict theme of sexual violence has been applied to *intraracial* rape as well. The writers in this case are generally associated with the feminist movement, and they argue that rape is symbolic of masculine power—not just physical power but also economic and political power. This is not to say that a significant number of rapists express overt political reasons for their behavior but that rape is the outcome of conflict encouraged by *cultural expectations.*

One of the first feminists to elaborate the conflict theme was Susan Griffin, who called rape the "All-American crime":

> Erotic pleasure cannot be separated from culture, and in our culture male eroticism is wedded to power. Not only should a man be taller and stronger than a female in the perfect love-match, but he must also demonstrate his superior strength in gestures of dominance which are perceived as amorous. . . .
> The scenario is even further complicated by the expectation that, not only does a woman mean "yes" when she says "no," but that a really decent woman ought to begin by saying "no," and then be led down the primrose path to acquiescence. . . .
> To regard the rapist as the victim, a man driven by his inherent sexual needs to take what will not be given him, reveals a basic ignorance of sexual politics. For in our culture heterosexual love finds an erotic expression through male dominance and female submission. A man who derives pleasure from raping a woman clearly must enjoy force and dominance as much or more than the simple pleasures of the flesh.[127]

Rape, then, according to the feminist, is not a *sexual* act that happens to be violent, but a *violent* act that happens to be sexual. Its ultimate purpose is to restrict the freedom of women and to ensure that they remain dependent on men for protection:

> Rape is a form of mass terrorism, for the victims of rape are chosen indiscriminately, but the propagandists for male supremacy broadcast that it is the women who caused rape by being unchaste or in the wrong place at the wrong time—in essence, by behaving as though they were free.[128]

During the 1970s the feminist movement was responsible for a national antirape campaign in the United States. Among its accomplishments were substantial changes in the rape laws: the enactment of legislation recognizing rape among spouses, rulings that the defendant's previous sexual activities could not be used as evidence for the defense, and so on. Other accomplishments were increased sensitivity by police in dealing with rape victims; the formation of rape crisis centers and community programs to counsel and assist rape victims; and greater public recognition of the medical, legal, and social aspects of rape.[129] In the meantime, a feminist theory of rape emerged and was increasingly accepted as the explanation of the offense. The feminist theory can be briefly described by three propositions:

1. The primary and ultimate factor behind rape is the social tradition of male domination in important sociopolitical and economic activities.
2. Because women are largely excluded from power positions in important sociopolitical and economic activities, they are regarded as being unequal to men in interpersonal relationships, and, at the extreme, they are viewed and view themselves as male property.
3. Rape is a male response to the unequal social status of females and to the interpretation of this status.[130]

Research attempting to validate this theoretical approach is in short supply. The best study to date was conducted by Lee Ellis and Charles Beattie, who compared rape rates in 26 cities (data drawn from the NCS) with measures of social inequalities between the sexes (e.g., male and female differences in median earnings, mean education, percentage employed in selected occupations, and so on). The assumption of the study was that if the feminist theory is valid, cities in which the sexes are most equal should be cities with the lowest rape rates. The results failed to support the feminist position. If anything, the study indicated that cities in which sexes are most equal are cities with *higher* rape rates.[131]

What do these findings mean? Supporters of the feminist approach may well argue that the available measures of sexual inequality are too imprecise for validating the theory. Others may respond that the theory overplays the violence of rape while underplaying its sexual nature. Ellis and Beattie recognize that their study is not the definitive test of the feminist theory; it is apparent, however, that the feminist theory of rape cannot yet be accepted without qualification. New feminist theories are more extreme. Susan Estrich, herself a rape victim, states that until women are fully empowered, even their consent to sex may not mean yes.[132] Neil Gilbert disputes the views of the feminists and questions much of the research done on the incidence of rape. In "The Phantom Epidemic of Sexual Assault," he claims that much of the research has been conducted with very broad definitions of rape. He states, regarding the data cited earlier by Koss, that "Koss takes a strict legal definition of rape and gives it a loose empirical interpretation." He cites an example:

> After having a drink, a young man and woman, sitting on a couch, kissing in a tight embrace; she offers no objection, perhaps she even offers some encouragement. As he embraces her, with the thought of having intercourse in mind, the man touches the woman's genitals. She pushes his hand away, and breaks out of the embrace. Although the man stops and sheepishly apologizes, he has already committed a sexual act that involves alcohol, forced intent to penetrate, and lack of consent. Many would say that the young man misbehaved. As Koss would have it, this encounter qualifies as attempted rape.[133]

Gilbert continues by suggesting that

> under these definitions of rape and sexual coercion, the kaleidoscope of intimate discourse—passion, emotional turmoil, entreaties, flirtation, provocation, demureness—must give way to cool-headed contractual sex: "Will you do it, yes or no? Please sign on the dotted line below."[134]

He concludes by stating that Koss and her fellow researchers are advocates of consciousness-raising:

> Advocacy numbers on sexual assault may resonate with their feelings of being, not literally raped, but figuratively "screwed over" by men. If this is the case, it will require more objective analysis to dispel the phantom epidemic of sexual assault.[135]

For explaining rape, perhaps we should conclude with a look at the latest research that focuses on a sociosexual model and a punishment model. The study, conducted by Richard B. Felson and Marvin Krohn, finds that

> rape, like other forms of violence, has a variety of motives. For rapes involving older offenders and victims, and estranged couples, it appears that rape and physical attacks are more likely to be used to punish the victim. For rapes involving younger offenders and victims, it appears that rape is more likely to be sexually motivated. For these rapes, violence tends to be used strategically in an attempt to complete the crime.[136]

CRITICAL THINKING EXERCISES

1. Compared to nations around the world, the United States has relatively high violent crime rates. Do you feel that you live in a violent society? What characteristics of U.S. culture might explain the U.S. tendency toward violent behavior?

2. Handguns are plentiful in the United States and easy to obtain. In your opinion, is there a relationship between handgun availability and high homicide rates? What would happen to the homicide rates if all handguns were destroyed?

3. What is meant by the statement "Rape is not a sexual act that happens to be violent, it is a violent act that happens to be sexual"? Discuss the different motivations for the crime of forcible rape.

CHECK IT OUT ON THE WEB

The Internet addresses listed below are intended to provide the reader with understanding of a wide range of perspectives on the subject matter discussed in this chapter. Some sites may contain objectionable material. The list is not intended to reflect the viewpoints or opinions of the authors or the publisher.

http://www.crimespider.com
    homicide case studies

http://vpc.org/studies/wherfadv.htm
    Violence Policy Center/handgun violence
http://www.silentwitness.net
    domestic violence homicides
http://wwwchronline.org
    gay homicide victims
http://www.daywilliams.com/homicide.html
    homicide investigation
http://www.eeoc.gov/facts/fs-sex.html
    sexual assault information
http://www.dsaoc.com/index.html
    support site for sex assault victims

ENDNOTES

1. U.S. Department of Justice, Bureau of Justice Statistics and Office of Community Policing Services, *Criminal Victimization and Perceptions of Safety in 12 Cities, 1998* (Washington, DC: U.S. Department of Justice, 1999), p. 12, Table 9.

2. Some of these examples were taken from Richard J. Meislin, "Fear of Crime Is Now Woven into Fabric of New York Life," *The New York Times,* January 31, 1982, pp. 1, 19.

3. CBS News, 524 West 57th Street, New York, NY 10019.

4. U.S. Department of Justice, Federal Bureau of Investigation [FBI], *Crime in the United States, 2002: 2002 Uniform Crime Reports* (Washington, DC: U.S. Government Printing Office, 2003), pp. 3, 19, 31.

5. Richard Lacayo, "Law and Disorder," *Time,* April 1, 1991, p. 16.

6. U.S. Department of Justice, FBI, *Crime in the United States, 2002, 2002 Uniform Crime Reports* (Washington, DC: U.S. Government Printing Office, 2003), pp. 3–31.

7. FBI, *Uniform Crime Reporting: National Incident-Based Reporting System,* vol. 1, *Data Collection Guidelines* (July 1, 1988), p. 14.

8. Timothy Hart and Callie Rennisan, *Reporting Crime, 1992–2000,* U.S. Department of Justice, Bureau of Justice Statistics, (Washington, DC: U.S. Government Printing Office, March 2003), p. 1–3.

9. U.S. Department of Justice, Bureau of Justice Statistics, *Violent Crime in the United States* (Washington, DC: U.S. Government Printing Office, March 1991), p. 2.

10. U.S. Department of Justice, Bureau of Justice Statistics, *Criminal Victimization in the United States, 1988* (Washington, DC: U.S. Government Printing Office, December 1990), p. 1.

11. See the U.S. Department of Justice's Fact Sheet NCJ-122705, *The Nation's Two Crime Measures.*

12. U.S. Department of Justice, Bureau of Justice Statistics, *Crime and the Nation's Households, 1990* (Washington, DC: U.S. Government Printing Office, August 1991), pp. 1, 2.

13. Patsy Klaus, *Crime and the Nation's Households, 2002,* U.S. Department of Justice, Bureau of Justice Statistics, (Washington, DC: U.S. Government Printing Office, February 2004), p. 1.

14. U.S. Department of Justice, Federal Bureau of Investigation [FBI], *Crime in the United States, 1993, Uniform Crime Reports* (Washington, DC: U.S. Government Printing Office, 1994), p. 6.

15. Bureau of Justice Statistics, See http://www.ojp. usdoj/bjs/correct.htm

16. Samuel Walker, *Sense and Nonsense about Crime: A Policy Guide,* 2nd ed. (Pacific Grove, CA: Brooks/Cole Publishing Co., 1989), p. 14.

17. Ibid., p. 15.

18. David J. Pittman and William Handy, "Patterns in Criminal Aggravated Assault," *Journal of Criminal Law, Criminology, and Police Science, 55* (December 1964), pp. 462–470.

19. Bureau of Justice Statistics, *Violent Crime in the United States,* p. 6.

20. Conversation with David W. Jones, Administrator, State of Kentucky, Medical Examiners Office, October 31, 1991.

21. Anastasia Toufexis, "Coroners Who Miss All the Clues," *Time, 134* (August 14, 1989), p. 61.

22. Trudy Knicely Henson, "Trends in Medicolegal Legislation—1980" (paper delivered at the annual meeting of the American Society of Criminology, November 7, 1980), p. 11. See also Henson, "Coroner/Medical Examiners and the Production of 'Manner of Death' Statistics" (Ph.D. diss., Bowling Green State University, 1978).

23. Alex Prud'homme, "Did They All Have to Die?" *Time,* August 12, 1991, p. 28.

24. Alex Prud'homme, "The Little Flat of Horrors," *Time,* August 5, 1991, p. 26.

25. Vern E. Smith, "A Killer's Confessions," *Newsweek, 118* (August 26, 1991), p. 23.

26. James S. Kunen, "Florida Cops Say Seven Men Met Death on the Highway When They Picked Up Accused Serial Killer Aileen Wuornos," *People Weekly, 35* (February 25, 1991), p. 44.

27. Nancy R. Gibbs, "Murders They Wrote," *Time,* April 1, 1991, p. 29.

28. Evan Thomas, "Day and Night: He Lived Two Lives. An Inside Look at O. J. Simpson's World," *Newsweek,* August 29, 1994, pp. 42–49.

29. U.S. Department of Justice, Federal Bureau of Investigation [FBI], *Crime in the United States, 2002, Uniform Crime Reports* (Washington, DC: U.S. Government Printing Office, 2003), p. 19.

30. Donald J. Mulvihill and Melvin M. Tumin, *Crimes of Violence,* staff report submitted to the National Commission on the Causes and Prevention of Violence, vol. 11 (Washington, DC: Government Printing Office, 1969), p. 54. For an attempt to assess homicide rates from earlier data, see Margaret A. Zahn, "Homicide in the Twentieth-Century United States," in *History and Crime: Implications for Criminal Justice Police,* ed. James A. Inciardi and Charles E. Faupel (Beverly Hills, CA: Sage Publications, 1980), pp. 111–131.

31. U.S. Department of Justice, Federal Bureau of Investigation [FBI], *Crime in the United States, 1999, Uniform Crime Reports* (Washington, DC: U.S. Government Printing Office, 2000), p. 281, Table 5.2.

32. James Allen Fox and Marianne W. Zawitz, U.S. Department of Justice, Bureau of Justice Statistics, *Homicide Trends in the United States* (last revised January 4, 2003). [Online]. Available: http://www.ojp.usdoj.gov/bjs/pub/pdf/htus00.pdf

33. FBI, *Crime in the United States,* 1999, p. 14.

34. Fox and Zawitz, *Homicide Trends in the United States, Trends by Race.*

35. Elliott Currie, "Reflections on Crime and Criminology at the Millenium." *Western Criminology Review, 2:* 1 (1999). [Online]. Available: http://wcr.sonoma.edu/v2n1/currie/html

36. John J. Donohue III and Steven D. Levitt, *The Impact of Legalized Abortion on Crime.* Stanford Law School, John M. Olin Program in Law and Economics. Working Paper No. 177, 2000, p. 2.3. [Online]. Available: http://papers.ssrn.com/paper.taf?abstract_id=174508

37. This refers primarily to lower-class homicides. For a discussion of social class differences, see Edward Green and Russel P. Wakefield, "Patterns of Middle and Upper Class Homicide," *Journal of Criminal Law and Criminology, 70* (Summer 1979), pp. 172–181.

38. FBI, *Crime in the United States, 2002,* p. 22.

39. David F. Luckenbill, "Criminal Homicide as a Situated Transaction," *Social Problems, 25* (December 1977), pp. 179–181.

40. Based on Mulvihill and Tumin, *Crimes of Violence,* pp. 225–226. Victim-precipitated homicide was first investigated by Marvin E. Wolfgang in *Patterns of Criminal Homicide* (Philadelphia: University of Pennsylvania Press, 1958), pp. 252–265.

41. See http://www.niaa.nih.gov/extramural/prevention.htm#violence

42. Lawrence A. Greenfeld, U.S. Department of Justice, Bureau of Justice Statistics, *Alcohol and Crime,* (Washington, DC: U.S. Government Printing Office, April 1998), p. v.

43. Ibid., p. 30.

44. Kai Pernanen, "Theoretical Aspects of the Relationship Between Alcohol Use and Crime," and Stephanie W. Greenberg, "Alcohol and Crime: A Methodological Critique of the Literature," both in *Drinking and Crime: Perspectives on the Relationships Between Alcohol Consumption and Criminal Behavior,* ed. James J. Collins, Jr. (New York: Guilford Press, 1981), pp. 11–43 and 70–109, respectively. This anthology contains several chapters detailing the theory and evidence on alcohol and criminal behavior.

45. William G. Doerner, "The Impact of Medical Resources on Criminally Induced Lethality: A Further Examination," *Criminology, 26* (November 1988), pp. 176, 177.

46. James R. Lasely, "Drinking Routines and Predatory Victimization: A Causal Analysis," *Justice Quarterly, 6:* 4 (December 1989), p. 540.

47. Bureau of Justice Statistics, *Violent Crime in the United States,* p. 17.

48. U.S. Department of Justice, Bureau of Justice Statistics, *National Update,* vol. 1, no. 2 (Washington, DC: U.S. Government Printing Office, October 1991), p. 6.

49. Fox and Zawitz, *Homicide Trends in the United States, Homicide Type by Age.*

50. Margaret A. Zahn, "The Female Homicide Victim," *Criminology, 13* (November 1975), pp. 400–401; Margaret A. Zahn and Glenn Snodgrass, "Drug Use and the Structure of Homicide in Two U.S. Cities," in *The New and the Old Criminology,* ed. Edith E. Flynn and John P. Conrad (New York: Praeger, 1978), pp. 134–150; and Zahn, "Homicide," p. 128.

51. Arnold L. Lieber and Carolyn R. Sherin, "Homicide and the Lunar Cycle: Toward a Theory of Lunar Influence on Human Emotional Disturbance," *American Journal of Psychiatry, 129* (July 1972), pp. 60–74.

52. Richard R. Bennet and James P. Lynch, "Does a Difference Make a Difference? Comparing Cross-National Crime Indicators," *Criminology, 28* (February 1990), pp. 165–169.

53. Philip Taft and Philip Ross, "American Labor Violence: Its Causes, Character, and Outcome," in *Violence in America: Historical and Comparative Perspectives,* ed. Hugh Davis Graham and Ted Robert Gurr (Beverly Hills, CA: Sage Publications, 1979), p. 187.

54. This discussion drew upon Richard Maxwell Brown, "Historical Patterns of Violence in America," in *Violence in America: Historical and Comparative Perspectives,* Report to the National Commission on the Causes and Prevention of Violence, vol. 1, ed. Hugh Davis Graham and Ted Robert Gurr (Washington, DC: Government Printing Office, 1969), pp. 35–64; and Ted Robert Gurr, "Political Protest and Rebellion in the 1960s," in *Violence in America,* ed. Graham and Gurr (1969), pp. 53–57.

55. Mulvihill and Tumin, *Crimes of Violence,* p. 201.

56. The following discussion draws upon Joe E. Frantz, "The Frontier Tradition: An Invitation to Violence," in *Violence in America,* ed. Graham and Gurr (1979), pp. 101–119.

57. Richard Maxwell Brown, "The American Vigilante Tradition," in *Violence in America,* ed. Graham and Gurr (1979), pp. 153–185.

58. Michael T. Kaufman, "Canada: An American Discovers Its Difference," *The New York Times Magazine,* May 15, 1983, p. 82 (emphasis added).

59. In Brown, "American Vigilante Tradition," p. 167.

60. Monica Blumenthal, Robert L. Kahn, Frank M. Andrews, and Kendra B. Head, *Justifying Violence: Attitudes of American Men* (Ann Arbor, MI: Institute for Social Research, 1972), p. 243.

61. Ibid., p. 101.

62. Ibid., p. 250.

63. Mark A. Deturck, "When Communication Fails: Physical Aggression as a Compliance-Gaining Strategy," *Communication Monographs, 54* (March 1987), p. 67.

64. University of Chicago, National Opinion Research Center, *General Social Surveys, 1972–1989: Cumulative Codebook* (July 1991), p. 270.

65. Wolfgang, *Patterns of Criminal Homicide,* pp. 188–189.

66. Marvin E. Wolfgang and Franco Ferracuti, "Subculture of Violence—A Socio-Psychological Theory," in *Studies in Homicide,* ed. Marvin E. Wolfgang (New York: Harper & Row, 1967), pp. 277–278.

67. Paraphrased and simplified from David F. Luckenbill, "Criminal Homicide as a Situated Transaction," *Social Problems, 25* (December 1977), pp. 176–186. Also see Ken Levi, "Homicide as Conflict Resolution," *Deviant Behavior, 1* (April–September 1980), pp. 281–307; and Richard B. Felson and Henry J. Steadman, "Situational Factors in Disputes Leading to Criminal Violence," *Criminology, 21* (February 1983), pp. 59–74.

68. Paraphrased and simplified from David F. Luckenbill and Daniel P. Doyle, "Structural Position and Violence: Developing a Cultural Explanation," *Criminology, 27* (August 1989), pp. 419–436.

69. Ibid., p. 420.

70. George D. Newton, Jr., and Franklin E. Zimring, *Firearms and Violence in American Life,* Report to the National Commission on the Causes and Prevention of Violence (Washington, DC: U.S. Government Printing Office, 1969), p. 1.

71. Kathleen Maguire and Ann L. Pastore, eds., *Sourcebook of Criminal Justice Statistics,* [online] http://www.albany.edusourcebook, 17 Jul 04, Tables 2.60, 2.61.

72. For a discussion of a recent survey on gun ownership, see Philip J. Cook and Jens Ludwig, "Guns in America: National Survey on Private Ownership and Use of Firearms National Institute of Justice Research in Brief, May 1997 [Online]. Available: http://www.ncjrs.org/txtfiles/1654476 Also see Philip J. Cook, "The Role of Firearms in Violent Crime: An Interpretive Review of the Literature," in *Criminal Violence,* ed. Marvin E. Wolfgang and Neil Alan Weiner (Beverly Hills, CA: Sage Publications, 1982), pp. 238–241.

73. U.S. Department of Health and Human Services, Centers for Disease Control and Prevention, *DC Factbook 2000/2001* (Washington, DC: Government Printing Office, 2001), pp. 1029–1034.

74. Gary Fields, "Gun Conundrum: More on Streets, Fewer Incidents," *Wall Street Journal,* December 11, 2000, A1, A6.

75. David Lampo, What Many Don't Know About Guns: These Statistics Might Surprise Control Advocates," *Sacramento Bee,* May 17, 2000, p. B9.

76. "Michigan Judge Orders Boy Shooter to Foster Care," *Washington Post,* August 4, 2000, p. A5.

77. Tom W. Smith, "The 75% Solution: An Analysis of the Structure of Attitudes on Gun Control, 1959–1977," *Journal of Criminal Law and Criminology, 71* (Fall 1980), pp. 300–301.

78. See Tom W. Smith, http://www.norc.uchicago/online/gunsol.pdf, p. 18.

79. Jens Ludwig and Philip J. Cook, "Homicide and Suicide Rates Associated with Implementation of the Brady Handgun Violence Prevention Act," *JAMA 284* (February 2000), pp. 585-591.

80. Thomas Sowell, "Gun Control Hypocrisy," *Jewish World Review,* June 1, 2000/27 Iyar, 5760.

81. Richard Harris, "Annals of Legislation: If You Love Your Guns," *New Yorker,* April 20, 1968, p. 57.

82. Newton and Zimring, *Firearms and Violence,* p. 48.

83. Robert Sherrill, *The Saturday Night Special* (New York: Charterhouse, 1973), p. 99.

84. Gary Kleck, "School Lesson: Armed Self-Defense Works," *Wall Street Journal,* March 27, 2001, p. A22.

85. See Wright and Rossi, *Weapons, Crime, and Violence,* pp. 13–20; and Cook, "Role of Firearms," pp. 251–264, 273–285.

86. FBI, *Uniform Crime Reporting,* pp. 35–37.

87. Callie Marie Rennison, Ph.D. and Michael R. Rand, U.S. Department of Justice, Bureau of Justice Statistics. *Criminal Victimization, 2002* (Washington, DC: U.S. Department of Justice, August 2003), p. 11.

88. U.S. Department of Justice, FBI, *Crime in the United States, 1976: 1977 Uniform Crime Reports* (Washington, DC: U.S. Government Printing Office, 1977), p. 16. This statistic is not available from subsequent issues of the *Uniform Crime Reports.*

89. Camille E. Legrand, "Rape and Rape Laws: Sexism in Society and Law," *California Law Review, 61* (May 1973), pp. 928, 929. For a more recent discussion of these factors, demonstrating that things have not changed much, see Lisa Frohman, "Discrediting Victims' Allegations of Sexual Assault: Prosecutorial Accounts of Case Rejections," *Social Problems, 38* (May 1991), pp. 213–226. Also, for an account of how jurors react to personality characteristics of rape victims and defendants, see research by Gary LaFree, Barbara Reskin, and Christy Visher, reported by Jeff Meer, "Rape Victims on Trial (Study of Jurors' Attitudes)," *Psychology Today, 19* (October 1985), p. 73.

90. Kurt Weis and Sandra S. Borges, "Victimology and Rape: The Case of the Legitimate Victim," *Issues in Criminology, 8* (Fall 1973), pp. 103–104.

91. Caroline Wolf Harlow, *Female Victims of Violent Crimes,* U.S. Department of Justice, Bureau of Justice Statistics (Washington, DC: U.S. Government Printing Office, January 1991), p. 9.

92. Helen M. Eigenberg, "The National Crime Survey and Rape: The Case of the Missing Question," *Justice Quarterly, 7* (December 1990), pp. 655–667.

93. Ibid., pp. 664–665.

94. FBI, *Crime in the United States, 2002,* pp. 29.

95. Ibid., p. 6.

96. Callie Marie Rennison and Michael Raun, U.S. Department of Justice, Bureau of Justice Statistics, *Criminal Victimization 2002* (Washington, DC: U.S. Government Printing Office, August 2003), pp. 2.

97. Ibid., p. 8.

98. In Harlow, *Female Victims of Violent Crimes,* p. 10.

99. Ibid., p. 8.

100. Callie Marie Rennison, U.S. Department of Justice, Bureau of Justice Statistics, *Criminal Victimization 2000: Changes 1999–2000 with Trends 1993–2000* (Washington, DC: U.S. Government Printing Office, June 2001), p. 8.

101. Bonnie S. Fisher, Francis T. Cullen, and Michael G. Turner, U.S. Department of Justice, National Institute of Justice, *The Sexual Victimization of College Women* (Washington, DC: U.S. Government Printing Office, December, 2000), p. 17.

102. Queen's Bench Foundation, *Rape: Prevention and Resistance,* as reprinted in *Crime and Society,* ed. Leonard D. Savitz and Norman Johnston (New York: John Wiley, 1978), pp. 773–774 (emphasis added).

103. Diana Scully and Joseph Marolla, "Riding the Bull at Gilley's: Convicted Rapists Describe the Rewards of Rape," *Social Problems, 32* (February 1985), pp. 251–263.

104. Ibid., p. 773; Paul H. Gebhard, John H. Gagnon, Wardell B. Pomeroy, and Cornelia V. Christenson, *Sex Offenders: An Analysis of Types* (New York: Harper & Row, 1965), p. 194; Mulvihill and Tumin, *Crimes of Violence,* pp. 642–649; and Menachem Amir, *Patterns of Forcible Rape* (Chicago: University of Chicago Press, 1971), pp. 98–100.

105. "Can a Woman Who Drinks Be Raped?" *Glamour,* July 1991, p. 59.

106. Ibid.

107. Eloise Salholz, Karen Springen, Nonny De La Pena, and Deborah Witherspoon, "A Frightening Aftermath: Concern About AIDS Adds to the Trauma of Rape," *Newsweek,* July 23, 1990, p. 53.

108. For subcultural approaches to rape by blacks, see Amir, *Patterns of Forcible Rape,* pp. 319–326; and Lynn A. Curtis, *Violence, Rape, and Culture* (Lexington, MA: Lexington Books, 1975). For a critique of Amir's argument, see Kurt Weis and Sandra S. Borges, "Rape as a Crime Without Victims and Offenders? A Methodological Critique," in *Victims and Society,* ed. Emilio C. Viano (Washington, DC: Visage Press, 1976), pp. 230–254.

109. David J. Maume, Jr., "Inequality and Metropolitan Rape Rates: A Routine Activity Approach," *Justice Quarterly, 6* (December 1989), pp. 523–524. For another explanation, see Robert M. O'Brien, "Sex Ratios and Rape Rates: A Power Control Theory," *Criminology,* February 29, 1991, pp. 99–114.

110. Eugene J. Kanin, "Reference Groups and Sex Conduct Norm Violations," *Sociological Quarterly, 8* (Autumn 1967), pp. 495–504.

111. Mary P. Koss, Christine A. Gidycz, and Nadine Wisniewski, "The Scope of Rape: Incidence and Prevalence of Sexual Aggression and Victimization in a National Sample of Higher Education Students," *Journal of Consulting and Clinical Psychology, 58* (February 1987), pp. 162–170.

112. William Goode, "Violence Among Intimates," in Mulvihill and Tumin, *Crimes of Violence,* p. 971.

113. Amir, *Patterns of Forcible Rape,* p. 266.

114. Eugene J. Kanin, "Date Rape: Unofficial Criminals and Victims," *Victimology: An International Journal, 9* (1984), pp. 105–106.

115. Kurt Weis and Sandra S. Borges, "Victimology and Rape: The Case of the Legitimate Victim," *Issues in Criminology, 8* (Fall 1973), pp. 79, 80.

116. Gebhard et al., *Sex Offenders,* pp. 177–178, 205.

117. Kanin, "Reference Groups," p. 502. See also Amir, *Patterns of Forcible Rape,* pp. 249–252.

118. Diane E. H. Russell, "Rape and the Masculine Mystique" (paper delivered at the annual meeting of the American Sociological Association, 1973), p. 3.

119. Weis and Borges, "Victimology and Rape," pp. 87–89; and Goode, "Violence Among Intimates," p. 971.

120. Kathleen Maguire and Anna L. Pastore, eds., *Sourcebook of Criminal Justice Statistics,* p. 191.

121. Richard B. Felson and Marvin Krohn, "Motives for Rape," *Journal of Research in Crime and Delinquency, 27* (August 1990), pp. 223–241.

122. Robert W. Dumond, "Inmate Sexual Assault: The Plague That Persists," *The Prison Journal* (December 2000), p. 407.

123. Alan J. Davis, "Sexual Assaults in the Philadelphia Prison System," in *The Sexual Scene,* ed. John H. Gagnon and William Simon (Chicago: Aldine, 1970), pp. 107–124.

124. Ibid., pp. 123–124.

125. Eldridge Cleaver, *Soul on Ice* (New York: McGraw-Hill, 1968), p. 14.

126. Gary LaFree, "Male Power and Female Victimization: Toward a Theory of Interracial Rape," *American Journal of Sociology, 88* (September 1982), pp. 311–328.

127. Susan Griffin, "Rape: The All-American Crime," *Ramparts,* September 1971, p. 28.

128. Ibid., p. 35.

129. Vicki McNickle Rose, "Rape as a Social Problem: A Byproduct of the Feminist Movement," *Social Problems, 25* (October 1977), pp. 75–89.

130. Paraphrased from Lee Ellis and Charles Beattie, "The Feminist Explanation for Rape: An Empirical Test," *Journal of Sex Research, 19* (February 1983), pp. 75–76. For a critique of the feminist writings on rape, see Gilbert Geis, "Introduction," in *Forcible Rape: The Crime, the Victim, and the Offender,* ed. Duncan Chappell, Robley Geis, and Gilbert Geis (New York: Columbia University Press, 1977), pp. 1–30.

131. Ellis and Beattie, "The Feminist Explanation," pp. 83–90.

132. Quoted in "When No Means No," *National Review,* June 10, 1991, pp. 12, 13.

133. Neil Gilbert, "The Phantom Epidemic of Sexual Assault," *The Public Interest, 104* (Summer 1991), pp. 54–65.

134. Ibid., p. 59.

135. Ibid., pp. 64, 65.

136. Felson and Krohn, "Motives for Rape," p. 239.

5 Crime in the Streets— Against Property

Despite people's concern over murder and nonnegligent manslaughter, aggravated assault, and forcible rape, these offenses represent a small proportion of the index crimes known to the police. According to the 2002 *Uniform Crime Reports* (UCR), these crimes made up only 12 percent of all index crimes. Robbery, burglary, larceny-theft, and motor vehicle theft made up the remaining 88 percent.[1] (The total number of arson offenses was not included.) Thus the crime picture, insofar as the police and FBI are concerned, is dominated by offenses against property. In this chapter we will briefly consider the dimensions of these crimes and some of the social factors contributing to them.

Robbery

The UCR defines robbery as "the taking or attempting to take anything of value from the care, custody, or control of a person or persons by force or threat of force or violence and/or by putting the victim in fear." The National Crime Victimization Survey (NCVS) defines it as "completed or attempted theft, directly from a person, of property or cash by force or threat of force, with or without a weapon." In writings on robbery the reader will often find the term *strong-armed robbery*. This simply refers to offenses in which no weapon is used. Approximately half of all robberies are strong-armed.[2] In our discussion, however, we will not make a distinction between armed and strong-armed robbery.

Dimensions of Robbery

Information about robberies and robbers is even more scarce than it is for rape. Therefore, the reader is again cautioned to approach the following "facts" with care. Because most robberies involve strangers and evoke some degree of anger and fear in the victims, one would assume that a high proportion of offenses would be reported. This assumption is apparently unfounded. According to the NCVS, 71 percent of *all* robbery offenses are reported to police, but reporting depends to some extent upon the characteristics of the offense. If there is no injury to the victim, fewer victims report. If there is an injury classified as "resulting from a serious assault" (broken bones, loss of teeth, loss of consciousness, or any injury by a weapon), then the reporting increases 14 percent.[3] Keep these reporting inconsistencies in mind as we now turn to the facts of robbery.

Fact 1. The robbery rate has dramatically declined in the last few years according to both the UCR and the NCVS. The reader may recall that the UCR and the NCVS do not always report similar trends, but in this case there is little doubt that they are in agreement. According to the UCR, in 2002 the rate declined to 145.9 per 100,000 inhabitants, the lowest rate recorded since 1973 and 2 percent lower than the previous year.[4] This represents a decline of 36 percent from the 1993 level. The NCVS reported a similar drop of over 63 percent during the same period. It is also interesting to note that this represents the lowest robbery rate ever recorded by the NCVS, which began issuing reports in 1973.[5]

Fact 2. Robbery is disproportionately high among young, lower-status nonwhite males. The pattern established in homicide and rape persists for robbery: Offenders are predominately nonwhite males who are unemployed or are involved in low-skill occupations. According to the 2002 UCR, 90 percent of those arrested for robbery were males, 54 percent were black, and 62 percent of the males were under the age of 25.[6] A Bureau of Justice Statistics report concluded that violent crime was largely intraracial for black and white victims, with 66 percent of white victims and 76 percent of black victims victimized by an offender of the same race.[7]

In several respects the victims of robbery are similar to their offenders. Two-thirds of the robbery victims are males, and while it is estimated that most robbery victims are white (73 percent), the highest victimization *rates* occur for nonwhites between ages 12 and 34.[8] In Table 5.1 we find that generally, the rate of robbery decreases as income rises. Victims of robbery are those who can least afford the loss, and these people are often poor, nonwhites, frequently male. Males were also robbed at rates more than twice that of females.

One can deduce from this discussion that robbery offenses are, to a degree, *intraracial*. According to NCVS findings, 66 percent of white robbery victims perceived the offenders to be white, and 76 percent of blacks perceived the offenders to be black.[9]

Fact 3. The majority of robberies are committed by strangers. The percentage of robberies involving strangers was over 64 percent, according to NCVS data.[10] Add to this the finding that well over half the robberies occur on a street, in a parking lot, and so on,[11] and the reality of robbery closely matches the public image of "crime in the street."

Fact 4. The role of alcohol and other drugs in robbery is unclear. This is not an especially enlightening statement. But the few available studies of the possible relationship

TABLE 5.1 Estimated Rate of Victims of Robbery per 1,000 Persons, Age 12 and Over, and Annual Family Income, 1999

	Family Income						
Crime	*Less than $7,500*	*$7,500– 14,999*	*$15,000– 24,999*	*$25,000– 34,999*	*$35,000– 49,999*	*$50,000– 74,999*	*$75,000– or More*
Robbery	6.3	4.1	2.9	2.9	2.2	2.1	1.0

Source: Adapted from U.S. Department of Justice, Bureau of Justice Statistics, *Criminal Victimization in United States, 2002,* Table 8, "Victimization Rates for Persons age 12 and over, by Type of Crime and Annual Family Income of Victims."

between alcohol and robbery simply do not offer hard evidence beyond the fact that robbers often have drinking problems.[12] One of the more controversial issues in criminology concerns the association between drug addiction and criminal activity. This will be discussed in detail in Chapter 8, but for now the reader should be aware that some addicts support expensive drug habits that they cannot afford. Because they often work in low-paying jobs or are unemployed, they must turn to one or more of a very limited number of alternative sources of funds: selling drugs, prostitution, or some form of theft. It appears that addicts who steal prefer an activity such as shoplifting that does not involve direct confrontation with the victim. But robbery does have the virtue of being a fast and direct means to money, and the addict's preference may mean little when he or she faces an emergency shortage of drugs. Thus some researchers argue that the stereotype of the passive drug user avoiding crimes of confrontation, such as robbery, is a myth. Instead, the addict is often willing to take the risk of any crime so long as financial gain is likely.[13]

Some indication of the part drugs may play in robbery comes from an Oakland, California, study. From interviews with offenders the researchers found the following:

1. Nearly one-quarter of the adult offenders said they were addicts and were robbing for drugs.
2. One-quarter of all the offenders interviewed reported being high on drugs or a combination of drugs and alcohol at the time of the robberies. Thirteen percent more were drunk at the time.[14]

Fact 5. The majority of robberies do not involve injury to the victims. The UCR divides the index into "crimes of violence" and "crimes against property." Robbery is included in the first category along with murder and nonnegligent manslaughter, forcible rape, and aggravated assault. Although it is true that approximately half the offenses involve the use of a weapon—guns, knives, and other weapons in about equal proportions—and that the threat of harm is, by definition, always a part of robbery, its classification as a violent crime is misleading. Despite the potential for violence, the great majority of offenses appear motivated only by financial gain; the desire to inflict harm is, at most, a secondary consideration.

The NCVS data indicate that only about a third of robberies involve injury to the victims. Furthermore, the likelihood of injury is related to the type of weapon employed:

1. The victim of a robbery in which no gun is used is much more likely to be injured seriously—defined as needing medical treatment or being hospitalized overnight. The gun robbery victim requires medical treatment in 5 percent of the incidents; knife robberies, 10 percent; other weapon, 13 percent; and unarmed, 10 percent.
2. For robberies involving guns, the victim is attacked in about 20 percent of the cases. In knife robberies, the attack rate is 36 percent. Robberies involving weapons other than knives or guns show a 56 percent attack rate. In unarmed robberies, the victim is attacked in 71 percent of the cases.[15]

Force is not absent in most robberies—people get shoved, knocked to the ground, and poked hard with a weapon—but the force itself is not an end; rather, it is a deliberate means toward a goal. Violence in most robberies is simply a necessary tool for accomplishing important phases of the job: frightening victims into giving up valuables with minimal argument and reducing chances of pursuit by enraged citizens.[16] According to Andre Normandeau,

> robbers . . . are primarily thieves who occasionally, though rather rarely, use force to achieve their objects. The display of violence in this context is on the whole an isolated episode. It is general persistence in crime, not a widespread specialization in crimes of violence, which is the main characteristic of robbers. The term "violent offender class" could not be applied to robbers without distorting the factual data to fit preconceived ideas. Violence is only an occupational risk of a career of nonviolent crime.[17]

Are we to assume, then, that attempting to understand the traditions of violence in the United States will contribute nothing to our understanding of robbery? The difficulty with such an assumption is that it overlooks the inherent potential for violence in the robbery situation. The very presence of a weapon indicates a willingness to use it "if necessary." Perhaps robbery is fundamentally a property offense. But since offenders obviously accept its "occupational risk" of violence, robbery appears consistent with the U.S. value of using physical aggression as a problem-solver.

Types of Robbers

Classifying offenders into neat pigeonholes or types is a dangerous game. As with any individuals who have been officially tagged (robbers, murderers, or parking ticket violators), there are no assurances that they represent the great numbers of people outside the legal system who do the same things. Furthermore, typologies can easily oversimplify the complexity of motives and situations that contribute to deviant behavior and to the cessation of such behavior.[18] Nevertheless, we shall present one typology of robbers that clarifies the dimensions of robbery just discussed. Typologies will also be used to describe other offenders in this chapter (burglars, auto thieves, and shoplifters) and in the chapter to follow (child and spouse abusers).

The author of the robber typology is John E. Conklin, who drew his information from interviews with 67 inmates in Massachusetts prisons.[19] The four types are listed in decreasing order according to the amount of planning involved in their offenses.

1. Professional robbers. As the term implies, these people make their living by robbery. They exhibit more skill than other robbers and focus on the large scores—a minimum of $500. Before the offense, they carefully plan how to overcome security measures (such as those found in financial institutions) and how to make a sure escape. According to Conklin, not all these professionals engage exclusively in robbery; some get involved in other property crimes such as burglary (for a discussion of the distinction between the two types of offenses, see below). In general, the professionals can be distinguished from others by a high degree of commitment to a career of stealing in one form or another.

Researchers investigating professional property criminals find that their lives are supported by verbalized motives that make the crimes seem reasonable to them. Werner J.

Einstadter, who studies armed robbers, found that professionals often avoid robbing individuals or small businesses. Instead, their targets are establishments that are insured and can recover the losses—presumably, nobody is out anything.[20] The professionals' general philosophy is derived from their view of the essential dishonesty of society and the interest group conflicts behind that dishonesty. One professional expressed his motives this way:

> "The way I see it a guy has several ways to go in this world. If he's not rich in front, he can stay honest and be a donkey. Only this way he works for someone else and gets fucked the rest of his life. They cheat him and break his back. But this guy is honest.
>
> "Now another way is he can start cheating and lying to people and maybe he can make himself a lot of money in business, legally I mean. But this guy isn't honest. If he's honest and tries to make it this way, he won't get nowhere.
>
> "Another way he can make it and live a halfway decent life and still be honest is to steal. Now I don't mean sneaking around and taking money or personal property from assholes who don't have nothing. I mean going after big companies. To me this is perfectly honest, because these companies are cheating people anyway. When you go and just take it from them, you are actually more honest than they are. Most of the time, anyway, they are insured and make more money from the caper than you do.
>
> "Really, I think it is too bad it is this way. I mean it. I wish a guy could make a decent living working, which he can't do because those people who have it made got that way fucking the worker. And they are going to keep it that way. And all the crap about having to have laws protecting property. These are just laws set up by those people who got all the property and are going to make sure they keep it."[21]

2. Addict robbers. As this term implies, these offenders rob as a result of drug habits that require funds to maintain. Unlike the professionals, they do not think in terms of big scores; they worry only about getting enough for the next fix. Because they know that they must have money by a certain time, some planning takes place, but it is not nearly as involved as that done by professionals. Addicts may attempt to lessen the risk through planning; however, their desperation can result in carelessness and lead to arrest.

3. Opportunist robbers. According to Conklin, these are probably the most common type of robbers. For them the situation plays an important role in the offense; little prior planning takes place, and the robbery's occurrence depends greatly upon the availability of vulnerable victims: drunks, old women, people in isolated places, and so on. The "take" is often less than $20 and is spent for extras to elevate the robber's lifestyle a bit. For the opportunists robbery is not a frequent activity, although they may occasionally be involved in other forms of property crime. Robbery is primarily a matter of convenience, not a long-term commitment.

4. Alcoholic robbers. For these the situation is the paramount factor precipitating the offense. The robbers have no commitment to theft as a way of life; nor do they plan at all in advance for the robberies, even to the extent of seeking out a vulnerable victim. For them the offenses "just happen" while they are under the influence of alcohol. Often they occur as afterthoughts to assaults or other contacts with victims. Consider one example provided by Conklin:

> [The] offender had just asked a clerk in a liquor store for a bottle of whiskey, and when he handed the clerk money to pay for the bottle, the clerk asked if there was anything else he

wanted. The alcoholic at that moment decided that there was, and told the clerk to give him all his money. After a fight the alcoholic took some money and fled.[22]

Burglary

The UCR defines burglary as "the unlawful entry of a structure to commit a felony or theft. The use of force to gain entry is not required to classify an offense as burglary." The NCVS defines it as the "unlawful or forcible entry of a residence, usually, but not necessarily, attended by theft." The distinctions among robbery, burglary, and a third category, larceny-theft (to be discussed later) are confusing at times. As a rule, the reader can distinguish them as follows: *Robbery* involves an offender using *force or a threat of force* against a *person; burglary* involves an offender being illegally present at a *place;* and *larceny-theft* is a grab-bag category involving most other forms of theft that do not involve fraud.

Perhaps an example will help. If an offender rings your apartment doorbell, you answer, and he demands your money or else, that is *robbery*. But if he rings the bell when you are not at home, and he enters (forcefully or otherwise) and takes your valuables, that is *burglary*. If you invite him into the apartment and he pockets something of value while you are out of the room, and then takes your bicycle parked in the driveway, both are instances of *larceny-theft*.

Dimensions of Burglary

As we depart from offenses that involve face-to-face contacts between offenders and victims, the data on offenders become particularly suspect because we must rely less on the victims' accounts and more on arrest data. In short, the NCVS is not helpful in describing offender characteristics. There are other problems in describing the facts about burglary, as we shall see.

Fact 1. The burglary rate is declining and has been doing so for a decade. The problem here goes beyond the usual difficulty in comparing offenses known to police with offenses recalled by victims: Namely, the UCR data include burglaries against both households and businesses, whereas the NCVS includes only household burglaries.

According to the UCR, the burglary rate dropped and the NCVS report reductions in burglaries. The UCR reports that the national offense rate for burglary in 2002 was 742 offenses per 100,000 inhabitants, the lowest since 1966 and a 24 percent decline from the 2002 figure. According to the NCVS, household burglaries continued to decline, falling 52 percent between 1993 and 2002, with these reported to police only 58 percent of the time.[23]

Fact 2. The majority of persons arrested for burglary are young, white males. Statistics from the UCR indicate that the arrestees for robbery and burglary are overwhelmingly male: 90 percent for robbery and 87 percent for burglary. Arrested male burglars are especially young, as are arrested male robbers: 63 percent of the burglars are under 25 years of age, while 62 percent of the robbers were under 25. Blacks are overrepresented in robbery arrests when one compares their 54 percent with the proportion of blacks in the total population—12 percent.[24] It appears, however, that whites are far more involved in burglary than robbery.

The reader is again reminded to regard these statistics with caution because of possible biases in reporting and arresting. We know from the NCVS that only about half of all household burglaries are reported to police, and we know from the UCR that police make an arrest for only 14 percent of the reported burglaries.[25] Obviously, there is much room for error in determining who is burglarizing. But let us assume that the statistics reasonably reflect reality. Although it is understandable that a socially and economically depressed minority would be overrepresented in crime statistics, what can we make of the racial variation among offenses? One conjecture is that the higher concentration of nonwhites in robbery is consistent with the subculture of violence viewpoint. Interpersonal violence is disproportionately high among nonwhites; thus, it is not surprising to find them more involved in violent than in nonviolent property offenses.

The World of Burglary

Probably no other crime enjoys the romantic aura often attached to burglary. Movies and television portray the cat burglar as dashing, clever, brave, and rich from his theft of gems. Presumably, he is everything that the common criminal is not. Some burglars in fact are not common, and the mass media image has a basis in reality. Historically, the king of American burglars was Armand, who made as much as $200,000 a year, owned a Ferrari and a Jaguar (the car not the cat), and lived in a high-rent, five-room Manhattan apartment.[26] He acquired all this as a result of six or seven carefully planned jobs a year. Scarcely one to argue that crime does not pay, Armand has definite opinions about his work:

> "You might laugh, but I'm for law and order. What I do is my business. I don't hurt anyone, and anyway most of the people who lose stuff are insured, and I could tell you about the way they inflate their losses. But this mugging on the streets and the rapes and the way they have to coddle these creeps makes me sick."[27]

Armand is, of course, an exceptional burglar. But we know nearly as much about the exceptions as we do about commonplace offenders. The more detailed studies of burglary concentrate on various demographic characteristics of offenders, offenses, victims, and the legal system's response. Other studies deal primarily with professionals—those offenders characterized by relatively high skills, by a commitment to a career in burglary, and by a livelihood made in crime.[28] But our knowledge about the motivations of nonprofessional burglars is deficient, and this is a critical lack because burglary appears to be a very *rational* crime. That is, it is rarely a purely situational offense. To execute a burglary, some degree of planning is undertaken by even the most inexperienced offender. Furthermore, the crime is rational because the potential payoff is high in comparison to what many could earn in noncriminal pursuits. Economists have concluded that on the basis of economic considerations alone, burglary pays. This is particularly the case for youths who are poorly paid in the conventional labor marketplace.[29]

Another rational aspect of burglary is its interrelationship with the legitimate world. Successful burglary not only victimizes this world, but also relies upon a variety of more or less respectable individuals for social support. Neal Shover provides a description of three types of such individuals:[30]

1. Bondsmen and attorneys. These people are part of the legitimate world and may actually assist the burglar in minimizing the risk of prosecution and punishment. They are accepted within the legal establishment, and the veteran burglar relies upon good relationships with them to avoid confinement. The burglar needs the trust of the bondsman who will provide bail for release after arrest and the trust of the lawyer who will seek to delay trial, who bargains with prosecutors, and who has the legal skills to gain the burglar the best possible outcome:

> When the good burglar [one with a reputation for being competent and trustworthy] is arrested—as he frequently is—he can count upon receiving the services of both a bondsman and an attorney, even if he has virtually no ready cash. In lieu of a cash down payment, the thief will be able to gain his release from confinement, and also preliminary legal representation, on the basis of his reputation and a promise to deliver the needed cash at a later date. He will then search for one or more suitable burglaries (or some other type of crime) which holds out the promise of a quick and substantial reward—so that he can pay his attorney and bondsman.[31]

In some cases the attorney may be able to obtain a "fix"—a venerable U.S. custom whereby police, witnesses, prosecutors, or judges are persuaded to ignore, forget, or withdraw evidence necessary for a conviction—for a price, of course.

2. Tipsters. A burglar does not become successful in selecting his or her targets by luck or accident. Without X-ray vision the burglar can only guess what valuables a residence contains, where they are located, and what security measures are active—that is, unless he or she has an information source. People who are willing to tip off burglars about potentially lucrative scores may work in the nonlegitimate world of gambling and prostitution, but they may also come from many walks of legitimate life: watchmen, attorneys, jewelers, repairpersons, beauticians, bartenders, detectives, and so on. Since some are paid and some are not, we can only guess at their motives, but tipsters make substantial contributions to the success of burglaries.

3. Fences. Once the burglar has made a score, if the loot is other than cash, someone is needed to purchase the goods. Standing on a corner trying to sell video recorders and snow tires is a risky business, so the burglar needs an outlet. Fortunately for the burglar, there are people who deal in stolen goods with no questions asked. Fences are the middlepersons in the world of property crime. Like bona fide retailers in the legitimate world, fences purchase goods for resale to the final users.

Purchasing stolen merchandise is just one function that fences fulfill for burglars. Fences can also instruct them on how to recognize the most marketable items, how to improve thieving techniques, and how to locate out-of-work burglars who might be helpful for the next big score. But by far the most important function of fences is being a ready and convenient market for stolen goods. Without this invaluable service, burglary would be a much more hazardous operation.[32]

Let us not forget the final element in the web of social support for burglary: the fences' *customers.* These are the people who really make burglary work. We do not know much about the customers except that most engage in legitimate occupations and usually have no illusion about the "retailer" with whom they are dealing. Because so many "good" people believe that getting a "deal" is more important than worrying about where the merchandise came from, fences stay in business—and so do burglars.

Motor Vehicle Theft

The sixth index crime in the UCR is motor vehicle theft, simply defined as "the theft or attempted theft of a motor vehicle." This includes automobiles, trucks, buses, motorcycles, motor scooters, and snowmobiles. According to the NCVS, about 86 percent of these thefts are reported to police—the highest reporting rate for any crime.[33] And according to the UCR, 75 percent of all reported motor vehicle thefts involve automobiles.[34]

Dimensions of Motor Vehicle Theft

This offense is not trivial. The FBI claims that 1 out of every 126 registered vehicles is stolen annually and that the total national loss amounts to $8 billion.[35] But despite its frequency and its cost, motor vehicle theft has not been extensively researched, so the facts are few.

Fact 1. The motor vehicle theft rate is stable. As is the case with robbery, the UCR and NCVS measures are not comparable. The UCR police report data include *all* vehicles, both business and private, while the NCVS victimization data include only private vehicles. Nevertheless, the NCVS reports a dramatic decline of over 50 percent since 1993 to a rate of 9 per 1,000 persons aged 12 and over, while the UCR reports a similar reduction of 20 percent for the period of 1993–2002, with a rate of 432 per 100,000 inhabitants for 2002.[36]

Fact 2. Most people who are arrested for motor vehicle theft are young, white males. Motor vehicle theft is the index crime most likely to be reported. Does this mean that we know a great deal about the offenders? Unfortunately not. Although victims are likely to report the crime to the police, chances are small that the police will arrest the offenders; in 2002 a dismal 14 percent of all reported motor vehicle thefts resulted in an arrest.[37] Nearly 90 percent of those arrested were male, 60 percent were white, and 50 percent of the males were under 21 years of age.[38] These figures are nearly identical to those for arrested burglars.

Fact 3. Approximately two-thirds of the locally stolen vehicles are recovered. Unfortunately, we have no information on the condition of these recovered vehicles—some, no doubt, are fit only for a junkyard. Nevertheless, this statistic indicates a unique feature of auto theft. Unlike other theft, in which property is taken for long-term use or resale, cars are often stolen for short-term use, after which the thieves abandon them. Thus, unlike victims who lose office equipment (8 percent recovered) or televisions, stereos, and other electronics (5 percent), the victims of auto theft stand a far better chance of seeing their property again. However, this chance appears to be declining. In 1955 approximately 95 percent of stolen vehicles were recovered; by 1973 the recovery rate had dropped to approximately three-quarters, and by 2002 it was down to the two-thirds figure.[39] This decline indicates another unique feature of auto theft: It is a crime whose *nature is shifting.* We will elaborate on this point a bit later.

Joyriders, Professionals, and Others

Until recently, sociological interest in motor vehicle theft was restricted to research on one type of thief: the *joyrider.* The joyrider was characterized as a white male teenager from a middle-class background who stole a car in moment of impetuousness, spent a few hours or a weekend with it, and finally abandoned it. But sociological preoccupation with auto theft as "favored-group" delinquency (i.e., white and middle class)[40] led to the neglect of other types of auto theft. Charles H. McCaghy, Peggy C. Giordano, and Trudy Knicely Henson categorized auto thieves into five types:[41]

1. Joyriders. These are the youngest of the auto thieves, usually in their mid-teens. Their offenses probably depend less upon planning than upon unanticipated opportunities such as finding keys left in the ignition. Their motives are *recreational* and *status-seeking:* entertainment from driving at high speeds or status from driving a specific type of automobile. For joyriders the duration of the ride often depends upon how much gasoline is found in the tank.

2. Short-termers. People often need a car in a hurry. They are late for an important engagement, they find that it is raining after a concert and the buses are full, or they just have to "get out of town—now!" One solution is to "borrow" a car. Like joyriders, short-termers probably depend upon available opportunities to steal, and they eventually abandon the car. But unlike joyriders, they have *practical* motivations.

3. Felony-motivated thieves. These types are similar to short-termers to the extent that their thefts occur for the purpose of accomplishing a task, after which the cars are abandoned. The factor that distinguishes these thieves is the nature of their task, which is to assist in the *commission of a crime.* Robbers, burglars, kidnappers, rapists, and murderers often use stolen autos to confuse victims, witnesses, and authorities. These thieves are less likely than joyriders and short-termers to rely upon opportunity, however.

4. Long-termers. Since they all abandon the cars they have stolen, the three types of thieves discussed so far contribute to the greater likelihood of victims recovering their vehicles.

But the remaining two types of thieves steal for the purpose of exploiting the cars to the maximum. As the name "long-termers" implies, these offenders steal with the intention of keeping the cars for *extended personal use.* Little is known about these types, but we can conjecture that advance planning is important, because a desirable car must be selected with an eye toward how it will be stolen and modified. Should the victim be fortunate enough to recover a vehicle from a long-termer, he or she may find it in better shape than when it was stolen.

5. Profit-motivated thieves. This final type consists primarily of the thieves known as *professionals*—those who make a living from the theft and sale of cars or their parts. Professional car theft involves a variety of actors, beginning with those who are paid from $250 to $500 for each stolen car. According to authorities, 10 to 15 percent of stolen cars are resold intact or with minor modifications to individual customers, retailers, or shippers who move them across the Mexican border or to South America by cargo vessels. Fifty percent end up in "chop shops"—garages where in 28 minutes a car can be dismantled into its component parts. Why parts? Because parts are harder to identify than the whole machine and because the sum of the individual parts is worth up to four-and-a-half times as much as the assembled car.[42]

In short, a professional can take a $500 investment and, in less than a half-hour, turn it into $40,000 worth of products.

In discussing the facts about motor vehicle theft, we mentioned the increase of its rate and the shifting nature of the offense as indicated by the falling recovery rate. These two facts are interrelated, as the following brief history reveals. Until 1970 it was relatively easy to steal a car; if a door was unlocked, all you needed was a little knowledge of ignition systems to start the engine. Consequently, even young, inexperienced joyriders had little trouble in finding targets. Then, in 1970, manufacturers introduced steering column locks that were not so easily defeated, at least by many potential joyriders. As cars with these locks replaced the earlier models, the motor vehicle theft rate leveled off, although it now is increasing; but the recovery rate began dropping and continues to do so. We can logically conclude that while the locks decreased thefts by joyriders and others who are not mechanically sophisticated, much of that decrease was counteracted by increased activity by professionals who are not deterred by the locks.

This inference about the growth in professional auto theft is understandable in light of the profit that can be made. There is also less moral and legal condemnation of this crime than of many others. Certainly, a car is expensive, and its loss an inconvenience. Nevertheless, compared with the potential danger from a robbery or the assault on one's privacy that occurs in a burglary, auto theft does not seem so bad. And is there any feeling of loss over a particular car that cannot be remedied by a good insurance settlement? Of course, there will be additional technological innovations designed to discourage the professional, and there will be continued calls for stronger laws and enforcement drives. In contrast, however, to the fear that other crimes generate, many people probably agree with the verbalized motives of one professional, who describes his work this way:

> "What I do is good for everybody. First of all, I create work. I hire men to deliver cars, work on the [identification] numbers, paint them, give them [forged documents], maybe drive them out of state, find customers. That's good for the economy. Then I'm helping working people to get what they can never afford otherwise. A fellow wants a Cadillac but he can't afford it; his wife wants it but she knows he can't afford it. So I get this fellow a car at a price he can afford; maybe I save him as much as $2000. Now he's happy. But so is the guy who lost his car. He gets a nice new Cadillac from the insurance company—without the dents and scratches we had to take out of it. The Cadillac company—they're happy too because they sell another Cadillac.
>
> "The only people who don't do so good is the insurance company. But they're so big that nobody cares *personally*. They got a budget for this sort of thing anyway. So here I am, a guy without an education, sending both my kids to college, giving my family a good home, making other people happy. Come on now—who am I really hurting?"[43]

Larceny-Theft

Larceny-theft, the seventh category of index crimes in the UCR, is a catch-all for all unlawful taking of property without force or fraud. This does *not* include embezzlement, forgery, confidence games, or the writing of worthless checks, all of which involve fraud. Although any one of these crimes may involve a tremendous loss of money, the FBI did not consider them serious enough for inclusion among the index crimes (this is being changed by the introduction of the National Incident-Based Reporting System). The larceny-theft category does include shoplifting, pocket-picking, purse-snatching, thefts from cars (accessories or cargo), bicycle thefts, and thefts from coin machines.

Statistics for this category must be regarded with extreme caution; according to the NCVS, only about one-quarter of larcenies from the home are reported to police.[44] Since the UCR larceny-theft category is a miscellaneous collection plagued by major statistical problems, nothing would be gained by treating it as a single-offense type such as burglary or motor vehicle theft. Instead, we will concentrate on one crime: shoplifting. This particular offense constitutes only 17 percent of all larcenies reported to police. The most frequently reported offenses are theft of motor vehicle accessories (11 percent) and theft from motor vehicles (26 percent).[45] Shoplifting has been researched sufficiently, however, to allow for some elaboration.

The Extent of Shoplifting

The retailing industry's accountants constantly deal with a concept known as *inventory shrinkage,* or *shrink,* as it is sometimes called. This refers to merchandise that cannot be accounted for by inventory lists, sales receipts, damage, and so on—the merchandise has simply vanished. The extent of shrinkage is not inconsequential; it can range from 1.2 percent of sales to a high of 8 percent in major cities.[46] One author believes that the average retailer loses "as much as 5 percent of sales to shrinkage, and in some departments, such as costume jewelry, shrinkage can be as high as 30 percent."[47]

Some shrinkage can be accounted for by bookkeeping errors, but most is attributed to two other sources: theft by employees and theft by customers. Naturally, the breakdown of how much each of these sources contributes to shrinkage is not completely certain, but it is generally agreed that bookkeeping errors constitute less than half—perhaps as little as one-fifth; employees may be responsible for most, perhaps as much as 80 percent.[48] The National Retail Survey conducted in 2001 determined that approximately 1.80 percent of the total gross retail sales were lost due to shrinkage. Respondents reported that they believed that the single largest cause of shrinkage was employee theft ($15 billion), followed by shoplifting ($10 billion) and bookkeeping errors ($5 billion), with the remainder attributed to vendors and other causes.[49]

How many customers shoplift? Conservative estimates say about 1 in 61. But an observational study conducted in a Manhattan department store found that of 500 people selected at random, one out of ten took merchandise without paying for it.[50] In another study, it was determined that

> enough food is stolen annually from supermarkets across the U.S. to feed every man, woman, and child in both San Francisco and Boston for a full year. Adding insult to injury, the store's shopping carts often serve as the get-away vehicles. The problem of losses in supermarkets approaches monumental proportions. Industry sources report that 48 percent of all customers shoplift at one time or another, while 58 percent of all employees help themselves to an occasional apple or pack of cigarettes. Employee theft of all kinds, including shoplifting, cash shortages, and inventory losses, accounts for 66 percent of a supermarket's total shrinkage.[51]

Obviously, the number of shoplifters "patronizing" a store depends greatly upon the type of store. Supermarkets and discount stores are easier targets than are stores that exercise more control over accessibility to merchandise. Supermarkets lose a shopping cart every 90 seconds in the United States, and that adds up to 1.8 million carts worth $175 million annually. Stores are now installing sensor systems in the carts that lock the wheels of the cart if it is taken past the parking lot's edge.[52]

Types of Shoplifters

Like the property offenders discussed earlier in this chapter, shoplifters can be categorized as either professionals or amateurs. Professionals, or *boosters,* steal in volume, primarily for purposes of resale; amateurs, or *snitches,* take goods intended for personal use.

Boosters, like other professional property offenders, have a high degree of skill, a commitment to earning a livelihood through criminal behavior, and connections with attorneys, bondsmen, and fences to make shoplifting as risk-free and profitable as possible.[53] The term "booster" refers not only to the shoplifter but also to the devices the shoplifter uses. The more common of these are as follows:

1. **Booster box.** A box wrapped and tied with string. One end is hinged to flip inward so that merchandise can be quickly inserted.
2. **Drop bag.** A cloth bag pinned or sewn into a coat lining. Merchandise is slipped inside the coat and dropped into the bag.
3. **Booster purse.** A purse with a false bottom into which merchandise can be inserted.
4. **Slashed pocket coat.** A coat with pockets removed so that a hand inserted into a pocket can reach out to grab merchandise and then hang it on a hook or a drop bag sewn inside the coat.[54]

But boosters do not live by devices alone. Hefty women can become adept at a practice known as *crotchwalking*—hiding items between their thighs without any change in their normal walk. Real experts can handle even a small television set with this technique. One legendary crotchwalker outran two detectives and scaled an eight-foot fence, all while carrying a 15-pound ham between her legs.[55]

The majority of shoplifters are amateurs. These are the legions of teenagers, housewives, office workers, and other "respectable" folks who steal for a wide variety of reasons: a budget sorely strained by unemployment, irritation over lines at checkout counters, anger at not finding a clerk when one needs one, and just plain thrills. Amateur shoplifters come from virtually every segment of society: the rich, the poor, the young, and the old. In a survey conducted on 740 shoplifters apprehended at a department store, the "average" shoplifter turned out to be an 18-year-old white female who had taken merchandise valued at $86.[56] The profile of the typical shoplifter is important because it forces us to recognize that criminal behavior is not monopolized by the socially and politically disadvantaged. The young woman would not dream of sticking a gun in a clerk's face for a bottle of perfume, yet she can in good conscience relieve the store of its perfume without payment just as surely as if she were carrying that gun.

Shoplifters vary greatly in the degree of skill and amount of planning that go into their shoplifting. Many amateur thefts undoubtedly are the result of situational factors, such as deserted store aisles and attractive displays of items that suddenly assume an importance unmatched by one's budget. But impulse does not characterize all shoplifters. There is a class of amateurs known as *shadow professionals,* so named because their methods are similar to the boosters'. Their techniques are innovative; their thievery is systematic and carefully planned. They differ from professionals because they do not steal for a living but rather for little luxuries and thrills that relieve the dullness of their jobs and lives.[57]

One of the most thorough studies of shoplifters is based on arrest data from the 1940s. The author, Mary Owen Cameron, describes one type of amateur who might be called a shadow professional:

> Normally, he has no criminal association or connections; yet he (in department stores, more often she) comes into the store usually equipped with a large handbag, brief case, shopping bag, "bad bag" [a paper bag with the store's imprint that can be used to conceal merchandise], or sometimes even booster bloomers [garments designed to hold merchandise on hooks or pockets] or a booster bag in which to carry off merchandise. She may have scissors or a razor blade to snip off price tags. She deliberately directs the sales clerk's attention elsewhere and slips various items into her bag when she believes herself unobserved. She may even bring . . . a shopping list of items she wants to steal. . . . [Such shoplifters] are deliberate thieves who manifest intent to steal by preparation beforehand and who carry out their crimes with system and method. They are sufficiently practiced that only by considerable interrogation can they be differentiated [from] professional thieves. Although they are . . . almost always technically "first offenders" when apprehended by store police, their behavior indicates only that they have not been *caught* before; it does not indicate that they have not previously shoplifted—quite the contrary.[58]

One other type of shoplifter needs mentioning. Store security personnel place drug addicts in a category separate from boosters and shoplifters.[59] Addict-shoplifters are the easiest to spot: high-school-aged males loping down store aisles looking for enough unguarded merchandise to pay for their habit. They are in an obvious hurry and exercise little caution; they are likely to simply grab and run. In large urban areas, addicts probably constitute about 5 percent of all apprehended shoplifters, although another study stated that evidence of drug use was detected among 46 percent of customer thieves.[60]

The motivations of boosters and addict-shoplifters are obvious. But what of the snitches? Why do otherwise apparently respectable people steal from stores? (It would be naive to assume that all snitches are otherwise respectable, but many are.) The little research that exists on this question has used samples limited to students.[61] One consistent finding is that shoplifting is regarded by students as a *rational* act. That is, students do not excuse their offenses as actions beyond their control or as matters of impulse. They accept responsibility for taking something because they *want* it and because they regard shoplifting as an *acceptable means* for taking it.

But why is shoplifting acceptable? That remains unanswered. We can speculate that it is simply an indication of a U.S. belief that organizations are easily legitimized as victims. William Henry Vanderbilt, president of the New York Central Railroad in the mid-1800s, once said, "The public be damned." Today, the U.S. public often feels this way toward business, an attitude that will be discussed further in the section below entitled "Larceny in the American Heart."

Reactions to Shoplifting

Much of the sociological research on shoplifting deals with the *reaction of audiences,* both customers and store employees, who witness shoplifting incidents. This emphasis is consistent with the *labeling perspective* on deviance that we discussed in Chapter 3. The labeling perspective concerns the *production of deviance*—the process by which officials and agencies translate rule-breaking behavior into deviant behavior. One implication of this perspective is pointed out by Darrell J. Steffensmeier and Robert M. Terry:

> Much of the literature in the [labeling] perspective has argued that differential treatment is accorded persons with poor social backgrounds, less than perfect social identities, or "bad" reputations. Many analyses of deviant categories are founded on the assumption that particular classes of people are more likely to perform deviant acts and to be particular types of deviant persons. Such studies are highly consistent in arguing that respectability decreases the likelihood of deviant imputation, whereas "unrespectability" has the opposite effect.[62]

When looking at shoplifting from the labeling perspective, the question is to what degree does respectability protect a person from being labeled as a shoplifter? To answer this question, Steffensmeier and Terry staged incidents in which a "thief" openly shoplifted in front of a customer. The "thieves" were varied according to sex and appearance. Appearance was either "hippie"—soiled jeans, denim jacket, no socks, unruly hair, and so on—or straight—neatly dressed and groomed. Results indicated that customers were more likely to report the incident to a clerk if the hippie were involved. The sex of either the thief or the customer had little influence on reporting rates.[63] The researchers concluded that clear support exists for the contention that assigning a label of deviance depends not only upon the act but also upon the actor's identity, a major tenet of the labeling perspective.

This conclusion, however, is made less certain by a similar study conducted by a team of psychologists led by Donald P. Hartmann and Donna M. Gelfand. These researchers used only a female "thief" who varied her appearance between hippie and straight. But they found that appearance had little effect on reporting rates.[64] Although the two studies are not identical in design, the conflicting results raise questions about the importance of appearance in assigning labels to shoplifting.

In one respect, both studies are in agreement: *Fewer than 30 percent of the customers reported the incident to store employees without prompting or encouragement.* Hartmann and his associates conclude that a widespread indifference exists toward the store as a victim. Indeed, it is far more convenient for onlookers to minimize the theft or to deny responsibility than it is to get involved in something that may be time-consuming, embarrassing, or worse should there be a mistake. When shoplifting, the offender apparently need not be overly concerned about witnesses, since thievery is protected by a shield of indifference. In fact, some data are alarming: The National Retail Security Survey of 1991 notes that less than 4 percent of shoplifters are reported by other customers.[65] One might feel a twinge of moral indignation when some scruffy individual runs off with a bag of kitty litter—but so what?

Other studies of audience reaction toward shoplifting have investigated the *reaction of store personnel.*[66] The great majority of apprehended shoplifters are caught by clerks or by private security guards employed by the store. If a shoplifting incident is reported to or seen by employees, those employees must decide on the course of action—release or referral to police. Among the several studies dealing with this question, all agree that the most important factor in determining whether an offender is referred to police is the *value of the item(s) stolen*. Furthermore, all find that *sex* is *not* an important variable. Beyond these findings, the studies' results are inconsistent: Some find that age and race are related to the likelihood of being referred to police; others find that age and race are irrelevant. Thus the labeling perspective remains an open issue as far as shoplifting research is concerned.

Arson

The original seven index crimes of the *Uniform Crime Reports* were stipulated by the International Association of Chiefs of Police in 1928 and remained unchanged until 1978. That year Congress approved legislation adding a new index crime, arson; in 1979 the FBI began collecting data on "any willful or malicious burning or attempt to burn, with or without intent to defraud, a dwelling house, public building, motor vehicle or aircraft, personal property of another, etc." Because the inclusion of arson as an index crime is more recent, there are few things we can say about it with certainty, and even the FBI is cautious.[67] Too, Patrick G. Jackson examined data on arson by conducting surveys of fire departments. His findings are somewhat astonishing, for "the survey results indicate that 56% of the 683 responding fire departments reported information to the UCR, 17% did not report, 27% did not know whether they reported, and 1% did not answer the question (data not shown)."[68] Jackson notes reasons for the reporting problems, and they are understandable; they include the facts that arson is not always immediately apparent, that arson may not be determined until after a lengthy investigation, and that arson may not fall under police jurisdiction.[69]

The majority of people arrested for arson are young, white males. Specifically, 86 percent of the arrestees are male, 74 percent are white, and 70 percent of the males are under 25 years old (54 percent were under 18).[70] According to the UCR, arson is notable in that 48 percent of all 1996 arson clearances involved solely young people under age 18.[71]

Does this mean that arson is a disproportionately juvenile crime? The major problem in answering that question is the low arrest rates for arson: Only 15 percent of all arsons known to police are cleared by arrest. One could speculate that juveniles are less likely than adults to plan their fire-setting carefully, with the consequence that juveniles run a far higher risk of being apprehended. Unlike the other index crimes, a well-planned arson is difficult to distinguish from an accidental fire. Even if investigators can establish that the fire was deliberately set, it is quite another matter to prove who is responsible. The smart building owner intent on fraud will plan to be in a remote Caribbean resort while a hired "torch" does the job. Making a connection between the owner and an unknown fire-setter is difficult indeed. Thus arrest statistics on arson do not spark confidence.

Despite the problems with official statistics, we do know that arson is a costly and diverse crime. Most arson targets are buildings, but not all types of buildings are equally victimized. Only an estimated 7 percent of one- and two-family dwelling fires are attributed to arson, but an astonishing 75 percent of fires in schools and colleges are so attributed. About half the fires in churches and one-third of those in storage buildings, offices, banks, and restaurants are due to arson. Buildings are not the only targets; many experts believe that a quarter of all forest fires and over half of the motor vehicle fires are deliberately set.[72]

Losses from arson amount to nearly $3 billion yearly, although that is a conservative figure.[73] In addition, there are other costs as well:

1. Deaths (approximately a thousand annually) and injuries to citizens and firefighters
2. Increased insurance premiums
3. Increased taxes to support fire services
4. Loss of jobs at arson sites
5. Loss of revenues to businesses
6. Loss of public facilities, especially schools
7. Loss of housing
8. Loss of municipal tax base[74]

Types of Arsonists

The variety of targets and the apparently high number of juveniles involved give some indication that arson is a complex crime. While people usually rob and burglarize for one reason—money—the motivation for arson is not so simple. The following scenarios are typical:

> The landlord of a large apartment building with high costs (in a market that will not bear high rents) applies for a section 8 award from [the U.S. Department of Housing and Urban Development] to subsidize low income residents after renovation. The present tenants protest the section 8 award because they are too well off to qualify for subsidy but too poor to afford the higher rents that will be charged after renovation. Fires are set to "burn them out" so renovations can take place.
>
> Real estate speculators buy a property at a low price from a white family and sell [it] at a high price to a minority family with an FHA mortgage. Operating costs are high, the new owner becomes unemployed and is forced to abandon the home. The property joins the city's growing list of vacant buildings and becomes a target for vandals who set fires for the thrill of watching the fire department at work.
>
> A fire in a multi-family home is set by a 15-year-old who is slow in school, overweight, has learning disabilities and family problems at home. The child has been previously responsible for small fires in the home but these have been covered up by the mother.[75]

Thus the motivations for arson range from economic to emotional. They fall generally into five broad types:[76]

1. Pyromania. This refers to an emotional condition in which individuals obtain psychological satisfaction—such as reducing anxiety or generating excitement—from setting and watching fires. Usually, this type of arsonist works alone. But there are exceptions. One case involved the fire chief of the Dickson City, Pennsylvania, volunteer fire department and 15 of his men. Over a six-year period they set approximately 59 fires because "they enjoyed fighting them."[77] According to the experts, anywhere from 6 to 25 percent of all arsons can be classified as stemming from pyromania.

2. Vandalism. This form of arson is usually committed by juveniles who are either expressing anger against a symbol—such as a school—or are responding to group pressures by burning vacant cars or abandoned buildings. Since a search for excitement is often associated with the latter type of vandalism, it is not always clear how this category can be distinguished from pyromania. Estimates of the prevalence of this type range from 35 to 50 percent of all arsons.

3. Revenge. From 18 to 30 percent of all arsons are apparently motivated by spite or revenge. Rejected spouses or lovers, persons attacking those from different racial groups, and friends and relatives involved in interpersonal disputes often resort to burning homes, barns, or cars, thus producing more heat than light.

4. Crime concealment. Persons involved in criminal conduct occasionally attempt to destroy evidence by setting a fire. The evidence can range from financial records to fingerprints to a body. Approximately 7 to 10 percent of all arsons are believed to be so motivated.

5. Arson for profit. Since this type of arson is more likely than the others to involve careful planning, estimates on its incidence are more questionable. Expert opinions range from 3 to 19 percent nationally and as high as 40 percent for some specific urban areas. The arsonists' specific goals are highly diverse: to frighten away tenants, to force a business to comply with strikers' demands, to obtain insurance payoffs for redecorating, to clear land for development, and to show a loss for tax purposes.

The alert reader will have noticed that the given estimated percentages total 69 to 134 percent. This indicates the limits of current knowledge about arson. One hopes that in the future researchers will be ignited to clear away the smoke obscuring this topic.

Larceny in the American Heart

Throughout our discussion of property crimes we have been confronted with a paradox. People fear crime and take all kinds of precautions to frustrate those who would rob, burgle, and steal—yet the victimized usually do not report the incidents. Why is there, on one hand, this fear of crime and, on the other hand, an indifference toward seeking official remedy? The NCVS data show that property crime victims who fail to report often think that nothing can be done or that the offense is too unimportant to warrant being reported.[78]

Although it is lamentable that the public does not have more confidence in its law enforcement system, the lack of confidence is not unreasonable. The police record is adequate in solving cases of murder, aggravated assault, and even rape, when they are reported. In 2002 police cleared by arrest over half of these offenses—that is, they identified some people as offenders, presumably had sufficient evidence to charge them with an offense, and took them into custody. Because the victims and the offenders in these crimes were often acquaintances, the police success is not surprising. Crimes against property are another matter: The clearance rate was 26 percent for robbery, 13 percent for burglary, 14 percent for motor vehicle theft, and 18 percent for larceny-theft.[79] Thus there is no real incentive to report property crimes, aside from a desire to go on record for insurance purposes, a feeling of civic responsibility, and so on.

Public apathy toward reporting crime is understandable in light of official inefficiency. But also underlying the reluctance to report property offenses may be a concession that such acts are an unavoidable part of everyday American life. People who relieve others of their property are part of our heritage—from the settlers who seized Indian lands to the fraudulent businesspeople who bamboozle the public by selling products to restore a youthful appearance, to obtain sexual potency, to cure arthritis, and simply to get rich in a hurry. American heroes are those who have shown extraordinary courage, diligence, and initiative in science, industry, politics, entertainment, sports—and crime. Our heroes walk on the moon, hit record numbers of home runs, and rob banks. Historically, Jesse James and Al "Scarface" Capone have been as heroic to the U.S. public as have Thomas Edison, Mark McGwire, or Hank Aaron. Despite the bluster over crime in the streets, theft is considered tolerable if it is done with class and if violence is kept to a minimum. Theft is most tolerable to American sensibilities if it is gentle and unassuming, without threats and the waving of guns. Shoplifting nicely fits these requirements and can be thought of as an only slightly distorted miniature picture—a microcosm—of the streak of larceny running through U.S. society. (If shoplifting involves as many as one in ten store customers, it is difficult to argue that it is not representative of American theft.) Shoplifting is a fraternity and sorority, a common meeting ground for all religions, classes, and races. Shoplifters are stumbling junkies, secretaries, professional thieves, coeds, housewives, well-to-do people, and teenagers. In short, shoplifters are at once the respectable and the unrespectable, the bad and the beautiful.

It is ironic that "good" citizens should be part of the crime problem, that all that distinguishes them from "criminals" is the degree of violence used. Much of this distinction has to do with opportunity. Criminals must break into buildings or point guns because they may have few other alternatives. Good citizens, however, have a wider range of alternatives: Their respectability permits them a form of violence-free theft inaccessible to the poor and the unemployed.

A good example of the larceny in the American heart is theft from hotels and motels. An estimated one in three guests steals something from his or her room. This includes sheets, Bibles, ashtrays, towels, lamps, television sets, and, on occasion, the wallpaper. As in all forms of theft, there are both amateurs and professionals. Although the professionals are rare, they can get the contents of an entire room into a truck in a matter of minutes. The amateurs' souvenir collecting is less organized, but it is costly. One first-class New York hotel must replace over 2,000 towels every month. Of course, the amateurs have verbalized motives that justify theft:

> A woman who travels frequently and who has not purchased a sheet or towel for years: "I've paid for those things. The places I've stayed at haven't lost anything because they jack up their prices so."
>   A woman with a closet full of hotel "souvenirs": "There's nothing wrong with taking little things from hotels. I think they expect you to take at least a towel. Anyway, if you have something marked with their crest, it's good publicity for them. After all, I show off these things to my friends."[80]

The Rip-off Philosophy

At the foundation of much of U.S. theft is the notion that organizations are more legitimate targets than are individuals. The reader will recall that professional thieves claim that since what they steal is insured, their victims do not suffer significantly, if at all. Although there is no scientific evidence to prove it, we are probably safe in assuming that most amateur thieves would agree that stealing from large chain stores is far more justifiable than is stealing from small, privately owned "Mom and Pop" operations. A classic study of how organization size affects attitudes toward stealing was conducted by Erwin O. Smigel in the early 1950s.[81] He found that although most of the U.S. public disapproved of stealing, they also felt that if one must steal it should be from large businesses or government rather than from small businesses. One can deduce that had "individuals" been an option, they would have been considered even less justifiable victims than small businesses.

Government and large businesses are seen as logical victims of theft because they can make adjustments in taxes or prices to accommodate losses. Smigel also found that the public's selection of preferred victims stemmed from *resentment* and *distrust*. The inefficiency, ruthlessness, and impersonality of large bureaucracies all were given as reasons for stealing from government and business. These reasons indicate that a conflict exists between organizations and those who sense that they are being exploited by those organizations. This is not to suggest that the everyday amateur shoplifter is making a profound political statement by lifting a CD. But there is an ideological undercurrent that says that business deserves whatever it suffers at the hands of the public.

Ripping off is a term for stealing that emerged with the youth culture of drugs and rock music in the late 1960s. It then had intense political connotations—theft was to be a means by which wealth would be redistributed from capitalist institutions. The bible of the rip-off philosophy was written by Abbie Hoffman and appropriately entitled *Steal This Book*. The book is a catalog of means, both legal and illegal, of obtaining free food, lodging, education, and so on. It includes chapters on shoplifting, street fighting, and collecting welfare and unemployment payments. Hoffman explains his ideology:

> [*Steal This Book*] implies that the reader already is "ideologically set," in that he understands corporate feudalism as the only robbery worthy of being called "crime," for it is committed against the people as a whole. Whether the ways it describes to rip-off shit are legal or illegal is irrelevant. The dictionary of law is written by the bosses of order. Our moral dictionary says no heisting from each other. To steal from a brother or sister is evil. To *not* steal from the institutions that are the pillars of the Pig Empire is equally immoral.[82]

The premise of the rip-off philosophy is that U.S. society itself is a rip-off and that the major corporations in particular and capitalism in general are guilty of far greater crimes than any individual. Thievery thus becomes political behavior that incidentally allows the individual to survive while working against, instead of for, the system. According to Hoffman,

> all our rip-offs together don't equal one price-fixing scheme by General Electric [an event that we will discuss in Chapter 7]. What we have to create is a nation of revolutionary outlaws and do away with the concept of money entirely. We want a society where your birth certificate is your passport, and everything is free.[83]

Whether one views business as too evil, too big, or simply too incompetent, the result is the same. The rip-off philosophy provides a morality in which one can violate the law and victimize institutions without a sense of guilt. At the time of Hoffman's writing, a favorite target was the telephone company. Hoffman claimed that "ripping off the phone company is an act of revolutionary love."[84] In one year it was estimated that nearly $22 million free phone calls were made at the expense of American Telephone & Telegraph.[85] Since AT&T was making about $10 billion annual profit at the time, it may be that indignation was limited to hardened capitalists and/or stockholders. Nevertheless, for years, revolutionaries and nonrevolutionaries alike have challenged the ingenuity of the phone company with slugs, phony credit cards, and electronic tampering.

One of the most resourceful devices designed to cheat the phone company was the *blue box,* which emitted signals that allowed one to tap into long-distance systems. Its owner could make calls to anywhere in the world without paying. The more sophisticated users, known as *phone phreaks* (see Chapter 11), held extended conference calls with one another, tapped into the lines of unsuspecting callers, and talked to acquaintances in many foreign countries free of charge.[86] Phreaks were generally not revolutionaries; they had no interest in destroying the phone company, only in meeting its challenges:

> "Did you ever steal anything?"
> ["Well, yes, I—"]
> "Then you know! You know the rush you get. It's not just knowledge, like physical chemistry. It's forbidden knowledge. You know. You can learn about anything under the sun and be bored to death with it. But the idea that it's illegal. Look: you can be small and mobile and smart and you're ripping off somebody large and powerful and very dangerous."[87]

As technology advances, we also have advances in more schemes that determined thieves use to defraud. Cellular telephones, now abundant and inexpensive, have their codes ripped off by special instruments. These codes are then sold, and the unsuspecting cellular phone owner receives huge bills.

Finally, with the advent of computers and the Internet, we have the *computer hacker* and an array of other computer-based deviants. These individuals, for reasons stated above, enjoy manipulating computers. (This new phenomenon creates a wonderful opportunity for criminologists. They get to view the formation of laws to deal with the problem. As the result of a number of media scares on computer hacking, legislation was enacted to stem the problem.)[88] In Chapter 10, "cyberdeviance" is discussed in detail.

A spirit of thievery, of rip-offs, is present not only among the poor and disadvantaged but in nearly every segment of society, particularly when the target is seen as powerful and bureaucratic. Furthermore, this spirit is supported by a variety of motives ranging from excessive prices to class warfare to the unpolitical motive of pure adventure.

But if those who aspire to giant killing are not innocent, what of the "respectable" giants? Their deviance is usually surrounded by secrecy and subtlety—they do not use guns to rob—and their acts will not be found in the *Uniform Crime Reports.* In a later chapter we will find that the deviance of giants may ultimately cost more in dollars and human suffering than all the index property crimes combined.

C R I T I C A L   T H I N K I N G   E X E R C I S E S

1. How do bondsmen and attorneys participate in the burglar's world? What is a tipster? What is a fence? How does the thief or burglar depend on these people?

2. Describe the different types of auto thieves. In your opinion, should the courts treat the different types differently? Would your opinion change if your car were stolen and never recovered?

3. Describe the different types of shoplifters. In your opinion, is there a strong connection between shoplifting and drug consumption? Explain.

4. What is *pyromania?* What motivates this type of offender?

CHECK IT OUT ON THE WEB

The Internet addresses listed below are intended to provide the reader with understanding of a wide range of perspectives on the subject matter discussed in this chapter. Some sites may contain objectionable material. The list is not intended to reflect the viewpoints or opinions of the authors or the publisher.

http://www.bankersonline.com
    property crime security training
http://www.effga.com/evwap/
    victims' rights
http://www.robberycria.org
    robbery investigation
http://www.crimedoctor.com
    property crime prevention

ENDNOTES

1. U.S. Department of Justice, Federal Bureau of Investigation [FBI], *Crime in the United States, 2002 Uniform Crime Reports* (Washington, DC: U.S. Government Printing Office, 2003), p. 9.

2. U.S. Department of Justice, Bureau of Justice Statistics, *Criminal Victimization in the United States, 2002* (Washington, DC: U.S. Government Printing Office, February 2003), p. 11. The NCVS also breaks "robbery" into "robbery with injury" and "robbery without injury."

3. Bureau of Justice Statistics, *Criminal Victimization in the United States, 2002,* p. 11.

4. FBI, *Crime in the United States, 2002,* p. 31. See also Bureau of Justice Statistics, *Criminal Victimization in the United States, 1996,* p. x; and U.S. Department of Justice, Bureau of Justice Statistics, *Crime and the Nation's Households, 1992* (Washington, DC: U.S. Government Printing Office, August 1993), p. 2.

5. Callie Marie Rennison, *Criminal Victimization, 2002:* U.S. Department of Justice, Bureau of Justice Statistics (Washington, DC: U.S. Government Printing Office, August 2003), pp. 5. Additionally, this report as well as links to the UCR can be found at http://www.ojp.usdoj.gov/bjs/

6. FBI, *Crime in the United States, 2002,* p. 35.

7. Callie Marie Rennison, *Violent Victimization and Race, 1993–98,* U.S. Department of Justice, Bureau of Justice Statistics (Washington, DC: U.S. Government Printing Office, March 2001), p. 10.

8. Callie Marie Rennison, *Criminal Victimization in the United States, 2002,* pp. 6.

9. Callie Marie Rennison, *Criminal Victimization 1999: Changes 1998–99 with trends,* p. 10.

10. Ibid., p. 8.

11. FBI, *Crime in the United States, 1999,* p. 28, Table 2.20.

12. James J. Collins, Jr., "Alcohol Careers and Criminal Careers," and Judy Roizen, "Alcohol and Criminal Behavior Among Blacks: The Case for Research on Special Populations," both in *Drinking and Crime: Perspectives on the Relationships between Alcohol Consumption and Criminal Behavior,* ed. James J. Collins, Jr. (New York: Guilford Press, 1981), pp. 152–206, 207–252, respectively. Bureau of Justice Statistics, *Criminal Victimization in the United States, 1990* (p. 58) reports that nearly 25 percent of robbery victims believed the offender was under the influence of drugs or alcohol. For a study on

drug use and relationship to crime, see David Altshuler and Paul J. Brounstein, "Patterns of Drug Use, Drug Trafficking, and Other Delinquency Among Inner City Adolescent Males in Washington, DC," *Criminology, 29* (November 1991), pp. 589–622.

13. Edward Preble and John J. Casey, Jr., "Taking Care of Business—The Heroin User's Life on the Street," *International Journal of Addictions, 4* (March 1969), pp. 1–14; see also Altshuler and Brounstein, "Patterns of Drug Use," pp. 608–610.

14. Floyd Feeney and Adrianne Weir, "The Prevention and Control of Robbery," *Criminology, 13* (May 1975), p. 104.

15. "Gun Wielding Bandits Injure Fewer Victims," *Law Enforcement Administration Agency Newsletter, 8* (February 1979), p. 5.

16. John E. Conklin, *Robbery and the Criminal Justice System* (Philadelphia: J. B. Lippincott, 1972), pp. 1, 102–122; Arnold Sagalyn, *The Crime of Robbery in the United States* (Washington, DC: U.S. Department of Justice, Law Enforcement Assistance Administration, National Institute of Law Enforcement and Criminal Justice, 1971), pp. 8–10. For a discussion of victim confrontation in bank robbery, see Peter Letkemann, *Crime as Work* (Englewood Cliffs, NJ: Prentice-Hall, 1973), pp. 107–116; and James F. Haran and John M. Martin, "The Armed Urban Bank Robber: A Profile," *Federal Probation, 48* (December 1984), pp. 47–53.

17. Andre Normandeau, "Patterns in Robbery," *Criminologica, 6* (November 1968), p. 12. For analyses of force in robbery, see Philip J. Cook, "A Strategic Choice Analysis of Robbery," in *Sample Survey of the Victims of Crime,* ed. Wesley G. Skogan (Cambridge, MA: Ballinger, 1976), pp. 173–187; and David F. Luckenbill, "Patterns of Force in Robbery," *Deviant Behavior, 1* (April–September 1980), pp. 361–378.

18. For a discussion of the pitfalls of typologies, see Clayton A. Hartjen and Don C. Gibbons, "An Empirical Investigation of a Criminal Typology," *Sociology and Social Research, 54* (October 1969), pp. 56–62.

19. Conklin, *Robbery,* pp. 63–78.

20. Werner J. Einstadter, "The Social Organization of Armed Robbery," *Social Problems, 17* (Summer 1969), pp. 80–81.

21. Quoted in John Irwin, *The Felon* (Englewood Cliffs, NJ: Prentice-Hall, 1970), p. 11.

22. Conklin, *Robbery,* p. 76.

23. FBI, *Crime in the United States, 2002,* p. 45 and Callie Marie Rennison, *Criminal Victimization, 2002:* p. 3.

24. FBI, *Crime in the United States, 1999,* p. 29, 43. Additional information is contained in the Arrest Tables, pp. 222–232.

25. Ibid., p. 43.

26. This discussion is based on Nicholas Pileggi, "1968 Has Been the Year of the Burglar," *The New York Times Magazine,* November 17, 1968, pp. 54–80.

27. Quoted in ibid., pp. 54–80.

28. For a variety of typologies of burglars and their offenses, see Thomas A. Reppetto, *Residential Crime* (Cambridge, MA: Ballinger, 1974), pp. 23–26; Marilyn E. Walsh, *The Fence: A New Look at the World of Property Theft* (Westport, CT: Greenwood, 1977), pp. 61–65; and Carl E. Pope, *Crime-Specific Analysis: An Empirical Examination of Burglary Offense and Offender Characteristics,* Utilization of Criminal Justice Statistics Project, Analytic Report 12 (Washington, DC: U.S. Department of Justice, Law Enforcement Assistance Administration, National Criminal Justice Information and Statistics Service, 1977). For discussions of the professional, see Harry King (as told to and edited by Bill Chambliss), *Box Man: A Professional Thief's Journey* (New York: Harper & Row, 1972); and Letkemann, *Crime as Work,* pp. 49–89.

29. William E. Cobb, "Theft and the Two Hypotheses," Gregory Krohm, "The Pecuniary Incentive of Property Crime," and J. Patrick Gunning, Jr., "How Profitable Is Burglary?," all in *The Economics of Crime and Punishment,* ed. Simon Rottenberg (Washington, DC: American Enterprise Institute for Public Policy Research, 1973), pp. 19–38. For a discussion on the value of crime, see James Q. Wilson and Richard J. Herrnstein, *Crime and Human Nature* (New York: Simon & Schuster, 1985), pp. 412–416; and for an examination of the relationship of income inequality and crime, particularly concerning burglary rates that are higher in areas with large youthful populations, see E. Britt Patterson, "Poverty, Income Inequality, and Community Crime Rates," *Criminology, 29* (November 1991), pp. 755–776.

30. Neal Shover, "Structures and Careers in Burglary," *Journal of Criminal Law, Criminology, and Police Science, 63* (December 1972), pp. 540–549; and Neal Shover, "The Social Organization of Burglary," *Social Problems, 20* (Spring 1973), pp. 499–514.

31. Shover, "Social Organization," p. 510. For a review of how this entire process works (or doesn't), see Samuel Walker, *Sense and Nonsense About Crime: A Policy Guide,* 2nd ed. (Belmont, CA: Brooks/Cole Publishing Company, 1989), pp. 36–54, 70–71.

32. For a variety of analyses of fencing, see Ted Roselius and Douglas Benton, "Marketing Theory and the Fencing of Stolen Goods," *Denver Law Journal, 50:* 2 (1973), pp. 177–205; Carl B. Klockars, *The Professional Fence* (New York: The Free Press, 1974); and Walsh, *The Fence.*

33. Callie Marie Rennison, *Criminal Victimization 1999: Changes 1998–99 with Trends 1993–99,* p. 11.

34. FBI, *Crime in the United States, 1993,* p. 50.

35. Ibid.

36. Callie Marie Rennison, *Criminal Victimization 2002,* p. 10; and FBI, *Crime in the United States, 2002,* p. 53.

37. FBI, *Crime in the United States, 2002,* p. 55.

38. Ibid.

39. FBI, *Crime in the United States, 2002,* p. 53.

40. William W. Wattenberg and James Balistrieri, "Automobile Theft: A 'Favored Group' Delinquency," *American Journal of Sociology, 57* (May 1952), pp. 575–579.

41. Charles H. McCaghy, Peggy C. Giordano, and Trudy Knicely Henson, "Auto Theft: Offender and Offense Characteristics," *Criminology, 15* (November 1977), pp. 367–385.

42. This discussion is based on John Russell, "Organized Crime Seen in Auto Thefts," *Automotive News,* June 16, 1980, p. 43; Richard Paton and Jon Chavez, "Stolen Car Can Become Hot Parts in 28 Minutes," *The Blade* (Toledo, Oh), November 30, 1980, pp. 1, 8; and Chitra Ragavan and David E. Kaplan, *Why Auto Theft Is Going Global,* U.S. News Online. [Online]. Available: http://www.usnews.com/usnews/issue/990614/auto.htm

43. Quoted in Peter Hellman, "Stealing Cars Is a Growth Industry," *The New York Times Magazine,* June 20, 1971, p. 45; see also Ruth Gastel, Editor, "Auto Theft," *III Insurance Issues Update 2004,* May 2004.

44. Callie Marie Rennison, *Criminal Victimization 1999: Changes 1998–99 with Trends 1993–99,* p. 11.

45. FBI, *Crime in the United States, 2002,* p. 52.

46. William E. Cobb, "Shoplifting," in *Crime in Society,* ed. Leonard D. Savitz and Norman Johnston (New York: John Wiley, 1978), pp. 924–925; Isador Barmash, "Pilferage Abounds in the Nation's Stores," *The New York Times,* October 28, 1973, sec. 3, p. 9; Isador Barmash, "In Retailing, Shrinkage Is Outdistancing Profits," *The New York Times,* April 12, 1970, sec. 3, p. 1; Calmetta Coleman, "Sticky Fingers: As Thievery by Insiders Overtakes Shoplifting, Retailers Crack Down," *The Wall Street Journal,* September 8, 2000, p. A1; see also Kelly Norton, "Cashing in on CCTV Technology," *Security Management,* March 1992, special supplement, p. 26A.

47. Steve Lottes, "What's in Store with EAS?" *Security Management,* March 1992, special supplement, p. 20A.

48. Norton, "Cashing in on CCTV Technology," p. 26A.

49. http://web.soc.ufl.edu/SRP/NRSS_2001.pdf

50. Barmash, "In Retailing," p. 1; and Hellman, "One in Ten," p. 34.

51. "The Siege on Supermarkets," *Security Management,* March 1980, p. 7.

52. "Shop Till You Stop," *The Sacramento Bee,* October 6, 2000, p. 18A.

53. Mary Owen Cameron, *The Booster and the Snitch: Department Store Shoplifting* (New York: The Free Press, 1964), pp. 39–60.

54. Cobb, "Shoplifting," pp. 929–930.

55. Ibid., p. 929.

56. P. James Carolin, Jr., "Survey of Shoplifters," *Security Management,* March 1992, special supplement, p. 11A.

57. Hellman, "One in Ten," p. 34; and Read Hayes, "Tailoring Security to Fit the Criminal," *Security Management 43:* 7 (July 1999), pp. 111–116.

58. Cameron, *The Booster and the Snitch,* pp. 59–60; for a discussion on females and shoplifting, see also Meda Chesney-Lind and Randall G. Shelden, *Girls, Delinquency, and Juvenile Justice* (Pacific Grove, CA: Brooks/Cole Publishing Company, 1992), pp. 42–44.

59. Hellman, "One in Ten," pp. 34, 39; cf. Cameron, *The Booster and the Snitch,* p. 49.

60. "Retail Shrinkage," *Security,* April 1991, p. 10; and for a recent Canadian study of this issue, see Benedikt Fischer, Wendy Medved, Maritt Kirst, Jurgen Rhem, and Louis Gliksman, "Illicit Opiates and Crime: Results of an Untreated User Cohort Study in Toronto," *Canadian Journal of Criminology, 43:* 2 (April 2001), pp. 197–217.

61. Robert E. Kraut, "Deterrent and Definitional Influences on Shoplifting," *Social Problems, 23* (February 1976), pp. 358–368; and Kevin B. Bales, "Contrast and Complementarity in Three Theories of Criminal Behavior," *Deviant Behavior, 3* (January–March 1982), pp. 155–173.

62. Darrell J. Steffensmeier and Robert M. Terry, "Deviance and Respectability: An Observational Study of Reactions to Shoplifting," *Social Forces, 51* (June 1973), p. 418.

63. Ibid., pp. 422–424. For an analysis of other variables from the same study, see Robert M. Terry and Darrell J. Steffensmeier, "The Influence of Organizational Factors of Victim Store on Willingness to Report a Shoplifting Incident: A Field Experiment," *Sociological Focus, 6* (Fall 1973), pp. 27–45.

64. Donald P. Hartmann, Donna M. Gelfand, Brent Page, and Patrice Walder, "Rates of Bystander Observation and Reporting of Contrived Shoplifting Incidents," *Criminology, 10* (November 1972), pp. 247–267. For a related study, see Leonard Bickman and Helen Helwig, "Bystander Reporting of a Crime: The Impact of Incentives," *Criminology, 17* (November 1979), pp. 283–300.

65. Barton Weitz, Richard Hollinger, and Read Hayes, *National Retail Security Survey, 1991,* p. 10.

66. Lawrence Cohen and Rodney Stark, "Discriminatory Labeling and the Five-Finger Discount: An Empirical Analysis of Differential Shoplifting Dispositions," *Journal of Research in Crime and Delinquency, 11* (January 1974), pp. 25–39; Michael J. Hindelang, "Decisions of Shoplifting Victims to Invoke the Criminal Justice Process," *Social Problems, 21* (April 1974), pp. 580–593; and Richard J. Lundman, "Shoplifting and Police Referral: A

Reexamination," *Journal of Criminal Law and Criminology, 69* (Fall 1978), pp. 395–401.

67. FBI, *Crime in the United States, 1999,* p. 55.

68. Patrick G. Jackson, "Assessing the Validity of Official Data on Arson," *Criminology, 26* (February 1988), p. 185.

69. Ibid., pp. 182–183.

70. FBI, *Crime in the United States, 1999,* p. 56.

71. Ibid.

72. John F. Boudreau, Quon Y. Kwan, William E. Faragher, and Genevieve C. Denault, *Arson and Arson Investigation: Survey and Assessment* (Washington, DC: U.S. Department of Justice, Law Enforcement Assistance Administration, National Institute of Law Enforcement and Criminal Justice, 1977), pp. 5–12.

73. This material is taken from the National Fire Protection Association Web site, http://www.nfpa.org/PressRoom/NewsReleases/ArsonDrops/ArsonDrops.asp, media release.

74. Paraphrased from *Arson Prevention and Control: Program Model* (Washington, DC: U.S. Department of Justice, Law Enforcement Assistance Administration, National Institute of Law Enforcement and Criminal Justice, 1980), p. 5; see also National Fire Protection Association Web site in note 73.

75. *Arson Prevention and Control,* pp. 1–2.

76. Paraphrased from ibid., pp. 7–9.

77. "16 Pennsylvania Firemen Face Arson Charges," *Daily Sentinel-Tribune* (Bowling Green, OH), February 4, 1983, p. 3.

78. See annual National Crime Victimization Survey Reports on the Bureau of Justice Web site, http://www.ojp.usdoj.gov/bjs/pub/ascii/cvus92.txt, for an explanation of why people fail to report crime to the police.

79. FBI, *Crime in the United States, 2002,* pp. 222.

80. This discussion and the quotations are from Michael S. Lasky, "One in 3 Hotel Guests Is a Towel Thief, Bible Pincher, or Worse," *The New York Times,* January 27, 1974, sec. 10, pp. 1, 18–19.

81. Erwin O. Smigel, "Public Attitudes Toward Stealing as Related to the Size of the Victim Organization," *American Sociological Review, 21* (June 1956), pp. 320–327; and Melanie Payne, "Worker Theft Rising Concern for Businesses," *The Sacramento Bee,* November 27, 2000, p. D1.

82. Abbie Hoffman, *Steal This Book* (New York: Pirate Editions, 1971), p. iv.

83. Quoted in Michael Drosnin, "Ripping Off, the New Life-Style," *The New York Times Magazine,* August 8, 1971, p. 52.

84. Hoffman, *Steal This Book,* p. 75.

85. Drosnin, "Ripping Off," p. 13.

86. Ron Rosenbaum, "Secrets of the Little Blue Box," *Esquire, 75* (October 1971), pp. 117–125, 222–226.

87. Quoted in ibid., p. 223. Also see Steven Levy, "The Miserable Life of a Phone Hacker," *Rolling Stone,* September 27, 1984, p. 91.

88. Richard C. Hollinger and Lonn Lanz-Kaduce, "The Process of Criminalization: The Case of Computer Crime Laws," *Criminology, 26* (February 1988), pp. 101–126.

6 Assaults against Children and Spouses

This chapter concerns child abuse—both physical and sexual—and spouse abuse. In one respect, these acts are similar because they involve at least the implicit threat of violence, as in the case of child molestation, which usually is not blatantly forceful. The theme of violence makes the acts similar to the assaults discussed in the last chapter. But they are also different because these acts are particularly private and secret; they are typically insulated from outsiders' knowledge and interference. This isolation is understandable when we consider the contexts of many of these assaults: they are not "street crimes"; rather, they occur in the home or in other situations in which the victims could assume that they are among friends. The participants usually are not strangers but people who have special bonds to one another. And the victims do not readily seek the help of outsiders because the victims are indifferent or ignorant, feel powerless, fear retaliation, or are reluctant to do anything that jeopardizes their relationship with the assaulters. Adding further to the isolation surrounding these assaults is most outsiders' reluctance to meddle in other people's "personal" matters.

Of course, one's spouse and children are about as personal as one can get. That is why the topics of this chapter are so difficult to study and to characterize. Homes and families are sanctuaries—places of immunity from many of the restrictions of society. Yet society's members must be protected from harm and exploitation, wherever they may be. At what point is societal interference in personal matters justified? When does a child's "discipline" or a family "spat" become a matter of social concern? When does a father's or uncle's "affection" for a child reach the point at which personal matters should become public ones? The assaults discussed in this chapter involve both special victims and special circumstances. While they share the theme of violence with other types of assaults, they are unique in their dynamics and in what they tell us about social institutions.

Physical Abuse of Children

The following verse is found in Lewis Carroll's classic work *Alice in Wonderland:*

> *Speak roughly to your little boy,*
> *And beat him when he sneezes:*
> *He only does it to annoy,*
> *Because he knows it teases.*

Carroll did not dislike children. He was parodying a popular poem of the time, the mid-1800s, when the death rate for children was considerably higher than it is now. Included among its verses is

Speak gently to the little child!
Its love be sure to gain;
Teach it in accents soft and mild;
It may not long remain.[1]

Although the poem deserves Carroll's ridicule, his humor may hit a sour note today, a time of increased awareness of children as victims. An idealistic view of children is that they lead carefree lives as objects of parental love and joy. But realistically, they are simply part of the adult world with all its stresses and frustrations. Despite their innocence, children become victims of the same outrages afflicting adults: They are cheated, beaten, and sexually violated. Paradoxically, it is perhaps *because* of their innocence that children are victimized. After all, they are potentially ideal victims. Relative to most adults, they are physically weaker, more easily persuaded, and less understanding of the nature and consequences of behavior. In short, children have few personal resources with which to defend themselves upon being victimized. Furthermore, children may not recognize their situation as victims. Young incest victims, for example, may accept father-daughter sexual relations as normal—a perception that incestuous fathers often encourage.

The vulnerability of children is obvious. Less obvious is what fosters the exploitation and harm of children in a society that characteristically esteems them. As the reader will soon discover, a satisfactory explanation is not available. This is due in large part to the recency of the problem. This is not to say that the abuse of children is a new development; rather, it is the *social perception of the problem* that is new.

The bulk of research on physical abuse of children has been published within the past three decades, and while research on sexual molestation has a somewhat older history, that topic has also received its greatest public attention recently. As a result, most studies of child abuse are descriptive—they provide information of incidence, offender characteristics, and victim characteristics. The theoretical explanations are tentative and untested. However, our knowledge about child abuse has grown rapidly and offers insights concerning possible causes.

Child abuse has quickly become a visible, serious issue for two reasons. First, there has been a growing awareness that victims, of all kinds, were frequently victimized a second time by an uncaring criminal justice system. Victims of even horrific crimes never heard a word concerning the status of the police investigation. They were not informed of plea bargains and frequently found out about the disposition of an offender in the newspaper or on the TV news. Too, the victim was never compensated for losses.[2] As the most "innocent" of victims, children as victims and the entire issue of child abuse received a great deal of attention.

Second, our distress over child abuse and neglect is magnified by the understanding that this violence repeats itself (this is called the "cycle of violence"). Abused children may become child abusers or spouse abusers. This assertion may be valid or not; more research must be conducted.[3] We do have research that clearly demonstrates that there is evidence that childhood abuse and neglect may foster adult criminal behavior. For example, a recent report on women offenders finds that nearly 44 percent of women in state prisons, in local jails, or on probation had experienced physical or sexual abuse at some time in their lives. Specifically, 69 percent of women prisoners reported experiencing abuse before age 18.[4] Cathy Spatz Widom summarizes her study by stating that

> the current findings indicate that being abused as a child significantly increases one's risk of having an adult criminal record (and, for males, of having an adult record for a violent crime); however, the pathway from childhood victimization to adult criminal behavior is far from inevitable. While 29% of the abused and neglected subjects had adult criminal records, the majority (71%) did not.[5]

Research in this area, however, is still in its early stages.[6]

Problems of Definition

We will divide our discussion of assaults on children into two sections: physical abuse and sexual contacts. To the casual reader these may appear sufficiently precise to outline the problem. In one instance the problem is physical injury of children; in the other it is sexual conduct between adults and children. But defining child assaults is really not so simple, because a child can be victimized in a great variety of ways.

Some writers approach the issue in a grand manner. David G. Gil, for example, believes that society should not merely protect the child from harm but should provide the best possible environment for the child's development. Consequently, his definition of child abuse is comprehensive:

> Every child, despite his individual differences and uniqueness, is to be considered of equal intrinsic worth and hence should be entitled to equal social, economic, civil and political rights, so that he may fully realize his inherent potential and share equally in life, liberty and happiness. Obviously, these value premises are rooted in the humanistic philosophy of our Declaration of Independence.
>
> In accordance with the value premises, then, any act of commission or omission by individuals, institutions, or society as a whole, and any conditions resulting from such acts or inaction, which deprive children of equal rights and liberties, and/or interfere with their optimal development, constitute, by definition, abusive or neglectful acts or conditions.[7]

Gil's definition is highly idealistic; but more important, it is imprecise: applied to an individual case, it might be difficult to prove that "optimal development" had been interfered with. Furthermore, the definition assumes that someone—the state, social workers, or whoever—knows better than the parents what is best for a child. This is an unwarranted assumption, and a dangerous one insofar as parental autonomy is concerned.

Gil's definition is not uniquely imprecise. According to Mary Porter Martin,

> one of the central issues in the field of child abuse and neglect is that of defining the problem. The vagueness and ambiguities that surround the definition of this particular social problem touch every aspect of the field. The way in which one defines abuse and neglect affects what is reported and how many reports are made, which in turn affects the effort to assess an incidence rate. . . . Using a broad definition, abuse and neglect include all acts that

interfere with the optimal development of children. This definition leaves open the issue of what is the optimal development of a child and what acts interfere with this development. At the other extreme, abuse and neglect include only those acts that result in observable injuries, a definition that excludes an uncomfortably large number of children who do not exhibit observable injuries yet are abused and neglected.[8]

Each state even has its own definition of child abuse and unique requirements on reporting and investigation, although "child abuse" is now a general term that refers to both actual physical abuse and neglect.[9] Fortunately, when the search for an adequate definition fails, the labeling perspective becomes especially helpful. (See the discussion of labeling in Chapter 3.) Instead of "What is child abuse?" the more plausible question is "What acts are identified as child abuse?" The emphasis thus shifts from the abstract and idealistic toward real events that are designated as requiring official reaction.[10] Toward this end, Jeanne M. Giovannoni and Rosina M. Becerra surveyed professionals—lawyers, social workers, police, and pediatricians—to ascertain the types of behavior they perceive as mistreatment of children. Nine general categories emerged from the data.[11] These categories and some selected examples of behavior are shown in Table 6.1.

As the reader can see, professionals dealing with abuse cases are concerned with more than direct assaults. There are also varying concerns with several forms of *neglect* and even with the *moral climate* of the households, as indicated by the category of parental sexual mores in Table 6.1. Although professionals agree on the relevance of a *general* category, they may disagree over specific behaviors fitting that category. For example, professionals may regard parents' sexual habits as indicating the potential for mistreatment. But not all professionals would agree that the homosexuality of a single parent warrants intervention, because there is no evidence that a parent's sexual orientation in itself jeopardizes a child. Disagreement occurs even for the category of physical abuse. Whereas professionals concur on the seriousness of severe injuries, they dispute whether some forms of physical punishment, such as hitting a child with a stick, constitute mistreatment.[12]

In light of all situations that may—or may not—be interpreted as mistreatment, one can see why a precise definition of child abuse is elusive and why it is likely to remain so. In this chapter, we will concentrate on instances in which abuse seems most evident: those involving violence or sexual activities. We begin with a discussion of how physical abuse was "discovered."

The Discovery and Medicalization of Physical Abuse

As mentioned, official concern over the abuse of children is a recent matter. It is important to understand that social perceptions of children have changed over time. In fact, the very notion of *childhood* itself is relatively new. Until the 1600s babies were regarded as noisy, undomesticated animals; after they had passed the total dependency stage of infancy, they were treated as essentially miniature adults who were expected to contribute to the support of the family. The idea that a special phase exists between infancy and adulthood has developed over the past 300 years, during which time children, particularly those of the middle and upper classes, have been increasingly seen as innocent and dependent creatures needing skilled guidance and protection. Instead of automatically becoming adults, children had to be carefully prepared for adulthood by both the family and the state.[13]

TABLE 5.1   Categories of Child Abuse and Neglect, in Declining Order of Seriousness, as Perceived by Professionals

General Category	Selected Examples
Physical abuse	Parents burn child on buttocks and chest with a cigarette. Parents usually punish child by spanking with a leather strap.
Sexual abuse	On one occasion, the parent and child engage in sexual intercourse. Parents have intercourse where child can see them.
Fostering delinquency	Parents make child steal small articles from the supermarket. Parents make child take stolen merchandise to store that sells it illegally.
Supervision	Parents regularly leave child alone outside the house after dark, often as late as midnight. Parents live in an old house. Two windows in the living room where the child plays have been broken for some time, and the glass has very jagged edges.
Emotional mistreatment	Parents dress their son in girl's clothing, sometimes putting makeup on him. They keep long curls on him. Parents constantly compare child with younger sibling, sometimes implying that the child is not really their own.
Drug/alcohol	Parents always allow child to stay around when they have friends over to experiment with cocaine. Parents leave bottles of whiskey around the house in places where child can get to them.
Failure to provide	Parents ignore the fact that child is obviously ill, crying constantly, and not eating. Parents do not wash child at all.
Educational neglect	Parents frequently keep child out of school. Parents never see to it that children do any homework. They let them watch TV all evening.
Parental sexual mores	Parents permit a relative who is a prostitute to bring customers to their house.

Source: Adapted from Jeanne M. Giovannoni and Rosina M. Becerra, *Defining Child Abuse* (New York: The Free Press, 1979), pp. 264–270.

Reflecting children's status up until the nineteenth century is the absence of laws specifically dealing with children:

There were, for example, no special laws relating to homicide or assault and battery of children: rather, children were assumed to be protected from such events by the same laws that protected adults. The same was true of sexual assault and incest, although definitions of rape did include a lower age limit for consenting females. Under the poor laws children enjoyed no special status. As public charges they were disposed of in the most efficient way, as were adults. . . . Finally, children were subject to the same criminal laws and punishments as adults, though here there was a demarcation: the "age of reason," which is essentially a

religious concept rather than a legal one. . . . In effect, deviant acts by or against children were handled pretty much as they were for adults.[14]

In short, until recently, children were not regarded as being legally special.

The most dramatic changes in children's legal status in connection with abuse began in the second half of the nineteenth century.[15] A well-publicized trial concerning cruelty to an 8-year-old girl led to the founding of the New York Society for the Prevention of Cruelty to Children (SPCC) in 1874. This was the first organization designed to seek out mistreated children, remove them from their homes, and undertake legal action to punish the mistreaters. Today, the idea that abused children can be taken from the control of their families is not an unusual one. But in the 1800s such actions by the SPCC set a precedent that departed from the legal assumption that the family was inviolate from state interference. The SPCC and other reform groups argued that some family situations were not satisfactory environments for children's development and health. Thus in some cases the state should intervene for the good of the children and, ultimately, for the good of society.

In the decades that followed, the SPCC and other child protective groups incorporated under the American Humane Association lobbied for state laws creating a class of children for which states were responsible: the "ill treated." The eventual legal definitions of ill-treated children differed from state to state, but they usually included references to child labor; endangered health; torture; deprivations of shelter, food, or clothing; sexual abuse; and several moral matters ranging from having habitually drunken parents to being allowed to beg.[16]

Despite this legislative activity, however, interest in child abuse as a social issue declined during the first half of this century. The reasons are varied and complex, but two appear especially relevant. First, the philosophy of the times was, "Any home is better than no home at all." Thus there was judicial reluctance to remove children from the home except in cases where the children themselves were delinquent. In short, the courts felt that except in the most extreme cases the family knew best how to handle children. Second, with the emergence of professional social work, an emphasis was placed on the *prevention* of abuse. As a result, social workers asked for court action against the family only as the last resort. In any event, both judicial and public interest in child abuse practically disappeared until its revitalization following World War II.

According to Stephen J. Pfohl, concern over physically abused children during the first half of this century was simply part of a more general interest in children's welfare. There was no focus on physical abuse as a separate child protection issue distinct from problems of neglect, delinquency, and especially poverty.[17] In the 1950s, however, the discovery of the "battered child syndrome" resulted in defining physical abuse both as a *specific form of deviance* and as a *disease.*

The battered child syndrome was discovered not by social workers or police but by pediatric radiologists—physicians specializing in children's X-rays. They found young children displaying a variety of hidden injuries (e.g., internal hemorrhages, certain types of bone fractures) that were unexplainable by children's normal activities and that came to be associated with the parents' use of force. The idea that children are sometimes injured by their parents was scarcely a revelation to social workers, but the physicians' research on the subject provided a new dimension. The most highly respected profession—medicine—had found a new "disease"—child abuse.

The emergence of child abuse as a medical issue was not a fortuitous event. Pfohl claims that hospital physicians and pediatricians logically should have discovered child abuse long before the radiologists did, since they are first to see injured children, especially in hospital emergency rooms. But three factors forestalled earlier medical recognition:

1. Many physicians were unwilling to believe that parents would abuse their children. This was consistent with the cultural assumption that parents can do little wrong when it comes to handling their children.
2. Physicians were concerned about violating the confidentiality of the physician-patient relationship. While technically the child was the patient, there was also the possibility that a diagnostic error could result in legal repercussions from the parents. Thus physicians were discouraged from claiming that abuse had probably occurred.
3. Physicians were reluctant about becoming involved in the legal process. Time-consuming judicial proceedings and defense counsel's attempts to discredit the evidence were inconveniences physicians felt they could do without.[18]

Radiologists, on the other hand, had few of these reasons to restrain them. Because radiologists interpret X-rays without direct contact with the patients, they had the luxury of being removed from the subjective and emotional aspects of physician-family relationships. Furthermore, according to Pfohl, radiologists comprised an *interest group* with much to gain from their discovery of child abuse. First, radiology was a marginal and low-prestige specialization within the medical community because it entailed research, not "working with people." This changed with the discovery of child abuse; now radiologists' skills became a crucial aspect in patient diagnosis. Second, the discovery meant that the lower-status radiologists could form an alliance with higher-status pediatricians and psychiatrists. This triple coalition benefited all parties: The radiologists helped the pediatricians spot abusive families whom the psychiatrists could treat. Third and finally, radiologists gained stature in the medical community by finding a new "disease." What might have been regarded as a legal and social issue became a medical one complete with appropriate medical terminology: the disease was called the "battered child syndrome."

According to Pfohl,

> a diagnostic category had been invented and publicized. Psychological obstacles in recognizing parents as capable of abuse were eased by the separation of normatively powerful parents from non-normatively pathological individuals. Problems associated with perceiving parents as patients whose confidentiality must be protected were reconstructed by typifying them as patients who needed help. Moreover, the maintenance of professional autonomy was assured by pairing deviance with sickness. This last statement is testimony to the power of medical nomenclature. It was evidenced by the fact that (prior to its publication) the report which coined the label "battered child syndrome" was endorsed by a Children's Bureau conference which included social workers and law enforcement officials as well as doctors.[19]

Publicity about the newly discovered disease brought an avalanche of activity. Within four years (1963–1966), all 50 states passed laws requiring that suspected abuse cases be reported by physicians.[20] The most dramatic result was in Florida, where new laws, a statewide toll-free telephone number, and a public information campaign shot the number of reported abuse cases from 17 to 19,120 in a single year.[21] In addition, federal and state agencies began funding research on the extent, cause, and treatment of abuse. By the early 1970s results from the research began pouring forth. Child abuse had been solidly established as a major public problem.

Extent

What does research tell us about the dimension of child abuse? In seeking to answer this question, the reader should remember that in practice the concept of abuse is a matter of interpretation by those in positions to say authoritatively, "This child has (or has not) been abused." As Richard J. Gelles points out, child abuse is a *social construction:*

> All the cases that make up the data on incidence, all the explanatory analyses, and all the prevention and treatment models are influenced by the *social process* by which individuals and groups are labeled and designated as deviants. In other words, there is no objective behavior we can automatically recognize as child abuse. . . .
>
> When I speak of the social construction of abuse, I mean the process by which: (a) a definition of abuse is constructed; (b) certain judges or "gatekeepers" are selected for applying the definition; (c) the definition is applied by designating the labels "abuse" and "abuser" to particular individuals and families.[22]

Because child abuse lacks a precise definition and because it is a social construction, the reader will not be surprised to learn that estimates of its extent are highly variable. The first national survey on abuse was conducted in 1965.[23] Respondents were asked whether during the last year they "personally knew families involved in incidents of child abuse resulting in physical injury." From this study, it was estimated that 4 million such cases occurred annually. The survey subjects were also asked if they *themselves* had abused children. On the basis of their responses the estimate was dropped to 2.5 million cases annually. In a reanalysis of the survey data, the estimate was again dropped to between 200,000 and 500,000 children abused each year.[24] Estimates from other studies range from as low as 30,000 to 1.5 million.[25]

A more comprehensive survey of parental violence against children was conducted in 1976. The researchers—Murray A. Straus, Richard J. Gelles, and Suzanne K. Steinmetz—sidestepped the problem of defining abuse by focusing on a range of violent acts. From interviews with 1,146 parents the researchers found that 63 percent had engaged in at least one violent act against their children during the year prior to the interviews. Does this mean that 63 percent of the parents were "abusive"? Not exactly. The researchers used a broad definition of violence—so broad that some might question whether a few of the acts included are violent. The researchers defined violence as

> an "act carried out with the intention, or perceived intention, of causing physical pain or injury to another person." The "physical pain" can range from slight pain, as in a slap, to murder. The basis for the "intent to hurt" may range from a concern with a child's safety (as when a child is spanked for running into the street) to hostility so intense that the death of the other is desired.[26]

It appears that the researchers found that defining violence has as many pitfalls as defining abuse. They decided to make the term *violence* all-inclusive:

We chose . . . to employ a broad definition that includes acts which are not normally thought to be violent because we wanted to draw attention to the issue of people hitting one another in their own families. We call this hitting "violence" because we would like to have people begin to question the acts which traditionally they have taken for granted as necessary, useful, inevitable, or instinctive.[27]

This (if you will excuse the pun) smacks of moral crusading, but it does not make the survey's results any less interesting. The following are the percentages of parents reporting episodes of violence against children over the year-long period studied:

58.2 percent slapped or spanked
40.5 percent pushed, grabbed, or shoved
13.4 percent hit with something
 5.4 percent threw something
 3.2 percent kicked, bit, or hit with a fist
 1.3 percent beat
 0.1 percent threatened with a knife or gun
 0.1 percent used a knife or gun[28]

The researchers considered the last four categories as the most dangerous forms of violence. By combining them, Straus and his colleagues estimated that between 1.4 and 1.9 million children were "vulnerable" to injury during the survey year. Of course, being "vulnerable" does not mean being "abused," so the figures are probably *over*estimates of abuse. But the researchers insist that they *under*estimated the extent of abuse because the data were based on self-admissions and do not include information on some severe forms of violence such as burning or torturing. Furthermore, the sample did not involve single-parent families and children under 3 years of age, both of which are associated with relatively high rates of abuse.[29] In 1988 Gelles and Straus conducted another national survey and determined that serious abuse had declined, but the estimate of 1.5 million remained.[30] Some recent data, derived from a survey conducted by the National Child Abuse and Neglect Reporting System, determined that 2,600,000 referrals were made in 2002. Of these, three-fifths were transferred for investigation or assessment, and two-fifths were screened out.[31] These data may be getting close to the real figure. But owing to the nature of this crime, the true extent of abuse is really impossible to calculate. While we may be finally getting closer to establishing the incidence of abuse, the studies by Straus and others do provide insights into some characteristics of U.S. family violence against children.

Characteristics

The reader will recall that child abuse was "discovered" as a "disease" in the 1960s. Consistent with the disease model, much research focused on abusive parents as people suffering from mental illness. This is a seductive model: It assumes that there must be something wrong with anyone who would act in such a wrongful way. But research findings have not supported the model. There seems to be no single common psychological trait or set of traits that consistently characterizes abusers. Indeed, it appears that abusers cannot adequately be described without reference to sociocultural and situational factors.[32]

Which sociocultural and situational factors reliably describe abusers? In light of the difficulties in identifying *what* abuse is, it is not surprising to find little consensus about *who* abusers are. The best—although not necessarily conclusive—evidence indicates that abusers seem to be disproportionately numerous among the following:[33]

Females who are single parents and who are employed outside the home
Parents who are socially isolated from their neighbors and community
Families with four to seven children
Families with children who were born premature, physically handicapped, or mentally retarded
Parents with unrealistic expectations about their children's capabilities
Parents who are inconsistent in disciplining children
Parents who themselves were abused as children
Lower-income families
Families under stress—emotional, physical, or economic

There may also be a connection between child abuse and biological relationships. On October 20, 1998, CNN News reported on Dr. Michael Stiffman's finding, based on his study of children under the age of 5 in 1992–1995, that children are eight times more likely to die from injuries in homes where a biologically unrelated adult, usually a live-in boyfriend, is present.[34]

What do these findings tell us about the sources of abuse? Not as much as they might seem to at first glance. In the first place, the great majority of studies producing these conclusions are methodologically inadequate. Their samples of abusing families are small and unrepresentative and are rarely contrasted to data on nonabusing families. In the second place, it appears that abusing families are far more diverse than the findings imply. It would be impossible to select any combination of these characteristics and say with assurance that they distinguish abusing from nonabusing families.[35] It may be true, for example, that lower-income parents who were abused themselves and who have a mentally defective child may abuse that child in a relatively high number of cases. But this finding's value in explaining abuse is considerably diminished when one realizes that most parents with these characteristics do not abuse their children and that the great majority of abusing parents are not so characterized. In short, distinguishing families who abuse from those who do not is an uncertain art, and, as a consequence, explaining abuse remains tentative. Despite the doubtfulness of the data, many researchers anticipate that one variable ultimately will emerge as the underlying cause of child abuse: *stress.*

Stress, Power, and Culture

One of the first writers to hypothesize stress as a crucial child abuse variable was David G. Gil, whom we mentioned earlier in connection with his comprehensive definition of abuse. Gil expresses concern over the relatively high number of reported rates of physical abuse among nonwhite and lower-income families.[36] He claims that although biased reporting procedures might be partly responsible for this finding, they cannot explain away the relationship between social class and abuse, because underreporting is widespread for all groups. He postulates that tensions associated with limited economic resources, frustrations generated by discrimination, large numbers of children, and limited living space may produce stress, which, in turn, weakens self-control over aggression against children. Gil argues that in the context of a society that supports physical force as an aspect of child-rearing, stress may be the catalyst for abuse.

Gelles elaborates on stress in discussing his "social psychological model of the causes of child abuse."[37] He outlines the following categories of stress: (1) stress between parents (e.g., marital disputes); (2) structural stress (e.g., a large number of children, unemployment, social isolation, and so on); and (3) child-produced stress (e.g., an unwanted child or a problem child who is physically deformed, mentally retarded, and so on). Gelles is careful to point out, however, that stress is only one component of the model, which also includes such factors as the parents' socialization experiences (being abused as a child, for instance), social position, and community or subcultural standards regarding violence.

In a survey of family violence, stress was examined as a major variable. Using a "stress index" of 18 items (such as serious sickness or injury, troubles with the boss, in-law troubles, and financial difficulties), Straus, Gelles, and Steinmetz found that the more stress events experienced by a family, the greater the likelihood that a parent would be abusive toward a child.[38] But—and a big "but" it is—they also found that

> stress among the very poor and the well-to-do has no effect in terms of increasing the chances of child abuse within these families. But for the middle income families—those with earnings between $6,000 and $20,000—increased stress does raise the risk of a child's being physically abused.[39]

The researchers go on to say that this finding indicates that stress is a matter of "business as usual" for the poor:

> The poor, by virtue of being poor, encounter stress as a normal part of their lives. For the poor, stress is life, it is not a major crisis. An increase in stress is often considered inevitable. [Furthermore] the rates of violence for the poor are already high. It would take much more extreme crisis to push the rates higher still.[40]

The problem is that if social class and stress are interrelated, can it be assumed that stress is the crucial variable in explaining abuse? No, because that conclusion requires more rigorous designs than researchers have used. According to Audrey M. Berger,

> stress may be an important antecedent to abuse. However, since lower class families experience a disproportionate number of stressors, and since most identified abusing families are from the lower social classes, stress and socioeconomic class are confounded. Since most lower class families do not abuse their children, it cannot be concluded on the basis of most available data that the stressors associated with poverty cause child abuse.
>
> A number of approaches could, however, be taken to investigate the role of environmental stressors in child abuse. One would be to show that abusing families experience more and/or different types of stressors than matched nonabusing lower class families. Another would be to identify particular types of stressors that are found with greater frequency in abusing families

of all social classes. A third would be to show that certain types of crises (i.e., sudden exacerbation of stress or new severe stressors) consistently precede abusive episodes.[41]

Finally, Robert Burgess and Patricia Draper find higher rates of abuse in low-income families and suggest that it occurs because raising children simply requires a very large percentage of their resources. More financially successful parents may not suffer as much stress, because a smaller percentage of their income is devoted to this.[42]

While final judgment on the importance of stress awaits definitive research methodology, a few sociologists have turned to more general theories of family violence. One theory is based on the concept of *power.* Timothy B. Dailey explains that unlike other relationships, such as those between employers and employees, family relationships are relatively one-sided.[43] Parents have nearly absolute authority over their children, which matches the parents' nearly total responsibility for their children's behavior. When children challenge this parental authority, resolution of the conflict takes place within the family, more or less as the parents see fit. Unlike employer-employee conflicts, "there are no unions, no one to vote on new rules, and one cannot fire one's child."[44] Since children are regarded as essentially incompetent to make decisions about their own behavior, the burden is on parents to ensure that their children perform well in school, do not get into trouble, and generally behave in ways that reflect favorably on the parents. In short, parents are expected to maintain control over their children, but *how* they maintain that control is unspecified and generally free from outside interference or assistance.

According to Dailey, the authority structure of the family holds the potential for violence against children. Children are viewed as incompetents who must be taught how to behave and who are in no position to resist whatever measures are deemed necessary to teach them. Of course, children are in no practical position to resist, owing to both their ignorance and the lack of alternatives. Under these circumstances, the use of violence fulfills at least two functions for the parents. First, the resulting pain and fear can gain compliance with the parents' wishes. But more important for our discussion, violence can reinforce the authoritative position of the parents. When violence is used by parents, it is tangible evidence of who is in charge; and the legitimate imbalance of power between parents (the competents) and children (the incompetents) is restored or maintained.

Dailey's explanation of child abuse differs from stress-oriented versions in one important respect. The assumption behind stress explanations is that abuse is the result of frustration—troubles mount until something snaps and the child becomes an innocent target. Dailey admits that at times abuse may serve to lessen parents' frustrations, but he is primarily concerned with violence that is "routine and passionless." The child is not a *substitute* target for the boss or society, but the *real* target for reinforcing the family's authority structure. Dailey cites violence by mental hospital staff against patients and by police against arrestees as instances supporting his thesis. Such acts may seem to be "needless and gratuitous," but they are actually acts in which the powerful are simply demonstrating their authority over those perceived as incompetent. In the case of parents, violence is but one *alternative* by which authority may be asserted. Violence is a matter of *choice,*

the outcome of a process of selection of methods and priorities. In certain cases the parent will perceive violence as the simplest way to be authoritative, especially in the context of a structure such that no other readily available conflict resolution mechanisms exist, and the child is perceived as a legitimate target of violence because of his low status.[45]

It is Dailey's contention that the parental authority structure facilitates violence and that perhaps the greater the power imbalance within that structure, the more likely it is that violence against children will occur.

Child abuse theories based on stress and power seem plausible, but they are only tentative until adequate research tests their validity. In the meantime, we are left with the basic question of why violence that is labeled as abusive exists in some families as an alternative to less damaging violence or to no violence at all. It is instructive to know that violence is widespread among U.S. families. But that does not explain why high degrees of violence against children are more likely to occur within families of the lower class—the same class that has a disproportionally high rate of homicide. In Chapter 4 we described the "subculture of interpersonal violence," a concept denoting that within some segments of society the quick resort to serious violence is tolerated, if not expected, in certain situations. If rationales supporting violence are culturally based, then an explanation of child abuse may depend ultimately less on measuring situational stress than on understanding situational definitions.[46]

Clinical indicators of abusing family profiles and the long-term consequences of family violence for children and spouses have been the subjects of research at the University of Kentucky's College of Medicine. Thomas W. Miller and his associates report that victims of family violence may suffer symptoms similar to the post-traumatic stress disorder (PTSD) experienced by some combat soldiers.[47]

Spouse Abuse

Although the physical abuse of children may frequently be ignored, once it is recognized, the victims usually elicit sympathy. The same cannot be said for other targets of family violence. Wives who are attacked by their husbands may be accused of provoking the assaults ("She must be bringing it on herself"), of being weak-willed ("Why doesn't she just leave?"), or of being masochistic ("She probably likes it").[48] Beaten wives have even been subjects of humor:

> *A woman, a dog, and a walnut tree*
> *The more you beat, the better they be.*[49]

When it comes to humor, however, it is the beaten husband who evidently causes the most laughs. Long-running gags in several comic strips—the most notable today is "Snuffy Smith"—have wives armed with frying pans or rolling pins awaiting their husbands' return from a night on the town. The concluding panel inevitably contains a scene of mayhem in which the husband is bombarded with housewares.[50] But reality is less amusing for both victimized husbands and wives. And, as in the case of child abuse, today's public concern over spouse abuse is of recent origin.

The Discovery of Spouse Abuse

As with child abuse, the attention that spouse abuse—particularly wife abuse—receives today does not reflect any known increase in the actual violence. Rather, it is the result of a "discovery." To understand this discovery better, let us first examine the issue from a historical context.

According to feminist writers, wife-beating is hardly new. If anything, it is a tradition consistent with the notion that husbands are lords in their houses and can assume the right to discipline their wives who fail to "honor and obey." Feminist writers argue that wife abuse has its roots in the continued subordination of women not only in the home, but in economic and political spheres as well.[51] This theme, which will recur in our discussion of theories of spouse abuse, is linked to the issue of the *legal status* of spouse abuse. Feminist writers claim that man's domination of woman is reflected in the history of laws related to marital violence. Terry Davidson elaborates upon this theme by asserting that in the United States wife-beating has been a legal "privilege":

> When we consider our own nation's 200 years of growth and progress, it is a shock to read laws from the 1800s which regulated wife beating: not criminalized it, but permitted it. Expected it. Accepted it. Before 1871, a husband was able to go unpunished for "beating [his wife] with a stick, pulling her hair, choking her, spitting in her face, kicking her about the floor." Marital violence was his "privilege." It was, in fact, an "ancient" privilege which would be long honored. The first case decided in the United States court acknowledging the husband's right of "chastisement" occurred in 1824 in the Supreme Court of Mississippi. And the law, in this new democracy, would not allow the battered wife to "vex or discredit or shame" the family name by seeking legal protection or relief. Such was the status of married women in the fledgling democracy, founded "under God."[52]

While Davidson's arguments are persuasive, Elizabeth Pleck interprets the tenor of nineteenth-century U.S. law quite differently.[53] From her research on the period, she finds that most states passed unqualified laws against wife-beating and that in some instances the punishments were quite harsh. In Maryland, for example, the offender could receive 40 lashes or a year in prison; in New Mexico he could get five years in prison. Furthermore, Pleck finds that states without wife-beating laws and court rulings supporting the husband's right physically to chastise his wife (the same ruling Davidson uses to buttress her position) were clearly *exceptions* to the legal situation nationally. If one were to choose selectively among Pleck's findings, one could draw a picture of the nineteenth-century United States as being more severe with wife-beaters than it is today:

- At the 1886 American Bar Association meeting, there was a resolution favoring the whipping of wife-beaters.
- Church ministers preached against wife-beating, interfered in families where it occurred, and if unable to stop it, expelled the offender from the congregation.
- Among vigilante groups—the Regulators of South Carolina, the White Caps, and the Ku Klux Klan—wife-beaters were prime targets regardless of color. A tactic of the White Caps was, while on Saturday night patrol, to leave a note on the doorstep: Stop mistreating your family or get whipped.

■ There are numerous other examples of women reformers, police, and other officials who expressed the need for action against spouse abusers.

It is not Pleck's intent to prove that in the nineteenth-century Americans were especially sympathetic toward battered wives. Nor does she deny that both then and now, males primarily determine the laws and how they will be enforced. Nevertheless, she points out that, contrary to feminist claims, during the 1800s there was an *awareness* of wife-beating and that it was *disapproved* and *illegal.* In her words:

> It has been claimed that society has made progress in its punishment of wife-beaters: at one time physical chastisement of a wife was legal and appropriate behavior, and now it is illegal and considered by most Americans to be inappropriate. It has been argued here that wife-beating was illegal in most states by 1870 and considered by many nineteenth-century Americans as inappropriate. *The difference between the past and the present was not a modern intention to prohibit wife-beating but a change in the manner of regulation.* A century ago the system for formal regulation against wifebeaters was relatively weak and cumbersome whereas the mechanisms for informal regulation were relatively vigorous and extensive; today the opposite is more nearly the case.[54]

Whatever the intent of nineteenth-century lawmakers and enforcers, however, one cannot deny that until recently legal reaction to wife-beating was weak. Even when the victims found the courage to report offenses, police were reluctant to make arrests, district attorneys were reluctant to prosecute, and judges were reluctant to do more than issue warnings or impose trivial sentences. Furthermore, victims who overcame the social pressures to stay in the home and "stick by" their husbands usually had no place to go, since social service agencies offered little help or protection. In short, beaten wives were made captives in their own homes because of an indifferent legal and social service system.

The movement to counteract this indifference started in 1971 in London, where a shelter house was opened for beaten women who had fled their homes.[55] In 1972 a telephone crisis hotline service began in St. Paul, Minnesota, to counsel battered women. This initiated a battered women movement in the United States, a movement that began gathering considerable momentum in 1975.

According to Kathleen J. Tierney, who analyzed the movement, its greatest impact occurred in four areas:

1. **Services.** Shelters, crisis hotlines, and various other programs to assist battered women in their relationships with police, courts, and other agencies were established by 1978. For example, more than 170 shelters opened between 1975 and 1978.
2. **Legislation.** By 1980, 45 states and the District of Columbia had enacted new laws specifically directed at wife-beating cases. These laws made it more difficult for justice agencies to ignore cases and stiffened the penalties against offenders. Five states—California, Florida, Montana, Ohio, and Pennsylvania—imposed a surcharge on marriage licenses to support shelters.
3. **Federal funding.** Funds were made available, especially in the late 1970s, to finance local and state programs providing services to battered women.

4. **Research and information.** Federal money was poured into research projects, conferences, and information services relating to domestic violence.

Thus, in less than a decade spouse abuse was "discovered" and became the focus of research and official action. Tierney points out that the battered women movement did not result from a wave of public sentiment. If anything, the public was ignorant of the women's plight. The sentiment came from existing interest groups, especially feminist groups such as the National Organization of Women (NOW) and reform groups concerned with social services. The movement was aided considerably by the mass media. Without newspaper, television, and magazine coverage—which had increased dramatically by 1977—the movement probably would not have been as successful as it was.

According to Tierney, the topic had the drama and timeliness that especially appealed to the mass media:

> Wife beating was a good subject for the media. It was a "new" problem for the public, although certainly not for its victims. It was controversial. It mixed elements of violence and social relevance. It provided a focal point for serious media discussion of such issues as feminism, inequality, and family life in the United States—without requiring a sacrifice of the entertainment value, action, and urgency on which the media typically depend.[56]

The movement succeeded after much specific research and study and resulted in the passage of the federal Violent Crime Control and Law Enforcement Act of 1994, including specifically a section called the "Violence Against Women Act." This legislation was designed to educate members of the criminal justice system concerning the special needs of women victims; encouraged arrest policies in cases of domestic abuse; and provided services, shelters, rape prevention, and education. Evaluations of this legislation are only now being conducted.

Extent

One obvious question is: How common is spouse abuse? The best initial estimate was based on the study by Straus, Gelles, and Steinmetz, who asked a national sample of 2,143 couples about the instances of violence within their homes.[57] The reader may recall from our discussion of child abuse that these researchers avoid defining abuse; instead, they rely on eight forms of violence ranging from "threw something" to "used a knife or gun." In connection with violence between spouses, the researchers used the five most serious forms to construct a "beating index": kicked or punched, hit or tried to hit with something, beat up, threatened with a knife or gun, and used a knife or gun. Some of their findings are as follows:

1. For 16 percent of the couples, at least one violent act of some kind is committed against a spouse in a given year.
2. For 28 percent of the couples, at least one violent act of some kind is committed against a spouse during the course of the marriage.
3. For 4 percent of the couples, a knife or gun is used against a spouse sometime during the marriage.

4. Using the "beating index," 4 percent of wives and 5 percent of husbands are beaten every year.
5. For 13 percent of the couples, there is at least one spouse-beating during the marriage.
6. Approximately 65 percent of both husband-beaters and wife-beaters beat their spouses twice or more a year.

One can draw at least three conclusions from these findings. First, spouse abuse is not rare in the United States; second, when spouse abuse occurs in a marriage, it tends to recur; and, third, husbands are abused as often as wives. Whatever one may have anticipated from a spouse abuse survey, the last finding is probably the most surprising. Does it mean that the comic-strip women armed with rolling pins and waiting in ambush for their husbands portray real wives after all? That characterization seems too bizarre. What *can* we conclude from the finding? The researchers themselves disagree. According to Steinmetz, the data show that in the home, women are as violent as men.[58] Not so, say her co-researchers. Gelles and Straus claim that the data are biased, since husbands are more likely than wives to report being victimized. They further argue that violence by husbands is more dangerous, since they are stronger and are more inclined toward serious forms, such as using a knife or gun, and that violence by wives is often in response to assaults initiated by husbands.[59] Kerrie James concludes that women's violence is most often an act of self-defense or an expression of stress and frustration and only rarely an attempt to control or dominate.[60]

Unfortunately, the data are not adequate for resolving the researchers' disagreement. Patsy A. Klaus and Michael C. Rand conducted a study on family violence and concluded that, on average, 260,000 violent incidents were committed by spouses or ex-spouses annually.[61]

What can be said about the extent of spouse abuse generally? Straus and his colleagues entitled one of their chapters "The Marriage License as a Hitting License." Although a catchy phrase, it seems to be an exaggeration. We can see from their data that in only a small minority of marriages do spouses act violently against one another with any regularity. Even allowing for underreporting of violent acts, the implication that marriage legitimizes violence for a substantial proportion of Americans is not yet substantiated. On the other hand, there is some recent evidence that marriage is a haven from at least one form of violence: homicide. In a study of Chicago homicides, Franklin E. Zimring, Satyanshu K. Mukherjee, and Barrik Van Winkle found that murders are less likely to occur between legally married persons than between those in common-law marriages or those who are just "romantically involved." These authors conclude that a legal marriage is "life insurance."[62]

Whether marriage is a "hitting license," "life insurance," or perhaps both, there is no doubting that for some couples, marriage is a battleground. And for many, marriage insulates the violent offender from the social reactions that the unmarried might anticipate. Marriage provides both opportunity for and toleration of activities that would be unthinkable on the "outside." In short, marriage may facilitate violence, but does it *promote* violence? That is a theoretical issue to which we will return shortly.

Characteristics

Unfortunately, we know little about the processes of family violence—what precipitates it, how it escalates or deescalates, and what its outcomes are. Pioneering research by Richard

Gelles in the early 1970s does provide us with a typology of violent situations.[63] Strictly speaking, these situations are not "characteristics" in the traditional sense, but they do bring us as close as we can get to comprehending the circumstances under which family violence arises.

The first type of family violence is directed against inanimate objects rather than against a person. The purpose is to impress the spouse with what is in store if things do not change. The violence is a *threat.* The husband puts his fist through a wall or door, or the wife throws a dish through a window to indicate, "This is what will happen to you if . . ."

Gelles calls the second type of family violence *normal violence.* It is aimed at achieving a specific short-term goal. It is "normal" in that not only does the offender feel justified in committing the violence, but the victim also agrees. In short, the victim admits, "I asked for it." Gelles describes a typical justification by the husband:

> I have slapped her on the arm or in the face a few times to shut her up. Not really an argument, it's usually when the kids get hurt. She just goes completely spastic. She just doesn't know what to do. She just goes wild so you've got to hit her or something to calm her down so she'll come to her senses.[64]

Secondary violence, Gelle's third category of family violence, arises when there is concern over violence against a third party. The most likely situation is when one parent is spanking a child in a manner that provokes the other parent to react violently in defense of the child.

Protective reaction, the fourth type, involves defensive tactics. For example, the wife who anticipates violence from the husband may beat him to the punch. Or a spouse may retaliate for past victimizations. The media has focused on several cases in which abusive spouses were killed by their victims. In most cases the murderers were females. These are two examples:

> Jennifer Patri, a 32-year-old Waupaca, Wisconsin, farm wife, shot her husband Robert, buried the corpse in the smokehouse, then set fire to the smokehouse. Made desperate by the husband's assaults, sexual abuse, and molestation of their 12-year-old daughter, Jennifer Patri bought a 12-gauge shotgun. Although she had felt dutybound to her marriage vows, she finally began divorce proceedings. Her husband, who had gone to live with another woman, threatened to kidnap his daughter or to kill her. When he arrived to visit the children, his wife shot him in the back. . . . Francine Hughes of Jackson, Michigan, poured gasoline around her sleeping husband James [and] then ignited it. The couple was divorced after seven years of marriage, but Francine returned to help nurse Hughes back to health after he suffered a near-fatal automobile crash. [James had beaten his wife throughout the marriage; on the day of his death he assaulted her several times.] Francine, 30 years old, was attending business school to . . . support herself . . . when her ex-husband forced her to burn her textbooks in the back yard.[65]

Not all these cases involved husband-killing. Eddie King of Jacksonville, Florida, shot his wife after four years of violence that included the wife throwing potash into his face, twice stabbing him in the back, and slashing him across the face with a carpet knife.[66]

(Although the issue is not directly relevant to this discussion, the reader probably has recognized that these cases raise the legal issue of what constitutes self-defense and justifiable homicide. Tactics by defense lawyers and decisions by the courts have been inconsistent on the matter.[67] In the cases cited, Jennifer Patri was convicted of first-degree murder and was sentenced to ten years, Francine Hughes was found not guilty by reason of temporary insanity, and Eddie King had all charges against him dropped by the prosecuting attorney.)

Volcanic violence is a fifth type of marital violence described by Gelles. It apparently results from stress and frustration and provides a tension release from outside pressures and failures, such as the loss of a job. Obviously, not all stress originates outside the family. Gelles notes that there may be a relationship between a wife's pregnancy and the likelihood that she will become a target of violence. Thus it is possible that family stress accompanying pregnancy could be related to volcanic violence.

The two remaining types of violence are essentially self-explanatory: *alcohol-related* cases, in which the husbands attack only when they are intoxicated, and *sex-related* attacks, which stem from jealousy and accusations of cheating.

Another form of violence should be added: *marital rape.* In the criminal law in some states, this is a contradiction, but in most states, husbands can be prosecuted for raping their wives. The source of the immunity in certain states dates from a British court decision of 1736, which reads in part that "the husband cannot be guilty of a rape committed by himself upon his lawful wife, for by their mutual matrimonial consent and contract the wife hath given up herself in this kind unto the husband which she cannot retract."[68]

But whether technically illegal or not, the behavior is real for the women who experience it. As in the case of practically all forms of family violence, the "discovery" of marital rape came in the early 1970s. Consequently, a great deal of research has been conducted in this area and a related one: intimate partner violence (an *intimate* is defined as a spouse, ex-spouse, boyfriend/girlfriend, or ex-boyfriend/girlfriend). For example, in a 1978 study the researcher, Dianna E. H. Russell, found, on the basis of a telephone survey of 644 San Francisco women, that 14 percent had experienced at least one rape or attempted rape by their husbands or ex-husbands. And in addition to the UCR and the NCVS we have the Centers for Disease Control and Prevention and the National Institute of Justice cosponsored National Violence Against Women Survey (NVAWS) and frequent Bureau of Justice Statistics Reports on Intimate Partner Violence. These all provide additional information on the scope of marital rape and violence in relationships. Recently, according to the NCVS, intimates committed 20 percent of all rapes and sexual assaults; the most recent Intimate Partner Violence Report provides a rate of 55.6 per 100,000 females as victims of rape and sexual assault. In a recent NVAWS report, 91 percent of women surveyed reported that they had been married or lived as a couple with a member of the opposite sex, and 4.5 percent of these reported having been raped by a current or former marital/opposite sex cohabiting partner at some time in their lifetime.[69]

Stress and Power—Again

Why do spouses assault one another? One might consider the question unnecessary, since it can be answered by answering a more general inquiry: Why do people who are personally acquainted, whatever their relationship, assault one another? We saw in Chapter 4 that people murder not only their husbands and wives, but also their lovers, friends, and neighbors. The outstanding characteristic of ordinary homicide is that offender and victim often know one another. In short, it can be argued that marriage is not so different from many other close relationships. Mary Riege Laner and Jeanine Thompson, for example, found that among 371 courting couples, 60 percent experienced "abusive or aggressive behavior" and that the more involved the couple, the more frequently the abusive behavior occurred.[70] Nevertheless, the working assumption of researchers studying marital violence is that marriage provides a unique situation that both fosters violence and shields the aggressor.

In his work, Gelles theorizes that violence against spouses stems from the same conditions that are responsible for child abuse, namely, *stress* and *learning patterns* supporting violence. He recognizes that, like child abuse, spouse abuse is disproportionately concentrated in the lower class. It is this class that is more likely to be exposed to stressful situations but that is least likely to have the resources to handle such situations. This condition plus greater experience with and exposure to physical aggression is a combination that makes the lower class the prime location of spouse abuse.[71]

Straus and others have also concentrated on the conditions underpinning wife abuse. There are, he says, cultural norms approving such violence. They are manifested by family members' acceptance of "normal violence" (see the discussion in the previous section) and by official legitimation of family violence: police, prosecutors, and judges who refuse to move against offenders. (This was beginning to change, with studies conducted that seemed to determine that requiring arrests in all domestic violence cases coupled with mandatory programs, such as therapy or, if therapy was refused, prosecution, improved things. Now we are uncertain whether arrest deters in this instance, with some suggesting that it may make matters worse.)[72] But much of the problem is rooted in the sexist nature of U.S. society.[73] To support his argument, Straus describes nine sexist aspects of violence:

1. **Male authority.** There is a presumption that males are superior. In the face of a challenge to their authority, males often resort to physical violence to maintain or restore their positions.
2. **Compulsive masculinity.** Physical aggressiveness is linked with the identity of being a "man." To be passive is to be womanlike, a shameful trait in a "real" man.
3. **Economic constraints.** There are few alternatives for women seeking economic independence. Physical assaults are therefore often tolerated because of women's lack of prospects outside marriage.
4. **Burdens of child care.** Women are given the primary responsibility for raising children. Occupational discrimination against women and the lack of other resources that would allow them to support their children independently lock women into marriage.
5. **Myth of the single-parent household.** There is a widely held assumption that a woman alone cannot adequately raise her children.
6. **Preeminence of the wife role.** Whereas men have a wide range of acceptable roles from which to select, women are expected to concentrate on becoming wives and mothers.
7. **Negative self-image.** Women regard themselves as inferior and are therefore tolerant of male aggressiveness.
8. **Women as children.** The husband is defined as the "head of the household," while the wife is presumed to be under his control, just like the children. In short, husbands are seen to have a moral right to discipline their wives as they do their children.

9. **Male orientation of the justice system.** Justice in the United States is run by males for males. Consequently, victimized wives can anticipate little help from the system, and offending husbands can anticipate little trouble.[74]

Straus concludes his discussion by asserting that only when sexism and its inequities are eliminated will violence in the home begin disappearing.

A third theoretical approach to wife-beating is offered by two British researchers, R. Emerson Dobash and Russell Dobash, who believe that it can be understood only within a historical context. Their analysis emphasizes the traditional subordinate status of women in religious, economic, and political institutions but especially in the family structure that has dominated Western history: *patriarchy*. The structure of patriarchy is one in which the wife is relegated to a position of power and privilege inferior to that of the husband. He is in control; she is to be obedient. From this structure has emerged the ideology that women are not the equals of men.

The Dobashes' analysis of patriarchy begins with early Rome, but they believe that the current situation started to solidify in the sixteenth century. At that time the rise of industry began to break up the family as an economic unit: The man worked outside the home, while the wife was isolated in the home. In addition to the rise of industry, the rise of Protestantism emphasized loyalty between spouses and the home as the spiritual center of life:

> The head of the household inherited much of the authority and power of the priest, and his increased authority had a moral or sacred quality imparted to it by religious support. The church also supported affective ties between husbands and wives as a means of keeping marriages together, sanctified and glorified married love, and rejected divorce as a means of ending an unsatisfactory relationship. . . .
>
> The sanctification of marriage made the lowly position of wives a holy one and the idea of married love and loyalty further ensnared wives and supported husbands by making the wife's submission a moral duty.[75]

During this time, according to the Dobashes, a husband was justified in using violence against his wife if she did not live up to the duties expected of her. Not only did communities approve such violence as long as it remained within certain bounds, but also the law recognized that certain situations called for "chastisement" of wives (rarely of husbands). In England the law giving husbands the right to chastise their wives was not abolished until 1829. In the United States the right was specifically abolished in 1894 by the last state whose statutes approved of it: Mississippi. (The reader may recall from our discussion of the discovery of spouse abuse that the legal status and community acceptance of wife-beating in the nineteenth-century United States are matters of contention among researchers. Some claim that others exaggerate the toleration of wife abuse. This is a matter that cannot be resolved here.)

According to the Dobashes, historical tolerance for wife-beating is only part of the story. Equally important is the process in which girls discover that they ultimately are to become wives and mothers. During this process, they learn attitudes of love, respect, deference, and dependence that suit them for a subordinate position in matrimony. Boys, by contrast, do not learn how to be married. Their real destinies lie outside the home, and it is those destinies for which they must train. Even during dating and courtship the authority position of the male is asserted and reinforced. For example, men tend to monopolize and make demands of women that men would resent if made of them. And women become more isolated from their friends as relationships with men develop, whereas men's contacts with friends are less likely to diminish. Marriage and the arrival of children further this isolation for women at the same time that women's dependence on their husbands increases.

According to the Dobashes,

> when a woman becomes a wife, she must give up most of her activities and aspirations and adjust her identity. She must schedule her work and pastimes around the work and leisure of other family members. She must fit herself into the nooks and crannies which are left after everyone else has been cared for, cleaned, served, fed, and nurtured. The woman becomes increasingly isolated and segregated as her husband's sense of possession grows and as household tasks mount and demands for service become greater. These demands are heavily laced with the ideas of duty and morality and they take on an almost religious character. . . . Failures to meet the husband's expectations do not just cause him inconvenience, annoyance, or disappointment: they are seen as affronts to the moral order and to his authority. . . . [She is] in a secondary position with respect to him and invests him with the right and indeed the obligation to control her behavior by the various means available to him. Physical coercion is simply one of those means.[76]

Thus in a real sense women learn to accept the possibility of violence as part of marriage. And when violence does first occur, a husband's reaction often is that he is sorry but that the wife was asking for it or at least deserved it. The wife's response will usually complement this interpretation: He could not possibly hit her for nothing, so she must be to blame for provoking the outburst. She sees her "guilt," forgives her husband, and seeks to change her behavior so he has no reason to hit her again.

> Thus, the first violent episode is played down, isolated, solved, defined as insignificant, and forgotten. But the factors that give rise to it are much wider reaching than a late meal, too much to drink, or an admiring glance, real or imagined, from another man. The first episode clearly illustrates a growing sense of possessiveness, domination, and "rightful" control and these are the factors that lead to the continuation of violence.[77]

The Dobashes argue that battered women are the legacy of the patriarchal family system in which man is the authority and provider while woman is obedient and dependent. They claim that the end of violence against wives will not come from simply identifying the characteristics of violent families but from eliminating women's subordination.

Sexual Abuse of Children

In contrast to the other topics of this chapter, curious things are happening regarding adult–child sexual encounters. The reader will recall that both physical child abuse and spouse abuse were "discovered" in the early 1970s; that is, they lost their secrecy and became public issues. There followed substantial increases in publicity and research that focused public awareness on the problems. A similar but not identical pattern emerged in the case of child molestation. The number of writings and research projects on the topic increased considerably during the 1970s, but this was not due to any revelation that children can be sexually victimized. Unlike the cases of physical child abuse and spouse abuse, several substantial research projects had explored molestation years earlier. In addition, anthropologists and psychiatrists had maintained a more or less steady output of theoretical articles on incest for several decades. So in a sense child molestation was "rediscovered" as a consequence of interest group and media attention on feminist and family issues.

More curious is the recent situation in which molestation is a problem being turned on its head. Physical child abuse and spouse abuse are "new" problems for which interest groups are demanding remedies; although these demands might meet with indifference, there is no organized effort to deny their legitimacy. Molestation, however, is an "old" problem for which some interest groups are requesting that remedies be eased and have publicized their reasoning on the Internet. In short, these groups are asking for more tolerance toward adult–child sexual contacts. They are not politically powerful; however, the groups' very existence is remarkable in light of current concerns over protecting the vulnerable. This is a matter to which we will return later.

As the reader might guess, adult–child sexual contacts are specifically prohibited everywhere in the United States. This is reflected in the state criminal codes that specify an "age of consent"—usually 16 or 18—below which legislators have assumed that persons are not intellectually equipped or "responsible" enough to deal with sex. In most states, sentences are especially harsh if one partner is quite young.

Despite the severe legal reactions against adult–child sexual contacts in the United States, the reader should not assume that such contacts are condemned everywhere. Anthropologists have found societies in which "molestation" is not only tolerated but, under certain circumstances, expected. For example, among the Aranda of Australia and the Big Nambas of the New Hebrides, homosexual relationships between men and boys may be maintained for years with community approval; in other societies brief homosexual relationships are permitted during puberty rites when boys are initiated into adulthood.[78] Among the Lepchas, who live in the Himalayas between India and Tibet, the sex lives of females begin as early as age 8 to 10, when they have intercourse with adults. The Lepchas believe that such experiences are necessary if the girls are to develop secondary sex characteristics.[79] Although no society allows its adults to have unrestricted sexual access to children,[80] it is evident that adult–child sexual contacts are not universally taboo. Indeed, early marriage of female children, by choice or arrangement, has been common in many cultures around the world.

Extent

Despite persistent scientific interest in adult–child sexual contacts, research on their prevalence is not definitive. The reader should remember that the National Crime Victim Survey excludes questioning children under 12 years of age. As David Finkelhor and Patricia Y. Hashima note in a chapter of a recent book, "There is no single source for the statistics on child victimizations"; they present categories of abuse, including rape/sexual assault and sexual abuse as well as sources where it may be possible to glean some information.[81] In an earlier effort David Finkelhor and Jennifer Dziuba-Leatherman conducted a national telephone survey of 2,000 children aged 10 to 16 years. The findings are revealing. Sexual abuse was much more common among girls, with 3.2 percent reporting incidents while boys reported 0.6 percent.[82] The study also reports that this abuse was committed by a family member over 18 years and older in 11 percent of the victimizations and by a family member under 18 years old in 3 percent of the cases. (In this particular study, contact incidents include a perpetrator touching the sexual parts of a child under or over the clothing, penetrating the child, or engaging in any oral-genital contact with the child.)[83]

Earlier efforts attempted to gather some information on sexual abuse by studying other groups that may not be representative of the general population. For example, some of these studies of the extent of victimization present problems because their samples consist exclusively of college students.[84] Such samples invariably underrepresent lower-income segments of the population. In a study by David Finkelhor, the sample was obtained from six New England colleges and universities. He found that among 530 women, 11.3 percent had had sexual experiences with adults 18 and older when they were under age 13. Among 266 men, 4.1 percent had had such experiences.[85] (Finkelhor's findings also included his subjects' experiences as children with adolescent partners and as adolescents with adult partners at least 10 years older. If all the subjects' sexual experiences when under 17 are combined, the total proportion having such experiences is 19.2 percent of the women and 8.6 percent of the men.) Diana Russell found that 16 percent of women surveyed reported sexual abuse by a relative, with another 4.5 percent reporting abuse by a father or stepfather.[86]

Another effort, using information gathered by the National Child Abuse and Neglect Data System for 2002, reports that the child sexual abuse rate was 10 percent, a drop in previous rates.[87] These prevalence rates, even if declining, are still alarming.

Characteristics

Contrary to what many think, child molesters are rarely dirty old men hanging around schoolyards, clutching bags of candy. Such characters exist, but most molesters do not fit this description. In fact, no single type can be said to represent child molesters. The only general observation that can be made about molesters concerns the nature of their offenses, which are typically *nonviolent, noncoital acts between lower-status adult males and underaged girls with whom they are acquainted.*

The last statement may sound as though it could be chiseled in stone, but it should not be. Because data on adult–child sexual behavior are based on biased samples—mostly middle-class victims, convicted offenders, or cases coming to the attention of social service agencies—little is certain.[88] To say that the typical offense is nonviolent is not to say that the victims actively cooperate. The unique relationship existing between adults and children makes children ideal victims in several respects. If quite young, they are naive and impressionable; adults can easily elicit compliance from them merely by arousing their curiosity. Children can often be cowed into compliance simply by an adult's authoritative stance. Even children's perceptions that they risk angering adults may be sufficient to overcome resistance. Therefore violence is seldom used in molesting offenses because it is seldom necessary.

The following comments by convicted molesters point up the advantages of children as victims:

To me a boy is more scared; it's always running through his mind that he'll get hit.

A child's mind is easily led.

If they are young there is no need for high pressure salesmanship.[89]

To characterize adult–child sexual contacts, we must look to surveys on victims, because less serious offenders are unlikely to show up in offender samples. Coincidentally, Finkelhor's sample of female victims indicates that fewer than 5 percent of the offenses involved coitus or genital-genital sexual contacts.[90] Finkelhor found that one-fifth involved only exhibition. Nevertheless, it appears that the great majority of molestations involve genital display, petting, or oral contacts.

Turning to the offenders themselves, studies have consistently shown that the majority fall into the unskilled and semiskilled occupational levels and may be acquaintances of the victim.[91] Finkelhor's female sample of victims reported that only 24 percent of their molesting experiences involved strangers; the male sample reported only 30 percent.[92] A recent study using National Incident-Based Reporting System data concerning juvenile sexual assault victims revealed that 34.2 percent of offenders were family members and 58.7 percent were acquaintances, only 7 percent being strangers.[93] Of course, those in the lower socioeconomic levels hold no monopoly on molesting offenses; as we shall see, offenders do come from upper occupational levels, and this group is more likely to be in positions to molest more children more frequently. That the offenders are overwhelmingly male is no surprise.

Types of Molesters and Their Offenses

With some reservations, then, one can characterize the *"typical" molestation offense:* nonviolent, noncoital sexual contact between acquaintances. But describing the *"typical" molester* is impossible, because one does not exist. Molesters are as varied as robbers or any other offenders. By turning to a typology of molesters, we can see their diversity and acquire some insight into the circumstances of their offenses.[94]

Incestuous Molester. The concept of incest includes more than molestation. In the anthropological literature on preliterate societies, for example, the concept is used primarily to describe the restrictions on who may marry whom. In the United States all states forbid parents marrying their children, siblings marrying one another, and grandparents marrying their grandchildren; most forbid aunts and uncles marrying their nephews and nieces.[95] But incest also refers to any sexual activities between close relatives without benefit of marriage. This is the meaning that interests us, particularly when one partner is an adult and the other a child.

Incestuous behavior is regarded as especially odious because we usually assume that incest violates a universal taboo. But like so many of our cherished beliefs, this isn't necessarily so. Historical and anthropological studies indicate that in some situations marriages between close relatives have been accepted as a means of preserving certain arrangements. For example, in ancient Egypt kings married their daughters and sisters for political purposes. Egyptian commoners also married their siblings to prevent family estates from being broken up. As another example, marriages between fathers and daughters and between siblings were frequent among Mormons in Utah less than a hundred years ago.[96] In short, the incest taboo is *not* universal.

To judge by estimates of its prevalence in the United States, one can also say that incest must not be universally taboo because there is so much of it. How much? Terms such as "rampant" and "epidemic" are often used. More objectively, Finkelhor estimates that 1 percent of female children are molested by their fathers.[97] As the reader might suspect, such estimates must be approached with great caution. But whatever the prevalence of such offenses, the offenders involved in father–daughter sexual contacts constitute a large, if not the largest, category of molesters. This large category also lacks homogeneity, and thus we have difficulty even in describing the typical incestuous molester.

In an exploratory study conducted in 1996 researchers examined specific characteristics of families referred for incestuous abuse. Although the sample size was not large, it produced some interesting results:

> Approximately half (48%) of the accused offenders were natural fathers of the victims, and 19% were stepfathers. . . .
>
> Victim's ages at the time of abuse ranged from 2 to 18 years. . . .
>
> Almost one-half (49%) of the offenders and non-offending spouses indicated . . . a marital relationship in which extreme emotional separateness was the modus vivendi. . . .
>
> Approximately half of the families in the study defined the highest level of parents' employment as skilled (47%), 22% were classified as unskilled, 13% were professional, and in 17% of families both parents were unemployed.
>
> Over one-third (36%) of the families in this study were identified as socially isolated from the outside environment with another 43% identified as moderately socially isolated.[98]

The above study illustrates the complexity of the situation, however. Real offenders come from a wide variety of families. At one extreme are families that "reek of normalcy": small, tight-knit, middle-class, religious, and abstinent from alcohol. At the other extreme are large, lower-class, "disorganized" families in which violence, unpredictability, and concern over survival are daily occurrences and in which sexual abuse—heterosexual and homosexual—may be initiated by more than one male and may involve both siblings and children.[99]

One way to make sense out of the variety of incest offenders is suggested by Blair Justice and Rita Justice, who classify them into four major personality groups.[100] The first and most prevalent group contains several subgroups:

1. **Symbiotic personalities.** The offender relies heavily on the child to supply the affection and warmth he lacks from other sources. According to the Justices, these personalities constitute as many as 85 percent of all incest offenders.
   a. **Introvert.** He has few social contacts outside the family except during work. The family is a shelter where he is the boss; his wife and daughters "belong" to him. Incest often results when the wife, because of illness or other circumstances, no longer supplies the love the offender craves.
   b. **Rationalizer.** He carries the notion of love for his children to extremes. Justifications or verbalized motives for this type of abuse take several forms, including claims that he just "loves her so much," that he is "educating" her on what love and

sex are all about, that he is "protecting" her by seeing that her sexual needs are met at home instead of on the street, and that father-daughter sex is just another form of "liberation" in an uptight world.

c. **Tyrant.** He sees his wife and children as being in debt to him because he is a man and the breadwinner. He loves his daughter but also believes she should furnish him with sex on demand. He is very authoritarian, macho, and jealous of anyone, male or female, who competes with him for the daughter's love.

d. **Alcoholic.** He feels very dependent on his family and uses alcohol as a "lubricant" for getting closer to them. He often drinks before the sexual contacts to gain courage; he often drinks afterward to ease his guilt. (Whether this type is technically an alcoholic or simply a drinker is unclear. In any case, alcohol is frequently associated with both incestuous and nonincestuous adult–child sexual contacts.)

2. **Psychopathic personalities.** The reader may recall from the first chapter that the term *psychopathic* is not an especially helpful label. In this instance the Justices refer to those incest offenders seeking "stimulation, novelty, and excitement." Unlike the symbiotic personalities who use incest as a means for gaining closeness to someone they love, the "psychopath" professes neither love nor guilt.

3. **Pedophiliac personalities.** This type consists of persons who have sexual cravings for children whether related to them or not. According to the Justices, these offenders rarely marry and have children; but if they do, incestuous sexual contacts are likely.

4. **Psychotic personalities.** A small number of offenders suffer from brain damage, which may result in hallucinations and delusions promoting incestuous behavior.

5. **"Subcultural."** The Justices do not name this type, but they mention isolated families of the Appalachian and Ozark mountains where traditionally "the oldest daughter is expected to assume her mother's role, both in the kitchen and the bed."

Incest has fascinated social scientists of all types for a long time. There is no shortage of theories about its causes; explanations range from overcrowding to alcoholism to stress to unconscious hostility toward grandmothers.[101] But the reader may have noticed a theme running through most of the offender types just described: that the male assumes almost a total right of control over his daughter. She is viewed less as a person than as an item of property. According to Judith Lewis Herman, this property relationship between father and daughter is very real and is the reason that sex between father and daughter is the most common form of incest.

Herman's argument is similar to the feminist theory of wife abuse. The paternal rule of the family facilitates the father's sexual dominance over its members, and society's sex roles encourage males to regard and use women as property:

Whereas male supremacy creates the social conditions that favor the development of father-daughter incest, the sexual division of labor creates the psychological conditions that lead to the same result. Male supremacy invests fathers with immense power over their children, especially their daughters. The sexual division of labor, in which women nurture children and men do not, produces fathers who are predisposed to use their powers exploitatively. The rearing of children by subordinate women ensures the reproduction in each generation of the psychology of male supremacy. It produces sexually aggressive men with little capacity to nurture, nurturant women with undeveloped sexual capacities, and children of both sexes who stand in awe of the power of fathers.[102]

High-Interaction Molester. In addition to incestuous molesters, there are several other types who are unrelated to their victims. Some of these offenders are distinguished from most others by their higher socioeconomic status, above-average interaction with children outside the home, and a higher probability that the victims will be male. These offenders' occupations and/or hobbies often involve children: these are the scout leaders, the dance instructors, the elementary school teachers, the choir master, or any number of other people who use their positions as a means to molest. It is impossible to say whether these adults became sexually interested in children before or after they attained their positions. They probably have always had a general interest in interacting with children, and their subsequent involvement and rapport with some individuals eventually led to sexual interest. The child victims are usually ones for whom the adults have a special regard:

> "The boys I liked were always more active; they were more willing to learn quicker."

> "It depended on the sexual appeal of the kid, how much the kid liked me, his appearance and behavior. He was always outstanding in sports and intellectual achievement."[103]

Because these relationships are based on affection, if not subtle manipulation, the children do not feel coerced. Consequently, the offenses occur frequently and often over prolonged periods without being detected. Both their social position and the nature of their offenses shield the high-interaction molesters; they may operate with impunity for many years.

Asocial Molester. These molesters are more likely to have criminal records for both sexual and nonsexual offenses. However, their records indicate little or no previous involvement with child victims. Their one or two molesting offenses are simply segments in a law-violating career. They are from the lowest socioeconomic status and are likely to be divorced or never married. Their offenses are opportunistic and spontaneous and are often preceded by drinking. An example is the case of a common laborer who felt pestered by a 9-year-old: "The kid would hang on me all the time. I'd tell her to go home all the time. . . . I wouldn't go across the street to get it but she was always crawling around. 'I want to love you as a daddy,' she'd say. She got on my nerves."

Aged Molester. As the name implies, the outstanding feature of these offenders is their advanced age. Because their child victims are rarely coerced, the offenders are likely to have several noncoital contacts with several neighborhood children before the behavior becomes known to other adults. Most of the offenders are in their 60s, but one of the authors knows of an instance in which the offender was 87 and the girl was 11. The offenders' age does not necessarily mean that their behavior is directly linked to senility or brain deterioration. Such factors may be relevant but in the context that the men may become extraordinarily attached to children in the absence of adult friends.

Career Molester. One popular image of the molester is the adult who frequents playgrounds to prey on children. Although we have seen that this image is inaccurate for the great majority of molesters, the stereotype does have a basis in reality. There are men with long records of molesting offenses who seek out victims in a deliberate, systematic fashion.

Unlike most of the offenders discussed so far, the career molesters' victims tend to be strangers. Also, the victims are likely to be younger: 9 years old or under. The offenders are also less discriminating regarding the victim's sex; whether they are boys or girls seems to depend less on the offenders' preferences than on the available opportunities.

Career molesters rarely use force. They rely on their affability and powers of persuasion as well as the gullibility of their very young victims. A typical tactic is to lure victims to isolated locations, some offenders even going so far as to use a monkey or a puppy as bait or to have the child help look for a lost kitten. This type of molester displays no affectional interest in children except as sexual objects.

Spontaneous-Aggressive Molester.   The offenses of these men are not typical of molesters but are the sort parents fear most. The offenses can be most concisely defined as forcible rapes. The victims are usually strangers, and the offenses are spontaneous in the sense that there is little or no attempt at persuasion. The offenders pull children into cars or deserted buildings or, if in an isolated area, simply approach them and proceed with an attack. The attack itself is likely to involve penetration of the genitals.

In general, spontaneous-aggressive molesters exhibit a total disregard for the victim's youth—the child is treated as an adult. The molesters have a low regard for children; the selection of children as their victims is a matter of circumstance and opportunity, not necessarily preference. The molesters' explanations of their victim choice are not paragons of clarity, but they leave the impression that age is of no consequence. Here are two such "explanations":

> I saw her walking alone on the street late at night. It was late and she was alone. It wouldn't have made any difference what age she was.

> It was just one of those things. She was walking down the road with no houses around. What's a young guy going to think?

What indeed?

The foregoing typology of molesters is undoubtedly incomplete and inexact in many instances. But it demonstrates that molesting offenses are highly diverse in circumstances, victim characteristics, offender characteristics, and motivation. Until recently, one could easily end the discussion of molestation here, with the final caution that "more research is needed." Today, however, the issues of molestation in general and molesters' motives in particular have become matters of controversy. Whereas traditionally the question has been "Why do they do it?," now some are asking, "Why shouldn't they?"

Adult–Child Sex: A Matter of Liberation?

A troubling issue has been the impact of molestation on the victims. Because most offenses are nonviolent and noncoital, some have argued that the *social definitions* of the experiences have a greater negative impact than do the experiences themselves. One can imagine the situation of a small girl solemnly announcing at the dinner table, "Today Mr. Brown took my panties off." The father storms from his chair and threatens to "kill the bastard"; the mother gets all the details and promptly phones every relative for miles around and relates the story to each. In the child's mind, what was a trivial incident has now become monumental. Anthony Mannarino and Judith A. Cohen expressed it this way in a recent study:

> These results may reflect the possibility that parents who are very upset about the abuse are less able to effectively utilize their parenting skills which, in turn, contributes to increased behavioral difficulties. . . .[S]ome parents feel so guilty about the abuse that they resist setting limits on sexual and other inappropriate behaviors. . . .[A] sexually abused child becomes distressed when she perceives that her parent is very troubled by the abuse disclosure and related events.[104]

The literature on the effects of molestation is plagued by the same problem of sampling faced by any of the research on molestation. To that basic problem we must add another: How can the researcher be certain that an adult difficulty (for example, sleeplessness or depression) is definitely linked with an early sexual experience and that no other factor substantially contributed to the situation?[105] Individual horror stories about the long-term effects of molestation are not hard to find, but we still lack solid evidence on the outcomes of various types of molesting experiences. In a study that reviewed a number of models and explanations of the long-term effects of child sexual abuse, two researchers, Paul E. Mullen and Jillian Fleming, delineated the complex factors involved in this process. They conclude by stating "that there is a wide range of potential adverse adult outcomes associated with child sexual abuse. . . .[C]hild sexual abuse is best viewed as a risk factor for a wide range of subsequent problems.[106]

Finkelhor later found in his sample of college students that only two factors were linked to "traumatic reaction": force and an age discrepancy greater than five years between offender and child.[107] Larry L. Constantine reviewed 30 studies—good and bad—conducted between 1937 and 1981, and he concluded that

> the research literature shows there to be no inbuilt or inevitable outcome or set of emotional reactions to incest or to sexual encounters of children with adults. The more negative outcomes are associated with ignorance of sexuality; with negative attitudes toward sex; with tense situations; with force, coercion, or brutality; and with unsupportive, uncommunicative, or judgmental adult reactions.[108]

However, Meda Chesney-Lind and Randall G. Shelden reviewed the literature and concluded that girls (who are more likely to be victims of sexual abuse, often with a relative, and for longer periods of time) may experience more severe trauma than boys. This can result in fear, anxiety, depression, anger and hostility, and inappropriate sexual behavior. Running away from home and delinquency can also result.[109] Too, Finkelhor suggests that boys who have been molested by men may become homosexuals or child abusers.[110] For some, then, there may be definite negative effects. Is there another alternative, namely, that the effects might be *positive?* Some authorities argue that childhood sexual experiences with adults are not necessarily "bad" and might even be "good."

This is a highly charged emotional issue; it is not easy to explore it in an objective way. Clearly, the assumption underlying most past research was that the effects of molesting were either negative or nonexistent. No thought was given to the possibility of positive effects. Some current researchers consider this an oversight and are attempting to remedy it. As you might guess, their projects suffer from enormous sampling problems; nevertheless, the results indicate that substantial numbers of younger partners in adult–child sexual relationships find the relationships satisfying and beneficial.[111] It is premature to draw conclusions or even to speculate about the proportion of "victims"—the term seems inconsistent here—who react in this manner:

> Perhaps you cannot imagine this but, when I was 12, I was very much in love with a man of 50 and he with me. I don't know who made the first move now, but we stroked each other and experienced a sexuality together. It relaxed me wonderfully. . . . One day my parents found out and the police were called in. The examination was terrible, I denied and denied again. Then I gave in. My older friend was arrested. My parents, after my forced confession, made out a formal complaint. Nothing then could be of help any more. I have never been able to forget this. It wasn't just. It could have been such a beautiful memory. I am married and have four children. I would not object to their having sexual contacts with adults. I regard it as positive. . . .

> When I [a male] was 7, I came into contact with a man who was especially nice to me. He used to take me to his attic, sit me on his lap, and play with me sexually. I thought it was very nice and enjoyed it. I always looked forward to Wednesday afternoons, the day when we saw each other. This lasted a long time. . . .
>
> Now, at almost 68, after a good life, I can see those former contacts as very positive to my development. I would not have wanted to have missed them, and I do not envy the people who never had these opportunities.[112]

Studies that explore the possible benefits to be derived from early sexual experiences with either peers or adults are part of what is variously called the "children's liberation movement" or the "children's rights movement." Unlike other such movements, this one is not led by those most directly affected: children.[113] Instead, it is supported on children's behalf by a diverse group of social scientists, some of whose work we have just mentioned, and other interested parties whom we will discuss shortly. Perhaps the most outspoken social scientist connected with the movement is Constantine. His perspective can be summed up as follows:

1. Contrary to conventional belief, sexuality or sexual "drives" do not begin with the onset of puberty. They are present at significant levels in children. Furthermore, children are physiologically capable of engaging in and enjoying nearly all the sexual activities of adults.
2. Children have the right to be free from the sexual anxiety fostered by society. This means that they have "the right to *know* about sexuality, the right to *be* sexual, the right of *access* to educational and literary sexual materials."
3. Although children probably prefer peers as sexual partners, adult–child sexual contacts should be permitted under certain circumstances. These circumstances would include the child who is knowledgeable about the nature of the sexual behavior and who is not compelled by physical force or psychological pressure.[114]

There are also organizations that vigorously support the children's sexual rights movement. Their interest appears to be immediate and personal, for these groups openly advocate changes in the laws regarding the age of consent. Although the groups usually deny that their members are having sexual contact with children, the tenor of their literature indicates otherwise. Such organizations are probably more numerous than the reader suspects; there are several in Europe and two of note in the United States: the Rene Guyon Society and the North American Man–Boy Love Association (NAMBLA). The Rene Guyon Society is the older group and appeals primarily to those interested in heterosexual contacts, including incest. Its slogan is "Sex by Year Eight or Else It's Too Late!"

But NAMBLA has recently attracted more public attention. Founded in 1979, its membership of about 500 promotes homosexual contacts.[115] The philosophy of organizations such as NAMBLA is summarized by Florence Rush:

> Boy-lovers or pederasts today as in ancient Greece claim that they raise their young lovers to be courageous, upstanding citizens who will be released before maturity to marry. They point to a long list of esteemed emperors, kings, politicians, militarists, artists, and such who enjoyed young boys, and to other cultures where, to this day, virile bold men make womanly use of a beardless boy. Fortified by history, tradition and experts, pederasts have organized to find kindred spirits and, encouraged by our sexual revolution, have lobbied to rescind legislation which prohibits sex with minors, to lower or eliminate the legal age of consent and to halt apprehension and imprisonment of boy-lovers.[116]

The children's sexual liberation movement is growing, judging by the increasing numbers of research articles, books, and conferences on the topic. Nevertheless, we should not overestimate the movement's influence or its likelihood of success in the face of formidable opposition. The great majority of Americans are simply not ready to accept adults having sex with 10-year-olds. But that is little reason to ignore the issues raised by the movement. Assuming that sweeping changes could be made in the laws regarding sexual behavior, are the movement's arguments persuasive?

To a point, they are. The legal age of consent—usually 16 or 18—is unrealistic in terms of the onset of sexuality; most adolescents are interested in sex long before those ages. The negative effects of noncoerced adult–child sexual contacts have probably been exaggerated, and the shroud of mystery and shame with which parents often surround sex may be less beneficial to a child than a more open approach. Yet there is a difficulty that the movement's advocates have not resolved: the problem of the *differential power* inherent in adult–child relationships. As Herman points out,

> power, according to Constantine, is "a subtle element of interpersonal relations." On the contrary, there is nothing subtle about the power relations between adults and children. Adults have more power than children. This is an immutable biological fact. Children are essentially a captive population, totally dependent upon their parents or other adults for their basic needs. Thus they will do whatever they perceive to be necessary to preserve a relationship with their caretakers.[117]

In calling for the "sexual freedom" of children, sexual rights activists assume that children are in a position to give or withhold consent. But the ability to consent becomes questionable when the participants in a sexual relationship are unequal. In such cases, the burden is on the adults to protect children. If anything, children have the right to be free from situations in which a power differential can so easily lead to exploitation:

> Unless we understand that children, though not easily duped, lack the capacity to resist adult pressure, granting a child the so-called "right" to freely choose an adult sex partner is much like liberating the chicken from its coop only to be devoured by the fox.[118]

Finally, two other items should be mentioned with regard to child sexual abuse. The Internet, with its huge capacity for global and anonymous communication, has greatly enhanced the ability of potential sexual child abusers to share information and perhaps more. According to a March 2001 *Newsweek* article detailing the use of the Internet for the distribution of child pornography, the U.S. Postal Inspection Service found that since 1997, 36 percent of all child pornography investigations turned up pedophiles with criminal records.[119] And in what cannot be the finest hour of the American Civil Liberties Union (ACLU), the organization represented NAMBLA in a wrongful death case arising from the 1997 torture and murder of a 10-year-old boy. One of the killers, Charles Jaynes, was a member of NAMBLA and allegedly used its Web site to obtain "how to" information. The ACLU suggested that the case raised serious First Amendment issues and then, fearing unfavorable headlines, asked for a gag order. The child's family is, of course, suing NAMBLA and states that the Web site literature played a role in their son's death. The outcome of this case is still pending at the time of this writing, but it demonstrates the difficulty and complexity of the entire child sexual abuse issue.[120]

CRITICAL THINKING EXERCISES

1. Criminal behavior by children is often linked to abuse or neglect of those children by others. Explain why abuse of a child would increase the likelihood for that child to be involved in crime.

2. Adolescent suicide is a topic that receives much attention today, and the claim is often made that children face an increasingly wide range of stressors in their lives. What are these stressors? Do you believe that they cause suicide?

3. Why would neighbors, or even police officers, be reluctant to report possible child abuse if they suspected that it was happening? How would *you* report it?

4. How does culture influence domestic violence? With America's wide range of cultural diversity and tradition, does culture ever conflict with law regarding domestic violence? Why have spouse abuse laws changed in the United States in the last 100 years?

CHECK IT OUT ON THE WEB

The Internet addresses listed below are intended to provide the reader with understanding of a wide range of perspectives on the subject matter discussed in this chapter. Some sites may contain objectionable material. The list is not intended to reflect the viewpoints or opinions of the authors or the publisher.

http://www.4children.org
    support site for abusers and abused persons
http://www.bwss.org
    support for battered women
http://www.bwjp.org
    legal advocates for battered women
http://www.keepmedia.com
    relevant articles from *Psychology Today*

ENDNOTES

1. Lewis Carroll, *The Annotated Alice,* ed. Martin Gardner (New York: Bramhall House, 1960), p. 85.

2. Samuel Walker, *Sense and Nonsense About Crime: A Policy Guide,* 2nd ed. (Pacific Grove, CA: Brooks/Cole Publishing Company, 1989), pp. 167–176; for a discussion of the resulting victim compensation programs, some even for child abuse, see Robert J. McCormack, "Compensating Victims of Violent Crime," *Justice Quarterly, 8* (September 1991), pp. 329–346.

3. For a discussion and review of the literature, see Cathy Spatz Widom, "Child Abuse, Neglect, and Violent Criminal Behavior," *Criminology, 27* (August 1989), pp. 251–271.

4. Lawrence A. Greenfield and Tracy L. Snell, *Women Offenders,* Special Report, U.S. Department of Justice, Bureau of Justice Statistics (Washington, DC: U.S. Government Printing Officer, December 1999), p. 8.

5. Widom, "Child Abuse," pp. 266–267.

6. Ibid., p. 267.

7. David G. Gil, *The Challenge of Social Equality* (Cambridge, MA: Schenckman Publishing, 1976), p. 130.

8. Mary Porter Martin, *1977 Analysis of Child Abuse and Neglect Research* (Washington, DC: National Center on Child Abuse and Neglect; U.S. Children's Bureau; Administration for Children, Youth, and Families; U.S. Department of Health, Education, and Welfare, 1978), p. 1. For discussions of definitional problems, see Jeanne M. Giovannoni and Rosina M. Becerra, *Defining Child Abuse* (New York: The Free Press, 1979), pp. 1–23, 77–94.

9. For a typical example of the laws, reporting, agencies involved, and investigation of child abuse and neglect, see Cecil L. Willis and Richard H. Wells, "The Police and Child Abuse: An Analysis of Police Decisions to Report Illegal Behavior," *Criminology, 26* (November 1988), pp. 695–716.

10. Richard J. Gelles, "The Social Construction of Child Abuse," *American Journal of Orthopsychiatry, 45* (April 1975), pp. 363–371.

11. Giovannoni and Becerra, *Defining Child Abuse,* pp. 77–156.

12. Ibid., pp. 242–254.

13. The history of childhood is best described in Philippe Aries, *Centuries of Childhood: A Social History of Family Life,* trans. Robert Baldick (New York: Vintage Books, 1962). The relationship between the discovery of childhood and abuse is summarized in Peter Conrad and Joseph W. Schneider, *Deviance and Medicalization: From Badness to Sickness* (St. Louis: C. V. Mosby, 1980), pp. 145–171; and Catherine J. Ross, "The Lessons of the Past: Defining and Controlling Child Abuse in the United States," in *Child Abuse: An Agenda for Action,* ed. George Gerbner, Catherine J. Ross, and Edward Zigler (New York: Oxford University Press, 1980), pp. 63–81.

14. Giovannoni and Becerra, *Defining Child Abuse,* p. 43.

15. This is a much abbreviated account of the changes in children's legal status. Reformatories and orphanages as well as the notions of delinquent and destitute children have a longer history that is intertwined with the discovery of "abuse." The reader is referred to ibid., pp. 31–66; Conrad and Schneider, *Deviance and Medicalization,* pp. 146–155; and Stephen J. Pfohl, "The 'Discovery' of Child Abuse," *Social Problems, 24* (February 1977), pp. 310–315. The following discussion is based on these works; see also Clifford K. Dorne, *Crimes Against Children* (Albany: Harrow and Heston, 1989); and Randall G. Shelden and Lynn T. Osborne, "For Their Own Good: Class Interests and the Child Saving Movement in Memphis, Tennessee," *Criminology, 27* (November 1989), pp. 747–768.

16. Giovannoni and Becerra, *Defining Child Abuse,* pp. 48–50.

17. Pfohl, "The 'Discovery' of Child Abuse," pp. 310–315.

18. Ibid., p. 316. Pfohl discounts a possible fourth factor: the unawareness of physicians. Some injuries are too obvious to be ignored.

19. Ibid., p. 319.

20. Eli H. Newberger and Richard Bourne, "The Medicalization and Legalization of Child Abuse," *American Journal of Orthopsychiatry, 48* (October 1978), pp. 596–597.

21. Saad Z. Nagi, *Child Maltreatment in the United States: A Challenge to Social Institutions* (New York: Columbia University Press, 1977), pp. 35–36; for a discussion on the effect of information and media campaigns, see Ray Surette, *Media, Crime, and Criminal Justice: Images and Realities* (Pacific Grove, CA: Brooks/Cole Publishing Company, 1992).

22. Gelles, "The Social Construction of Child Abuse," pp. 364–365.

23. David G. Gil, *Violence Against Children* (Cambridge, MA: Harvard University Press, 1970), pp. 49–70.

24. Richard J. Light, "Abused and Neglected Children in America: A Study of Alternative Policies," *Harvard Educational Review, 43* (November 1973), pp. 556–578.

25. For reviews on the various estimations, see Martin, *1977 Analysis,* pp. 7–13; and Charles P. Smith, David J. Berkman, and Warren M. Fraser, *Reports of the National Juvenile Justice Assessment Centers: A Preliminary National Assessment of Child Abuse and Neglect and the Juvenile Justice System—The Shadows of Distress* (Wash-

ington, DC: National Institute for Juvenile Justice and Delinquency Prevention; Office of Juvenile Justice and Delinquency Prevention; Law Enforcement Assistance Administration; Department of Justice, 1980), pp. 8–13.

26. Murray A. Straus, Richard J. Gelles, and Suzanne K. Steinmetz, *Behind Closed Doors: Violence in the American Family* (Garden City, NY: Anchor Press, 1980), pp. 20–21.

27. Ibid., p. 21. Also see ibid., pp. 53–60; and Richard J. Gelles, "Violence Toward Children in the United States," *American Journal of Orthopsychiatry, 48* (October 1978), p. 584.

28. Gelles, "Violence Toward Children," p. 586.

29. Straus, Gelles, and Steinmetz, *Behind Closed Doors,* pp. 63–65.

30. Richard J. Gelles and Murray A. Straus, *Intimate Violence* (New York: Simon & Schuster, 1988), pp. 108–109.

31. For highlights of this study and links to related material and information, see the Web site http://www.acf.dhhs.gov/programs/cb/publications/cmreports.htm

32. Edward Zigler, "Controlling Child Abuse: Do We Have the Knowledge and/or the Will?" in *Child Abuse,* ed. Gerbner, Ross, and Zigler, pp. 18–19; and Audrey M. Berger, "The Child Abusing Family—I: Methodological Issues and Parent-Related Characteristics of Abusing Families," *American Journal of Family Therapy, 8:* 3 (1980), pp. 57–59.

33. The following are derived from Zigler, "Controlling Child Abuse," pp. 16–21; Straus, Gelles, and Steinmetz, *Behind Closed Doors,* pp. 65–72, 174–190; Berger, "The Child Abusing Family—I," pp. 53–66; and Audrey M. Berger, "The Child Abusing Family—II: Child and Child-Rearing Variables, Environmental Factors, and Typologies of Abusing Families," *American Journal of Family Therapy, 8:* 4 (1980), pp. 52–68.

34. LEXIS-NEXIS 1998 Academic Universe Report, October 20, 1998; CNN byline, Daryl Kagan and Don Knapp.

35. For an idea of the difficulties, see Widom, "Child Abuse," pp. 251–254.

36. Gil, *Violence Against Children,* pp. 134–139.

37. Richard J. Gelles, "Child Abuse as Psychopathology: A Sociological Critique and Reformulation," *American Journal of Orthopsychiatry, 43* (July 1973), pp. 617–619.

38. Straus, Gelles, and Steinmetz, *Behind Closed Doors,* pp. 181–183.

39. Ibid., p. 189.

40. Ibid.

41. Berger, "Child Abusing Family—II," pp. 60–61. For a viewpoint that poverty-associated stress is behind abuse, see Leroy H. Pelton, "Child Abuse and Neglect: The Myth of Classlessness," *American Journal of*

Orthopsychiatry, 48 (October 1978), pp. 608–617; for a discussion on the relationship of socioeconomic status to delinquency, see Robert E. Larzelere and Gerald R. Patterson, "Parental Management: Mediator of the Effect of Socioeconomic Status on Early Delinquency," *Criminology, 28* (May 1990), pp. 301–324.

42. Robert Burgess and Patricia Draper, "The Explanation of Family Violence," in *Family Violence,* ed. Lloyd Ohlin and Michael Tonry (Chicago: University of Chicago Press, 1989), pp. 58–116.

43. Timothy B. Dailey, "Parental Power Breeds Violence Against Children," *Sociological Focus, 12* (October 1979), pp. 311–322.

44. Ibid., p. 315.

45. Ibid., p. 319.

46. For an attempt to integrate several theories that might add to an understanding of child and family abuse, see Richard J. Gelles and Murray A. Straus, "Determinants of Violence in the Family: Toward a Theoretical Integration," in *Contemporary Theories About the Family,* vol. 1, ed. Wesley R. Burr, Reuben Hill, F. Ivan Nye, and Ira L. Reiss (New York: The Free Press, 1979), pp. 549–581; also see Joan McCord, "Family Relationships, Juvenile Delinquency, and Adult Criminality," *Criminology, 29* (August 1991), pp. 397–417.

47. Thomas W. Miller et al., eds., *Children of Trauma: Stressful Life Events and Their Effects on Children and Adolescents,* Monograph 8, Stress and Health Ser. (Madison, CT: International Universities Press, 1998), pp. 61–75.

48. Mildred Daley Pagelow, *Women-Battering: Victims and Their Experiences* (Beverly Hills: Sage Publications, 1981), pp. 54–68. The quotations are hypothetical.

49. A "vintage American limerick," cited by Julia R. Schwendinger and Herman Schwendinger, "Rape, the Law, and Private Property," *Crime and Delinquency, 28* (April 1982), p. 289.

50. For an early discussion of marital violence in comic strips, see Gerhart Saenger, "Male and Female Relations in the American Comic Strips," in *The Funnies: An American Idiom,* ed. David M. White and Robert H. Abel (Glencoe, IL: The Free Press, 1963), pp. 219–231.

51. For a review of the feminist orientation, see Sally S. Simpson, "Feminist Theory, Crime, and Justice," *Criminology, 27* (November 1989), pp. 605–631.

52. Terry Davidson, "Wifebeating: A Recurring Phenomenon Throughout History," in *Battered Women: A Psychosociological Study of Domestic Violence,* ed. Maria Roy (New York: Van Nostrand Reinhold, 1977), p. 4.

53. Elizabeth Pleck, "Wife Beating in Nineteenth-Century America," *Victimology, 4:* 1 (1979), pp. 60–74.

54. Ibid., p. 71 (emphasis added).

55. The following discussion is based on Kathleen J. Tierney, "The Battered Women Movement and the

Creation of the Wife Beating Problem," *Social Problems, 29* (February 1982), pp. 207–220.

56. Ibid., pp. 213–214. For an in-depth account of the movement against domestic violence, see Susan Schechter, *Women and Male Violence: The Visions and Struggles of the Battered Women's Movement* (Boston: South End Press, 1983); for an example of the media reporting of domestic violence, see Ellen Steese, "Battered Families, Voices of the Abused," *The Christian Science Monitor,* July 14, 1988, pp. 25–26, and July 15, 1988, pp. 23–24.

57. The following discussion is based on Straus, Gelles, and Steinmetz, *Behind Closed Doors,* pp. 32–44. For another study using the same measures but a less representative sample, see Mark Schulman, *A Survey of Spousal Violence Against Women in Kentucky* (Washington, DC: U.S. Department of Justice, Law Enforcement Assistance Administration, July 1979).

58. Suzanne K. Steinmetz, "The Battered Husband Syndrome," *Victimology, 2:* 3–4 (1977), pp. 499–509.

59. Richard J. Gelles, "The Truth About Husband Abuse," *Ms.* (1979), reprinted in *Family Violence,* ed. Richard J. Gelles (Beverly Hills, CA: Sage Publications, 1979), pp. 137–142; and Murray A. Straus, "Wife-Beating: How Common and Why?" in *The Social Causes of Husband-Wife Violence,* ed. Murray A. Straus and Gerald T. Hotaling (Minneapolis: University of Minnesota Press, 1980), pp. 31–33; see also Scott L. Feld and Murray A. Straus, "Escalation and Desistance of Wife Assault in Marriage," *Criminology, 27* (February 1989), pp. 141–161.

60. Kerrie James, "Truth or Fiction: Men as Victims of Domestic Violence?" *Australia and New Zealand Journal of Family Therapy, 17:* 3 (September 1996), pp. 121–125.

61. Patsy A. Klaus and Michael C. Rand, *Family Violence* (Washington, DC: U.S. Department of Justice, Bureau of Justice Statistics, 1984), p. 3.

62. Franklin E. Zimring, Satyanshu K. Mukherjee, and Barrik Van Winkle, "Intimate Violence: A Study of Intersexual Homicide in Chicago," *University of Chicago Law Review, 50* (Spring 1983), pp. 910–930; for current statistics, see Callie Marie Rennison, *Intimate Partner Violence,* U.S. Department of Justice, Bureau of Justice Statistics (Washington, DC: U.S. Government Printing Office, May 2000), pp. 2–6.

63. Richard J. Gelles, *The Violent Home: A Study of Physical Aggression Between Husbands and Wives* (Beverly Hills: Sage Publications, 1974), pp. 58–85; see also Feld and Straus, "Escalation and Desistance," pp. 141–161.

64. Gelles, *The Violent Home,* p. 61.

65. Nancy Wolf, "Victim Provocation: The Battered Wife and Legal Definition of Self-Defense," *Sociological Symposium, 25* (Winter 1979), pp. 101–102. For several examples of similar homicides, see Diana E. H. Russell, *Rape in Marriage* (New York: Macmillan, 1980), pp. 273–285. Also, an excellent discussion of this topic may be found in Sue Titus Reid's *Criminal Law,* 4th ed. (Boston: McGraw Hill, 1998), pp. 121–125.

66. "Murder Charge Is Dropped Against Battered Husband," *Daily Sentinel-Tribune* (Bowling Green, OH), October 28, 1980, p. 12.

67. N. Fiora-Gormally, "Battered Wives Who Kill—Double Standard Out of Court, Single Standard In?" *Law and Human Behavior, 2:* 2 (1978), pp. 133–165.

68. Russell, *Rape in Marriage,* p. 17.

69. Quoted in ibid., pp. 44, 173, 240; and see Callie Marie Rennison, *Criminal Victimization, 1999: Changes 1998–99 with Trends 1993–99,* U.S. Department of Justice, Bureau of Justice Statistics (Washington, DC: U.S. Government Printing Office, August, 2000), p. 8.; Callie Marie Rennison, *Intimate Partner Violence,* p. 2.; and Patricia Tjaden and Nancy Thoennes, "Prevalence and Consequences of Male-to-Female and Female-to-Male Intimate Partner Violence as Measured by the National Violence Against Women Survey," *Violence Against Women, 6* (February 2000), p. 147.

70. Mary Riege Laner and Jeanine Thompson, "Abuse and Aggression in Courting Couples," *Deviant Behavior, 3* (April-June 1982), pp. 229–244.

71. Gelles, *The Violent Home,* pp. 188–189.

72. Murray A. Strauss, "Sexual Inequality, Cultural Norms, and Wife Beating," *Victimology, 1* (Spring 1976), pp. 63–68; Walker, *Sense and Nonsense About Crime,* Samuel Walker, *Sense and Nonsense About Crime and Drugs: A Policy Guide,* 5th ed (Belmont, CA: Wadsworth/Thompson Learning, 2001) pp. 118, 181.

73. An example of a treatment approach dealing with this assumption of the problem is found in Richard A. Stordeur and Richard Stille, *Ending Men's Violence Against Their Partners: One Road to Peace* (Newbury Park, CA: Sage Publications, 1989).

74. Paraphrased from Murray A. Straus, "Sexual Inequality, Cultural Norms, and Wife-Beating," *Victimology, 1* (Spring 1976), pp. 63–68.

75. R. Emerson Dobash and Russell P. Dobash, *Violence Against Wives: A Case Against the Patriarchy* (New York: The Free Press, 1979), pp. 52, 56.

76. Ibid., pp. 92–93.

77. Ibid., p. 96. This discussion is based on ibid., pp. 31–96. For other works of similar theoretical tenor, see Russell P. Dobash and R. Emerson Dobash, "Community Response to Violence Against Wives: Charivari, Abstract Justice, and Patriarchy," *Social Problems, 28* (June 1981), pp. 565–581; and Dorie Klein, "Can This Marriage Be Saved? Battery and Sheltering," *Crime and Social Justice, 12* (Winter 1979), pp. 19–33.

78. Clellan S. Ford and Frank A. Beach, *Patterns of Sexual Behavior* (New York: Harper & Brothers, 1951),

p. 132; and Tom Harrisson, *Savage Civilization* (New York: Alfred A. Knopf, 1937), pp. 409–410.

79. Geoffrey Gorer, *Himalayan Village* (London: Michael Joseph, 1938), pp. 175, 330; John Morris, *Living with the Lepchas* (London: William Heinemann, 1938), p. 236; and Ford and Beach, *Patterns of Sexual Behavior,* p. 191. For a review of anthropological literature on adult–child sexual contacts, see Charles H. McCaghy, "Child Molesters: A Study of Their Careers as Deviants" (Ph.D. diss., University of Wisconsin, 1966), pp. 8–17. Also see Julia S. Brown, "A Comparative Study of Deviations from Sexual Mores," *American Sociological Review, 17* (April 1952), pp. 135–146.

80. Clyde Kluchhohn, "Sexual Behavior in Cross-Cultural Perspective," in *Sexual Behavior in American Society,* ed. Jerome Himelhoch and Sylvia Fava (New York: W. W. Norton, 1955), p. 336.

81. David Finkelhor and Patricia Y. Hashima, "The Victimization of Children and Youth: A Comprehensive Overview," in *Handbook of Youth and Justice,* ed. Susan O. White (New York: Kluwer Academic/Plenum Publishers, 2001), pp. 49–78, with this discussion from p. 54 and Table 4. For an example of recent research that summarizes rates of early childhood sexual abuse, see Kimberly A. Tyler, Dan R. Hoyt, and Les B. Whitbeck, "The Effects of Early Sexual Abuse on Later Sexual Victimization Among Female Homeless and Runaway Adolescents," *Journal of Interpersonal Violence, 15:* 4 (March 2000), pp. 235–250.

82. David Finkelhor and Jennifer Dziuba-Leatherman, "Children as Victims of Violence: A National Survey," *Pediatrics, 94:* 4 (October 1994), p. 414.

83. Ibid., pp. 416, 419.

84. Judson Landis, "Experiences of 500 with Adult Sexual Deviants," *Psychiatric Quarterly Supplement, 30* (1956), pp. 91–109; and David Finkelhor, *Sexually Victimized Children* (New York: The Free Press, 1979).

85. Finkelhor, *Sexually Vicitimized Children,* pp. 55–56.

86. Diana Russell, *Sexual Exploitation: Rape, Child Sexual Abuse, and Workplace Harassment* (Beverly Hills, CA: Sage Publications, 1984).

87. U.S. Department of Health and Human Services, Administration on Children, Youth and Families. *Child Maltreatment 2002* (Washington, DC: U.S. Government Printing Office, 2003), Table 2.9.

88. The following discussion is based on Finkelhor, *Sexually Victimized Children,* pp. 53–72, 154–156; Judith Lewis Herman, *Father-Daughter Incest* (Cambridge, MA: Harvard University Press, 1981), pp. 12–15; see also Kristin A. Danni and Gary D. Hampe, "An Analysis of Predictors of Child Sex Offender Types Using Presentence Investigation Reports," *International Journal of Offender Therapy and Comparative Criminology, 44* (August 2000), pp. 490–504.

89. Quoted in McCaghy, "Child Molesters," p. 112.

90. Finkelhor, *Sexually Victimized Children,* p. 62.

91. Norman S. Hayner, "Characteristics of Five Offender Types," *American Sociological Review, 26* (February 1961), p. 100; Paul H. Gebhard, John H. Gagnon, Wardell B. Pomeroy, and Cornelia V. Christenson, *Sex Offenders: An Analysis of Types* (New York: Harper & Row, 1965), p. 51; McCaghy, "Child Molesters," pp. 115–116; and David Finkelhor, *Child Sexual Abuse: New Theory and Research* (New York: The Free Press, 1984), p. 83.

92. Finkelhor, *Sexually Victimized Children,* p. 58.

93. Howard N. Snyder, *Sexual Assault of Young Children as Reported to Law Enforcement: Victim, Incident, and Offender Characteristics,* U.S. Department of Justice, Bureau of Justice Statistics (Washington, DC: U.S. Government Printing Office, July, 2000), p. 10.

94. The following discussion is based on McCaghy, "Child Molesters," pp. 230–248. For other typologies of molesters, see Gebhard et al., *Sex Offenders,* pp. 73–81, 151–153, 225–229, 294–296; and J. W. Mohr, R. E. Turner, and M. B. Jerry, *Pedophilia and Exhibitionism* (Toronto: University of Toronto, 1964).

95. For an analysis of state incest laws, see Karl G. Heider, "Anthropological Models of Incest Laws in the United States," *American Anthropologist, 71* (August 1969), pp. 693–701; and Joseph J. Costa and Gordon K. Nelson, *Child Abuse and Neglect: Legislation, Reporting, and Prevention* (Lexington, MA: DC Heath, 1978).

96. For a discussion of the exceptions to the incest taboo, see Christopher Bagley, "Incest Behavior and Incest Taboo," *Social Problems, 16* (Spring 1969), pp. 505–519. See also Russell Middleton, "Brother-Sister and Father-Daughter Marriage in Ancient Egypt," *American Sociological Review, 27* (October 1962), pp. 603–611.

97. Finkelhor, *Sexually Victimized Children,* p. 86. See also Herman, *Father-Daughter Incest,* pp. 12–19.

98. Discussion and statistics from Terry S. Trepper, Dawn Niedner, Linda Mika, and Mary Jo Barrett, "Family Characteristics of Intact Sexually Abusing Families: An Exploratory Study," *Journal of Child Sexual Abuse, 5:* 4 (1996), pp. 1–18.

99. Ibid., pp. 1–18.

100. The following discussion is based on Blair Justice and Rita Justice, *The Broken Taboo: Sex in the Family* (New York: Human Sciences Press, 1979), pp. 59–92.

101. D. James Henderson, "Incest: A Synthesis of Data," *Canadian Psychiatric Association Journal, 17:* 4 (1972), pp. 299–313; and Patricia Beezley Mrazek, "The Nature of Incest: A Review of Contributing Factors," in *Sexually Abused Children and Their Families,* ed. Patricia Beezley Mrazek and C. Henry Kempe (New York: Pergamon Press, 1981), pp. 97–107.

102. Herman, *Father-Daughter Incest,* p. 62.

103. This discussion and the quotations are derived from McCaghy, "Child Molesters"; Charles H. McCaghy, "Child Molesting," *Sexual Behavior, 1* (August 1971),

pp. 16–24; and Charles H. McCaghy, "Social Sources of Verbalized Motives for Adult–Child Sexual Contacts," in *Childhood and Sexuality: Proceedings of the International Symposium,* ed. Jean-Marc Samson (Montreal: Editions Etudes Vivantes, 1980), pp. 712–725; for highly visible examples, see Barbara Kantrowitz and Debra Rosenberg, "The School for Scandal: An Exeter Drama Teacher Faces Child-Porn Charges," *Newsweek,* August 17, 1992, p. 60; and Titus Aaron, "The Civil Liability of Churches for Sexual Misconduct," *Social Justice Review, 83* (March/April 1992), pp. 45–47.

104. Anthony P. Mannarino and Judith A. Cohen, "Family-Related Variables and Psychological Symptom Formation in Sexually Abused Girls," *Journal of Child Sexual Abuse, 5:* 14 (1996), p. 113.

105. For an example that demonstrates this type of research and some of the difficulties, see Beth E. Molnar, Stephen L. Buka, and Ronald C. Kessler, "Child Sexual Abuse and Subsequent Psychopathology: Results from the National Comorbidity Survey," *American Journal of Public Health, 91:* 5 (May 2001), p. 753.

106. Paul E. Mullen and Jillian Fleming, "Long-Term Effects of Child Sexual Abuse," *Issues in Child Abuse Prevention, 9* (Autumn 1998), [Online]. Available: http://www.aifs.org.au/nch/issue9/html

107. Finkelhor, *Sexually Victimized Children,* pp. 30–33, 97–108.

108. Larry L. Constantine, "The Effects of Early Sexual Experiences: A Review and Synthesis of Research," in *Children and Sex: New Findings, New Perspectives,* ed. Larry L. Constantine and Floyd M. Martinson (Boston: Little, Brown, 1981), p. 238. This book contains several other chapters detailing research efforts on the molesting effects. For a rejoinder to Constantine's conclusions, see Herman, *Father-Daughter Incest,* pp. 22–35.

109. Meda Chesney-Lind and Randall G. Shelden, *Girls, Delinquency, and Juvenile Justice* (Pacific Grove, CA: Brooks/Cole, 1992), pp. 32–33.

110. Finkelhor, *Child Sexual Abuse,* pp. 47–48, 191–196.

111. See the following in Constantine and Martinson, eds., *Children and Sex:* Joan A. Nelson, "The Impact of Incest: Factors in Self-Evaluation," pp. 163–174; Michael Ingram, "Participating Victims: A Study of Sexual Offenses with Boys," pp. 177–187; and Frits Bernard, "Pedophilia: Psychological Consequences for the Child," pp. 189–199. See also Theo Sandfort, *The Sexual Aspect of Paedophile Relations: The Experience of Twenty-Five Boys* (Amsterdam: Pan/Spartacus, 1982).

112. Quoted in Bernard, "Pedophilia," pp. 194–195.

113. Bennett M. Berger, "Liberating Child Sexuality: Commune Experiences," in *Children and Sex,* ed. Constantine and Martinson, pp. 251–254.

114. Larry L. Constantine, "The Sexual Rights of Children: Implications of a Radical Perspective," in *Children and Sex,* ed. Constantine and Martinson, pp. 255–263. The quotation is from M. S. Calderone, "Sexual Rights," *SIECUS Report,* May 1977, p. 5.

115. For examples of publicity concerning NAMBLA, see "A New Furor over Pedophilia," *Time,* January 17, 1983, p. 47; and Allan Sonnenschein, "Child Molesters and Their Victims: Close Encounters of the Worst Kind," *Penthouse,* April 1983, pp. 60ff.

116. Florence Rush, *The Best Kept Secret: Sexual Abuse of Children* (New York: McGraw-Hill, 1980), p. 172.

117. Herman, *Father-Daughter Incest,* p. 27.

118. Rush, *The Best Kept Secret,* p. 187. For a demurral to this argument, see Dennis Altman, *The Homosexualization of America, the Americanization of the Homosexual* (New York: St. Martin's Press, 1982), pp. 198–202.

119. Rod Nordland and Jeffrey Bartholet, "The Web's Darkest Secret," *Newsweek,* March 19, 2001, p. 47.

120. Al Knight, "ACLU Priorities Are Bizarre," *The Denver Post,* July 25, 2001, p. 7B.

CHAPTER

7

Deviance and Organizations

In 1939 Edwin H. Sutherland directed sociologists' attention to what he called "white-collar crime."[1] In his presidential address to the American Sociological Society, Sutherland declared that the profession's single-minded concern over persons officially designated as criminal—who are, of course, primarily from the lower class—resulted in misleading theories about the causes of crime that focused on feeble-mindedness, slums, unstable families, and so on. These theories ignored the criminality of business, professional, and political persons—those who are respected and looked up to. Upper-class individuals may not commit armed robbery, but they do bribe public officials, misrepresent products in advertising, embezzle, defraud the Internal Revenue Service, and generally cost society incredible sums of money. "Respectable" people are involved in what Al Capone, an organized crime figure of the 1920s, called the "legitimate rackets."

Because white-collar crimes were clearly not the result of poverty or of any known individual malady, Sutherland concluded that such crime existed because of *differential association,* a process whereby behavior is learned in association with those who define the behavior favorably and in isolation from those who define it unfavorably (see Chapter 2). As examples, Sutherland provided cases in which mastering the art of "practical business" often involves the learning of unethical or illegal procedures from those who have been successful:

> He [the beginner in business] learns specific techniques of violating the law, together with definitions of situations in which those techniques may be used. Also, he develops a general ideology. This ideology grows in part out of the specific practices and is in the nature of generalization from concrete experiences, but in part it is transmitted as a generalization by phrases such as "we are not in business for our health," or "no business was ever built on the beatitudes." These generalizations, whether transmitted as such or abstracted from concrete experiences, assist the neophyte in business to accept the illegal practices and provide rationalizations for them.[2]

Sutherland points out that businesspeople not only are exposed to definitions favorable to white-collar crime, but also are *isolated* from contrary definitions because business is generally shielded from criticism of its practices. At the extreme, to criticize business is to invite accusations of being un-American. But for the most part, criticizing business is a futile exercise because business interests are economically and politically powerful and are interwoven with the only element of society that can successfully challenge them: government.[3]

The concept of white-collar crime as originally formulated by Sutherland was limited to "crime committed by a person of respectability and high social status in the course of his occupation."[4] This definition, however, omitted the many respectable people besides the highly esteemed who are involved in occupationally related deviance: service station employees who make unnecessary car repairs, salespeople who sell ill-fitting clothes to gullible customers, and dentists who yank perfectly sound teeth out of unsuspecting heads. The color of the collar, whether white, blue, or pink, makes no difference, because nearly all occupations provide opportunities for deviance. An example of "white-collar" crime that applies to any individual or business that has vehicles and pays insurance on them is the following:

> The insurance industry has formed an organization . . . [—] the National Insurance Crime Bureau (NICB) [—that] will unify the industry's efforts to cut down on the estimated $17 billion a year insurers pay in false and inflated claims and the more than $8 billion a year they pay for vehicle theft. . . . According to NICB, an estimated 15 percent of all vehicle theft claims are fraudulent. Recent results from a Roper Poll conducted for the Insurance Research Council show that 23 percent of the respondents believe padding an auto claim is acceptable to make up for collision deductibles.[5]

Clearly, color of the collar is not relevant when it comes to some deviance or crime.

The term *crime* is misleading, however, since many acts of deviance in an occupation may not violate the traditional criminal code.[6] This is particularly true for organizations such as corporations. Many of the regulations that govern corporate operations are promulgated by federal regulatory agencies such as the Securities and Exchange Commission and the Federal Communications Commission. When a corporation breaks the rules that define matters such as unfair labor practices, unfair competition, false advertising, or patent infringement, these regulatory agencies are empowered to impose sanctions. If, for example, a furniture manufacturer advertises a pine chest of drawers as being constructed of "Indonesian mahogany," the Federal Trade Commission (FTC) is responsible for investigating complaints and instituting remedies. The FTC can recommend that certain acts be prosecuted in criminal courts, where the perpetrators will presumably be treated with the same evenhanded justice dispensed to muggers. As we shall see, however, the penalties imposed on corporations are usually minor at best. Few cases even reach the criminal court. In the instance of false advertising, a corporation's promise that it will desist from further publication of its fraudulent claims is usually sufficient as far as the FTC is concerned.[7] Imagine yourself under arrest for shoplifting—just try to tell the police that prosecution is unnecessary because you promise to desist from further illegal appropriation of merchandise. Good luck.

Despite problems with Sutherland's definition, the central point is inescapable: Well-to-do people commit acts of deviance that are related to their occupational positions. These positions provide them with opportunities to engage in behaviors that are not available to less well-off people.[8] Sutherland's work also focused upon *organizations* as important elements in the study of deviance. Sociologists have long been interested in *organized crime*— businesses set up specifically for the purpose of making profit from illegal enterprises—but Sutherland forces us to recognize that legitimate organizations as well as legitimate individuals can also be involved in a network of deviance.[9] While organizations may be victimized, they may also victimize.

One of the more comprehensive classifications of crime and organizations is provided by Herbert Edelhertz, part of which is presented here:

I. Crimes in the course of their occupations by those operating inside business, government, or other establishments in violation of their duty of loyalty and fidelity to employer or client.

   A. Commercial bribery and kickbacks, i.e., by and to buyers, insurance adjusters, contracting officers, quality inspectors, government inspectors and auditors, etc.

   B. Embezzlement or self-dealing by business or union officers and employees.

   C. Securities fraud by insiders trading to their advantage by the use of special knowledge, or causing their firms to take positions in the market to benefit themselves.

   D. Employee petty larceny and expense account frauds.

   E. Frauds by computer, causing unauthorized payouts.

   F. "Sweetheart contracts" entered into by union officers.

   G. Embezzlement or self-dealing by attorneys, trustees, and fiduciaries.

   H. Fraud against the government.

      1. Padding of payrolls.

      2. Conflicts of interest.

      3. False travel, expense, or per diem claims.

II. Crimes incidental to and in furtherance of business operations but not the central purpose of the business.

   A. Tax violations.

   B. Antitrust violations.

   C. Commercial bribery of another's employee, officer, or fiduciary (including union officials).

   D. Food and drug violations.

   E. False weights and measures by retailers.

   F. Violations of Truth-in-Lending Act by misrepresentation of credit terms and prices.

   G. Submission or publication of false financial statements to obtain credit.

   H. Securities Act violations, i.e., sale of nonregistered securities to obtain operating capital, false proxy statements, manipulation of market to support corporate credit or access to capital markets, and so on.

   I. Collusion between physicians and pharmacists to cause the writing of unnecessary prescriptions.

   J. Deceptive advertising.

   K. Commercial espionage.

III. White-collar crime as a business or as the central activity.

   A. Medical or health frauds.

   B. Advance fee swindles.

   C. Phony contests.

   D. Bankruptcy fraud, including schemes devised as salvage operations after insolvency of otherwise legitimate businesses.

   E. Securities fraud and commodities fraud.

    F. Chain referral schemes.
    G. Home improvement schemes.
    H. Land frauds.
    I. Charity and religious frauds.
    J. Personal improvement schemes.
        1. Diploma mills.
        2. Correspondence schools.
        3. Modeling schools.
    K. Insurance frauds.[10]

In this chapter we will discuss examples of deviance that roughly correspond to Edelhertz's three categories. We will begin with two types of occupational deviance in which respectable individuals violate the trust of their positions: employee theft and police corruption. Then we will consider organizational deviance in which legitimate firms are deviant to increase profits. This corresponds to Edelhertz's category II and is closest to what Sutherland had in mind when he first described white-collar crime. The chapter's final section will deal with organized crime, which in many respects approximates category III: white-collar crime as a business.

Employee Theft

As you are already aware, statistics on theft are based more on creative guesswork than on hard data. Nevertheless, they hold a fascination for us if only because numbers seem to indicate a kind of reality and give us something concrete to discuss. The FBI estimates that in 2002 robbery cost U.S. citizens $539 million, burglary $3.3 billion, and larceny-theft $4.9 billion.[11] If the magnitude of those numbers is staggering, it may surprise you to learn that their total of approximately $8 billion barely matches the lowest estimated annual loss from employee theft alone: from $5–10 billion to $25 billion.[12] Even if this estimate is exaggerated, it seems safe to assume that employee theft is one of the most costly, if not *the* most costly, offense by individuals in the United States. A survey of supermarket employees found that the average employee admitted to stealing approximately $143 per year, and the respondents estimated that their average co-worker stole another $1,176 per year.[13] Software piracy—the illegal copying of software packages—was estimated to be $3.6 billion annually for North America and Canada, and one in every three business software applications in use each year may have been pirated.[14] Finally, when discussing the costs of these crimes, it is worthwhile to remember that expenditures to combat them have risen dramatically. One report notes that private security is now an almost $20-billion-a-year industry, employing 2 million people.[15]

    For purposes of our discussion we shall divide employee theft into two types: *pilferage,* which refers to the theft of goods, and *embezzlement,* which refers to the misappropriation or misuse of funds entrusted to one's care. This distinction is necessary because studies of employee theft have concentrated on one or the other rather than both, and because embezzlement is generally a lone offense, whereas pilferage can involve several persons working in concert. In addition, nearly all employees, regardless of position, can pilfer, but employees who embezzle must hold special positions of trust that allow them access to funds.

Pilferage

Pilferage occurs among all types of employees and involves practically any item of value one can imagine. Recently, television shows with hospital settings, such as "ER," became popular. One consequence was that scrub suits (V-neck pullover tops and baggy drawstring pants) became hot items for jogging, sailing, and dancing at rock clubs. The suits began disappearing from hospitals; the situation has deteriorated to the point that hospitals have been forced to lease antitheft vending machines at a cost of $1,500 a month. In some hospitals the suit shortage was so great that doctors often stood around in their underwear before surgery while staff frantically searched for a scrub suit. On a less amusing note, a well-known researcher and author on the Blackfoot Indian tribe stole over a million dollars worth of artifacts from the museum in which he worked. In another case an individual known as a "family man, helpful neighbor, successful engineer, and plant manager" with "an unblemished 26-year record of advancement" in high-technology firms sold his employer's vital trade secrets to competitors all around the world. The secrets were worth millions.[16]

What and how employees steal vary greatly and depend, of course, upon their positions and access to goods. Without question, a considerable degree of innovation is often involved. In one interesting case an airline employee stole expensive, small electronic parts from the airline's facility. He then shipped them to a friend, who formed a supply company. The airline employee then "ordered" the parts from his friend's company, who happily sold the parts to the airline.[17]

Among the common techniques of pilferage are the following:

1. Cashiers who ring up a lower price on single-item purchases and pocket the difference or who ring up lower prices for friends going through the checkout.
2. Clerks who do not tag some sale merchandise, sell it at the original price, and pocket the difference.
3. Receiving clerks who have duplicate keys to storage facilities and return to the store after hours.
4. Truck drivers who make fictitious purchases of fuel and repairs and split the gain with truck stop employees.
5. Employees who simply hide items in garbage pails, incinerators, or trash heaps and retrieve them later.[18]

Let us not forget a form of pilferage available mainly to executives and traveling sales personnel: expense account padding. Most padding, such as using a bus while billing the company for taxi fare, requires little imagination. But some requires genuine creativity:

> A stockbroker in Fort Lauderdale regularly turned in chits for visits to a massage parlor as "physical therapy." The parlor's operator gave him the receipts.

> A Houston farm equipment executive, who treated a group of friends to a few games of bumper pool at the local Playboy Club, put in for $30. He described the expense as the cost

of "researching the mobility of spherically shaped objects in juxtaposition with vertical sides of felt-covered shale." He got away with it.

A Los Angeles art director charged his company for pornographic books and wrote them off as "art references."[19]

In a survey of 47 corporations including department stores, general hospitals, and electronics firms, one-third of the employees reported that they had stolen company property. The survey also found that pilferage within a company was linked to worker dissatisfaction with immediate supervisors and worker perceptions of the company's indifferent attitude toward the workforce. "Employees who felt that their employers were genuinely concerned with the workers' best interests reported the least theft."[20]

But worker dissatisfaction does not in and of itself explain pilferage. It is not simply a matter of individual soreheads running off with whatever is not nailed down in the shop. Sociological research indicates that while pilferers usually act alone and in secret, pilferage itself is a *group-supported activity* with norms that regulate what and how much may be taken. One of the earliest studies of this phenomenon was conducted by Donald N. M. Horning in an electronics assembly plant. He found that the workers defined property in three categories: company property (power tools, machinery, testing equipment), personal property (items owned by workers and marked as personal), and property of uncertain ownership. The stealing of items in this last category was collectively considered legitimate by the workers: unmarked clothing, small tools, and most items that were small, plentiful, and individually inexpensive—nails, screws, electrical tape, scrap metal, wipe rags. Horning found no widespread justification for large-scale theft from the company, but as long as the stealing was confined to property of uncertain ownership that was not sold but was taken only for personal use, pilferage was defined as acceptable:

> "Most of [the equipment] belongs to the Company—but there are some things that are furnished by the Company which ya might say we own—for instance, I got me a little electric fan that I made from junk I found out there—I've got my name painted on it. . . . It's mine."[21]

Alfred N. Weiner claims that drug addiction, other economic pressures, and simply the desire to own something are common motivations for pilferage. He concludes that pilferage on a large scale is a reflection of management ineffectiveness in hiring procedures, loss prevention programs such as spontaneous audits, and general internal security.[22] Most forms of motivation disappear with diligent adherence to the proper practices. Sue Titus Reid echoes the same thought but instead argues for the effectiveness of vigorous civil procedures to recover property and to establish an environment of strong managerial commitment to loss prevention.[23]

Subsequent research has consistently shown that the work group indeed sets limits on pilferage. For example, Gerald Mars studied dockside pilferage by longshoremen. He found that the work crews not only define the types of cargo that may be stolen but also set a "value of the boat" that dictates how much cargo can be taken from a particular ship.[24] And, as one might suspect, research has also shown that the informal sanctions of the work group exert more influence than do the formal sanctions of management in controlling pilferage.[25]

Why do norms favoring pilferage or expense account padding exist in the first place? A possible clue to answering that question is suggested in a study of embezzlement.

Embezzlement

Pilferers come from many stations within organizations, from janitors to executives. They steal everything from pencils to 20-ton cranes. But the real stars among employee thieves are the embezzlers. In most cases they occupy positions in the middle or upper echelons of the organization, they are trusted beyond question, and they are stealing the organization blind. *Embezzlers are people who use their positions of trust to acquire the employer's money for their own use.* The following example represents the range of individuals who embezzle.

For example, a former Norwest Bank employee embezzled more than $7.1 million over 12 years from the branch in Sauk Rapids, Minnesota. Most of it went to pay for her gambling addiction. The judge in this case chided the bank, saying that they "must have been leaving the safe open at night." In a recent article concerning employee theft, John Conley notes that the average organization loses 6 percent of its annual revenues to employee fraud with an annual price tag of $400 billion. Interestingly, even with losses ranging from $40 to $25 million, only two-thirds of these cases were reported to law enforcement authorities, the victims "preferring to sweep the crime under the rug rather than risk a blemish on their reputation."[26]

The very best of people can become embezzlers. Indeed, they would have to be the best of people to be in a position to embezzle. Why do they do it? Is it a matter of fast lovers and slow horses or of keeping up with the neighbors? The closest answer to these questions comes from Donald R. Cressey, who sought to determine the sequence of events that occurs when people violate their positions of financial trust. After eliminating from his sample those who had not taken their positions of trust in good faith—that is, those who intended to embezzle even before taking the job—he concludes that

> trusted persons become trust violators when they conceive of themselves as having a financial problem which is nonsharable, are aware that this problem can be secretly resolved by violation of the position of financial trust, and are able to apply to their own conduct in the situation verbalizations which enable them to adjust their conceptions of themselves as trusted persons with their conceptions of themselves as users of the entrusted funds.[27]

As you can see, the process of trust violation involves three steps. The first, the *nonsharable financial problem* refers to money difficulties that the individual believes must be kept secret because he or she feels ashamed. These difficulties are extremely varied, according to Cressey, but all are related to worries over *social status*. But seeking to maintain or increase one's standard of living and respectability will not cause embezzlement unless it creates a nonsharable problem for the individual. It matters not whether a person faces debt because of gambling, a new swimming pool, or a business setback; it is the failure to reveal the problem to anyone that can lead to embezzlement. Cressey cites the case of a banker who feared financial difficulty because his salary did not meet the ordinary expenses of his family:

> "No, [my wife] didn't know about it. I never told her. I took care of all the finances in the family. It wasn't her job. When it was all over she said I should have told her, that she could have cut down on a lot of things. She never knew how much I made. That's one thing, if I had it all to do over again I'd tell her all about everything."[28]

Failure to reveal financial problems to others does not alone cause embezzlement, however. The individual must also *perceive that funds entrusted to her or his care can be used to relieve the financial problem.* Many times this is learned as part of acquiring the skills of the job. As one auditor put it,

> "by the time an accountant has done some auditing work he learns what an auditor is for—it becomes common knowledge to him. Naturally, I knew I shouldn't take it, but still the fact that I was the only one making the reports, I knew I shouldn't be found out."[29]

Once the individual has defined a financial problem as nonsharable and realizes the possibility of resolving it by embezzlement, a third and last step remains: The individual must *adjust the concept of herself or himself as a trusted employee with the concept of a person violating that trust.* This adjustment involves verbalized motives—what Cressey calls "vocabularies of adjustment." The particular motives found among embezzlers center especially on the idea that they simply were "borrowing," not stealing, the money; the funds would be used to clear up some difficulties and then returned, with no one harmed or any wiser. Other motives define the embezzlement as justified because the employer paid too little salary or was crooked or both. In other instances a kind of to-hell-with-it attitude emerges in which a combination of financial woes, drink, and other difficulties gets to be too much.[30]

Cressey is careful to point out that these motives are not dreamed up to account for long-past behavior. Instead, trusted individuals acquire the motives from the culture *in advance* and apply them to their own specific situations. These reasons for violating a trust are available to all:

> [Verbalized motives] are not something invented by embezzlers (or anyone else) on the spur of the moment. Before they can be taken over by an individual, these verbalizations exist as group definitions in which the behavior in question, even crime, is in a sense *appropriate.* There are any number of popular ideologies that sanction crime in our culture: "Honesty is the best policy, but business is business"; "It is all right to steal a loaf of bread when you are starving"; "All people steal when they get in a tight spot." Once these verbalizations have been assimilated and internalized by individuals, they take a form such as: "I'm only going to use the money temporarily, so I am borrowing, not stealing," or "I have tried to live an honest life, but I've had nothing but troubles, so to hell with it."[31]

In James W. Coleman's assessment of the recent research on embezzlers, he attributes the growing number of women involved in this behavior to their increased access to book-keeping and accounting positions as well as their increased responsibility for family finan-cial support. Another interesting conclusion seems to be that many people simply grow accustomed to living beyond their financial means and then turn to embezzlement to cope with heavy credit card and other personal debt. Rationalizing the crime of embezzlement is apparently becoming less complex. Coleman also discusses "collective embezzlement," which is defined as the expenditure of company funds for purely personal use by top exec-utives, and focuses on groups of such people who use their authority to loot the corporation. The implication is that this too is a growing phenomenon, although the same activity may have been classified differently in the past.[32]

Another area of concern is the use of computer systems (see Chapter 11) for large-scale embezzlement. FBI data demonstrate that sophisticated computer criminals can take advantage of new electronic banking systems to steal from financial institutions. With little personal risk, computer-based thieves average between $400,000 to $560,000 per crime, while traditional bank robbers get only a few thousand and are caught more frequently.

Organizations as Victims

So far we have concentrated on two forms of deviance—pilferage and embezzlement—in which individuals within organizations victimize them by violating a trust. This deviance represents a borderline between the "crime in the streets" discussed in earlier chapters and the deviance of organizations themselves, to be discussed shortly. With few exceptions pilfering and embezzling are actions by "respectable" people. Their respectability generally shields them from detection and from the embarrassment of being regarded as common criminals if they are detected.

We are left with the question of why there is in the United States an undercurrent of public indifference, if not resentment, toward organizations and their property. In particular, why do organizations constantly face the problem of their otherwise honest employees taking company supplies and padding expense accounts? Are we to take at face value the employees' claims of inadequate pay and of the companies' ability to afford the losses?

The lack of employee responsibility toward organizations is perhaps understandable in light of two factors. First, the impersonality of large organizations makes it difficult for employees to form strong allegiances to the company. Employees' workdays are spent with co-workers; the company provides only the context in which work occurs. True, the company pays one's salary, but that can stop at any time. The company exists for one thing: to make a profit. When you as an employee cease being profitable, you are likely to cease being an employee. The only tangible evidence of regret over your leaving will come from co-workers. If you have allegiances to anyone in the organization, it is likely to be your work group, not the organization itself. It is not surprising, then, that the pilfering norms of the work group are more influential than are the formal regulations of the company.

Second, relationships among individuals and organizations have traditionally been based on conflict. As we mentioned in Chapter 7, the U.S. labor movement has a stormy history. Attempts to unionize workers and to obtain shorter hours, higher pay, and better working conditions frequently met with violent resistance from companies. The antagonistic relationship did not disappear with the end of open warfare between labor and management, however. Workers are still interested in job security, workplace safety, and a good wage; companies are still interested in extracting from workers as much as possible for as little as possible.

This is, of course, an oversimplified version of a very complex situation. Nevertheless, the conflict between workers and employers is reenacted continuously in strikes. In most cases strikes are symbolic affairs in which the two sides suspend contact with one another while negotiations take place between their representatives. In extreme cases strikes become nasty—property, usually the company's, is damaged; a few people get shot at; and each side vows to bring the other to its knees. Workers have ample precedent for viewing their employer as an enemy or as someone who only grudgingly provides increased extra pay or a better pension plan. Consequently, there is little obvious reason to treat the employer's property with much more than indifference.

The conflict between individuals and organizations extends beyond labor-management quarrels. A long-standing U.S. business principle is *caveat emptor.* Literally translated as "let the buyer beware," this means that sellers of products or services have no responsibility for quality, unless something is specifically guaranteed by a warranty. In short, what you buy is what you get. The fine print of contracts and many instances of outright fraud against customers have led to misunderstanding, resentment, and cynicism toward business. Offenses committed by organizations will be discussed later, but it should be said here that individuals, both customers and employees, know that companies can be guilty of their own particular brand of immorality. The ethical standards expected of individuals are often not met by employers. Thus the property of organizations is less than sanctified, and the theft of that property is more easily justified.

Police Corruption

> *I like policemen. It gives me a very secure feeling, knowing that it's that blue uniform that is all that stands between me and him robbing and killing me.*
> —Woody Allen

There was a time when the police radiated an image akin to sainthood. Calendars given away by lumber stores in small towns carried pictures of a ruddy-cheeked officer stopping traffic to allow a duck and her brood to cross the road—at a plainly marked crosswalk, of course. Times change, however. In the 1960s the image for many Americans was the bull-necked, potbellied policeman clubbing a bloody, helpless figure—a white student or any black person. The 1970s brought still another image: In several U.S. cities the appropriate calendar illustration might have depicted two officers stealing television sets through a store's rear door, while out front another policeman stands lookout as he casually takes a bribe from a heroin pusher. The police image for the 1980s and the 1990s comes primarily from television. A major police scandal over extortion in Philadelphia, scandals in other cities, the March 1991 beating of Rodney King by members of the Los Angeles Police Department (LAPD), and the LAPD Rampart scandal (with 65 officers facing charges that they routinely beat, robbed, framed, and sometimes shot suspects) now shape our image of police.[33]

Police in disrepute project an image that does not accurately portray most officers. But the "thin blue line" protecting us from crime becomes definitely crooked at times. And much of the crookedness is related to the nature of police work: It is a job uniquely surrounded by temptations and pressures toward several forms of deviance. Police swear to "enforce and uphold" all laws within their jurisdiction, and they must know not only what behaviors or conditions are illegal but also how legally to deal with offenders. Consequently, they may violate their oath and public trust in many ways: They may ignore violations; they may act illegally when making arrests or controlling individuals; and, of course, they may break laws just as other citizens do. The following discussion of police deviance will concentrate on *corruption.* Police brutality and the use of illegal means to apprehend offenders or obtain evidence will not be examined.[34] Omission of these topics is not meant to minimize their importance. But however distasteful these behaviors may be, they are at least consistent with the general goal of police work: controlling criminal activity.[35] Our concern is with *actions that exploit law enforcement powers to obtain personal benefit.*[36]

According to Michael Johnston, there are four major categories of police corruption:

1. Internal corruption. This usually does not involve the public. It refers to actions within departments such as making payoffs to obtain choice duties and selling drugs among police personnel.

2. Selective enforcement or nonenforcement of laws. Police officers who witness a crime can often exercise discretion in deciding whether to make an arrest. Although there are many situations in which an offender's arrest would plainly not benefit the individual or the society, corruption creeps in when arrest decisions are based on friendship, political pull, or bribery.

3. Active criminality. Police personnel have access to and knowledge about places vulnerable to crime. Armed and in two-way radio communication with other officers, police can be a potent force for or against burglary. (During a Des Moines scandal over a police burglary ring, it was widely rumored that the physical fitness tests for police recruits included a 100-yard dash with a television set under each arm.)

4. Bribery and extortion. Bribery refers to payoffs initiated by the citizen; extortion refers to payoffs demanded by the police. These practices vary widely, and they range from individual officers who occasionally accept bribes to highly organized groups of officers who are paid to protect illegal businesses.[37]

Meat- and Grass-Eaters

A wave of police corruption scandals began in 1970 on both the east and west coasts. In Seattle it was discovered that police officers were receiving at least $144,000 a year from a vice ring; in New York City *The New York Times* reported that the police were systematically being paid off by gamblers, narcotics peddlers, and other law violators and that police officials and city administrators had been informed of the corruption but had failed to take action. There followed a procession of similar scandals across the country: Chicago, Atlantic City, Albany, Philadelphia, and Indianapolis. Even small cities were not spared: Bowling Green, Ohio, and Newburgh, New York, dismissed sizable proportions of their police forces because of various forms of corruption.

The offenses involved in the scandals ranged from the mildly amusing to the grotesque:

- In Albany police broke into parked cars if they saw something they wanted inside. On occasion they jacked cars up and stole the tires.
- Also in Albany, Trixie's House of Prostitution paid police $600 a week to remain open. On Fridays, payoff day, the traffic of detectives and uniformed officers coming in to get protection money was so heavy that the brothel was closed to customers from 5:30 to 9:00 P.M.
- Still in Albany, officers collecting money from parking meters "nickeled and dimed" the city out of over $36,000 a year.

■ In Atlantic City a hotel operator paid $10,000 annually to more than 60 city police-men to ensure that his hotels would not be closed for violations of health and fire reg-ulations. One patrolman asked that he be notified immediately of any death in the hotels so he could get whatever money was in the dead person's pockets.[38]

The situation has not gotten better, with charges of corruption in Miami, New York City (again), Philadelphia, and Boston.[39] The scandal that received the greatest national attention was in New York City. Events leading up to the scandal began in the mid-1960s, when two officers took information of serious police corruption to several highly placed officials.[40] The officials essentially ignored the information, however. In 1970, after *The New York Times* published the charges, Mayor John V. Lindsay authorized the establishing of the Commission to Investigate Allegations of Police Corruption and the City's Anti-Cor-ruption Procedures. This commission came to be known as the Knapp Commission after its chairman, Judge Whitman Knapp.

The commission found that corruption was widespread in the New York City police force and that it was not confined to the lower ranks but reached into the upper echelons.[41] As with all forms of thievery, police corruption can be roughly divided into "amateur" and "professional" categories, depending on the degree of commitment. The great majority of corrupt police officers in New York were described as *grass-eaters:* They accepted what-ever payoffs their work happened to throw their way. They took under-the-table payments and gifts but did not aggressively pursue them. *Meat-eaters,* by contrast, spent many of their working hours seeking out situations that they could exploit for large financial gain. For them, a single payoff might range from $5,000 to $50,000.[42]

A model meat-eater testified before the Knapp Commission. William Phillips—owner of five private airplanes on a $12,000 patrolman's salary—described himself as a "super thief."[43] Money came to Phillips from many sources: gamblers, pimps, loan sharks, illegal liquor dealers, owners of bowling alleys, garages, and so on. An unusual source was an undertaker who paid 10 percent of the funeral price for any new body he heard about from Phillips. After a phone call from Phillips the undertaker would rush to the relatives of the recently deceased to say, "I understand there's been a tragedy in the family."

One of the best indicators of Phillips's professionalism was his ability to find out, merely by a phone call, whether any specific officer on the force could safely be approached with a corrupt proposal. That he could do this also indicated the extent to which corruption had permeated the New York City police department—Phillips had innumerable contacts scattered throughout the force who were corrupt and knew whoever else was corrupt.

The Knapp Commission found that the principal opportunities for police corruption came from the following sources:

1. **Gambling.** To avoid police intervention in their operations, gamblers paid a form of insurance:

   The heart of the gambling payoff system was found to be the plainclothes "pad." In a highly systemized pattern . . . plainclothesmen collected regular bi-weekly or monthly payoffs from gamblers. . . . The pad money was picked up at designated locations by one or more bagmen who were most often police officers but who occasionally were ex-policemen or civilians. The proceeds were then pooled and divided up among all or virtually all of the division's plainclothesmen. . . . Division plainclothesmen generally met once a month to divide up the money and to discuss matters concerning the pad—i.e., inviting plainclothes-men newly assigned to the division to join, raising or lowering the amounts paid by various gamblers, and so forth.[44]

The average monthly share per man in these operations ranged from $400 to $1,500, depending on the area of the city.

2. **Narcotics.** Patterns of corruption involving drugs were many. Here are a few beyond the usual bribe-taking:
   a. Keeping money and/or narcotics confiscated at the time of an arrest or raid
   b. Selling narcotics to addict-informants in exchange for stolen goods
   c. Passing on confiscated drugs to police informants for sale to addicts
   d. "Flaking," or planting narcotics on arrested persons to have evidence of law violations
   e. "Padding," or adding to the quantity of narcotics found on arrested persons to upgrade arrests
   f. Introducing potential customers to narcotics pushers
   g. Revealing the identities of government informants to narcotics dealers
   h. Providing armed protection for narcotics dealers
   i. Offering to obtain hit men to kill potential witnesses

3. **Prostitution.** It is an unwritten rule among police that taking money from prostitutes is risky business because prostitutes are considered unreliable and are likely to become informants. Nevertheless, brothels, prostitution bars, and streetwalkers often had to make payoffs to New York City police.

4. **Construction.** The Knapp Commission described a "dizzying array" of ordinances in connection with construction work. It found that building construction in New York City required a minimum of 40 permits and licenses. In addition, ordinances covered a variety of related problems: noise, dust, double parking, obstruction of sidewalks, and so on. The inspection for certain permits and the enforcement of construction ordinances are the responsibility of police. The result was that construction work provided an opportunity for police corruption—it was easier for contractors to make payoffs than it was to comply with all the ordinances. For example, $50 to $100 a week was paid to allow double parking of concrete trucks. According to testimony received by the commission, the cost of buildings may be increased by as much as 5 percent because of bribes paid to police.[45]

5. **Bars.** The commission estimated that payoffs from construction and from liquor establishments were the most common sources of illegal income for police. Bars were vulnerable to extortion if they catered to prostitutes, drug users, gamblers, or homosexuals. After-hours and unlicensed operations were also prone to extortion, but even legitimate bars might have trouble. For example, some patrolmen threatened bar owners with flushing soap down the toilet and then writing a summons for having no soap in the rest room.

The Knapp Commission found many forms of police corruption and many sources of temptation for police. The essential question is: Why do police violate their trust by yielding to these temptations?

Rotten Apples or Rotten Barrels?

Traditional explanations of police corruption begin with the assumption that the great majority of police and the police system itself are good. Nevertheless, a small minority of cops still turn bad. The usual metaphor employed is apples. The logic is that one is apt to find a few rotten apples in any barrel and that the important thing is to screen them out before they contaminate the others.

To this explanation are often added complaints about apathy or hostility toward police. Police receive little support from the public they serve; they are poorly paid (average starting salary was around $29,840 per year in 1999),[46] they work long hours, and the public is indifferent about the standard required of them. In short, police just do not get any respect. According to the rotten apple theory, corruption will be minimized by better screening of police applicants, higher standards for recruits, better pay, and more effective police-community relations.

It is difficult to argue with any of these claims about the characteristics of police work and public attitudes toward police. It would be unrealistic to argue that the foregoing proposals would not improve police effectiveness. But as an explanation of police corruption, the rotten apple theory fails to confront a crucial reality, namely, that while isolated instances of corruption may be attributed to inadequate recruiting and training, *the theory does not explain corruption that spreads throughout the hierarchy of a department*. The Knapp Commission was especially emphatic about laying to rest the rotten apple theory when it pointed out that New York City police corruption was not only widespread and included upper-level officers but also had been ignored by administrators and "good" police for years. In New York City the corrupt policeman (no women were involved) was not isolated; rather, he was "only one part of an apparatus of corruption."[47] Thus the *barrel itself* is suspect, and support for corruption is built into the law enforcement system. The three main sources of that support are public encouragement of corruption, police solidarity, and laws that encourage corruption.

1. Public encouragement of corruption.

> A police officer and his partner stop for lunch at a small diner. Both in uniform, they sit at the counter and eat a full meal. When they are done, they wave at the owner and leave, paying nothing. Neither the owner nor the police officers give the matter much thought, for the owner routinely gives free lunch to the officers working the district.[48]

Many police officers have become sensitive to the ethical issues associated with traditional gratuities and gifts, and an increasing number of departments have changed their standard operating procedures to minimize any suggestion of corrupt behavior. Indeed, in some areas officers seek out restaurants that *refuse* to give price breaks to police. However, old habits don't die easily for some, and civilians continue to accept (perhaps grudgingly) the concept of gratuities for police as a "perk" of the job. In addition to free meals, there are free hotel rooms, free drinks, Christmas payments, free merchandise, and miscellaneous tips for services rendered:[49]

> The fact is that the public by and large does not regard gratuities as a serious matter. While some may be offended by the occasionally arrogant way in which some police officers

demand what they consider to be their due, most people are willing to allow a police officer who spends long hours providing protection for an area to stop in for a quick free meal or cup of coffee at an eating establishment which enjoys the benefit of his protection.[50]

Of course, the public does not approve of police robbing or blackmailing citizens; but with regard to gratuities the public does, in its own way, encourage graft, however petty and grass-eating it may seem. The free cup of coffee, the whiskey at Christmas, and the discount on purchased goods are offered with the best of intentions: respect and appreciation. But they are also offered as incentives to pay a little more attention at night to places of business. In still other cases they are offered in gratitude for overlooking minor infractions such as overparking or double-parking by customers. There is also the "gratuity" offered by citizens who, when stopped for speeding, hand over their driver's licenses along with a $20 bill as an inducement not to write a summons.

In a three-city survey (Boston, Chicago, and Washington, DC) the researcher found that one-third of all businesses in high-crime areas openly admitted giving favors to police in the form of free merchandise or services; at the very least they gave discounts. Observers riding in squad cars found that one-third of all officers on duty did not pay for their meals:[51]

> Many officers reported large discounts on purchases of durable goods. On most occasions, free goods or discounts are not solicited, largely because officers know well which businesses offer them and which do not. The informal police networks carry such information, obviating in most cases open solicitation. . . . These transactions are viewed as "favors" by the line and tacitly approved by their superiors.[52]

Buying favors—that is what most police corruption is about. While a distinction can be made between accepting an occasional free meal and taking bribes in connection with narcotics and prostitution, the difference is a matter of degree. The end result is the same: Some police are being bought.

2. Police solidarity. In nearly all the scandals that make headlines, many honest police were aware of the widespread corruption in their departments, but extremely few were willing to do anything about it. The heavy, meat-eating corruption was viewed with distaste, but it went on for years, along with the milder grass-eating variety, because honest colleagues looked the other way.

This indifference of police toward corruption in their own ranks is not simply the result of misplaced loyalty. Rather, it indicates the solidarity of police that emerges as a necessary element of the job.[53] Few occupations are as close-knit as police work. In large part, this is a result of police isolation from the rest of society. Although the public may appreciate the protection that police offer, there is also an underlying resentment of their authority. The police are obliged to regulate other people's lives: They ticket speeders, pick up drunks, investigate suspicious behavior, and affect others' lives in many ways. Because of their authority and their peculiar working conditions, police are not readily integrated into the social world of others. Some find that they must rely almost exclusively upon the supports available within their occupational group. At the same time many police view the rest of society as being unsympathetic and unable to comprehend the nature of police work.[54]

Another element that contributes to police solidarity is the dangerousness of the job. Although the typical police day is filled with routine and boredom, the threat of danger is always present. Since the ordinary citizen is unlikely to help a policeman or policewoman in trouble, when things get rough, police offers can rely only on each other:

> The ordinary citizen does not assume the responsibility to implicate himself in the police-man's required response to danger. The element of danger in the policeman's role alienates him not only from populations with a potential for crime but also from the conventionally respectable (white) citizenry, in short, from the segment of the population from which friends would ordinarily be drawn.[55]

Police work in tight, informal groups and see themselves as operating alone against an indifferent, if not hostile, world. Any illegal practices that emerge within police groups can develop into secret standards for the groups. These standards are perpetuated by being passed on to recruits coming into the ranks. Should a recruit resist participation, group acceptance will be withheld, and the recruit will experience isolation because of his or her lack of group "loyalty." To remain completely honest under such conditions is difficult enough. To "blow the whistle" on one's colleagues is almost impossible. Thus the honest police officer overlooks corruption in order to avoid rejection, to protect the cohesiveness of the force, and to avoid interference from outsiders who do not understand police work.[56]

3. Laws that encourage corruption. The reader will recall from our discussion of the Knapp Commission that the principal opportunities for police corruption come from gambling, narcotics, prostitution, construction, and bars. The laws that regulate these activities have one thing in common: They are difficult to enforce because *there are no victims who will complain.* Participants in gambling, narcotics dealing, and prostitution generally act voluntarily, whether as sellers or buyers. Construction contractors are merely trying to cut through a maze of red tape to build more efficiently and profitably, and bar owners who violate the law are simply providing convenience for their customers.

Whether gambling, prostitution, and after-hours drinking cause harm is essentially irrelevant to the police. Laws prohibit the behavior, and police are responsible for enforcing them. But there is no urgency about enforcing these laws, as there is with the laws against homicide, rape, and robbery. It is this lack of urgency that fosters corruption. The combination of large demand for the illegal services—which results in large money—and the lingering question of whether something so wanted should be illegal means that bribe money does not have the taint of something "serious."

The Knapp Commission believed that the dangers of corruption from gambling and similar laws often outweighed any dangers from the behaviors themselves.[57] It recommended that criminal laws against gambling be repealed and that other means be undertaken for handling prostitution and narcotics.[58] About other opportunities for police corruption, the commission categorically stated that

> as a simple matter of efficiency there is no justification for using the police—with all their powers and prerogatives—in the enforcement of many miscellaneous regulations. It is ridiculous to have an armed officer wasting his time (and that of his partner and supervising sergeant) checking restaurant washrooms to find out whether they are properly supplied with soap. We believe that the police should be taken out of bars and restaurants and away from building sites and returned to their principal job of protecting lives and property.[59]

Police corruption stems from more than just a few misplaced and misguided individuals. It has its roots in the organizational context of police work: isolation, solidarity, and unrealistic law enforcement goals. But we must not fail to mention the respectable public's collusion. The public makes its own payoffs to police and provides most of the customers for prostitution, after-hours bars, and gambling. Since the public often wants the police to "look the other way," it should not be surprised when they do just that.

Corporate Deviance

Competition brings out the best in products and the worst in men.

—David Sarnoff

The reader will recall from our earlier discussion that Edwin H. Sutherland defined white-collar crime as violations of the law by persons of respectability and high status in the course of their occupations. Most of the crimes mentioned by Sutherland involve the illegal attempts of business to increase profits and gain competitive advantage.[60] So far in this chapter we have discussed the deviant behavior of individuals acting against the interest of the organization. Now we shall turn to individuals acting on behalf of an organization, specifically a corporation. A corporation is

> an organization formed under a state statute for the purpose of carrying on an enterprise distinct and separate from the persons who control it; " . . . an artificial being, invisible, intangible, and existing only in contemplation of law." . . .
>
> In a corporation—particularly a large corporation with many stockholders—those who have contributed to the capital of the business do not ordinarily conduct its affairs. Management is concentrated in the hands of a Board of Directors, elected by the stockholders, who may own only a small portion of the stock. Stockholders cannot bind the corporation by their acts merely because they are stockholders.[61]

The individuals of concern to us are not the stockholders, however, but any number of individuals within a corporation who make and implement decisions about planning, manufacturing, distribution, pricing, and advertising. They can range from members of the board of directors to department heads, and down to the great array of lesser-ranked managers *who act for and in the name of the corporation* when dealing with other employees, other companies, customers, and the general public. These are the individuals who may cause a corporation to engage in such illegal behaviors as (1) undermining collective bargaining efforts by unions, (2) conspiring with competitors to keep prices uniform or not to cut prices on certain products, (3) failing to report dangerous working conditions or the sale of dangerous products to the public, (4) drastically cutting prices in only one product area for the purpose of eliminating competition, (5) misrepresenting products in advertising or in sales practices, and (6) engaging in practices that damage the environment.

Despite advertised claims to the contrary, the foremost goal of any business in a capitalist society is to make a profit. Without profit—or at least a government subsidy—no business can long survive. The roads to profit are many. Ideally, the best road is to provide a superior product or service that the public needs at a price consistent with the quality. But some products are difficult to make better than those of one's competitors. One can make a better automobile, but how does one improve a golf tee so that customers abandon the competition in droves? Microsoft has been involved in defending itself against monopolistic practices for years. Already facing remedies for antitrust violations concerning some past practices, Microsoft's antitrust violations should be quickly addressed by a lower court because it has recently released a new version of its "monopoly operating system," according to government attorneys. Windows XP continues the practice of bundling software programs, giving Microsoft an edge, critics say.[62]

But antitrust violations and even price fixing are rather trivial in comparison with other methods that companies use to sustain their profit margins:

> An explosion killed 15 miners in the Dutch Creek No. 1 Mine near Redstone, Colorado. In the previous five years the mine had been cited for 1,133 health and safety violations.[63]

> Dow Chemical knew that defoliants containing dioxin might injure and even kill people, but the company kept the information secret and continued selling the products to the government and the public. Dioxin was used in Agent Orange, an herbicide used during the Vietnam war. Some 20,000 veterans of that war have filed suit against Dow, claiming that their exposure to the chemical has injured them.[64]

> A. H. Robins Company sold some 4.5 million Dalkon Shields, a birth control device, that resulted in 5 percent of the users becoming pregnant. An estimated 60 percent of the women who conceived with the Shields in place lost their unborn. The Food and Drug Administration did nothing to protect Shield wearers for nine years, from the time the Shield went off the market in 1974 until 1983, when a study by the Centers for Disease Control incriminated the device. The FDA never acted on a petition filed by the National Women's Health Network in April 1983 for a recall, to be paid for by Robins, to ensure retrieval of the Shield.[65]

> In what is perhaps the most remarkable case (the company president actually went to prison), in 1991 a fire broke out in a poultry-processing plant in Hamlet, North Carolina, after a hydraulic line burst, spraying flammable material onto a chicken fryer. The management of the company, Imperial Food Products, fearing the pilfering of processed chickens, had locked the emergency exits. Twenty-six people were killed, and 56 were seriously injured.

> Finally, Bridgestone/Firestone, Inc. very reluctantly announced a recall of some tires in August 2000, after it become public that some Ford Explorer SUVs equipped with the tires had crashed and rolled over. As of August 2001 there had been 203 deaths and at least 700 injuries. Bridgestone/Firestone has blamed Ford, citing design flaws inherent in the vehicle.[66]

Most of the lawsuits against Bridgestone/Firestone and Ford have been settled quietly, but the list of corporate wrongdoing is long and can easily be expanded. In fact, according to one report, over half of the 25 largest U.S. corporations have been convicted of or have settled serious criminal charges against them in recent history.[67] The point of the list is to impress on the reader that corporate deviance is not a trifling issue—it is often calculated, expensive, and dangerous. In the following section we will discuss in detail other examples of corporate deviance. Some of them are expensive, some dangerous, and all calculated.

Price-Fixing: A Fact of American Industry?

In the late 1800s the U.S. economy was moving toward what Karl Marx termed "monopolistic capitalism." Great trusts arose in which vast and diverse industries were concentrated in the hands of a few combinations such as John D. Rockefeller's Standard Oil. One result of these monopolies was the virtual elimination of competition based on prices; instead, prices were fixed by agreement of the companies under control of the same trust. But price-fixing was only part of the problem:

> Producers of raw material were compelled to accept whatever the trust chose to pay, for there was no other buyer; labor was forced into line by the closing of troublesome plants, and by the circulation of blacklists that prevented agitators from obtaining employment; politicians were influenced by free railroad passes, by campaign contributions, and by outright bribes. Powerful lobbies became the "third house" of Congress.[68]

Eventually, the public, particularly labor organizations, farmers, and small businesses, demanded that something be done about a situation in which wealth and power were increasingly concentrated in the hands of a very few. The result was the Sherman Act of 1890, which made illegal the monopolizing of trade and any contract, combination, or conspiracy attempting to eliminate competition. Although the Sherman Act and subsequent antitrust laws were instrumental in breaking up some monopolies—Standard Oil was broken into 38 units in 1911—the concentration of power in the hands of a few corporations has recently accelerated.[69] In 1960, 450 corporations controlled half the nation's manufacturing assets; thirty years later, those corporations controlled nearly three-quarters of the assets.[70]

Even with monopolies, price-fixing between competitors has not vanished. The best-documented example began in the mid-1940s, when various heavy electrical equipment manufacturers decided to fix prices among themselves. What has come to be known as the "Electrical Conspiracy" involved twenty-nine companies controlling 95 percent of the industry.[71] Most prominent were General Electric and Westinghouse, but companies such as Allen-Bradley, Allis-Chalmers, and McGraw-Edison were also involved.

The conspirators—all executives—met in the best tradition of gangsters scheming to knock off a large bank. They gathered in obscure places, they did not dine together while at the same hotels, their communications were sent in plain envelopes to home addresses, they used only public telephones, and they even devised a code for telephoning about aspects of their plots. Essentially, their task was to fix prices on equipment and to agree on what company should submit the lowest bid on contracts about to be let. By the time the ax fell on the operation in 1960, prices had been fixed and bids rigged for an estimated $7 billion worth of equipment. The loss to the public is estimated at $1.7 billion.

The genuinely outraged judge sentenced seven of the conspirators to 30 days in jail; twenty-one others were given suspended 30-day sentences. Someone who broke into a parking meter might spend more time in jail, but you must recognize that locking up executives for antitrust violations was an unprecedented move at the time. The lawyer for a General Electric vice president begged that his client not be put "behind bars with common criminals who have been convicted for embezzlement and other serious crimes." Still another attorney argued, "Why punish these men? It is a way of life—everybody's doing it."[72]

No top executives were implicated, and one General Electric attorney stressed that the case really involved only certain individuals, not the company—a kind of rotten apple theory transplanted from police corruption explanations. But the judge was not convinced: The companies were fined a total of $1.8 million. Never underestimate the ingenuity and power of U.S. business, however. Top executives of the companies persuaded the Internal Revenue Service that all legal expenses, fines, and damages could be written off as "ordinary and necessary" expenses of doing business. Senator Philip A. Hart questioned whether a bank robber could likewise deduct his legal expenses.[73] What do you think?

How widespread is price-fixing? This is impossible to answer accurately, of course, but a sizable proportion of the business community believes that it is common. A survey of the presidents of the 1,000 largest manufacturing corporations were asked whether many engage in price-fixing. Among presidents of the top 500 firms, 47 percent believed that such was the case; of the next 500 firms, 70 percent believed the same.[74]

We mentioned earlier that having a few companies control the major portion of an industry was a contributing factor to price-fixing, for it facilitates getting together and eventually reaching agreements.[75] But the basic motivations of the participants remain unexplored. Gilbert Geis, in his analysis of the "Electrical Conspiracy," suggests that individuals and the corporations they represent are drawn into trust activities because of the attractiveness of a secure market:

> The elimination of competition meant the avoidance of uncertainty, the formalization and predictability of outcome, the minimization of risks. It is, of course, this incentive which accounts for much of human activity, be it deviant or "normal."[76]

Geis also points out that for individual conspirators three conditions appear to be crucial to their participation:

1. **A perception of gains** stemming from the behavior, such as advancement within the corporation or a more efficient means of carrying out duties.
2. **Verbalized motives** that allow executives to violate the law and still maintain an image of themselves as law-abiding and respectable persons. These motives assume the theme that nothing wrong has occurred: "I do not know that it is against public welfare because I am not certain that the consumer was actually injured by this operation," or "We did not fix prices . . . All we did was recover costs."
3. **Market conditions** in which competition is particularly strong, enforcement of antitrust statutes is weak, and company demand for profits is high.[77]

Sally S. Simpson and Christopher S. Koper studied companies that were already "prior offenders" and found that "it seems that a firm's cultural and economic climates exert more influence toward reoffending than the legal environment exerts against reoffending."[78]

It would appear, then, that the concentration of industry provides a situation conducive to deviance by corporations that are beset by profit-making pressures. But there is more to corporate deviance than that, as an examination of the automobile industry will show.

"Would You Buy a Used Car from This Person?"

Not long ago this question was a humorous way of implying that an individual's scruples were highly suspect. This is unfair to the honest used car dealers, of course. A more appropriate question is "Would you let this person make, sell, or repair your car?" This is not as catchy a phrase, but it conveys the notion that the entire auto industry, from manufacturers to new car dealers to repair personnel, often gouges the U.S. public. And the public knows it:

> A cross section of American adults were asked to pick the industries they thought were doing a poor job in serving customers. "Garages and auto mechanics"—one category—came out in a tie for first place with auto manufacturers. . . . They were followed . . . in fourth place by used car dealers. Another poll . . . asked a cross section of American household heads to rank 31 industries (not including auto repairmen) according to their job performance. Ranked lowest was another industry related to auto repairs: auto insurance companies (auto dealers came in 29th, auto manufacturers 26th, and oil and gas companies 25th).[79]

Does the auto industry—manufacturers, dealers, and so on—deserve public dissatisfaction? It certainly seems so. For example, a former Federal Trade Commission chairman called auto repairs the "granddaddy of consumer problems." And one student of the situation claims, "There's probably a greater chance you'll be robbed by driving into an auto repair shop than by walking through New York City's Central Park at 3:00 in the morning." Among the many horror stories this observer tells is the experience of the Nashville television reporters who altered a car so that it had a loose bolt on the front tie-rod clamp and loose front-wheel bearings. They took the car to fifteen repair shops. Only one repairman found both problems, and he tried to sell the driver some other unneeded part.[80]

In the case of auto repair, it is often impossible to separate deliberate fraud from sheer incompetence. A mechanic may make unnecessary repairs simply because he or she is poorly trained or careless. But incompetence cannot be used as an excuse in other areas of the auto industry. One of the first sociological studies of auto dealers was conducted by William N. Leonard and Marvin Glenn Weber. They found that many questionable dealer practices were precipitated by manufacturer practices:

1. **Forcing accessories.** New cars arrive at the dealers with accessories that buyers did not order but must pay for to get the cars.
2. **High used car markups.** Since dealers receive low returns on the sales of new cars (around $200 in 1968, the time of the study), they try to compensate by large markups on used cars.
3. **Service gouging.** This simply refers to overcharging for service, another method of making up for the low returns on new cars. For example, dealers may charge for more labor time than is actually used, charge for repairs not made, and replace parts unnecessarily.

4. **High finance charges.** Dealers may finance cars themselves by borrowing from a bank and lending the money to buyers at higher interest rates. Occasionally, a dealer will recommend a poor credit risk to a loan shark and receive a commission in return.

5. **Parts pushing.** This involves overcharging for parts or using rebuilt parts while charging for new ones. Sometimes mechanics will use a new part when the old one could be repaired more cheaply.[81]

Why do such practices arise? Leonard and Weber argue that they grow out of the excessive power of automobile manufacturers, both generally and more specifically in their relationship to dealers. In 1921 there were 88 automobile manufacturing firms in the United States. Today there are 3. The keystone company is General Motors (GM), having the largest market share for domestic cars. GM has withstood several attempts to break it up, and there is little likelihood it will be dissolved in the near future or, because of the tremendous costs involved, that any new domestic competitors will emerge.

Leonard and Weber claim that the concentrated market power of auto manufacturers adversely affects other aspects of the industry. Specifically, they find that unethical or illegal behavior on the part of dealers stems directly from manufacturer pressures over which the dealers have no control. In short, *the dealers are coerced into patterns of deviant behavior.* At the heart of the problem is the intense pressure placed on dealer franchises to be *sales oriented*—bonuses and other rewards come only with increased sales; service is simply a necessary evil.

Dealers have other problems besides the manufacturers' intense emphasis on sales. One problem involves the warranties issued by manufacturers to increase sales. Warranties supposedly protect the motorist by guaranteeing that certain defects will be repaired at no cost if they are detected within a certain period or before a specified number of miles have been driven. According to Leonard and Weber, warranties are just another sales gimmick, and their burden falls upon the dealers:

> Manufacturers used the warranty to limit their liability under the law and further limited the effectiveness of the warranty by establishing cumbersome paperwork and procedures for dealers and by compensating the dealers in labor and parts below the levels charged for regular repairs. As a result, dealers tended to avoid warranty work, or provided poor service to new car owners. Dealers made motorists wait for service, often failed to work on cars brought into the shop or told owners they could not fix them, sometimes "discovered" additional repairs which could be charged, and padded bills. The improper behavior of dealers . . . reflects the market power of manufacturers, who unilaterally drafted the warranties . . . but then undermined warranty service by creating conditions which induced dealers to operate unethically in providing repairs.[82]

But the role that manufacturers play in pressuring dealers toward deviance is not the end of the story. Manufacturers themselves stoop to tricks that would embarrass a high-class swindler. For example, when Joseph Siwek took his Oldsmobile to a mechanic for a routine repair, the mechanic discovered a small problem: Siwek's *Oldsmobile* had a *Chevrolet* engine. It seems that GM sort of ran out of Oldsmobile engines and "substituted" the Chevrolets—some 30,000 of them, in fact. General Motors claimed that this was nothing to get excited about because one engine was just as good as another. But many owners of the "Chevymobiles" had purchased the cars on the basis of GM advertisements about the superiority of the Oldsmobile engine.[83] It should not be surprising to the reader that once again, in 1999, the two top major consumer complaints were auto sales and car repair. Perhaps things have improved, but in 1989 the comments about GM made by Martin Stein, then president of the Society of Automotive Analysts, led William H. Davidow and Bro Uttal to conclude that

> except in the case of Cadillac, General Motors takes a "cosmetic" approach to service. It sends service members through a training program—or charm school—where they learn to refuse customer requests for service politely, and uses 800 numbers to field complaints. "This approach backfires," says Stein. "Customers say that General Motors is 'supercilious' and that 'they are overly courteous but don't want to fix your car.' "[84]

There is a much more serious pattern of deviance among auto manufacturers: their willingness to jeopardize human life in the pursuit of profits. Even with current technology it would be difficult to build economically a totally injury-free vehicle. But when a vehicle is especially dangerous, is it unrealistic to assume that purchasers will be warned or, better still, that the vehicle will be pulled off the market? Recent history indicates that such an assumption *is* unrealistic. For example, the Ford Motor Company recently settled a lawsuit paying to replace defective ignition systems in millions of cars that could stall on highways and across railroad tracks. This could cost as much as $1 billion. Ford is also facing at least $2.4 billion in claims from owners of Bronco sport utility vehicles who said that a faulty design increases the chance of rollovers.[85]

The classic case of dangerous cars is the Ford Pinto, which was designed to sell in the early 1970s for under $2,000.[86] Forty tests were conducted in which the car was subjected to a rear-end collision at over 25 miles per hour (mph); in each test, the fuel tank ruptured. The company settled on 20 mph as the standard for the tank. A ruptured fuel tank is a serious matter: It means spilled gasoline that can be easily ignited in a crash by a spark from scraping metal. The testers found that minor, inexpensive modifications to the tank considerably increased its ability to withstand a collision. But none of the modifications was adopted because each meant more weight and expense, thus making the $2,000 price limit doubtful. How much expense was involved? For merely $6.65 per car the fuel tank could have withstood a 30-mph collision. Had the Pinto been designed like other subcompacts at that time, it could have withstood collisions up to 50 mph without a fire risk.

Why didn't Ford make the Pinto safer? Simply because it would have cost too much. In an internal Ford Company memorandum it was calculated that an $11-per-car improvement would prevent 180 "burn deaths" and 180 "serious burn injuries" annually. The $11 was deemed too expensive. By 1977 an estimated 500 to 900 burn deaths had resulted from rear-end collisions involving Pintos.

We have mentioned the efforts of the insurance industry to control fraud from inflated claims for damaged vehicles. Paul E. Tracy and James Alan Fox designed an experiment to determine the extent of this type of crime. Specifically, they wondered whether a car covered by insurance would cost more to repair than an uninsured car. They reported that "repair estimates under the insured condition were 32.5% higher than under the noncovered condition."[87] If that figure alone is not disturbing, realize that we may be talking about one-third of perhaps $20 billion dollars. Put another way, one-third of your insurance premium goes to offset fraud in the insurance industry.

"You Are What You Eat"

The auto industry is not alone in having a persistent history of deviance. One industry that affects everyone except vegetarians is the meatpacking industry, which has the dubious distinction of being the target of some of the earliest government investigations. In 1899 a Spanish-American War general charged that "embalmed meat" sold to the Army by Armour, Swift, Wilson, and other companies had killed more troops than enemy bullets. Theodore Roosevelt is quoted as saying that he would have preferred to eat his hat than canned meat during that war.[88]

The meatpacking industry also inspired a sensational novel, *The Jungle,* written by Upton Sinclair at the turn of the century as a criticism of capitalism in general and the Chicago stockyards in particular. Sinclair described in stomach-wrenching detail how rats overran piles of meat stored under leaking roofs. In an attempt to be rid of the pests, packinghouse workers put out poisoned bread. Little attempt was made to separate the components that eventually went into the sausage hopper: poisoned bread, dead rats, rat dung, and, of course, some meat.

President Theodore Roosevelt secretly commissioned a study of Chicago meatpackers that found Sinclair had not exaggerated the situation.[89] An outraged public overcame the opposition of the House Agriculture Committee, and in 1906 Roosevelt signed into law the Meat Inspection Act.

Interpretations differ on the meatpackers' view of the law. Gabriel Kolko finds that the major meatpacking companies supported rather than resisted the passage of the Meat Inspection Act. According to Kolko, insofar as the large packers were concerned, the law had two benefits. First, it established an inspection program at government expense that would certify meat for foreign export—a market that U.S. packers were finding difficult to enter because of their reputation for low-quality meat. Second, it extended regulations to smaller competitors, thus making it difficult for them to survive. In short, the act enhanced the interests of the large companies.[90]

The Meat Inspection Act covered only meat sold in interstate commerce. As late as 1967, nearly 15 percent of the meat slaughtered and 25 percent of the meat processed in the United States were not inspected according to federal standards. Surveys of packinghouses in Delaware, Virginia, and North Carolina found the following tidbits in meat: animal hair, sawdust, flies, abscessed pork livers, and snuff spit out by the meat workers. To add more flavoring, packinghouses whose meat did not cross state lines could use 4-D meat ("dead, dying, diseased, and disabled") and chemical additives that would not pass federal inspection. Not all such plants were minor operations; some were run by the giants—Armour, Swift, and Wilson.

In 1967 consumer groups began agitating for legislation that would make federal inspection mandatory even for plants not engaged in interstate commerce.[91] They argued that because the states had refused to take responsibility, the federal government must. Opponents included the Secretary of Agriculture and the meatpackers, who were working to "preserve our free enterprise system." Eventually, the Wholesome Meat Act was signed into law in December 1967. It specified that, unless state standards matched federal standards, the states' meatpacking industries would fall under federal inspectors' jurisdiction.

Of course, a law's mere existence does not guarantee compliance. The industry continued violations that could result in disease and death. For example, a perennial problem is Number 2 meat. If meat is returned by a retailer to a packer, it can be resold as Number 2 meat to a different customer if it meets standards of wholesomeness. One 1969 case involved a Los Angeles–area Hormel plant:

> When the original customers returned the meat to Hormel, they used the following terms to describe it: "moldy liverloaf, sour party hams, leaking bologna, discolored bacon, off-condition hams, and slick and slimy spareribs." Hormel renewed these products with cosmetic measures. . . . Spareribs returned for sliminess, discoloration, and stickiness were rejuvenated through curing and smoking, renamed Windsor Loins, and sold in ghetto stores for more than fresh pork chops.[92]

This situation persisted because the U.S. Department of Agriculture (USDA) inspector chose to look the other way. The fact that Hormel paid him $6,000 annually for "overtime" no doubt helped. Lack of sufficient inspectors, however, probably contributes to offenses more often than bribery does:

> Inspectors in North Carolina report that companies repackage unsold meat without having it rechecked by the inspector. An Associated Press reporter, visiting three meat packaging plants in August 1971, saw bacon, hams, wieners, and cold cuts which were rotten—a solid green with mildew—stacked on return tables. Since federal inspectors only spot check the packaging plants, the meat can be cleaned up and sold as new stock with no one the wiser.[93]

But that was years ago. Surely things are better now? This is from a recent newspaper article:

> There is little mystery about how salmonella gets into ground beef. When slaughterhouse workers rush to keep up with the high-speed production line, they can make mistakes. Manure can spill onto the meat. If that meat is turned into ground beef, bits of fecal matter are widely distributed throughout it. Salmonella in that manure thrives in uncooked meat. . . . In the 10 months the USDA had tested ground beef intended for schools, roughly 5 million pounds were rejected for contamination. . . . Yet our food-safety system remains decentralized, underfunded and chaotic. A dozen federal agencies are responsible for food safety. The welter of competing bureaucracies leads to enforcement gaps and absurdities. The FDA . . . has just 400 inspectors to oversee food safety at nearly 60,000 U.S. plants.[94]

More food for thought: Although companies that process food *may* rigorously comply with federal standards for their products, consumers may be surprised at what goes into the food they eat. The following are permissible according to federal guidelines:

1. Sixty aphids, thrips, and/or mites per 100 grams (just over a quarter pound) of frozen broccoli
2. Sixty insect fragments or one rodent hair per 100 grams of chocolate
3. Six percent of rot in potato chips
4. Thirty drosophila fly eggs, or five drosophila fly eggs and one drosophila maggot, or two maggots per 100 grams of pizza sauce
5. One rodent excreta pellet in six 10-ounce consumer-sized packages of popcorn[95]

In addition, even when food contaminated to an unacceptable degree is discovered and recalled, such as meat containing *Escherichia coli* bacteria, processors are allowed to reprocess and redistribute it.

Before we bid you *bon appétit,* consider a final word from Robert Sherrill on what the government lets us eat:

> The consumer is . . . confronted by such *pièces de résistance* as the hot dog, which by law can contain 69 percent water, salt, spices, corn syrup and cereal, and 15 percent chicken; that still leaves a little room for goat meat, pigs' ears, eyes, stomachs, snouts, udders, bladders and esophagus—all legally okay. There is no more all-American way to take a break at the old ball game than to have water and pigs' snouts on a bun, but you might prefer to go heavier on the mustard from now on.[96]

The Badness of Good Business

The examples of corporate deviance that we have provided may seem isolated and unique to some readers. Unquestionably, most American businesses operate conscientiously and within the bounds of legality and ethics. But a great number are consistently and deliberately involved in blatantly illegal acts, and it is important not to underestimate their impact. The conclusion of anyone who has studied the matter is that *the cost to society of corporate crime far exceeds the cost of other property crimes.*

An investigation into the extent and cost of corporate deviance was conducted by *U.S. News & World Report.* The investigators found that

1. In the 1970s, 12 percent of the 500 largest firms were convicted of or did not contest at least one crime; and an additional 11 percent were penalized for serious noncriminal offenses.
2. In the late 1970s, seven of the twenty-five largest firms were convicted of or did not contest at least one crime; an additional seven were forced into settlements of major noncriminal charges.
3. In the 1970s, almost 2,700 corporations were convicted of federal criminal offenses.
4. Corporate crimes in the form of price-fixing; poisoned air, land, and water; corruption of officials; and tax evasion cost the U.S. public as much as $200 billion a year.[97]

The 1980s saw takeovers, mergers, and buyouts financed with junk bonds, with deals done for the sake of fees and stock payoffs. The result: Thousands of people lost their jobs. In a subsequent poll asking, "How much do you trust Wall Street bankers and brokers to do what is best for the economy?" the answers were: not at all—30 percent; a little—33 percent; somewhat—30 percent; and a great deal—4 percent.[98] The savings and loan scandal of the 1990s, whether due to fraud or mismanagement, ultimately cost U.S. taxpayers about $1 trillion.[99] By comparison, index property crimes known to police cost about $10 billion a year.

In addition to its financial costs, corporate deviance may cost more in lives and physical injury than traditional crime:

1. Since 1900 over 100,000 men have died in coal mines. It is argued that most could have been saved if safety laws had been obeyed.
2. About 200,000 disabling injuries result from industrial safety violations annually.
3. About 100,000 deaths result each year from industrial diseases.

4. Each year approximately 150,000 people suffer serious injuries from product safety violations.
5. Untold numbers of deaths and injuries occur from misrepresented drugs, violations of automobile safety standards, violations of pollution laws, and so on.[100]

Why are respectable businesses lawless? It is tempting to lay the faults of business at the doorstep of profit. Without the profit incentive, business need not involve itself in most of the practices we have mentioned. Even though the profit argument considerably over-simplifies a very complex matter and ignores the great number of businesses and their exec-utives who operate within the bounds of legality, we still must say the *pressure for profit* remains the single most compelling factor in behavior deviance by industry.

The profit motive, or the "bottom-line philosophy," often dictates a company's actions when economic stresses build in the fact of "produce or perish."[101] Competition is supposedly the heart of business, but it can make a company's survival problematic and tempt its executives into questionable, if not illegal, practices. On a small scale, the influ-ence of competition upon deviance is illustrated by Earl Richard Quinney's study of phar-macists. Quinney found that the orientation of pharmacists toward their occupation varied according to whether they viewed themselves as being in a *business* role (i.e., being good salespeople and successful businesspeople) or in a *professional* role (i.e., being active in pharmaceutical rather than business matters). The business-oriented pharmacists were much more likely to engage in illegal prescription practices because the professional norms represented by prescription laws had little relevance for business behavior.[102]

The goal of business is to provide a product or a service that will produce a profit for the owners or stockholders. Any businessperson who ignores that goal is derelict in her or his role. The problem for the sociologist is: Under what conditions does the pursuit of profit translate into illegal and unethical practices? Marshall B. Clinard attempted to answer this question by investigating the deviant activities of the 582 largest U.S. corporations during a two-year period. About 40 percent of the companies had not been charged with violations by any of twenty-four federal agencies. At the other extreme, 8 percent had been charged with ten or more violations—one company had sixty-two cases initiated against it.

Clinard hypothesized that the number of a firm's violations is related to market con-ditions and to the firm's organizational characteristics such as size, financial performance, degree of product diversification, and growth rate. As expected, he found that firms with poor financial performances tended to have more violations than did companies not facing financial strains. Nevertheless, the relationship between financial condition and number of violations was weak; Clinard and Peter C. Yeager concluded that company and industry characteristics were not strong predictors of corporate deviance:

> Taken together, the results suggest that, compared to nonviolating corporations, the violating firms are on average larger, less financially successful, experience poorer growth rates, and are more diversified. However, the relationships were of moderate strength at best. When combined in statistical models to maximize our ability to predict the extent of firms' illegal behavior, the corporate characteristics examined proved not to be strong predictors. Indeed, knowledge of a firm's growth, diversification, and market power added virtually no predictive power when combined with size and financial measures. . . . Information on firm financial performance and structural characteristics is, by itself, insufficient for explaining corporate crime.[103]

Thus the question of why some corporations become involved in deviance while others do not remains unanswered. We are especially confused by one of Clinard's major findings: that oil, pharmaceutical, and motor vehicle industries are more chronically criminal than are any others—in fact, they account for nearly half of all violations.[104] Why do these particular industries have a disproportionately high offense rate? Is there a "subculture of industrial deviance," similar to a subculture of violence, in which some business personnel are socialized into illegally responding to certain situations? Only by studying criminal businesspeople, as we have studied other criminals, will we know for certain.

According to Clinard and Yeager, one factor clearly promotes business deviance: the immunity of executives from being held personally responsible for corporate actions. In only 1.5 percent of the cases were corporate officers convicted for failing to carry out their responsibilities. Of these a quarter were sent to jail for an average of 37 days. There is rarely any punishment by the corporation itself. Because neither courts of law nor employers respond negatively to white-collar offenses, it is hardly surprising that executives seldom think of themselves as being criminals or as being morally responsible for the harm they have caused:

> This reaction perhaps reflects the executive's perspective on the value of the law he has violated, his general attitude toward government regulation of the private business sector, and the social and business environment in which he lives and works. This point of view was expressed by one of the convicted electrical company executives: "No one attending the gathering [of the conspirators] was so stupid he didn't know the meetings were in violation of the law. But it is the only way a business can be run. It is free enterprise."[105]

Clinard and Yeager make several recommendations for controlling corporate deviance. These include the development of a stronger business ethic, federal rather than state chartering of corporations, deconcentration of corporate giants, stiffer penalties for violations, wider publicity concerning offenses, and, as a last resort, federal ownership or nationalization of certain corporations (corporate sentencing guidelines are being developed).[106] Given the close ties between government and business, the enactment and effectiveness of many of these measures seem unlikely, whatever their merits. Radical sociologists argue that even if implemented, the recommendations would be ineffectual because corporate deviance is inherent in capitalism. And capitalism encourages the maximization of profits and the concentration of wealth—the prime motivations behind corporate deviance. According to T. R. Young, to ignore the concept of *capitalism* in a discussion of corporate deviance "is much like talking about child abuse apart from the concept of the authoritarian family structure."[107]

However, we know that corporations can operate successfully without breaking the law. In the absence of the drastic changes suggested by Clinard and Yeager, perhaps the best weapon against white-collar offenders is a knowledgeable and outraged public—a public that demands that businesspeople accept responsibility for their offenses and that they be treated as law violators. According to Gilbert Geis,

> corporate offenses . . . do not have biblical proscription—they lack, as an early writer noted, the "brimstone smell." But the havoc such offenses produce, the malevolence with which they are undertaken, and the disdain with which they are continued, are all antithetical to principles we as citizens are expected to observe. It is a long step, assuredly, and sometimes an

uncertain one, from lip service to cries of outrage; but at least principled antagonism is latent, needing only to be improved in decibels and fidelity. It should not prove impossible to convince citizens of the extreme danger entailed by such violations of our social compact.[108]

Organized Crime

MAFIA STAFF CAR—Keepa You Hands Off!!

—Bumper Sticker

This sums up rather well what most Americans "know" about organized crime: it is run by Italians, and they are not to be trifled with. The "Mafia" is familiar to most as an association of closely knit "families" who exert nearly total control over illegal gambling, who have a strict code of honor, and who kill a lot of people. The most famous example of the last is the St. Valentine's Day Massacre in February 1929, when five of Al "Scarface" Capone's "boys" lined up seven mobsters belonging to George "Bugs" Moran and machine-gunned them down.

It is difficult to separate fact from fiction about organized crime. Obviously, it thrives best in secrecy, and even expert observers disagree over several of its characteristics. What is known about organized crime definitely places it in our category of an organization (or organizations) whose central activity is crime. Technically speaking, most criminologists do not consider organized crime as white-collar crime, but the similarities between it and legitimate businesses are too important to ignore. Organized crime is conducted like a *business,* like business its goal is *profit,* and its means to that end is to establish a *monopoly* by destroying the competition.[109] (That is why Bugs Moran's associates met an untimely end: They were victims of the free enterprise system in a dispute over who should control a market.)

Both legitimate business and organized crime seek freedom from governmental meddling by offering favors to persons in key positions who can exert influence on the organization's behalf. The only difference is that, for business, this process is achieved through *lobbying,* whereas for organized crime it is achieved through *corruption.* Finally, as we shall see, organized crime often works hand in glove with legitimate business. If "every man is like the company he is wont to keep," then gangsters are more respectable than is usually acknowledged.

Characteristics and Structure

Before proceeding to a detailed discussion of organized crime, we should offer a definition of exactly what we will be examining. This is not a simple matter. Organization alone is not the key variable. Burglars, shoplifters, and even rapists might work together as teams, but their organization, no matter how formal, would usually not qualify them as organized criminals.[110] A presidential commission described organized crime as follows:

> The core of organized crime activity is the supplying of illegal goods and services—gambling, loan sharking, narcotics, and other forms of vice—to countless numbers of citizen customers. But organized crime is also extensively and deeply involved in legitimate business and in labor unions. Here it employs illegitimate methods—monopolization, terrorism,

extortion, tax evasion—to drive out or control lawful ownership and leadership and to exact illegal profits from the public. And to carry on its many activities secure from governmental interference, organized crime corrupts public officials. . . .

What organized crime wants is money and power. What makes it different from law-abiding organizations and individuals with those same objectives is that the ethical and moral standards the criminals adhere to, the laws and regulations they obey, the procedures they use are private and secret ones that they devise themselves, change when they see fit, and administer summarily and invisibly.[111]

Several characteristics of organized crime alluded to in the foregoing definition are worth emphasizing. First, *organized crime provides illegal goods and services.* The exact nature of those goods and services will be discussed later, but for the purpose of describing the enterprise, it is important to note that the customers are a blend of both the respectable and the not-so-respectable. In the absence of a demand for commodities not legally available, organized crime would be a marginal operation at best. This points up a fundamental distinction between ordinary crime and organized crime: Few people would grieve over the sudden disappearance of rapists, robbers, burglars, and so on, but if organized crime were to vanish, a great number of people would be very unhappy.[112] This is not to say that gangsters are not predatory; many are, as is evidenced by the commission's reference to extortion and terrorism. But organized crime does owe much of its continuing existence to the public *demand* that it satisfies.

A second characteristic of organized crime is *corruption.* To carry on business freely, it is necessary for organized criminals to minimize the effectiveness of law enforcement.[113] The forms of possible corruption vary, but they include outright bribery, campaign contributions, and promises to deliver voters. The favors of organized crime can taint the low and the high. Those beholden to its wishes range from police on the beat to their supervisors, from city prosecutors to judges, from news reporters to publishers, and from city council members and mayors to state and federal legislators. Should anyone doubt the extent of organized crime's influence on the entire political scene, consider this: An estimated 15 percent of the costs of local and state political campaigns are financed by organized criminals.[114]

So important is corruption to organized crime that each of the major crime families has at least one position devoted specifically to that purpose:

The person occupying this position bribes, buys, intimidates, threatens, negotiates, and sweet-talks himself into a relationship with police, public officials, and anyone else who might help "family" members maintain immunity from arrest, prosecution, and punishment. . . .

In one or, perhaps, two instances, a single corrupter does all the "fixing" for his "family," which means that he is responsible for the political dishonesty of a geographical territory. More commonly, one corrupter takes care of one subdivision of government, such as the police or city hall, while another will be assigned a different subdivision, such as the state alcoholic-beverage commission. A third corrupter might handle the court system by fixing a judge, a clerk of court, a prosecutor, an assistant prosecutor, a probation officer.[115]

Like the public demand for illegal goods and services, the corruption of legal and political officials is not merely an incidental characteristic but a critical element for the survival of organized crime. And like other organizations that become deviant, organized crime does not exist in isolation from other segments of society. Organized crime needs corruption to continue; it continues because it reaches the corruptible. To understand organized crime, then, it is important to recognize that it is not a collection of families forcefully imposing their wills on society. *It is part of an alliance between some government personnel and criminals.*[116]

This alliance poses perhaps the greatest danger from organized crime. As Donald R. Cressey points out,

> [organized crime] functions as an illegal invisible government. However, its political objective is not competition with the established agencies of legitimate government. . . . It is not interested in political and economic reform. Its political objective is a negative one: nullification of government.
>
> Nullification is sought at two different levels. At the lower level are the agencies for law enforcement and the administration of criminal justice. When a [gangster] bribes a policeman, a police chief, a prosecutor, a judge, or a license administrator, he does so in an attempt to nullify the law-enforcement process. At the upper level are legislative agencies, including federal and state legislatures as well as city councils and county boards of supervisors. When a "family" boss supports a candidate for political office, he does so in an attempt to deprive honest citizens of their democratic voice, thus nullifying the democratic process.[117]

The third and final characteristic of organized crime is the *use of violence for enforcement.* A business dealing in illegal goods and services is in no position to appeal to the legitimate government for a redress of grievances. Individuals who violate a trust or otherwise fail to meet expectations must be disciplined from within the organization. This is not to be confused with so-called gang wars. The St. Valentine's Day Massacre was part of a dispute over control of alcohol bootlegging operations. More recent was the war between the Joseph Profaci gang and the Gallo mob. Profaci monopolized vice in Brooklyn, and the Gallo upstarts wanted some of the action. One result was eight deaths and three "disappearances" between 1961 and 1965. Even into the 1970s, well after the main characters went to their eternal rewards, sporadic killing continued on both sides.

Gang wars, which are rare today, do not distinguish organized criminals from any number of individual entrepreneurs, such as pimps or pushers, squabbling over markets; organized criminals just do their killing on a larger scale. What sets organized crime apart is *its own equivalent of criminal law.* When someone violates that "law" by failing to pay back a loan or by skimming from funds entrusted to him, sanctions are imposed to impress upon the offender and all others that such errors in judgment will not be tolerated. Organized crime thus functions not only as a business but also as a government.[118]

The term *government* must here be used cautiously. Some students of organized crime conceive of its structure as a tightly knit bureaucracy with a ruling national commission—in short, a structure similar to what one would expect in any formal government. These students, as well as the press and most law enforcement officials, refer to organized crime as the *Mafia* or *Cosa Nostra* (Our Thing)—a more complex, more bureaucratic form of the earlier Mafia.[119] A leading proponent of the Cosa Nostra theory is Cressey, who claims that organized crime is structured as follows:

1. A nationwide alliance of at least twenty-four tightly knit "families" of criminals exists in the United States. (Because the "families" are fictive, in the sense that the members are not all relatives, it is necessary to refer to them in quotation marks.)

2. The members of these "families" are all Italians and Sicilians, or of Italian and Sicilian descent, and those on the eastern seaboard, especially, call the entire system "Cosa Nostra." Each participant thinks of himself as a "member" of a specific "family" and of Cosa Nostra (or some equivalent term).

3. The "families" are linked to each other, and to non–Cosa Nostra syndicates by understandings, agreements, and "treaties," and by mutual deference to a "Commission" made up of the leaders of the most powerful of the "families."[120]

Cressey's position is the one usually presented by law enforcement officials and by the press: Organized crime is a unified entity with Italians and Sicilians pulling the important strings. Despite the popularity of this "godfather" version of organized crime, several critics question its assumptions about the relationships among crime families and about the role played by persons of Italian and Sicilian descent. Some writers claim that evidence for the existence of a highly centralized organization is simply not convincing. According to Joseph L. Albini, organized crime operates not as a formal organization but as a "system of power relationships." Its leaders at any given time are those who exert the most influence over legal agencies and who provide the most lucrative opportunities for making money:

Rather than being formally structured organizations, the syndicates in the United States are informally structured systems of patron-client relationships. The patron is the individual who has achieved a power position where he can grant favors to those beneath him in the underworld. He also serves as a client to those legal power sources who can offer him protection in return for his pay-off services. This system of patron-client relationships—a system which, by its very nature is one constantly immersed in conflict, cooperation, and accommodation—is, in our view, the nature of the structure and functioning of syndicated crime in the United States.[121]

Albini goes on to say that the official version of the unity of organized crime is the product of wishful thinking:

There is no doubt that police probably wish that such a rigidly structured organization did exist, since it would be easier to destroy. If it were truly centrally organized, then all that would be necessary to destroy it would be to remove its top echelon. . . . The power of syndicates in the United States rests in the fact that they are not structured in this fashion. If a powerful syndicate figure is incarcerated all that has really been severed is his position as a patron to his clients. If it so happens that another individual is in a position to assume this role, the clients may continue in this enterprise. If not, they simply must develop their own enterprises or find new patrons to whose enterprises they can attach themselves.[122]

Dwight C. Smith and Richard D. Alba suggest that

adherents of the Mafia view have spent so long mapping the presumed organizational details of a single national conspiracy that they are frequently unable to observe the actual coalitions of men and women which form (and occasionally reform) to exploit specific entrepreneurial possibilities. Many features of the coalitional structures can be better understood as responses to particular marketplaces. After all, one cannot do business in such areas as narcotics, numbers, and bookmaking without some degree of organization or coordination of the activities necessary for successful operation.[123]

Considering that there may be no national structure or no "commission," it is inaccurate to speak of organized crime in the singular. Clearly, there are organized crime families, and they may be linked by common interests and occasional intermarrying.[124] But to accept the official portrait of a monolithic crime bureaucracy may be to miss a crucial point: Organized crime is more ingrained in U.S. life than we would like to believe.

What about the Italians? Since there are so many of them in organized crime, does that not indicate a foreign influence, an alien conspiracy to undermine the American way? Alan A. Block and William J. Chambliss found that only 16 percent of convicted organized crime figures are of Italian or Sicilian background. This means that for every Umberto Anastasio there are six others with names like Guy Harmon, R. M. Rodriquez, Isadore Eisenstein, Edward Gallagher, Young Ah Fook, and Glenn Smith.[125] These sound less like Mafiosi than like a bomber crew in a World War II movie.

Today, organized crime is a worldwide phenomenon, with highly sophisticated international relationships and cooperative participating by groups as diverse as motorcycle gangs and former Soviet police. Life in the United States is influenced by South American drug manufacturers, Central American and Canadian traffickers, Asian document forgers, Caribbean bankers, European software pirates, and virtually any combination of persons with plans to supply the massive market for illegal goods, services, and activities. To think of organized crime solely in terms of the Sicilian Mafia family is not accurate and never really has been, as U.S. history demonstrates.

From Muscle to Respectability

On January 16, 1920, the Eighteenth Amendment of the U.S. Constitution went into effect. It prohibited "the manufacture, sale, or transportation of intoxicating liquors within, the importation thereof into, or the exportation thereof from the United States and all territory subject to the jurisdiction thereof, for beverage purposes." In short, alcoholic beverages were illegal. Thus began Prohibition, a period that lasted nearly fourteen years, during which time, many people erroneously believe, organized crime had its birth.

Unquestionably, without Prohibition organized crime would not have gained the power it has today, but its origins go back to the early nineteenth century. Gus Tyler describes the development of organized crime as an evolutionary process in which illegal violence moved from the streets of urban slums into the world of business and finance.

The earliest gangs in New York City were Irish immigrants, who emerged during a conflict among ethnic, political, and economic groups and dominated from 1820 to 1890. The Irish gangs made their own rules and enforced them with their fists. Their principal activities were idling and fighting—"free-floating chunks of violence," in Tyler's words. With names like the Bowery Boys, Dead Rabbits, and Shirt Tails, their first targets were other ethnic groups and whoever was reckless enough to invade their territory. These gangs provided the raw material for the genesis of organized crime, for they soon discovered that money could be made with muscle.

Starting with the extortion of whorehouses, gambling houses, and opium dens, gangs soon began selling their muscle to whoever could afford it. They were mercenary armies whose skills with their fists and disdain for the law placed them in demand for such activities as breaking up union picket lines, terrorizing voters, marching in protest demonstrations, kidnapping, stuffing ballot boxes, and so on. These gangs prompted Jay Gould, a nineteenth-century financier, to brag, "I can hire one half the working class to kill the other half."

By 1850 the gangs of New York had become an important force in city politics. With a gang in his pocket a politician could be assured that voting at election time would go his way. If a politician chose to operate bars, gambling houses, or whorehouses in his district, as many ward leaders did, the gang could guarantee that no outsiders would disrupt their smooth operation.

By the end of the nineteenth century the Irish had begun losing their grip as gang leaders in New York. Jews from Eastern Europe were taking over. At the same time gang operations began shifting from protection, extortion, and violence toward actual control of prostitution and gambling. The gangster-as-businessman had arrived on the scene.

The dominance of Jews in organized crime was short-lived. By 1920 the more recently immigrated Italians were replacing them, and these newcomers could not have arrived at a better time. With the ratification of the Eighteenth Amendment, gangs had another commodity to sell besides violence, sex, and gambling. But alcohol was a commodity with a difference. First, it was a bulk product that had to be manufactured, transported, and distributed. This required giant breweries and distilleries, vast warehouses, tank cars, trucks, and outlets. There had to be interstate and sometimes international alliances if alcohol were to be smuggled into the country. And, of course, there had to be a high degree of cooperation among police, politicians, and the public. In short, dealing in alcohol required a degree of *organization* that gangs had never needed before.

In addition to providing an impetus for greater organization, Prohibition gave the gangsters *respectability.* In the Roaring Twenties the United States was a nation of outlaws enjoying bathtub gin (homemade gin), speakeasies (illegal taverns), and hip flasks (designed for discreet portability). The Prohibitionists had grossly miscalculated: Americans were thirsty. The bootleggers who satisfied that thirst were accepted as part of the public scene. There were few raised eyebrows as politicians, businessmen, and all manner of good citizens openly rubbed elbows with gangsters. The funerals of major bootleggers brought out mourners from the highest echelons of government and finance. According to Tyler, "prohibition did more to give organized crime respectability than any other single force in our national history."[126]

With the repeal of the Eighteenth Amendment in 1933 organized crime lost its biggest moneymaker but not its respectability or organization. Its organization, in fact, was further aided by the gangs' decision to cooperate more and fight less. With the enormous profits made from bootlegging, gangs were able to expand their gambling operations and move into other areas such as real estate, industrial racketeering, and control of labor unions. Organized crime could no longer be characterized by the gangster who had only violence to sell. Now it was a full-scale business.[127]

Ethnic Succession

In our discussion of the passage from muscle to respectability, we mentioned another transition experienced by organized crime: the changing ethnic backgrounds of its members. In

New York control shifted from the Irish to Eastern European Jews to Italians. Nationally, almost every ethnic group—including the Chinese and Australians on the west coast—had been involved in organized crime at one time.

New migrants to the urban United States found that the streets were not paved with gold. The road to success was rocky because of discrimination and a lack of economic resources and because many legitimate avenues were already occupied by those who had come before. But politics and crime were immediate alternatives to the slow climb that most other jobs entailed. As Stuart L. Hills points out,

> historically, organized crime, along with the political machine, has represented an important means to obtain wealth, power, and fame. Each major immigrant group has taken its turn successively in the upper echelons of syndicated crime. With the rags-to-riches paths pre-empted by earlier arrivals, opportunities in organized crime have provided shortcuts to the great American dream of individual success. When the members of each group found increasing opportunities in more conventional forms of enterprise as discriminatory barriers declined, the group itself became less prominent in the world of gangs and rackets.[128]

The survival of Italians and Sicilians in organized crime is the result of a historical accident, not of any unique ethnic characteristics. These two groups were among the last of the large-scale immigrations, and they found even city politics already dominated by other groups. Although the Italians began arriving in the 1890s, no potent Italian political bloc rose in major northern cities until the late 1930s.[129] Because they were primarily from rural areas and generally lacking in occupational skills, the Italians and Sicilians found it especially difficult to break out of the slums and into positions of power. Their first signs of strength came from within the ranks of organized crime. Prohibition brought gangsters into contact with established politicians who needed money and who in turn were needed for protection of the gangsters' bootlegging operations. Once Italian and Sicilian gangsters got their feet into political doors, it was simply a matter of time before politicians from these ethnic groups began to emerge. Meanwhile, the gangsters remained remarkably democratic in their support of politicians. Many Irish and Jews, as well as Italians, owed their political lives to organized crime.

If organized crime is a stepping-stone to respectability for immigrant groups, who will be its next leaders? The logical successors should be the current inhabitants of the urban slums—African Americans, Hispanics, Russians, and Vietnamese. It appears that some of the brightest African Americans and Puerto Ricans are entering organized crime, and at least one Mexican American crime family can be found in California.[130] Today, families of Italian and Sicilian descent are still involved in much of the organized crime throughout the country. But there are signs that these traditional families are being replaced by newcomers. Organized crime will not disappear in the process, because organized crime is not Italian—it is American.

Sources of Profit

As we have seen, organized crime's first product was muscle power. Then it expanded into gambling, prostitution, and bootleg alcoholic beverages. Today, it is involved in many enterprises, which can be grouped as follows: (1) illegal goods and services, (2) thievery and fraud, (3) racketeering, and (4) infiltration of legitimate business.[131]

Illegal Goods and Services.   This category remains the principal source of income for organized crime. Within the category, *narcotics* are the greatest moneymaker. Just how much money is, of course, subject to the usual guessing game, but experts estimate that marijuana and cocaine revenues may be as high as $63 billion annually. Most narcotics operations are located in the major drug entry points: Florida, Texas, Arizona, and California. At these locations a kilogram of cocaine costing $20,000 in Colombia is worth $40,000. It jumps in value to $80,000 when "cut" (diluted) by wholesalers. The cocaine is cut again by retailers at the street level, and by the time it reaches its snorting consumers, the kilo has attained a value of $800,000 (this is an example; prices vary and in fact have dropped below this level, in some cases dramatically, indicating that more cocaine than ever is available).

Beginning with its extortion of opium dens in the late nineteenth century, organized crime has always been involved in the narcotics trade to some degree. Following World War II, the importation and distribution of narcotics were practically monopolized by organized crime, but in the 1970s the gangsters limited their involvement to handling overseas shipping arrangements and providing capital for large-scale purchases.[132] In the 1980s, however, the old crime families began to increase their involvement in narcotics. The money was too great to resist, and the changing ethnic composition of organized crime was too threatening:

> The dominance of the traditional groups [in organized crime] is fading fast. The growth in narcotics has been so great that it has replaced gambling as organized crime's number one source of income, and, in the process, introduced a number of dynamic newcomers to the structure of the business. Until a few years ago, the traditional crime families left the drug trade to others. They may have financed it, but they let others do the dirty work—blacks, Cubans, Chinese, Puerto Ricans, Mexicans. But nowadays the traditional families are beginning to move into the drug traffic themselves. To an extent, they had to: The newcomers don't need them anymore. They have the clout and the financial resources to operate on their own.[133]

The second largest moneymaker for organized crime is *gambling,* with revenues estimated at $22 billion a year. As indicated in the preceding quotation, gambling provided the greatest profits between the end of Prohibition and the recent rise of the narcotics trade. Although some gambling profits come from large bettors and from gang-controlled casinos, the bulk comes from small gamblers, most of whom are poor slum dwellers. The most lucrative operation historically has been the *numbers* or *policy* racket. In the 1970s, an estimated 75 percent of all adult and late-teenaged slum residents in New York's Harlem, South Bronx, and Bedford-Stuyvesant bet on the numbers.[134]

Numbers or policy is a form of lottery usually based on horse-racing results. The name derives from the time when the poor bet with money they had saved to pay insurance policy premiums. A participant bets 50 cents or more to pick a winning number. The simplest variation involves selecting a three-digit number that corresponds to a set of figures taken from the win, place (second place), and show (third place) totals of racetrack parimutuels. For example, if a track paid out $73.80 for the third and fourth races, $80.40 for the fourth and fifth races, and $108.00 for the fifth and sixth, the winning number would be 308—the first figures immediately to the left of the decimal points in sequence. The odds of winning are 1 in 1,000, and the payoff is 600 to 1.

As the reader is probably aware, many states have instituted their own lotteries as revenue-producing ventures. Have these cut into organized crime's gambling profits? There is no evidence that they have. Considering the advantages of gambling via organized crime, there is no reason, aside from moral or legal ones, why the bettor should switch to the state: Organized crime gives better odds, offers more conveniences (e.g., providing loans, placing bets by telephone), doesn't check age, and issues no statements to the IRS about big winnings.[135]

The third largest moneymaker for organized crime—an estimated $20 billion a year—is *usury* or *loan-sharking*. For the individual who needs money in a hurry with no questions asked, this is a valuable service. But there is a price: Interest rates are high, ranging from 1 to 150 percent a week. Most small borrowers pay 20 percent a week, or $60 to repay a $50 loan. The money is quick, but collection can get a bit sticky, because no legal action can be taken against tardy borrowers. But mobs have ways to encourage clients, ranging from thinly veiled threats against one's family to burly collectors like the one in Chicago known as "The Leg Breaker"—a name undoubtedly more effective than "Acme Collection Agency."

In many cases the lenders care little whether loans are collected, because people who are in debt to organized crime may prove beneficial in several ways. For example, when the spiraling interest engulfs a small businessperson beyond all hope, the gang may take over the business as a "partner," milk it dry, and have the businessperson declare bankruptcy. The result will be greater profit for the gang than the loan repayment would have been. Indebted individuals can also be persuaded to aid gangsters: A longshoreman provides information on the arrivals of valuable cargo that can be hijacked, a businessperson becomes a fence, and a government official awards a garbage collection contract to a gang-controlled company. In short, the debts produced by its loan-sharking operations become levers that allow organized crime to further its interests and expand its influence into the legitimate world.[136]

Finally, under the heading of illegal goods and services, there is an assortment of other organized crimes such as arson-for-hire, prostitution, cigarette bootlegging, and miscellaneous services such as hazardous waste disposal. The first two are self-explanatory. The third, cigarette bootlegging, involves the purchase (or theft) of cigarettes in South Carolina, North Carolina, Kentucky, and Virginia and their subsequent resale in states with high tobacco taxes, such as Florida, Massachusetts, New York, and Pennsylvania. Appropriate tax stamps are forged, and in some cases the cigarettes are sold by mob-owned vending machine companies. Organized crime then pockets the prospective tax revenues along with the sales profits.

The involvement of gangsters in hazardous waste disposal is a recent innovation and a further indication that organized crime often works hand in hand with segments of conventional society. In the late 1970s federal legislation was passed requiring strict controls over the dumping of poisonous and explosive industrial wastes. Proper disposal is expensive: It costs $40,000 to send a tank-truck load of chemicals to a legitimate disposal site. A mob will dump it in the New Jersey Pine Barrens in eight minutes for just half the cost.[137] Or maybe they will simply leave a tap open on the truck and spread the contents across the countryside at three o'clock in the morning or dump the waste in a sewer. Whatever the method, the cause is the same: a desire for profit motivates businessperson and gangster alike.

Thievery and Fraud.   Organized crimes also range from stealing and marketing automobiles to hijacking cargo from trucks, warehouses, and docksides to manipulating securities on Wall Street. The following example will be of interest to any student who is highlighting passages of this book with a Magic Marker:

> The mob was very much in control in [a] stock market fraud prosecuted . . . by the Department of Justice's Philadelphia Strike Force, this one in a substantial public company: Magic Marker. That was financed by Miami Beach hotel owner and [Meyer] Lansky cohort Yiddy Bloom and run by a Kansas City real estate operator named Jack Silbiger. The scheme involved the collusion of employees at several brokerage houses (including one headed by the president of Magic Marker), the Magic Marker specialist on the National Stock Exchange, and an analyst with the Value Line investment survey. The brokerage houses used most of the stock manipulation devices known to man. The specialist would tell them how much stock they'd need to buy each day to get the price closing on an uptick. The company president promoted the stock. The Value Line analyst wrote a favorable piece on the company. All beautifully orchestrated. By carefully restricting the float, they were able to balloon the stock from around $5 to over $30 in less than a year. When they had unloaded their shares, the stock dropped back to under $6.[138]

Racketeering.   As we mentioned in our discussion of the history of organized crime, one of its earliest operations was the extortion of funds from illegal businesses such as brothels. Today, organized crime is more involved in legitimate businesses. In its simplest form, racketeering is the sale of "insurance" to proprietors to ensure that their companies remain free of unusual "accidents" such as delivery people being beaten up, store windows being broken, merchandise being vandalized, and so on. One example that came to light occurred in the Fulton Fish Market in downtown Manhattan. For nearly seven years, wholesalers in that area paid out about $100,000 to the Fulton Patrol Service, a protection racket controlled by Carmine Romano. The payoffs were made in a variety of forms, including "parking fees," $300 Christmas gifts, and the "renting" of cardboard union shop signs for $25 a month.[139]

In one of its more elaborate forms, racketeering involves labor unions. By infiltrating the upper levels of a union hierarchy, gangsters are in a position to manipulate both management and workers. The gangsters can keep companies in line by threats of strikes or walkouts, and, at the same time, keep the companies relatively happy by allowing contracts that hold labor costs to a minimum. In return for these "sweetheart contracts," organized criminals receive considerations from management, such as under-the-table payoffs or increased company contributions to the union pension fund, which the gangsters systematically loot or use to their personal advantage.

In a manner of speaking, labor racketeering is another illegal service provided by organized crime. Employers who wish to gain competitive advantage by obtaining the cheapest available labor or by short-circuiting a union's bargaining power can do so with the assistance of gangsters—for a price. The real loser in the arrangement is the weakest party: the workers, whose interests are undermined by the coalition of management and mob. Two radical criminologists, Alan A. Block and William J. Chambliss, argue that this coalition has existed for decades as a means by which businesses could be assured of labor stability and increased profits. Block and Chambliss assert that "labor racketeering" is a misnomer:

Clearly, "labor racketeering" is a most inappropriate and misleading term for describing what takes place in the corruption of unions and in the arena of "labor-management relations." Business co-optation of the labor movement through corruption and violence to protect the short term interests of business and union leaders is a more apt description. But the tenacity of the term "labor racketeering" . . . points out how deeply ingrained are the myths of private enterprise as the engine of public good. Labor unions are per se suspect; criminal capitalists are simply the bad bananas of an otherwise efficient, if not benevolent, bunch. Consequently, social scientists and popular writers alike focus on the "racketeers" and on the "rackets" rather than on the symbiosis between business and corrupt labor practices.[140]

The premier example of gangster infiltration of a labor union involves the International Brotherhood of Teamsters. There are several ways in which organized crime has exploited its position in this union. But the most profitable has been its control of the Central States Pension Fund—a $2.8 billion fund that has been used to invest hundreds of millions into Las Vegas hotels and casinos and into a sizable share of Bally Corporation, which makes slot machines. One of the first investments was the $25 million that went to Morris "Moe" Dalitz to build the Stardust Hotel in 1960. Moe was known to have mob connections. There followed the Desert Inn, the Four Queens, the Aladdin, the Circus, Caesar's Palace, the Dunes, and many more. In 1981 the U.S. Justice Department claimed that at least $300 million of the Teamsters' Central States Pension Fund had been improperly loaned to gambling casinos and gangster-controlled real estate developments. Furthermore, two of the union's last three international presidents have been convicted of corruption. It has been truly said that the Teamsters "is not really a labor union in the traditional sense. It is more like a motorcycle gang that has taken over a bank."[141]

Infiltration of Legitimate Business.   One of the greatest concerns of those studying organized crime is its acquisition of legitimate businesses. Already, its holdings are said to be worth tens of billions of dollars.[142] The reasons for this infiltration are threefold. First, a legitimate business can be simply another way to make a profit. But organized crime has the advantage of applying gangster tactics in suppressing competitors and establishing a monopoly. One example is the takeover of many pizza enterprises in New York, New Jersey, and Pennsylvania by the Gambino and Bonanno crime families. These enterprises included the manufacturers of mozzarella cheese, the distributors of pizza ingredients, and the retail shops. According to one report,

> organized crime has acted to stifle competition from legitimate operators and suppliers by a variety of tactics, including arson, death threats and start-up loans to shops to guarantee business for the distributor-lender after the loans are made. In addition, . . . some pizzeria owners cut business costs by "skimming" large amounts of cash from their businesses to avoid taxes. These owners are also said to staff their pizzerias with underpaid illegal aliens smuggled in the country through Canada.[143]

Second, the enormous sums made from illegal activities have to be placed where they will not appear too conspicuous and will not cause embarrassing problems with the Internal Revenue Service should it inquire about the source of such funds. Legitimate businesses thus serve not only as outlets for money, but also as facades of respectability and as fronts for additional illegal operations if necessary. By reporting ill-gotten gains as the profit realized in a legitimate enterprise, the money becomes "laundered" in the sense that it may be reinvested without suspicion in other legitimate ventures.

Third, the acquisition of legitimate businesses by organized criminals may represent an attempt to phase into respectability the younger generations of the crime families. In short, business enterprises by gangsters may not always be shady. There may be difficulty, of course, for businesses competing against gangster-financed firms. For example, in one city organized crime gained a monopoly on garbage collection by lowering its prices and then using cash reserves to offset temporary losses. The legitimate businesspersons simply did not have the resources to compete and were driven out of business.[144]

Federal authorities, working closely with state and local officials, have utilized the Racketeer Influence and Corrupt Organizations (RICO) Act to reduce the influence of these crime families:

> Not one of the nation's 24 Mafia families has escaped successful prosecution in recent years and only a few are left with leadership intact. . . . Today, gangs such as the Jamaican posses, Chinese *tongs* and Colombian drug dealers are all more violent or much wealthier than La Cosa Nostra. None of these groups, however, has so far managed to have the Mafia's success at infiltrating legitimate businesses, labor unions and government. And other immigrant-based criminal organizations have disappeared as their ethnic groups have assimilated; during the past half-century the Mafia has hung on stubbornly. Partly that's because some of the public has tolerated the Mafia and even conferred folkhero status on its leaders.[145]

The Japanese *Boryokudan* have, however, been successful at integrating crime profits with ventures in legitimate business in their native land and are beginning to appear more frequently in commerce around the world. They are known generally as *Yakuza*, after the self-imposed nickname *ya-ku-sa* (8-9-3), which apparently is a losing number in an Asian dice game. They run an interesting array of gambling, vice, drug (primarily amphetamines), soft extortion, smuggling, and labor racketeering operations to meet domestic and regional demand, and have business ties in Hawaii and other states. They are a well-established, and perhaps necessary, part of Japanese society, and are not aggressively persecuted by Japanese law enforcement as long as their activities do not become overtly violent. Also, criminal triads of Chinese origin, Latin American cartels, and even outlaw motorcycle groups patterned after and affiliated with U.S. motorcycle gangs have been steadily increasing their involvement in legitimate business around the world.

After all is said and done, the differences between organized crime and legitimate businesses are largely differences of degree, not of kind. Both pursue profit by providing a product or service in response to a demand. Both endeavor to eliminate competition to maximize profits and stabilize the market demand. Even the gangster practices of arson and death threats in connection with the pizza industry takeover are hardly unknown in the history of U.S. business. True, legitimate businesses have the approval of government. But without an alliance with government created by political corruption, organized crime could not exist either. Furthermore, government inadvertently creates a monopoly for organized crime by means of the criminal law. The suppression of trade in commodities or services that are in demand primarily affects the small, less efficient illegal operators, whereas the powerful ones become even stronger.

Drawing parallels between legitimate and illegitimate business is not meant to obscure or diminish the dangers of organized crime to the functioning of society. But it should be recognized that both forms of business develop within a competitive economy in response to real demands and that their deviance derives from the same context. Deviance by organizations is often a rational response to conflicts of interest, whether between legitimate business competitors or between the government that sets standards of conduct and those who refuse to comply with those standards.

CRITICAL THINKING EXERCISES

1. What is a nonsharable financial problem? Have you ever had one? How might it have a relationship to white-collar crime?

2. How are embezzlers different from other types of thieves? Why might a banking institution be reluctant to prosecute an employee for embezzlement?

3. How does the public or the business community encourage police corruption? Write a detailed definition of police corruption according to your own opinions about police conduct. Would you accept a free cup of coffee if you were a cop? Why or why not?

4. Why is price-fixing against the law? Who is victimized by it? How is it an advantage to businesses?

5. How did early immigrant groups use organized crime to succeed in the United States? Why did some remain involved while others went on to legitimate lifestyles?

6. How have computers and the Internet changed organized crime?

CHECK IT OUT ON THE WEB

The Internet addresses listed below are intended to provide the reader with understanding of a wide range of perspectives on the subject matter discussed in this chapter. Some sites may contain objectionable material. The list is not intended to reflect the viewpoints or opinions of the authors or the publisher.

http://www.geocities.com/CapitolHill/9295/index.html
      articles on police misconduct
http://www.ckfraud.org/whitecollar.html
      types of white-collar crime
http://www.securitieslaw.com
      stock market fraud
http://www.wccfighter.com
      investigating white-collar crime
http://www.cfenet.com
      professional fraud investigators
http://www.americanmafia.com
      current news about American organized crime
http://Gomexico.about.com/cs/drugcartels
      Mexican organized crime

ENDNOTES

1. Edwin H. Sutherland, "White-Collar Criminality," *American Sociological Review, 5* (February 1940), pp. 1–12.

2. Edwin H. Sutherland, *White Collar Crime* (New York: Holt, Rinehart and Winston, 1949), p. 240.

3. Ibid., pp. 247–249; for an example of how government challenges business, see Victoria L. Swigert and Ronald A. Farrell, "Corporate Homicide: Definitional Processes in the Creation of Deviance," in *Social Deviance,* 3rd ed., ed. Victoria L. Swigert and Ronald A. Farrell (Belmont, CA: Wadsworth Publishing Company, 1988), pp. 155–165.

4. Sutherland, *White Collar Crime,* p. 9.

5. "Bureau Beats the Cheats," *Security Management, 36* (April 1992), p. 10.

6. The controversy over the proper definition of white-collar crime is best described in a series of articles found in Gilbert Geis and Robert F. Meier, eds., *White-Collar Crime: Offenses in Business, Politics, and the Professions,* rev. ed. (New York: The Free Press, 1977), pp. 253–335. Also see Steve Blum-West and Timothy J. Carter, "Bringing White-Collar Crime Back In: An Examination of Crimes and Torts," *Social Problems, 30* (June 1983), pp. 545–554; Darrell Steffensmeier, "On the Causes of 'White-Collar' Crime: An Assessment of Hirschi and Gottfredson's Claims," *Criminology, 27* (May 1989), pp. 345–358; and Travis Hirschi and Michael Gottfredson, "The Significance of White-Collar Crime for a General Theory of Crime," *Criminology, 27* (May 1989), pp. 359–371.

7. For a discussion of guidelines on this subject, see Sally S. Simpson and Christopher S. Koper, "Deterring Corporate Crime," *Criminology, 30* (August 1992), pp. 347–375; and Marianne Hilbert, "Pushing Business Toward Ethics: The New Corporate Sentencing Guidelines," *Ethics Journal,* May-June 1991, pp. 1, 4–5.

8. For suggestions on expanding the concept to include blue-collar workers, see Richard Quinney, "The Study of White-Collar Crime: Toward a Reorientation in Theory and Research," *Journal of Criminal Law, Criminology, and Police Science, 22* (June 1964), pp. 209–210. For a discussion of the scope of the definition, see Steffensmeier, "On the Causes of 'White-Collar' Crime," pp. 347–348; Hirschi and Gottfredson, "The Significance of White-Collar Crime," pp. 362–363; and Kathleen Daly, "Gender and Varieties of White-Collar Crime," *Criminology, 27* (November 1989), pp. 769–794.

9. For an early statement concerning deviance in organizational contexts, see Albert J. Reiss, Jr., "The Study of Deviant Behavior: Where the Action Is," *Ohio Valley Sociologist, 32* (Autumn 1966), pp. 1–12; and for a work on the organizational aspects of illegal organiza-

tions, see Mark H. Haller, "Illegal Enterprise: A Theoretical and Historical Interpretation," *Criminology, 28* (May 1990), pp. 207–235.

10. Herbert Edelhertz, *The Nature, Impact, and Prosecution of White Collar Crime* (Washington, DC: U.S. Department of Justice, Law Enforcement Assistance Administration, 1970), pp. 73–75. Edelhertz has a fourth major category not shown here: crimes by persons operating on an individual ad hoc basis. This includes credit card frauds, bankruptcy frauds, individual income tax violations, and others.

11. U.S. Department of Justice, Federal Bureau of Investigation [FBI], *Crime in the United States, 2002: Uniform Crime Reports* (Washington, DC: U.S. Government Printing Office, 2003), pp. 32, 46, 50.

12. John P. Clark and Richard C. Hollinger, *Theft by Employees in Work Organizations: Executive Summary* (Washington, DC: U.S. Department of Justice, National Institute of Justice, 1983), p. i; and Richard Hollinger, from his Web site of the National Retail Security Survey, http://web.soc.ufl.edu./SRP/Frequently%20asked%20questions.html

13. "Picking out the Bad Tomatoes: The Second Annual Report on Employee Theft in the Supermarket Industry: 1990," *Security Management,* March 1992, special supplement, p. 6A; for recent statistics, see Bob Ingram, "Shrink Has Shrunk, Two Surveys Find," *Supermarket Business, 55*: 9 (September 15, 2000), p. 65.

14. Peter Beruk, SIIA, Press Release, http://www.siia.net/sharedcontent/press/2000/5-24-00.html. This Web site also contains information on applicable legislation and measures aimed at curtailing and reducing the problem.

15. Terence J. Mangan and Michael G. Shanahan, "Public Law Enforcement/Private Security: A New Partnership," *FBI Law Enforcement Bulletin, 59* (January 1990), pp. 19–22.

16. Rich Hein, "Scrub Thieves Beware," *The Chicago Sun-Times,* January 10, 2000, p. 4; For another example of employee theft, see Calmeta Coleman, "Sticky Fingers: As Thievery by Insiders Overtakes Shoplifting, Retailers Crack Down," *The Wall Street Journal,* September 8, 2000, p. A1.

17. Henry K. Lee, "2 Indicted in Scheme to Sell Parts Back to Airline," *The San Francisco Chronicle,* April 17, 2001, p. A17.

18. Derived from Monty Hoyt, "The Artful Dodgers," *Toledo Blade Sunday Magazine,* June 24, 1973, pp. 4–7; "The Case of the Missing Bucks," *Investor's Reader, 56* (January 6, 1971), pp. 24–25; and Karen M. Hess and Henry M. Wrobleski, *Introduction to Private Security,* 2nd ed. (St. Paul, MN: West Publishing Co., 1988), pp. 119–142.

19. Candance E. Trunzo, "Cracking Down on Creative Padding," *Money,* November 1982, p. 214.

20. "A Third of Workers Steal from Firms, Survey Finds," *The Blade* (Toledo, OH), June 11, 1983, p. 4. The article does not name the researchers—John P. Clark and Richard C. Hollinger.

21. Quoted in Donald N. M. Horning, "Blue-Collar Theft: Conceptions of Property, Attitudes toward Pilfering, and Work Group Norms in a Modern Industrial Plant," in *Crimes Against Bureaucracy,* ed. Erwin O. Smigel and H. Laurence Ross (New York: Van Nostrand Reinhold, 1970), p. 50.

22. Alfred N. Weiner, *How to Reduce Business Losses from Employee Theft and Customer Fraud* (Vestal, NY: Almar Press, 1997), pp. 15–21.

23. Sue Titus Reid, *Crime and Criminology,* 8th ed. (Guilford, CT: McGraw-Hill, 1997), p. 324.

24. Gerald Mars, "Dockside Pilferage: A Case Study in Occupational Theft," in *Deviance and Social Control,* ed. Paul Rock and Mary McIntosh (London: Tavistock, 1974), pp. 209–228.

25. Richard C. Hollinger and John P. Clark, "Formal and Informal Controls of Employee Deviance," *Sociological Quarterly, 23* (Summer 1982), p. 342.

26. John Conley, "Knocking the Starch out of White Collar Crime," *Risk Management, 47:* 11 (November 2000), pp. 14–22. The first example is drawn from Pam Louwagie, "Sauk Rapids Bank Embezzler Sentenced to 5 Years in Prison," *Star Tribune,* May 3, 2001, B6.

27. Donald R. Cressey, *Other People's Money: A Study in the Social Psychology of Embezzlement* (Belmont, CA: Wadsworth, 1953), p. 30.

28. Quoted in ibid., p. 43.

29. Ibid., p. 83.

30. Ibid., pp. 114–138.

31. Donald R. Cressey, "The Respectable Criminal," *Transaction, 3* (March/April 1965), p. 14. For research whose results are contrary to Cressey's findings, see Gwynn Nettler, "Embezzlement Without Problems," *British Journal of Criminology, 14* (January 1974), pp. 70–77. For research applying Cressey's model to pilferers, see Gerald D. Robin, "The Nonshareable Problem Theory of Trust Violation," *Criminologica, 7* (February 1970), pp. 48–57.

32. James W. Coleman, *The Criminal Elite: Understanding White-Collar Crime,* 4th ed. (New York: St. Martins Press, 1997), pp. 17–21.

33. Lance Morrow, "Rough Justice," *Time,* April 1, 1991, pp. 16–17; "Judge Releases Former Officer Involved in LA Police Scandal," *Arizona Republic,* July 25, 2001, p. A6.

34. For an excellent discussion of the various types of deviant police behavior, see Thomas Barker and David Carter, *Police Deviance* (Cincinnati: Anderson Publishing Co., 1986), in which the authors consider such topics as perjury, brutality, sex on duty, drinking on duty, and sleeping on duty.

35. A different rationale for distinguishing between police brutality and corruption is found in Barbara Raffel Price, "Police Corruption: An Analysis," *Criminology, 10* (August 1972), pp. 161–162; for discussions on police brutality and violence, see Andrew H. Malcolm, "Police Brutality Cases: Once a Minority-Area Concern, Now Found Widely," *The New York Times,* July 30, 1985, p. A19; and David Bayley and James Garofalo, "The Management of Violence by Police Patrol Officers," *Criminology, 27* (February 1989), pp. 1–27.

36. This definition was suggested by Michael Johnston, *Political Corruption and Public Policy in America* (Monterey, CA: Brooks/Cole Publishing Company, 1982), p. 75.

37. Paraphrased from ibid., pp. 75–78.

38. The examples are from Ronald Sullivan, "25 Atlantic City Policemen Are Indicted," *The New York Times,* August 31, 1973, p. 29; Ralph Blumenthal, "Officer in Albany Says Fellow Police Joined in Thievery," *The New York Times,* September 21, 1973, p. 54; Ralph Blumenthal, "Ex-Patrolman Testifies He Committed 16 Break-ins with Other Albany Police," *The New York Times,* September 20, 1973, p. 47; and Ralph Blumenthal, "A Policeman's Plot: The Wolves Patrol the Sheepfold," *The New York Times,* September 30, 1973, sec. 4, p. 8.

39. Robert J. McCormack, "Confronting Police Corruption: Organizational Initiatives for Internal Control," in *Managing Police Corruption: International Perspectives,* ed. Richard J. Ward and Robert J. McCormack (Chicago: University of Chicago Press, 1987), pp. 151–165.

40. Peter Maas, *Serpico: The Story of an Honest Cop* (New York: George Braziller, 1973), pp. 1–3.

41. *The Knapp Commission Report on Police Corruption* (New York: George Braziller, 1973), pp. 1–3.

42. Ibid., pp. 65–66.

43. Ibid., pp. 51–56; and Michael Blaine, "Please Don't Eat the Slips," *Village Voice,* December 13, 1973, p. 103.

44. *Knapp Commission,* p. 74.

45. "Police: Cops as Pushers," *Time,* November 8, 1971, p. 17.

46. For results of the latest salary survey conducted by the International City/County Management Association, see http://www.icma.org/download/cat15/grp120/sgp224/pfs1999.pdf; the site also contains average maximum salary, both as of January 1, 1999.

47. *Knapp Commission,* p. 7. For a theory of police corruption encompassing characteristics of police work, the community, police organization, and other variables,

see Lawrence W. Sherman, "Introduction: Toward a Socio- logical Theory of Police Corruption," in *Police Corruption: A Sociological Perspective,* ed. Lawrence W. Sherman (Garden City, NY: Anchor Press, 1974), pp. 1–39. See also Lawrence W. Sherman, "Three Models of Organizational Corruption in Agencies of Social Control," *Social Prob- lems, 27* (April 1980), pp. 478–491; and Johnston, *Political Corruption and Public Policy,* pp. 79–101.

48. Johnston, *Political Corruption and Public Policy,* p. 72.

49. *Knapp Commission,* pp. 170–182.

50. Ibid., p. 181.

51. Albert J. Reiss, Jr., *The Police and the Public* (New Haven: Yale University Press, 1971), pp. 161–162.

52. Ibid., p. 162.

53. This discussion is based on Jerome H. Skolnick, *Justice Without Trial: Law Enforcement in Democratic Society* (New York: John Wiley, 1966), pp. 49–62; and Ell- wyn R. Stoddard, "The Informal 'Code' of Police Deviancy: A Group Approach to 'Blue-Coat Crime,'" *Journal of Criminal Law, Criminology, and Police Sci- ence, 59* (June 1968), pp. 202–204; see also Egon Bittner, *The Function of Police in a Modern Society* (Cambridge, MA: Oelgeschlager, Gunn & Hain, 1980), p. 63.

54. For a discussion of this, see Michael K. Brown, *Working the Street* (New York: The Russell Sage Founda- tion, 1981); and Hans Toch and J. Douglas Grant, *Police as Problem Solvers* (New York: Plenum Press, 1991), pp. 1–26.

55. Skolnick, *Justice Without Trial,* p. 54; for a more recent discussion, see Richard Lacavo, "Law and Disor- der," *Time,* April 1, 1991, pp. 18–21.

56. Lawrence W. Sherman, "Learning Police Ethics," *Criminal Justice Ethics,* Winter-Spring 1982, pp. 10–19; for a review of the extremes to which some departments have gone, see Gary T. Marx, *Undercover: Police Surveil- lance in America* (Berkeley: University of California Press, 1988).

57. *Knapp Commission,* pp. 18–19, 89–90, 112–115, 122.

58. For a discussion of possible results of this "decriminalization," see Samuel Walker, *Sense and Non- sense About Crime: A Policy Guide,* 5th ed. (Pacific Grove, CA: Brooks/Cole, 2001), pp. 239, 270–275.

59. Ibid., p. 20.

60. Sutherland, *White Collar Crime,* pp. 83–88.

61. *Prentice-Hall Encyclopedic Dictionary of Busi- ness Finance* (Englewood Cliffs, NJ: Prentice-Hall, 1960), pp. 174–175; for an expanded explanation, see Len Young Smith, G. Gale Roberson, Richard A. Mann, and Barry S. Roberts, *Smith and Roberson's Business Law,* 7th ed. (St. Paul, MN: West Publishing Company, 1988), Index I, p. 199.

62. Brier Dudley, "Feds Say Further Delay Is Harm- ful," *The Seattle Times,* August 11, 2001, p. E1.

63. "Mine That Claimed 15 Lives Was Cited for Vio- lations," *The Blade* (Toledo, OH), April 22, 1981, p. 18.

64. "Speak Softly About Dioxin," *The New York Times,* July 10, 1983, sec. 4, p. 7.

65. Morton Mintz, "At Any Cost, Corporate Greed, Women, and the Dalkon Shield," in *Deviant Behavior and Human Rights,* ed. John F. Galliher (Englewood Cliffs, NJ: Prentice-Hall, 1991), pp. 248–303.

66. These examples are taken from Charlie Morgan, "Murder Incorporated," *Risk Management* (March 2001), p. 80; and John O'Dell and Terril Yue Jones, "Tire Recall Had Brought Many Changes in the Name of Safety," *Los Angeles Times,* August 9, 2001, Business Section, Part 3, p. 1.

67. "Grim Statistics on Employee Theft," *Corporate Security,* March 15, 1992, p. 3.

68. Ovid Demaris, *Dirty Business: The Corporate- Political Money-Power Game* (New York: Harper's Maga- zine Press, 1974), p. 13.

69. For a discussion of the history of antitrust legisla- tion, see Mark J. Green, *The Closed Enterprise System: Ralph Nader's Study Group Report on Antitrust Enforce- ment* (New York: Grossman, 1972), pp. 47–60. For more recent developments, see David Eckert, "Sherman Act Sentencing: An Empirical Study, 1971–1979," *Journal of Criminal Law and Criminology, 71* (Fall 1980), pp. 244–254; and Donald W. Scott, "Policing Corporate Collusion," *Criminology, 27* (August 1989), pp. 559–587.

70. David R. Simon and D. Stanley Eitzen, *Elite Deviance* (Boston: Allyn and Bacon, 1982), pp. 70–71; and Scott, "Policing Corporate Collusion," pp. 562–563.

71. This discussion is based on Richard Austin Smith, "The Incredible Electrical Conspiracy," *Fortune,* April 1961, pp. 132–180, and May 1961, pp. 161–224; Green, *Closed Enterprise System,* pp. 153–157; and Demaris, *Dirty Business,* pp. 10–13.

72. Demaris, *Dirty Business,* p. 10.

73. Ibid., p. 12.

74. Green, *Closed Enterprise System,* pp. 149–150, 472; see also Scott, "Policing Corporate Collusion," pp. 560–565.

75. William N. Leonard and Marvin Glenn Weber, "Automakers and Dealers: A Study of Criminogenic Mar- ket Forces," in *Deviant Behavior and Human Rights,* ed. John F. Galliher (Englewood Cliffs, NJ: Prentice-Hall, 1991), pp. 193–220; see also Scott, "Policing Corporate Collusion," p. 563.

76. Gilbert Geis, "The Heavy Electrical Equipment Antitrust Cases of 1961," in *White-Collar Criminal: The Offender in Business and the Professions,* ed. Gilbert Geis (New York: Atherton Press, 1968), p. 116.

77. Ibid., pp. 108–112, 116–117.

78. Simpson and Koper, "Deterring Corporate Crime," p. 367.

79. Arthur P. Glickman, *Mr. Badwrench: How You Can Survive the $20 Billion-a-Year Auto Repair Rip-Off* (New York: Wideview Books, 1981), p. 6.

80. Ibid., pp. 6–7.

81. Paraphrased from Leonard and Weber, "Automakers and Dealers," p. 198. See also Harvey Farberman, "A Criminogenic Market Structure: The Automobile Industry," in *Deviant Behavior and Human Rights,* ed. Galliher, pp. 205–220.

82. Leonard and Weber, "Automakers and Dealers," pp. 200–201.

83. Caroline E. Mayer, "Consumer Grievances Ranked," *The Washington Post,* November 24, 1999, p. E3; and "Jury Orders G.M. to Pay $10,000 in Switch of Engines," *The New York Times,* June 28, 1981, p. 30.

84. William H. Davidow and Bro Uttal, *Total Customer Service: The Ultimate Weapon* (New York: Harper Perennial, 1989), p. 62.

85. Stephen Labaton and Lowell Berman, "Settlement Seen by Ford in Suits over Ignitions," *The New York Times,* August 13, 2001, p. A1.

86. This discussion is based on Mark Dowie, "Pinto Madness," *Mother Jones,* September/October 1977, pp. 18–32; and "Safer Pinto Tank Cost $6.65, Engineer Says," *The Blade* (Toledo, OH), February 8, 1980, p. 14. For an analysis of reactions to the Pinto case, see Swigert and Farrell, "Corporate Homicide," pp. 155–165.

87. Paul E. Tracy and James Alan Fox, "A Field Experiment on Insurance Fraud in Auto Body Repair," *Criminology, 27* (August 1988), pp. 589–603; the quotation is on p. 602.

88. Demaris, *Dirty Business,* pp. 6–7.

89. Harrison Wellford, *Sowing the Wind: A Report from Ralph Nader's Center for Study of Responsive Law on Food Safety and the Chemical Harvest* (New York: Grossman, 1972), pp. 3–6.

90. Gabriel Kolko, *The Triumph of Conservatism: A Reinterpretation of American History, 1900–1916* (New York: The Free Press, 1963), pp. 99–108.

91. Wellford, *Sowing the Wind,* pp. 8–25.

92. Ibid., p. 69.

93. Ibid., pp. 70–71.

94. Eric Schlosser, "Why You're at Risk from Contaminated Food," *USA Today,* June 28, 2001, p. 15A.

95. U.S. Department of Health, Education, and Welfare, "Food Defect Action Levels," as cited in *National Lampoon,* August 1980, p. 88.

96. Commentary by Robert Sherrill, *The New York Times Book Review,* March 4, 1973, p. 3.

97. "Corporate Crime: The Untold Story," *U.S. News & World Report,* September 6, 1982, p. 25.

98. Greenwald, "Predator's Fall," p. 47.

99. "The 'Moral Hazard' in the Savings and Loan Crisis," *Ethics Journal,* January/February 1991, p. 1.

100. John Braithwaite, "Challenging Just Desserts: Punishing White-Collar Criminals," *Journal of Criminal Law and Criminology, 73* (Summer 1982), pp. 742–747; see also David R. Simon and D. Stanley Eitzen, *Elite Deviance,* 2nd ed. (Boston: Allyn and Bacon, 1986), pp. 97–98, 109–111.

101. Irwin Ross, "How Lawless Are Big Companies?" *Fortune,* December 1, 1980, p. 62.

102. Richard Quinney, "Occupational Structure and Criminal Behavior: Prescription Violations by Retail Pharmacists," *Social Problems, 11* (Fall 1963), pp. 179–185.

103. Marshall B. Clinard and Peter C. Yeager, *Corporate Crime* (New York: The Free Press, 1980), p. 132. For additional examples of corporate crimes, many of them transnational, see the Mother Jones Web site at http://www.motherjones.com and read about the recent scam in the moving industry in Cindy Skrzycki, "The Regulators Traditional vs. Online Movers," *The Washington Post,* June 19, 2001, p. E1.

104. Clinard, *Illegal Corporate Behavior,* pp. 104–107.

105. Clinard and Yeager, *Corporate Crime,* p. 298.

106. Ibid., pp. 299–325. Also see Simpson and Koper, "Deterring Corporate Crime," pp. 347–375; and Hilbert, "Pushing Business Toward Ethics," pp. 1–5.

107. T. R. Young, "Corporate Crime: A Critique of the Clinard Report," Redfeather Institute for Advanced Studies in Sociology, unpublished paper (May 1980), p. 9.

108. Gilbert Geis, "Deterring Corporate Crime," in *Corporate Power in America,* ed. Ralph Nader and Mark J. Green (New York: Grossman, 1973), p. 189.

109. For an excellent review of the intermingling of legitimate enterprise and organized crime, see Andrew Szasz, "Corporations, Organized Crime, and the Disposal of Hazardous Waste," in *Deviant Behavior and Human Rights,* ed. Galliher, pp. 286–302.

110. The problem of distinguishing "crime that is organized" from "organized crime" is discussed in Thomas C. Schelling, "What Is the Business of Organized Crime?" *Journal of Public Law, 20:* 1 (1971), pp. 71–84. See also Joseph L. Albini, *The American Mafia: Genesis of a Legend* (New York: Appleton-Century-Crofts, 1971), pp. 35–48; and Jay Albanese, *Organized Crime in America,* 2nd ed. (Cincinnati: Anderson Publishing, 1989).

111. The President's Commission on Law Enforcement and Administration of Justice, *Task Force Report: Organized Crime* (Washington, DC: U.S. Government Printing Office, 1967), p. 1.

112. Donald R. Cressey, *Theft of the Nation: The Structure and Operations of Organized Crime in America* (New York: Harper & Row, 1969), pp. 72–74; see also Roy Rowan, "The 50 Biggest Mafia Bosses," *Fortune,* November 10, 1986, pp. 24–38.

113. Cressey, *Theft of the Nation,* pp. 248–289; Albini, *American Mafia,* pp. 67–77; see also Haller, "Illegal Enterprise," pp. 209–214.

114. Cressey, *Theft of the Nation,* p. 253. For a typology of organized crime payoffs, see Denny F. Pace and Jimmie C. Styles, *Organized Crime: Concepts and Controls,* 2nd ed. (Englewood Cliffs, NJ: Prentice-Hall, 1983), pp. 27–31.

115. Cressey, *Theft of the Nation,* pp. 250–251; for the organizational aspects, see Rowan, "The 50 Biggest Mafia Bosses," pp. 24–38.

116. William J. Chambliss, "Vice, Corruption, Bureaucracy, and Power," in *Deviant Behavior and Human Rights,* ed. Galliher, pp. 177–192; and William J. Chambliss, *On the Take: From Petty Crooks to Presidents* (Bloomington: Indiana University Press, 1978), pp. 169–188; see also William J. Chambliss, "State Organized Crime," *Criminology, 27* (May 1989), pp. 183–208.

117. Cressey, *Theft of the Nation,* p. 248.

118. For a current assessment of violence and organized crime, see Rod Nordland, "The 'Velcro Don': Wiseguys Finish Last," *Newsweek,* April 13, 1992, pp. 34–35.

119. Robert T. Anderson, "From Mafia to Cosa Nostra," *American Journal of Sociology, 71* (November 1965), pp. 302–310; see also Stephen Fox, *Blood and Power: Organized Crime in Twentieth-Century America* (New York: William Morrow and Company, 1989), esp. pp. 391–420.

120. Cressey, *Theft of the Nation,* pp. x–xi. Only selected characteristics are quoted here, and they have been renumbered. In "The 'Velcro Don,' " p. 34, Nordland states there are 24 Mafia families in the nation; for a different perspective, see Alan Block, *East Side/West Side* (New Brunswick, NJ: Transaction Books, 1983). For the newer trends in organized crime, see Fox, *Blood and Power,* pp. 411–420.

121. Albini, *American Mafia,* p. 258; cf. pp. 264–267, 300–302.

122. Ibid., p. 285.

123. Dwight C. Smith and Richard D. Alba, "Organized Crime and American Life," in *Deviant Behavior and Human Rights,* ed. Galliher, p. 173.

124. John E. Conklin, "Organized Crime and American Society," in *The Crime Establishment: Organized Crime and American Society,* ed. John E. Conklin (Englewood Cliffs, NJ: Prentice-Hall, 1973), p. 13.

See also Francis A. J. Ianni, *A Family Business: Kinship and Social Control in Organized Crime* (New York: Russell Sage Foundation, 1972), pp. 87–106, 109–110; and

Smith and Alba, "Organized Crime and American Life," pp. 174–175.

125. This discussion is based on Alan A. Block and William J. Chambliss, *Organizing Crime* (New York: Elsevier, 198\1), pp. 195–196, 212–213. Parts were influenced by John Galliher, "Tale of Two Mafias," *Crime and Social Justice, 17* (Summer 1982), p. 106. The latter contains a review of the Block and Chambliss book.

126. Gus Tyler, ed., *Organized Crime in America: A Book of Readings* (Ann Arbor: University of Michigan Press, 1962), p. 150; see also Fox, *Blood and Power,* pp. 7–51.

127. The discussion in the foregoing section is based primarily on Tyler, ed., *Organized Crime,* with emphasis on Tyler's editorial comments and his reprinted selection from Herbert Asbury, *The Gangs of New York* (New York: Alfred A. Knopf, 1927), pp. 89–178. See also Albini, *American Mafia,* pp. 177–211; and Fox, *Blood and Power,* pp. 53–76.

128. Stuart L. Hills, *Demystifying Social Deviance* (New York: McGraw-Hill, 1980), p. 87.

129. For discussions of why Italians are prominent in contemporary organized crime, see Daniel Bell, "Crime as an American Way of Life: A Queer Ladder of Social Mobility," in *The End of Ideology,* rev. ed., ed. Daniel Bell (New York: The Free Press, 1962), pp. 127–150; Ianni, *A Family Business,* pp. 54–59; and Peter A. Lupsha, "Individual Choice, Material Culture, and Organized Crime," *Criminology, 19* (May 1981), pp. 3–23; see also Fox, *Blood and Power,* pp. 61–76.

130. Francis A. J. Ianni, *Black Mafia: Ethnic Succession in Organized Crime* (New York: Simon & Schuster, 1974), pp. 313–330; and George H. Lewis, "Social Groupings in Organized Crime: The Case of La Nuestra Familia," *Deviant Behavior, 1* (January-March 1980), pp. 129–143.

131. These categories are suggested by Gus Tyler, "The Crime Corporation," in *Current Perspectives on Criminal Behavior: Original Essays on Criminology,* ed. Abraham S. Blumberg (New York: Alfred A. Knopf, 1974), pp. 198–205.

132. Nicholas Gage, "Organized Crime in City Bleeds Slums of Millions," *The New York Times,* September 27, 1970, p. 85; see also Fox, *Blood and Power,* pp. 362–366, 391–392.

133. James Cook, "The Invisible Enterprise," *Forbes,* September 29, 1980, p. 64. The discussion of the narcotics trade is based on this article, pp. 60–71.

134. Gage, "Organized Crime in City," p. 85.

135. Commission on the Review of the National Policy Toward Gambling, *Gambling in America* (Washington, DC: U.S. Government Printing Office, 1976), p. 71.

136. This discussion is based on Cressey, *Theft of the Nation,* pp. 77–91; and Tyler, "The Crime Corporation," pp. 201–202.

137. Jack Anderson, "Mob Dumping Hazardous Waste," *The Blade* (Toledo, OH), November 15, 1980, p. 9; and Ralph Blumenthal, "Illegal Dumping of Toxins Laid to Organized Crime," *The New York Times,* June 5, 1983, pp. 1, 21; see also Szasz, "Corporations, Organized Crime, and the Disposal of Hazardous Waste," pp. 286–302.

138. Cook, "The Invisible Enterprise," p. 67.

139. Stanley Penn, "On the Waterfront: New York Fish Market Points Up Pattern of Extortion and Fear," *The Wall Street Journal,* April 14, 1982, pp. 1, 16.

140. Block and Chambliss, *Organizing Crime,* pp. 86–87.

141. Joe Conason and Jack Newfield, "John Cody, the Mega-Mafia, and the Teamsters," *Village Voice,* May 13–19, 1981, p. 11. The discussion has drawn upon this article and Joe Conason, "Laying Odds on the Teamsters," *Village Voice,* June 10–16, 1981, pp. 1, 11–15.

142. Ianni, *A Family Business,* p. 6. For a description of one "family's" legitimate business interest, see ibid., pp. 87–106.

143. Donald Janson, "Pizza Industry Linked to the Mob," *The New York Times,* August, 24, 1980, p. 1.

144. The President's Commission, *Task Force Report,* p. 5; see also Rowan, "The 50 Biggest Mafia Bosses," pp. 24–38.

145. Nordland, "The 'Velcro Don,' " pp. 34–35.

PART THREE

Deviant Behavior in Contemporary Society

The last five chapters of the text deal with thorny issues: deviant drug use, mental disorders, cyberdeviance, and sexual deviance. Drug use, alcohol use and abuse, and the war on drugs form the basis for Chapter 8. This chapter provides clear examples of the dynamic nature of deviance and the interest group conflicts that characterize U.S. society. Massive efforts to reduce illegal drug use have largely been ineffective, yet they remain in place.

Chapter 9 focuses on mental disorders, another area characterized by shifts in what is deviance and what is not. It discusses the debate on mental illness and the issues of whether mental illness is a disease, a label, or a myth. Sexual psychopath laws and involuntary commitment again provide ample evidence that deviance is a thorny concept.

Chapter 10 covers the topic of suicide in contemporary society, beginning with a history of suicide and the development of attitudes toward suicide. Relevant sociological theories are discussed along with the risk factors and statistical correlates associated with suicide. The chapter concludes with a discussion of warning signs and how suicide may be anticipated and prevented.

Chapter 11 is a discussion of the rapidly developing realm of cyberdeviance. Included in this chapter are descriptions of emerging computer-based subcultures and of the variety of unusual motives and opportunities that instant worldwide communication has facilitated. The chapter ends with a consideration of sexual deviance in cyberspace.

Finally, Chapter 12 discusses sexual deviance. Sexual deviance or deviant sexual behavior may not differ in form from nondeviant behavior except in context. Exposing oneself in public may result in arrest or hospitalization, while performers in a bar down the street may be paid for a similar act. Prostitution and homosexual behaviors are also addressed. Both are excellent examples of the continued conflict over deviant behavior in the United States.

8   Deviant Drug Use

"Nobody in the United States is more than a handshake away from virtually any drug they [sic] want."

Norman Zinberg[1]

In his new book *How to Ruin Your Life*, satirist and former presidential speech writer Ben Stein suggests, "use drugs and alcohol freely."[2] Binge drinking is currently widespread on college campuses, over one-third of students have used marijuana at least once, and .4 percent have used heroine.[3] Why do so many of our "best and brightest" use drugs?

It all starts inside our brains, in the complex chemical and electrical processes that determine how we experience pleasure. Research done by Dr. Hans Breiter of Massachusetts General Hospital and others shows how drugs, good food, sex, winning in sports, and other enjoyable events activate responses in the sublenticular extended amygdala and nucleus accumbens (we will call this *the pleasure circuit*) in the human brain.[4] Pleasure circuits utilize the chemical neurotransmitters, such as dopamine, and the ways in which neurotransmitters are produced and received by neurons in the brain. Amphetamines increase dopamine production, while some drugs, like cocaine, inhibit reabsorption of dopamine so that it remains in place to continue firing the pleasure circuit longer. Alcohol causes the release of serotonin, increasing the sense of well-being. When dopamine receptors on neurons are "clogged" or eliminated, users required greater dosages to achieve the expected effects.[5] Hard-core addicts of any type may be unable to stimulate the pleasure circuit at all and be reduced to using the drugs in an attempt to avoid the pain.

The term *drug* is a broad and nebulous one. *A drug is any substance other than food that by its chemical nature affects the structure or function of the living organism.*[6] This definition is so inclusive that all we can say with certainty about people who use drugs is that they are taking something other than food that alters them in some manner. Only when we specify the intended effects of the drug use do we come closer to understanding the user and reactions to the user. For instance, your feelings about your instructor may be different if you find that he or she is taking antihistamines to control a runny nose, drinking several belts of Scotch to ease end-of-day tensions, or using amphetamines to stay awake for late-night examination grading.

Which, if any, is *deviant* drug use? The use of antihistamines to avoid cold symptoms seems unlikely to be defined as deviant unless the user is a Christian Scientist or a member of any one of several other religions that advocate treating disease by spiritual means only. Drinking alcohol is permitted in our society, but its manufacture and sale were once illegal nationwide, and in some areas it is still illegal to sell alcoholic beverages. Everywhere else in the United States the distribution and sale of alcohol are highly regulated by laws specifying where, when, and to whom it may be sold. Amphetamines are widely available through medical prescription, but taking them without a prescription makes one liable to imprisonment for using a dangerous drug. "Deviant" drug use is a flexible term, depending on many social, political, and ethical variables.

Drug Use as Deviance

From the legal standpoint, most deviant drug use in the United States involves *psychoactive drugs—substances with the capacity to influence behavior by altering feeling, mood, or other mental states.* There are two fundamental means of modifying one's relationship with the environment: Change either the environment or the perception of that environment. The former is generally more satisfying, but the latter is often more convenient or realistic. There are several ways in which to change one's perception, such as through religion, political beliefs, or general life philosophy. Another means is the use of psychoactive drugs. Distraught parents and employees gulp mood-altering drugs so that unpredictable, ungrateful children and bosses become more bearable. Long-distance truck drivers and cramming students find that amphetamines keep them attentive to their monotonous tasks.

Barbiturates and amphetamines are psychoactive drugs, as are alcohol, caffeine, nicotine, tranquilizers, heroin, marijuana, and cocaine. They all have the *capacity* to alter one's mental state. As Erich Goode points out, however, the consequences of taking a particular drug are not based solely on the properties of the drug's chemical components but also on an individual's expectations of any experiences with the drug:

> All drugs will have a range of physiological [consequences], will touch off a number of physiological responses in the organism. But it takes a human consciousness to react to these effects subjectively—that is, to internally *experience* and *reflect on* these "effects." Some of these effects may be ignored; others will be enjoyed and sought out under the influence. . . . Users learn that certain effects are "supposed" to happen and that others will not. These expectations and group definitions of drug effect have a powerful influence on what the user experiences under the influence.[7]

The variability of drug effects is easily exemplified by people under the influence of alcohol: Some become lively and outgoing, others become morose and withdrawn, and still others become belligerent and aggressive. Furthermore, the social influences of drug effects make it difficult to translate the results of tests on laboratory animals to humans. For example, research indicates that mice and rats under the influence of the active chemical in marijuana lose interest in food and sex, while many humans find that smoking marijuana increases their interest in both.[8]

Classification of Drugs

Keeping in mind this variation in their effects on human behavior, we can divide the psychoactive drugs into the following categories: *narcotics, depressants, stimulants, hallucinogens,* and *marijuana.*[9] This classification system sorts out common *physiological* responses to the great array of drugs, but within each category the drugs vary both in their potential for affecting mental states and in their particular effects, depending upon the individual user and the context of drug use. For example, caffeine and cocaine are both stimulants, but cocaine has a much greater capacity for altering perception and behavior. Also, persons using morphine (a drug derived from opium) will vary in their perceptions of the physiological experience depending on whether they are using it to kill pain or to get high.

The various types of psychoactive drugs operate in different ways:

1. Narcotics are derived from opium or a synthetic substitute. They include drugs such as morphine, methadone, codeine, and heroine. They are effective for the relief of pain and thus are essential in medicine. They may produce euphoria, reduce vision, cause drowsiness, and decrease physical activity. Except in large doses, there is no loss of motor coordination or slurred speech.

2. Depressants include the benzodiazepines or Valium-type drugs, barbiturates such as phenobarbital, and other central nervous system drugs such as methaqualone and chloral hydrate. These drugs lower the activity of the central nervous system. They can produce relaxation, drowsiness, deadening of pain, and easing of anxiety. They can also cause death at high dosage levels. For some users, depressants cause euphoria, belligerence, or even depression.

3. Stimulants include cocaine, caffeine, Ritalin, and amphetamines such as dexedrine, and benzedrine. They cause behavior opposite to that caused by depressants: increased activity, alertness, and excitation. Depending on the individual user, stimulants may result in feelings of elation, intellectual brilliance, euphoria, irritability, or anxiety.

4. Hallucinogens include LSD, DMT, MDA, PCP, MDMA (Ecstasy), DOM (STP), PCP, mescaline (peyote), psilocybin (magic mushrooms), nutmeg, belladonna, jimsonweed, and certain designer amphetamines.[10] As the term suggests, these drugs produce sensory experiences that represent a "reality" not verifiable to those who are not under the influence of the drug. Generally, however, the user recognizes the experiences as being connected with the drug. The effects can be quite dramatic: feeling that time is no longer measurable or relevant, reacting emotionally to objects that otherwise would be unnoticed and unimportant (fly specks on a window or lint on a rug), or losing one's identity in the universe or the woodwork.[11] Some user's experience "synesthesia," a crossing over of senses during which they, e.g., perceive "seeing music" or smelling or "tasting colors."[12]

A user of a psilocybin describes his experience this way:

When I opened the door of the freezer, I had a strong temptation to run my fingers over everything inside and feel different textures of the frozen foods. . . . [Mike and I] both had great fun feeling the fried chicken . . . , for it was at once greasy, crisp, and frozen, and we could feel these qualities separately as well as all at once. I then bit into a pea. . . . I could taste the ice and the pea as distinct properties and also noticed a great change in taste and texture as the pea thawed. Mike then tried one. "It tastes green," he said. I tasted another. "Yes, green, too."[13]

5. Cannabis, or **marijuana,** has been classified as a hallucinogen, a stimulant, and even a narcotic, but today researchers and the government place it in a class by itself. The active ingredient in cannabis is tetrahydrocannabinol (THC). The amount of THC varies from about .5 percent to about .8 percent depending on the type of plant, where it is grown, and how it is processed. Hashish, a highly concentrated product of cannabis secretions, may contain 10 percent THC; "hashish oil" may contain as much as 20 percent THC.[14] When used at sufficient strength, it can produce effects associated with hallucinogens: a loss of time sense and a feeling of increased sensory perception. Goode describes the most common effects mentioned by users:

> Euphoria; relaxation; a sense of one's mind wandering, a kind of stream of consciousness; a sensation that time is slowed down; . . . an impairment of one's short-term memory; a feeling of ravenous hunger; a strong increase in the enjoyment of one's senses—food tastes better, music sounds richer, more exciting, touch becomes sensuous, one's sexual orgasm becomes more intense; one feels a kind of "floating" sensation; there is a reduced and impaired ability to think logically, rationally, in a linear fashion; one finds it difficult or impossible to read well or at all.[15]

The terminology used to describe the characteristics of psychoactive drugs is relevant to why some drug use is regarded as deviant. One term is *tolerance*. This refers to the ability of the human system to adapt to and to build up resistance to the effects of some drugs. A person is building up tolerance when he or she increases the dosage to obtain the effects experienced earlier with smaller dosages. Heroin has an especially high potential for tolerance. Long-term heroin users may habitually take doses that would kill others who are not experienced with the drug.

A second term of importance is *physical dependence*. The body adapts to prolonged use of a drug so that *withdrawal symptoms* occur when use is stopped. Depressants and narcotics all have the potential for physical dependence; however, the symptoms differ somewhat among barbiturates and narcotics. Many drugs are controlled substances and therefore are illegal without a medical prescription, although some, particularly the hallucinogens, are not even available legally. Alcohol, which we will discuss later, is legal for adults but is also a central nervous system depressant. For alcohol the withdrawal symptoms include tremors, sweating, nausea, rapid heartbeat, rise in temperature, and jerky reflexes; in cases in which large amounts have been consumed over a long period, convulsion and delirium tremens may occur. Delirium tremens is characterized by confusion, delusions, and vivid hallucinations. This is often jokingly referred to as "seeing pink elephants." Victims rarely laugh about it.

Heroin withdrawal can cause anxiety, restlessness, body aches, insomnia, yawning, tears, runny nose, perspiration, contraction of the pupils, gooseflesh, hot flushes, nausea, diarrhea, rise in body temperature and respiratory rates, abdominal cramps, ejaculations, and loss of body weight.[16] It should be noted, however, that withdrawal from heroin is not always the wrenching agony portrayed by the mass media. In many respects it resembles the effects of the flu, and its intensity varies according to the individual and to the strength of the usual drug dosage. Some heavy users kick their habit, temporarily at least, with minor irritations, while some light to moderate users seem to be at death's door. In short, psychological as well as physiological influences operate in the withdrawal process.

Now that we have discussed the terms tolerance and physical dependence, we can tackle the term *addiction*. Most readers probably assume that addiction is a widely accepted scientific term. It is not. For one thing, the term has strong moral and emotional overtones. For another, the term lacks precision because of the variety of patterns that characterize drug use. The term is supposed to describe *compulsive, repetitive drug use associated with increased dosages to overcome tolerance and physical dependence stemming from withdrawal symptoms.*

Part of the problem with the term *addiction* stems from the very slippery notion of compulsion. "Compulsion" assumes a loss of control—the user *must* have the drug, the pursuit and use of the drug completely *dominate* the user's life, and *no alternative* behaviors are open except as dictated by the drug. Although some people seem to exhibit compulsive behavior, it is difficult, if not impossible, to identify its presence. Regardless of how often a drug is used or how many risks are taken to obtain the drug, when can a person's behavior be accurately described as resulting from a loss of control rather than from a rational, informed decision?

To complicate matters, the term *addiction* is usually associated only with drugs having a high potential for physical dependence. However, apparent compulsive use can also arise with drugs that do not cause physical dependence. The differences between individuals who *must have* that cup of coffee, cigarette, sundae, tranquilizer, or shot of heroin are only a matter of degree. As Steven Wisotsky puts it,

> conventional terminology does not describe cigarette smokers as "addicts," because their drug is cheap, legal, and readily available. Is not "addiction" then a function of law and custom rather than medicine or physiology? Is not "addiction" a value judgment applied selectively to stigmatize those who make socially the defiant choice to habituate to an illegal drug? . . .
>
> "Addiction" conveys some rough conception of enslavement to a drug by a mechanism (biological, psychological, or otherwise) so powerful that freeing oneself is impossible or exceptionally difficult. Only the clinical cases fit that paradigm. Most others do not. In the final analysis, to call cocaine or any other drug "addicting" requires both blindness to evidence and the adoption of a conceptual apparatus of victimization.[17]

For now, at least, it appears that drug users are most accurately categorized according to their *dependence* on drugs. Such dependence cannot be automatically measured by anything we know about the drug itself. Regardless of the chemical qualities of a drug, the effects it produces, its ability to build tolerance, or the likelihood of withdrawal symptoms, the way the drug is used varies tremendously from one individual to another. In short, *patterns of drug use are more contingent upon personality and social factors than upon attributes of the drugs.*[18]

There is a recognition that the use of illegal drugs may, for many, never become a problem or "addiction" at all. Nevertheless, the official U.S. drug policy is to eliminate nonmedical drug use.[19] The implementation of this policy is surrounded by inconsistencies, however. For example, alcoholic beverages, coffee, and tobacco contain psychoactive drugs and are used by the public as psychoactive substances, not as medicine. (As comedian W. C.

Fields said, "Always carry a flagon of whiskey in case of snakebite and furthermore always carry a small snake.") In addition, some Americans obtain by prescription drugs that they use as mind-altering substances in addition to alcohol and tobacco.

Large numbers of Americans drink alcohol, smoke cigarettes, and use innumerable "nutritional supplements," and over-the-counter and prescription drugs to make life more pleasant. Is there no contradiction between the official effort to suppress the illegal drug trade and the multibillion-dollar drug industry that constantly advertises how helpful drugs can be? In this chapter we shall discuss drug use as deviance. Focusing on alcohol, heroin, marijuana, and cocaine, we shall also consider how interest group conflict contributes to the labeling of drugs as deviant. We will also discuss perscription drug abuse and use of performance-enhancing drugs.

Alcohol

It has been estimated that "the annual beer consumption of American college students is just short of *four billion cans*. If these 'college beer' cans were stacked end-to-end upon each other, the stack would *reach the moon* and . . . beyond. . . ."[20] Drinking may be seen as congenial, disgusting, escapist, or pitiful, depending upon one's perspective. The cocktail party is an American institution at which people find refuge from the trials of everyday drudgery; the conversation becomes increasingly witty as pleasant people sample hors d'oeuvres along with margaritas and Scotch. But skid row is an American institution too. Here the company is less attractive; men in urine and vomit-stained clothes lounge about swigging cheap wine wrapped in brown paper bags. The one thing that cocktail parties and skid row have in common is alcohol. No psychoactive drug is so frequently used, and none brings about so much joy and misery at the same time.

It was not until 1857 that the chemical origins of alcohol were discovered by Louis Pasteur, but the social origins reach far into history. Sometime in our dimmest past, someone discovered that fruit juices provided unusual effects after being exposed to the air in a warm place. It was probably about the same time or shortly thereafter that someone discovered that a broth made of cereals ferments into an interesting liquid if malt is added—thus the basis of beer and ale was found. The more potent beverages—whiskey, gin, brandy, and so on—had to await the discovery of the distillation process around A.D. 800, but the wine and beer of earlier times attracted an enthusiastic following. Egypt had a brewery flourishing in 3700 B.C., and taverns were so common in Babylonia that around 2300 B.C. King Hammurabi issued regulations concerning their management. The ancient Greeks had a specific god, Bacchus, just for wine. The Bible contains several references to wine, ranging from the Psalms—"Wine that maketh glad the heart of man" (Psalms 104:15)—to Timothy, "Drink no longer water, but use a little wine for thy stomach's sake and thine often infirmities" (I Timothy 5:23).[21] and Ephesians, "Do not get drunk on wine, which leads to debauchery" (Ephesians 5:18).[22]

Alcohol as a Drug

Despite its link to the gods, alcohol is inescapably a psychoactive drug, and as its dosage is increased, it affects the performance of the human system. The terms we usually associate with the extreme result are *intoxicated, drunk, plastered, blotto,* and others that we are not at liberty to write here. As we have pointed out, alcohol acts as a depressant on the central nervous system. Alcohol is not digested but, rather, is absorbed into the bloodstream through the walls of the stomach and small intestine. The blood then rapidly carries it to the brain. As the level of alcohol in the blood rises, coordination, reaction time, vision, and general skilled performance levels are affected. When enough alcohol reaches the brain, one begins to stagger, weave, and speak with a slur. It is possible to drink so much as to suppress even automatic functions such as breathing, after which, of course, death occurs.[23]

Thus intoxication is a matter of degree. With the development of devices to measure quickly the amount of alcohol in the blood, however, state legislatures relied on them to provide a quantitative measure of intoxication. Today, throughout the United States a blood-alcohol level of .08 percent or more has been legislated to be too high for driving a motor vehicle. There is uncertainty about what blood-alcohol level invariably results in detectable influences on reflexes, reaction time, and other skills; however, it is generally agreed that .03 to .05 percent produces obvious changes.

It is important to note that the level of alcohol in the blood at any given moment in the drinking process depends on factors such as what you are drinking (e.g., 1.5 oz of spirits or brandy, 2.5 oz of liqueur, 3.5 oz of sherry, 5 oz of table wine, 8.5 oz of malt liquor, or a 12 oz beer or wine cooler all have the same alcohol content.[24] Blood alcohol content is also affected by speed of drinking, body weight, sex, presence of food in the stomach, rate of metabolism, and type of beverage (distilled products are absorbed more rapidly than wine, and wine more rapidly than beer).[25]

Carbonated drinks are absorbed more rapidly and drinks mixed with water less rapidly. Taken together, we can assume that the person most likely to get drunk would be a small female drinking scotch and Pepsi on an empty stomach. The least likely would be a large, muscular male who has been eating cheese pizza and drinking watered-down beer.[26] (For a custom-tailored blood alcohol content calculator, see www.ou.edu/oupd/bac.htm.)

Increased blood-alcohol levels are associated with more than reduced efficiency and physical performance, as we all know. People "under the influence" act in a variety of ways: Some want to fight, some want to seduce or be seduced, some become sad and philosophical, some laugh, some curse, some sing, and so on. Such social behaviors are usually explained by the notion that alcohol impairs the higher brain functions by lowering inhibitions. Typical of this interpretation is the following:

> The apparent "stimulation" from alcohol is the result of the lower brain centers being released from higher brain controls. This reduces inhibitions, and behavior which is untoward when the individual is sober becomes acceptable. For example, . . . an always proper, ladylike woman may become obscene and promiscuous when intoxicated.[27]

This is a particularly attractive notion. If alcohol erodes an individual's reason and conscience, then all kinds of unwanted behavior by others and by ourselves become more acceptable, or at least more understandable. Although people may be chided for *getting* drunk, behavior *while* drunk must be excused because drunkenness presumes a "loss of control." The utility of this argument is often recognized by child molesters, who are usually reluctant to claim that they were "normal" when the offense occurred. An especially popular explanation among molesters is that they had been drinking or were drunk at the time of the offense. Armed with this excuse, they point out that if they have any problem it is not a *sex* problem but a *drinking* problem: "This would have never happened if I hadn't been drinking."[28]

Craig MacAndrew and Robert B. Edgerton challenged the assumption that alcohol incapacitates morals as well as sensorimotor skills. They argue that while differences between sober and drunken behavior are often great and quite obvious, the behavioral changes are inconsistent and vary from one time to another for a single individual, to say nothing of the differences between individuals. In contrast to the diversity of drunken behavior in the United States, in smaller, more homogeneous societies, individuals get very drunk indeed, but there is no indication that they lose their inhibitions. In other societies drunken behavior actually has changed over time, and in still others the behaviors vary according to the situation. MacAndrew and Edgerton claim that the thesis that alcohol neutralizes social control cannot explain these patterns. More likely, societies teach individuals how to behave when drunk as well as when sober:

> Persons learn about drunkenness what their societies impart to them and comporting themselves in consonance with these understandings they become living confirmations of their societies' teachings. We would propose that this formulation is similarly applicable to our own society, but with this difference: our society lacks a clear and consistent position regarding the scope of the excuse and is thus neither clear nor consistent in its teachings. Because our society's teachings are neither clear nor consistent, we lack unanimity of understanding; and where unanimity of understanding is lacking, we would argue that uniformity of practice is out of the question. Thus, although we all know that in our society the state of drunkenness carries with it an "increased freedom to be one's other self," the limits are vague and only sporadically enforced, and hence what (if anything) the plea of drunkenness will excuse in any specific case is similarly indeterminate. In such a situation, our formulation would lead us to expect that what people actually do when they are drunk will vary enormously; and this is precisely what we find when we look around us.[29]

Alcohol Use and Deviance

Despite the many social and personal benefits that alcohol provides, it is a dangerous drug. It impairs physical performance, people under its influence often behave erratically and bring harm to themselves and others, and its continued use can lead to high degrees of dependence, physical deterioration, and great personal expense to self and to social relations. Consider these facts about alcohol in the United States:

1. Most Americans drink alcoholic beverages, and small but significant proportions drink very heavily and report problems related to drinking. Two-thirds of Americans drink sometimes, even if their drinking is limited to a drop of sherry on holidays and at weddings. The average annual consumption, however, is staggering (if you will excuse the pun): 300 cans of beer, 15 bottles of wine, and 10 quarts of distilled spirits for each American 14 years of age and older. An even more remarkable statistic is that 10 percent of the drinkers drink 50 percent of the alcohol consumed annually. Furthermore, 20 percent of drinking males and 10 percent of drinking females report signs of dependence on alcohol; about half of these claim that drinking has led to serious consequences such as loss of job and family problems.[30] And an estimated 7 percent meet the diagnostic criteria for alcoholism.

2. A large proportion of serious street crime is related to alcohol use. As we pointed out earlier, the majority of homicides and aggravated assaults and a significant proportion of rapes are alcohol related. Recent research on victimizations indicates that nearly one-fourth of victims of violent crimes reported that offenders had been drinking or were under the influence of alcohol at the time of their offenses. Our knowledge of the dynamics of alcohol use and crime is inadequate, but the consistent relationship between alcohol use and so many offenses should, encourage more research.[31]

3. Alcohol-related offenses constitute the largest single arrest category. In 2002, 572,735 arrests were made for drunkenness, despite the fact that most states no longer have laws allowing criminal prosecution solely because of a person's intoxicated appearance in public. Almost a million and a half arrests were for driving under the influence of alcohol, and more were for disorderly conduct and vagrancy—classifications that are often used instead of a drunkenness charge. This means that one-fourth of all arrests involve people who get into legal difficulty because of drinking. Add another 5 percent of arrests for violation of liquor laws—selling to minors, violating closing hours, and so on—and one can see that an enormous amount of police time and energy are spent on alcohol-related activities.[32]

One qualifying statement must be made with regard to these statistics: The percentage of arrests for alcohol-related offenses has been *decreasing.* In 1960, for example, 36 percent of all arrests were for drunkenness alone. Adding that year's arrests for disorderly conduct, vagrancy, and driving under the influence, the total arrests for all alcohol-related offenses came to 56 percent.[33] This does not mean that fewer people are getting drunk today; it simply reflects changes in legal policy. Since 1960 many states have decriminalized public intoxication, and many cities have established special medical facilities for the publicly intoxicated. People who would have been arrested and jailed a few decades ago are now turned over by police to detoxification or alcohol rehabilitation centers. This represents a considerable improvement over the situation exemplified by the case of Benson Begay of Phoenix, Arizona. Between December 1948 and mid-1973 (with a gap of four years in the Army), he was arrested 396 times for being drunk. As one officer put it, "Benny was doing a life sentence on the installment plan for liking beer."[34]

The Benson Begays have not disappeared, however. Whether under arrest or in treatment, they still constitute a considerable drain on the legal system.

4. A large proportion of automobile fatalities and injuries are related to alcohol use. The following data from the National Highway Traffic Safety Administration are self-explanatory:

   a. Fifty percent of people who die in accidents while driving passenger cars, light trucks, or vans have been drinking.
   b. Forty percent of fatally injured motorcyclists have blood alcohol above the legal limits at the time of death.
   c. Over 30 percent of fatally injured pedestrians age 16 and over have a blood-alcohol level of 0.10 or more at the time of their accidents.[35]

5. Alcohol is also involved in a large proportion of other types of accidents. Studies estimate that up to 38 percent of the accidental drownings and submersions are related to alcohol, 35 percent of fatal falls are alcohol-related, 45 percent of the fire accidents resulting in deaths are related to alcohol. Nearly one-third of all suicides involve the use of alcohol.[36] In all, there are twenty-five times more deaths from alcoholism than from illegal drugs.[37]

6. Alcohol may be especially harmful to college-age adults. Research indicates that the adolescent brain may be uniquely susceptible to alcohol impairments. In addition, the National Institutes of Health estimate that, each year:

  a. Five hundred thousand students under the influence of alcohol are accidentally injured, and more than 600,000 are assaulted by someone who has been drinking.

  b. Over 70,000 are victims of alcohol-related sexual assault.

  c. Over 150,000 develop health problems related to their drinking.

  d. Approximately 25 percent report that drinking has resulted in such things as missed classes, poor performance on exams, and lower grades.[38]

7. Drinking is also implicated in physical deterioration and illness. Until recently, alcohol and physical problems were assumed to be only indirectly related. The accepted explanation was that a preoccupation with alcohol led to neglect of one's diet, which, in turn, made the drinker more prone to physical problems. In short, it was believed that alcohol-associated diseases were the result of malnutrition. Research still supports the link between heavy drinking and malnutrition, but it also shows that alcohol itself increases the risk of the following:

  a. Heart ailments such as: cardiomyopathy (a disease of the heart muscle), arrhythmia (irregular heartbeat), and other heart ailments such as high blood pressure and coronary artery disease.

  b. Cancers of the tongue, mouth, esophagus, larynx, and breast.

  c. Brain cell loss.

  d. Decreased functioning of the immune system.[39]

  e. Infertility and osteoporosis in women.

  f. Birth defects.[40]

Alcohol use during pregnancy is the leading cause of mental retardation and can produce babies with fetal alcohol syndrome.[41] The following letters show the devastating effect fetal alcohol syndrome can have on children and their families:

A Letter from Andy's Parents

Dear Friends,

When we adopted Andy 35 yeas ago, it was love at first sight. He had a few physical problems, but he was a beautiful baby boy with long eyelashes and curly brown hair. What a gift we were given in adoption! I felt that God had chosen us to be his parents. But we soon found that Andy was different. Then, we saw a TV program about children who looked and acted just like Andy. They had misshapen jaws and teeth, small eyes, and low-set ears. They were mildly retarded and could be very warm and loving, but they could become very agitated and at times even aggressive. Many had seizures.

Andy has fetal alcohol syndrome. Andy's birth mother drank before and during her pregnancy. And that has made all the difference in his life and in ours. We had such positive dreams for our son. We dreamed of him growing up to play football or being in the band in high school. What happy dreams we had: good health, fun, enjoyment, and various achievements growing up. Then college and a satisfying career doing something he loved and making a real contribution to his community. We dreamed of his wedding day and grandchildren. All those dreams have had to be set aside because his birth mother drank during her pregancy. The sad part is that all of THIS WAS 100% PREVENTABLE![42]

Letter from Andy

Teachers, Students, Faculty, Ladies and Gentlemen:

It is a very high privilege for me to write to you all today about not drinking while you all are pregnant or this is what will happen to your child. This is what my birth mother did to me when she was pregnant with me. Some things that I cannot do are go to high school and go to college and get a degree of what I want to do. I can't drive a car or be part of the fire department like I would want to be part of them.

If I could have come to your college, maybe I could be like all of you. Maybe I could have been in the band or part of the pep squad because I know that would be a dream come true if I could have done those things and if I could walk across the stage at graduation and get my diploma like all of you.

My adoptive parents are very good to me and we try very hard to let people know how important it is not to drink (or do drugs either) when you are pregnant. Then you will not have a child with all of the things wrong like I have with me. If I could see my birth mother, I would say to her why did you do this to me?

Your friend,

Andy (age 35)[43]

Given all these horrors, dare anyone drink at all? Remember that problems with alcohol are rarely of concern for light or moderate drinkers (although being intoxicated always increases the risk of accidents). Indeed, it appears that the risk of coronary artery disease may be less for light drinkers than for abstainers. Nonetheless, it is inescapable that more deaths, disease, and financial and emotional loss result from alcohol use than from all of the other psychoactive drugs combined. Add to these costs the expenses of medical care and lost production and the intangible and unmeasurable expenses of disrupted families, desertions, and countless other social and psychological problems that arise from drinking. Alcohol clearly constitutes the greatest drug problem in the United States.

Alcoholism, Disease, and Problem Drinking

The problems associated with alcohol have nothing to do with Aunt Lucy and Uncle Ricky sipping their evening sherries or with the vast majority of drinkers whose alcohol use never gets them into difficulty with their health, their employer, their family, or the law. They have nothing to do with cousin Charlie who is one of a generation of freshmen entering college reporting record low rates of alcohol consumption.[44] As one might infer from the previous section, a hard core of drinkers is the principal source of alcohol-related problems.

The common term applied to this group of drinkers is "alcoholics." It is, however, about as scientifically precise as the term "wacko" used to describe the mentally disordered. One of the reasons for the imprecision is a continuing controversy over whether alcoholism is a disease.

The major pioneer of the disease concept of alcoholism was E. M. Jellinek. Jellinek defined alcoholism very loosely as "any use of alcoholic beverages that causes any damage to the individual or society or both."[45] He was purposely broad in his definition to impress upon his readers the many species of alcoholism. He suggested at least five specific types but considered the most prominent type in the United States to be *gamma alcoholism,* characterized by tolerance, withdrawal symptoms, craving, loss of control, and the progression from psychological to physical dependence.[46]

Jellinek's description of gamma alcoholism clearly dominates both the medical and the popular views of alcoholism. Included in both views is the perception of alcoholism as a *progressive disease* characterized by a *compulsion to drink.* Excessive drinking is seen not as a matter of personal weakness or lack of will power but as a consequence of *innate, predisposing factors* within the individual.

In abbreviated form, these are the progressive phases of gamma alcoholism outlined by Jellinek:

1. **Prealcoholic symptomatic phase.** The prospective alcoholic begins drinking socially and discovers drink gives relief from tensions. Within a period of six months to two years the individual's tolerance for tension decreases, and he or she drinks more frequently to obtain relief.
2. **Prodromal phase.** This phase begins with the onset of blackouts—amnesia or loss of memory about what occurred while drinking. The individual becomes more preoccupied with alcohol at social gatherings, drinks ahead of time to ensure that he or she gets enough, tries to get more drinks without the knowledge of others, and begins to develop some guilt about drinking.
3. **Crucial phase.** The drinker loses control, thus marking the beginning of the "disease process." This does *not* refer to *why* the individual begins drinking—that is attributed to the original psychological factors. Instead, it means that once drinking begins the individual has no ability to control the quantity of drinks until the supply is exhausted or the individual becomes too intoxicated to continue.
4. **Chronic phase.** This phase begins with the onset of "benders"—prolonged bouts of uncontrolled drinking that last for days. This is followed by ethical deterioration, impairment of thinking, loss of alcohol tolerance, indefinable fears, tremors, and recognition of defeat by alcohol.[47]

With the growing acceptance of Jellinek's disease model, medical and hospital interest groups moved to include the alcoholic as their responsibility. In 1967, in an unprecedented action, the American Medical Association (AMA) decided by formal vote that "alcoholism must be regarded as within the purview of medical practice."[48] The AMA's position is reflected in the following statement by the chair of its Committee on Alcoholism:

Today the physician is equipped to help care for these sick people [alcoholics]. . . . Doctors can prescribe drugs to alleviate physical symptoms. In physical complications from excessive drinking, proper diet, vitamins and drugs can be used to restore the patient physically and usually he can return to his former physical fitness. When underlying psychological reasons can be discovered to account for the patient's escape into alcoholic oblivion, corrective therapy can be applied. Anxieties due to insecurity in financial, domestic or physical matters may be alleviated by psychotherapy. In his relationship with the physician, the alcoholic may be relieved of fears that have no foundation in fact, thus obviating the need for escape through alcohol. . . .

It must be remembered that alcoholism is a disease, that habitual excessive drinking is an illness which the physician is ready to treat.[49]

Despite the widespread acceptance of Jellinek's scheme, there has always been skepticism that alcoholism is a disease. Peter Conrad and Joseph W. Schneider argue that the scientific claims for the disease concept do not hold. According to Conrad and Schneider:

1. There is no evidence of characteristics that consistently differentiate persons labeled alcoholics from nonalcoholics. Particularly fruitless has been the search for an "alcoholic personality" that might be used to explain excessive drinking.
2. There is no evidence supporting Jellinek's notion of a progression of symptoms. Unless alcoholism is unlike any other disease, its symptoms should be relatively uniform and consistent in sequence. But research shows this is not the case. In some longitudinal studies, for example, it was found that for substantial numbers of young men, problem drinking was not predictive of problem drinking in later life.
3. There is doubt that people labeled as alcoholics "lose control" once they begin drinking. It is a key hypothesis of the disease model that an alcoholic cannot consciously regulate his or her intake of alcohol and that to be "cured," the alcoholic must abstain totally and permanently from drinking. Of all the disease model's components, this is the most volatile; to challenge it is to strike at the very heart of the model and at the basic philosophy of Alcoholics Anonymous: "Once an alcoholic, always an alcoholic." The issue is so emotionally charged that researchers who dare to suggest that alcoholics can drink socially have been vilified by those who support the model.[50]

To date, regarding alcoholism as a disease has proven of no value in describing *what alcoholism is, what causes it,* or *what cures it.* No physiological or psychological factor has been isolated that accounts for "loss of control," itself a phenomenon that may or may not exist. Compounding the problem of the disease concept of alcoholism is the fact that the best-known "cure" for drinking problems is Alcoholics Anonymous (AA), an organization that employs not medicines or surgery but social and theological influences.[51] AA relies on group support and "a power greater than ourselves" to reinforce abstinence. In a sense alcoholism is a "disease" that a Christian Scientist can appreciate far more than a physician can. As a president of the American Medical Association stated, the "ultimate" solution to the alcoholic's problem

> may have to come from his religious counselor, his employer, his family, his friends, from social workers or other dedicated people trained to deal with this kind of person. I know of no other medical or health problem in which so many groups and so many individuals outside of the medical profession can contribute so much toward its solutions.[52]

One alcohol researcher responded, "That, to put it mildly, is strange medical practice."[53]

This is not to imply that calling alcoholism a disease is without consequences. If people are "sick," they are relieved of some responsibility. Being labeled "sick" affects the *social response* toward the persons so labeled. For people with drinking problems the disease label has resulted in profound changes, the most notable being the widespread decriminalization of public intoxication. In short, the disease concept has taken problem drinkers out of jails and put them into hospitals. But treating people as patients rather than as criminals has brought us no closer to understanding why they drink too much too often. As one critic of the disease concept points out,

> the major advantage of defining alcoholism as an illness is social. It legitimates social support for rehabilitation of the alcoholic instead of punishment. To say that alcoholism is an illness should not be construed as a statement about the etiology [the cause or origin] or treatment of alcoholism.[54]

Oakley Ray suggests the following:

> An *alcoholic* is an *individual who uses alcohol to such an extent, and in such a way, that it interferes with his personal, social, or occupational behavior.* This is obviously a psychosocial definition, since it does not talk of blood alcohol levels, medical problems, or quantities of alcohol consumed. It does not say the alcoholic is suffering from an illness. It just says that when alcohol mucks up a person's life in any way, let's call him an alcoholic and see if the problem can't at least be reduced. . . .[55]

A growing number of researchers support this view. In addition, a growing number are coming to view alcohol use as a falling along a continuum. You will recall that earlier in this chapter we rejected the notion of addiction in favor of a continuum of drug dependence. As one approaches extreme dependence (the compulsive type), the more likely it is that one will conform to what is usually thought of as the *alcoholic*—the person who drinks because he or she must. But researchers are now questioning how many of those labeled as "alcoholics" are really at this end of the continuum.

In the final analysis, *problem drinking* is a concept preferable to *alcoholism* because the latter is burdened with too many difficulties. How do we define "problem drinking?" Perhaps we should simply consider one of the least complicated definitions of problem drinking, that of the Cooperative Commission on the Study of Alcoholism: "Problem drinking is a *repetitive use of beverage alcohol causing physical, psychological, or social harm to the drinker or to others.*"[56]

Correlates of Problem Drinking

The literature on drinking habits is enormous, diverse, and often inconclusive, but one finding is consistent: Drinking problems vary from one social group to another. The differences among ethnic groups are especially striking. For example, the impact of drinking among primitive societies ranges from nil to highly disruptive.[57] Among modern cultures the Irish and French have many drinking problems, but Jews, Italians, and Chinese have few.[58]

One of the more sophisticated studies of drinking patterns among ethnic groups was conducted by Richard Jessor and his associates. Known as the Tri-Ethnic Study, it involved a small Colorado community of Hispanic, American Indian, and Anglo-American members. The researchers' goal was to identify the interrelationships between problem drinking and both social and personality variables.[59] The social variables were based on the concept of *anomie* as suggested by Robert K. Merton and others (see Chapter 2). The researchers proposed that the probability of problem drinking increases in groups characterized by (1) lack of opportunities for group members to obtain the valued goals of U.S. culture, (2) lack of group consensus on appropriate norms, and (3) opportunities to learn and engage in deviant behavior.

The personality variables were based on a social learning theory similar, but not identical, to the *differential association theory* of Edwin H. Sutherland (see Chapter 2). Here the researchers proposed that the probability of problem drinking increases in groups characterized by (1) the perception that the opportunity structure will not fulfill personal goals through socially acceptable means, (2) alienation—feelings of isolation and powerlessness, and (3) personal toleration for deviant behavior and a tendency toward immediate gratification.

Jessor and his associates found that ethnic differences in problem drinking (Anglos having the fewest problems and Indians the most) were related to each of the variables listed. When the variables were used in combination, they appeared to explain even more of the ethnic differences than when used singly. The researchers concluded that a consideration of both social and personality variables is necessary to understand problem drinking.

The findings of the Tri-Ethnic Study are supported in part by a study that we shall refer to as the *national survey*. This survey, conducted by Don Cahalan and others, was based on intensive personal interviews with adults representing the total population of the United States. In the first stage of the study, over 2,700 were interviewed;[60] approximately two years later a subsample of over 1,300 was reinterviewed to detect any emerging drinking problems. These problems could be any of the following: binges; behavior associated with Jellinek's gamma alcoholism; feelings of psychological dependence on alcohol; and alcohol-related problems with relatives, friends, employment, the law, health, and finances.[61]

The national survey found drinking problems to be associated with the following variables:

1. Favorable attitudes toward drinking.
2. Environmental support for heavy drinking as measured by items on how many friends and relatives drink heavily, parents' attitudes toward drinking, parents' drinking habits, and so on.
3. Alienation and maladjustment as measured by several items concerning feelings of helplessness, unhappiness, and so on.
4. Impulsivity and nonconformity as measured by items similar to Jessor's toleration of deviant behavior and tendency toward immediate gratification.
5. Unfavorable expectations of the future.
6. Looseness of social controls as measured by items concerning ties to family and friends.[62]

The survey results indicated that all these variables are related to drinking problems but that some are clearly more predictive of problems than others. For both sexes *attitude toward drinking* is especially important. For males, who are more likely to have drinking problems, *environmental support* is also crucial; for females *alienation and maladjustment* constitute the second most important variable.

Cahalan, Cisin, and Crossley sum up the conclusions of the national survey:

> In general, the findings bear out the conclusion that both sociological and psychological factors are important in the development of problem drinking. The sociological—that is to say, the external environmental—factors determine whether the individual is encouraged or permitted to drink heavily; and the psychological factors can operate to help to bring about or to maintain a level of drinking which may be above that normally encouraged or permitted for the person's environment. Thus if one sets aside the major factor of attitude toward drinking, it was found that for men the external environmental factors played a more conspicuous role among the correlates of problem drinking . . . while for women the variable of alienation and maladjustment appeared to be more influential than the sociological factors. . . . It is speculated that it takes more psychological pressures for a woman than for a man to persist in problem drinking, in the face of general disapprobation of heavy drinking for women.[63]

The fact that both the Tri-Ethnic and national surveys focus on the interaction between sociological and psychological variables should not mislead the reader into believing that such an approach predominates in problem-drinking studies. The amount of research in the area is, to put it mildly, vast. But if any single theme is paramount, it is that problem drinking is symptomatic of maladjustment in individuals.[64] Although some recognition is given to social factors, the major thrust is that the individual cannot cope with his or her situation and turns to alcohol as a way out. A popular example is the dependency approach to problem drinking, which, put most simply, ascribes great significance to *oral-dependency needs*. Alcohol gratifies these needs while allowing the individual to maintain a facade of adult independence and assertiveness.[65] Another individual-centered approach is the *power need* hypothesis suggested by David C. McClelland and his associates. They claim that males, at least, drink primarily to feel strong and that those who drink excessively have excessive power concerns and low inhibitory tendencies at the outset.[66]

These individual-centered approaches fail to recognize that the meaning drinking has for individuals is at least partly the result of a social learning process. One learns from others *how* to drink and *why* to drink, as well as *when* drinking is appropriate and when it is not. A primary example is the well-documented finding that alcohol problems among Jews are consistently low despite the high proportion of Jews who drink.

According to Barry Glassner and Bruce Berg, there are four learning processes that effectively insulate Jews from problem drinking:

1. Jews learn from childhood that excessive drinking is something that non-Jews do, whereas Jews drink only in moderation. In short, Jews define themselves as not having alcohol problems—a definition that acts as a self-fulfilling prophecy.
2. Jews learn that drinking is a ritual process limited primarily to family, religious, and other social occasions. Drinking is thus a symbolic act rather than an end in itself. Jews do not drink to experience the sensations of alcohol but to punctuate the significance of an event.

3. Jews tend to have friends who only drink in moderation. therefore, they experience relatively little peer pressure to engage in deviant drinking and significant support for drinking only in moderation.

4. Jews learn a variety of techniques for avoiding heavy drinking when exposed to heavy drinking situations. These include "nursing" and diluting drinks and developing convincing "lines" about why they should not drink more.[67]

Some years ago, Robert F. Bales presented a theory to account not only for the Jewish problem-drinking rates but also for most of the variations in such rates across cultures worldwide. He hypothesized that problem-drinking rates were linked to three factors:

1. **The extent to which a culture produces inner tensions in its members.** Bales suggests that a culture can induce feelings of guilt, conflict, anxiety, and sexual tension. Jessor's use of anomie as a social correlate of problem drinking is consistent with this hypothesis.

2. **The types of attitudes toward drinking that the culture produces.** Bales claims that there are four alternative attitudes:

    a. **Complete abstinence.** By definition this should prevent problem drinking. However, when people do drink in cultures that prohibit the behavior, they lack any guidelines or directives on *how* to drink. Thus on an individual level, drinking can result in serious consequences.

    b. **Ritual attitude.** In this instance alcohol is consumed in rigorously defined situations, especially religious ceremonies. The place of alcohol in the culture is clearly defined to its members. Jewish drinking customs would fit in this category.

    c. **Convivial attitude.** This is closest to what is commonly referred to as *social drinking.* Alcohol is seen as a means of putting people at ease and producing congeniality in group settings. Drinking alcohol together is viewed as a means of fostering social unity and goodwill.

    d. **Utilitarian attitude.** This refers to drinking that serves personal rather than social interests. It includes drinking for medicinal purposes—to ease a hangover, for example—and for purposes of forgetting one's troubles, of gaining courage to face difficult situations, and so on. Such an attitude, according to Bales, can often evolve from convivial attitudes and is the one attitude most likely to result in drinking problems.

3. **The extent to which a culture provides suitable substitutes for alcohol for easing culturally produced tensions.** Bales does not specify what such substitutes might be in the United States.[68] However military bases provide a good example. Traditionally, the center of social life, the club bars are today frequently nearly empty. Crowded fitness centers have taken their place.

As Bales insists, these factors have little explanatory value individually; they must be considered in concert. Even then, the Bales model admittedly provides only the barest outline of a complex issue. Eventually, however, it will probably be a similar theoretical approach that explains cross-cultural differences in problem drinking. Currently, research on alcoholism continues, with much of the research considering the above factors. As E. te Wierik points out, many other possible causes of alcoholism are being studied as well. These include:

- Hereditary or constitutional [physiological] studies
- Trait studies, also called "psychological studies," or investigations of the specific character features of the alcoholics
- Psychoanalytic studies that reconstruct the alcoholic's development
- Learning theories
- Sociocultural studies
- Studies focusing on an interaction model[69]

Even researchers involved in discovering how alcoholism may be genetically transmitted suggest that

> environmental or psychological factors—or some combination of the two—appear to be responsible for differences in the expression of genetic influences. In light of these recent developments, the identification of environmental, psychological, and biological factors responsible for the transmission of alcoholism across generations takes on an added importance.[70]

Perhaps we are getting close to an integration of the myriad explanations of alcoholism.

If there is an obvious answer to problem drinking, it lies in the values attached to drinking. How can these values be altered so that problem drinking declines? We are unlikely to answer that question until the setting for alcohol research moves from the hospitals and into the world where people learn *how, why,* and *when* to drink. If there is an answer to how we can help them stop, it appears to lie in social support. Ironically, it may lie in drug support as well. In July 2004, the Food and Drug Administration approved a drug, campral (acamprosate), which acts on the brain pathways that are related to alcohol abuse and aids recovering alcoholics in abstaining from drinking.[71] In the meantime, if you are interested in a personal evaluation of your drinking or if you are concerned about a friend, go to http://www.med .unc.edu/alcohol/prevention/signs.html or http://www.indiana.edu/~adic/friend.html.

Heroin

For years, to many people the *drug problem* meant the *heroin problem.* Heroine is one of the most widely abused illegal drugs with perhaps as many as 15,000,000 users worldwide.[72] Heroin is a far more potent drug than is alcohol: Its euphoric effects are greater, the human system is capable of building an extremely high tolerance for heroin, and the likelihood of developing patterns of physical dependence and continual use is high.

The raw material of heroin is *opium,* which is simply the dried juice of the unripened seed pods of the opium poppy. Opium's effects were known at least as early as 4000 B.C. to the Sumerians, who lived in what is now southern Iraq and who called the opium poppies "joy plants." In 1803 the chief active ingredient of opium was chemically isolated. It was appropriately named *morphine* after the Greek god of dreams, Morpheus, because it proved to be the greatest pain reliever the world had known. But once it was discovered that using morphine, like using opium, often resulted in physical dependence, a search was undertaken for a substitute.

One result was the development of heroin, a derivative of morphine, in 1898. Heroin proved to be an extremely potent drug: It doubles or triples the strength of morphine (heroin actually turns into morphine once in the body), and its effects are particularly rapid when it is injected by a hypodermic needle. But it, too, often results in dependence. Today, heroin is regarded as having no unique medical qualities and is outlawed in most countries.

Whereas heroin is rarely used for medical purposes, no satisfactory substitute has been found for the medical qualities of morphine. Therefore opium poppies are cultivated in various areas throughout the world to supply both the pharmaceutical and illegal markets. Because of political turmoil in some of these countries, the size of the annual harvest is difficult to estimate.

From the small farmer's field in Afghanistan or Myanmar, the opium trail to the United States leads first to a laboratory where the opium is transformed into heroin, thereby reducing its volume by a ratio of 10 to 1. The heroin is then shipped in its concentrated form to the United States, where it most likely enters the country through either New York City or Detroit. Once in the United States, the product begins to increase in volume as it passes through a series of dealers, each of whom dilutes the heroin's strength. By the time it reaches its eventual users, the product consists of about 6 percent heroin. Heroin users thus pay considerable overhead for their habits. According to one estimate, the retail cost of heroin in the United States is *two hundred times* more than it would be if its sale were not hampered by law.[73] Notice that the word used here is "hampered," not "excluded." By following a few words of good advice, anyone can buy heroin—a half-million Americans do it every day. The problem is not its availability but its expense.

The regular heroin user may make up to 1,400 buys annually, and his or her habit may average $100 a day or more.[74] The persistence of use despite the drug's price suggests something of the nature of heroin dependence. The motivations for heroin use are particularly strong, and intensified or compulsive use is extremely difficult to alter. To understand better the nature of heroin dependence—the process of being "hooked"—let us explore what the drug does for its users.

Heroin as a Drug

As indicated, heroin is a narcotic—it is particularly effective in blocking pain, and it creates drowsiness, lethargy, and an inability to concentrate. In themselves these effects scarcely explain dependence, however. Heroin use as a habit can be discussed only in terms of three factors that characterize individuals' experiences with the drug: the *initial impact,* or *rush;* the *euphoria,* or *high* or *nod;* and the *withdrawal symptoms.* The initial impact is experienced when heroin is injected into a vein. This sensation has been variously described as ranging from a sudden flush of warmth in the stomach to a huge orgasm. The rush is followed by a more prolonged state of euphoria known as the high or nod. It is in this phase that one may attain a sense of well-being and a loss of anxiety. The following statements by occasional heroin users convey their impressions of the high:

It gives you a real warm, mellow feeling . . . puts everything at ease and relaxes your nerves.

It's the ultimate in escape. Nothing bothers you.

Life passes swiftly as if you're in a dream.

It stimulates the freedom of my ideas.[75]

Although these effects seem to be identifiable, first experiences with the rush and the high may be anything but pleasurable. Some people have feelings of fear and sickness instead. The reason is that positive responses to the effects of heroin are neither automatic nor inherent in the chemical properties of the drug. One's responses to the drug are *learned*. Most first experiences with heroin occur in the company of others who encourage a favorable interpretation of the drug's effects.[76] This influence may counteract even the most distasteful initiation.

But learning to enjoy the euphoric effects of heroin is only the first step in the process of becoming hooked. The individual must also decide whether he or she should continue its use and risk joining the ranks of those for whom heroin has become an absolute need. Does a person *decide* to become dependent on heroin? Apparently not. Instead, the person decides that he or she is immune from such a fate:

> The individual user never believes he himself will become addicted. Perhaps we see here the same mechanism that allows a soldier on a battlefield to surge forward and continue fighting while he sees soldiers around him dying from wounds. One can be firmly set in the belief that the self is inviolable, unique, and not subject to suffering, accident, or death. . . . One no more decides to become an addict than one decides to die on the battlefield.[77]

Although group influence and euphoric effects play important roles in the initiation and continuation of heroin use, addiction—or, in our terminology, intensified or apparently compulsive dependence—is created in large part by *withdrawal symptoms*. Heroin is characterized by both *tolerance* and *physical dependence*. The first term refers to the consequence of continued drug use whereby a person becomes accustomed to the drug's effects and, to experience euphoria, requires steadily larger doses. But as the regular user increases the dosage, the body adjusts to the drug and now requires it for normal functioning. Should the user abstain, certain physical symptoms occur until the body adapts to the new state. These withdrawal symptoms include yawning, runny nose, and perspiration in the early stages and fever, chills, and vomiting in the later stages. As we mentioned, the severity of the symptoms is influenced by the attitudes and other personality factors of the individual user, but generally it is related to the strength of the dosage to which the body has adjusted.[78] Apparently, there is no limit to the degree of tolerance that can be developed; a regular user may eventually take dosages that would be fatal to less experienced users.

If there is such a thing as an invariable sequence in becoming hooked, we are ignorant of it. However, for most cases the process probably approximates that suggested by Troy Duster, which goes something like this:

> An individual first tries heroin, usually on the spur of the moment. The introduction takes place in a group of friends if the individual is male, but a female is more likely to be intro-

duced by someone with whom she has an intense emotional relationship, such as her husband or her lover. After the first or subsequent attempts, the person decides that the drug experience is both physically (the rush) and emotionally (the high) pleasurable. After using the drug, the novice notices a slight headache or nausea, but it passes quickly. The same result occurs after the next few experiences. The user connects these negative symptoms with the drug, but they are considered a small price to pay. Since the user concludes that this minor discomfort is all that withdrawal will involve, he or she feels insulated from becoming dependent.

This state of affairs continues for a few months until the user begins to recognize that the original dosage is no longer supplying the wanted effects. This is no problem; the dosage can be increased, and the only inconvenience will be that the headaches and nausea will be a little stronger. But the sequence intensifies. The dosages get larger, and the symptoms progress to vomiting, hot flushes, diarrhea, and so on. Now the user begins to take the drug to get relief from the symptoms and is hooked.[79]

This progression is not inevitable; some people use heroin on an occasional basis for years without becoming involved in the dependence spiral. However, the high potential of heroin for producing extreme dependence cannot be denied. From this fact has arisen a controversy over the degree to which euphoria and withdrawal symptoms contribute to the dependence. For over a quarter of a century, the prevailing sociological view was that proposed by Alfred R. Lindesmith.

According to Lindesmith, there is a definite distinction between the heroin *user* and the *addict*. This distinction entails what he calls a "reversal of effects":

> In the beginning phases of addiction, the pleasurable effects of drugs, other than those that occur at the time of injection [rush], tend to diminish and vanish. As this occurs, and as withdrawal distress increases, the psychological significance of the doses changes. Whereas they at first produced pleasure, their primary function becomes that of avoiding pain, that is withdrawal. The addict seems to continue the use of the drug to avoid the symptoms which he knows will appear if he stops.[80]

For the addict, then, according to Lindesmith, all that heroin provides is the rush and the avoidance of pain; the high is a thing of the past. A more recent interpretation of this matter by William E. McAuliffe and Robert A. Gordon casts doubt on Lindesmith's contention. They find evidence that even among hard-core addicts, euphoria remains a positive factor that reinforces continued use of the drug. If these users have just enough drug to avoid withdrawal, they will be satisfied with that. However, should a larger supply be available, they will use it to obtain positive effects beyond merely feeling normal. McAuliffe and Gordon suggest that it is this ability of all addicts to enjoy euphoria that recruits others to try heroin and to continue use even after any initial unpleasant effects:

> Their own enjoyment, in turn, leads these recruits to continue use until they themselves become physically dependent. Once dependent, the promise of euphoria holds the addict to his habit and the pursuit drives up his tolerance, increases the high overhead cost of his addiction, and depletes his legitimate resources. If he remains determined to pursue euphoria at a maximum level in the face of these developments, rather than contenting himself merely with avoiding the abstinence syndrome, he must commit himself more completely to the life-style of the criminal addict.[81]

According to the McAuliffe-Gordon thesis, continued heroin use involves a complex interrelationship of two goals: avoiding withdrawal symptoms and reexperiencing the pleasures of the drug. The relative importance of each of these goals will be subject to controversy and research. Whether Lindesmith or McAuliffe and Gordon are more accurate in their assessment, one fact remains incontrovertible: the incentive to continue heroin use is great.

Heroin Use and Deviance

It is impossible to discuss heroin use as deviant behavior without considering the historical context of the laws regarding heroin. Before we do that, let us briefly indicate some features of heroin dependence.

1. **Treatment programs to end user drug dependence have been generally disappointing.** There is a saying, "Once a junkie, always a junkie." An indication of the truth behind this adage is *methadone maintenance,* one of the more successful "treatment" programs that simply substitutes another drug for heroin. Methadone is a synthetic drug similar in chemical structure to heroin; it was developed in Germany during World War II as a replacement for scarce opium-based drugs. Taken orally, methadone produces no rush or high, but it takes the place of heroin in the human system, thus halting withdrawal symptoms; it also blocks the euphoric effects of opiates used in low dosages. The body acquires a tolerance for methadone just as it does for any opiates, but there is a difference: Methadone is *legal* and therefore cheap. In short, methadone users are not "cured" of drug dependence, but they can abandon the criminal subculture so necessary to continued heroin use and can take their places in respectable society—at least that is the theory. The problem is that entering a methadone program means surrendering the junkie lifestyle and its values. The program will be most successful for those who obtain the least emotional and physical satisfaction from heroin.[82] As one dropout from the program put it, "The reason I didn't stay on it was that I missed the excitement of using dope. I missed all the glamour of hustling and beating on people."[83]

Whereas many studies of treatment programs are discouraging, study of a methadone maintenance program found promising results. Researchers determined that even coerced clients showed improvement. By coerced, we mean an individual on probation or parole who was "forced" or "encouraged" to receive treatment as a condition of parole or probation or otherwise was in the program as part of some legal procedure. They summarize by stating that "the major findings from this study were that criminal and drug use behavior, as well as social functioning, were significantly improved during treatment for the three groups and remained improved following treatment."[84]

If anything truly "cures" heroin dependence, it is *aging.* Many users simply quit when they reach their mid-thirties. The reason for the relationship between advancing age and termination of heroin use is unclear. Possibly it has less to do with a waning desire for the drug's effects than with a growing weariness with the lifestyle: the continuous risks from financing and finding fixes, concern about overdoses, and the dangers from other junkies and the law. Whatever the reason, it is evident that junkies can and do quit.[85] But they may do it only when they are ready to and on their own terms, sometimes permanently, sometimes not, as we shall see next.

2. Heroin use is neither permanent nor continuous. This statement is related to the preceding discussion on the disappointing results of treatment programs. These programs are based on a disease concept of heroin addiction that views addiction as something over which the sufferer has no control—he or she is compelled to continue using the drug to avoid fearsome consequences. It is presumed that "treatment" of these individuals is the only way to break the vicious circle of continuing use and growing tolerance. We have already mentioned that heroin dependence is not permanent—many users quit as they grow older. Recent evidence indicates that many addicts permanently stop using heroin even at an early age and that still other addicts quit and later use the drug regularly without again becoming dependent. In short, it appears that heroin users have far more control over the drug than was once believed.

This conclusion is supported by evidence that the majority of users do not use the drug on a daily basis over an entire year. Many discontinue use because their habit has become too expensive. They go through withdrawal and then resume use with lower dosages and lower costs. Others simply quit for a while because they tire of the strenuous junkie life. Still others may quit for important engagements such as a forthcoming trial. Studies of U.S,. soldiers in Vietnam support this. Many used high-potency heroin on a daily or frequent basis, yet over 90 percent of them ceased upon their return to the United States.[86] Thus there is increasing evidence that the image of the junkie locked into his or her compulsive daily search for drugs is a myth.

3. In comparison with other psychoactive drugs, heroin appears to be physiologically harmless. This may come as a surprise to those who have heard horror stories about overdoses and heroin-related deaths. And many readers are undoubtedly familiar with the image of the addict as a dirty, skinny person with rotten teeth and running sores. In reality, heroin is a relatively safe psychoactive drug; prolonged use results in no disease or damage to organs or cells.[87] There are some minor short-term effects: diminished sexual potency, menstrual irregularities, constriction of pupils, constipation, and excessive sweating. In the long run, cigarette smoking and alcohol drinking are far more dangerous than heroin use—they cause physical problems; heroin does not.

Furthermore, if the user's primary motivation is to avoid withdrawal distress, he or she can take just enough heroin to do that and can still behave normally; that is, the user can work, drive, and think lucidly, even while using very large dosages. A good example of this is one of the hidden drug-dependent populations: medical personnel. According to Oakley Ray, "Many physicians and other biomedical people become addicted and continue their normal activities for years. Physicians have a high addiction rate, 1% or 2%, compared to the general population."[88]

How does the claim of the harmlessness of heroin square with the fact that, in the United States, three to four thousand deaths occur each year from heroine overdoses and still more from heroine-related causes?[89] There is no doubt that the death rate among users is high. However, many are due not to the drug itself but to the *conditions under which its users live.*[90] Imagine the situation if you were a junkie—a slum junkie, not a physician junkie. You have a habit you cannot afford because its illegality has driven the price beyond what you can earn. Much of your time is spent getting funds, one way or another, for drugs, not food. Furthermore, you are forced to purchase drugs about which you have no guarantee as to quality or composition. They could even be laced with arsenic, a practice not unknown in the drug world. Finally, you take a fix with a needle a friend has had wrapped in his dirty handkerchief. Now you can settle back to enjoy yourself until you have to worry once more about where the next fix will come from—if you should live so long.

Such conditions lead to malnutrition, tetanus, hepatitis, pneumonia, AIDS, and gangrene. What about an "overdose"? Does heroin kill in that instance? Yes. Because of the illegal nature of heroin, there is no quality control or standardization of the amount of heroin in any dose. It is possible for even a long-term user to purchase a dose that is too powerful to handle.[91] Thus it can be argued that the danger to the user stems not from the drug itself, but from the conditions created by its illegal status.

It should be noted, however, that dangers to involuntary, secondary users may be substantial. Babies born to heroine-addicted mothers have problems such as anemia, hepatitis, pneumonia, heart disease, and low birth weight (a risk factor for yet more problems.) They cry more than other babies and do not eat or sleep as well. According to the National Institute on Drug Abuse, these infants frequently require medication to alleviate symptoms of neonatal abstinence syndrome.[92]

4. Criminal behavior among heroin users is extensive, but the relationship between drug use and criminal behavior is unclear. It is axiomatic among big-city dwellers that addicts are responsible for a large percentage of crime. But how much crime? John C. Ball and his associates conducted an interview study of 243 male opiate addicts identified by the Baltimore Police Department. The researchers found that only 6 addicts had committed no crime in an 11-year period and that the remaining 237 had committed more than a half-million crimes! About two-thirds (156) of the addicts engaged primarily in theft, 45 in drug sales, and 36 in other types of crime. The researchers also found that the subjects were not continuously dependent on drugs; rather, they had periods of dependence followed by periods of abstinence. Most startling was the discovery that when the subjects were drug dependent, the number of their offenses increased sixfold.[93]

Ball's research and other studies make it clear that crime is an important aspect of the drug user's life, but it is also evident that portraying addicts as people in constant, frantic pursuit of drugs is an inaccurate stereotype. To say that a person has a "$100-a-day habit" is misleading if the implication is that, day in and day out, he or she has to come up with $100 acquired through crime. Paul J. Goldstein found that while crime may be the largest single source of income for drug users, they also survive through the help of friends and relatives, by the assistance of drug sellers, and by legitimate employment. Furthermore, according to Goldstein, users' daily drug expenses are highly variable, ranging from nothing to what the users idealize them to be:

> When addicts are asked how much heroin they have used . . . they may very well respond in terms of the "ideal" addict—the one they would like to be but, in fact, approximate only infrequently. They may forget about those days when they . . . used little or no heroin. An opiate user who likes to use $50 worth of heroin per day, but may only do so one or two days a week, may still maintain the self-image of a $50-a-day addict, even though his actual consumption may average out to $20 per day or less. Thus, the generally erratic and unstable patterns of generating income . . . are complemented by generally erratic and unstable patterns of heroin consumption.[94]

Goldstein goes on to say that the connection between drug dependence and crime is difficult to fathom because sometimes users commit crimes for reasons unrelated to their habits.

How, then, are drugs and crime linked? James A. Inciardi suggests four possible patterns:

1. Most users are of the criminal element anyway, and drug dependence is simply one aspect of their criminal careers.
2. Drug effects predispose otherwise law-abiding users to crime.
3. Users are driven to crime to support their habits.
4. Users are forced to associate and cooperate with criminal elements to have access to drugs.[95]

At this stage of knowledge it is impossible to say which of these patterns is most accurate. Probably some combination will eventually provide an explanation of the drugs-crime connection. For now, at least, researchers are disproving some myths about drug dependence, and that is an important step toward answering some crucial questions.

Before leaving the issue of drugs and crime, we must mention one other facet of heroin use. The traditional belief has been that heroin users are unlikely to commit violent crimes. Presumably, users want their fixes with the least amount of trouble, and once high they become uninterested in their surroundings. In recent years, however, researchers have noted an increasing amount of violent crime among these users. Certainly, the pharmacological effects of heroin are inconsistent with violence: The nervous system is depressed, and the user feels tranquilized. However, "The irritability resulting from withdrawal symptoms has been known to lead to violence," and Howard Abadinsky, who dealt with heroine addicts for fourteen years,["found many, if not most, to be quite capable of committing violent acts including homicide [and that] they were frequently convicted of violent crimes."[96] In addition, the world of drug *dealing* is anything but tranquil. The drug sale is an act that can be highly charged with suspicion. The seller tries to sell the lowest quality product at the highest price and worries about the customer's likelihood of stealing from him. The buyer tries to buy the highest quality product at the lowest price and worries about the seller's adulterations.[97] In addition to these seller–buyer suspicions, there are purely capitalistic problems among competing dealers. Seller–buyer and seller–seller disputes in the drug world cannot be referred to the police, so they are often resolved by violence. The problem of violence among heroin users thus stems not from the drug itself but from the social setting of drug use.

Correlates of Heroin Use

It should be clear from this discussion that there are few inherent dangers involved in heroin use aside from the strong likelihood of dependence and the temporary disabilities accompanying its euphoric effect. Heroin scarcely seems to deserve all the concern surrounding its use, especially in a society already saturated with psychoactive drugs.

While many people link heroin use to neighborhood devastation, conflict theorists argue that the history of the U.S. response to heroin has been one of overreaction and heavy-handedness. This history is an excellent example of interest group conflict and the process by which behavior becomes labeled as deviant.[98]

"Thou shalt not use opium or any derivative thereof" is not one of the Ten Commandments; it is a legal philosophy that developed to solve a perceived problem. The origins of that problem date back to the mid-nineteenth century. Opiates were easily available then. Physicians wrote prescriptions for them; they were available in drug, grocery, and general stores; and they could even be ordered through the mail. Countless patent medicines containing opium could be purchased for a variety of symptoms, ranging from teething to coughing and menstrual difficulties. Toward the end of that century, the use of morphine was encouraged by physicians as a substitute for alcohol on the theory that morphine was considerably less dangerous.[99] Heroin was introduced as a "safe and reliable," nonaddicting substitute for morphine in treatment of some illnesses.

Of course, the possibility of dependence upon opiates was recognized, and in some circles, their use was regarded as immoral. But the *reaction* to dependence then in no way resembled that of today:

> Employees were not fired for addiction. Wives did not divorce their addicted husbands, or husbands their addicted wives. Children were not taken from their homes and lodged in foster homes or institutions because one or both parents were addicted. Addicts continued to participate fully in the life of the community. Addicted children and young people continued to go to school, Sunday School, and college. Thus, the nineteenth century avoided one of the most disastrous effects of current narcotics laws and attitudes—the rise of a deviant addict subculture, cut off from respectable society and without a "road back" to respectability.[100]

There was, then, a toleration for opiate-dependent individuals. They were not viewed as a menace to society, nor is there any evidence that they were a menace. In fact, the typical addict of the nineteenth century was a middle-aged, middle-class female. What happened? Why did the users become criminal, and why did the characteristics of the user population change?

The first law concerning opiates in the United States was a San Francisco ordinance against opium dens passed in 1875. Opium smoking had been introduced to the United States by the Chinese, who were imported to work on railroad construction crews. Ostensibly, the rationale for the ordinance stemmed from public alarm over the rich, idle adults and young white girls who frequented the Chinese opium dens.[101]

But conflict theorists argue the moral indignation had less to do with opium than with the Chinese. They posed a threat to the white labor market; this engendered racial prejudice, and the public was ready to believe anything about the Chinese. Several other cities adopted ordinances against opium dens (but not against opium smoking itself) and Congress progressively increased the tariff on opium prepared for smoking. By 1909 the importation of smoking opium was prohibited altogether.

The passage of federal laws also had little to do with concern over the U.S. Chinese addict population but was the result of a curious combination of prejudice against the Chinese in general and a desire to obtain the diplomatic goodwill of China, which was then waging its own war against opium.[102] In 1912 a multinational conference on opium control was held in the Netherlands. Several countries, including the United States, agreed to limit the trade and production of opiates to medical and scientific purposes to solve the opium problems of Asia, particularly China. Despite great pressure by the patent medicine interests, congressional concern about meeting the international obligation of the United States led to the passage of the Harrison Narcotics Act in 1914.

On its face the Harrison Act was not prohibitory. It was basically a tax law requiring anyone who handled or manufactured opium products to register, pay a fee, and keep records of their transactions. There was no mention of addiction; patent medicines could still contain a small portion of opiates, including heroin; and more important, physicians retained control over the prescribing of opiates. Thus two powerful interest groups were satisfied: The pharmaceutical industry could still manufacture many of its opiate medicines, and physicians were assured that their professional activities would not be tampered with.[103]

But these interest groups had not reckoned with the power of another interest group: law enforcement agencies. What had started out as a revenue act to control the nonmedical use of opiates soon evolved into a weapon to suppress addiction.

Because the Harrison Act was a revenue act, its enforcement was the responsibility of the Treasury Department, whose Narcotics Division in the very earliest days of the act made clear its intention to eliminate drug addiction. As part of its crusade, the division forbade physicians to prescribe opiates to users for the purpose of maintaining their habits. In short, the Narcotics Division adopted the moral position that opiate use for any nonmedical purpose—even preventing withdrawal symptoms—must be stopped. By harassing physicians through a series of complicated regulations and arrests, the division quickly disillusioned the medical profession.[104] Less than nine months after the effective date of the Harrison Act, the medical establishment began realizing that it had miscalculated in supporting the legislation. This editorial appeared in *American Medicine* in 1915:

> Narcotic drug addiction is one of the gravest and most important questions confronting the medical profession today. Instead of improving conditions, the laws recently passed have made the problem more complex. Honest medical men have found such handicaps and dangers to themselves and their reputations in these laws . . . that they have simply decided to have as little to do as possible with drug addicts or their needs. . . . The druggists are in the same position and for similar reasons many of them have discontinued entirely the sales of narcotic drugs. [The addict] is denied the medical care he urgently needs, open, above-board sources from which he formerly obtained his drug supply are closed to him, and he is driven to the underworld where he can get his drug, but of course, surreptitiously and in violation of the law. . . .
>
> Abuses in the sale of narcotic drugs are increasing. . . . A particular sinister sequence . . . is the character of the places to which [addicts] are forced to go to get their drugs and the type of people with whom they are obliged to mix. The most depraved criminals are often the dispensers of these habit-forming drugs. The moral dangers, as well as the effect on the self-respect of the addict, call for no comment. One has only to think of the stress under which the addict lives, and to recall his lack of funds, to realize the extent to which these . . . afflicted individuals are under the control of the worst elements of society.[105]

What had originally been defined as a medical problem was now transformed into a legal one: "Patients" became "criminals" practically overnight. In a few years a black market for drugs was in operation, and crimes began to be connected with drug use. In the meantime the Narcotics Division solidified its position by (1) launching a public information campaign portraying drugs as a crucial factor in a crime wave and as an evil to be stamped out at any cost and (2) undertaking a series of court cases to broaden the division's powers.[106]

Exactly how much influence the division had on the public's image of opiate use is impossible to say. It seems that the nation was ripe for modifying its tolerant attitudes, however. The Harrison Act was passed in an era that included World War I, the emergence of Prohibition, and increasing nationalism fanned by fears of anarchism and communism. It was a period of reform and reevaluation of national priorities. It was also a time of social crisis for the old white middle class as new immigrants, labor unions, and radical ideas threatened the old order.[107]

In a series of decisions between 1919 and 1922, the U.S. Supreme Court ruled in favor of the Division's interpretation of the Harrison Act. It was decided that a doctor could not prescribe drugs at a level to maintain an addiction. Thus a user could no longer legally obtain drugs unless he or she were undergoing treatment in an institution. A later decision (*Linder* v. *U.S.*, 268 U.S. 5 [1925]) modified this stand when the Court held that addiction was a disease and that a physician acting in good faith could administer moderate amounts of a drug to relieve withdrawal symptoms. In practice, however, the Narcotics Division for decades carried on an enforcement policy consistent with the earlier decisions. As Charles Reasons concludes,

> by focusing upon judicial decisions, rather than Congressional action, the Narcotics Division circumvented the strong lobbies of physicians and pharmacists and was able to create a whole new class of criminals, i.e., the addicts. The Treasury Department drew up its regulations based upon these early decisions, instructing doctors when and when not to give narcotics. The judgment had been made that addiction was essentially not a disease, but a willful indulgence meriting punishment rather than medical treatment. Those invested with enforcing the law and the dominant moral order would prove to be very capable in maintaining such an approach.[108]

But explaining how a medical problem gets redefined as a criminal problem does not explain the change in the typical opiate user between the late nineteenth and the mid-twentieth century. Why did addicts change from respectable middle-aged, middle-class white females to criminal, young, lower-class black males? Part of the answer lies in the fact that the former were mostly prescription-related addicts, and doctors and patients had become increasingly aware of the dangers of opiates. In addition, some writers speculate that making opiates illegal created an addict subculture in the lower class where black market supplies were available and new users were recruited.[109] There is no question that transforming drug users from patients to criminals created more problems than it solved. Unfortunately, the criminalization of psychoactive drugs did not solve the problem of herione addiction.

Marijuana

The U.N. Office on Drugs and Crime reports that, throughout the world, marijuana is the drug most widely produced, trafficked, and consumed.[110] Despite the fact that there has been a 30 percent decrease in worldwide usage since the 1970s, data indicate that over half of young Americans age 18 to 25 have tried marijuana at least once.[111]

The source of marijuana is the Indian hemp plant, *Cannabis sativa,* which provides not only a drug but also rope fiber and other useful by-products. The drug is prepared by drying and chopping the leaves and flower tops of the plant. Another, more potent drug, known as *hashish,* is produced from drying the resins of the hemp plant. The potency of both marijuana and hashish varies greatly according to the type of seed and the source of the plants. For example, a significantly stronger preparation can be obtained from plants grown in Mexico as compared with those in the United States. Usually, marijuana and hashish are smoked in the United States; however, they can also be eaten blended in food or drink.

As with alcohol and opium, marijuana has a long history. There is evidence that it may have been used as a medicine around 2700 B.C. in China. There is extensive documentation of its widespread use for its psychoactive effects in Asia and Africa by 500 B.C. Later, Muslims readily accepted the drug as a substitute for forbidden alcohol.[112] Marijuana smoking was probably introduced into the United States by Mexican laborers in the early twentieth century and by merchant seamen frequenting the Port of New Orleans in the 1920s.[113]

Today, the plant grows almost everywhere in the world. Tens of thousands of acres in the United States are infested with a wild variety, and thousands of acres are under cultivation. The majority of the world's marijuana is grown in the Western Hemisphere.

Marijuana has been used as a medicine by many cultures around the world, and indeed, over half of the states in the United States have officially, at one time or another, recognized the medical value of marijuana in the treatment of pain and muscle spasms, nausea and loss of appetite caused by chemotherapy, and glaucoma.[114] It is unlikely, however, that the Food and Drug Administration (FDA) will recognize and approve marijuana as a medicine. A plant in its natural form cannot be patented and the dosage cannot be precisely controlled. Perhaps more importantly, it is usually smoked, and no FDA-approved drug is delivered in that manner.[115] Ironically, this may be one of its greatest potential benefits to nauseated chemotherapy patients.

Marijuana as a Drug

When smoked, marijuana passes quickly into the bloodstream. The immediate physical effects are minimal: An increase in pulse rate and reddening of the eyes are the most obvious. Like other psychoactive drugs, marijuana most noticeably affects one's mental processes and the responses directed by those processes. The nature and extent of impairment of the processes is related to the size of the dosage and experience with the drug.

> The immediate effect of marijuana on normal mental processes is a subtle alteration in state of consciousness probably related to a change in short-term memory, mood, emotion, and volition. This effect on the mind produces a varying influence on cognitive and psychomotor task performance that is highly individualized, as well as related to dosage, time, complexity of the task and experience of the user. The effect on personal, social and vocational functions is difficult to predict. In most instances, the marijuana intoxication is pleasurable. In rare cases the experience may lead to unpleasant anxiety and panic, and in a predisposed few, to psychosis.[116]

Marijuana, like alcohol and heroin, is largely a *social* drug. For the great majority of users, their *introduction* to and *continued use* of the drug occur within a group context. Friends and relatives not only usually provide the drug, they also provide encouragement, guidance, and a spirit of companionship, making the experience worthwhile.[117] According to Howard S. Becker, the process of becoming a marijuana user involves three steps:

1. Learning the technique of producing the effects. One must discover the correct manner of smoking, or the effects of the drug will not be obvious.
2. Learning to recognize the effects and connecting them with the drug. Some sensations, such as feeling hungry or elated, are not always perceived as stemming from the drug; one learns from others what the high is.
3. Learning to enjoy the effects of the drug. At first, the sensations are not automatically perceived as pleasant; reassurance that all is well can come from the group.[118]

In addition, the initiate acquires from the group the verbalized motives necessary to overcome any reluctance to try something that is illegal or about which he or she may have heard many horror stories. As Becker points out, to become a regular user, it is not enough to learn to recognize the drug's effects. One must also learn to set aside fears. The group can help do this:

> A person will feel free to use marihuana to the degree that he comes to regard conventional conceptions of it as the uninformed views of outsiders and replaces those conceptions with the "inside" view he has acquired with the drug in the company of other users.[119]

In the early 1980s, the Institute of Medicine assembled a committee to analyze the existing evidence about its health hazards. Although committee members concluded that the drug's use "justifies serious national concern," they also pointed out great areas of ignorance about its effects. In any case most negative effects were linked to long-term, heavy use.[120]

Research into long-term effects of marijuana use continues. Early findings linking daily use and cerebral atrophy (brain shrinkage), chromosomal damage, and lowered immunity have not held up to further scrutiny.[121] However, research cited by the National Institutes of Health and others indicates a variety of health risks associated with marijuana use.

1. Chronic use has been found to increase the risk of head and neck cancer and impair lung capacity.[122] Because marijuana smoke contains over 50 percent more carcinogens than tobacco, it may also increase the risk of lung cancer.[123]

2. There is evidence that smoking marijuana causes acute changes in the heart and circulation. A recent study indicates possible significantly increased risk of heart attack immediately after smoking marijuana.[124]

3. Although there is evidence that heavy usage is linked with mental disorders, it is unknown whether the usage is a cause or a result of the disorders.[125] However, chronic, heavy use can lead to "persistent and troublesome behavioral changes in some users"[126] as well as "depression, anxiety, and personality disturbances"[127] and even paranoia.[128]

4. Heavy users can suffer attention, memory, and learning problems, and marijuana use has negative effects on school and job performance.[129]

5. Mothers who use marijuana during pregnancy produce children who "during infancy and preschool years . . . have more behavioral, . . . visual perception, language comprehension, sustained attention, and memory"[130] problems than unexposed children. "In school, these children are more likely to exhibit deficits in decision-making skills, memory, and the ability to remain attentive."[131]

6. The body builds tolerance for marijuana, and mild withdrawal symptoms do occur: restlessness, irritability, mild agitation, and insomnia. Long-term use can lead to psychological dependence in some people and even compulsion.[132] Miami Dolphins football player Ricky Williams, for example, retired from the National Football League after repeatedly failing tests for the drug. This may not be evidence of dependency or addiction, but it surely is an indication of a very strong preference for marijuana over a multimillion dollar job.[133]

Still, some contend that marijuana is a "relatively nontoxic drug" with fewer proven ill effects and posing less danger to the user than alcohol and tobacco. Indeed, marijuana has much in common with alcohol and tobacco.[134]

Marijuana Use and Deviance

As is the case with alcohol, driving an automobile under the influence of marijuana is dangerous because it impairs coordination and reaction time. We also know that regular users—20 or more times in 30 days—tend to do poorly in school because they are absent more frequently than are irregular users or nonusers.[135] The cause–effect relationship is not clear, however. Perhaps those who skip class are more likely to be frequent users rather than vice versa. Do these kinds of problems warrant making the drug illegal? Or are we missing something? For example, is marijuana linked to other crimes: homicide, rape, and so on? According to the National Commission on Marijuana and Drug Abuse, *"The only crimes which can be directly attributed to marihuana-using behavior are those resulting from the use, possession or transfer of an illegal substance."*[136] In short, the crimes stemming from marijuana are the same crimes that would stem from butter if it were made illegal.

But marijuana leads to the use of heroin and other dangerous drugs, doesn't it? Isn't it a "gateway drug"? As Earleywine puts it, "There is no evidence that cannabis creates physiological changes that increase the desire for drugs. The idea that marijuana causes subsequent drug use appears unfounded. . . . Evidence for the association of marijuana and other drugs remains limited.[137] There is no question that studies comparing marijuana users with nonusers find that users are more likely to use heroin. But it is one thing to say that persons who use marijuana are more likely to try heroin; it is quite another thing to say that marijuana use leads to heroin use. It must be recognized that coffee drinkers, aspirin takers, tobacco smokers, and alcohol drinkers are all more likely to use illegal drugs than are noncoffee drinkers, nonaspirin takers, and so on. In fact, any user of any drug, legal or illegal, is more likely than a nonuser to use any other drug.[138] Erich Goode puts it, "In this sense, there is a kind of drug-taking "disposition."[139]

In addition, the criminal status of marijuana also isolates users to some degree from conventional society and incorporates them into a drug-taking subculture with its own particular norms and verbalized motives supporting all kinds of drug-taking. It is possible, he suggests, that removing the illegal status of marijuana might decrease the number of persons turning to heroin because it would neutralize the influence of this criminal drug-taking subculture.

Correlates of Marijuana Use

Word about marijuana first emerged in the legislative halls as early as 1911 during hearings that resulted in the Harrison Act of 1914. It was then suggested that marijuana be subject to the same controls as opiates and cocaine because some experts believed it to be habit-forming. But the pharmaceutical industry was firmly opposed; it used the drug in corn plasters and animal medicines, and the drug scarcely seemed to pose a threat that would warrant such restrictions. Consequently, marijuana was not included in the Harrison Act.[140]

However, fears over marijuana were soon to build. Rumbles of concern came from California, where large numbers of immigrants from India were believed to be initiating Anglos into a habit. Even more feared were the Mexican migrant laborers in the Southwest. Murder, mayhem, and rape, to say nothing of the corruption of children, were all attributed to the migrants' use of the weed. During the Depression in the early 1930s, when jobs were scarce, Mexicans were even less welcome. The problem of marijuana and the problem of Mexican immigration became one.

In addition to marijuana's association with a powerless minority group, stories about the drug's link to violent and perverted crimes were spread. By 1936, for example, 68 percent of all crimes committed in New Orleans were attributed to marijuana users. Political pressure for the federal prohibition of marijuana grew as its presumed link with race and crime was increasingly publicized. Spurred by ignorance, hysteria, and not a small amount of vested interest, a propaganda campaign was launched with the support of the Bureau of Narcotics to warn the public. An illustrated poster was prepared for trains, buses, and streetcars:

> BEWARE! Young and old people in all walks of life! This marihuana cigarette may be handed to YOU by the *friendly stranger*. It contains the Killer Drug Marihuana in which lurks MURDER! INSANITY! DEATH!—WARNING! Dope Peddlers are shrewd! They may put some of this drug in the teapot or in the cocktail or in the tobacco cigarette.

The stream of misinformation about the drug is exemplified by this excerpt from a pamphlet issued by the International Narcotic Education Association:

> The habitual use of this narcotic poison always causes a very marked mental deterioration and sometimes produces insanity. . . . While the marihuana habit leads to physical wreckage and mental decay, its effects upon character and morality are even more devastation. The victim frequently undergoes such degeneracy that he will lie and steal without scruple; he becomes utterly untrustworthy. . . . Marihuana sometimes gives man the lust to kill unreasonably and without motive. Many cases of assault, rape, robbery, and murder are traced to the use of marihuana.[141]

The evil dimensions of this drug were becoming clear: Once used only by Mexicans, it was now spreading to blacks and lower-class whites and turning them into drug-crazed criminals. As its presumed link with race and crime was increasingly publicized, political pressure for the federal prohibition of marijuana grew. In 1937 another revenue bill, the Marihuana Tax Act, became law. This placed an extremely high tax on the drug, and responsibility for the law's enforcement was assigned to the Bureau of Narcotics. Another class of criminals was created.

Cocaine

Cocaine is the latest drug to capture national attention. But what is it? It clearly is a stimulant, and the federal government even calls it that, but then it classifies it as a narcotic under the Controlled Substances Act, Title II of the Comprehensive Substance Abuse Act of 1970. What this means is the government is clearly convinced it is dangerous. Cocaine comes from the leaves of the coca shrub that thrives in several regions of South America. The leaves have been chewed for over 2,000 years by some Peruvians and Bolivians. Cocaine, the main ingredient in the leaves, was isolated in the 1880s. It was used as an anesthetic for eye, nose, and throat surgery, because it would constrict the blood flow and limit bleeding, and was an ingredient in a number of patent medicines. Sigmund Freud used it (which may explain things) and it was also marketed in a variety of wines, champagnes, and the original Coca-Cola (original, not Classic). The majority of its medical uses are now obsolete, with the development of newer and safer drugs.

Coca leaves are refined into a coca paste, usually in the countries of origin. The paste needs to be processed, so it is generally moved to a lab, usually in Colombia, and mixed with ether and acetone. It changes from paste to a base and then into cocaine hydrochloride. The cocaine hydrochloride, a pure white powder, is then smuggled into the United States, where it is diluted and passed on to wholesalers and dealers.[142] Principal sources for cocaine are Bolivia, Colombia, and Peru. Although other countries, such as the producers and especially Europe, receive some of the drug, most finds its way to the United States. We have estimates that 4.6 percent of U.S. college students used cocaine in 1998, with 1.7 percent reporting recent use.[143] The motivations to use cocaine are extremely strong, and it is seemingly easy to become psychologically dependent on the drug.

Cocaine as a Drug

As we have said, cocaine is a stimulant. It stimulates the nervous system and affects the cardiovascular system, raising the heart rate. It also raises blood pressure. At high doses cocaine can be toxic, producing seizures or cardiovascular collapse. Adverse physical effects may be sleep problems, fatigue, headaches, and nausea. Cocaine, as a white powder, can be taken by nasal inhalation, mixed and taken by injection, or freebased (purified with ether and then smoked). The stimulant effect, producing euphoria, diminishes quickly, in one to two hours, as it is metabolized by the liver. A number of individuals turn cocaine into "crack," which is simply made by mixing cocaine with baking soda, heating it, and then smoking the residue in a pipe or mixing it with plant material and smoking it in a "joint." Inhaling the fumes, in particular, produces a rush that is reported to be very intense but brief.

Cocaine has the potential to create psychological dependency, but tolerance for the toxic effects of the drug never develops. Some studies report that repeated use may even lower tolerance for the drug.[144] One longitudinal study found that cocaine users generally follow a continuum pattern (as we have suggested) of using the drug experimentally and then moving into sociorecreational use, to more intensified use, and eventually back to sociorecreational use. There does seem to be a proportion of cocaine users (10 to 20 percent, a proportion similar to those who fall victim to alcoholism) who do become compulsive. In the United States, it is the drug with the heaviest treatment demand.[145]

Stories reported about the successful businessman, husband, civic leader, and so on, who "threw" everything away for cocaine, are common.[146] Thus cocaine may be very psychologically addicting. Recognizing that the term "addiction" has problems, we can conclude only that for some individuals, cocaine may cause dependency. There does seem to be no clear evidence that it produces withdrawal symptoms, although this is debated.[147] The cocaine high produces euphoria, a feeling of self-confidence, and an increase in energy. For a number of years cocaine was regarded as an expensive yet playful habit, with many enjoying it frequently. However, a number of studies now link cocaine use to physical and psychological problems[148] such as sleeplessness, irritability, depression, irrational behavior, and paranoia. Extreme reactions can include muscle spasms, chest pains, hallucinations, and delirium. Abadinski observes that in a small percentage of genetically predisposed users, large doses can lead to strange paranoid agitation and even death.[149]

As with alcohol and heroine, drug use by pregnant women has a negative effect on their babies. Some of this may be attributed to the mother's lifestyle, but some is the result of blood and oxygen deprivation related to the drug. Crack babies, babies of mothers who use the smokable form of cocaine, suffer from such things as low birth weight (which is related to a variety of other problems), lower IQ, language development difficulties, and motor skills problems.[150] In addition, they are more prone to serious emotional difficulties and behavior problems.[151]

Cocaine Use and Deviance

Cocaine use would not be considered deviant if it were not illegal. Laws regarding cocaine will be discussed, but we must mention other concerns regarding the drug. Too, the issues raised previously about heroin and marijuana and deviance are relevant here. First, we do know that cocaine users present some difficult problems for treatment centers, since those seeking treatment are often heavy users of other drugs, such as alcohol. These individuals are considered to be *polydrug users.*[152] Second, there may be some relationship between cocaine and crime, similar to that discussed for heroin. Committing crime to obtain resources to purchase cocaine may occur.[153] But, enforcement of cocaine laws no doubt causes much of the deviance and crime. The vast sums used to purchase cocaine create problems. Listing just a few may be enlightening: tax evasion, corrosion of the work ethic, corruption of officials, violence, and disrespect for the law. The high price of cocaine may encourage individuals to deal to provide for their needs, corrupt others, and so on. Thus, the deviance linked to cocaine can most readily be attributed to drug laws.

Correlates of Cocaine Use

As it did with opium, the Harrison Act of 1914 required all persons handling cocaine to register and report all transfers and to pay a special tax. The Narcotic Drug and Import and Export Act of 1922 forbade the dispensing of cocaine to patients (much of the concerns raised about heroin apply here). But cocaine remained, underground. It seems to have been available to those in "café society," as reflected in songs of the 1930s. For example, the Cole Porter song "I Get a Kick Out of You" contains the line "I get no kick from cocaine." Factors such as amphetamine availability led to a decline in cocaine use for a number of years. It did see a return from the 1960s on, until it again became a prominent drug of choice. Perhaps successes at interdicting marijuana contributed to this. Cocaine is much easier to transport and more profitable. Nevertheless, cocaine use peaked around 1982 and has since declined, despite plentiful supplies and falling prices. Concern over cocaine became greatest perhaps in the 1980s, when the popular press noticed the scourge and began reporting it with such cover stories as "Middle-Class High" and "Crashing on Cocaine." High-profile celebrities and athletes were reported to be using and occasionally dying from cocaine. The result of all this was an unprecedented "war on drugs" on a national and international scale.[154]

Prescription Drug Abuse

As you will recall, much of U.S. opium dependence during the mid-nineteenth century was the result of prescription and over-the-counter drug use. In the mid-twentieth century, famous sportscaster Bill Stern refocused our attention on prescription drug abuse in his autobiography, *The Taste of Ashes.* Recovering from a severe injury, he started using powerful prescription drugs to ease the pain. After some time, he was using because he could not stop. At the beginning of the twenty-first century, 3 percent of drug overdose, hospital emergency room admissions were for misuse of prescription drugs.[155]

A report issued in 2003 by NHSDA indicated that an estimated 35 million Americans had used prescription drugs for nonmedical purposes at some time in their lives.[156] Their reasons include relief of withdrawal symptoms and enhancement or simulation of the effects of illegal drugs. Benzodiazepines may be used, for example, to relieve the discomfort of alcohol withdrawal, tranquilizers may be used to ease withdrawal from cocaine or heroine, and the synthetic narcotic oxycodone (Percocet) may be used to create a high similar to that of heroine.[157]

In addition, it is not uncommon for prescription drug abusers to seek the narcotic or pain-relieving effects of drugs such as Demerol, codeine, methadone, or Darvon. In a recent government survey, 20 percent of teens reported abuse of prescription painkillers and about one in ten reported abuse of stimulants such as Ritalin or dexedrine. Prescription tranquilizers such as Valium, Xanax, and Soma are also sometimes diverted to nonprescription use as are sedatives and hypnotics such as Halcion, Dalmane, and Restoril.[158]

There are currently about 1,500 drugs "and more than 10,000 prescription products sold in the United States."[159] Doctors, law enforcement, the government, and health insurance companies, who pay much of the costs of these drugs, agree that they should be regulated. Large segments of the U.S. public (especially those who do not have term papers due tomorrow) agree. However, pharmaceutical companies continue to advertise the benefits of their products and encourage their use. The drugs are legal (with prescriptions), providing them to those with medical needs is essential, and the confidentiality of the doctor/patient relationship must be maintained. In addition, finding and prosecuting miscreant medical professionals and drug-abusing patients is difficult. Moreover, relatively little funding has been directed at the prescription drug abuse issue, and states that have set up monitoring systems have been accused of adding to an already costly and inefficient healthcare bureaucracy. This will not be an easy problem to solve. Further examination of the issue might send many of us to the medicine cabinet for an aspirin.

Performance-Enhancing Drugs

Most people who use drugs for nonmedical purposes are seen as acting outside existing values—or, at least, outside existing laws. At the other end of the continuum, however, is a group of drug users whose use is related to what might be seen as an overcommitment to certain U.S. values. In the worlds of competitive sports, body building, and male modeling, for example, increased pressure to be better and better against greater and greater competition for more and more rewards has led some to seek a competitive advantage through the use of performance-enhancing drugs. In the spring of 2004 Congress heard testimony from a wide range of medical and sports professionals. At the same time, the United States Anti-Doping Agency (USADA), in cooperation with a federal investigation of a California nutrition company, launched an investigation of over three dozen world class and Olympic athletes. One of the general findings of both investigations was that performance-enhancing drugs are readily available, and athletes with the assistance of manufacturers and even coaches have used a wide variety of means to take advantage of them while keeping ahead of testing requirements and technology.[160]

Concern has focused on a group of drugs called anabolic steroids. These synthetic substances related to male sex hormones are available by prescription for the treatment of delayed puberty, impotence, and the wasting effects of diseases such as MS and AIDS.[161] In the 1950s, some state-sponsored sports programs experimented with their use, and it was discovered that their ability to stimulate the production of tissue mass could give athletes in sports such as wrestling, weight lifting, and women's swimming a significant advantage. Currently, major league baseball, track and field, football, body building, wrestling, swimming, and most sports that rely on size and strength are at high risk for steroid use.[162] Recently, one seller of steroid-type supplements blatantly advertised on the Internet that, in sports such as professional body building, the incidence of use is virtually 100 percent. The "Monitoring the Future" studies of the University of Michigan's Institute for Social Research have tracked a steadily increasing use among high school athletes as well. The trend in "past year use" appears to have peaked in the early 2000s at a rate of under 3 percent, however. This is fortunate because, although long-term effects of steroid use are not fully understood, they have been shown to cause such things as premature termination of the adolescent growth spurt, and some of the effects of steroid use (such as decreased stature) appear to be irreversible.

Some of the other possible health consequences of anabolic steroid use include reduced sperm production, impotence, testicle shrinkage, and breast enlargement in males. In females, health consequences include reduced breast size, increased facial and body hair, and menstrual problems. Steroid use can lead to increased risk of blood clots, liver damage, cancer, and male pattern baldness in both males and females as well as high blood pressure (which can lead to heart attack or stroke in athletes as young as 20 or 30.)[163] Behavioral effects of the drugs can include extreme mood swings, paranoid jealousy, delusions, extreme irritability, and insomnia. Withdrawal symptoms can include depression, fatigue, restlessness, reduced sex drive, headache, muscle and joint pain, loss of appetite, and insomnia.[164] Animal studies indicate that long-term use of anabolic steroids might even shorten one's life.[165]

Merton's anomie theory describes deviant "Innovators" who accept the goals of the society but go beyond socially accepted means to attain them. If you will recall, we used a sports quotation to describe their philosophy of life. Although the rate of intercollegiate athletes using anabolic steroids has fallen in recent years and still remains low, investigations into world-class and professional athletes are revealing a disappointing amount of "Innovation" among this group of role models for U.S. youth.

CRITICAL THINKING EXERCISES

1. Write a description of an "alcoholic" person. How is this person different from someone who drinks alcohol but is not an alcoholic? Do you know any students at this college who would be classified as alcoholic by your description? How will their futures be different because of alcohol use? What would they have to do to change?

2. What is the most dangerous drug, in your opinion? Why? What substance poses the greatest threat to the well-being of our way of life in the United States?

3. The United States has been described as the world's greatest marketplace for illegal substances. Why is our nation different from other countries in the tendency to consume drugs?

4. Have anti-drug policies in the United States been a success? What would you have done differently if you had been calling the shots?

5. List the arguments for and against the legalization of marijuana. Do you believe that recreational marijuana use will be legalized in your lifetime? Explain.

6. If we legalized all drugs tomorrow, what would happen to the vast numbers of people involved in the drug trade? Can we assume that they would all be able or want to find legal employment?

CHECK IT OUT ON THE WEB

The Internet addresses listed below are intended to provide the reader with understanding of a wide range of perspectives on the subject matter discussed in this chapter. Some sites may contain objectionable material. The list is not intended to reflect the viewpoints or opinions of the authors or the publisher.

http://www.mhri.edu.au/pda/
      psychotropic drug advisory service
http://www.druglibrary.org/schaffer/heroin/methadone/selfmed.htm
      methadone
http://www.usdoj.gov/dea/pubs/s
      counterarguments to medicinal marijuana use
http://www.dying.about.com
      marijuana for the dying (enter "marijuana" in the Search area)
http://law.about.com
      medicinal marijuana debate/law
http://www.pbs.org/wgbh/pages/frontline/shows/heroin/brain
      heroin and the brain
http://www.niaaa.nih.gov
      National Institute on Alcohol Abuse and Alcoholism
http://www.clubdrugs.org
      information on club drugs
http://www.whitehouse drug policy.gov/streetterms
      street names for drugs

ENDNOTES

1. "Thoughts on the Business of Life, " *Forbes* (July 26, 2004), p. 188.

2. Ben Stein, *How to Ruin Your Life* (London: Hay House, 2002).

3. Daniel Ari Kapner, The Higher Education Center for Alcohol and Other Drug Prevention, *Infofacts Resources: Alcohol and Other Drugs on Campus, The Scope of the Problem,* June 2003, p. 2.

4. Sharon Begley, "Fighting Addiction," *Newsweek,* February 12, 2001, pp. 40–42.

5. Ibid., p. 42.

6. National Commission on Marihuana and Drug Abuse, *Drug Use in America: Problem in Perspective* (Washington, DC: U.S. Government Printing Office, 1973), p. 9; see also James Willis, *Drug Use and Abuse* (London: Faber and Faber Limited, 1989), p. 20.

7. Erich Goode, *The Drug Phenomenon: Social Aspects of Drug Taking* (Indianapolis: Bobbs-Merrill, 1973), p. 39; see also U.S. Department of Justice, Drug Enforcement Administration [DEA], *Drugs of Abuse, 1989 Edition* (Washington, DC: U.S. Government Printing Office, 1989), pp. 12, 25–26, 37, 45–46, 49–50.

8. Goode, *The Drug Phenomenon*, p. 39; for a review of the research on whether marijuana use causes increased sexual activity or whether the increase is based on social expectations, see Ernest L. Abel, *Marijuana, Tobacco, Alcohol, and Reproduction* (Boca Raton, FL: CRC Press, 1983).

9. There is considerable debate on what constitutes a realistic classification of psychoactive drugs insofar as human use is concerned. Practically every author on the subject has his or her own system. For example, see Goode, *The Drug Phenomenon*, pp. 8–9; Ronald L. Akers, *Deviant Behavior: A Social Learning Approach*, 2nd ed. (Belmont, CA: Wadsworth, 1977), p. 74; and Oakley Ray, *Drugs, Society, and Human Behavior*, 3rd ed. (Saint Louis: C. V. Mosby, 1983), *passim;* for the way the federal government classifies drugs, see DEA, *Drugs of Abuse, 1989*, pp. 5, 6, 11–53.

10. Glen Hanson and Peter Venturelli, *Drugs and Society* (Boston: Jones and Bartlett, 2001), p. iv-viii; Patricia Stevens and Robert L. Smith, *Substance Abuse Counseling Theory and Practice* (Upper Saddle River, NJ: Merrill Prentice Hall, 2001).

11. Goode, *The Drug Phenomenon*, p. 13; see also DEA, *Drugs of Abuse, 1989*, pp. 49–52.

12. Ibid., p. 340.

13. Richard Jones, " 'Up' on Psilocybin," *The Harvard Review, 1* (Summer 1963), as cited in *Their Own Behalf: Voices from the Margin*, 2nd ed., ed. Charles H. McCaghy, James K. Skipper, Jr., and Mark Lefton (Englewood Cliffs, NJ: Prentice-Hall, 1974), pp. 68–69; see also DEA, *Drugs of Abuse, 1989*, pp. 49, 50.

14. Howard Abadinsky, *Drugs: An Introduction* (Belmont, CA: Wadsworth, 2001).

15. Goode, *The Drug Phenomenon*, p. 10; see also DEA, *Drugs of Abuse, 1989*, p. 45.

16. Richard R. Lingeman, *Drugs from A to Z: A Dictionary* (New York: McGraw-Hill, 1969), pp. 244–245; see also DEA, *Drugs of Abuse, 1989*, p. 12.

17. Steven Wisotsky, *Beyond the War on Drugs* (Buffalo: Prometheus Books, 1990), pp. 204, 227.

18. Ibid., pp. 24–30, 204–209.

19. Ibid., p. 1.

20. Lewis D. Eigen, *Alcohol Practices, Policies, and Potentials of American Colleges and Universities* (Washington, DC: U.S. Department of Health and Human Services, Office for Substance Abuse Prevention, n.d.), although Eigen uses 1990 data (emphasis added).

21. This discussion is based on Norman Taylor, *Narcotics: Nature's Dangerous Gifts*, rev. ed. of Norman Taylor, *Flight from Reality* (New York: Dell, 1963), pp. 67–95. Also see Joel Fort, *Alcohol: Our Biggest Drug*

Problem (New York: McGraw-Hill, 1973), pp. 43–48; and Jerome David Levin, *Alcoholism: A Bio-Psycho-Social Approach* (New York: Hemisphere Publishing Corporation, 1990), pp. 54–56.

22. *The Holy Bible, New International Version* (Colorado Springs: International Bible Society, 1984).

23. Hanson and Venturelli, Op. cit. pp. 108–194.

24. Karen Springen and Barbara Kantrowitz, "Alcohol's Deadly Triple Threat," *Newsweek,* May 10, 2004, pp. 88, 91–92.

25. National Institute of Mental Health, *Alcohol and Alcoholism: Problems, Programs, and Progress*, rev. ed. (Rockville, MD: National Institute of Mental Health, 1972), p. 4; and Ray, *Drugs, Society, and Human Behavior,* pp. 166–168; see also Levin, *Alcoholism*, pp. 1–14. For the differences in types of alcohol beverages, see W. G. Vrij-Standhardt, "Differences Between Alcoholic Beverages," in *Biomedical and Social Aspects of Alcohol Use: A Review of the Literature*, ed. Dirk G. van der Heij and Gertjan Schaafsma (Wageningen, The Netherlands: Centre for Agricultural Publishing and Documentation, 1991), pp. 190–203.

26. Hanson and Venturelli, *Drugs and Society,* pp. 108–194.

27. Morris E. Chafetz and Harold W. Demone, Jr., *Alcoholism and Society* (New York: Oxford University Press, 1962), p. 9, as cited in Craig MacAndrew and Robert B. Edgerton, *Drunken Comportment: A Social Explanation* (Chicago: Aldine, 1969), pp. 6–7; see also Levin, *Alcoholism*, pp. 9–14.

28. Charles H. McCaghy, "Drinking and Deviance Disavowal: The Case of Child Molesters," *Social Problems, 16* (Summer 1968), pp. 43–49.

29. MacAndrew and Edgerton, *Drunken Comportment*, pp. 165, 172. The discussion is based on ibid., pp. 13–135; see also Levin, *Alcoholism*, pp. 48–60.

30. This discussion is based on material from the U.S. Department of Health and Human Services, *Alcohol and Health* (Washington, DC: U.S. Government Printing Office, 1998); National Institute on Alcohol Abuse and Alcoholism (NIAAA) press release, 2004.

31. U.S. Department of Justice, Federal Bureau of Investigation [FBI], *Crime in the United States, 1996: Uniform Crime Reports* (Washington, DC: U.S. Government Printing Office, 2002), p. 243.

32. Ibid., pp. 243–244.

33. U.S. Department of Justice, FBI, *Crime in the United States, 1960: Uniform Crime Reports* (Washington, DC: U.S. Government Printing Office, 1961), p. 90.

34. Jack West, "Drunk Loses 'Home' After 396 Arrests," *Arizona Republic* (Phoenix), March 18, 1974, pp. 1–2.

35. Task Force of the National Advisory Council on Alcohol Abuse and Alcoholism, *A Call to Action: Changing the Culture of Drinking at U.S. Colleges,* (Washington, DC, U.S. Department of Health and Human Services, 2002), pp. 4, 7.

36. Frederick S. Stinson and Samar Farha Debakey, "Alcohol-Related Mortality in the United States," *British Journal of Addiction, 87* (May 1992), pp. 777–783.

37. National Institute on Alcohol Abuse and Alcoholism, *Alcohol and Health,* p. 5.

38. Daniel Ari Kapner, The Higher Education Center for Alcohol and Other Drugs Prevention, *Alcohol and Other Drugs on Campus,* p. 1; National Institute on Alcohol Abuse and Alcoholism, *A Call to Action,* pp. 4, 7.

39. National Institute on Alcohol Abuse and Alcoholism [NIAAA], *NIAAA Information and Feature Service,* November 30, 1978, IFS No. 53, p. 4; Alcohol, Drug Abuse, and Mental Health Administration [ADAMHA], *ADAMHA News, 19* (September 19, 1980), p. 1; NIAAA, *NIAAA Information and Feature Service,* May 31, 1978, IFS No. 48, p. 5; and Stinson and Debakey, "Alcohol-Related Mortality," pp. 777–799.

40. Springen and Kantrowitz, *Alcohol's Deadly Triple Threat,* pp. 88, 91–92.

41. Hanson and Venturelli, *Drugs and Society,* pp. 108–194.

42. Letter from Barth and Sandy to Sandra Carey, August 2004.

43. Letter from Andy to Sandra Carey, August 2004.

44. L. J. Sax, A. W. Astin, J. A. Lindholm, W. S. Korn, V. B. Saenz, and K. M. Mahoney, *The American Freshman: National Norms for Fall 2003* (Los Angeles: The Higher Education Research Institute, UCLA Graduate School of Education and Information Studies, 2004), p. 1.

45. E. M. Jellinek, *The Disease Concept of Alcoholism* (New Haven, CT: Hillhouse, 1960), p. 35.

46. Ibid., pp. 37–38.

47. Derived from E. M. Jellinek, "Phases of Alcohol Addiction," in *Society, Culture, and Drinking Patterns,* ed. David J. Pittman and Charles R. Snyder (New York: John Wiley, 1962), pp. 356–368.

48. National Institute of Mental Health, *Alcohol and Alcoholism,* Public Health Service Publication No. 1640 (Washington, DC: U.S. Government Printing Office, n.d.), p. 6.

49. Marvin A. Block, "Alcoholism Is a Disease," pamphlet distributed by the National Council on Alcoholism, Inc., reprinted from *Today's Health* (n.p., n.d.), pp. 6–8.

50. Peter Conrad and Joseph W. Schneider, *Deviance and Medicalization: From Badness to Sickness* (St. Louis: C. V. Mosby, 1980), pp. 103–106; see also Stanton Peele, "Through a Glass Darkly," *Psychology Today,* April 1983, pp. 38–42.

51. For an example of the Alcoholics Anonymous effort, see Hal Bernton, "Now Their Children Can Smile," *Anchorage Daily News,* August 14, 1988, p. A1.

52. D. L. Wilbur, "Alcoholism: An AMA View," in *Proceedings of the 28th International Congress on Alcohol and Alcoholism,* vol. 2, ed. M. Keller and T. G. Coffey

(Highland Park, IL: Hillhouse, 1969), p. 15, as cited in Conrad and Schneider, *Deviance and Medicalization,* p. 102.

53. Selden D. Bacon, "The Problems of Alcoholism in Society," in *Social Disability,* ed. D. Malikin (New York: New York University Press, 1973), p. 23, as cited in Conrad and Schneider, *Deviance and Medicalization,* p. 102.

54. E. Mansell Pattison, "Comment on 'The Alcoholic Game,' " *Quarterly Journal of Studies on Alcohol, 30* (December 1969), p. 953.

55. Ray, *Drugs, Society, and Human Behavior,* pp. 173–174 (emphasis added).

56. Thomas F. A. Plaut, *Alcohol Problems: A Report to the Nation by the Cooperative Commission on the Study of Alcoholism* (New York: Oxford University Press, 1967), pp. 37–38 (emphasis added).

57. Robert F. Bales, "Cultural Differences in Rates of Alcoholism," in *Drinking and Intoxication: Selected Readings in Social Attitudes and Controls,* ed. Raymond G. McCarthy (Glencoe, IL: The Free Press, 1959), pp. 263–277; see also Levin, *Alcoholism,* pp. 49–54.

58. For collections of the various studies, see Pittman and Snyder, eds., *Society, Culture, and Drinking Patterns;* and McCarthy, ed., *Drinking and Intoxication.*

59. Richard Jessor, Theodore D. Graves, Robert C. Hanson, and Shirley L. Jessor, *Society, Personality, and Deviant Behavior: A Study of a Tri-Ethnic Community* (New York: Holt, Rinehart and Winston, 1968), pp. 50–115, 233–331. The terminology and discussion of these variables have been simplified.

60. The first-stage interviews resulted in a description of patterns of drinking behavior. See Don Cahalan, Ira H. Cisin, and Helen M. Crossley, *American Drinking Practices: A National Survey of Behavior and Attitudes* (New Brunswick, NJ: Rutgers Center of Alcohol Studies, 1969).

61. Ibid., pp. 27–34.

62. Ibid., pp. 81–85.

63. Ibid., pp. 141–142.

64. Edwin M. Lemert, "Sociocultural Research on Drinking," in *Human Deviance, Social Problems, and Social Control,* 2nd ed., ed. Edwin M. Lemert (Englewood Cliffs, NJ: Prentice-Hall, 1972), pp. 207–217.

65. For a discussion of this approach, see Sharon C. Wilsnack, "The Needs of the Female Drinker: Dependency, Power, or What?" in *Proceedings of the Second Annual Alcoholism Conference of the National Institute on Alcohol Abuse and Alcoholism,* ed. Morris E. Chafetz (Washington, DC: National Institute of Mental Health, 1973), pp. 65–83.

66. For discussions of this approach, see David C. McClelland, "Drinking as a Response to Power Needs in Men," and Ozzie G. Simmons, "Discussion: Alcohol and Human Motivation," both in *Proceedings,* ed. Chafetz, pp. 47–64 and 84–91, respectively.

67. Barry Glassner and Bruce Berg, "How Jews Avoid Alcohol Problems," *American Sociological Review, 45* (August 1980), pp. 647–664.

68. Bales, "Cultural Differences," pp. 263–277.

69. E. te Wierik, "Factors Influencing Behaviour in Relation to Alcohol," in *Biomedical and Social Aspects of Alcohol Use: A Review of the Literature,* ed. Dirk G. van der Heij and Gertjan Schaafsma (Wageningen, The Netherlands: Centre for Agricultural Publishing and Documentation, 1991), pp. 204–227.

70. Sean O'Connor, Victor Hesselbrock, and Lance Bauer, "The Nervous System and the Predisposition to Alcoholism," *Alcohol Health and Research World, 14: 2* (1990), pp. 90–97.

71. U.S. Food and Drug Administration, *FDA Talk Paper, TO4–27, FDA Approves New Drug for Treatment of Alcoholism* (Washington, DC: Department of Health and Human Services, 2004).

72. United Nations Office on Drug Abuse and Crime, *World Drug Report 2004,* June, 2004, p. 7; Hanson and Venturelli, *Drugs and Society,* p. 234.

73. Kaplan, *The Hardest Drug,* p. 99; see also Louis Kraar, "The Drug Trade," *Fortune,* June 20, 1988, pp. 27–38; United Nations Office on Drug Abuse and Crime, *The Opium Economy in Afghanistan: An International Problem,* January, 2003; The United Nations Office on Drugs and Crime, *The Opium Economy in Afghanistan: An International Problem* (Vienna: The United Nations, 2003).

74. Ray, *Drugs, Society, and Human Behavior,* p. 356.

75. Douglas H. Powell, "A Pilot Study of Occasional Heroin Users," *Archives of General Psychiatry, 28* (April 1973), pp. 587–589; see also DEA, *Drugs of Abuse, 1989,* p. 12; Abadinsky, *Drugs: An Introduction,* pp. 79–80.

76. There is little consistency in descriptions of exactly what feelings are experienced by people who knowingly or unknowingly use heroin for the first time and by people who have used it for long periods. Furthermore, the means of using the drug also seem to influence the perceived effects. For example, inhaling heroin or injecting it under the skin rather than mainlining it into the vein appears to eliminate the rush. The discussion in this text deals only with mainlining and is drawn from Edward M. Brecher, *Licit and Illicit Drugs* (Mount Vernon, NY: Consumers Union, 1972), pp. 12–15; Alfred R. Lindesmith, *Addiction and Opiates* (Chicago: Aldine, 1968), pp. 23–45; William E. McAuliffe and Robert A. Gordon, "A Test of Lindesmith's Theory of Addiction: The Frequency of Euphoria Among Long-Term Addicts," *American Journal of Sociology, 79* (January 1974), pp. 795–803; and James V. Delong, "The Drugs and Their Effects," in *Dealing with Drug Abuse: A Report to the Ford Foundation,* ed. Patricia M. Wald, Peter Barton Hutt, et al. (New York: Praeger, 1972), pp. 78–85.

77. Troy Duster, *The Legislation of Morality: Law, Drugs, and Moral Judgment* (New York: The Free Press, 1970), pp. 70–71. See also Alan G. Sutter, "The World of the Righteous Dope Fiend," *Issues in Criminology, 2* (Fall 1966), p. 191.

78. Delong, "The Drugs and Their Effects," pp. 81–84; and Ray, *Drugs, Society, and Human Behavior,* pp. 349–351.

79. Duster, *The Legislation of Morality,* pp. 69–75.

80. Lindesmith, *Addiction and Opiates,* pp. 31–32; Abadinsky, *Drugs: An Introduction,* p. 81.

81. McAuliffe and Gordon, "A Test of Lindesmith's Theory," p. 831. For recent examples see Peter Katel and Mary Hager, "Rockers, Models, and the New Allure of Heroin," *Newsweek, 128*(9) (August 26, 1996), pp. 50–54.

82. Kaplan, *The Hardest Drug,* pp. 220–221. For discussions of methadone program success, see ibid., pp. 213–225; and Ray, *Drugs, Society, and Human Behavior,* p. 367.

83. Quoted in "Medicine," *Time,* January 4, 1971, p. 60, as cited in Ray, *Drugs, Society, and Human Behavior,* p. 367.

84. M. Douglas Anglin, Mary-Lynn Brecht, and Ebrahim Maddahian, "Pretreatment Characteristics and Treatment Performance of Legally Coerced Versus Voluntary Methadone Maintenance Admissions," *Criminology, 27* (August 1989), pp. 537–557.

85. This discussion is based on Kaplan, *The Hardest Drug,* pp. 34–43.

86. Wisotsky, *Beyond the War on Drugs,* p. 27.

87. For discussions of this point, see Brecher, *Licit and Illicit Drugs,* pp. 21–32; Goode, *The Drug Phenomenon,* pp. 40–44; and Delong, "The Drugs and Their Effects," pp. 71–85, 116.

88. Ray, *Drugs, Society, and Human Behavior,* pp. 351–352.

89. Hanson and Venturelli, *Drugs and Society,* pp. 236.

90. See T. Premkumar, Walter Cuskey, and Johannes Ipsen, "A Comparative Study of Drug-Related Deaths in the United States," *International Annals of Criminology, 11: 2* (1972), pp. 501–527; for an example of drug deaths in comparison to deaths from alcohol, see Rice et al., *The Economic Costs of Alcohol and Drug Abuse and Mental Illness,* p. 19.

91. There is a theory that overdoses are actually very rare. The argument is that such deaths are caused either by the adulterants used in the heroin or by the interaction of heroin with other drugs being used at the same time, for example, alcohol. See Brecher, *Licit and Illicit Drugs,* pp. 101–114.

92. Abadinsky, *Drugs: An Introduction,* p. 82.

93. John C. Ball, Lawrence Rosen, John A. Flueck, and David N. Nurco, "The Criminality of Heroin Addicts: When Addicted and When Off Opiates," in *The Drugs-Crime Connection,* ed. James A. Inciardi (Beverly Hills,

CA: Sage Publications, 1981), pp. 39–65; for a more recent study, see David M. Altschuler and Paul J. Brounstein, "Patterns of Drug Use, Drug Trafficking, and Other Delinquency Among Inner-City Males in Washington, DC," *Criminology, 29* (November 1991), pp. 589–622.

94. Paul J. Goldstein, "Getting Over: Economic Alternatives to Predatory Crime Among Street Drug Users," in *The Drugs-Crime Connection,* ed. Inciardi, p. 82.

95. Paraphrased from James A. Inciardi, "The Vilification of Euphoria," *Addictive Diseases, 1*(3) (1974), p. 245; see also Altschuler and Brounstein, "Patterns of Drug Use," pp. 589–622, esp. pp. 607–617.

96. Abadinsky, *Drugs: An Introduction,* pp. 226–227.

97. Duane C. McBride, "Drugs and Violence," in *The Drugs-Crime Connection,* ed. Inciardi, pp. 112–113.

98. The history of drug control legislation in the United States is discussed in Brecher, *Licit and Illicit Drugs,* pp. 3–63; Alfred R. Lindesmith, *The Addict and the Law* (Bloomington: Indiana University Press, 1965); David F. Musto, *The American Disease: Origins of Narcotic Control* (New Haven, CT: Yale University Press, 1973); Conrad and Schneider, *Deviance and Medicalization,* pp. 110–130; and David T. Courtwright, *Dark Paradise: Opiate Addiction in America Before 1940* (Cambridge, MA: Harvard University Press, 1982), pp. 62–86.

99. Brecher, *Licit and Illicit Drugs,* pp. 8–11.

100. Ibid., pp. 6–7.

101. Courtwright, *Dark Paradise,* p. 78.

102. Musto, *The American Disease,* pp. 5–6.

103. Charles Reasons, "The Politics of Drugs: An Inquiry in the Sociology of Social Problems," *Sociological Quarterly, 15* (Summer 1974), pp. 393–394.

104. Musto, *The American Disease,* pp. 121–128.

105. "Editorial Comment," *American Medicine, 21,* o.s.; *10,* n.s. (November 1915), pp. 799–800, as cited in Brecher, *Licit and Illicit Drugs,* p. 50.

106. Donald T. Dickson, "Bureaucracy and Morality: An Organizational Perspective on a Moral Crusade," *Social Problems, 16* (Fall 1968), pp. 149–151.

107. Musto, *The American Disease,* pp. 134–134, 244–249.

108. Reasons, "Politics of Drugs," p. 398.

109. Conrad and Schneider, *Deviance and Medicalization,* p. 127; and Courtwright, *Dark Paradise.*

110. United Nations Office on Drug Abuse and Crime, *World Drug Report,* pp. 1, 7.

111. United Nations Office on Drugs and Crime, *Global Illicit Drug Trends,* p. 5; National Institute on Drug Abuse, INFOFACTS, p. 1.

112. For histories of marijuana, see Brecher, *Licit and Illicit Drugs,* pp. 397–430; and Allen Geller and Maxwell Boas, *The Drug Beat* (New York: McGraw-Hill, 1969), pp. 3–42.

113. Richard R. Lingeman, *Drugs from A to Z: A Dictionary* (New York: McGraw-Hill, 1969), p. 144.

114. Hanson and Venturelli, *Drugs and Society,* p. 384.

115. Lester Grinspoon and James Bakalar, "Marijuana: The Forbidden Medicine," in Roxbury *The American Drug Scene: An Anthology,* 3rd ed., ed. James Inciardi and Karen McElrath (Los Angeles: 2001), pp. 95–101.

116. National Commission on Marihuana and Drug Abuse, *Marihuana: A Signal of Misunderstanding* (Washington, DC: U.S. Government Printing Office, 1972), p. 59.

117. *A Call to Action,* pp. 4–5.

118. Howard S. Becker, *Outsiders: Studies in the Sociology of Deviance* (New York: The Free Press, 1963), pp. 41–58.

119. Ibid., p. 78.

120. Paraphrased from Institute of Medicine, *Marijuana and Health* (Washington, DC: National Academy Press, 1982), pp. 2–4, 26–27; see also Erich Goode, *Drugs in American Society,* 2nd ed. (New York: Knopf, 1984), pp. 116–117.

121. Hanson and Venturelli, *Drugs and Society,* p. 382.

122. Ibid.

123. National Institute on Drug Abuse, *NIDA INFOFACTS,* June, 2004, p. 2.; Erich Goode, *Deviant Behavior* (Upper Saddle River, NJ: Prentice Hall, 2001), p. 186.

124. *NIDA INFOFACTS,* 2004, p. 2.

125. Institute of Medicine, *Marijuana and Health,* pp. 2–4, 26–27.

126. Hanson and Venturelli, *Drugs and Society,* p. 382.

127. National Institute on Drug Abuse, *NIDA INFOFACTS,* 2004, p. 3.

128. Goode, *Deviant Behavior,* p. 186.

129. Ibid.

130. Ibid., p. 3.

131. Ibid.

132. Goode, *Deviant Behavior,* p. 186; *NIDA INFOFACTS,* 2004, p. 3.

133. Associated Press Release, "Williams Files Papers to Retire," New York, Tuesday, August 2, 2004.

134. Goode, *Deviant Behavior,* p. 186.

135. Institute of Medicine, *Marijuana and Health,* p. 43.

136. National Commission, *Drug Use in America,* p. 159 (emphasis added).

137. Mitch Earlywine, *Understanding Marijuana: A New Look at the Scientific Evidence* (New York: Oxford University Press, 2002), pp. 63–64; Marshall B. Clinard and Robert F. Meier, *Sociology of Deviant Behavior* (Belmont, CA: Wadsworth/Thompson Learning, 2004), pp. 260, 262–264.

138. This discussion is based on Goode, *The Drug Phenomenon,* pp. 44–48; and Institute of Medicine, *Marijuana and Health,* p. 42. See also National Commission, *Marihuana,* pp. 45–49; and Stanley E. Grupp, *The Marihuana Muddle* (Lexington, MA: D. C. Heath, 1973), pp. 101–111.

139. Goode, *The Drug Phenomenon,* pp. 47–48. Cf. Eric Single and Denise Kandel, "The Role of Buying and Selling in Illicit Drug Use," in *Drugs, Crime, and Politics,* ed. Arnold S. Trebach (New York: Praeger, 1979), pp. 118–128.

140. This discussion is based on Musto, *The American Disease,* pp. 216–229; Geller and Boas, *The Drug Beat,* pp. 23–33; Brecher, *Licit and Illicit Drugs,* pp. 410–421; Becker, *Outsiders,* pp. 135–146; Dickson, "Bureaucracy and Morality," pp. 151–156; and Charles E. Reasons, "The 'Dope' on the Bureau of Narcotics in Maintaining the Criminal Approach to the Drug Problem," in *The Criminologist: Crime and the Criminal,* ed. Charles E. Reasons (Pacific Palisades, CA: Goodyear, 1974), pp. 144–155. These authors, although more or less in agreement on most matters of fact, differ greatly in their interpretations. The principal point of contention is the role of the Federal Bureau of Narcotics. Was its agitation for legislation an independent action or a response to outside pressures? The discussion here represents a combination of these differing interpretations. Cf. John F. Galliher and Allynn Walker, "The Politics of Systematic Research Error: The Case of the Federal Bureau of Narcotics as a Moral Entrepreneur," *Crime and Social Justice,* 10 (Fall–Winter 1978), pp. 29–33.

141. Quoted in Geller and Boas, *The Drug Beat,* pp. 24–26.

142. Sources for this discussion are Tullis, *Handbook of Research,* pp. 1–21; Kraar, "The Drug Trade," pp. 27–38; DEA, *Drugs of Abuse, 1989,* p. 37; and Willis, *Drug Use and Abuse,* pp. 76–77.

143. Bureau of Justice Statistics, *Sourcebook of Criminal Justice Statistics—1998,* p. 237.

144. The foregoing discussion was based on DEA, *Drugs of Abuse, 1989,* pp. 37, 40; Willis, *Drug Use and Abuse,* pp. 78–79; and Wisotsky, *Beyond the War on Drugs,* pp. 20–30.

145. United Nations Office on Drugs and Crime, *Global Illicit Drug Trends,* p. 116.

146. Wisotsky, *Beyond the War on Drugs,* p. 189.

147. For an excellent discussion of this issue, see P. F. Mannaioni, "The Cocaine Risk: Toxicity, Dependency, and Treatment," in *Cocaine Today: Its Effects on the Individual and Society,* ed. Francesco Bruno (Rome: United Nations Interregional Crime and Justice Research Institute, 1991), pp. 55–62.

148. Ibid., pp. 58–59.

149. Howard Abadinsky, *Drugs: An Introduction,* p. 115.

150. Hanson and Venturelli, *Drugs and Society,* p. 277.

151. Howard Abadinsky, *Drugs: An Introduction,* pp. 16, 116–117.

152. H. Khalsa and M. D. Anglin, "Treatment Effectiveness for Cocaine Abuse," in *Cocaine Today,* ed. Bruno, pp. 89–98.

153. Altschuler and Brounstein, "Patterns of Drug Use," pp. 608–609.

154. This discussion is based on ibid., pp. 110–111; Mary H. Cooper, "Does the War on Drugs Need a New Strategy?" *Editorial Research Reports,* February 23, 1990, p. 5; and Ethan A. Nadelmann, Mark A. R. Kleiman, and Felton J. Earls, "Should Some Illegal Drugs Be Legalized?" *Issues in Science and Technology,* Summer 1990, p. 45.

155. Bill Stern, *The Taste of Ashes* (New York: Hillman Books, 1961).

156. Department of Health and Human Services, *National Household Survey on Drug Abuse Report: Non-medical Use of Prescription-Type Drugs among Youths and Young Adults,* (Washington, DC: U.S. Government Printing Office, 2003).

157. Hanson and Venturelli, *Drugs and Society,* pp. 224–225.

158. U.S. Department of Health and Human Services, *Youth Attitute Tracking Survey 2002* (Washington, DC: U.S. Government Printing Office, 2002).

159. Ibid.

160. Mark Starr, "Running on Dope," *Newsweek* (May 31, 2004), pp. 58–59.

161. National Institute on Drug Abuse, *NIDA INFO-FACTS-Steroids* (Washington, DC: U.S. Department of Health and Human Service, 2004), p. 2.

162. Joan Sosin, "The Real Dope on Youth and Steroids," *The Rotarian* (June, 2004), p. 16.

163. National Institute on Drug Abuse, *NIDA Community Alert Bulletin – Anabolic Steroids* (April, 2000), p. 4.

164. Ibid., p. 5.

165. National Institute on Drug Abuse, *NIDA Research Report Series – Anabolic Steroid Abuse,* (Washington, DC: U.S. Department of Health and Human Services, 2002).

9 Mental Disorders

What we have learned, our personal experiences, and our "common sense" tell about the levers that move the world of human behavior. In our culture, we assume a rational, logical universe capable of being comprehended. We assume that much of what happens may be understood by putting ourselves in someone else's place and understanding his or her motives, feelings, and intent. When an out-of-shape middle-aged man puts on a Batman suit and climbs the front of Buckingham Palace, the behavior at first appears so much beyond anything we would think of doing (at least until we get into better shape) that we conclude, "He must be crazy." When a group of political/religious fanatics takes over an elementary school in Russia, we at first think, someone who would go to this extreme must be desperately trying to send a political message. However, when we see Batman's hand-lettered sign pleading for increased rights for divorced fathers, we can at least understand his motivation. When we hear that the radicals have denied the children water and bathroom privileges, we have difficulty understanding their behavior. When we see them blow up a school full of parents, teachers, grandparents, children, and themselves, the action is so far from our comprehension that we conclude the political message they are trying to send is, "We are crazy!"

In the last chapter, we discussed how people use psychoactive drugs to alter their perception of the environment. But differences in both perceiving and responding to one's surroundings are not limited to drug users. When the differences become obvious and the actions cannot be attributed to the temporary effects of drugs or explained in some other logical way, we become uncomfortable. "What's so funny?" breaks up your friend. And "Are you crazy or something?" has him or her rolling on the ground in uncontrolled mirth.

When people act "inappropriately" for reasons we cannot readily explain—and perhaps they cannot explain either—we place them into the "crazy-or-something" category. No doubt many readers have had personal experiences with someone so classified. Your great-aunt Minnie talks to herself a lot, and your father says she is "not dealing from a full deck." Your neighbor Waldo goes to bed one day and refuses to get up and go to classes for a whole week; he then spends some time in a hospital. And your best friend's mother always seems so nervous about nothing at all and starts screaming over the smallest things, but she is taking some special drugs and is much calmer lately.

We are, of course, talking about behavior referred to as *mental illness*. It was once called *madness, craziness,* and *insanity.* Today "madness" and "craziness" are considered unflattering unless used in jest, and "insanity" is strictly a *legal* term designating a lack of responsibility for what otherwise would be criminal behavior.

Mental disorders, in all forms, are the second leading cause of disability in industrialized nations, accounting for lost productivity and premature death at rates similar to cancer and heart disease.[1] The U.S. Surgeon General reports that one of every two Americans will suffer a mental health problem at some time in his or her life. Each year nearly 20 percent of Americans will suffer some sort of mental disorder, and about 15 percent of adult Americans will use mental health services of some sort.[2]

Whether a person is or was "insane," on the other hand, is a decision made by courts—in most cases, juries—and the basis for the decision varies from one jurisdiction to another. One example of this is convicted mass murderer Jeffrey Dahmer, who attempted to use the insanity defense at his Milwaukee jury trial. As one writer notes, "focusing on the sensational, the media raised the prospect of a cannibal being let off the hook because of a legal loophole."[3] Federal courts and some states, for example, have adopted the following definition of insanity, which incorporates the term *mental disease:*

> A person is not responsible for criminal conduct if at the time of such conduct as a result of mental disease or defect he lacks substantial capacity either to appreciate the criminality (or wrongfulness) of his conduct or to conform his conduct to the requirements of law.[4]

Another way in which "insanity" has been handled by the courts is demonstrated by the "guilty but mentally ill" statute, which essentially separates the concepts of mental illness and insanity.[5]

People with mental problems are labeled and classified in many ways, in a range of different perspectives. An individual's inability to make an expected social adjustment might earn him or her the "psycho" label and exacerbate the person's adjustment problems. A report on mental health in the United States, released in 2000 by the Surgeon General of the United States, stresses the connection between good mental health and physical health generally.[6] Mental health is broadly defined as

> the successful performance of mental function, resulting in productive activities, fulfilling relationships with other people, and the ability to adapt to change and to cope with adversity; from early childhood until late life, mental health is the springboard of thinking and communication skills, learning, emotional growth, resilience, and self esteem.[7]

The Surgeon General discusses all manner of mental disorders under the heading of "mental illness." Despite its widespread use, the term *mental disease* (or *mental illness*—the terms are used interchangeably) is controversial. We shall elaborate on this controversy later, but the reader should be aware that the term has no precise, objective definition. Instead, it is usually employed in the context of highly relative concepts such as "lack of social adjustment" and "deviations from normality."[8] Unlike physiological illness, mental illness is defined in terms of norms, ethics, and law. It is a matter of *social definition* whether the behavior in question will be acceptable to whoever makes such judgments. Nachman Ben-Yehuda states it well: "The nature of mental illness, especially the nonorganic, functional type, is very problematic. Determining who is mentally ill or abnormal is largely a question of social norms."[9] It has also been a question of social roles and has changed over time. In the 1960s, when sociologists first began to study gender roles, researchers Broverman and Broverman looked at stereotypical male, female, and adult (sex unspecified) behavior expectations. They found that the "adult" expectations were so highly correlated with the "male" role that one could not be both a mentally healthy adult and a mentally healthy adult female![10]

To say that certain behavior is evidence of an illness tells us nothing about the *cause* of the behavior. It does tell something about the *effect* of the behavior, because observers have defined the behavior as being socially unacceptable and as warranting a reaction appropriate to a disease. And those who are ill become patients who go to a hospital or a doctor for treatment rather than to a jail, a church, or some other institution designed to change behavior.

There is no conclusive evidence, however, that most of what is called mental illness is any more a medical issue than is alcohol dependence or any other form of deviance discussed in previous chapters. Thus for purposes of consistency and clarity, we shall use the term mental *disorder* rather than mental *illness.* The substitution is not entirely satisfactory, but it is less likely to mislead the reader about what is known about the source of the behavior.

What Is Mental Disorder?

Mental disorders are defined as "diagnosable conditions that impair thinking, feeling, and behavior and interfere with a person's capacity to be productive and enjoy fulfilling relationships."[11] It is important at the outset to distinguish between two major categories of mental disorder: that associated with physical disorders of the brain and that not so associated. The forms in the first category, *organic mental disorders,* are more or less linked to known physiological causes. Among the behaviors associated with organic disorders are hallucinations, lack of control over impulses, and loss of memory. In such cases the brain may have been affected by any of a variety of factors such as syphilis, lead poisoning, encephalitis, tumors, malnutrition, overexposure to carbon monoxide, and head injuries. Because of the aging of the U.S. population, recent attention has focused on organic mental disorders associated with older people, particularly Alzheimer's disease. The course of dementia of the Alzheimer's type tends to be slowly progressive.[12]

In the early stages, some people may show personality changes or increased irritability as well as memory problems and difficulty with routine tasks, organizing a meal, driving, finding one's way home. A common course of the disease is an insidious early onset with losses in short-term memory followed, over a period of years, by gradual inability to understand spoken or written language, perform purposeful movements, and recognize objects— or loved ones. The disease is characterized by the buildup of plaques of a sticky protein called amyloid. Scientists have made great strides in the last fifteen years, and exciting new brain imaging techniques are now available to detect these plaques and evaluate the effects of drugs designed to attack them or discourage their formation. These techniques will also give us additional information about how brain function relates to mental disorders.[13]

Also included among organic disorders are behaviors linked to psychoactive drug use. For example, an individual withdrawing from alcohol after extended bouts of intoxication may have auditory hallucinations—such as hearing voices discussing the hallucinator in the third person. Almost all the psychoactive drugs such as barbiturates, opiates, amphetamines, and cocaine may result in behavior labeled as an organic mental disorder.

The organic disorders are not particularly important to our discussion, but one historical footnote is relevant. The first scientific advances in the study of mental disorders, made in the late nineteenth century, examined the link between brain damage by syphilis and a disorder known as *general paresis*. Because brain damage was found to underlie one kind of behavioral disorder, there emerged a belief that all such disorders would ultimately be connected to brain pathologies. One result was that the field of medicine gained a firm foothold as a discipline that possessed expertise in the area of mental disorders. More about this later.

It soon became apparent that for most disorders a neat link to physiological damage could not be demonstrated. Such disorders are usually called *functional mental disorders* and are assumed to stem from psychological rather than physical origins. The following abbreviated classification of the major functional disorders and their associated symptoms is taken from the latest edition of the *Diagnostic and Statistical Manual of Mental Disorders* (fourth edition), published by the American Psychiatric Association.

Known as the DSM-IV, this manual contains the following 16 primary categorizations, 10 more than in the previous edition, the DSM-III-R (1987).

1. **Disorders usually first diagnosed in infancy, childhood, or adolescence.** This category includes disorders such as mental retardation, learning disorders, communication disorders, and attention-deficit/hyperactivity disorders.

2. **Delirium, dementia, and amnestic and other cognitive disorders.** This group refers to problems such as substance intoxication, Alzheimer's disease, and Parkinson's disease.

3. **Mental disorders due to a general medical condition not elsewhere classified.** Persons suffering from personality changes and echolalia (the uncontrollable repeating or "echoing" of other people's words) would be included in this category.

4. **Substance-related disorders.** These prevalent disorders involve cocaine and opiate dependence as well as the more common alcohol- and caffeine-related disorders.

5. **Schizophrenia and other psychotic disorders.** This group refers to disorders such as delusions and hallucinations.

6. **Mood disorders.** This category involves the fairly common depressive disorders (e.g., those commonly called "depression") and bipolar disorders (formerly called *manic-depression*).

7. **Anxiety disorders.** These include panic disorders, obsessive-compulsive disorders, posttraumatic stress disorders, and phobias.

8. **Somatoform disorders.** This group involves physical distress that cannot be explained by a medical condition, such as pain disorders, hypochondriasis (fear that one has a serious disease), and body dysmorphic disorders (exaggeration of defects in one's physical appearance).

9. **Factitious disorders.** Psychological or physical symptoms that are intentionally feigned in order to appear sick are grouped under this heading.

10. **Dissociative disorders.** This classification includes dissociative amnesia as well as dissociative identity disorder.

11. **Sexual and gender identity disorders.** Sexual desire, sexual arousal, and sexual pain disorders are located in this category.

12. **Eating disorders.** Both anorexia nervosa and bulimia nervosa are classified as eating disorders.

13. **Sleep disorders.** This heading refers to problems such as primary insomnia (inability to sleep), narcolepsy (tendency to fall asleep), nightmare disorders, and sleepwalking disorders.

14. **Impulse-control disorders not elsewhere classified.** Fairly well-known disorders like kleptomania (gratification through theft), pyromania (gratification by setting fires), and pathological gambling are included here.

15. **Adjustment disorders.** This category involves emotional and/or behavioral difficulties that result from an attempt to adjust to increased stressors.

16. **Personality disorders.** This group includes disorders such as antisocial personality disorders, narcissistic personality disorders, and dependent personality disorders.

The symptoms described in the DSM-IV may seem obvious, but in practice behaviors are seldom so clear-cut and magnified, and diagnoses often turn out to be very hit-and-miss affairs. Although the diagnostic system of the DSM-IV may be much improved over the older systems, traditionally psychiatric diagnoses are very *unreliable;* that is, there is little agreement from one psychiatrist to another about the proper diagnosis for a given set of symptoms when dealing with real patients.[14]

Diagnosis in psychiatry is often tantamount to one physician telling you that you are suffering from appendicitis while another says that you have a broken leg. Although this analogy may be slightly far-fetched, the state of diagnostic reliability does not inspire confidence in the statistics that purport to describe the distribution of mental disorders. Nor does it inspire confidence in the treatment procedures that are presumably based on diagnoses.

In one study, referred to as the Midtown Manhattan Survey, researchers attempted to diagnose a random sample of adults through interviews. By interpreting claims of restlessness, nervousness, and other behaviors as symptoms of disorder, the researchers arrived at some startling conclusions: Only 18 percent of the sample was mentally *well,* 23 percent had marked symptoms of disorder, and the remainder had moderate or mild symptoms.[15] In viewing these findings, one must wonder: If the great majority of a city's residents are found to be in need of psychiatric help, what has really been measured—the extent of disorder, or the researchers' opinions about city dwellers?

The DSM-IV has been criticized from all angles, and it seems that no category is safe from complaint in the psychiatric community. Some argue that value judgments and even politics have affected what has been included and how it has been stated.[16] Others criticize what has been left out. Wakefield, for example, challenged the exclusion of bereavement as a criterion for a classification of major depressive disorder (under mood disorders) because it is "normal" depression.[17] It could be that the consequences of normal bereavement are much more far-reaching than assumed and may easily be the equal to major stressors such as divorce, job loss, and terminal illness.[18] Erich Goode's excellent discussion of the range and depth of challenges to the DSM-IV is daunting.[19] It illustrates and amplifies the extreme diversity in the field and the lack of agreement among practitioners regarding causes, effects, and the categorizing of mental disorders.

But even though diagnostic procedures are inconsistent, misleading, and lacking in explanatory value, we must also recognize that countless individuals do behave in ways that jeopardize their health and social relationships and that lead to their being labeled as mentally disordered. Occasionally, this labeling process is initiated by the individuals themselves. In Mexico or in the U.S. Latino community, one may consult a *curandero,* a person who may help find the cause of one's problems in spells and the supernatural. Americans are most likely to seek help from their clergy. Even the nearly 25 percent who have the most serious disorders are unlikely to go on to seek a physician or mental health professional as well.[20] However, many people do commit themselves to mental hospitals or clinics, consult various types of mental health professionals, or periodically attend therapy sessions whose purposes range from getting to know one's body better to improving one's emotional outlook on growing old, getting a divorce, enjoying sex, or tolerating idiotic co-workers.

The majority of "mentally ill" individuals are defined so by others, however. They seek help only after encouragement or pressure to do so, and in many cases they are forced to submit to various control and treatment measures because their behavior has been perceived as extraordinarily inappropriate or burdensome. Thus the question "Who is mentally disordered?" is not necessarily answered simply by diagnostic procedures; it also involves a labeling process that precedes diagnosis:

> The early definitions of mental illness, especially in middle-class populations, are likely to take place in the groups within which the person primarily operates; evaluations are made by family, fellow employees, friends, and employers. If symptoms appear and are not recognized as such by members of the individual's more primary groups, it is unlikely that he will become accessible to psychiatric personnel unless his symptoms become visible, and disturbing enough to lead to his commitment to some treatment center by external authorities. . . .
>
> The basic decision about illness is usually made by community members and *not professional personnel.*[21]

Correlates of Mental Disorder

If one of the authors were to claim he had spoken with "shadow people" or extraterrestials, what would result? Would he be locked up in a rubber room or be asked to go on a lecture tour? In our society both results are possible, since he could be defined either as someone having hallucinations or as the discoverer of a new form of being. If your gray-haired grandmother carries on lengthy conversations with God, is she a candidate for sainthood or for sedation? These examples may seem far-fetched, but they illustrate that the appropriateness of behavior is a matter of interpretation. Thus from a practical standpoint the question of who is designated as mentally disordered may depend as much upon the actor's audience as upon the actor's behavior. Obviously, if one audience defines a particular behavior as "disordered" while another audience defines it as "normal," there are going to be problems in discovering what causes "mentally disordered behavior." Despite this obstacle, however, researchers have consistently found striking relationships between certain social characteristics and the likelihood of being defined as mentally disordered. We will investigate these. First, however, we must deal with the issue of genetics.

Genetics

Early in the last century, it was found that untreated, advanced syphilis led to the development of mental illness. In addition, the recreational drug use of the 1960s provided evidence that chemicals could produce effects mimicking those of mental illness. Since then, there has been a continuing search for physiological bases of mental disorder. There remains a widespread belief that even the so-called functional disorders have some organic explanation. Few observers believe that the relationship between all mental disorders and physical causes will be found to be as direct and as simple as the syphilis–insanity connection. Rather, scientists suspect that certain physiological conditions increase the *risk* of or *susceptibility* to contracting disorders.

Support for this hypothesis comes from a number of studies of the brain[22] as well as the consistent research finding that persons who are biologically related to someone diagnosed as schizophrenic stand an increased chance of also developing the disorder. There is some evidence that this result occurs even when the related individuals have had no personal contact.[23] Numerous genetic studies have used various types of samples (e.g., parents and children, identical and fraternal twins) to investigate the nature of the link between genetic factors and this mental disorder. Recent studies indicate that while children in the general population have a 1.2 percent probability of developing the disorder, children with one schizophrenic parent have a 12 percent chance and a child with two schizophrenic parents a probability of 35 percent. A twin also faces a relatively high risk for developing schizophrenia if the other twin has it.[24] A genetic link is clearly indicated and promising research is being conducted with the help of new tools ranging from brain imaging techniques to genetic studies of the isolated population of Iceland. Still, the exact nature of the link is not full understood.[25] However, it appears that whatever contribution genetics makes to mental disorder, there are links with nongenetic variables as well.

Social Class

One of the most recurrent patterns in mental disorder research is the high correlation between social class and the diagnosis of serious mental disorder. The pioneering study in this area was conducted by Robert E. L. Faris and H. Warren Dunham, who examined the distribution of persons admitted to mental hospitals in Chicago from 1922 to 1934. Using procedures similar to the ecological studies by Clifford Shaw on crime and delinquency (see Chapter 2), Faris and Dunham found that rates of hospital admission for psychosis were highest for people who resided in the city's center—the area of lowest economic status. As the distance from the city center increased and the economic status rose, rates of hospitalization fell off. These findings clearly indicated to Faris and Dunham that social factors must play a role in mental disorder, and like Shaw, they described those factors in terms of *social disorganization.* They concluded that areas characterized by culture conflict and the breakdown of old normative structures produce a disproportionate amount of mental disorder.

August B. Hollingshead and Frederick C. Redlich in New Haven, Connecticut, improved upon the work of Faris and Dunham. While the Chicago researchers studied only hospitalized individuals and based their definition of social class on area of residence, Hollingshead and Redlich instead included in their sample all patients in both public and private psychiatric institutions as well as patients not institutionalized but under the care of private practitioners. Their gauge of social status was based upon an index that included area of residence, occupation, and education. The results confirmed those of Faris and Dunham, however: *An inverse relationship exists between the occurrence of psychoses and social class.*[26] For a variety of mental disorders, a strong relationship continues to exist.[27]

Other findings from the New Haven study are also of interest. First, Hollingshead and Redlich found that neuroses—less serious disorders now called anxiety disorders—were concentrated in the *upper* classes. The authors concluded that a neurosis is a "state of mind" involving not only the patient but his or her social status and the therapist as well:

> A diagnosis of neurosis is a resultant of a social interactional process which involves the patient, the doctor, and the patient's position in the status structure of the community.
>
> It seems likely that the most important role in diagnosing "neurosis" is played by the individual who bears the label. Just how and why he accepts this designation is a fascinating question. In a very literal sense, the individual usually decides whether he is neurotic. The old saw, "Anyone who goes to a psychiatrist should have his head examined," is applicable here. The degree to which he accepts or rejects the role he plays or is assigned in his social milieu often determines whether or not he considers himself neurotic or accepts others' appraisal of his being disturbed.[28]

Further, different social classes apparently experience not only different *types* of mental disorders but also different *reactions,* by others, toward the disorders. For example, Hollingshead and Redlich found that even among those diagnosed as psychotic, the higher the social class, the less time spent in hospitals and the more intensive the treatment. Lower-class psychotics, on the other hand, were more likely to be confined without treatment or to be subjected to lobotomies and various forms of shock treatment administered primarily to control rather than to cure.

Many subsequent studies have explored the relationship between social class and mental disorder. Each is distinctive in its methods of sampling, its measurement of social class, and its criteria of mental disorder. But even accounting for these variations and recognizing that psychiatric diagnosis is often unreliable and some mental disorders are more equal opportunity than others, the conclusion is escapable. As social status decreases, a greater proportion of individuals are diagnosed as suffering from some form of serious mental disorder.[29]

Two general explanations are suggested for the inverse relationship between social class and rates of mental disorder. The first is the *drift hypothesis.* This view states that people who develop or are likely to develop emotional difficulties stay in the lower class or even descend into the lower class because they experience difficulties with employment and other social relationships. In short, the drift hypothesis emphasizes individual vulnerabilities rather than environmental influences as causes of mental disorder. The second explanation, the *social causation model,* assumes that environmental characteristics are the key determinants of mental disorder. This model claims that experiences in the lower strata of society make individuals more susceptible to mental disorder. Currently, there appears to be more evidence for social class as cause of mental disorders than as result.[30] However, most researchers acknowledge that both characteristics of the person and circumstances of the social class play a role. Before discussing these theories further, we must touch on some related issues.

Minorities and Mental Health

Social class research is complicated by the fact that minorities are unevenly distributed among the social classes. The questions of who is labeled mentally disordered and why are even more difficult to address in the minority population. Cultural differences may obscure mental health problems, and minority members are even more unlikely than majority Americans to seek mental health treatment. Those who seek help or those who try to help them find help encounter barriers such as language, lack of insurance, low income, and cultural actions and stigma against mental disorders and treatment. They may also find that not only the mental health system, but also the research, techniques, and therapies on which it is based are oriented almost exclusively toward Anglo Americans. Ideally, treatment should be conducted in an atmosphere acknowledging definitions of "normal" and "deviant" in both cultures. Unfortunately, this rarely occurs.[31]

Family Setting

Obviously confounding the relationship between genetics, other variables, and mental disorder is the role of the family in transmitting behavior patterns. Does one learn from relatives (or close nonrelatives, for that matter) behaviors that eventually are defined as evidence of mental disorder?

Research findings in this area are inconclusive, but some variables that appear to contribute to schizophrenia are (1) serious medical problems of the mother, (2) blurring of identities in family roles (child sees self as similar to parents, or parents see selves as similar to child), and (3) the parents' general lack of communication and reasoning skills.[32]

Factors that appear to be linked to children's depressive and anxiety disorders include (1) depressive disorders of a parent, (2) anxiety disorder of a parent, and (3) family history of these disorders. Studies of adjudicated juvenile delinquents have also found correlations between mental disorders and (1) physical, emotional, and sexual abuse; (2) physical neglect; and (3) family history of mental illness. In addition, there is some evidence that children growing up in other than intact, two-parent families also tend to be at higher risk for mental disorders than their counterparts who have not experienced parental divorce.[33]

It is not only the children's mental health that is affected by the family setting. Married adults appear to be happier, more satisfied, and more "mentally healthy" than are those never married, widowed, or divorced. In their classic research on mental health and marriage, Walter R. Gove, Michael Hughes, and Carolyn Briggs Style indicate that marital status is as powerful a predictor of mental disorder as is social class. Furthermore, they provide some evidence that for males, *marriage itself* is a strong insulator from mental disorder; for females, however, the *quality of marriage* as measured by *marital happiness* is a stronger insulator than is marriage itself. Gove and his colleagues speculate that "this pattern holds because males gain more instrumentally out of marriages, e.g., the house is cleaned and meals are prepared, than do females, whereas females tend to be more emotionally invested in marriage than are males."[34]

Although challenged, Gove's findings have held for decades. More recently, Robin Simon conducted an extensive test of these theories using data from the National Survey of Families and Households. Simon's findings indicate that today, (1) "Research consistently indicts that marriage is associated with enhanced mental health for (both) men and women"; (2) "mental health is a consequence as well as a cause of marital status"; and (3) because of the mental health indicators they have used, most studies have tended to "overestimate the extent of women's distress and underestimate men's."[35] Researchers Waite and Lehrer did a critical review of the literature on the effect of marriage on mental health that provides additional insight. Even controlling for the fact that people who are more mentally healthy might be more likely to get and stay married, they found "persistent evidence" that getting married improved emotional well-being and "getting and staying married (to the same person) is associated with better mental health . . . and overall happiness." Studies indicate that rates of bipolar disorder and major depression, for example, are higher for unmarried individuals and rates for disorders such as schizophrenia may be as much as three times higher.[36]

Sociologically, the physical and mental health benefits of marriage may be traced to the social integration and support marriage provides. Marriage is likely to provide security, stability, and a continuing source of companionship, friendship, intimacy, love, and emotional support. According to Waite and Lehrer, this "emotional support on a regular basis . . . [decreases] depression, anxiety, and other psychological problems, and [improves] overall mental health," and physical health as well.[37] Marriage and the long-term commitment it implies also link people with a wider support network of individuals, groups, and institutions. This has "additional positive effects on both spouses and on their children."[38]

Male/ Female Differences

Despite greater equality than ever before and a blurring of the gender roles, U.S. men and women still live in somewhat different social worlds. Their biology is different, many of their experiences are different, and society's expectations of them differ as well. In short, women are not just small men and men are not just large, muscular women. It is not surprising, therefore, that the incidence of various mental disorders varies by sex. Evaluation of sex-related differences is complicated by the way mental disorder is defined in various studies. It is also complicated by the fact that men are only about half as likely to seek help. Women are more open to acknowledging a need for help and are more likely to discuss their problems with others. They are also more likely to see counseling and psychotherapy in a more favorable light than do men. They are, therefore, more likely to seek help and to be counted in mental health statistics.[39]

However, the preponderance of evidence indicates that overall rates of mental disorders are essentially similar for both sexes. But, the manner in which men and women express their distress varies. Women have higher rates of affective or mood disorders such as depression and anxiety disorders.[40] Men are more likely to evidence problems related to impulsiveness, substance abuse, antisocial behavior, and violence.[41] World Health Organization data indicate that these differences are not culture-specific.[42] Some may have a biological basis. Studies conducted at Stanford University using MRIs of brain functions suggest, for example, that women store memory and linked emotions together, while men store them in the same part of the brain but in two different spots.[43] Studies of schizophrenics indicate that cerebral blood flow and glucose metabolism are probably different in male and female schizophrenics.[44]

Some of the differences between males and females may be explained in terms of the sociology of emotion. Just as there have been appropriate gender roles spelled out in U.S. society, some argue that ideas about appropriate male and female emotional styles are strongly rooted in U.S. emotional culture. Simon states that "a consequence of gender-related emotional socialization is that females learn to express distress through internalizing emotional problems, such as depression, while males learn to express distress [by] externalizing emotional problems, such as substance abuse."[45] If this reasoning holds, we might, for example, anticipate greater predisposition toward violence among women as emotional styles of males and females follow the course of U.S. gender roles and begin to converge. With the emergence of such things as "girl gangs," this is what we are seeing.

Stress

One factor may underlie most, if not all, of the variables we have mentioned as being associated with mental disorder: genetics, social class, minority group status, family setting, sex, and marital status. That factor is *stress:* anxiety caused by real or imagined problems. It is easy to conjecture, for example, that in the lowest social classes, feelings of economic uncertainty and political powerlessness alone can create great stress. But a bad situation becomes even more intolerable in the event of serious family illness, death of a loved one, loss of employment, marital conflict, loneliness, or any of a variety of social difficulties and frustrations. In reaction to stress and its attendant anxieties, one may become depressed to the point of inactivity. Fatigue and indifference to job, family, and other social obligations result. One may even reach the point of constructing another "reality" that is preferable to the "real" one with all its distresses.[46]

There is evidence that stress is related to the incidence of mental disorder, but it is also obvious that stress does not invariably result in disorder.[47] So how do all these variables related to disorder—social class, genetics, family setting, and so on—come together with stress? One theory is suggested by Melvin L. Kohn. Restricting his theory to the causes of schizophrenia, Kohn argues that there is sufficient evidence that some persons are genetically vulnerable to mental disorder and that such persons are disproportionately concentrated in the lower class. So far, his theory is consistent with the drift hypothesis that we discussed earlier. However, Kohn also claims that most disorders in this class stem not from vulnerability alone but from vulnerability combined with other characteristics of lower-class life. In short, his theory is a combination of the drift hypothesis and the social causation model.

According to Kohn, lower-class people generally experience stress-producing situations over which they have *less personal control* than do those in higher social classes. Their lack of power and money allows them fewer resources for coping with illness, unemployment, and so on. In addition to a lack of control over stressful situations, the impact of the situations themselves may be influenced by *conceptions of reality and self.* This is the area in which the lower-class family plays a strategic role in the mental disorder process. Kohn argues that many lower-class families transmit a life orientation that is too rigid and limited for successfully dealing with stress. This is not to say that what the family teaches is unrealistic; indeed, the conceptions of reality transmitted to the children may be quite consistent with actual experience. If parents know from their own past that there are limited means to deal with stress, there is no reason for their children to learn otherwise.

Kohn has attempted to bring together the research findings concerning the relationships between schizophrenia and class, genetics, family, and stress. In his words,

the thrust of the argument is that the conditions of life experiences by people of lower social class position tend to impair their ability to deal resourcefully with the problematic and the stressful. Such impairment would be unfortunate for all who suffer it, but would not in itself result in schizophrenia. In conjunction with a genetic vulnerability to schizophrenia and the experience of great stress, however, such impairment could well be disabling. Since both genetic vulnerability and stress appear to occur disproportionately at lower social class levels, people in these segments of society may be at triple jeopardy.[48]

Kohn's theory remains conjectural at present. Testing is a formidable task. Doubtlessly, the variables that constitute different types of vulnerability—genetics, family experiences, and so on—will be difficult to untangle one from the other. Sociological research to date, however, indicates that Kohn may be at least partially correct. Ronald C. Kessler and Paul D. Cleary examined data from 720 interviews conducted in New Haven, Connecticut, and concluded that "lower class people are more responsive emotionally to the stresses they experience, even when these stresses are no more common among them than among persons who occupy higher social positions."[49] In short, Kessler and Cleary are claiming that the principal reason for high rates of mental disorder among lower-class persons is their vulnerability and that we will not be able to fully understand class differences until we more fully understand differences in responsiveness.[50]

But for many sociologists the really important issues about mental disorder do not concern the whys and wherefores of how people behave. To these sociologists the problems of value judgments, imprecision, and the lack of reliability in psychiatric diagnosis are too formidable to ignore. They argue that mental disorder is not like the disease of leprosy. You know that either you have leprosy or you don't. Whether you have a mental disorder, however, depends upon *how you get along*. Thus the decision processes surrounding a person's disorder may be based less upon the presence or absence of a disease than upon the degree to which her or his behavior is disruptive or inconvenient for the decision makers.[51]

Disease or Label?

Our discussion thus far has dealt with mental disorder from the perspective of the *medical model*. Most simply stated, this model assumes that certain behaviors are symptomatic of disease, and, depending upon one's particular theoretical orientation, that the disease stems from either organic causes (e.g., a chemical imbalance) or psychological causes. For over a hundred years now, doctors and scientists have known that infections of the brain can cause mental disorders. The dementia, mental deterioration, paralysis, and death associated with paresis, the advanced state of syphilis in brain tissue, was controlled and virtually eliminated with antibiotics following World War II. The dementia associated with HIV-related infections in the brain appears to be the result of deterioration from toxic *macrophages* borne by the blood to the brain.[52] Conversely, doctors also know that symptoms of illness have causes "in the psyche or in the patient's social, vocational, marital, or even political environment," rather than in the physical body.[53] The role of social definitions is considered minimal within this model. The individual's symptoms are regarded nearly as invariable and inevitable as those of someone suffering from whooping cough or athlete's foot. Although some observers may or may not recognize the symptoms, or may pretend not to recognize them, the disease is not significantly affected by the social reaction to the sufferer. In short, the individual experiencing mental disorder is seen as acting within a social vacuum. The medical model can be illustrated by the following axioms that underlie the psychiatric conception of schizophrenics:

1. Schizophrenics differ fundamentally from the rest of humanity; their experiences—the images, delusions, and logic—are so unreal that others never encounter them except possibly in dreams. Schizophrenics are nearly inhuman, alien creatures.
2. The schizophrenic disease process progressively strips individuals of all social learning so they eventually have little left of what could be called "civilized characteristics."
3. Schizophrenics have no control over their illness. They are weak and ineffective. Consequently, they do not *make* things happen; things happen *to* them.[54] Thus the medical model, by focusing on the individual, portrays the source of mental disorder as almost exclusively *within* the individual; her or his behavior is independent of social judgment or influence, as is any physiological disease.

In contrast to the medical model of mental disorder is the *labeling model.* Advocates of the labeling model do not totally reject research findings based on the medical model, but they do disagree with the medical model's assumptions about the nature of mental disorder. The dispute centers on the *role of social reaction* toward people who behave in ways considered to be disagreeable.

As we have mentioned, those of the medical persuasion minimize the importance of social reaction. They may allow that social reactions can aggravate behavioral difficulties, but they believe that the principal source of the difficulties is a clearly definable phenomenon whose symptoms can become progressively severe and finally require professional assistance. Purists of the labeling persuasion claim that mental disorder is not a disease at all, but a form of rule-breaking.

Mental Disease as a Myth

One of the forerunners of the labeling approach to mental disorder was not a sociologist but a psychiatrist, Thomas S. Szasz. Szasz has directly attacked the fundamental core of the medical model by asserting that mental disease does not exist—it is a myth, he argues. The assumption that disorders are evidence of disease stems from the early association of brain damage with certain problems of behavior (e.g., syphilis leading to paresis). Anxiety, depression, conflict, and other such problems do indeed exist and are common in the human condition, but they are not diseases in the pathological sense. Thus the medical profession established itself as having expertise in the area not only of physical symptoms and their physical causes but also of *behavior,* regardless of whether the behavior was related to physical causes. Szasz asserts that it is an error to conceptualize an individual's beliefs or ideas in the same way as one would characterize a physical defect. The appropriateness of particular beliefs or ideas is instead a matter of judgment and communication.[55]

To say, for example, that chronic hostility is a sign of mental disorder merely reflects a judgment that people should be kind and sweet to each other. How often have you heard, "Anyone who commits suicide must be mentally ill"? This simply indicates that the speaker disapproves of suicide and cannot understand those who would disagree—unless they are crazy, of course. According to Szasz, judgments about similar *normative* matters have been entrusted to the psychiatric profession in the mistaken belief that psychiatry is value-free because it "treats disease."[56]

If what we have been calling *mental disorders* are not illnesses, then what are they? According to Szasz, they are "problems of living": problems of expressing unacceptable ideas and behaving in unacceptable ways—unacceptable, that is, to those who must interact with the individuals, and perhaps unacceptable even to the individuals themselves. They boil down to "moral conflicts in human relations" that cannot be cured by disposing of an individual malady. Szasz contends that medical terminology obscures the true nature of mental disorder and places psychiatrists in the role of social control agents. He maintains that the very practice of psychiatry is dependent on being able to label someone as mentally ill.[57] Michael S. Goldstein interprets Szasz's work as follows:

> [Szasz] argues that the use of a medical or psychiatric vocabulary mystifies and often explicitly denies that [psychiatry functions as a social control mechanism]. . . . The mystification becomes critically important as psychiatrists (and other psychotherapists) are increasingly employed by third parties such as the armed forces, universities or business organizations, as well as increasingly apt to claim that they work for individual clients while being paid directly or indirectly by a third party such as an insurance company or the government. Szasz feels these psychotherapists must inevitably defer to needs and values of their employers while overtly maintaining that they are the agents of the patient. . . . Because a true contract between patient and doctor does not exist, their relationship becomes biased. "As a result, bureaucratic, as contrasted with entrepreneurial, medical care ceases to be a system of curing disease and becomes instead a system of controlling deviance." Thus Szasz sees a collectivistic social control function substituted for an individualistic healing relationship.[58]

Szasz alludes to collaboration between the pychiatric community and government in the formation of a "therapeutic state," which serves to control inappropriate behavior.[59] Medical controls replace traditional checks such as family, church, and the legal system.[60] He believes that the practice of regarding behavior such as illegal drug use, promiscuity, gambling, racial bigotry, smoking, and shoplifting as forms of disease or symptoms of disease is wrong and discourages individual responsibility. The eventual result could be more invasive government control in the form of "coercive paternalism."[61]

A Labeling Theory of Mental Disorder

Just because I'm paranoid doesn't mean that I'm not being followed.
—Anonymous

The reader may recall from our discussion of the labeling perspective in Chapter 3 that the proponents of the perspective attach little significance to the original causes of deviant behavior, particularly if the behavior is tolerated and can be incorporated into an otherwise nondeviant image. Such behavior is termed *primary deviance* or *rule-breaking;* it might stem from any one of a variety of causes, social or emotional.

Of principal concern to the labeling theorists are the reactions of others toward persons whose behavior is defined as deviant. This reaction is important because it can reinforce the deviant behavior by isolating the individual from the nondeviant world, and it can impress upon the individual that he or she is the kind of person who becomes involved in such behavior. In short, acquiring a deviant status can set off a career sequence in which the individual ends up in *secondary deviance*—deviant behavior that is a means of defense, attack, or adjustment to the problems caused by social reaction.

The application of this perspective to mental disorder produces quite a different framework from that of the medical model. The emphasis shifts from the deviant actors and the initial causes of their behaviors to the issues of how certain behaviors come to be regarded as evidence of disorder and of how the reactions to the behaviors can lock the actors into careers of mental disorder.

A theory of mental disorder based on the labeling perspective has been proposed by Thomas J. Scheff. Scheff states his theory in propositional form, and we shall enumerate the propositions shortly. Before we do, however, two points should be emphasized. First, the reader should not be misled by Scheff's occasional use of the term *mental disease.* Scheff agrees with Szasz that mental disease is a myth, and he uses the term for the sake of convenience only. Second, the term *residual rule-breaking* requires some explanation.

In Chapter 3 we described how Howard Becker makes a distinction between *rule-breaking* and *deviance,* with rule-breaking being the violations on norms and deviance being those behaviors against which there is a social reaction. People "break" rules all the time—they lie, steal, clean their ears in public—but a wide range of behavior is tolerated, and, according to the labeling perspective, true deviance depends not only on rules but also on the reaction to their violation. Indeed, it is even possible that some individuals will be treated as deviants even though they have broken no rules.

Within a cultural group, rule-breaking behavior is variously classified according to the kinds of rules broken: crime, bad manners, and so on. But some rule-breaking behaviors do not fit nicely into established categories; they are *residual* behaviors because they defy classification into the normal types of rule-breaking. Consider, for example, someone who is distracted all the time and does not seem to be listening when you speak to him or someone who gets upset easily and seems always to be on the verge of flying off the handle. These behaviors are not consistent with what we think of as appropriate conduct. But what rules have been broken? It is from this residual category, according to Scheff, that what is called *mental disorder* is drawn. The violations seem so unusual, weird, or inexplicable that they are seen as evidence of a mental problem.[62] Scheff's first proposition concerns the origins of residual rule-breaking:

1. Residual rule-breaking arises from fundamentally diverse sources. There are many reasons why persons might hear, see, or otherwise experience things that others cannot. These reasons might include things such as the genetic, family, and stress factors we discussed in connection with the medical model. Others suggested by Scheff include psychoactive drug use, starvation, fatigue, and deliberate attempts to rebel against the conventional. He cites as an example of the latter the French Impressionist painters, whose colors were seen by some contemporary critics as evidence of madness.

2. Relative to the rate of treated mental illness, the rate of unrecorded residual rule-breaking is extremely high. This simply means that many people do or imagine culturally inappropriate things, but their behavior goes unrecognized, is ignored, or is rationalized as being eccentric. *Denial* is the term used in the mental disorder literature for this pattern of inattention to or rationalization of unusual behavior among others.[63]

3. Most residual rule-breaking is "denied" and is of transitory significance. In total, this proposition claims that most examples of what could be regarded as madness are acts of primary deviance, but that observers attach no particular significance to the behaviors. The proposition has two parts, however. The first recognizes the general reluctance of people to shift their judgment of someone they know from "well" to "sick." One can easily get the impression that presumed symptoms of mental disorder will always be readily recognized as such. Instead, most people make extraordinary efforts to interpret unusual behavior on the part of others as normal. One study of women whose husbands were diagnosed as mentally disordered found these examples:

> [Some] wives describe their husbands as spoiled, lacking will-power, exaggerating little complaints and acting like babies. This is especially marked where alcoholism complicates the husband's symptomatology. For example, Mrs. Y., whose husband was chronically alcoholic, aggressive and threatening to her, "raving," and who "chewed his nails until they almost bled," interprets his difficulty thus: "He was just spoiled rotten. He never outgrew it. He told me when he was a child he could get his own way if he insisted, and he is still that way." . . .
>
> Many recall their early reactions to their husbands' behavior as full of puzzling confusion and uncertainty. Something is wrong, they know, but, in general, they stop short of a firm explanation. Thus Mrs. M. reports, "He was kind of worried. He was kind of worried before, not exactly worried." . . . She thought of his many physical complaints; she "racked" her "brain" and told her husband, "Of course, he didn't feel good." Finally, he stayed home from work with "no special complaints, just blah," and she "began to realize it was more deeply seated."[64]

In practice, many do not recognize the symptoms of mental disorder in people they know until a third party—an employer or a physician, for example—redefines the situation by suggesting illness as an explanation.

The second part of Scheff's proposition—that most residual rule-breaking is "of transitory significance"—is important because it claims that although persons may exhibit symptoms of mental disorder, it does not necessarily follow that they will develop the full-blown, incapacitating characteristics associated with psychoses. But what about the small proportion of residual rule-breakers who are persistent? This is the question that the remaining propositions attempt to answer.

4. Stereotyped imagery of mental disorder is learned in early childhood. Evidence is meager on this point, but the impression is that children soon grasp what kinds of behavior are associated with terms like *crazy, nuts,* and *not all there.* Once learned, these stereotypes of the mentally disordered are reinforced throughout life.

5. The stereotypes of insanity are continually reaffirmed, inadvertently, in ordinary social interaction. Has anyone ever said to you, "I am crazy about you"? This seems flattering, of course, but the speaker is also implying that he or she has lost his or her reason. As George Bernard Shaw wrote about marriage,

> when two people are under the influence of the most violent, most insane, most delusive, and most transient of passions, they are required to swear that they will remain in that excited, abnormal, and exhausting condition continuously until death do them part.[65]

When people do things we find very difficult to explain, we frequently diagnose them as "crazy." We constantly use terms referring to mental disorder in everyday situations: in advertising (on the east coast, one "Crazy Eddie" advertised his "record and tape asylums"—"His prices are insane!"); in humor (Asylum inmate: "What are you going to do with that manure?" Farmer: "Put it on my strawberries." Inmate: "I put cream and sugar on mine, and they got me in here!"); and in ordinary conversation ("They get along fine; she is just as weird as he is.").

But the stereotypes are not always so innocuous. The mass media often use the notion of mental disorder as an explanation of disapproved conduct. How often have you seen headlines similar to "Police in Shootout with Ex-Mental Patient"? This only serves to reinforce the conception that once a person is found to be mentally disordered, you can never trust them again.[66] The common acceptance of this stereotype was clearly demonstrated during the 1972 election campaign, when a vice-presidential candidate was forced to resign his nomination after it was revealed that he had once been a psychiatric patient. No assurances about his present state of mind could alter the fact that he was seen as unpredictable and untrustworthy.

Thus, while most residual rule-breaking is denied, it is also widely known how the mentally disordered are "supposed" to act. According to Scheff, the individual begins to stabilize his or her career of residual rule-breaking once observers decide to deny the behavior no longer:

> In a crisis, when the deviance of an individual becomes a public issue, the traditional stereotype of insanity becomes the guiding imagery for action, both for those reacting to the deviant, and at times, for the deviant himself. When social agents and persons around the deviant react to him uniformly in terms of the traditional stereotypes of insanity, his amorphous and unstructured rule-breaking tends to crystallize in conformity to these expectations, thus becoming similar to the behavior of other deviants classified as mentally ill, and stable over time.[67]

6. Labeled deviants may be rewarded for playing the stereotyped deviant role. Once a person is labeled as *ill,* there are pressures to accept that as fact. For example, the person who voluntarily enters a mental hospital will be complimented for "doing the right thing."

7. Labeled deviants are punished when they attempt to return to conventional roles. Once a person is labeled, it is difficult to revert back to a "normal" status. People may refuse to allow the individual to resume former responsibilities. Would you want an "ex-mental patient" to marry your sister, babysit your children, or shave the back of your neck?

8. In the crisis that occurs when a residual rule-breaker is publicly labeled, the deviant is highly suggestible and may accept the proffered role of the insane as the only alternative. It is easy to imagine the confusion, anxiety, and shame you would feel if your family wanted you committed to a mental institution. Should you fight it because family members don't understand you or may using mental disorder as a ploy to achieve their own selfish ends? Or is there *really* something wrong with you?

9. Among residual rule-breakers, labeling is the single most important cause of careers of residual deviance. This final proposition clearly separates Scheff's theory from the medical model of mental disorder. It is not the *disease* that distinguishes the mentally disordered from others—it is the *reaction* that closes off other behavioral alternatives and thus forces the individual into the role of the mentally ill.

As you have probably guessed, Scheff's theory has generated considerable controversy and several attempts to test its validity empirically. No doubt the ultimate explanation of mental disorder—if there is one—lies somewhere between the extremes of the medical and the labeling models. In the meantime, the principal point of contention is the relative importance of the *causes of behavior* versus the *reactions* that tend to stabilize the behavior. In short, is labeling the single most important factor behind a career of mental disorder, as Scheff claims?

One unique study often cited in support of the labeling approach was conducted by D. L. Rosenhan. He titled it, "On Being Sane in Insane Places." Eight subjects gained admission to twelve mental hospitals by claiming that they had been "hearing voices." After admission to each hospital—which proved to be remarkably easy—the pseudopatients behaved "normally." Although several of the real patients in the wards had their suspicions, none of the staff did:

> Despite their public "show" of sanity, the pseudopatients were never detected. Admitted, except in one case, with a diagnosis of schizophrenia, each was discharged with a diagnosis of schizophrenia "in remission." The label "in remission" should in no way be dismissed as a formality, for at no time during any hospitalization had any question been raised about any pseudopatient's simulation. Nor are there any records that the pseudopatient's status was suspect. Rather, the evidence is strong that, once labeled schizophrenic, the pseudopatient was stuck with that label. If the pseudopatient was to be discharged, he must naturally be "in remission"; but he was not sane, nor, in the institution's view, had he ever been sane. . . .
>
> Beyond the tendency to call the healthy sick—the tendency that accounts better for diagnostic behavior on admission than it does for such behavior after a lengthy period of exposure—the data speak to the massive role of labeling in psychiatric assessment. Having once been labeled schizophrenic, there is nothing the pseudopatient can do to overcome the tag.[68]

Criticisms and Contributions of Labeling Theory

One study rarely proves a theory in social research. Instead, a theory is usually supported or eventually rejected by the combined results of several works that, in a piecemeal fashion, examine different implications of the theory. Few theories of deviant behavior have generated as much research as has Scheff's labeling approach to mental disorder. And while it is premature to say that his theory has been proven or disproven, it is fair to say that, so far, the preponderance of evidence does not favor Scheff's theory.

The major critic of Scheff and the principal chronicler of the research that tests the labeling approach to mental disorder is Walter R. Gove. Gove concedes that labeling theory alerts us to some important processes by which people are designated as disordered and by which social reactions may affect one's career as a mental patient. But he regards these processes as less important today than when the labeling approach was formulated in the 1950s. In short, he argues that reactions toward the mentally disordered have changed and that Scheff's theory is out-of-date. What has happened?

1. Changes in treatment policies. It appears that 1955 was the high-water mark for chronically ill populations in state mental institutions. That year and the period leading up to it can be characterized as a time when the hospitals were dumping grounds for people whose behavior was no longer tolerated by their families or by authorities. Once committed, patients were expected to remain for a long time; the more seriously disordered ones were sedated or otherwise restrained, placed on "back wards," and ignored until they died.

Since 1955, however, the resident population of mental institutions has declined. Rather than retaining patients, hospitals are releasing them much sooner than previously. As one author puts it, a "psychiatric revolution" has occurred.[69] The revolution comprised two major developments. The first was the introduction of a new breed of *drugs* that controlled the symptoms of mental disorder without disabling the patients in other ways. For example, lithium arrests the mood swings found in bipolar disorders (previously called manic-depressive behavior); various antipsychotic medications dispel disordered thoughts and violent episodes associated with some forms of schizophrenia; and several types of tranquilizers decrease anxiety and depression.

The second component of the psychiatric revolution was the increased reliance on shorter-term treatments in general hospitals, community mental health centers, and Veterans Administration hospitals to replace long-term inpatient care in state institutions for the mentally disordered. Regardless of the treatment setting, the average length of hospitalization declined considerably after 1955, and the practice of long-term institutionalization has been replaced by a trend toward *deinstitutionalization.* According to Gove,

> given the changes in the setting and the brevity of treatment, it is difficult to imagine that most mental patients are in the formal role of the mental patient for a long enough period of time to be socialized into the role of the chronically ill in the manner suggested by the labeling theorists.[70]

2. Increased legal rights for patients. One of the horror stories during the 1960s was the ease by which individuals could be labeled "disordered" and committed against their will to a mental institution. The philosophy seemed to be that if someone wanted someone else put away, there must be a good reason for it. For example, the following situation existed in New York until 1973:

> The standard civil commitment procedure . . . does not require or authorize a judicial hearing prior to commitment. Commitment for 60 days is generally based on the certificate of two physicians, who do not have to be psychiatrists. And *emergency* commitment for 30 days can be based on nothing more substantial than the unsworn and perhaps fraudulent allegation of a layman, unsupported and unconfirmed by any doctor, and unexamined, either prior or subsequent to commitment, by any court. . . .
> The emergency, or 30-day, patient has very few rights. If he requests release, he can be held for 10 days and then administratively converted from emergency to non-emergency status and held for an additional 60 days. Only after he has been converted does he have the right

to request judicial review, and that review, when it comes, will be limited to the need for his *retention.* It will not examine the legality or propriety of his emergency commitment.[71]

In the early 1970s a series of court cases specified that nondangerous individuals cannot be involuntarily committed if they are capable of safely surviving by themselves or with the help of willing friends or relatives. In conjunction with these decisions, states passed laws that severely restricted the conditions under which civil commitments may occur. In all states, prospective patients have a right to a lawyer. For a civil commitment to occur in some states the individuals must be severely mentally ill and a danger to self or others; in other states the persons may be committed if they are gravely disabled and/or dangerous; and in a few states, persons may be committed if they pose a serious threat to property and/or are dangerous.[72]

As a consequence of more stringent civil commitment legislation, the number of involuntary commitments to mental institutions has decreased considerably since the early 1970s. Thus the "residual deviant" is not so readily exposed to official labeling as in the past.

3. Changes in attitudes toward the mentally disordered. One of the assumptions of labeling theory is that to be labeled "mentally ill" is to be stereotyped in a derogatory way and, as a result, stigmatized and isolated from conventional social interaction. Gove concedes that such stereotyping probably was common in the 1950s when people didn't talk about their mental health and attributes it to public ignorance. Today, however, public education efforts, the transitory nature of most disorders, and more effective treatment have moderated negative public attitudes about the disordered and consequently diminished their isolation. In addition, outstanding individuals such as former First Lady Barbara Bush, football great Terry Bradshaw, and Olympic gold medalist Ian Crocker have openly discussed their battles with depression, and TV anchorwoman Jane Pauley has talked publicly about her bipolar disorder. These and others have helped to put a human face on mental disorders. According to Gove, research now shows that

a. While being labeled mentally ill *may* be stigmatizing and produce an exclusionary reaction, being labeled an ex-mental patient does not.

b. Persons who have had experience in dealing with the mentally ill are less rejecting than persons without such experience.

c. Family members tend not to be particularly rejecting of the mentally ill because close ties override the stigma and enable one to see positive qualities in the individual.

d. In general, families experience little fear, shame, anger or guilt regarding a family member who is mentally ill. . . .

e. [Despite their expressed prejudice] against the mentally ill, the evidence suggests that employers do not discriminate against ex-mental patients in their hiring practices.

f. [Evidence indicates] that a substantial majority of hospitalized mental patients have favorable attitudes toward the mental hospital and their treatment.[73]

4. Development of the belief that the mentally ill are intrinsically different. Finally, labeling theorists contend that the primary difference between the "ill" and the normal is the result of social reaction. Not so, argues Gove. He feels that the evidence of a genetic link in schizophrenia and the relationship between lower-class stress and disorder clearly indicate that the mentally disordered are intrinsically different from individuals who are not so labeled. Their behavior leads to labeling, not the other way around.

In sum, then, Gove is convinced that while labeling theory sensitizes us to some possible consequences of social reaction, the theory has outlived its usefulness. Current evidence goes overwhelmingly against it both as an explanation of *who* is labeled mentally disordered and as an explanation of *why* the disordered behavior emerges or persists.[74]

Conflict and the Therapeutic State

Any political state develops means by which it deals with persons who, for one reason or another, are regarded as troublesome. The most obvious means is the criminal justice system with its laws, enforcement agencies, courts, and places of confinement for those defined as "criminal." Being convicted of a crime is not the only way one can lose freedom, however. One can also be diagnosed as "mentally ill" and thereby qualified for *involuntary commitment*. The state's ability to confine individuals to mental institutions without their permission is crucial to the operation of the *therapeutic state*.[75] This term refers to an ideology that "treatment," not punishment, should be society's response to its disruptive or dangerous members. This ideology applies not only to persons who are or might become engaged in criminal behavior, but also to all sorts of suffering, disorganized, or "sick" individuals whose ailments prevent them from leading happy, productive lives. Furthermore, these individuals should be treated whether they want to be or not.

It is tempting to applaud the benevolent goal of the therapeutic state. Who could possibly argue against the elimination of conflict and unhappiness? But apparent humanitarianism becomes suspect once you examine the assumptions and consequences of the therapeutic state. If a treatment is proposed for dealing with a condition, the assumption is that objective means exist for diagnosing and predicting outcomes for both the treated and the untreated condition. We have already seen, however, that the diagnosis of mental conditions is a normative decision; it is anything but an exact science. As for treatment, it is obviously difficult to treat that which is not consistently recognized as a condition to be treated. An indication of how slippery diagnosis of mental conditions can be is evident from a study of changing psychiatric diagnoses over twenty years. Jeffery D. Blum found that similar behaviors were diagnosed differently depending upon the time and place. He concludes that

> the central finding of the current research project is quite simple: that the interpretation of similar symptomatology may differ over time. Just as British psychiatrists find manic-depressive illness where Americans find schizophrenia, so 1970s clinicians seem to diagnose affective disorders where 1950s clinicians found anxiety neurosis. In brief, *diagnosis is relative to the historical era in which the diagnosticians perform their task.*[76]

If diagnoses vary from place to place and over time, it is not surprising to find that they vary with the political climate. The best contemporary example of politics in the therapeutic state is the former Soviet Union, where nearly all political dissidents underwent psychiatric examinations. Most were diagnosed as having a "psychopathic personality with paranoid tendencies, paranoid development, sluggish schizophrenia." Their symptoms were their "reformist ideas, bizarre behavior, emotional flatness, emotional inadequacy, inappropriate reaction to situations, tendency to moralize, conviction of [their] own rightness, and uncritical attitude towards the situation." Leonid Plyushch, a Soviet mathematician who was arrested for writing letters on behalf of two dissident writers, was diagnosed as suffering from "sluggish schizophrenia." The psychiatrists informed him, "Your abnormality is shown by the way you have always, from an early age, been concerned with things that were none of your business."[77]

That was Soviet Russia, of course. Could it happen here? Strange things have happened here because of the combination of psychiatric power and incompetence:

> In 1962 Leonard Frank disturbed his parents because of his new-found religious and political views, which included vegetarianism and a refusal to cut his hair or beard. Frank was forcibly committed to a mental hospital, labeled "paranoid schizophrenic," and subjected to insulin coma and electroconvulsive therapies. He was released with his memory of the previous two years wiped out and with only partial recall of his earlier life. Not surprisingly, he is now active in an organization fighting the "disease model" of mental illness which forces therapy on persons who are not regarded as dangerous.[78]

> In 1964, at age 15, Edmund Kemper murdered two of his grandparents. From 1964 to 1969 he was committed to an institution for the criminally insane and then released as "cured." In 1972 he initiated proceedings to have his criminal records sealed, a process which would involve his being examined by psychiatrists. In the meantime he murdered and dismembered two teenaged girls. Three days later court-appointed psychiatrists declared him no longer a danger to society. He then killed two more girls. In 1973 he killed three more girls and his mother. (Afterwards he called the police; at least *he* knew he was dangerous.) Later, several psychiatrists admitted they had no way of predicting Kemper's behavior. One said, "Most of this work is a matter of an educated guess, plain common sense."[79]

Common Mental Disorders

As we mentioned at the beginning of the chapter, mental disorders are not uncommon. They range in severity from transient unpleasantness to debilitating illness. In this section, we will discuss two of the most common mental disorders, depression and phobias.

Depression

Depression has been called the "common cold of mental illnesses." Things in our physical environment cause physical illnesses such as colds, and things in our social and emotional environment can lead to mental illnesses such as depression. Physical illnesses also have a social-psychological component. Research indicates that we are more susceptible to physical illnesses such as colds, for example, when we are under psychological stress[80] and we all know that when we have colds, we are not our usual cheery selves. Similarly, mental disorders such as depression can have genetic and physiological components. Although . . . "there is no sound biochemical theory of depression at the present time,"[81] research indicates that brain chemicals such as serotonin probably play an important role. Support for this assertion is provided by the widespread use and success of antidepressants such as the selective serotonin reuptake inhibitors (SSRIs) in combating this disorder.[82]

Depression is a mood disorder. It can range from "the blues" to a life-threatening Major Depressive Disorder with multiple, severe, long-lasting symptoms. The *Encyclopedia of Mental Health* and National Institutes of Health publications note that the term is used in a variety of ways. For example, it may be used to describe: (1) the normal feelings of temporary sadness we all have from time to time; (2) a pervasive, overriding feeling of gloom that can last a few hours up to a few days; (3) a long-term depressive illness called "dysthymia," that does not disable, but keeps the suffer from living up to potential and enjoying life; or (4) a major depression, a combination of severe symptoms that not only interferes with one's ability to live and enjoy life, but is also disabling.[83]

Risk factors for depression include stressful life events, lack of social support, family history of depression, medical problems, alcohol or substance abuse problems, and having had a depressive disorder in the past. Women are at higher risk in the postpartum period following childbirth.[84] Warning signs vary from culture to culture and from age group to age group. Common symptoms include persistent sadness, lack of interest or pleasure in activities usually considered interesting and pleasurable, loss of energy, persistent fatigue, loss of self-esteem or feelings of unwarranted guilt, and difficulty thinking, focusing, and making decisions. Symptoms can also include significant increases or decrease in appetite, weight, and time spent sleeping. They can include recurring thoughts of death or suicide.[85] When these symptoms persist over several weeks, and when symptoms are severe enough to cause problems with work and social relations, it is an indication of clinical depression.

The good news about depression is that this disorder is highly treatable and perhaps as many as 80 to 90 percent of people seeking help can be treated successfully.[86] There is a wide variety of treatment options available ranging from medication to self-help groups, counseling, and psychotherapy. There is also a wide range of help groups eager to provide information and support. These include Depression/Awareness, Recognition, Treatment (D/ART) of the National Institute of Mental Health; National Alliance for the Mentally Ill (NAMI), and the National Depressive and Manic Depressive Association. Confidential assistance may also be accessed at http://www.mentalhealth.com.

The bad news is that nearly two-thirds of the people who could benefit from treatment continue to suffer. Some still fear being labeled as mentally ill, others are misdiagnosed, still others just try to "tough it out." This is unfortunate because it may be more difficult to "just snap out of" a major depression than it is to cure oneself of pneumonia. For the do-it-yourselfer with mild to moderate depression determined to try to begin to fight it him or herself, however, there are books such as Copeland and Copans *Recovering from Depression: A Workbook for Teens.* Emphasizing that taking back one's life from depression is a process rather than a "quick fix," the authors offer a variety of "wellness tools." These include a list of depression warning signs such as weepiness, grumpiness, and negativity. They also include tips for recognizing triggers of depression such as conflict, rejection, loss, and even major reminders of past losses. Wellness and stress-reduction strategies that are suggested include improving diet, sleep, and exercise; "developing dreams and goals"; involving oneself in pleasurable activities; and developing a support network of friends and trained peer counselors. The authors also provide information on managing suicidal thoughts and making suicide safety plans; finding a mental healthcare provider; and, if necessary, getting the appropriate medication.[87]

Phobias

When one of your authors was on a speaking trip to Australia, her hosts treated her to a beautiful room with floor-to-ceiling windows on the forty-second floor of a new hotel. While she insists she is not phobic, she never got within five feet of the windows. She also made a lot of new friends waiting by the elevator until she could find someone to go up or down with her chatting to keep her mind off the ride.

According to the National Institute of Mental Health, phobias are the most common form of mental illness. Somewhere between 5 percent and one-fifth of Americans suffer these disorders. *Phobia* comes from the Greek word for *fear,* and phobias are irrational fears that cause those who have them (phobic individuals) to feel anxious, change their behavior, experience severe anxiety, and even suffer panic attacks. Some studies have even found higher rates of coronary heart disease related to deaths among women with high scores on phobic anxiety tests.[88] Most people with phobias are aware that their fears are irrational. They are aware, for example, that more people are killed in helicopter accidents than in elevator accidents and that the fact that they love helicopters and hate elevators makes no sense. Nevertheless, they may suffer intense anxiety when even thinking about something they know poses little real danger.

The source of phobias is not fully understood.[89] In many cases the fear has some possible justification: Aviophobics read about people being killed in airplane crashes, arachnophobics know that people have been bitten by spiders, claustrophobics are aware that people have suffocated in confined spaces. The source of our phobias may be biochemical, but people appear to be more likely to develop them if they are anxious and under a great deal of stress. The source may be genetic.[90] However, even though phobias tend to run in families, it is still unclear whether the cause is inherited characteristics, learned behavior or both.[91] Natalie Schor and Jerilyn Ross, in separate research, propose similar explanations of how phobias take hold of us. Schor states that, "People tend to be in a susceptible state before they become phobic."[92] This may be caused by life stresses or changes or by something as specific as a panic attack. (This may have a biological basis.) Ross theorizes that while in this susceptible state, something interesting occurs. "Like a chick that imprints . . . upon the first thing it sees, following a human . . . it believes to be its mother, those biologically predisposed to phobias become instantly sensitized to the environment—or some aspect thereof—in which their terror first occurs." Rather than deal with an uncontrollable situation, they attempt to alleviate their anxiety by making "an almost magical agreement with themselves . . . , 'If I don't go into the subway, I'm not going to feel the panic again.' "[93] This possible explanation seems to help explain all types of phobias. Phobias are classified into three major types: (1) specific phobias, (2) social phobia, and (3) agoraphobia.

Specific Phobias.   A person can develop an irrational fear of almost anything. Phobias are designated by a Greek (or Latin) word for the focus of the fear and adding "phobia." The Greek word for *water,* for example, is *hydro,* so an irrational fear of water is *hydrophobia. The Encyclopedia of Phobias, Fears, and Anxieties* contains over 2,000 entries.[94] Time has published an online list of *Phobias from A to Z,* compiled by Don Powell of the American Institute for Preventive Medicine. This list contains approximately 350 of the most common and interesting.[95] These include:

- Claustrophobia. 24 percent of women and 17 percent of men admit to experiencing some degree of discomfort when "closed in" or crowded.
- Ophidiophobia. Women are more likely to fear snakes than anything else.
- Dentophobia. 48 percent of people fear dentists.
- Glossophobia. Speaking in public ranks very high for both men and women.
- Acrophobia. Fear of heights is another top-ranking phobia.[96]

Interesting, though less common, phobias include: Achluophobia, fear of darkness; ailurophobia, fear of cats; androphobia, fear of men; aviophobia, fear of flying; caligynephobia, fear of beautiful women; diaskaleinophobia, fear of school; enochlophobia, fear of crowds; gamophobia, fear of marriage; necrophobia, fear of death; philophobia, fear of falling in love; testaphobia, fear of taking tests; and zoophobia, fear of animals.[97]

In one survey, more people reported fear of the Internal Revenue Service (57%) than fear of God (30%). Zeusophobia, or fear of God, is a phobia, but fear of the IRS and some other things commonly referred to as phobias are not usually considered clinical phobias. Homophobia (fear of homosexuals) and xenophobia (fear of strangers or the unknown), for example, are more likely to be symptoms of ignorance, hatred, narrow-mindedness, or prejudice than of an anxiety disorder. Hydrophobia is more likely to be a symptom of the disease rabies than an actual anxiety disorder relating to fear of water.[98]

Social Phobias. The National Institute of Mental Health and the Surgeon General estimate that between 4 and 7 percent of Americans suffer from a social phobia.[99] This phobia is characterized by overwhelming anxiety, excessive self-consciousness, worry about saying or doing something embarrassing, and a fear of making a mistake and of being judged, evaluated, and humiliated in public. Social phobias may be associated with depression or any of the other types of phobias. They make social interaction stressful and make it difficult for individuals to do such things as join groups and make friends. These phobias can produce physical affects ranging from blushing, trembling, and sweating to stomach upsets and even full-scale panic attacks. People with social phobias tend to avoid social events, find meetings stressful, and even dread meeting new people. Social phobias may occur twice as often in women as in men, but perhaps because of the negative affect this form of mental disorder can have on job performance, a higher proportion of men seek help.[100]

Agoraphobia. Agoraphobia has been called "the fear of fear itself."[101] More specifically, it is a fear of leaving one's safe, familiar surroundings and being alone in a public space— even a space filled with people—from which one might not be able to escape. It is not the space itself that is most threatening, but the potential for new social interactions that may not be avoided and have the potential to cause panic attacks. In severe cases, the agoraphobic increasingly avoids the places in which he or she is likely to feel fearful. His or her "safe space" becomes smaller and smaller until he or she is unable to leave the house and becomes dependent upon family members.[102] Agoraphobia is closely related to depression and other phobias and has the capacity to destroy lives. It is not uncommon for agoraphobics to confine themselves to their homes, obsess about their health, abuse alcohol, or become suicidal.[103]

Treatment

Most people with minor phobias avoid situations that trigger their anxiety or just "tough it out." When dealing with everyday anxieties, it is helpful to identify the source of the anxiety, address, it, and try to refocus. Rather than thinking about your fear or your anxiety and allowing it to consume your attention, exercise or concentrate on some concrete task (some suggest counting backwards by threes).[104] Learn how to manage stress. It may also be helpful to build up your general resistance by taking care of yourself and avoiding caffeine, nicotine, alcohol, and unprescribed drugs. Talking to a friend and finding a support group might also be helpful. However, when a phobia begins to demand too much attention or threatens to take over a significant portion of your life, or when it interferes with normal concerns such as family activities and your job, be aware that help is available.[105]

Specific phobias are more responsive to therapy than any other anxiety disorder and treatment for phobias, in general, is more likely to be successful than any other type of psychotherapy. Many recommend a combination of talk therapy, behavioral therapy, and possibly anti-anxiety medication as well.[106] The goal of this therapy is to change the way people think and react to the thing that makes them anxious. The goal of some new drug treatments is to accelerate the process.[107] In yet another type of treatment, the problem is addressed through a process of desensitization. By gradually increasing exposure to the source of the anxiety, the therapist helps the phobic to overcome his or her fears. People who fear flying, for example, discuss flying, visit an airport, go aboard an airplane, and eventually take a flight. A new form of this therapy is a videogame-type virtual desensitization in which people who are afraid to fly, for example, are guided through their fear in a controlled virtual reality environment. They may be gradually desensitized without ever actually leaving the ground. Of course, they still have to take that first flight.

The most important thing to remember about mental disorders is that we now know more about them than ever before. We also have more resources for dealing with them than ever before. Most people no longer have to suffer alone and in silence.

CRITICAL THINKING EXERCISES

1. Describe the difference between mental illness and mental disorder.

2. Read the list of mental disorders in the DSM-IV. Think of a person you know, other than your instructors, who might fit in each category.

3. Describe the differences between psychotic and psychopathic disorders. If you worked in a mental health institution, which type would be harder to predict? Which type would be harder to control?

4. Discuss the term *therapeutic state.* Do you believe that the United States will eventually become one? Why or why not?

5. Phobias and depression can both be debilitating. Discuss how this occurs and what can be done to prevent it.

CHECK IT OUT ON THE WEB

The Internet addresses listed below are intended to provide the reader with understanding of a wide range of perspectives on the subject matter discussed in this chapter. Some sites may contain objectionable material. The list is not intended to reflect the viewpoints or opinions of the authors or the publisher.

http://bmei.org
    medical ethics
http://www.surgeongeneral.gov
    government reports on mental health in the United States
http://www.nami.org
    Nation's Voice on Mental Illness

ENDNOTES

1. Staff Writer, "Surgeon General Cites Pervasive, Untreated Mental Disorders," *Clinician Reviews, 10* (March 2003), p. 953; David Satcher, "Mental Health Gets Noticed," *Psychology Today* (January 2000), pp. 32–37.

2. Presidential Task Force on People with Disabilities, *The President's New Freedom Initiative for People with Disabilities: The 2004 Progress Report* (Washington DC: U.S. Government Printing Office, 2004); Department of Health and Human Services press release, "Scientific Revolution in Mental Health Research and Services Declared in First Surgeon General's Report on Mental Health," pp. 1–3; Staff Writer, "Surgeon General Cites Pervasive, Untreated Mental Disorders," *Clinician Reviews, 10* (February 2002), p. 30.

3. Lincoln Caplan, "The Post-Dahmer Insanity Defense, Not So Nutty," *The New Republic,* March 30, 1992, pp. 18–20.

4. This is the test proposed by the American Law Institute's *Model Penal Code,* as cited in Herbert Fingarette, *The Meaning of Criminal Insanity* (Berkeley: University of California Press, 1972), p. 13; see also Norval Morris, *Crime Study Guide: Insanity Defense,* National Institute of Justice, U.S. Department of Justice (Washington, DC: U.S. Government Printing Office, 1986), p. 3; and U.S. Department of Justice, Bureau of Justice Statistics *Report to the Nation on Crime and Justice,* 2nd ed. (Washington, DC: U.S. Government Printing Office, 1988), p. 87.

5. *People* v. *Ramsey,* 375 N. W. 2d 297 (Mich. 1985).

6. Monica Preboth, "Surgeon General Releases Mental Health Report," *American Family Physician,* June 15, 2000, pp. 3739–3790.

7. Ibid., pp. 3739–3740.

8. David Mechanic, *Mental Health and Social Policy* (Englewood Cliffs, NJ: Prentice-Hall, 1969), pp. 1–33. For other terms used, such as "mentally disabled," see Samuel Jan Brakel, John Parry, and Barbara A. Weiner, *The Mentally Disabled and the Law,* 3rd ed. (Chicago: American Bar Foundation, 1985); for a discussion on the social aspects of the terms, see Nachman Ben-Yehuda, *The Politics and Morality of Deviance: Moral Panics, Drug Abuse, Deviant Science, and Reversed Stigmatization* (Albany: State University of New York, 1990), pp. 86–88.

9. Ben-Yehuda, *The Politics and Morality of Deviance,* p. 86.

10. I. K. Broverman, D. M. Broverman, F. E. Clarkson, P. S. Rosencrantz, and S. R. Vogel, "Sex-role Stereotypes and Clinical Judgments of Mental Health," *Journal of Counseling and Clinical Psychology, 34* (Winter 1970), pp. 1–7.

11. Presidential Task Force on People with Disabilities, *The President's New Freedom Initiative for People with Disabilities: The 2004 Progress Report.*

12. American Psychiatric Association (APA), *Diagnostic and Statistical Manual of Mental Disorders,* 4th ed. (Washington, DC: APA, 1994), pp. 141–142.

13. National Alzheimer's Association, "Powerful Advancement in Imaging Research in the Brains of Living People with Alzheimer's Disease," press release, January 23, 2004.

14. Kathleen J. Pottick, Jerome C. Wakefield, Stuart A. Kirk, and Xin Tian, "Influence of Social Workers' Characteristics on the Perception of Mental Disorder in Youths," *Social Service Review, 77* (September 2003), pp. 431–456.

15. Leo Srole, Thomas S. Langner, Stanley T. Michael, Marvin K. Opler, and Thomas A. C. Rennie, *Mental Health in the Metropolis: The Midtown Manhattan Study* (New York: McGraw-Hill, 1962), p. 138. For a critique of this study, see Frank E. Hartung, "Manhattan Madness: The Social Movement of Mental Illness," *Sociological Quarterly, 4* (Summer 1963), pp. 261–272.

16. Dean Frederick MacKinnon, "Descriptions and Prescriptions: Values, Mental Disorders, and the DSMs," *Perspectives in Biology and Medicine, 47* (Winter 2004), pp. 152–158; K. W. M Fulford, " 'What Is (Mental) Disease?': An Open Letter to Christopher Boorse," *Journal of Medical Ethics, 27* (April 2001), p. 80.

17. J. C. Wakefield, "Diagnosing DSM-IV-Part 1: DSM-IV and the Concept of Disorder," *Behavior Research and Theory, 7* (1997), pp. 633–649.

18. H. G. Prigerson, M. K. Shear, S. C. Jacobs, C. F. Reynolds, and P. K. Maciejewski, "Consensus Criteria for Traumatic Grief," *British Journal of Psychiatry, 174* (January 1999), pp. 67–73.

19. Erich Goode, *Deviant Behavior,* 6th ed. (Upper Saddle River, NJ: Prentice-Hall, 2001), pp. 372–377.

20. Philip S. Wang, Patricia Berglund, and Ronald C. Kessler, "Patterns and Correlates of Contacting Clergy for Mental Disorders in the United States," *Health Services Research, 38* (April 2003), pp. 647–674.

21. David Mechanic, "Some Factors in Identifying and Defining Mental Illness," *Mental Hygiene, 46* (January 1962), pp. 67, 69 (emphasis added); see Lloyd H. Rogler, Robert G. Malgady, and Warren W. Tryon, "Evaluations of Mental Health: Issues of Memory in the Diagnostic Interview Schedule," *The Journal of Nervous and Mental Disease, 180* (April 1992), pp. 215–222.

22. S. C. Baker, E. M. van der Meulen, et al., "A Whole-Genome Scan in 164 Dutch Sib Pairs with Attention-Deficit/Hyperactivity Disorder: Suggestive Evidence for Linkage on Chromosomes 7p and 15q," *American Journal of Human Genetics, 72* (May 2003), pp. 125–135; Dorothy E. Grice, "Genetics of Mental Disorders: A Guide for Students, Clinicians, and Researchers," *Journal of the American Academy of Child and Adolescent Psychiatry, 40* (October 2001), p. 1238.

23. John G. Gunderson, Joseph H. Autry III, and Loren R. Mosher, "Special Report: Schizophrenia, 1974," *Schizophrenia Bulletin, 9* (Summer 1974), pp. 24–27; Seymour Kessler, "The Genetics of Schizophrenia: A Review," in *Special Report: Schizophrenia 1980* (Washington, DC: U.S. Department of Health and Human Services, Public Health Service, 1981), pp. 14–26; Patricia McBroom, *Behavioral Genetics* (Washington, DC: U.S. Department of Health, Education, and Welfare; Public Health Service; Alcohol, Drug Abuse, and Mental Health Administration, 1980), pp. 59–83; and Susan L. Farber, *Identical Twins Reared Apart* (New York: Basic Books, 1981), pp. 142–166. For current research in this field, see Eckart R. Straub and Kurt Hahlweg, eds., *Schizophrenia, Concepts, Vulnerability, and Intervention* (Berlin: Springer-Verlag, 1990).

24. Encyclopedia Britannica, 1999–2000, "Mental Disorders." [Online]. Available: http://www.britannica.com

25. S. C. Baker, et al., "A Whole-Genome Scan in 164 Dutch Sib Pairs with Attention-Deficit/Hyperactivity Disorder: Suggestive Evidence for Linkage on Chromosomes 7p and 15q"; Dorothy E. Grice, "Genetics of Mental Disorders: A Guide for Students, Clinicians, and Researchers," *Journal of the American Academy of Child and Adolescent Psychiatry, 40* (October 2001), p. 1238.

26. August B. Hollingshead and Frederick C. Redlich, *Social Class and Mental Illness: A Community Study* (New York: John Wiley, 1958).

27. Roland Sturm and Carole Roan Gresenz, "Relations of Income Inequality and Family Income to Chronic Medical Conditions and Mental Health Disorders: National Survey in USA," *British Medical Journal, 324* (January 2002), p. 20–24.

28. Ibid.

29. Bruce P. Dohrenwend and Barbara Snell Dohrenwend, "Social and Cultural Influences on Psychopathology," *Annual Review of Psychology, 25* (1974), pp. 417–452. For other research on social class characteristics and paranoia, see John Mirowsky and Catherine E. Ross, "Paranoia and the Structure of Powerlessness," *American Sociological Review, 48* (April 1983), pp. 228–239.

30. William C. Cockerham, *Sociology of Mental Disorder,* 3rd ed. (Englewood Cliffs, NJ: Prentice Hall, 1995).

31. Luis Augusto Rohde, "ADHD in Brazil: the DSM-IV Criteria in a Culturally Different Population," *Journal of the American Academy of Child and Adolescent Psychiatry, 41* (September 2002), pp. 1131–1134.

32. Joan Huser Liem, "Family Studies of Schizophrenia: An Update and Commentary," in *Special Report: Schizophrenia 1980,* pp. 82–108; and Gunderson, Autry, and Mosher, "Special Report," pp. 27–30. See also William W. Eaton, *The Sociology of Mental Illness* (New York: Praeger, 1980), pp. 78–89; and J. Parnas, F. Schulsinger, and A. Mednick, "The Copenhagen High Risk Study: Major Psychopathological and Etiological Findings," in *Schizophrenia,* ed. Straub and Hahlweg, pp. 45–56.

33. Linda J. Waite and Evelyn L. Lehrer, "The Benefits from Marriage and Religion in the United States: A Comparative Analysis," *Population and Development Review, 29* (June 2003), pp. 255–280.

34. Walter R. Gove, Michael Hughes, and Carolyn Briggs Style, "Does Marriage Have Positive Effects on the Psychological Well-Being of the Individual?" *Journal of Health and Social Behavior, 24* (June 1983), p. 128. See also Paul D. Cleary and David Mechanic, "Sex Differences in Psychological Distress Among Married People," *Journal of Health and Social Behavior, 24* (June 1983), pp. 111–121; for a view that marriage is stressful, particularly in the middle years, see Carolyn Maltas, "Trouble in Paradise: Marital Crises of Midlife," *Psychiatry: Interpersonal and Biological Processes, 55* (May 1992), pp. 122–131.

35. Robin W. Simon, "Revisiting the Relationships Among Gender, Marital Status, and Mental Health,"

American Journal of Sociology, 107 (January 2002), pp. 1065, 1067, 1097–1099.

36. Staff writer, "Genetic Abnormality Linked to Panic Attacks, Phobias," *Genomics & Genetics Weekly* (May 18, 2001), p. 8.

37. Linda J. Waite and Evelyn L. Lehrer, "The Benefits from Marriage and Religion in the United States: A Comparative Analysis," pp. 255–257, 275–278.

38. Ibid.

39. Mary Ellen Copeland and Stuart Copans, *Recovering from Depression: A Workbook for Teens* (New York: Paul H. Brookes, 2002).

40. Robin W. Simon, "Revisiting the Relationships Among Gender, Marital Status, and Mental Health," pp. 1065, 1095–1097.

41. Jeffrey Kluger, "What's Sex Got to Do with It? Your Gender Can Determine a Lot—Including, Perhaps, Your Mental Health," *Time, 161* (January 20, 2003), p. 89.

42. Editors, "Gender, Culture, and Psychiatric Symptoms," *Harvard Mental Health Letter, 15* (October 1998).

43. Staff Writer, "Schizophrenia: Gender Connections," *Science News, 130* (December 20, 1986), p. 398.

44. Robin W. Simon, "Revisiting the Relationships Among Gender, Marital Status, and Mental Health," pp. 1065, 1067, 1097–1099.

45. Robin W. Simon, "Revisiting the Relationships Among Gender, Marital Status, and Mental Health," p. 1067.

46. For a discussion of a similar but more elaborate sequence of stress and mental disorder, see Lloyd H. Rogler and August B. Hollingshead, *Trapped: Families and Schizophrenia* (New York: John Wiley, 1965), pp. 410–412; and H. D. Brenner, S. Kraemer, M. Hermanutz, and B. Hodel, "Cognitive Treatment in Schizophrenia," in *Schizophrenia,* ed. Straub and Hahlweg, pp. 161–192.

47. H. Jick, J. A. Kaye, and S. S. Jick, "Antidepressants and the Risk of Suicidal Behaviors," *Journal of the American Medical Association, 292* (July 2004), pp. 379–381; Robert S. Eliot, *From Stress to Strength: How to Lighten Your Load and Save Your Life* (New York: Bantam Books, 1994); Lyle H. Miller, Alma Dell Smity, and Larry Rothstein, *The Stress Solutions* (New York: Putnam, 1987), pp. 13–14; Ronald G. Nathan, Thomas E. Staats, and Paul J. Rosch, *The Doctors' Guide to Instant Stress Relief* (New York: Putnam, 1987), pp. 37–41.

48. Melvin L. Kohn, "Social Class and Schizophrenia: A Critical Review and a Reformulation," *Schizophrenia Bulletin, 7* (Winter 1973), p. 74. The discussion on Kohn's theory is based on ibid., pp. 69–75.

49. Ronald C. Kessler and Paul D. Cleary, "Social Class and Psychological Distress," *American Sociological Review, 45* (June 1980), p. 476.

50. Ronald C. Kessler and Paul D. Cleary, "Reply to VanFossen et al.," *American Sociological Review, 46* (October 1981), p. 696.

51. Ibid.

52. U.S. Surgeon General, *2000 Mental Health: A Report of the Surgeon General,* Chapter 2. [Online]. Available: http://www.surgeongeneral.gov

53. Hilton P. Terrell, *Ethics and the Medical Model of Disease.* [Online]. Available: http://bmei.org/jbem/volum3/nhm4/terrell.htm

54. Paraphrased from Benjamin M. Braginsky, Dorothea D. Braginsky, and Kenneth Ring, *Methods of Madness: The Mental Hospital as a Last Resort* (New York: Holt, Rinehart and Winston, 1969), pp. 31–33; for an overview of this process, see Straub and Hahlweg, eds., *Schizophrenia,* pp. 1–6; and Sandra R. Arbetter, "Schizophrenia: Fact vs. Fantasy," *Current Health, 2* (September 1989), pp. 23–25.

55. Nick Haslam "Folk Psychiatry: Lay Thinking about Mental Disorder," *Social Research, 70* (Summer 2003), pp. 621–646; Thomas Szasz, "Mental disorders Are Not Diseases," *USA Today Magazine,* January 2000. [Online]. Available: http://www.findarticles.com

56. Ibid.

57. Thomas Szasz, "Mental Illness Is Still a Myth," in *Deviant Behavior* (Guilford, CT: Dushkin), pp. 200–205; Thomas S. Szasz, "Noncoercive Psychiatry: An Oxymoron—Reflections on Law, Liberty, and Psychiatry," *Journal of Humanistic Psychology, 31* (Spring 1990), pp. 117–125.

58. See also Michael S. Goldstein, "The Politics of Thomas Szasz: A Sociological View," *Social Research, 27* (June 1980), p. 573. The quotation is from Thomas S. Szasz, *The Theology of Medicine* (New York: Harper & Row, 1977), p. 115; see Mathis, "Psychiatric Diagnoses," pp. 253–261.

59. Thomas Szasz, "Mental Disorders Are Not Diseases."

60. John Elvin, "Is Mental Illness All in Your Head?" *Insight on the News,* July 31, 2000. [Online]. Available: http://findarticles.com

61. Jacob Sullum and Thomas Szasz, "Curing the Therapeutic State," *Reason,* July 2000. [Online]. Available: http://findarticles.com

62. This discussion is based on Thomas J. Scheff, *Being Mentally Ill: A Sociological Theory* (Chicago: Aldine, 1966), pp. 31–101.

63. Elaine Cumming and John Cumming, *Closed Ranks: An Experiment in Mental Health* (Cambridge, MA: Harvard University Press, 1957), pp. 91–108.

64. Marian Radke Yarrow, Charlotte Green Schwartz, Harriett S. Murphy, and Leila Calhoun Deasy, "The Psychological Meaning of Mental Illness in the Family," *Journal of Social Issues, 11: 4* (1955), cited in *Deviance: The Interactionist Perspective,* 4th ed., ed. Earl Rubington and Martin S. Weinberg (New York: Macmillan, 1981), pp. 35–36.

65. George Bernard Shaw, preface to *Getting Married,* in *The Collected Works of Bernard Shaw* (New York: William H. Wise, 1939), vol. 12, p. 201.

66. For an excellent discussion of the media and crime, see Ray Surette, *Media, Crime, and Criminal Justice* (Pacific Grove, CA: Brooks/Cole, 1992), pp. 1–105.

67. Scheff, *Being Mentally Ill,* p. 82.

68. D. L. Rosenhan, "On Being Sane in Insane Places," *Science, 179* (January 19, 1973), pp. 252–253. Critics of the labeling perspective point out, however, that this study has been severely criticized, especially by Robert Spitzer in "Move on Pseudoscience in Science and the Case for Psychiatric Diagnosis," *Archives of General Psychiatry, 33* (1976), pp. 459–470.

69. Gerald L. Klerman, "The Psychiatric Revolution of the Past Twenty-Five Years," in *Deviance and Mental Illness,* ed. Walter R. Gove (Beverly Hills, CA: Sage Publications, 1982), pp. 177–198.

70. Walter R. Gove, "The Current Status of the Labelling Theory of Mental Illness," in *Deviance and Mental Illness,* ed. Gove, p. 279.

71. Bruce J. Ennis, "Mental Commitment," *Civil Liberties, 264* (October 1969), p. 3.

72. Gove, "Current Status," pp. 281–282. Also see R. Kirkland Schwitzgebel, "Survey of State Civil Commitment Statutes," in *Civil Commitment and Social Policy: An Evaluation of the Massachusetts Mental Health Reform Act of 1970,* ed. A. Louis McGarry, et al. (Washington, DC: U.S. Department of Health and Human Services, Public Health Services, 1981), pp. 47–83.

73. Walter R. Gove, "Postscript," in *The Labelling of Deviance,* 2nd ed., ed. Walter R. Gove (Beverly Hills, CA: Sage, 1980), p. 103. For more recent evidence supportive of Gove's claims, see Bruce Link, "Mental Patient Status, Work, and Income: An Examination of the Effects of a Psychiatric Label," *American Sociological Review, 47* (April 1982), pp. 202–215; and Raymond M. Weinstein, "Labeling Theory and the Attitudes of Mental Patients: A Review," *Journal of Health and Social Behavior, 24* (March 1983), pp. 70–84.

74. The foregoing discussion on Gove was drawn from Gove, "Postscript," pp. 99–105; Gove, "Current Status," pp. 273–300; and Walter Gove, "Labelling Theory's Explanation of Mental Illness: An Update of Recent Evidence," *Deviant Behavior, 3* (July–September 1982), pp. 307–327.

75. Much of this debate is found in the works of Thomas S. Szasz. In particular, see his *Law, Liberty, and Psychiatry: An Inquiry into the Social Uses of Mental Health Practices* (New York: Macmillan, 1963), and *Ideology and Insanity.* See also Seymour L. Halleck, *The Politics of Therapy* (New York: Science House, 1971); and Nicholas N. Kittrie, *The Right to Be Different: Deviance and Enforced Therapy* (Baltimore: Penguin, 1971).

76. Jeffery D. Blum, "On Changes in Psychiatric Diagnosis over Time," *American Psychologist, 33* (November 1978), p. 1028 (emphasis added).

77. *Behavior Today,* February 9, 1976, pp. 4–5. See also Sidney Bloch and Peter Reddaway, *Psychiatric Terror: How Soviet Psychiatry Is Used to Suppress Dissent* (New York: Basic Books, 1977); August Stern, ed., *The USSR vs. Mikhail Stern* (New York: Urizen Books, 1978); and Ben-Yehuda, *The Politics and Morality of Deviance,* pp. 86–94.

78. "Ex-Mental Patient Fights Against Forced Treatment," *Daily Sentinel-Tribune* (Bowling Green, OH), January 13, 1981, p. 13.

79. "8 Murders Laid to a Californian," *The New York Times,* October 21, 1973, sec. 1, p. 44.

80. Sandra Harley Carey, *A Diachronic and Synchronic Analysis of the Relation between Cause Specific Mortality Patterns and Status Integration* (Austin: The University of Texas, 1979), unpublished doctoral dissertation.

81. Ronald W. Maris, Alan L. Berman, and Morton M. Silverman, *Comprehensive Textbook of Suicidology* (New York: Guilford Press, 2000), p. 369.

82. H. Jick, J. A. Kaye, and S. S. Jick, "Antidepressants and the Risk of Suicidal Behaviors," *Journal of the American Medical Association, 293* (July 2004), pp. 379, 380.

83. Bryan Tanney, Nancy DiNicolo, and SIEC Staff, "Depression: Some Pieces of the Puzzle," *Suicide Information and Education Center Alert,* #31 (August 1998), p. 1; Donald A. B. Lindberg, *Depression,* Medline Plus (Washington, DC: National Institutes of Health, U.S. Department of Health and Human Services, 2004) pp. 1–2.

84. Ibid.; U.S. Department of Health and Human Services, *Depression in Primary Care* (Washington, DC: Department of Health and Human Services, 1993).

85. David Satcher, *The Surgeon General's Report on Mental Health* (Washington, DC: Department of Health and Human Services, 1999); American Psychiatric Association, *Diagnostic and Statistical Manual-IV,* 4th ed. (Washington, DC: American Psychiatric Association, 1994).

86. Taney, "Depression: Some Pieces of the Puzzle," p. 1.

87. Mary Ellen Copeland and Stuart Copans, *Recovering from Depression: A Workbook for Teens* (New York: Paul H. Brookes, 2002).

88. Specific Phobia provided online at http://encyclopedia.thefreedictionary.com/Specific%20phobia accessed 9/16/04; U.S. Department of Health and Human Services. *Mental Health: A Report of the Surgeon General.* (Rockville, MD: U.S. Department of Health and Human Services, Substance Abuse and Mental Health Services Administration, Center for Mental Health Services, National Institutes of Health, National Institute of Mental Health, 1999), pp. 45–47; Robert Finn, "Phobic Anxiety Linked to Cardiac Death in Women," *Cardiovascular Medicine, 37* (July 2004), p. 60.

89. Mayo Clinic Staff, *Phobias: Signs and Symptoms* (Rochester, MN: Mayo Clinic, 2003), pp. 1–2.; Heidi

Splete, "Source of Phobias Elusive," *Clinical Psychiatry News, 30* (May 2002), p. 51.

90. K. W. M. Fulford, " 'What Is (Mental) Disease?': An Open Letter to Christopher Boose," *Journal of Medical Ethics, 27* (April 2001), p. 80; Xavier Estelevill, "Genetic Abnormality Linked to Panic Attacks, Phobias," *Genomics & Genetics Weekly* (May 18, 2001), p. 8; Staff Writer, "New Study Finds Thunderstorm Phobias May Be in Dogs' Genes," *PR Newswire, 29* (July 10, 2001), p. 4944.

91. Canadian Mental Health Association, *Anxiety Disorders and Phobias* (Thunder Bay, Ontario: Canadian Mental Health Association, 2001), p. 1.

92. Stephen Rae, "Who's Afraid of the Big Bad Phobia?" *Annual Editions: Deviant Behavior* (Guilford, CT: Dushkin, 1996), p. 216.

93. Ibid., p. 217.

94. Ron Doctor and Ada P. Kahn, *The Encyclopedia of Phobias, Fears, and Anxieties,* 2nd ed. (Washington, DC: The American Library Association, 2000).

95. Fredd Culbertson, *Phobias from A to Z,* provided online at Time.com, Science and Health at www.phobialist.com

96. Amber Smith, "Facts about Phobias," September 2004 report on a study done by Penn, Schoen & Berland Associates, Inc. for Discovery Health.

97. Ibid.

98. Doctor, *Encyclopedia of Phobias;* The Free Dictionary.com by Farlex.

99. Smith, "Facts about Phobias," p. 1

100. Ibid.; Mayo Clinic Staff, *Phobias: Signs and Symptoms,* pp. 1–3.

101. Canadian Mental Health Association, *Anxiety Disorders and Phobias,* p. 1; Smith, "Facts about Phobias," p. 1.

102. Ibid.; Mayo Clinic Staff, *Phobias: Signs and Symptoms,* pp. 1–3.; Doctor, *Encyclopedia of Phobias;* The Free Dictionary.com by Farlex.

103. Ibid.

104. Stephen Rae, "Who's Afraid of the Big Bad Phobia?" pp. 97, 216.

105. Mayo Clinic Staff, *Phobias: Signs and Symptoms,* pp. 1–3.

106. Ibid.

107. John Travis, "Fear Not: Scientists Are Learning How People Can Unlearn Fear," *Science News, 168* (January 2004), pp. 42–45; Carol A. Kemper, "Cycloserine for Phobics?" *Infectious Disease Alert, 23* (February 2004), p. 59.

CHAPTER

10 Suicide

Richard Cory

  by Edwin Arlington Robinson

Whenever Richard Cory went down town,
  We people on the pavement looked at him:
He was a gentleman from sole to crown,
  Clean favored, and imperially slim.

And he was always quietly arrayed,
  And he was always human when he talked;
But still he fluttered pulses when he said,
  "Good-morning," and he glittered when he walked.

And he was rich—yes, richer than a king—
  And admirably schooled in every grace:
In fine, we thought that he was everything
  To make us wish that we were in his place.

So on we worked, and waited for the light,
  And went without the meat, and cursed the bread;
And Richard Cory, one calm summer night,
  Went home and put a bullet through his head.

The United States has one of the world's highest standards of living. Science and technology have made life easier, and advances in medicine and public health have made it possible for us to live longer, healthier lives than ever before. We are surrounded by modern conveniences, entertainment of all kinds, plenty to eat and drink, and churches, clubs, and political parties eager to take us in. Recently, some enterprising entrepreneurs have even launched a business where strangers can be found to cuddle with us.[1] Why then do thousands (10.8 of each 100,000) of Americans each year decide that their lives are not worth living? Why then, is suicide the eleventh leading cause of death?[2] If "Richard Cory" speaks especially to you, you may already have some idea.

Definition

TV talk show host Phil Donahue has described suicide as "a permanent solution to a temporary problem." Others have described it as "a deadly decision rooted in biology and expressed in behavior."[3] Derived from the Latin, the word means literally a killing (*cide, cidium*) of oneself (*sui*). As the subject has been addressed by various writers representing a variety of fields; however, the definition has been elaborated and embellished to also include references to positive or negative acts, consciousness of the act, need state of the perpetrator, intentionality, murder, hatred, anger, guilt, hopelessness, solution seeking, lethality, and intent. Although we will discuss most of these variables, we prefer the simple definition used by The American Association of Suicidology (AAS), which defines *suicide* as "self-inflicted, intentional death."[4] In much of the literature, "suicide" can refer either to the act or to the person who commits it. It has also been used as a synonym for the verb "kill." We will use it only to refer to the act.

History of Suicide

Despite the presence of seemingly similar animal behavior, close examination indicates that suicide is a uniquely human behavior. It is also a behavior that has existed throughout human history. It is likely that some of the questions, feelings, and concerns we have on the topic today were shared by our earliest ancestors.[5]

Suicide was taboo in primitive societies because the defection of one of its members called into question the values of the society and its ability to care for and control its members. It also, by depriving the group of warriors, hunters, procreators, or other contributing members, threatened the very existence of the society. In addition, it also must have aroused in primitive people some of the same questions we are still dealing with today.[6]

The earliest document dedicated to the topic was written by the Egyptians and entitled *The Dialogue of a Misanthrope with His Own Soul*. This writing details a discussion that takes place between a man contemplating suicide and his reluctant soul. The soul's reservations center on its fear that the suicide will deprive the man of a "proper funeral" and the soul of its chance for what we would call heaven. The indication is that early Egyptians, as well as the primitives, felt suicide a threat to the group and had figured out ways to discourage it.[7]

There is ambiguity in other ancient writings on suicide, however. Attitudes toward self-killing vary among and within religions and among and within cultures. The ancient Chinese found suicide a good way to rid society of dependent, excess females when their husbands died, and the Hindus of India even offered incentives. Suicidal Hindu wives were promised that their self-sacrifice would atone for their husbands' sins and bring honor on their children.[8]

The ancient Greeks and Romans permitted, even extolled, suicide under the proper circumstances. While it was viewed as an offense against the state by both cultures, the Greeks saw suicide as an appropriate answer to unrequited love or dishonor, and they allowed it for relief of physical or mental pain.[9] Roman legal experts drew up a list of acceptable motives that included these reasons as well as despair, loyalty, fury, shame, consciousness of guilt, bringing a curse on an opponent, demonstrating contempt for death, sacrificing one's life for the benefit of the community, and "having had enough of life."[10] In ancient Rome, suicide was also an acceptable "loophole" for those sentenced to execution. If they killed themselves, their property would go to their heirs. If the state executed them, their property was confiscated by the state. Although suicide has been called "Roman Death," it appears to have been more rare in practice than in literature and philosophy.[11] The state especially sought to deter suicides, which deprived the state of valued assets. The battle-weary soldier who died by his own hand, for example, was condemned, since it deprived the state of a soldier's services. Those who attempted to commit suicide for other than acceptable reasons could, ironically, be punished by death.[12]

Much of the history of suicide is found in ancient religious literature. Here again we find ambivalence. The Koran and the teachings of Islam were constant in their condemnation of suicide. The Torah and the teachings of Judaism demanded respect for the Giver and sanctity of life, but did allow Jews to take their own lives in extreme circumstances. These included dishonor, disgrace, and torture. In one of the first recorded cases of mass suicide, Jews at Masada killed themselves and their children rather than submit to Roman conquest and religious conversion.[13] In general, however, suicide was punishable by denial of burial rights and the fear of punishment in the life hereafter.[14]

Some early Christians, secure in the promise of eternal life, saw suicide an escape from worldly woes to the joys of salvation. By the fourth century, however, the church had taken a strong stand against it. Elaborated in the writings of St. Thomas Aquinas, the Catholic Church defined it as unnatural and a "usurpation of God's" prerogative, a violation of the commandment "Thou shalt not kill," and ultimately, a mortal sin.[15] Under this guidance, suicide was rare from the fourth to the thirteenth centuries.

After the Reformation, protestant churches retained this prohibition. In the fourteenth and fifteenth centuries, however, the Renaissance brought with it an emphasis on individualism and personal freedom that allowed people to question church teachings and reignited the debate. Sixteenth-century French essayist Montaigne wrote that "The most voluntary death is the finest."[16] But the religious community stood firm and writers such as Lutheran pastor Johannes Nester reaffirmed the doctrine of suicide as sin. He excepted only those driven by melancholia or madness.[17]

During the seventeenth and eighteenth centuries, philosophers generally condemned suicide, but writers such as John Donne and David Hume continued to argue against them.[18] By the mid-eighteenth century writers such as Merian were venturing the opinion that suicide might be a problem of "mental derangement" rather than moral weakness.[19] Nevertheless, the major religions continued to condemn it, and the state followed suite. Suicide was considered a crime in Great Britain until 1961, in Canada until 1972,[20] and Ireland until 1993.[21]

Current Attitudes toward Suicide

If you discuss the topic with your friends and classmates, you will probably hear some of these same themes echoed today. The topic still stirs rational debate about such things as free will, rational choices, personal rights, quality of life, and personal as well as societal responsibility. The topic also elicits strong emotions of sadness, frustration, guilt, and even horror. Your discussion may be heated and will, almost certainly, tell you a great deal about the person with whom you are discussing the issue.

Public Opinion and Public Policy

In the recent past, public attitudes about suicide have softened somewhat, but it is still generally condemned. The great monotheist religions of Christianity, Judaism, and Islam all consider it a sin. Many still view it as resulting from mental illness as opposed to rational choice. The greatest difference we see in present-day attitudes is a strong conviction that we are capable of determining the dynamics of suicide, understanding it, and stopping it. In the United States and other nations there is a national commitment to at least try.[22]

Professional Opinion

Professionals from a wide range of disciplines are working to further our understanding of this behavior. One of the newest areas of exploration is the physical sciences. A pioneer in this area, J. J. Mann, has stated that, "Reduced serotonin input into this part of the brain [the ventral prefrontal cortex] may result in impaired inhibition and a greater propensity to act on powerful feelings such as suicidal or aggressive feelings."[23] Dopamine, another neurotransmitter, also appears to be involved.[24] Psychopharmacologists have had some success attacking mental disorders such as depression, bipolar disorder, and even drug and alcohol abuse with drug therapy. Since these disorders are frequently underlying or contributing causes of suicide, these professionals view chemistry as a source of answers to some of our questions about suicide and medication as a possible means of addressing the problem.

If some suicide can be explained in terms of brain chemistry, geneticists and some psychologists feel that there may well also be an inherited component to suicide. Some genetics researchers have found that people who are depressed and have suicidal thoughts are more likely to have a mutation in the gene encoding for a certain serotonin receptor. Follow-up studies indicated that people with a parent or sibling who committed suicide were two and one-half times more likely to commit suicide appear to bolster their theory of a physiological or genetic link.[25] Indeed, suicidologists have long observed a tendency for suicide to "run in families."[26] Maris summarized twin studies dating back to the middle of the last century and observed that the data indicate that genetic factors are at work. He theorizes that these factors increase vulnerability to suicide by increasing the risk of mental disorders associated with suicide.[27] This does not rule out the possibility of directly involved genetic factors, however, and some interesting research being done on adopted children in Copenhagen suggests that one might be found.[28]

Psychologists see the etiology of suicide in intrapersonal dynamics and mental illness. Psychoanalysts in the Freudian tradition see suicide as the result of inwardly directed aggression and hostility. Menninger dissected this "death instinct" and theorized that suicide was the result of aggression/revenge (the wish to kill), guilt/depression/hopelessness (the wish to die), and guilt/escape (the wish to be killed).[29] Self Psychology theorists see suicidal impulses as stemming from feelings of being alone and overwhelmed by negative self-judgments, unworthiness, and guilt.[30]

Suicidologists see all suicides as having some traits in common. Shneidman, for example, feels that there are eleven commonalities in all suicides. These include: (1) solution seeking, (2) an end to consciousness, (3) intolerable psychological pain, (4) frustrated psychological needs, (5) hopelessness/helplessness, (6) ambivalence about living, (7) narrowing of perceived alternatives, (8) a desire to escape, (9) cries for help, (10) aggression, and (11) chronic patterns of self-destructive attempts at "coping." According to this theory, suicide would be most likely to occur when "psychache" (pain), press (stress), and perturbation (agitation)" are at their highest.[31]

Social psychologists and family therapists are more likely to look at interpersonal dynamics than at intrapersonal dynamics. They look at the interaction of individuals in important personal relationships and see suicide as the result of stress and pain brought about by unhealthy and unsatisfying relationships with those closest to us.

Sociologists go beyond the individual and small group and seek explanation of suicide in societal factors and in the relationships of people and groups to the larger society. They search for answers by studying the influences of society and the roles individuals play in their societies. The major sociological theories of suicide will be discussed in the next section.

Sociological Theories of Suicide

Sociologists have sought to understand suicide not from the perspective of the individual psyche, but as the product of social forces acting on groups. Among the major sociological theories are the social integration theories of Durkheim and the status integration of theories of Gibbs and Martin.[32]

Social Integration

Over 100 years ago, French social philosopher Émile Durkheim laid the foundations for the sociological study of suicide by observing that suicide was the result of variations in social integration (i.e., social cohesion resulting from stable and durable social relationships) within the society.[33] He classified suicide into four types: altruistic, egoistic, anomic, and fatalistic. In altruistic suicide, the perpetrators have such a strong attachment to the group that they are moved to sacrifice themselves for the welfare of the group. These suicides have been seen as more common in primitive societies where the emphasis was on group welfare and survival. A frequently cited modern-day example has been the soldier who throws himself on a grenade to save his comrades. More recently, attention has focused on traditionally male suicide-bombers,[34] women following in their footsteps,[35] and others such as the children's suicide brigades of the Iran–Iraq war.[36]

At the other end of the continuum is the egoistic suicide. These suicides are seen as the result of inadequate integration, which not only may result in inadequate support for some group members but may also provide them the freedom to commit suicide for individualistic reasons. Examples are more likely to be found in modern societies and may include groups such as unemployed, elderly males.

Anomic suicide occurs because of a change in the nature of the society. In periods of societal disruption and change, the rules are no longer clear and aspirations are no longer clearly regulated or achievable. Society's control and guidance are weakened and suicide increases. Either positive or negative changes in society can result in suicide. Examples include deaths resulting from sudden economic crises such as those of individuals who lost everything during the great depression. Surprisingly, they also can include deaths resulting from sudden economic good fortune such as winning the lottery or becoming rock stars.

Durkheim wrote very little about fatalistic suicide. Suicides in this group result from excessive regulation, i.e., the fact that social status has closed off not only all hope of self-determination, but also all hope for the future. Groups at high risk for this type of suicide include slaves and some types of prisoners and mental hospital patients.[37]

Status Integration

The theory of status integration was developed by Gibbs and Martin to test Durkheim's theory of suicide. They reviewed Durkheim's statements on social integration and concluded that social relationships were the ties that bound individuals to society and that the strength of these ties could be measured by measuring the degree to which social relationships were stable, durable, and predictable.[38] In a highly integrated society, where knowledge of one status would be a good indicator of many other statuses, this could be taken as evidence of strong societal ties, and a low rate of suicide could be predicted. In a weakly integrated society, knowledge of one status would tell little about the others, groups would occupy conflicting combinations of statuses, there would be more role conflict, and social relationships would be more problematic.[39] There would also be more stress[40] and more suicide. For example, in a primitive society, knowing that women were 20 years old would also tell you almost certainly that they were also married, mothers, and the primitive equivalent of housewives. This would be evidence of a high degree of social integration and would predict low rate of suicide. In an advanced, industrial society such as twenty-first century America, knowing women are 20 years old tells you very little about their marital, parental, or occupational status. This would indicate a very much less integrated society and would predict much higher suicide rates.[41] Gibbs has tested the theory for more than thirty years, and the predictive power of at least one of his measures remains strong. The usefulness of his marital status integration measure has declined since the 1970s. However, ". . . tests of the theory now number in the hundreds, encompassing comparisons of the [suicide rates] of race-sex populations, age groups, marital statuses, occupations, metropolitan areas, and states," and it remains the most robust, statistically based predictor of suicide rates among populations.[42]

Community Migration

Investigating ties with the local community rather than the society as a whole, Stack has studied suicide and migration. He theorizes that if suicide is related to the degree to which people are tied to their societies, it should also be related to the degree to which they are tied to their communities. He used migration rates as an indicator of a disruption in these ties. Areas of greater interstate migration were predicted to have less social cohesion, weaker integration of their population into the community, and higher rates of suicide. Stack's research has supported this relationship.[43] Workgroups may be considered communities in many respects, so Stack also looked at migration between work groups. He looked at the relationship between job changes and suicide, for example, and found that ". . . work mobility . . . can affect suicide risk. Changes, especially if sudden, can result in a sense of disorientation and can elevate suicide risk." The changes need not be negative. Mobility can be horizontal or lateral, upward involving increases in career status, or downward involving losses in one's former prestige."[44]

Incidence of Suicide

Suicide is not always detectible or readily distinguished from accidental or other causes. In addition, there are, in many nations, cultural, religious, and even monetary motivations to not identify deaths as suicides. For these and other reasons, suicide statistics are almost certainly underreported. Underreporting according to some estimates may well exceed 25 to 33 percent. Since some countries have not always reported rates for women and some have reported surprisingly low rates for women, there may even be a systematic bias to the underreporting. In addition, there have been indications that international reporting organizations have been influenced to produce overly positive portrayals of some nation's data.[45] Nevertheless, nations around the world collect data on cause of death, albeit each using its own system and methods of certifying cause of death. The World Health Organization publishes these rates as number of deaths per 100,000 population per year.

International

Statistics indicate that, worldwide, about a million people each year die intentionally from voluntary, self-inflicted causes.[46] This represents an average rate of about 14.5 (per 100,000). Rates of suicide vary widely from country to country. Over the last century Hungary led the world in number of reported suicides, and in 1985 this nation reached an all-time high rate of 46.[47] This is in contrast to a rate of 0 reported by Egypt in 1987 and rates under 2 in New Guinea and Syria.[48] Countries such as Syria, Santa Lucia, Saint Vincent, and Dominica have also reported rates of rates of 0 for women.[49]

Currently, although the former Soviet Republic of Azerbaijan reported a rate of less than 1 in 2,000, other nations in this group are experiencing record high rates of suicide. For example, at the beginning of this century, Belarus reported a rate of 61 for males, 10 for females; Estonia 56 for males, 12 for females; Kazakhstan 46 for males, 9 for females; Latvia 57 for males, 12 for females; Lithuania 76 for males, 16 for females; the Russian Federation 63 for males and 12 for females; and Ukraine 52 for males and 10 for females.[50] Although this may well be the result of less politically influenced, more accurate reporting, it is also a part of what has been called a sensational increase in suicide around the world since the 1950s. The World Health Organization estimates that if the trend continues, global rates may increase by as much as 50 percent by the year 2020.

Of special concern is the trend toward rising rates for the young.[51] Why is the rate rising for those who would seem to have the most to live for? Similarly, why does Canada, a rich nation that consistently ranks among the top nations for quality of life, have a higher suicide rate than India?[52] Why also is China, whose "one child policy" would appear to make women a valued, scarce resource, the only nation where suicide is the leading cause of death for young women? Why is China the only country where rates are higher for women than for men?[53] The explanation probably lies in a lethal combination of social isolation, lack of access to medical care, and pesticides. We will address this later.

United States

The good news is that more than 98 percent of Americans survive the challenges of life in twenty-first century without resorting to suicide to resolve their problems.[54] However, approximately 1.3 percent of all deaths in the United States each year are the result of suicide. This means that more than 35,000 Americans die each year from suicides and with a rate of 10.8, suicide is the eleventh leading cause of death in the United States.[55] Suicide takes 50 percent more lives than homicide and twice as many lives as HIV/AIDS.[56] Firearms are used in about 55 percent of completed suicides. Other lethal means include suffocation/hanging 20 percent; poisoning/drug ingestion 17 percent; and jumping/falling, about 2 percent.[57] For each completed suicide, there are about 25 attempts.[58] For each death there are also about 5 hospitalizations and 22 emergency room visits.[59] In all, suicides and attempted suicides have touched the lives of nearly half of all Americans.[60]

In the United States the rate of suicide has been relatively stable over the past forty years. However, between 1990 and 2001, the rate generally declined slightly year by year to produce an overall decline from 12.4 in 1990 to approximately 10.8 in 2001.[61] Although suicide is an intensely personal matter, rates are correlated with micro-level factors such a where a person lives. Therefore, within the United States, as among nations, rates have also varied from region to region.[62] Rates have ranged from only a little over 7 percent in New Jersey to nearly 23 percent in Nevada. They are higher in the western part of the nation and highest in the mountain states.[63] Rates in the West have ranged from slightly over 11 percent in the Pacific region to over 17 percent in the Mountain region.[64]

Risk Factors and Correlates of Suicide

The incidence of suicide varies not only with geography, but also with gender, race, age, income level, and even occupation. Factors such as mental health, drug and alcohol use, time of the year, and even who else is doing it and how it is being reported have an effect on suicide rates. The U.S. Surgeon General's *National Strategy for Suicide Prevention* outlines the following important risk factors:[65]

Risk Factors for Suicide

Biopsychosocial Risk Factors
- Mental disorders, particularly mood disorders, schizophrenia, anxiety disorders and certain personality disorders
- Alcohol and other substance use disorders

- Hopelessness
- Impulsive and/or aggressive tendencies
- History of trauma or abuse
- Some major physical illnesses
- Previous suicide attempt
- Family history of suicide

Environmental Risk Factors

- Job or financial loss
- Relational or social loss
- Easy access to lethal means
- Local clusters of suicide that have a contagious influence

Sociocultural Risk Factors

- Lack of social support and sense of isolation
- Stigma associated with help-seeking behavior
- Barriers to accessing health care, especially mental health and substance abuse treatment
- Certain cultural and religious beliefs (for instance, the belief that suicide is a noble resolution of a personal dilemma)
- Personal knowledge or exposure through the media to the influence of others who have died by suicide[66]

Shea offers two acronyms to summarize clinical and statistical risk factors. They form what Shea calls his "No Hope Scale" and the "Sad Persons Scale" of Patterson, Dohn, Bird, and Patterson.

Psychological Risk Factors

The SAD PERSONS Scale

- Sex
- Age
- Depression
- Previous attempt
- Ethanol (Alcohol)
- Rational thought loss
- Social supports lacking
- Organized plan
- No spouse
- Sickness[67]

The NO HOPE Scale

- No framework for meaning
- Overt change in clinical condition
- Hostile interpersonal environment
- Out of hospital abuse recently
- Predisposing personality factors
- Excuses for dying to help others

How do these factors act on the individual to lead him or her to choose suicide? In the rest of this section, we will examine some of these variables and how they appear to influence suicide, suicide attempts, and suicidal ideation (the process of forming thoughts, ideas, and images of suicide).

Correlates of Suicide

In the search for greater understanding of suicidal behavior, literally hundreds of factors have been investigated. Suicide researchers have looked at the influence of such diverse factors as abortion, age, aggression, alcoholism, brain chemistry, climate, cranial injury, cultural attitudes, depression, diabetes, drug use, epilepsy, ethnicity, firearms legislation, genetics, geography, holidays, light/dark cycles, marital status, media coverage, mental disorders, menstruation, music, physiology, pregnancy, race, religion, sex, sexual orientation, sexual perversions, social class, substance abuse policies, sunspots, tuberculosis, unemployment, and weather.[68] In the following section we will review those that appear to be most highly correlated with suicide and a few that are merely interesting.

Depression. Seriously depressed people have described their suffering as "life in a dark room," devoid of joy or hope. Depression is not only a threat to one's quality of life; however, it is one of the most important risk factors for suicide. The American Association of Suicidology reports that depression is involved in about two-thirds of suicides and that over 6 percent of those who suffer from depression (1 percent of the women and 7 percent of the men) will eventually die by their own hand.[69] Some National Institute of Mental Health reports indicate that over 90 percent of all suicides are related to depression or some other mood or mental disorder.[70] People suffering from major depression are about twenty times more likely than the general population to die from suicide.[71] Although recurrent major depressive disorder is most strongly associated with suicide, there is a variety of other mental disorders that also place individuals at higher risk for suicide.[72] Recognizing depression and other mental disabilities and the important role they play in setting the stage for suicide will help us save lives. British researchers have concluded that "A fifth of suicides among people with mental illnesses are preventable."[73]

Age. Although teen age suicides are alarming and attract the most media attention, the highest U.S. suicide rates have traditionally been found among people over the age of 65. For more than fifty years, the rates for those 65 to 84 years old have been nearly twice the rates for the general population. Despite the fact that today's elderly are arguably the most prosperous generation that ever existed, this pattern persists. In 2001, the elderly made up just 12.4 percent of the population, but committed 17.6 percent of the suicides. Elderly white males are especially at risk. While suicide rates for other group tend to peak in midlife, rates for white males increase with age. In some years the suicide of elderly males has been four to six times the rate for the age-adjusted population as a whole.[74]

Some of the factors that contribute to high rates of suicide in among the elderly include "undiagnosed and untreated depressive disorder, social isolation and loss of spouse (through death or divorce), years of alcohol abuse, ready availability of firearms . . . , and conceptual rigidity and failure to adapt to changing life demands."[75] In addition, "Many common illnesses are independently associated with increased risk of suicide in the elderly [and] the risk is greatly increased" by multiple illnesses.[76] Contrary to popular belief, however, only about 3 percent are suffering from a terminal illness at the time of their attempt.[77] Factors unique to the elderly include loss of status and social roles: "My son-in-law is taking all my jobs." "My daughter is taking over my kitchen." They also include concerns about loss of independence and fear of institutionalization. In addition, some share the sentiments of one 85-year-old woman, "I am old and sick and all my friends are dead."

Older Americans actually attempt suicide less often, but they are more likely to die from their attempts.[78] The ratio of attempts to completed suicides for the elderly is 4:1 as compared to the ratio for the general population, which is estimated at about 25:1.[79] This is evidencing commitment and lethal intent. The ratio may also be influenced, however, by frail health, lesser recuperative abilities, and lack of potential rescuers available to those living in social isolation.[80] A variety of private and government programs ranging from Meals on Wheels to adult day care and senior action centers have targeted the problem of isolation in the elderly population and may be helping to ease this isolation. An encouraging sign is the fact that the suicide rate for the elderly has declined more than the rate for the total population since 1990.

At the other end of the spectrum is the youth population. We like to think of childhood as a happy time, free of problems and stress. We also think of childhood as a time of innocence with children as carefree beings with neither the motivation nor the maturity to think of suicide. Recent studies indicate, however, that even relatively young children have an understanding of suicide.[81] In addition, although children rarely kill themselves, there were 279 suicides of young people under the age of 15 in the United States in 2001.

Between maturity and childhood is the turbulent time we call adolescence. Suicide is currently the third leading cause of death of young adults (15–24), surpassed only by homicide (number two) and accidents (the leading cause of death for this group). Self-reports indicate that nearly 20 percent of high school students have seriously considered suicide during the past year. In fact, it is likely that in one of your high school classes there were two girls and one boy who had attempted suicide within the previous year.[82] Although the rate for adolescence is lower than that of the population as a whole (9.9 as compared to 10.8) and has been declining since 1990, it is a cause for concern.[83] For each completed suicide among this group there are an estimated 100 to 200 attempts. Approximately 7 percent of those in this age group attempt suicide; more than 40 percent of these will attempt it more than once.

Why would young people, arguably in the prime of their lives, attempt suicide? Child psychiatrists contend that "Adolescent suicide almost always occurs in the context of an active, often treatable, mental illness."[84] Other possible contributing factors appear to be poor parenting,[85] homes without fathers, unemployment, poverty, and physical or sexual abuse,[86] poor school performance, and high-risk behavior (e.g., smoking, getting drunk, having sex, fighting,[87] carrying a weapon to school, using marijuana,[88] and self-mutilation.)[89] Depression, other personality and psychiatric disorders, narcissistic and antisocial personality traits, substance abuse, shame, victimization, lack of resiliency, and limited problem-solving and coping skills also appear to play a role.[90] Additional risk factors include social isolation and loss of psychological support; early-onset and continuing negative life events; and friendship patterns in which they either had very few friends or friends who were not friends with each other.[91] Some clinicians note that depression may or may not be a factor and that adolescent suicide may, instead, be associated with aggressive and violent behavior.[92]

Protective factors for adolescence included feelings of connectedness to parents and family, emotional well-being (for girls), and high grade-point average (for boys). If at least three of these protective factors are present, suicide risk may be reduced by 70 percent to 85 percent.[93] Precipitating factors include: suicide of a friend or relative; severe stress, e.g., sexual orientation crisis; unplanned pregnancy; perceived significant loss; significant family loss; instability; or conflict. The AAS states that "Most adolescent suicide attempts are precipitated by interpersonal conflicts." They most often take place in the adolescent's home in the afternoon or early evening. The typical attempter is a young woman who takes pills. The typical completer is a young man who uses a firearm. "The intent of the behavior appears to be to effect change in the behaviors or attitudes of others."[94]

Sex.   Suicide is not an equal opportunity behavior. Throughout history and throughout the world, men have traditionally committed suicide in significantly greater numbers than women. In the United States, men consistently commit suicide four times as often as women. However, women attempt suicide three times more often than men. These differences may be accounted for, in part, by the fact that women are more likely to seek help and men are more likely to use guns. Males have been, or have been socialized to be, traditionally more violent, more aggressive, and more achievement oriented. "Freud interpreted suicide as an aggressive act toward oneself that often was really directed toward others."[95] Completing a suicide attempt would, therefore, be consistent with the male role. Completing it by using a weapon of violence, such as a handgun, would be seen as an appropriately masculine technique. Help-seeking, on the other hand, could be seen as a sign of weakness rather than a sign of wisdom. (Rather like the old cliché about men refusing to stop and ask for driving directions.) Studies of the relationship between sex role demands and suicide are hindered by the evolving nature of those sex roles. Some recent research suggests that the old assumption that women died for love and men for failure either never were or no longer are true and both men and women are now likely to be motivated by problems with relationships.[96] Interestingly, current indications are that such things as women's increasing labor force participation and increasing androgyny in the sex roles have not resulted in a predicted increase in women's overall suicide rates.[97] Perhaps the answer is biological. Biochemists have found that lower levels of serotonin are not only found in people with depression and increased risk of suicide. They are also found in men in general. So, more of the answer may be found in brain chemistry. The success of some medications in combating depression points in this direction.[98]

A key factor influencing suicide rates is choice of method. Women continue to be more likely to use less lethal means. U.S. women, for example, prefer pills to firearms. Currently, the higher suicide rates of rural Chinese women as compared to rural Chinese men may be partially explained by the ready availability of poisonous pesticides. Since the days of imperial China, when women of the court committed suicide by methods such as swallowing their earrings, poison has been seen as an appropriately feminine mode of death. In the United States, methods such as taking an overdose of some medication usually results in a suicide attempt (and perhaps the unpleasant process of having one's stomach pumped). In rural China, ingesting a powerful pesticide usually means an unpleasant death. The isolation of the female farmer makes it very difficult to get prompt medical attention and medical personnel are largely untrained in crisis care.[99]

Marital Status.   Being married and having children are protective factors against suicide. Traditionally, suicide rates increase in the following order: married with children, married, never married or single, divorced, and widowed. Marriage is especially protective for men and for whites. Married men are only 30 percent as likely as widowers and about 20 percent as likely as divorced men to commit suicide.[100] A notable exception to this pattern is adolescent marriage. It appears that, for this group, the attendant stresses of such things as premature parenthood, family conflict, and financial problems outweigh the benefits of the marital support system.[101] For reasons still undetermined, marriage is also less protective for women.[102]

We have seen that having children in the home is protective for black females. This is also true of parents in general, regardless of race or sex. There are also indications that the more children a woman has, the less likely she is to commit suicide. This may be related to the fact that the more children a woman has, the more likely she is to have a child under the age of 2. Having a child under the age of 2 is a protective factor for the mother. The vulnerability for families with children is that, if one of the children dies, the trauma can have a devastating affect on the family that increases the risk of suicide for both parents.[103]

Gay and Lesbian Youth.   In addition to the risk factors common to other adolescents, gay and lesbian youth face other stresses as well. Most experience some ambivalence, confusion, guilt, anxiety, and identity conflict. Those who do not profess their sexual identity may also suffer from the stress of secrecy.[104] Those who openly identify themselves as homosexual risk psychological stress such as hopelessness, despair, and other reactions to prejudice and discrimination. They may also suffer sociological stressors such as family rejection, alienation from society, religious condemnation, harassment, and increased risk of HIV/AIDS. All these factors would point to increased risk for suicide. Gay advocacy groups argue that as many as a third of adolescent suicide victims may be gay and lesbian youth. Some researchers have found that, although these adolescents may be as much as seven times more likely to attempt suicide, these attempts cannot be linked directly to sexual preference. Others researchers have found that, when other variables are controlled, the rates for homosexuals do not vary widely from those for heterosexuals. Research methods as well as political and emotional motives have been questioned.[105] Currently, there is no hard evidence of a higher rate of suicide among gay and lesbian adolescents. There are indications, however, that for some high-risk teenage homosexuals, the rates for attempted suicide may be two or three times higher than those for heterosexuals.[106] Some speculate that the differences in these rates may be the result of differences in incidence of mental disorders and substance abuse within the two groups.[107] Resolution of the issue awaits further carefully constructed studies that address important contributing factors such as substance abuse and AIDS.

Race and Ethnicity.   A "minority group is any group of people who, because of their physical or cultural characteristics, are singled out for differential and unequal treatment by the majority, and who are, thus, objects of collective discrimination."[108] Whether the differentiation is based on racial characteristics (i.e., inherited, physiological characteristics) or ethnic factors (i.e., nationality and cultural differences) members of identifiable minority groups are more likely to face adversity and less likely to share fully in the benefits of the host society. It would seem likely, therefore, that minority group members would have higher rates of suicide.

However, African American suicide rates have been consistently lower than those for whites and rates for black females are among the lowest for any group. The most recent rates are about 20 percent for white males and 5 percent for white females as compared to just over 9 percent for black males and under 2 percent for black females. In the early 1980s there was concern as rates for African American children and teens (especially young males) began to rise much more rapidly than those for their white counterparts.[109] There was also increased concern about their increased access to firearms.[110] During the last decade and a half, however, rates for nearly all gender and racial groups have continued to fall, and the relationship between African American and white rates persists.

What is it that appears to insulate African Americans—especially African American females—from suicide? Protective factors for black females include strong social support networks of family, friends, and church and the ability to seek help. They also are likely to include strength developed while caring for others and dealing with a variety of hardships. Other possible factors include religious values, which not only provide a source of comfort and strength, but also define suicide as "sinful and prideful."[111]

Maris suggests that lower rates for African American males compared to white males may be explained by the fact that "In the United States, black aggression is more likely to be other-directed (for example, in the form of assault and homicide)." As supporting evidence for his assertion, he notes the inverse relationship between black male suicide and homicide rates in the United States.[112] Because of this, there has been some concern that lower homicide rates for upper-class blacks might signal higher suicide rates. Carefully controlled studies have found this not to be the case.[113]

Hispanics also have lower overall suicide rates than non-Hispanic whites.[114] An area of concern, however, is the significantly higher rate of suicide attempts among Hispanic adolescent females. Centers for Disease Control and Prevention data indicate attempt rates of about 20 percent for Hispanic females as compared to nearly 11 percent for non-Hispanic white females and about 10.5 for black females. Young Hispanic women are also twice as likely as their black or Anglo counterparts to have harmed themselves seriously enough to require medical attention.[115] Significant relationships have been found between this behavior and factors such as suicide attempts by family members or friends, family history of physical and sexual abuse, and environmental stress.[116] Environmental stressors include lack of traditional Hispanic extended family support and the need to support parents who are new to U.S. culture[117] and may depend on their daughters to help bridge the gap between Hispanic and mainstream U.S. culture.

The racial/ethnic group that has the highest overall suicide rate is Native Americans.[118] It is important to note, however, that Native Americans are a diverse group and while tribes such as the Shoshone have high suicide rates, others such as the Navajos have rates lower than those for non-Indian residents of the states in which they live.[119] The most common risk factors for suicide among Native Americans are depression and alcohol abuse and the many personal, social, and financial problems related to these factors. Key contributing factors are unemployment, poverty, family disruption, and substance abuse.[120] Protective factors include, for example, a Navajo belief system that condemns suicide. In some cultures, it is seen not as a means of escape but as an act that leads to entrapment of the soul in a ghost state, forever imprisoned in its pain.[121]

Occupation and Social Status.   If you want to ask just one question that will tell you as much about a person as possible, you might ask, "What do you do?" One of the many things occupational status tells us about is suicide risk. Occupational status is also one of the key predictors used in suicide theories such as status integration theory. For this reason, it is somewhat surprising that there is not more research on occupation and suicide. Unfortunately, a disproportionate amount of this research has been done on professional occupations. Suicide rates are inversely related to education, and the rate of suicide appears to be twice as high among the least educated as compared to the highest educated groups.[122] Therefore, we have the most information on the groups that may well have the lowest rates of suicide. Nevertheless, some general patterns emerge. Not surprisingly, the unemployed have a suicide rate two or three times that of their employed counterparts[123] and times of prosperity and high employment bring decreases in the suicide rates.

Characteristics of specific occupations appear to play a role in the prevalence of suicide. Women in traditionally male occupations, for example, have higher rates of suicide than their male counterparts. Status integration theory would indicate that these rates may fall as more women enter occupations such as the military, physicians, chemists, and laborers, but women in these jobs are still probably working under the increased pressure of being "round pegs in square holes" and violating traditional expectations about people who fill these jobs. Self-selection, opportunity, and stress, also play a role in suicide rates for various occupations. Some fields such as art and psychiatry may recruit from more suicide-predisposed groups. Some, such as physicians, pharmacists, nurses, and agricultural workers in China have access to lethal chemicals that provide greater opportunity. Occupations such as physician, dentist, and lawyer are very stressful,[124] and women in these occupations may be under additional stress since they are working in traditionally male-dominated fields.[125] Lower-than-average suicide rates are found among U.S. school teachers and college professors. This may be related to greater self-determination and lower stress inherent in these occupations. Average suicide rates were found for accountants, engineers,[126] and—somewhat surprisingly—police officers.[127]

A few of the "higher than average rates" merit special attention. Researchers are currently investigating why the suicide rate for lawyers is twice the average, for pharmacists more than three times the average, for female chemists five times the average, and for dentists is more than six times the average rate for working-age adults.[128] They are also working to explain why those working in the "medical and allied professions" appear to be especially susceptible to suicide.[129]

Time Factors.   There is a myth that suicide rates are higher at Christmas time and on other holidays. Actually, research indicates that, in the United States, not only does the rate drop for Christmas, but that it is also lower just before and just after Christmas as well.[130] A similar pattern has been found in Europe.[131] Possible reasons include the increased social support provided by friends and relatives gathered for festivities, happy memories and hope rekindled by Christmas rituals, and the outpouring of community support that occurs at this time of the year.[132] That the fact that suicide rates are low for the month of December is especially surprising since the decreased number of hours of sunlight during this month could reasonably be expected to lead to more seasonal affective disorder (SAD) and depression.[133] Some writers have noted that since the Middle Ages, suicide has been more likely to occur in the spring.[134] In the United States today, rates are actually highest in the spring and summer months.[135] Contrary to some folk wisdom, suicide does not appear to be related to lunar phases. It is, however, more likely to occur on Mondays and during the first two weeks of the month[136] It is, for unknown reasons, less likely during the early morning hours of 0400–0800.[137]

Media Coverage and Copy Cat Clusters.   When Diana, Princess of Wales, died tragically a few years ago, the overall suicide rate for England and Wales rose by 17 percent, suicide in women increased 34 percent, and suicide in women of Diana's age increased more than 45 percent in the month following the funeral.[138] When a character in a popular British soap opera died of cervical cancer, cervical smear tests increased by 21 percent.[139] When Marilyn Monroe killed herself, there was a 12 percent increase in the suicide rate during the following month. Generally, there is an approximately 11 percent increase in the week following a widely publicized suicide and a 2 percent increase in the month following the press release.[140] Clearly people are influenced by the behavior of those around them even when—as in the case of the TV heroine—they are not real people.

"The exposure to suicide or suicidal behaviors within one's family, one's peer group, or through media reports of suicide . . . can result in an increase in suicide and suicidal behaviors." This phenomenon is called "suicide contagion."[141] Contagion is more likely in cases where there is deep grief, glorification of the victim, sensationalization of the death, and a supercharged emotional environment.[142] Adolescents and young adults and at-risk individuals such as those who have made previous suicide attempts are most likely to be affected. However, contagion has also been observed in the workplace, the military, rural communities, groups of psychiatric patients, and prison populations.[143] These "copycat" suicides are called "suicide clusters." Suicide clusters have been found throughout history. Early on, suicide contagion was called the "Werther Effect," after a character in a 1774 novel who shot himself and set off a string of similar suicides that eventually caused the book to be banned. This may have been our first realization that the media play an important role in suicide contagion.

Media coverage that tends to promote suicide contagion is more likely to be sensational, simplistic, and repetitive. It is more likely to glorify suicide or the suicide victim, portray suicide as an effective tool, and offer "how-to" advice. It is more likely to be exploitive and shocking. Some have argued that shocking depictions should discourage imitation. Ironically, evidence indicates that they may actually have an alluring appeal for at-risk individuals.[144]

Aware that the media can be either a part of the problem or a part of the solution, several key players in the public health arena have combined forces to draw up research-based recommendations for the media. The suicide prevention community is also attempting to pressure the media to be responsible in reporting and to provide important information that can help save lives. The recommendations include the caution to resist the temptation to overreport. Sensationalism sells, but the number and length of stories has been found to be directly correlated with an increase in suicides. Using these stories as lead stories in radio and TV broadcasts, placing them on the front page of a newspaper, or accompanying them with dramatic headlines can also increase rates of copy cat suicide. More detailed descriptions of the methods or locations can have a similar effect. The media are urged to exercise caution and not to idealize suicide victims, romanticize suicide or portray the act as somehow heroic. Dramatic portrayals of grieving friends and relatives are also discouraged since these might well inadvertently imply that attempting suicide might be a good way to get attention or revenge.[145] On the other hand, journalists are cautioned that suicide is a complex issue and should not be simplistically presented as having resulted solely from a failed relationship, job loss, stress, discrimination, or physical illness. Special care is urged for treatment of celebrity deaths because these are more likely to be imitated than other suicides.[146]

Failure to Seek Help

In athletics, business, and life, those with good coaches, mentors, healthcare providers, and other support personnel are more likely to succeed. World class and Olympic athletes have nutritionists, therapists, sports medicine specialists, and sports psychologists to help them. Similarly, research indicates that those who survive the challenges of adverse life events, suicidal ideation, and low levels of serotonin in their brains are likely to have assistance.[147] Key steps in help-seeking include (1) realizing there is a problem, (2) recognizing that you need help, and (3) reaching out and getting it.[148] Embarrassment, shame, fear, frustration, ignorance, and even arrogance can be barriers to rational help seeking. The most fundamental reason for not seeking help is failure to realize that there is a problem. The elderly may not see a need for help. "I have made it this many years without help, why should I need it now?" Adolescents naively or arrogantly may feel that they are the best ones to solve their problems.[149] One study of young people found that, even when they saw suicidal ideas as one of their biggest problems, 67 percent did not seek help.[150]

Even if at-risk individuals realize that they have a problem and need help, it may be hard for them to seek it. Some people fear that if they admit they are thinking about suicide, they are "crazy," that other people will think they are crazy, or that seeking counseling will prove they are crazy. Some fear they will be "locked up" or that their jobs or careers will be affected. Some are afraid they can't afford help. Others have had unsatisfactory dealings with healthcare professionals, fear loss of confidentiality, don't know where to turn, or just give up.[151] Actually, seeking help may be as easy as dialing a local hotline, logging on to http://www.hopeline.com., calling 1 (800) SUICIDE, or making an appointment at the health center. It may be much easier than being miserable or thinking about suicide.

Warning Signs

According to the American Association of Suicidology, "Nearly everyone at some time in his or her life thinks about suicide. (However, nearly) everyone decides to live because they come to realize that the crisis is temporary, but death is not."[152] Most come to realize that life offers alternatives, but death does not.

It is a myth that "People who talk about suicide, don't do it." Talking about suicide may be a warning sign. According to the AAS, signs that a person may be seriously considering suicide include the following:

- Talking about suicide, death, or the "fact" that there is no reason to live.
- Preoccupation with death and dying.
- Making statements such as, "I won't be a problem for you much longer" or "I'd be better off dead."
- Withdrawing from family, friends, and/or social activities.
- Recently suffering or fearing a significant loss.
- Experiencing drastic behavior changes.
- Losing interest in hobbies, work, school, and previously enjoyed activities.

- Making preparations for death.
- Giving away prized possessions.
- Having previously attempted suicide.
- Taking unnecessary risks, being reckless, and acting impulsively.
- Losing interest in personal appearance.
- Increasing use of alcohol or drugs.
- Expressing a sense of hopelessness and being overwhelmed.
- Being faced with failure or humiliation.
- Having a history of violence or hostility.
- Having been unwilling to "connect" with potential helpers.[153]

Other warning signs include changes in sleep patterns; changes in appetite and weight; sudden mood or behavior changes, feelings of restlessness and inability to concentrate; unshakable feelings of sadness, depression, or hopelessness; inability to think clearly and make decisions; tension, anxiety, or nervousness; impulsiveness; expression of feelings of guilt, low self-worth, and loss of control; pain seemingly without the possibility of relief; and sudden behavior changes, especially sudden calm after a period of anxiety.[154]

The New Zealand Ministry of Education guidelines for schools also lists warning signs teachers (and parents) may see. These include several of those mentioned above as well as:

- Failing performance and grades.
- The appearance in schoolwork of ideas and themes of depression, death, and suicide.
- Signs of significant grief or stress.
- Psychosomatic illnesses.[155]

Precipitating Events

When people are depressed, they may or may not even be capable of organizing a suicide plan. Ironically, sometimes the medication that helps relieve their distress also gives them the energy and focus that helps them to organize a suicide attempt. More frequently, some life event serves as the "last straw" and triggers a suicide attempt. Life events that serve as catalysts for suicide attempts may be real or imagined. Some of the common precipitating events include (1) loss or threatened loss of happiness, a close relationship or communication with a significant other; (2) disruption of an important relationship through, e.g., divorce, separation, death, or lover's breakup; (3) significant disappointment or humiliation; and (4) career failure or setbacks. These stressful events are less likely to lead to suicide attempts if those suffering them have a wide repertoire of healthy coping skills and can rely on a strong network of support. These events are more likely to result in suicide where these resources are not as developed. They are also more likely to result in suicide attempts in cultures where (1) expectations of individuality and self-sufficiency in problem solving are strong; (2) demands to display strength, competence, or effectiveness are great; and (3) individuals and institutions fail or refuse to provide help.[156]

Helping Someone Who Is Suicidal

Suicide is real, and it can happen to someone you know. Suicide is also preventable. The American Association of Suicidology and other organizations offer the following guidelines for those who know someone who needs help:

- Be aware that suicide is a reality. Learn the warning signs.
- Get involved. Become available. Show interest and support.
- Most people contemplating suicide give warnings. If you think you are getting a warning, find a private time and ask.
- Don't be afraid to be direct and talk openly about it. Talking doesn't hurt and not talking may.
- Listen calmly. Allow feelings to be expressed and be accepting of those feelings.
- Be aware that some of the things the person might be feeling include unrelenting pain, depression, and sadness; worthlessness; lack of control; inability to think clearly or make decisions; and that no one cares and there is no way out.
- Be nonjudgmental. Don't debate whether suicide is right or wrong or life is or is not worth living. Don't lecture.
- Never dare a person contemplating suicide to do it.
- Avoid the temptation to tell people what to do to solve their problems. There is a thin line between helping and meddling.
- Don't put people on the defensive by pushing them to explain "why" they would consider suicide.
- Try to offer empathy rather than sympathy.
- Don't act shocked. This may be taken by people in crisis as additional evidence of their unworthiness and may create distance between you.
- Refuse to promise not to tell anyone. Instead, try to find help and support.
- Offer hope that alternatives are available, but avoid statements such as, "It will all be better in the morning." This appears to trivialize the problem and indicates that you really don't understand and may not care.
- Take action! Try to get people to postpone any action for a while and offer to help them find help and support. (Therapists sometimes negotiate "no-suicide contracts" specifying such things as a specific time period and contingency conditions if the person feels compelled to break the agreement.)
- Take action! Remove things that might be used to implement a suicide attempt.
- Get help! Suicide crisis hotlines; community mental health agencies; school counselors, psychologists, or therapists; suicide prevention/crisis intervention centers; medical doctors; religious leaders and others are trained in crisis intervention and suicide prevention or can refer you to someone who is. Don't overlook family and friends as a possible source of help and support. Call 1 (800) 367-7287 or 1 (800) SUICIDE (784-2433).[157] There are also a variety of good books on suicide that may be helpful. Some of these are written by people who have intimate knowledge of suicide. These include: *How I Stayed Alive When My Brain Was Trying to Kill Me: One Person's Guide to Suicide Prevention* by Susan Rose Blauner (New York: Harper Collins Publishers Inc., 2002), and *Suicide: The Forever Decision: For Those Think-*

ing About Suicide, and for Those Who Know, Love, and Counsel Them by Paul G. Quinnett (New York: Crossroads Publishing Company, 2000).

Attempting Suicide

Each year, more than 765,000 Americans attempt suicide.[158] These attempts may not be dismissed as either indicating a lower level of commitment or as resolution of suicidal ideation. Between 20 and 50 percent of people who commit suicide have attempted suicide before.[159] Indeed, "Prior attempt is the strongest predictor of suicide."[160] In the year immediately following the attempt, the rate of completed suicide is 100 times greater among attempters than in the general population.[161] Research indicates that attempters may continue to be at increased risk fifteen[162] or twenty years after their initial attempt.[163] Indeed, a Finnish study that followed attempters for nearly four decades has concluded that "a history of a suicide attempt by self-poisoning indicates suicide risk over the entire adult lifetime."[164]

According to the Suicide Information and Education Center (SEIC), you can help someone who has attempted suicide by:

- Showing you are concerned and care.
- Offering your support and listening without judging or criticizing.
- Offering hope and reassurance.
- Ensuring a safe, suicide-proof environment.
- Facing your own fears and worries, taking care of yourself, and getting help if you need it.
- Assisting the attempter to identify and build a safety net of support that includes trusted friends, professionals, and community resources.
- Learning the suicide warning signs and intervention techniques.
- If the attempter is diagnosed with a psychiatric diagnosis, working with the attempter to seek and maintain treatment; being or finding an advocate for him or her.
- Providing reassurance, offering practical help and support, helping find ways of making changes or alleviating stress.[165]

Physician-Assisted Suicide

Although the issue of assisted suicide has received a great deal of public attention, research indicates that very few terminally ill people seriously consider ending their own lives. Nevertheless, the flamboyant advocacy of Dr. Jack Kevorkian has aroused considerable interest in the issue. A professional taskforce report on the topic concluded that "Nearly everyone can agree . . . that involuntary euthanasia is completely unacceptable and that no one should have to suffer intolerably in order to preserve life at all costs."[166] From that point, there has been extensive debate on moral, ethical, religious, public policy, personal freedom, and legal battlegrounds.

Physician-assisted suicide is the intentional termination of one's life by means of medicine and/or medical advice provided by a doctor. Assisted suicide is distinct from euthanasia, double-effect medication, and withholding or withdrawing life-sustaining treatment. Euthanasia, or "mercy killing," usually involves painlessly causing the death of a person with a painful, or incurable illness. Double-effect medication involves providing pain medication sufficient to relieve suffering even though death may be a side effect of the treatment. Withholding or withdrawing life-sustaining treatment is a course the patient or the patient's representative in consultation with the doctor may take when the treatment appears to be doing more harm than good, when it is, for example, prolonging the dying rather than prolonging the living.

Briefly stated, the position of those who favor a "right to die" is that this is an issue of personal freedom and an individual's right to control his or her destiny. In addition, medicine is incapable of relieving physical pain in some situations (terminal cancer, for example) or emotional pain in others (Alzheimer's disease, for example). In these cases, compassion requires that this alternative be made available.

The position of the group opposing assisted suicide is that involving physicians violates their oath and commitment to healing. They feel that patients should not attempt to involve their physicians in something many consider immoral and inappropriate. This group also feels that involving physicians undermines the physician/patient relationship and can lead to abuse. They note that Dr. Kevorkian, for example, has been inclined to answer the patient's request for life-ending treatment without considering what other treatments might be helpful in addressing the problem. They claim that, in at least some of the cases in which he has been involved, patients could have benefited greatly from better diagnosis and treatment.[167] One study found, for example, that depression, lack of social support, and lack of hope were better predictors of people who wanted to die than were pain and anxiety.[168] For those who were committed to ending their lives, they argue that hospice programs are available throughout the nation and that these resources in addition to better forms of pain control make suicide for relief of pain unnecessary.[169]

Assisted suicide is legal only in the state of Oregon.[170] It is interesting to note that even in that state, it is an alternative seldom selected. Indeed, terminally ill patients are currently twice as likely to end their lives by refusing food and fluids as by assisted suicide.[171]

Prevention and Protection

The National Strategy for Suicide Prevention identifies things we can do on the national level to reduce the level of suicide. These include making it easier for get help for physical, mental, and substance abuse disorders, which increase suicide risk, and making it harder to obtain lethal means. They also include encouraging strong family, medical, and mental healthcare relationships and promoting cultural and religious beliefs in opposition to suicide.[172]

The Suicide Information and Education Centre of the Canadian Mental Health Association also lists personal protective factors that should be nurtured. These include (1) a sense of self-worth and purpose, (2) effective communication and the ability to effectively "think things through," (3) a network of friends who do not use drugs, and (4) strong, healthy families with consistent parenting that serve as a training ground for learning resiliency. The SIEC report notes that "Teaching [children] how to cope is the greatest gift parents can give their children."[173]

The Centers for Disease Control have issued recommendations for a community plan for prevention of suicide contagion. It advises that communities develop response plans in advance, identify community resources, and determine how they will be used. When multiple suicides or suicides with strong contagion potential occur, plans should be activated taking care not to glorify or sensationalize the suicide or multiple suicides. High-risk individuals should be identified, screened, and referred to counseling. The media should be kept informed. Environmental risk factors and long-term issues should be identified and addressed.[174]

CRITICAL THINKING EXERCISES

1. Throughout history there has been a continuing debate concerning whether suicide is a question of free will or a usurpation of the prerogative of God or the state. What do you think and why?

2. What are some of the signs that a person is contemplating suicide?

3. What are some of the things you can do to help stop a friend who is contemplating suicide?

4. What are some of the factors that "insulate" against suicide? How do they work to keep people from attempting or committing suicide?

5. Construct a "Grand Theory of Suicide," using various theories presented in this chapter as building blocks.

6. Do you think that physician-assisted suicide should be legal? Defend your answer.

CHECK IT OUT ON THE WEB

The Internet addresses listed below are intended to provide the reader with understanding of a wide range of perspectives on the subject matter discussed in this chapter. Some sites may contain objectionable material. The list is not intended to reflect the viewpoints or opinions of the authors or the publisher.

http://www.who.int.whr2001/main/en/chapter2/002g.htm
        international data
http://www.hopeline.com
        help for those thinking about suicide
http://www.suicide hotline.com
        help for those thinking about suicide
http://www.save.org/depressed/checklist.html
        depression checklist
http://www.afsp.org
        information provided by the American Foundation for Suicide Prevention
http://www.siec.ca
        information provided by the Suicide Information and Education Center, Canada
http://www.suicidology.org
        alerts provided by the American Association of Suicidology
http://www.afsp.org/education/recommendations.5/l.htm
        media recommendations

http://www.hlm.nih.gov/medlineplus/print/ency/article/001554.htm
medical information in encyclopedia format
http://MayoClinic.com
information on depression and other health-related topics

ENDNOTES

1. Reuters News, *CNN News Website,* "Cuddling New Craze for New York's Singles," Monday, August 9, 2004 Posted: 11:47 AM EDT (1547 GMT).

2. John L. McIntosh, *U.S.A. Suicide: 2001 Official Final Data* (Washington, DC: American Association of Suicidology, 2003).

3. Shiloh S. Jiwnlal and Cathy Weitzel, "The Suicide Myth," *RN, 64* (January 2001), p. 33.

4. Personal communication with the administrative director, American Association of Suicidology, August 2004.

5. Ronald W. Maris, Alan L. Berman, and Morton M. Silverman, *Comprehensive Textbook of Suicidology* (New York: Guilford Press, 2000), p. 197.

6. Edward Sagarin and Fred Montanino, eds., *Deviants: Voluntary Actors in a Hostile World* (New York: General Learning Press, 1977), p. 506.

7. Ibid., p. 507.

8. Leonardo Tondo, MD, and Ross Baldessarini, *Suicide: Historical, Descriptive, and Epidemiological Considerations* (Golden, CO: Medical Education Collaborative, 2001), p. 4.

9. Sagarin and Montanino, *Deviants: Voluntary Actors in a Hostile World,* p. 507.

10. Ronald W. Maris, Alan L. Berman, and Morton M. Silverman, *Comprehensive Textbook of Suicidology,* p. 101.

11. Ibid., p. 103.

12. Ibid.

13. Leonardo Tondo, MD, and Ross Baldessarini, *Suicide: Historical, Descriptive, and Epidemiological Considerations,* p. 3.

14. Sagarin and Montanino, *Deviants: Voluntary Actors in a Hostile World,* p. 506.

15. Ibid., p. 508.

16. Maris, Berman, and Silverman, *Comprehensive Textbook of Suicidology,* p. 111.

17. Ibid., p. 112.

18. Tondo and Baldessarini, *Suicide: Historical, Descriptive, and Epidemiological Considerations,* p. 4.

19. Ibid., p. 3.

20. Sagarin and Montanino, *Deviants: Voluntary Actors in a Hostile World,* p. 509.

21. Ibid.

22. U.S. Surgeon General, *National Strategy for Suicide Prevention: Goals and Objectives for Action* (Washington, DC: U.S. Department of Health and Human Services, 2001), pp. 139, 614.

23. J. J. Mann, "The Neurobiology of Suicide," *Nature Medicine, 4* (Winter 1998), p. 26.

24. National Institute of Mental Health, *Frequently Asked Questions about Suicide* (Washington, DC: U.S. Government Printing Office 1999), pp. 2–3.

25. Ping Qin, Esben Agerbo, and Preben Mortensen, "Suicide Risk in Relations to Family History of Completed Suicide and Psychiatric Disorders: A Nested Case-Control Study Based on Longitudinal Registers," *The Lancet, 360* (Summer 2002), pp. 126–1130; Maris, Berman, and Silverman, *Comprehensive Textbook of Suicidology,* pp. 377–380.

26. National Institute of Mental Health, *Frequently Asked Questions about Suicide,* p. 3.

27. Maris, Berman, and Silverman, *Comprehensive Textbook of Suicidology,* pp. 379–380.

28. P. Wender, S. Kety, D. Rosenthal, and F. Schulsinger, "Psychiatric Disorders in the Biological and Adoptive Families of Adopted Individuals with Affective Disorders," *Archives of General Psychiatry, 43* (Summer 1986), pp. 923–929; S. Ketty, "Genetic Factors in Suicide: Family, Twin, and Adoption Studies," in S. J. Blumenthal and D. J. Kupfer, eds., *Suicide over the Life Cycle* (Washington, DC: American Psychiatric Press), pp. 127–133.

29. Maris, Berman, and Silverman, *Comprehensive Textbook of Suicidology,* pp. 52, 524.

30. Ibid., p. 524.

31. Ibid., p. 50.

32. Ibid., pp. 242–246.

33. Emile Durkheim, *Suicide,* Translated by John A. Spaulding and George Simpson (New York: The Free Press, 1897), p. 363.

34. Christoph Reuter with Helena Ragg-Kiry translator, *My Life as a Weapon: A Modern History of Suicide Bombing* (Princeton: Princeton University Press, 2004).

35. Barbara Victor, *Army of Roses* (Emmaus, PA: Rodale, 2003).

36. Ibid.

37. Emile Durkheim, *Suicide,* p. 276.

38. Jack P. Gibbs and Walter Martin, *Status Integration and Suicide: A Sociological Study* (Eugene: University of Oregon Books, 1964).

39. Sandra Harley Carey, *A Diachronic and Synchronic Analysis of the Relation between Cause Specific*

Mortality Patterns and Status Integration. Unpublished Doctoral Dissertation, 1979, pp. 31–34.

40. Ibid., pp. 3–36, 51.

41. Ibid., pp. 31–34.

42. Jack P. Gibbs, "Status Integration and Suicide: Occupational, Marital, or Both?" *Social Forces, 79* (December 2000), pp. 363–364.

43. Steven Stack, "Interstate Migration and the Rate of Suicide," *International Journal of Social Psychiatry, 26* (Winter 1980), pp. 17–26.

44. Steven Stack, "Work and the Economy," in Maris, Berman, and Silverman, *Comprehensive Textbook of Suicidology,* pp. 193–195.

45. Michael Phillips, Xianyun Li, and Yanping Zhang, "Suicide Rates in China, 1995–99," *The Lancet, 359* (March 2002), p. 13.

46. Tondo and Baldessarini, *Suicide: Historical, Descriptive, and Epidemiological Considerations,* p. 9.

47. A. Schmidtke, "Perspectives: Suicide in Europe," in A. A. Leenaars, R. W. Maris and Y. Takahashi, eds., *Suicide: Individual, Cultural, International Perspectives,* (New York: Guilford Press 1997), p. 128.

48. Ibid., p. 79.

49. Ibid.

50. World Health Organization data online at http://www.who.int/whr2001/2001/main/en/chapter2/002g.htm

51. Raj Persaud, "Suicide: An Unnecessary Death," *British Medical Journal, 323* (July 2001), p. 14.

52. Ibid., p. 114.

53. Zosia Kmietowicz, "A Fifth of Suicides among People with Mental Illness Are Preventable," *British Medical Journal, 322* (March 2001), p. 884; Michael Phillips, Xianyun Li, and Yanping Zhang, "Suicide Rates in China, 1995–99," *The Lancet, 359* (March 2002), p. 835.

54. Lawrence M. Salinger, *Deviant Behavior 96/97* (Guilford, CT: Duskin Publishing Group/Brown & Benchmark, 1996), p. 10.

55. David Taylor, "Medical Encyclopedia: Suicide and Suicidal Behavior," *Medline Plus,* U.S. National Library of Medicine and The National Institutes of Health (Washington, DC, 2003), p. 1; American Association of Suicidology, "Some Facts about Suicide and Depression,"(Washington, DC: American Association of Suicidology, 1999).

56. U.S. Department of Health and Human Services, Public Health Service, *National Strategy for Suicide Prevention: Goals and Objectives for Action,* (Washington, DC; U.S. Government Printing Office, 2001), pp. 52, 71.

57. John L. McIntosh, *U.S.A. Suicide: 2001 Official Final Data* (Washington, DC: American Association of Suicidology, 2003).

58. Ibid.

59. U.S. Department of Health and Human Services, *National Strategy for Suicide Prevention,* p. 87.

60. Susan Rose Blauner, *How I Stayed Alive When My Brain Was Trying to Kill Me: One Person's Guide to Suicide Prevention* (New York: HarperCollins, 2003), Publisher's note.

61. John L. McIntosh, *U.S.A. Suicide: 2001 Official Final Data.*

62. Ibid.

63. American Association of Suicidology, *Some Facts About Suicide in the U.S.A.* (Washington, DC: American Association of Suicidology), p. 1.

64. Tondo and Baldessarini, *Suicide: Historical, Descriptive, and Epidemiological Considerations,* p. 9.

65. U.S. Department of Health and Human Services, *National Strategy for Suicide Prevention,* p. 36.

66. Ibid.

67. Shawn Christopher Shea, *The Practical Art of Suicide Assessment* (New York: John Wiley & Sons, 1999), p. 100.

68. Austin L. Porterfield, "The Problem of Suicide," in Jack P. Gibbs, ed. *Suicide* (New York: Harper & Row 1968), p. 507; Tondo and Baldessarini, *Suicide: Historical, Descriptive, and Epidemiological Considerations,* p. 9.

69. American Association of Suicidology, "Some Facts about Suicide and Depression."

70. David Taylor, "Medical Encyclopedia: Suicide and Suicidal Behavior," p. l.

71. American Association of Suicidology, "Some Facts about Suicide and Depression," p. 1.

72. Margda Waern, "Mental Disorder in Elderly Suicides: A Case-Control Study," *Issues in Law & Medicine, 18* (Summer 2002).

73. Zosia Kmietowicz, "A Fifth of Suicides among People with Mental Illness Are Preventable," p. 633.

74. Ronald W. Maris, Alan L. Berman, and Morton M. Silverman, *Comprehensive Textbook of Suicidology,* p. 101; John L. McIntosh, *U.S.A. Suicide: 2001 Official Final Data.*

75. Ronald W. Maris, Alan L. Berman, and Morton M. Silverman, *Comprehensive Textbook of Suicidology,* p. 143.

76. D. N. Jouurlink, N. Herrmann, J. P. Szalai, A. Kopp, and D. A. Redelmeier, "Medical Illness and the Risk of Suicide in the Elderly," *Archives of Internal Medicine* 164 (June 2004), p. 1179.

77. American Association of Suicidology, *Elderly Suicide Fact Sheet,* (Washington, DC: American Association of Suicidology, October 2002), p. 2.

78. Ibid., p. 1.

79. John L. McIntosh, *U.S.A. Suicide: 2001 Official Final Data.*

80. Suicide Information & Education Center, SIEC ALERT #20, *Suicide Among the Aged* (Calgary, Alberta, Canada: Canadian Mental Health Association, February 1998).

81. Ibid.

82. Peter Lewinsohn, Paul Rohde, John Seeley, and Carol Baldwin, "Gender Differences in Suicide Attempts from Adolescence to Young Adulthood," *Journal of the American Academy of Child and Adolescent Psychiatry, 40* (April 2001), p. 427; American Association of Suicidology, *Youth Suicide Fact Sheet* (Washington, DC: American Association of Suicidology, 2003), pp. 1–2.

83. John L. McIntosh, *U.S.A. Suicide: 2001 Official Final Data.* David Taylor, "Medical Encyclopedia: Suicide and Suicidal Behavior."

84. David Shaffer, Michelle Scott, Holly Wilcox, Carey MasLow, Roger Hicks, Christopher Lucs, Robin Garfinkel, and Steven Greenwald, "The Columbia Suicide Screen: Validity and Reliability of a Screen for Youth Suicide and Depression," *Journal of the American Academy of Child and Adolescent Psychiatry, 43* (January 2004), p. 71.

85. Ronald W. Maris, Alan L. Berman, and Morton M. Silverman, *Comprehensive Textbook of Suicidology,* p. 143.

86. I. W. Borowsky, M. Ireland, and M. D. Resnick, "Adolescent Suicide Attempts: Risks and Protectors," *Journal of Developmental & Behavioral Pediatrics, 22* (August 2001), p. 1301; Simone Fullagar, "Wasted Lives: the Social Dynamics of Shame and Youth Suicide," *Journal of Sociology, 39* (September 2003), p. 291; Leonardo Tondo, MD, and Ross Baldessarini, *Suicide: Historical, Descriptive, and Epidemiological Considerations,* pp. 12–13.

87. Robert King, "Psychosocial and Risk Behavior Correlates of Youth Suicide Attempts and Suicidal Ideation," *Journal of the American Academy of Child and Adolescent Psychiatry, 40* (July 2001), p. 837.

88. A.D.S., "Adolescent Suicide Attempts: Risks and Protectors, *Journal of Developmental and Behavioral Pediatrics, 22* (August 2001), 261.

89. Tracey Guertin, Elizabeth Lloyd-Richardson, Anthony Spirito, Diedre Donaldson, and Julie Boergers, "Self-Mutilative Behavior in Adolescents Who Attempt Suicide by Overdose," *Journal of the American Academy of Child and Adolescent Psychiatry, 40* (September 2001), p. 1062.

90. Leonardo Tondo, MD, and Ross Baldessarini, *Suicide: Historical, Descriptive, and Epidemiological Considerations,* pp. 12–13; Simone Fullagar, "Wasted Lives: the Social Dynamics of Shame and Youth Suicide," p. 291; A.D.S., "Adolescent Suicide Attempts: Risks and Protectors," p. 261.

91. Ronald W. Maris, Alan L. Berman, and Morton M. Silverman, *Comprehensive Textbook of Suicidology,* p. 143; P. S. Barman and J. Moody, "Suicide and Friendships among American Adolescents," *American Journal of Public Health, 94* (January 2004), p. 93.

92. Christine Walrath, David Mandell, Qinghong Liao, E. Wayne Holden, Gary De Carolis, Rolando Santiago, and Philip Leaf, "Suicide Attempts in the 'Comprehensive Community Mental Health Services for Children and Their Families Program'", *Journal of the American Academy of Child and Adolescent Psychiatry, 40* (October 2001), p. 1197.

93. A.D.S., "Adolescent Suicide Attempts: Risks and Protectors, p. 261.

94. American Association of Suicidology, *Youth Suicide Fact Sheet* (Washington, DC: American Association of Suicidology, 2003), p. 2.

95. Lawrence S. Wrightsman, *Social Psychology* (Monterey, CA: Brooks/Cole Publishing 1977), p. 214.

96. Silvia Sara Canetto and David Lister, "Love and Achievement Motives in Women's and Men's Suicide Notes," *The Journal of Psychology, 136* (September 2002), p. 573.

97. U.S. Department of Health and Human Services, *National Strategy for Suicide Prevention,* pp. 167–168.

98. Lawrence M. Salinger, *Deviant Behavior 96/97* (Guilford, CT: Duskin Publishing Group/Brown & Benchmark, 1996), p. 10; National Institute of Mental Health, *Frequently Asked Questions about Suicide* (Washington, DC: U.S. Government Printing Office 1999), pp. 2–3.

99. Leonardo Tondo, MD, and Ross Baldessarini, *Suicide: Historical, Descriptive, and Epidemiological Considerations* (Medical Education Collaborative, 2001), p. 13; Michael Phillips, Xianyun Li, and Yanping Zhang, "Suicide Rates in China, 1995–99," *The Lancet, 359* (March 2002), pp. 1, 10; National Institute of Mental Health, *Frequently Asked Questions about Suicide,* p. 1.

100. American Association of Suicidology, *Some Facts About Suicide in the U.S.A.,* p. 1; Jack P. Gibbs, "Testing the Theory of Status Integration and Suicide Rates," *American Sociological Review, 47* (Winter 1982), pp. 227–237.

101. American Association of Suicidology, *Some Facts About Suicide in the U.S.A.,* p. 1; Ronald W. Maris, Alan L. Berman, and Morton M. Silverman, *Comprehensive Textbook of Suicidology,* p. 222.

102. Ronald W. Maris, Alan L. Berman, and Morton M. Silverman, *Comprehensive Textbook of Suicidology,* p. 252.

103. Karl E. Miller, "Parental Status and Risk of Completed Suicide," *American Family Physician, 69* (February 2004), p. 986.

104. W. Harrison, "Adolescent Homosexuality and Concerns Regarding Disclosure," *Journal of School Health, 73* (March 2003), p. 107.

105. Trevor Hazell, *Gay and Lesbian Youth Suicide* (Canberra, Australia: Hunter Institute of Mental Health, 1998), pp. 1–6.

106. Ronald W. Maris, Alan L. Berman, and Morton M. Silverman, *Comprehensive Textbook of Suicidology,* p. 160.

107. National Institute of Mental Health, *Frequently Asked Questions about Suicide,* p. 1.

108. Ibid., p. 171.

109. National Institute of Mental Health, *Frequently Asked Questions about Suicide,* pp. 2–3; American Association of Suicidology, *Youth Suicide Fact Sheet.*

110. Ibid., p. 1.

111. Ronald W. Maris, Alan L. Berman, and Morton M. Silverman, *Comprehensive Textbook of Suicidology,* pp. 176, 190.

112. Ronald W. Maris, Alan L. Berman, and Morton M. Silverman, *Comprehensive Textbook of Suicidology,* p. 174.

113. Ronald W. Maris, Silvia Sara Canetto, John L. McIntosh, and Morton M. Silverman, *Review of Suicidology, 2000* (New York: The Guilford Press, 2000), p. 248.

114. American Association of Suicidology, *Some Facts About Suicide in the U.S.A.,* p. 1.

115. Louis H. Zayas, Carol Kaplan, Sandra Turner, Kathleen Romano, Gladys Gonzalez-Ramos, "Understanding Suicide Attempts by Adolescent Hispanic Females," *Social Work,* 45 (January 2000), p. 53.

116. Lynn Rew, Nancy Thomas, Sharon Homer, Michael Resnick, Trisha Beuhrin, "Correlates of Recent Suicide Attempts in Triethnic Group of Adolescents," *Journal of Nursing Scholarship, 33* (Winter 2001), p. 361.

117. Louis H. Zayas, Carol Kaplan, Sandra Turner, Kathleen Romano, Gladys Gonzalez-Ramos, "Understanding Suicide Attempts by Adolescent Hispanic Females," pp. 53–54.

118. American Association of Suicidology, *Some Facts About Suicide in the U.S.A.*

119. Ronald W. Maris, Alan L. Berman, and Morton M. Silverman, *Comprehensive Textbook of Suicidology,* p. 191.

120. American Association of Suicidology, "Some Facts about Suicide and Depression," p. 1,

121. Ibid.

122. Evelyn M. Kitagawa and Philip M. Hauser, *Differential Mortality in the United States: A Study in Socioeconomic Epidemiology* (Cambridge, MA: Harvard University Press, 1973); Raj Persaud, "Suicide: An Unnecessary Death," *British Medical Journal.*

123. T. A. Blakely, S. C. D. Collings, and J. Atkinson, "Unemployment and Suicide. Evidence for a Causal Association?" *Journal of Epidemiology & Community Health, 57* (August 2003), p. 594.

124. Ronald W. Maris, Alan L. Berman, and Morton M. Silverman, *Comprehensive Textbook of Suicidology,* pp. 214–220.

125. Sandra Harley Carey, *A Diachronic and Synchronic Analysis of the Relation between Cause Specific Mortality Patterns and Status Integration.*

126. Ronald W. Maris, Alan L. Berman, and Morton M. Silverman, *Comprehensive Textbook of Suicidology,* pp. 214–220.

127. David Lester, "Suicide in Police Officers: A Survey of Nations," *Police Studies, 15* (Winter 1992), pp. 146–147.

128. Hawton, A. Clemets, C Sakarovitch, S. Simkin, and J. S. Deeks, "Suicide in Doctors: A Study of Risk According to Gender, Seniority, and Specialty in Medical Parishioners in England and Wales, 1979–1995," *Journal of Epidemiology & Community Health, 55* (May 2001), pp. 296–298; Ronald W. Maris, Alan L. Berman, and Morton M. Silverman, *Comprehensive Textbook of Suicidology,* pp. 214–220.

129. Stephen Platt and Keith Hawton, "Suicidal Behavior and the Labour Market" in K. Hawton and K. van Heeringen, *The International Handbook of Suicide and Attempted Suicide* (New York: John Wiley & Sons, 2000), p. 309.

130. D. P. Phillips and J. Liu, "The Frequency of Suicides Around Major Public Holidays: Some Surprising Findings," *Suicide and Life-Threatening Behavior, 10* (Spring 1980).

131. Leonardo Tondo, MD, and Ross Baldessarini, *Suicide: Historical, Descriptive, and Epidemiological Considerations,* p. 13.

132. Suicide Information & Education Center, SIEC ALERT #16, *Are Suicide Rates Higher at Christmas?* (Calgary, Alberta, Canada: Canadian Mental Health Association, December 1995), p. 1.

133. Alison McCook, "Suicide Rates Highest in Spring, Summer Months," *American Journal of Psychiatry, 160* (Winter 2003), pp. 793–795.

134. Leonardo Tondo, MD, and Ross Baldessarini, *Suicide: Historical, Descriptive, and Epidemiological Considerations,* p. 13; Alison McCook, "Suicide Rates Highest in Spring, Summer Months," p. 795.

135. American Foundation for Suicide Prevention, *Frequently Asked Questions,* p. 1.

136. Ronald W. Maris, Silvia Sara Canetto, John L. McIntosh, and Morton M. Silverman, *Review of Suicidology, 2000,* p. iii.

137. G. Maldonado and J. F. Kraus, "Variation in Suicide Occurrence by Time of Day, Day of the Week, and Month, and Lunar Phase," *Suicide and Life Threatening Behavior, 21* (Summer 1991), pp. 174–187.

138. Raj Persaud, "Suicides Rise After Diana's Death," *British Medical Journal, 321* (November 2000), p. 1243.

139. American Association of Suicidology, "Some Facts about Suicide and Depression," p. 498.

140. Mark Miller, "Tough Calls: Deciding When a Suicide Is Newsworthy and What Details to Include Are Among Journalism's More Sensitive Decisions," *American Journalism Review, 42* (December 2002).

141. National Institute of Mental Health, *Frequently Asked Questions about Suicide,* p. 4.

142. Suicide Information & Education Center, SIEC ALERT #36, *A Suicide Attempt is Meaningful and Significant* (Calgary, Alberta, Canada: Canadian Mental Health Association, July 2001), p. 42.

143. Ibid.

144. Ibid, p. 2.

145. Taskforce Representing: Centers for Disease Control and Prevention, National Institute of Mental Heath, Office of the Surgeon General, Substance Abuse and Mental Health Services Administration, American Foundation for Suicide Prevention, American Association of Suicidology, and the Annenberg Public Policy Center, *Reporting on Suicide: Recommendations for the Media* (Washington DC: U.S. Government Printing Office, 2001), p. 2.

146. Ibid., pp. 3–4.

147. Suicide Information and Education Center, SIEC ALERT #35, Barriers *to Help-Seeking* (Calgary, Alberta, Canada: Canadian Mental Health Association, May 1999), p. 1.

148. R. C. Kessler, R. L. Brown, and C. L. Broman, "Sex Differences in Psychiatric Help-Seeking: Evidence from Four Large-Scale Surveys," *Journal of Health and Social Behavior, 22* (March 1981), pp. 49–64.

149. Ibid.

150. E. F. Dubow, K. R. Lovko, and D. F. Kausch, "Demographic Differences in Adolescents' Health Concerns and Perceptions of Helping Agents," *Journal of Clinical Child Psychology, 19* (March 1990), pp. 44–54.

151. Suicide Information and Education Center, SIEC ALERT #35, *Barriers to Help-Seeking.*

152. American Association of Suicidology, *Some Facts about Suicide in the U.S.A.,* p. 2.

153. Adapted from American Association of Suicidology, *Understanding and Helping the Suicidal Individual* (Washington, DC: American Association of Suicidology); information provided by the Teen Education and Crisis Hotline, S. W. Johnson and L. J. Maile, *Suicide and the Schools: A Handbook fro Prevention, Intervention, and Rehabilitation* (Springfield, IL: Charles C. Thomas, 1987);and Shawn Christopher Shea, *The Practical Art of Suicide Assessment* (New York: John Wiley & Sons, 1999), p. 100.

154. David Taylor, "Medical Encyclopedia: Suicide and Suicidal Behavior."

155. Suicide Information and Education Center, SIEC ALERT #32, *Considerations for School Suicide Prevention Programs* (Calgary, Alberta, Canada: Canadian Mental Health Association, October, 1998), p. 1.

156. Adapted from S. W. Johnson and L. J. Maile, *Suicide and the Schools: A Handbook for Prevention, Intervention, and Rehabilitation* and Jeff Bauer, "Hospice Patients are More Likely to Stop Eating Than to Opt for Assisted Suicide."

157. Suicide Information & Education Center, SIEC ALERT #49, *No-Suicide Contracts: A Review of the Findings from the Research* (Calgary, Alberta, Canada: Canadian Mental Health Association, September 2002); Suicide Information & Education Center, SIEC ALERT #55, *Helping Someone Who May Be Suicidal* (Calgary, Alberta, Canada: Canadian Mental Health Association, July 2001).

158. John L. McIntosh, *U.S.A. Suicide: 2001 Official Final Data.*

159. American Federation of Suicide Prevention Website, "Danger Signs of Suicide."

160. K. Suominen, E. Isometsa, J. Soukas, J. Haukka, K. Achte, and J. Lonnqvist, "Completed Suicide After a Suicide Attempt: A 37-Year Follow-up Study," *American Journal of Psychiatry, 161* (March 2004), p. 562.

161. Gary R. Jenkins, Robert Hale, Maria Papanastassiou, Michael J. Crawford, Peter Tyrer, "Suicide Rate 22 Years After Para Suicide: Cohort Study, " *British Medical Journal, 325* (November 2002), p. 1155

162. Editor, "Risk of Suicide Remains High Fifteen Years After Deliberate Self-Harm," *Evidence-Based Mental Health, 6* (November 2003), p. 106.

163. Ibid.

164. K. Suominen, E. Isometsa, J. Soukas, J. Haukka, K. Achte and J. Lonnqvist, "Completed Suicide After a Suicide Attempt: A 37-Year Follow-up Study," pp. 562–563.

165. Suicide Information & Education Center, SIEC ALERT #45, *A Suicide Attempt Is Meaningful and Significant.*

166. "Report of the Committee on Physician-Assisted Suicide and Euthanasia," *Suicide and Life Threatening Behavior, 26* (Summer 1996).

167. John Donnelly, *Suicide* (Amherst, NY: Prometheus Books, 1998), pp. 225–261.

168. Elizabeth Mayfield Arnold, "Factors That Influence Consideration of Hastening Death among People with Life-Threatening Illnesses," *Health and Social Work, 29* (February 2004), p. 17.

169. Ibid.

170. Roxanne Nelson, "Oregon Court Upholds Assisted-Suicide Law," *The Lancet, 363* (June 2004), p. 1877.

171. Jeff Bauer, "Hospice Patients Are More Likely to Stop Eating Than to Opt for Assisted Suicide," *RN, 66* (September 2003), p. 98.

172. U.S. Department of Health and Human Services, *National Strategy for Suicide Prevention,* p. 35.

173. Suicide Information & Education Center, SIEC ALERT #40, *Suicide Prevention Doesn't Always Mean Talking About Suicide* (Calgary, Alberta, Canada: Canadian Mental Health Association, April 2000).

174. Suicide Information & Education Center, SIEC ALERT #36, A *Suicide Attempt Is Meaningful and Significant.*

11 Cyberdeviance

WITH JEFFREY ARBAUGH

At this moment we are in the midst of an era that will eventually be known as a technological revolution. Just as the Industrial Revolution changed the world in countless ways, the galloping technological developments of recent decades are transforming the ways in which we live: from how we go shopping and elect presidents to how we make money, receive medical attention, pay bills, socialize, communicate in our private and public lives, listen to music, and, yes, acquire an education. These are exciting times, as they say; there is no turning back from our "techno-revolution," and no end in sight to the possibilities for change that may occur.

The Internet and the use of cyberspace have been generally available to anyone on the earth who has access to a computer and phone line since, practically speaking, the late 1980s. Our lives have been enriched to such a degree that it is hard to imagine how we got along without these developments. There is a downside, of course, that accompanies the continuing technological enhancement of our quality of life. Criminals—*any type of criminal*—may utilize the same tools that put the world before us on a computer screen. Any traditional, familiar sort of crime or deviance may be perpetrated on a grand scale in cyberspace. People who are interested in traditional deviant behavior find a comfortable, anonymous environment in cyberspace and may pursue those interests by surfing Web sites and in chat room interaction without the restraints and inhibitions associated with open society. Along with the enormous opportunity that cyberspace provides for traditional crime and deviant behavior, esoteric forms of deviance that are unique to the computer environment have developed. Indeed, many of the determined geniuses who developed the technology necessary for the existence of cyberspace could be described as "deviant" from some perspectives. Steve Wozniak, for example, started out as a "phreaker" manipulating the telephone system and went on to become a founder of Apple Computers. Shawn Fanning was 18 years old when he dropped out of college and spent months, sometimes 60 hours at a stretch, writing the source code for the Napster file-sharing system that allowed Internet users to swap music files directly. In his book *Cybershock*,[1] Winn Schwartau describes the computer genius breed as often bored underachievers in school. They are likely to be highly intelligent, curious, and determined in pursuing certain types of challenges. Many have addictive personalities and narcissistic personality disorder from lack of attention and incomplete family life during adolescence.

Cyberdeviance is a fascinating mix of old crime and new opportunity, old deviance and new exposure, and revolutionary behavior trends unique to the complex world of the cyberspace environment.

The Computer Underground

Those who are intent upon using new technologies to take advantage of others through deception usually discover the weaknesses and vulnerabilities of those new technologies long before the agents of social control and law enforcement do.[2] A small subculture known as the *computer underground* grew out of the vast web that is the Internet, and over the years the media, law enforcement, and other government officials have incorrectly labeled the individuals involved as "hackers," probably because the term is universally associated with unauthorized computer manipulations of any sort.

In the early days of computers the first users referred to each other as hackers, reflecting the cooperative and collaborative atmosphere in which they operated.[3] Various groups of individuals banded together to share information and solve technological problems.[4] They would typically "hack" at a string of computer code, thereby improving it. The term *hacker* was thus originally intended to be a complimentary recognition of someone's computer skills.[5] In fact, the basic software beneath all e-mail and Web-browsing was created collaboratively by unpaid hackers around the globe, whom Steven Levy has designated the heroes of the computer revolution.[6]

These heroes, according to Levy, share the "hacker ethic," which contains the following basic propositions:

1. Access to computers—and indeed to anything that might teach us something about the way the world works—should be unlimited and total.
2. All information should be free.
3. Authority is to be mistrusted, and decentralization promoted.
4. Hackers should be judged by their hacking, not by bogus criteria such as degrees, age, race, or position.
5. Anyone can create art and beauty on a computer.
6. Computers can improve your life.[7]

Eric S. Raymond says that although most hackers subscribe to this ethic, it is by no means universal.[8] One deviation of the hacker's ethic is the belief that system-cracking for fun and exploration is ethical as long as the cracker commits no theft, vandalism, or breach of confidentiality.[9]

As was mentioned, the term *hacker* eventually came to be used incorrectly to describe computer users who commit crimes. Movies such as *WarGames* and *Hackers* fueled this misunderstanding. Furthermore, it is still common today, nearly two decades after the term was first used inaccurately, to see headlines reading, "Israeli Sought for Breaking into Military Computers: FBI Hunts 'Master Hacker,'"[10] or "Hacker Alert Sounded."[11] There is some difference of opinion about what a true hacker really is. For some a true hacker does not profit his or her computer skills or damage systems.[12] Schwartau, however, divides hackers into amateur and professional categories, the professional ones being formally trained, highly paid experts.[13] They can be found providing services to terrorists, organized criminals, or the FBI.[14]

A Typology of the Computer Underground

Early on, the computer underground was composed of actors adhering to one of five roles: *hackers, crackers, phreakers, warez d00dz,* or *lamers, leeches,* and *posers.* Understanding these roles answers many sociological questions concerning how the computer underground has become a subculture in itself, and how those within the subculture learn their behaviors, beliefs, and norms from other members. The importance of the various roles was explained by Gordon R. Meyer in his paper "The Social Organization of the Computer Underground."[15]

The Relevant Actors of the Computer Underground

It may be argued that Americans generally harbor misconceptions about the computer underground. As far as many people are concerned, evil hackers, bent on perpetrating all forms of cyber-mayhem, are the principal actors. The media, which generally make little distinction between different types of computer underground activity, have promoted this false understanding. Almost every criminal or mischievous act that involves computers— embezzlement to viruses—has been attributed to hackers. But by carefully considering the actual roles of the various participants in the computer underground, it is hoped that the word *hacker* will be freed of its negative connotations.

Hackers. Hackers are not the evildoers that the media claim. Hackers themselves prefer to be known as *wizards* or *computer wizards.* Unlike most computer users, who want to learn only the minimum necessary for a system's use, a hacker enjoys exploring the details of programmable systems and learning how to stretch their capabilities. Most of the time, a hacker's goal is to make a program or system perform with optimum efficiency. A hacker is one who programs enthusiastically and masterfully (even obsessively) or who enjoys programming rather than just theorizing about programming;[16] often a hacker is an expert at a particular program or operating system. A hacker is also seen to subscribe to some version of the hacker ethic, as described by Raymond.[17]

To others in the computer underground, "hacking" refers to gaining access to and exploring computer systems and networks without authorization. Since this means the hacker does not generally have access to the operating manuals and other resources that are available to legitimate users, the hacker must experiment with commands and explore various files to understand and use the system effectively. By examining files and perhaps by a little clever programming, the hacker may be able to obtain protected information or more powerful access privileges. Such a person may thereby become the malicious meddler, or *cracker,* who tries to discover sensitive information by trial and error.

Consider the following definitions of a hacker posted on the United Hackers Association's Web page:

Someone who can't resist exploring computers and communications networks to their fullest. It's an obsession, passion, disease—take your pick.

—Carolyn Meinel

I believe it's someone who watches over systems. They try to find a solution to a problem. They are constantly curious and try to learn as much as they can.

—Destiny

Hacker (hack' er) n. 1. a person who gathers information investigating computer systems using unconventional methods of exploration. 2. a person who learns the weaknesses and security holes of computer systems. 3. someone who understands and manipulates information gathered from computer systems. 4. someone that is exceptional in understanding technology and uses it to gather information.

—Leopard

A computer enthusiast who enjoys to learn, he does this by exploring other's systems, by gaining access to privileged accounts. Showing off to his friends is of no concern to him, he knows what he is and he doesn't need to publicize it very much, it's the path he takes to learn, and not as much the result he gets. He will never intentionally damage a system, however he will erase logs etc. . . . He will be very smart, not as in school smart but as in smart, and efficient thinking. He does not rely on programs to help him unless he has crafted those programs himself. He tries to learn as much about electronics as he can, constantly studying to keep up with the times, a hacker is never finished with learning once he becomes a guru at one O/s [operating system] he moves onto the next.

—AcidMEister[18]

In the paper she presented to the thirteenth annual National Computer Security Conference, Dorothy E. Denning uses the words of one hacker to summarize the group:

A hacker is someone that experiments with systems. . . . [Hacking] is playing with systems and making them do what they were never intended to do. Breaking in and making free calls is just a small part of that. Hacking is also about freedom of speech and free access to information—being able to find out anything. There is also the David and Goliath side of it, the underdog vs. the system, and the ethic of being a folk hero, albeit a minor one.[19]

Another individual had this to say about hackers:

A Hacker is any person who derives joy from discovering ways to circumvent limitations. I recognize that a class of criminals and juvenile delinquents has taken to calling themselves "hackers," but I consider them irrelevant to the true meaning of the word; just as the Mafia calls themselves "businessmen" but nobody pays that fact any attention.[20]

By examining these various definitions, one can see that "there seem to be at least two distinct threads [among hackers:] those concerned with figuring stuff out, and those who thrive on including some form of subversion in their activities."[21] Those concerned with "figuring stuff out" are true hackers, while those who engage in some form of "subversion" are individuals who want to be known as hackers but more often than not are, in fact, crackers or lamers, leeches, and posers.

Crackers.   A *cracker* is someone who breaks the security on a computer system either to browse through the information or to manipulate or damage files. The term *cracker* is almost always used in a derogatory way. The term reflects a strong revulsion against the theft and vandalism perpetrated by crackers.

There is far less overlap between hackerdom and crackerdom than the general public, misled by sensationalist journalism, might expect. Whereas crackers often like to describe themselves as hackers, most true hackers consider them to be a separate and lower form of life.

Crackers are the individuals who develop and implement computer viruses or new ways to break into computer systems. Simply stated,

> the long and short of it [is] that a cracker is a hacker with "Mens Rea"—the Latin term for guilty-mind or malicious intent. Hackers are more dedicated to figuring things out and writing their own programs than crackers. Crackers are more technique oriented and more likely to use programs written by other people and exploit holes found by others to carry out their disruptions or criminal activities.[22]

Crackers tend to gather in small, tight-knit, very secretive groups. They often take on nicknames that make them feel better about themselves, or that make them sound strong or powerful, such as AcidMaster, Exploiter, The GateKeeper, Baal, or SoulAssasin. Their group names include Cult of the Dead Crow (CoC), Death'n Decay (D'n'D), and the National Hackers Association.

Phreakers.   *Phone phreaking,* usually called just *phreaking,* is a term used to describe the different means of receiving telephone services without being billed. Phreaking can also be used to prevent, or at least inhibit, the possibility of calls being traced, thereby helping the phreaker to avoid being caught.

Phreaking was first widely publicized when the exploits of John "Cap'n Crunch" Draper, the "father of phreaking," were reported in a 1971 *Esquire* article.[23] Early phreaking methods involved electromechanical devices that generated key tones or altered line voltages in ways that tricked the mechanical switches of the telephone company into connecting calls without charging.[24] However, these devices were made obsolete with the advent of computerized telephone switching systems, which meant that phreaks had to learn more about computers.

For most members of the computer underground, phreaking is simply a tool that allows them to call long distance without getting enormous bills; many are interested in the phone system solely to the extent that they can exploit its weaknesses to pursue other goals. In this case phreaking becomes a means and not a pursuit unto itself. But dedicated phreakers have a deeper and more technically oriented interest in the "telco" (telephone company),[25] and want to master and explore a system that few outsiders really understand. To the phreaker the phone system is the most interesting, fascinating computerized entity. Since most of the information about the phone system is not made public, phreakers have to resort to legally questionable means to obtain the knowledge they want.[26]

Early on, phreaking was a fairly respectable activity among hackers and phreakers, who used it as an intellectual game of exploration. To this generation serious theft of telephone services was viewed as an unsavory act. There was in fact significant crossover between the hacker community and the hard-core phreakers. However, this ethos began to break down in the mid-1980s as wider dissemination of the techniques involved generated a class of less responsible phreaks. Around the same time changes in the phone network made old-style technical ingenuity a less effective way of cracking it, so phreaking came to depend more on overtly criminal acts such as stealing phone-card numbers.[27]

Warez D00dz.   In the computer underground the *warez d00d* (plural "warez d00dz") is an individual who pirates software through the unauthorized copying and distribution of copyrighted material. This activity used to center on computer bulletin board systems that specialize in "warez," an abbreviated form of the word *software* used by members of the computer underground. On the older bulletin board system, warez d00dz could share copies of commercial software, usually via a telephone modem.[28] Today, the warez d00dz use Web pages to advertise and distribute their product. It has become much easier for anyone to find and download pirated software: simply type "warez" in any search engine, and hundreds of links will appear.

Warez d00dz gain some sort of personal satisfaction by being the first to release a new program or game. The greatest coup for a warez d00d, it appears, is to emit *0-day warez,* that is, a pirated copy of commercial software that is cracked on the day it is released for retail sale.[29] Warez d00dz also hoard large amounts of software, collecting untold gigabytes of arcade-style games, pornographic pictures, and applications on their hard disks.

In *The New Hacker's Dictionary,* Raymond quotes one former warez d00d, Ozone Pilot, describing the group as follows:

> [BELONG] is the only word you will need to know. Warez d00dz want to belong. They have been shunned by everyone, and thus turn to cyberspace for acceptance. That is why they always start groups like TGW, FLT, USA and the like. Structure makes them happy. . . . Warez d00dz will never have a handle like "Pink Daisy" because warez d00dz are insecure. Only someone who is very secure with a good dose of self-esteem can stand up to the cries of fag and girlie-man. More likely you will find warez d00dz with handles like Doctor Death, Deranged Lunatic, Hellraiser, Mad Prince, Dreamdevil, The Unknown, Renegade Chemist, Terminator, and Twin Turbo. They like to sound badass when they can hide behind their terminals. More likely, if you were given a sample of 100 people, the person whose handle is Hellraiser is the last person you'd associate with the name.[30]

It may seem that the warez d00d is doing the public a favor, albeit an illegal one, by providing free copyrighted software. However, the warez d00d does this not only for a sense of personal satisfaction but also to make money by tricking individuals who arrive at his or her page into clicking on links that take them to another site, usually that of a sponsor. Each time a customer goes to a link, the warez d00d makes a small amount of money from the sponsor. It can take a considerable amount of time to move through all the links to arrive at the actual warez, which means that warez d00d will earn a nice sum in commissions.

Hackers, crackers, and phreakers do not necessarily support the activities of warez d00dz, and there is distrust and misunderstanding between them. Many hackers, crackers, and phreakers believe that warez d00dz indiscriminately abuse the telephone network in pursuit of the latest computer game or application;[31] many also view piracy as an *unskilled* activity. A possible exception to this are pirates who have the programming skills needed to remove copy protection from software.

Others in the computer underground complain that it is pirate calls made to upload large programs, not the ones placed by "telecommunications enthusiasts" (a popular euphemism for phreakers and hackers), that cost the telephone industry large sums of money. However, the data do not support the assertion that all warez d00dz phreak their calls. Phreaking is considered "very tacky" among elite pirates, and operators of pirate bulletin boards discourage phreaked calls because they draw attention to the system when they are discovered by the telephone company.[32]

Regardless of whether it is the warez d00dz' perceived lack of skills, reputation for abusing the network, or some other reason, there is indeed a certain amount of division between the world of hackers, crackers, and phreakers and that of warez d00dz. Although they coexist and share resources and methods within the computer underground, they function separately.

Lamers, Leeches, and Posers. Lamers, leeches, and posers can all be described by one word: wannabes; they want to be a part of the computer underground. Often, these are the individuals who watched the films *WarGames* or *Hackers* and decided that they wanted to be cool and become a hacker. They are likely to brag that they are hackers, phreaks, or warez d00dz, when they actually are not. These, too, are those who are most likely to use programs (such as "nukes," "floods," and "mail bombs") that attack and damage others' computers. Damaging systems by these methods makes them feel powerful, although they are in turn disrespected by the computer elite for using programs someone else created to do their work. A lamer, leech, or poser can also be someone who is just getting into the computer underground. They may sincerely want to learn more about the culture of computers but must carry the negative label until their skills are more highly developed.

Lamer is a term used most often by crackers, phreakers, and warez d00dz to describe individuals who want to be like them but do not understand what that really means. Crackers use the word to describe cracker wannabes. Phreaks apply it to those who scam codes off others rather than cracking them themselves. To warez d00dz, who highly value the ability to distribute cracked commercial software within days of its release to the commercial market, or even before release, the lamer might try to upload useless or free software or something incredibly old.[33]

A *leech* consumes knowledge without generating new software, cracks, or techniques. These individuals constantly press others for information and/or assistance but have nothing to contribute themselves.[34]

The term *poser* is used among crackers, phreakers, and warez d00dz to refer to a wannabe who is not yet particularly skilled, but it does not have the same negative connotation as *lamer* and *leech*. The word probably derives from a similar usage among punk rockers to criticize those who "talk the talk but don't walk the walk."[35]

These terms, as crackers, phreakers, and warez d00dz use them, carry the additional connotation of self-conscious elitism. To call someone a lamer, leech, or poser tends to make those doing the name-calling feel that they are among those who are "plugged in." In the computer world hackers are the true elite, and others in the computer underground like to think of themselves, or want to be known, as one of the same.

Subcultures of Deviance in the Computer Underground

The concept of *subculture* has typically been defined as a relatively cohesive cultural system that varies in form and substance from the dominant culture.[36] While loosely part of the dominant culture, a subculture maintains a unique set of values, beliefs, and traditions. Many theories regarding deviance are based upon the assumption that it arises from membership in a group whose beliefs and attitudes support such behavior. Although interpreted by outsiders as deviant, the behavior in question in fact conforms to the expectations of the particular subgroup or subculture (see Chapter 1). Classified under the rubric *subculture* are ethnic groups, delinquent gangs, and religious sects. Thus it is proposed here that the computer underground can also be classified as a subculture.

What makes the computer underground a subculture? Several years ago, there was an interesting debate on a bulletin board site known as The Well over whether the computer underground was indeed a true subculture. Established in 1985, The Well has been, as boards go, an anomaly from the beginning.[37] Most Well users (known as "Wellbeings") tend to work in the information industry: hardware, software, telecommunications, media, and entertainment. Librarians, academics, and journalists are also especially common participants. Wellbeings wander about a huge smorgasbord of conferences, each containing many discussion topics and each topic containing dozens and sometimes hundreds of comments or messages. The subculture debate was in the Hacking/Cracking conference. In any case there were mixed responses. Some hackers and others feared that classifying the computer underground as a subculture attached a criminal label to it. However, after reaching agreement on how to define "subculture" and why the computer underground was one, there were few participants in disagreement.

Hackers, phreakers, crackers, warez d00dz, lamers, leeches, and posers do form a subculture because they display the following traits that are generally considered distinguishing characteristics of subcultures, as outlined in Chapter 1:

1. A special vocabulary, or argot, usually concerning the activities that differentiate the group from those around it
2. A set of shared beliefs and norms, which contrast in direction or emphasis with the norms of other groups, such as the larger society
3. Contacts between members through which behavior is learned and membership in the group is confirmed
4. Sometimes a specialized way of dressing and acting that, like argot, serves to distinguish the members from those of other groups and to assist in identifying members to one another

Each of the four characteristics will be examined in light of its relevance to the computer underground.

Special Vocabulary. A subculture usually has a special vocabulary, or argot, that differentiates the group from those around it. The computer underground in fact creates and uses a tremendous amount of jargon, such as verb doubling, sound-alike slang, the "-P" convention, overgeneralization, spoken inarticulations, and anthropomorphization. Hackers more often use these types of jargon, but some others in the computer underground have also adopted them.

Verb doubling is used to make a concise, sometimes sarcastic comment on what the implied subject does or to terminate a conversation while remarking on the current state of affairs or what the speaker intends to do next:

> "The disk heads just crashed. Lose, lose."
>
> "Mostly he talked about his latest crock. Flame, flame."
>
> "Boy, what a bagbiter! Chomp, chomp!"[38]

With *sound-alike slang* hackers often make rhymes or puns to convert an ordinary word or phrase into something more interesting. It is considered particularly flavorful if the phrase is bent so as to include some other jargon word:

> Boston Herald = Boston Horrid (or Harried)
>
> Boston Globe = Boston Glob
>
> Microsoft = Microshaft[39]

The *"-P" convention* turns a word into a question by appending a "P":

> Q: "Foodp?"
>
> A: "Yeah, I'm pretty hungry."[40]

Overgeneralization takes many forms, but often it is the frequency with which hackers find amusing analogies for technical terms, such as names of program tools and command language primitives, in contexts outside of computing. For example, UNIX hackers often *"grep"* (the UNIX search command) for things rather than search for them. Many hackers also love to make nouns and verbs by extending a standard rule to nonuniform cases:

> mysterious = mysteriosity
>
> ferrous = ferrosity
>
> obvious = obviosity[41]

Others attach the suffix "-itude" to abstract a quality from just about any adjective or noun:

> win = winnitude
>
> loss = lossitude
>
> cruft = cruftitude
>
> lame = lameitude[42]

The generalization of an inflectional rule to cases in which it isn't normally considered to apply is not poor grammar but a playful form of grammatical creativity. It is done not to impress but to amuse and never at the expense of clarity.[43]

Spoken inarticulations occur when words such as "mumble," "sigh," and "groan" are said in places where their referent might more naturally be used. It has been suggested that this usage derives from the impossibility of representing such noises on a bulletin board system or in e-mail.[44]

Semantically, one rich source of jargon construction is the hackish tendency to *anthropomorphize* hardware and software in ways that suggest that they contain little people, each with intentions and desires, talking to one another. Thus one hears, "The protocol handler got confused," or that a program's "poor little brain couldn't understand *X,* and it died."[45]

Hackers have a general fondness for *form-versus-content language jokes* that shows up as they intentionally misspell words or write incorrectly. For example, one might comment, "This sentence no verb," "Too repetetive," "Bad speling," or "Incorrectspa cing." Similarly, intentional spoonerisms are often made, "dain bramage," for "brain damage," perhaps being the most common.[46]

Hackers also tend to use quotation marks incorrectly and also commonly place punctuation outside rather than inside the quotes. They do this, for example, when communicating command lines or small pieces of code, since any character that does not belong in the command or code should not be included within the quotes.[47]

It is also common for hackers and others in the computer underground to use all lowercase letters even when capitals would be proper. This usually occurs when they are typing something like a username or password (which is always lowercase) at the beginning of a sentence. Furthermore, a number of punctuation and emphasis conventions are frequently adapted to communications over the Internet. Many, for example, consider typing done in all caps, LIKE THIS, to be yelling and often will say, "Please stop shouting!" Also, it is common to see brackets or asterisks to signify emphasis ("What the *hell*?") or to indicate that an action is taking place or that a sound is being made (for example, *bang*, *hic*, *grin*, or <bang>, <hic>, <grin>).[48]

Hacker speech generally features extremely precise diction, careful word choice, a relatively large working vocabulary, and relatively little use of contractions or street slang. Dry humor, irony, puns, and a mildly flippant attitude are highly valued, but an underlying seriousness and intelligence are essential. One should use just enough jargon to communicate precisely and identify oneself as a member of the culture; overuse of jargon or a breathless, excessively assertive attitude is considered the mark of a loser or lamer.

Subcultures can also be distinguished from the main culture by their habit of constantly referring to the parent society.[49] The computer underground (excluding hackers) makes use of parody and mockery of the main society in the names they give their groups, such as the following list of "hacker" organizations:

> Apple Mafia, American Tone Travelers (AT&T), Bellcore, Catholics Anonymous, Chaos Computer Club, Chief Executive Officers, Feds-R-Us, IBM Syndicate, Justice League of America, Legion of Doom, Lunatic Labs, NASA Elite, The NATO Association, Secret Service, The United SoftWarez Force, and WASP.[50]

Shared Beliefs and Norms. Subcultures also have a set of shared beliefs and norms that contrast in direction or emphasis with those of other groups, such as the larger society. Despite their differences, most hackers, phreakers, crackers, warez d00dz, lamers, leeches, and posers generally hold one principle most dear: a belief that one should acquire as much knowledge as possible, that all information should be shared, and that all information should be free. Consider the words of the hacker known as The Mentor:

> We've been spoon-fed baby food at school when we hungered for steak. . . .The bits of meat that you did let slip through were pre-chewed and tasteless. We've been dominated by sadists, or ignored by the apathetic. The few that had something to teach found us willing pupils, but those few are like drops of water in the desert.
>
> This is our world now . . . the world of the electron and the switch, the beauty of the baud. We make use of a service already existing without paying for what could be dirt-cheap if it wasn't run by profiteering gluttons, and you call us criminals. We explore . . . and you call us criminals. We seek after knowledge, and you call us criminals. We exist without skin color, without nationality, without religious bias . . . and you call us criminals. You build atomic bombs, you wage wars, you murder, cheat, and lie to us and try to make us believe it's for our own good, yet we're the criminals.
>
> Yes, I am a criminal. My crime is that of curiosity.[51]

In *The Hacker Crackdown,* Bruce Sterling expressed a similar attitude:

> Pricing "information" is like trying to price air or price dreams. Well, anybody on a pirate board knows that computing can be, and ought to be, *free.* Pirate boards are little independent worlds in cyberspace, and they don't belong to anybody but the underground.[52]

A culture's beliefs, norms, and values can be learned not only from such statements but also from the behavior of its members. Every member of the computer underground performs some action that conveys his or her belief that information should be free.

In 1971, when Richard Stallman (head of the Free Software Foundation and founder of the GNU Project) started his career at MIT (the breeding ground for many of the old-school hackers), he worked in a group that used free software exclusively. Even computer companies often distributed free software. Programmers were free to cooperate with each other and often did. However, by the 1980s, almost all software was proprietary, which means that it has owners who forbid and prevent cooperation by users. In 1983 this gave rise to the GNU project, which developed a complete, free software system named "GNU." "Free" in this case refers to freedom, not price. You may or may not pay a price to get GNU software (you hardly ever do). But either way, once you have the GNU software, you have three specific freedoms in using it: (1) the freedom to copy the program and give it away to others, (2) the freedom to change the program as you wish by having full access to its source code, and (3) the freedom to distribute an improved version and thus help build the community.[53] Most hackers agree with Stallman that all software sources should be community property. Hackers who do not totally agree with him have nevertheless cooperated to produce large amounts of high-quality software for free redistribution through his Free Software Foundation. The operating system known as Linux was created this way.

Crackers, warez d00dz, and phreakers, by definition, believe in the freedom of information. They in fact stretch this belief to its very boundaries. Crackers, for example, bypass the systems' security to gain access to the information they hold. What they do with that information varies. Some will browse a system to obtain new knowledge; others may copy or destroy the information they find. Phreakers do much the same as the crackers, except that they are exploiting the phone system. They believe that phone companies are overpricing their services and thus limiting access to information. The warez d00dz go so far as to distribute illegal copies of copyrighted software. If the software has copy protection on it, they break the protection so others can copy the software.

As wannabes the lamers, leeches, and posers often seem to be the most enthusiastic in their belief that information should be free because, more than likely, they have just discovered that they can now obtain any software they want, without the hindrance of inadequate resources.

Currently, there is an ongoing debate online over the future of intellectual property, since information is so easily copied and distributed over the Internet (http://www.theatlantic.com/index-js.htm). On one side are those who want to make copyright rules even tighter, and on the other are those who wish to abandon copyright altogether. Many in the computer underground are uniting behind Stallman of the Free Software Foundation and John Perry Barlow, co-founder of the Electronic Frontier Foundation, a civil liberties group for Cyberspace. Charles P. Mann quotes Barlow as saying that "copyright's not about creation, which will happen anyway—it's about distribution."[54] Mann continues that

> in Barlow's view, copyright made sense when companies had to set up elaborate industrial processes for "hauling forests into Waldenbooks or encapsulating music on CDs and distributing them to Tower Records." To make such investments feasible, unauthorized copying had to be stopped. In the future, Barlow [argued], people will be able to download music and writing so easily that they will be reluctant to take the trouble to seek out hard copies, let alone want to pay for them. Musicians or writers who want to be heard or read will have to thumbtack their creations onto the Web for fans to download—free, Barlow insisted. Because distributing material on the Internet costs next to nothing, there will be no investment in equipment and shipping to protect. Record companies and publishers will be obviated, and the economic justification for copyright will vanish.[55]

However, belief in the freedom to share information runs counter to our mainstream society's position that information should be protected. Copyright laws have been with us since the creation of our government. On all levels, especially economic, our country values the economic success of the individual, which means that there must be some protection, in the form of copyright laws, for those whose livelihood depends upon the creation of intellectual property.

Contact between Members.   Contact between members of a subculture is required to confirm membership and to learn behavior. This was achieved within the computer underground by establishing centralized points for the communication of information, using the existing technologies of bulletin board systems, news groups, telephone bridges, loops, and voice mail boxes.[56] Each of these technologies will be described in turn.

Bulletin Board Systems and Newsgroups.   Bulletin board systems and newsgroups provide wannabes with preliminary socialization and instruction on the behavior and techniques of the computer underground, while also teaching more experienced members new techniques. Communication in the computer underground takes place largely at night and primarily through bulletin board systems. By calling these systems and "logging on" with an account number and password, individuals can leave messages for each other, download files and programs, and, depending on the number of phone lines into the system, type messages to other users who may have logged on at the same time (known as "chatting"). Newsgroups are huge collections of topic groups where individuals can respond to each other by posting messages. Although most bulletin boards and newsgroups cover rather mainstream topics, a number cater strictly to members of the computer underground. Over the years comprehensive patterns of interacting with others—including the specialized vocabulary described above—have developed as bulletin boards and newsgroups have become major means of communicating within the computer underground.

Bridges, Loops, and Voice Mail Boxes.   Bridges, loops, and voice mail boxes are generally the phreakers' preferred means of communication, used most often for recreation or sometimes to share technical information.

A "bridge" is a technical name for what is commonly known as a "chat line" or "conference system." The most familiar public form is the pay-per-minute group conversation systems advertised on late-night television. Many other bridge systems are owned by large corporations, which maintain them for business use during the day. Although the numbers to these systems are not public knowledge, many of them have been discovered by phreakers, who then utilize the systems at night.[57]

Phreakers have also become skilled at creating temporary, private bridges via AT&T's conference-calling facilities that allow for conversations among a self-selected group of phreakers/hackers.[58] These "conferences" usually last hours, with people joining and leaving throughout.

Phreakers likewise utilize "loops" to limit their conversations to just two people at a time. "Loop lines," which are actually telephone company test lines installed for internal use, consist of two telephone numbers that connect only to each other. They allow individuals to hold private conversations without exchanging telephone numbers and thus divulging their location or identity.[59]

Voice mail boxes (VMBs) function rather like a telephone answering machine, in that people can call in, listen to a recorded message, and then leave a message for the box owner. Like bulletin boards, VMBs disseminate information to a large number of users, and unlike the live telephone conversations of bridges and loops, they are available at any time of the day. Additionally, VMBs do not require use of a computer and modem; only a touch-tone phone is needed to call the box. Their usefulness is limited somewhat, however, because they play only one outgoing message at a time and because their transitory nature limits their reliability.[60] There are several commercial voice mail box systems throughout the country, and many are accessible via toll-free telephone numbers. VMB numbers are frequently posted on bulletin boards with invitations to "call if you have any good stuff."

They are often used by warez d00dz to exchange messages about new releases of software and by phreakers and crackers to trade account and access numbers. Additionally, some of the underground newsletters and journals obtain boxes so that users can call in news of arrests and other gossip.[61] The security of some VMB systems is notoriously poor, however, since many phreakers can create boxes for themselves that are unknown by the owner of the system. But the discovery and closure of such boxes are usually only a matter of time.

Specialized Way of Dressing and Acting. Another defining characteristic of subcultures is their specialized way of dressing and acting. According to Raymond, hackers generally dress casually, in a vaguely post-hippie style in which T-shirts, jeans, running shoes, and Birkenstocks are preferred. Long hair, beards, and moustaches are common. A substantial minority prefers such outdoors clothing as hiking boots, khakis, and lumberjack or chamois shirts. And from at least the late 1970s, backpacks have been more common than briefcases.[62] Others in the computer underground dress similarly to the hacker, although the style may vary depending on their geographical location and group affiliation.

Is the Computer Underground a Subculture?

In terms of the four characteristics that characterize a subculture, the computer underground can be said to fit the definition. Its members define themselves, and are defined by others, as belonging to this group, and as a consequence they gravitate toward others who share their interests. Admission to the subculture provides the individual with a more positive image and a greater opportunity to learn its skills, norms, and beliefs. In a way, it is a source of deviation from the norms of the mainstream society, and it supports the sort of behavior that differentiates itself from the main society.

Furthermore, by examining the computer underground in light of both the theory of differential association and the theory of differential reinforcement, we can see how its culture is transmitted. Individuals entering into the subculture learn and internalize its techniques, values, norms, and beliefs through intimate personal communications that take place in the many bulletin board systems, newsgroups, bridges, loops, and voice mail boxes serving their community. Finally, a series of positive and negative reinforcements ensures that the individual continues to be an active member in the computer underground.

Crime and the Internet

The Council of Europe Convention on Cybercrime (CECC), formed by the G-8 nations and the Council of Europe, has defined four categories of cybercrime in a logical manner that may eventually serve as a template for international law governing cyberspace.[63] In the draft treaty developed by the CECC, Internet crime includes the following:

1. **Offenses against the confidentiality, integrity, and availability of computer data and systems.** This category would include many of the hacking and cracking activities discussed in the preceding section and would prohibit such offenses as the coordinated attacks that deny service by overloading business and government sites, network intrusions, virus damage, and espionage.

2. **Computer-related offenses.** This category would include theft and fraud offenses committed with the aid of computers and Internet communication. The range of crime types in this category is enormous and would even include homicide, robbery, sexual assault, and other violent or stalking-type crime when the predation involves computer communication. Drug trafficking, prostitution, and other victimless offenses with computer communication elements would be included as well.
3. **Content-related offenses.** Pornography in all illegal forms and perhaps gambling offenses are the best examples of content offenses.
4. **Copyright-related offenses.** This category would include unauthorized copying of software, digital music, business information, and the like when there is infringement on proprietary interest.

It may be difficult to imagine, but crimes ranging from terrorism[64] and industrial extortion to real-time child pornography events and identity theft[65] are flourishing through the use of Internet tools. Virus software, from the novice level through expert source code programs,[66] is available for downloading.

The seemingly purposeless, destructive urges of virus writers may qualify them as a separate category of deviant. Sarah Gordon[67] describes motivation for writing and reworking destructive programs as sort of intellectual curiosity on one end to the adolescent urge to gain a reputation by "getting over" on the adult establishment without pausing to consider the consequences. Viruses such as the Chernobyl Virus of 1999 and the I Love You Virus of 2000 cause massive damage. Even China, where regulation of Internet use is attempted, reported losses of $291 billion in 1999.

Graham Cluley[68] reported in *Security* magazine that viruses as well as Trojan horse programs and worm programs are used to steal passwords, ATM PIN numbers, credit card numbers, online banking information, Social Security numbers, and other information that makes identity theft and property theft possible. Often, the invasive programs are placed on target computers by "spoofing" the user with a phony e-mail message that, when opened, allows the virus to gain access. The U.S. Secret Service estimates that over $1 billion annually is stolen from private computer users this way in the United States. A further $250 billion, according to the FBI's Economic Crimes Unit, is stolen in the form of intellectual property theft.[69]

Sexual Deviance and Cyberspace

In September 1998 Michael Grunwald of the *Washington Post* reported that law enforcement officials in the United States and 13 other nations had arrested suspects involved in an international, Internet-based child pornography ring known as the "Wonderland Club," who protected themselves with passwords and private cyberspace sites.[70] U.S. Customs officials described the participants as a "dangerous, dangerous crowd" that included people from all walks of life in as many as 49 countries.[71] Images traded via the Wonderland Club showed the sexual abuse and rape of children as young as 18 months, and some members had the technological means to record and transmit live sex shows. Club members could correspond during the shows to instruct the producers about what they wanted to see done to the child subjects. Authorities indicated that most of the participants probably wouldn't be caught at this point because of the sophistication of the encryption methods and codes used and the ease with which evidence may be erased by reformatting computer hard drives. They were, however, able to identify a number of users and confiscate computer records, which may be used to identify many more participants. Five of the arrested individuals had over 500,000 illegal pornographic images of children.

Technically, each such image represents the sexual assault of a child, and the simple act of downloading such an image to a computer hard drive is a felony under federal law. The prohibition includes virtual images such as animated characters and allows for imprisonment for as long as five years for possession.

Although child pornography might be described as the most insidious use of cyberspace for deviant sexual appetites, it is by no means unique. The range of groups involved in the exchange of images that might be criminal extends from explicit heterosexual pornography through a variety of homosexual acts to sadomasochism, bestiality, pyromania, necrophilia, and sex acts involving feces and urine. One of the most important reasons for the proliferation of these interest groups is the opportunity that cyberspace provides for *anonymous* communication.

Rod Nordland and Jeffrey Bartholet describe the proliferation of child sexual abuse in the form of pornography as the "darkest corner of the Internet."[72] Many of the perpetrators are known to the authorities but remain active online because of global regulation problems and the lack of laws prohibiting the behavior in some countries. In addition, there are active organizations, such as the Pedophile Liberation Front,[73] that defend pedophilia as a lifestyle and provide forums of support and political activism for pedophiles.

Opportunity for Sexual Deviance in Cyberspace

Curiosity about deviant sex is certainly not a new phenomenon, but it has normally been contained by the social consequences associated with attempting to satisfy it. A person could lose friendships, status in the community, employment, and even a family if an interest in some unusual sexual practice became publicly known. Participation might thus be practically limited to furtive commerce in the legally marginal world of adult books and films plus perhaps a few local contacts who are equally paranoid about remaining undiscovered. The risky behavior required to pursue such a perceived deviant interest could easily extinguish the individual's curiosity.[74]

The Internet has changed this dramatically. With privacy and anonymity people, including children, may investigate and discuss virtually any subject through connections in cyberspace. Inhibitions disappear with the anonymity and reinforcement, and involvement in socially discouraged or illegal activity may become possible and readily available. Such a situation has given rise to the following very real dangers:

1. The expanding market demand for child pornography may seriously increase the sexual exploitation of children.
2. Computer-literate children have access to sexually oriented sites, chat rooms, and bulletin boards, where they may be victimized by sexual predators.
3. Individuals, especially those with poor social skills, may develop problematic sexual behavior patterns that would otherwise not have occurred due to the opportunity and reinforcement experienced in cyberspace.

4. A class of socially dysfunctional "cybersex" addicts could become a serious mental health problem in the future.

To understand more fully how cyberspace can support and even encourage sexual deviance, consider the discussion below, which was generated by an interview with White Eagle, who has been involved in numerous heterosexual sadomasochistic (S&M) encounters, real and virtual, through contacts made on Internet sites.

An Interview with White Eagle

"White Eagle" is the cybernickname, or "nick," used for identification in S&M chat rooms by a 45-year-old male in the United States. In his real life White Eagle is a successful, upper-middle-class professional, currently single, whose hobbies include playing guitar and collecting antique firearms. He jokingly admits to being something of a "control freak" and believes that this personal characteristic probably contributed to the failure of "more than one" previous marriage.

White Eagle is skilled in the use of computer systems and has at his disposal the means to create, send, and receive pictures and video images. He demonstrates the ease with which a computer user may access sexually explicit material, converse with individuals having any imaginable sexual preference, purchase a wide variety of pornographic films and pictures, and join interest groups. By using any search engine and appropriate keywords and preferences, hundreds of sites become accessible in seconds. Many of the sites require credit card numbers and confirmation of adulthood prior to granting access and then charge for the products available.

White Eagle logs onto his favorite sadomasochism site, noting that the capital letters in his handle indicate that he plays the dominant role in sadomasochistic encounters. He explains that people interested in the submissive role outnumber the dominant players by five or six to one. Many of the nicknames also include an icon at the end, which further describe the individual. White Eagle's is followed by a large "shackle," which indicates that he has a certain level of S+M experience, that the site administrators have confidence in him, and that he maintains a private "shack" at the site, protected by passwords, in which he can meet others in cyberencounters that are not subject to general participation.

This particular site is organized into "chat zones" associated with different types of role-playing. Bondage, sadomasochism, and discipline are the most common, and the range of categories includes bisexual, gay and lesbian, and other combinations along with heterosexual titles. The cyberenvironment is supposed to resemble a bar with different areas to which the participants might move. Newcomers are encouraged to "lurk" and learn for a while to get comfortable with the interaction and rules of play and are repeatedly cautioned to keep their actual identities secret. They are also urged to read a list of publications that explain sadomasochistic lovemaking, along with novels on the subject. A bibliography of fiction and nonfiction is provided, along with sources of online information. Participation by minors is forbidden, and members must discontinue any scenario if a reference to a child pops up in any form and ignore any further communication with the individual who made the reference.

The conversations at this level of the site seem fairly normal, and it is obvious that many of the participants have been acquainted for some time. Some conversations center on descriptions of sex equipment used in the role-playing encounters, and there are frequent solicitations by vendors, who provide links to other sites where purchases could be made. Sometimes an invitation to meet in the "basement" is made, which White Eagle explains is an offer to engage in a virtual sexual encounter.

The "basement" is a second level of the site, and approval by the site administrator is required for admission. Here role-playing encounters take place in the various "chambers," which are equipped with virtual equipment for use by the participants, who usually have some idea about their partner's tastes and limits before an encounter begins. If invited, observers may become involved or voice support for a participant.

The third level of the site is composed of private "shacks" maintained by long-term participants. These are accessible by invitation only and are protected by passwords, which may be changed as often as the owner desires. White Eagle's shack is equipped with virtual whips, gags, and other bondage and torture equipment. He pays a fee to the site administrator to keep the shack and feels that it is money well spent. White Eagle has had a number of actual liaisons with people he has met in cyberspace. "It is like a very complex blind date," he says, "sometimes it is great, sometimes a disaster." Usually, the participants will agree to a meeting place midway between their homes. White Eagle prefers Las Vegas, where all of the necessary equipment and facilities are available for rent.

Thus it appears that deviant behavior of virtually any type may be facilitated by the existence of the Internet. The information superhighway, for all its benefit, is easily utilized for deviant purposes. If we are careful, however, the versatility of the Internet as a resource won't be inhibited by measures necessary for control of cyberdeviance.

CRITICAL THINKING EXERCISES

1. Describe the difference between hackers and crackers.

2. How has the existence of the Internet increased the opportunity for traditional types of crime? How might a burglar use the Internet to help commit crime?

3. Describe the motivation of people to write virus programs that destroy computer files. How could someone make money by creating new types of virus programs?

4. What is a pedophile? How is the Internet useful to this type of person?

CHECK IT OUT ON THE WEB

The Internet addresses listed below are intended to provide the reader with understanding of a wide range of perspectives on the subject matter discussed in this chapter. Some sites may contain objectionable material. The list is not intended to reflect the viewpoints or opinions of the authors or the publisher.

http://www.accessorl.net/~cyberwar/hackers.html
    becoming a hacker
http://www.pbs.org/wgbh/pages/frontline/shows/hackers
    hacker exploits

http://www.rent-a-hacker.com
     counterhacking advice
http://csrc.ncsl.nist.gov/virus
     virus security clearinghouse
http://www.hackerz.org
     advancement of the hacker's community
http://www.ncjrs.org
     National Criminal Justice Database
http://www.ncjrs.org/txtfiles/exploit.txt
     child sexual molestation
http://www.missingkids.org/
     laws and legislation (select "Child Pornography Issues" from the dropdown menu on the "About Us" page)
http://www.caughtbythe web.com
     informative Web site about pornography
http://www.ecpat.org
     World Wide Web site against child porn
http://www.usdoj.gov
     U.S. Department of Justice Web site
http://www.cyber-rights.org
     child porn laws and regulations
http://www.enough.org
     Internet Web site against pornography
http://m-net.arbornet.org
     anti-pornography activism

ENDNOTES

1. Winn Schwartau, *Cybershock* (New York: Thunder's Mouth Press, 2000).

2. Richard C. Hollinger, *Crime, Deviance, and the Computer* (Brookfield, VT: Dartmouth Publishing Company, 1997), p. xvii.

3. Steven Levy, *Hackers: Heroes of the Computer Revolution* (New York: Doubleday, 1984), pp. 23–24.

4. Hollinger, *Crime, Deviance, and the Computer,* p. xix.

5. Ibid.

6. Levy, *Hackers.*

7. Ibid., pp. 39–49.

8. Eric S. Raymond, *The New Hacker's Dictionary,* 3rd ed. (Cambridge, MA: MIT Press, 1997), p. 234.

9. Ibid.

10. Richard Cole, "Israeli Sought for Breaking into Military Computers: FBI Hunts 'Master Hacker,' " 1998. [Online]. Available: http://www.abcnews.com/sections/tech/DailyNews/hackers0308.html

11. Nick Wingfield, *"Hacker Alert Sounded,"* 1998. [Online]. Available: http://ne2.news.com/News/Item/0,4,2095,00.html

12. Oracle, "Hackers, Crackers, and Heroes," 2000. [Online]. Available: http://www.mfgraffix.com/oracle/infoprot/hackers.html

13. Schwartau, 2000, pp. 50–52.

14. Bryan Burrough, "Invisible Enemies," *Vanity Fair* (June 2000), pp. 173–175, 209.

15. Gordon R. Meyer, "The Social Organization of the Computer Underground," Northern Illinois University, unpublished paper (1989).

16. Raymond, *The New Hacker's Dictionary,* p. 233.

17. Ibid., p. 234.

18. United Hackers Association, "Hacker's Interview," (1998). [Online]. Available: http://www.uha1.com/

19. Dorothy E. Denning, "Concerning Hackers Who Break into Computer Systems" (paper presented at the 13th National Computer Security Conference, Washington, DC, October 1–4, 1990).

20. From message logs from computer underground bulletin board systems and e-mail, 1988–98.

21. Ibid.

22. From message logs from computer underground bulletin board systems and e-mail, 1988–98.

23. Ron Rosenbaum, "The Secrets of the Little Blue Box," *Esquire,* October 1971, p. 161.

24. Meyer, "The Social Organization of the Computer Underground," p. 22.

25. Ibid.

26. Ibid., p. 23.

27. Raymond, *The New Hacker's Dictionary,* pp. 355–356.

28. Meyer, "The Social Organization of the Computer Underground," p. 24.

29. Raymond, *The New Hacker's Dictionary,* p. 478.

30. Ibid.

31. Meyer, "The Social Organization of the Computer Underground," p. 26.

32. Ibid., p. 27.

33. Raymond, *The New Hacker's Dictionary,* p. 275.

34. Ibid., p. 277.

35. Ibid., p. 362.

36. Stanley D. Eitzen and Maxine Baca Zinn, *In Conflict and Order: Understanding Society,* 7th ed. (Boston: Allyn & Bacon, 1995), p. 141.

37. Bruce Sterling, *The Hacker Crackdown: Law and Disorder on the Electronic Frontier* (New York: Bantam, 1992), p. 226.

38. Raymond, *The New Hacker's Dictionary,* p. 9.

39. Ibid., p. 10.

40. Ibid., pp. 10–11.

41. Ibid., p. 11.

42. Ibid., p. 12.

43. Ibid., pp. 13–14.

44. Ibid., p. 13.

45. Ibid.

46. Ibid., p. 14.

47. Ibid., pp. 14–15.

48. Ibid., pp. 17–18.

49. Sterling, *The Hacker Crackdown,* p. 72.

50. Ibid., pp. 70–71.

51. The Mentor, "The Conscience of a Hacker," *Phrack, 1:* 7 (1986), Phile 3.

52. Sterling, *The Hacker Crackdown,* p. 82.

53. Free Software Foundation, "Overview of the GNU Project," 1998. [Online]. Available: http://www.fsf.org/gnu/gnu-history.html

54. Charles P. Mann, *Who Will Own Your Next Good Idea?* 1998. [Online]. Available: http://www.theatlantic.com/issues/98sep/copy.htm

55. Ibid.

56. Meyer, "The Social Organization of the Computer Underground," p. 33.

57. Ibid.

58. Ibid., p. 53.

59. Ibid., p. 54.

60. Ibid., p. 56.

61. Ibid., pp. 55–56.

62. Raymond, *The New Hacker's Dictionary,* p. 522.

63. Richard Power, Tangled Web: *Tales of Digital Crime from the Shadows of Cyberspace* (Indianapolis, Ind.: QUE Publications, 2000).

64. Robert Merkle, *The Ultimate Internet Terrorist* (Boulder, CO: Paladin Press, 1998).

65. John Schwartz, "Tapping into Grey Areas," *The Houston Chronicle,* February 16, 2001, p. 1F.

66. Dr-K, *A Complete Hacker's Handbook* (London: Carlton Books, 2000).

67. Sarah Gordon, "Who Writes Viruses?" 2000. [Online]. Available: http://www.commandcom.com/virus/writes.html

68. Graham Cluley, "The Security Application Service Provider," *Security* (March 2000), pp. 48–52.

69. Ibid, p. 48

70. Michael Grunwald, "14 Nations Join in Internet Child Porn Raid," *The Washington Post,* September 3, 1998, p. A3.

71. Elaine Shannon, "Main Street Monsters," *Time,* September 14, 1998, p. 59.

72. Rod Nordland and Jeffrey Batholet, "The Web's Dark Secret," *Newsweek Special Report,* March 19, 2001, pp. 44–52.

73. Ibid, p. 44.

74. John Bingham and Chris Piotrowski, "On-Line Sexual Addiction: A Contemporary Enigma," *Psychological Reports, 79* (1996), p. 257.

12 Sexual Deviance and Sexual Harassment

Humans possess many unique characteristics that set them apart from the rest of living things. No other animal has reached our proficiency in language, art, or war, for example. So too, our sexual practices are far more diverse and imaginative than are those of other species in the animal kingdom. But what is possible is not always permissible, and human societies impose many restrictions on sexual practices. In the United States "acceptable" sexual behavior is limited to a certain age established by state legislators. Furthermore, the sexual relationships may not occur with anyone "for hire," within sight of others, with coercion or by position of authority, and with more than one partner at a time. Even marriage does not confer complete sexual liberty, because certain "unnatural" sexual acts, whether occurring between wed or unwed people, are illegal in some states. And sexual taboos go beyond the law. For example, devices such as vibrators, whips, and other "marital aids" are not illegal, but few users leave them in full view when in-laws or friends visit.

Often what is labeled as deviant sexual behavior does not differ from nondeviant behavior in *form* but rather in *context.*[1] Take the case of being naked in public. Those who expose themselves to passersby in a park risk jail or a session with a psychiatrist. In a strip club, by contrast, performers are paid to expose themselves, but those who pay—the customers—are forbidden to do the same thing for free. Being an advertising model is a respectable and lucrative occupation that allows one to pose in one's underwear (or less) for millions of magazine readers. But the same models would be arrested for appearing in such dress (or undress) on Main Street. Thus it is often not what you do, but where you do it.

Queen Victoria is quoted as having declared, "I don't care what you do as long as you don't do it in the street and frighten the horses!" Similarly, in some states, sexual behavior behind closed doors is of minimal legal concern as long as it is screened from the public and the participants are unrelated, of legal age, and not subject to coercion. However, in other states, laws still limit who goes into bedrooms and what goes on there. Even when such laws remain unenforced—which is usually the case today—powerful social pressures act to restrain one's sexual behavior. In general, it is better to keep one's departures from sexual "normality" a secret.

An Interview with Tony

Tony Simon (not a real name) is 30 years old, lives in an urban area in the Southwest, and holds an administrative post in a large state university. He is on the smallish side physically, in excellent condition from a strenuous workout regimen, and bears a noticeable resemblance to the movie actor Jean-Claude Van Damme. He has a movie star smile and expensive tastes in clothes. Tony has developed considerable expertise with computers as part of his job and is quite adept at surfing the Web. During slow periods at work and often through the night, he prowls the gay chat rooms and gay support Web sites, often conversing for hours with new acquaintances and old friends. He is looking for a soulmate for life—and for evening customers in the meantime. For the past nine years, since the end of his last serious relationship, Tony has been a self-admitted "tramp," a well-paid homosexual prostitute.

Tony believes that his homosexuality is a biological phenomenon and that he was "born with it." As early as 6 or 7 years of age, he knew that he was attracted to males. His father was not distant or rejecting while he was growing up, and his mother could never have been described as "protecting and demanding," as some research has indicated to be characteristics of parents of gay men. Tony described his family life as normal, and he dated (and had sex with) females during high school even though he knew that he was gay. He did not "come out" as an openly gay man until he moved away from the small "hick town" where he grew up, primarily out of consideration for his family's reputation and to avoid causing trouble for his younger brother, who is heterosexual and was a varsity athlete in high school. Tony believes that his father (now deceased) suspected that he was gay, although they never discussed it. His mother knows now and is comfortable with it and proud of his career. Tony states that he has seen remarkable changes in the degree to which society accepts gay people in the last ten years. He has not been harassed by police officers (he has gay friends in the police department) or other officials, even though he is openly gay and displays the pink triangle and rainbow symbols of the gay community on his automobile. He has never experienced attempted blackmail, job or housing discrimination, or hate crime, although on one occasion some drunk teenagers shouted at him when they saw the symbols on his car.

Tony admits to being addicted to sex and freely discusses his promiscuity. He is extremely afraid of the AIDS virus, however, and insists on using protection at all times. He knows a number of gay men who are HIV-positive and had friends who died of AIDS, and he is highly critical of younger men who tend to want unprotected "bareback" sex. He believes that the Internet and the proliferation of gay chat rooms has dramatically increased the promiscuity among gay males because the anonymity of cyberspace circumvents shyness. Chat room conversations quickly turn to sexual preferences, explicit questions, and graphic detail that would probably not be discussed at all in a bar or over the telephone. All of the embarrassing detail has already been discussed and is out of the way when two people eventually agree to meet and "hook up" for casual sex. Plus, he says, "Men are pigs," whether they are gay or straight. They are driven by testosterone and generally have no need for any emotional attachment in a sexual encounter; therefore the courtship games don't have to be played out prior to the sex act. Neither partner expects anything beyond sex. Tony maintains that violent, "caveman" sex is quite popular and occasionally has such encounters with married men who can't be so rough with their wives.

Tony is skeptical on the topic of bisexuality and tends to believe that men who profess to be bisexual are either gay men trying to maintain a straight image or heterosexual men who sometimes want rougher sex than they can get with women.

Tony eased into prostitution after deciding not to meet with an older man with whom he had exchanged e-mail photos. The man began to plead with Tony and offer him money, and Tony finally agreed when the price was high enough. He has been exchanging sex for money ever since.

Prostitution

There are strong opposing beliefs about the so-called oldest profession. On the one hand are those who argue that prostitution is a social evil that spreads disease, promotes other crimes, and degrades both prostitute and patron. On the other hand are those who claim that prostitution is not only inevitable but also performs valuable social functions by providing sexual outlets for the perverse and lonely and that whatever ills accompany it are not inherent but stem from the way in which society treats prostitution.

Regardless of which position one takes, proof is difficult to find. As a consequence, arguments about the dysfunctions or functions of prostitution are usually based on ideology rather than evidence. The indisputable fact is that there is a demand for prostitutes and their services and probably always has been.

In the 1940s Alfred C. Kinsey and associates conducted the first large-scale study of sexual behavior of the American male. Although the study has been widely criticized for its nonrepresentative sampling, it has also been widely quoted. Kinsey found that 69 percent of his white male sample had had some experience with a prostitute. He notes, however, that only about 15 to 20 percent had had repeated contacts. In fact, *homosexual contacts accounted for more male sexual behavior than did contacts with female prostitutes.* In addition, Kinsey estimated that sex with prostitutes accounted for less than 10 percent of non-marital sex in the United States. Kinsey concluded that the attention given prostitution was highly disproportionate to its social significance.[2]

By the 1950s, Kinsey estimated the percentage had dropped to about half that found in his original research.[3] With the increasing availability of nonprofessional partners, indications are that the percentage has continued to decline during the last fifty years. In the 1990s, Janus and Janus estimated that only about 20 percent of adult males had experienced commercial sex.[4] A more recent study of sex in the United States does not address prostitution per se, but has implications for our discussion. In their carefully constructed study, Lauman and associates found strong indications that Americans may be much more conventional and conservative than the Kinsey data originally indicated. Among their findings, only a tiny fraction of Americans (about 5 percent of men and 1 percent of women) indicated that they found the idea of sex with a stranger appealing.[5] A study of 11,000 16 to 44-year-old men recently reported in the British medical journal *Lancet* estimates, however, that there may be a resurgence of interest in commercial sex. The researchers found that while only 2.1 percent men interviewed in 1990 reported having had sex with prostitutes in the previous five years; in 2000 the figure had more than doubled.[6] Still, while prostitute seeking is not considered inconsistent with the male role, most men do not use prostitutes' services or don't use them often.

Why do men go to prostitutes? Kinsey found that males go to prostitutes primarily because they provide easy and certain sexual outlet, they are cheaper than dates with non-prostitutes, they offer sexual contacts with no later responsibilities, and they provide services that are difficult to obtain from other women: bondage, oral or anal intercourse, and so on.[7]

Jennifer James expanded upon Kinsey's research and offered the following classification of clients:

1. **Quantity seekers.** They require many sexual experiences to prove their own sense of worth and potency.

2. **Variety seekers.** They want women with specific characteristics: long-legged women, large-breasted women, black women, fat women, or little-girl-like women. Prostitutes often cater to men who seek a specific variety by dressing to emphasize certain physical attributes or to project a certain image.

3. **Service seekers.** They want a variety of services not easily available elsewhere: oral and anal sex, use of oils and lotions, and so on.

4. **Specials.** They seek a greater degree of service. Also known as "freaks" or "perverts," they require the enactment of elaborate fantasies that rarely are fulfilled outside of prostitution. For example, the prostitute may dress up in a severe "governess" costume and discipline a "very naughty little boy" by verbal abuse and spanking.

5. **Impotents.** They need extraordinary stimulation to perform sexually. The prostitute knows and is willing to attempt a variety of techniques to overcome the men's problems. If the men fail anyway, they are safe because the prostitutes protect the male ego: "Honey, you're tired, you work so hard"; "All that tension from your job makes it difficult for you."

6. **Therapy seekers.** They often just want to talk with someone about personal problems. Prostitutes provide a sympathetic ear as the men spill out their troubles about love, work, and injustice. It is a joke among prostitutes that good whores and good shrinks have more business than they know what to do with.

7. **Uninvolved.** They seek sex without wasting time from dating and entertaining and without fearing such problems as a potential pregnancy or emotional involvement. They are men who want an orgasm with no games or hassles.

8. **Travelers.** They are salesmen, conventioneers, long-distance truckers, construction workers, and military personnel away from home and without socially acceptable sexual outlets.

9. **Disabled.** They are a wide variety of males whose characteristics severely limit sexual access to desirable females: the handicapped, the deformed, those of low intelligence, the aged. For these males prostitutes may be the only appropriate or available source of sexual release. Included in this category are those whose race or culture is restrictive in certain circumstances:

> Variety is not the issue here as much as cultural or class limitations. For instance, white males may feel that this is the only way to satisfy their desire for access to black or Asian women, and the reverse may also be true. Or a Jewish man may want a "shicksa" but would not date a non-Jewish woman because of cultural pressures against doing so. Even if they speak English well, male foreigners who work at international occupations or travel may have problems in gaining sexual access in a socially acceptable manner.[8]

10. Social bonders. They are the groups who hire prostitutes for a friend's first sexual experience or his last fling before marriage or as part of a night on the town. It is a socially integrating experience for males doing things together.[9]

Although most, but not all, of these types have sexual contacts as their primary goal, it is apparent that customers have a great variety of motivations for hiring prostitutes. For many—perhaps most—sex is only one component of being a trick. According to Harold R. Holzman and Sharon Pines, who interviewed 30 johns, being a trick is "a sexual fantasy tinged with elements of fear and adventure."[10] Even more revealing is their finding that when selecting a woman, johns are more concerned with her personality than with her appearance—they are buying more than sex:

> Most . . . were likely to rate a [prostitute] as physically acceptable if she possessed a "moderate" or "average" degree of attractiveness; few respondents required specific physical attributes, such as large breasts, blond hair, or youthfulness. They tended to look for personal warmth and friendliness. Although these men wanted to pay for sex, it seemed that they did not want to deal with someone whose demeanor constantly reminded them of this fact.[11]

The reasons for seeking the services of a prostitute are as varied as the customers. These have been found to include not only the stereotypical salesmen, servicemen, and college students, but also member of the clergy, Little League coaches, school bus drivers, day care workers, and strongly religious family men who had stated they thought prostitution was wrong. Although seldom studied, these customers are an important part of the equation.[12]

Sweden has recently focused new attention on customers in an attempt to curtail what the Swedish State Secretary for Gender Equality sees as a form of violence against women that threatens the balance of power between the sexes. In an attempt to reduce prostitution by reducing demand, Swedes have criminalized use of a prostitute as well as prostitution and are vigorously enforcing the law. Estimates indicate that the number of practicing prostitutes has declined 40 to 80 percent in the five years following passage of the laws.[13]

The Context of Prostitution

What is prostitution? This is not as easy to answer as it seems because there are many variations. For example, a person may be sexually available in exchange for one night's good time. Is he or she a prostitute? A male hires a man or woman to beat him with a whip and shout obscenities at him; he has an orgasm, but the whipper never undresses or is sexually touched by the customer. Is the whipper a prostitute? If you answered yes to either or both of these questions, you will not be in agreement with the definition proposed by two prominent students of the subject, Charles Winick and Paul M. Kinsie, who argue that prostitution "can generally be defined as the granting of nonmarital sexual access, established by mutual agreement of the woman, her client, and/or her employer, for remuneration which provides part or all of her livelihood."[14]

In the first example above, the remuneration of a "good time" scarcely constitutes a livelihood; in the second, being a whipper stretches too far the concept of "sexual access." Little would be gained by muddying the waters of definition any further, but the reader should be aware that sex and its sale occur in many forms, although most would probably fit the definition.

How much prostitution is there in the United States today? This is also a difficult question. Given the variety of forms prostitution currently takes, the difficulty of defining it precisely, and the fact that prostitutes are working illegally in a socially scorned occupation and frequently involved in other forms of illegal behavior as well, it is virtually impossible to tell how many prostitutes there are in the United States today. Experts estimate that about half a million women currently earn most or all of their in come from prostitution. UNICEF estimates that about 100,000 of these are actually children.[15] The State Department has estimated that each year, 50,000 women and children are brought to the United States from countries in Asia, Latin America, and the former USSR (voluntarily and involuntarily) as part of the international sex trade.[16]

Regardless of the amount of prostitution or the form it takes, all prostitution seems to have the following elements in common:

1. Activity that has sexual significance for the purchaser. This includes an entire range of behavior from sexual intercourse to cases in which the seller simply (and literally) walks all over the purchaser.

2. Economic transaction. Whether the sellers earn part or all of their livelihood from prostitution is inconsequential; something of economic value, which may or may not be currency, is exchanged for the activity, usually just prior to the service.

3. Emotional indifference. The behavior is limited to an exchange of service for economic consideration. The participants may or may not be strangers (some prostitutes have repeat customers), but their interaction has nothing to do with affection by the seller for the buyer (although the buyer may be attempting to buy affection).

Some might wish to add *promiscuity* to the list, the assumption being that the seller is indiscriminate with regard to customers. Although this may seem to be the case, some prostitutes, as we shall see, are highly discriminating, and *all* prostitutes must be discriminating to some degree, since their lives depend upon spotting and avoiding dangerous customers.[17]

Before describing the contexts in which prostitution occurs, we remind you that prostitutes are necessarily female. There are also *male* prostitutes like Tony. A small proportion of them live off the earnings and gifts of females. Such males, sometimes called *gigolos,* serve as escorts and sexual partners for middle-aged or elderly women. But the segment of male prostitution that they represent is very small. A far larger number of male prostitutes cater to other males. Research on this activity is scarce.[18] The discussion that follows deals primarily with female prostitution, but it will refer to male prostitution wherever information exists.[19]

Until 1939 much of U.S. prostitution flourished within brothels—popularly known as *whorehouses* or *cathouses.* These were buildings where, under the management of a *madam,* prostitutes lived and carried on their business. Typically, half the women's earnings went to the madam to pay for room, board, and other services provided by the house. The number of women per house ranged from two to sixteen; the houses themselves ranged from the sleazy to the luxuriously furnished, the latter having their own dance bands and bars and catering to well-to-do businessmen and politicians.[20]

In major cities brothels were often clustered in specific areas known as *red-light* districts:

> The phrase "red light" seems to have had its origin in Western railroad construction camps, where prostitutes outnumbered other women by as many as fifty to one. A brakeman visiting a prostitute would hang his red signal lamp outside her tent so that a dispatcher looking for the men to make up a crew could easily find him. On a busy night, a number of such tents that were close together became known as a red light district.[21]

The most famous of such districts were the Barbary Coast in San Francisco and Storyville in New Orleans. In the first decade of this century, Storyville contained as many as 230 brothels within its 36 square blocks.

Because the red-light districts and their brothels were so obvious, they were vulnerable whenever interest group wrath built up against prostitution. As we shall discuss, public agitation against the "social evil" destroyed brothels as a major aspect of prostitution by 1939. Among the large cities only Galveston, Texas, maintained a red-light district of any consequence into the 1960s. Prostitution, of course, was not eliminated along with the red-light districts. Today, the contexts in which prostitution occurs are extremely varied, limited only by the imagination and ingenuity of the sellers and their customers.[22]

Brothels and their madams have not completely disappeared, but the houses are generally much smaller and less conspicuous than they were in the past.[23] The most obvious contemporary brothels today are in Nevada—the one state that leaves the legality of prostitution up to county discretion. Ten counties currently allow prostitution and, in 2000, there were thirty-six licensed brothels in the state.[24]

A variation on the brothel is the *sadomasochistic parlor.* This is a small, specialized operation designed for customers who want to experience pain. An example came to light in Sacramento, California, with the arrests of a high school football coach; his wife, who was an assistant to the principal; and another woman, who was a teacher's aide. The coach and his wife had equipped part of their duplex home with whips, chains, racks, leather restraints, branding irons, and other instruments of torture. Customers were charged $80 an hour for whatever they wanted and could stand.[25]

Another innovation is the brothel catering to homosexuals. David J. Pittman found several in large cities; they are small, lodging one or two males, with another fifteen or more living outside.[26] The customers are typically affluent white professionals and businessmen, a large proportion of whom are married and who are probably unwilling to risk being recognized in more public homosexual settings.

Another variation on the brothel is the *call house* or *escort service.* The prostitutes do not live in the house but report in either regularly or whenever the madam phones them about a customer. The customer may be met at the house or at a place of his choosing. The call-house madam provides an answering and coordinating service for customers who call. One example of this was the Cloud Nine Escort Service of Berkeley, California. It was very "high tech," with state-of-the-art telephone and computer systems. The service maintained the names, addresses, credit card numbers, and sexual preferences of more than 50,000 clients.[27]

However, with the decline of brothels, prostitution often became a matter of individual entrepreneurship. The *call girl* and the *call boy* modes of operation exist in several forms, but all entail the solicitation of services by telephone rather than on the street, in a bar, or in other risky environments. In some cases the telephone allows a high degree of selectivity for the prostitutes: Their phone numbers are available only to customers who have been referred and recommended by other trusted customers or prostitutes. Some call prostitutes serve as escorts for an entire evening of dinner and nightclubbing. In fact, many firms hire such call girls to entertain visiting businessmen. As you might surmise, these women often are (or profess to be) college graduates or from middle-class backgrounds; they are attractive, articulate, well dressed, and well paid.

An example of a sophisticated call girl trade is the San Francisco ring that was so large that four people were needed to answer its 35-line telephone system. The operation employed nearly 200 prostitutes: housewives who worked during the day, and business-women who worked at night. The prostitutes charged $160 an hour for a hotel room visit; they kept $100, and the remainder went to the operation. All the women carried credit card imprinters on their rounds.[28]

The less sophisticated members of the call prostitute trade are available through advertisements in nearly every major American city, for example, *Screw* in New York City and *Pleasure Guide* in the San Francisco Bay area. The following ads are representative:

> "Boy Next Door." I am 24, have blue eyes, brown hair, am 5'11" and weigh 147 pounds. My body is lean, hard and well defined from hours in the gym and on a surf board. Because of my good, clean, wholesome looks I have been billed as the "boy next door" in several under-ground flicks and have appeared in several publications. I am versatile and cooperative.

> Attractive lady, former schoolmistress, well educated and very dominant, seeks submissive males in need of strict behavior training.

Another context in which prostitutes and customers meet is the bar. Many bars employ women primarily to push drinks. These *B-girls* approach customers with such come-ons as "Want to buy me a drink, honey?" If the customer assents, the woman may encourage him to order champagne. Ordering champagne in these places is a costly mistake usually committed only by the extremely gullible or the extremely drunk: A nonvintage New York State brand will cost upwards of $35 per bottle. Usually, however, the woman orders something such as sloe gin or some other high priced, low-alcohol concoction, on which she receives a commission.

The role that prostitution plays among B-girls varies according to the rules of the bar. Some bar owners prohibit soliciting, although the women may make after-hours arrange-ments at their own risk. In other bars, prostitution is an integral part of the job. In the crasser establishments customers may—for a price—fondle the women or be masturbated under the table or perhaps hire the women for "lap dancing," which involves an erotic dance per-formed while sitting on the customer's lap. Often the couple retires to a private room.

The closest counterpart to the B-girl among male prostitutes is the *bar hustler.* (*Hus-tling* is the preferred term among gays for prostituting.) The hustler is not employed by an establishment but systematically patrols gay bars in search of customers.

Another context for prostitution is the *massage parlor,* varying from the shabby to the luxurious. Toward the shabby end are storefronts advertising body rubs and massages. Inside, the customer learns from a sign on the wall what services are available ("body rub," "body shampoo," etc.) and that the masseuse's stage of dress is negotiable. Once in the "massage room," the customer briefly bargains for and receives services over and above the actual massage. Clifton Bryant regards these massage parlors as comparable to "fast-food" establishments: They are businesslike and efficient and even post a menu.[29]

For those with a great deal more money to spend, there are parlors complete with saunas and whirlpools. One establishment near Times Square in New York City has nine massage rooms, each with a different fantasy theme, including the Hall of Caesar with its "seductive slave girl," the House of the Geisha, the Western Bordello, and the completely mirrored Infinity Room.

Before turning our attention to one of the oldest but still most common types of prostitute, the *streetwalker,* we should remember that prostitution is found in nearly any situation in which potential customers exist. Historically, roving armies had their *camp followers.* Today, prostitutes are found near military installations, major truck stops, and large-scale construction projects. Prostitutes can easily be located in any large city by reading the local "adult newspaper" or by strolling through the areas occupied by pornography shops, adult movie theaters, strip joints, gentlemen's clubs bars, and so on. They are literally, "only a phone call away," and readily accessible by email. In the 2002, the FBI shut down an Internet sex services that had records indicating contacts with thousands of customers in the United States and worldwide.[30] In short, despite its illegality, prostitution thrives wherever a demand exists.

To meet this demand, new means of accommodating customers are often devised. One example occurred in Portland, Oregon, where a woman installed a massage parlor in a recreational vehicle. Said she, "We'd eventually like to go statewide. . . . The [motor homes] are so versatile that you can virtually go to the fisherman on the bank of a river and if he doesn't catch any fish he can just climb aboard and relax."[31]

Despite all the innovations of Infinity Rooms and motor homes, streetwalkers (or "kerb crawlers" as the British call them) remain a constant staple in the world of female prostitution. Probably outnumbering all others in the business, they are at the bottom of its prestige ladder. According to Gail Sheehy, three types of female streetwalkers can be found in New York City:

1. Daytimers. These are the classiest of the street trade, made up of white, out-of-work models and actresses and of housewives secretly supplementing their husbands' incomes. Daytimers work office buildings for contacts with executives at no less than $60 a trick.

2. Early evening girls. Usually finished by 11:00 P.M., these are full-time, independent professionals who work in and around hotels, especially during conventions. They may make as much as $300 to $400 per evening.

3. All the rest. This includes the old, the very young, the tough, the desperate, the unattractive, and any others not fitting into the other categories. They work far into the night and try to turn as many tricks as possible before the stream of customers simply runs out.[32]

There are also male streetwalkers who appeal to the homosexual market. Those in their early and mid-teens often do not regard themselves as homosexuals and prefer to be called *hustlers.* Despite their preference, however, the youngest boys are commonly referred to as *chickens* and their clients as *chickenhawks*. These hustlers are paid by adults for playing the "inserter" role in oral sex acts. These hustlers will be discussed further in the next section.

Another type of male hustler ranges in age from the late teens to the early twenties. These young men

> appeal to men of their own age group or older because they project an exaggeratedly and stereotypical masculine image. They stand on the street, in what is known as the "meat rack" and display their muscular arms, often tattooed, and they wear tight jeans to advertise their wares. The customer and the hustler negotiate the fact that there is a mutual interest in a sexual contact, that it will be for a given amount of cash, and that there is a place where they can go for the performance, and finally, they often negotiate the physical nature of that performance before it occurs. With the masculine types of hustler (often called "trade"), that may not be necessary: the customer believes, or wants to believe, that his partner is so masculine as to be straight and will not allow any contact except when he (the hustler) does the inserting.[33]

There also are males variously known as *female impersonators, drag queens,* and *transvestites* who become involved in prostitution. They dress and speak in imitation of females, and they perform oral sex on usually unsuspecting customers. These male prostitutes are most likely to be found in major cities, although they are occasionally found around truck stops, where convenience dictates quick sex without undressing.

Finally, perhaps the greatest opportunities for marketing, innovation, and participation in the sex trade exist in cyberspace. Anyone with something to sell, a wish to buy, or even idle curiosity can get connected or experiment with virtual encounters at Internet sites.

Becoming a Prostitute

As was mentioned, the literature on why women become prostitutes is voluminous. One of the oldest explanations is that women are forced into the profession, a practice known as *white slavery.* (This curious term implies that anyone forced into the profession must be white.) The usual story about white slavery involves gullible country girls who, arriving at big-city train and bus stations, are accosted by slick-talking pimps and lured into brothels. There the girls are repeatedly threatened, raped, or beaten until their spirit and sense of decency are broken.

In truth, the global trade in human beings for sex and pornography is flourishing. Young women, and sometimes young men, are traded internationally by criminal groups in the sex slave business.[34] In addition to conventional prostitution, "sex tourism" trips to Southeast Asia, Thailand, India, and Central America are popular among Western businessmen and wealthy Asians and Arabs and often involve sex with children. Organized criminal groups from Russia, Japan, the United States, the former Yugoslavia, and Thailand are heavily involved.[35] Poverty seems to be the root cause, as poor families sell children into prostitution or young women are lured away from home with promises of employment and then forced into sexual bondage.[36]

Kevin Bales tells the story of Siri. Sold by desperately poor parents into the thriving Thailand sex industry, she is a 15-year-old Thai prostitute. Reasons for selling female children range from saving the farm to purchasing a TV. Her parents may have believed she was being taken to the city to work in some menial job, but the presence in their village of retired women dying of AIDS means that they have reason to believe otherwise. Many Tai females enter the trade more or less voluntarily and work more or less independently. Siri, however, is one of the approximately 5 percent who are imprisoned in the brothel, raped, beaten, and exploited. Her recruiter, the pimp who stands guard, the brothel owner, even police and politicians make money from her services. Eventually, some will be sent home to Siri's parents to help ensure that one of her sisters will join her when she comes of age. Siri will see little of this money. This is an ugly side of capitalism.[37]

Another view of prostitution is presented by Denise Brennan. She studied sex workers in a small resort town in the Dominican Republic. "Sex workers in Sosua are at once independent and dependent, resourceful and exploited. They are local agents caught in a web of global economic relations. To the extent that they can, they try to take advantage of the men who are in Sousua to take advantage of them." The object of the game for these women is not only increase their standard of living (and that of their children) by working in the sex trade, but also to entice one of their clients into marriage and a ticket off the island.[38]

The degree to which U.S. women are initially forced to prostitute themselves seems minimal. The following are two exceptions. The first is a quotation from a pimp on how runaway girls are initiated:

"You've got to find out if they've got problems, if they're smart enough to say they are 18 when cops make a bust. . . . My partner's finding out everything about her, if she sniffs coke, he'll give her that. She's in a beautiful crib [apartment], a penthouse almost. It's heaven on earth—until tomorrow. Tomorrow the respect thing starts. A few blows. Some ass kicking. You've got to stomp her ass a few times to let her know where you're coming from. You've got to set the rules, make her show respect. . . . If she makes it through tomorrow, the process will take three days. We'll get her a wig, some clothes, then put $10 in her pocket and see if she tries to run. You watch her close, maybe send another girl out with her. If she turns her first trick and comes back smiling, you've got her."[39]

The following concerns the recruiting of chickens (young male prostitutes):

Since the most requested commodity by chickenhawks is a new face, the pimps are always looking for new boys. The pimps stand like vultures around the Port Authority Bus Terminal waiting to descend on runaways. A young boy needs only to get off the bus, a knapsack on his back, walk a few confused steps in the big city, before a nice man will offer him a free meal and a place to stay. Too often the boy accepts. By that night the boy has been broken in. He becomes the victim of what is called on the street the rape artist. The boy is beaten. Perhaps he is drugged. And he's working. All the money he makes goes to the pimp. All the child receives is a few meals and enough pills to keep him too stoned to resist. He is now part of the stable, a chicken sold from john to john until the pimp tires of him.[40]

Fortunately, such horror stories are the exceptions. As we shall see from the research, most prostitutes, female and male, enter the profession without coercion. This leaves us with the question: Why do people voluntarily become prostitutes? Because prostitution is deviant behavior, this question is seldom asked with the same detachment that is seen in asking why people become morticians, bookkeepers, or chicken-pluckers. Just as these individuals provide desired services, prostitutes provide services for a fee. True, they sell—actually, they "rent"—their bodies, but so do boxers, football players, and models. What if we were to reply that people become prostitutes in response to the capitalistic dictum of making the most money with the least effort in the shortest time? This would probably not satisfy those who expect an explanation based on an unhappy childhood, disturbed personality, low IQ, and so on. All these and a host of other possibilities have been suggested over the years, but no research conclusions come close to explaining the incredible variety of people engaged in the profession, ranging from junkies to housewives to secretaries to individuals like Sally Stanford, a madam who later became a successful restaurateur and politician in Sausalito, California.[41]

From the limited amount of research on the backgrounds of prostitutes, there emerges a set of three experiences common to many of the women engaged in the occupation on a full-time basis. (We know little about the backgrounds of part-timers.) These three career contingencies do not explain why specific women enter the occupation, but they do point to factors that make prostitution a logical behavioral alternative:

1. **Early and frequent promiscuous sexual experiences.** By "early," we mean from 10 to 13 years of age at the time of first sexual intercourse. "Promiscuous" is difficult to use without sounding moralistic, but there appears to be a pattern of sexual experiences with several men, often after the briefest of acquaintanceships. Childhood sexual abuse is linked to later imvolvement in prostitution, and there may be high correlations with repeated and persistent abuse.[42] For many women who become prostitutes—perhaps as many as half—the earliest sexual experiences involve incest or rape. Thus there may be at least two early life patterns that favor entering prostitution. In the first the girl learns that her sexuality is an efficient means for gaining affection and attention. In the second, early sexual victimization leads to a loss of self-esteem and to acceptance of a role as simply a sex object.

For many lower-class women both patterns may be reinforced: first in dating, when sexual intercourse is perceived as barter for the male's time and expense, and second in certain lower-status occupations, such as waitressing, in which women must be "sexy" to please the boss and the customers.

The reader should bear in mind that patterns of early sexual experience, either voluntary or coerced, and the often not-so-subtle encouragement of promiscuity by dates and employers may not necessarily distinguish women who become prostitutes from their peers who do not. Nevertheless, the patterns facilitate entry into prostitution because they establish an awareness of sex as a marketable commodity.[43]

2. **Acquisition of verbalized motives favorable to prostitution.** With few exceptions it appears that becoming a prostitute involves associations with others who encourage undertaking the career. These associations may be with prostitutes or with pimps who extol the life as fast and glamorous—a life of expensive clothes, independence, and excitement. (Among prostitutes already working for a pimp, there is an incentive to recruit: bringing others into the stable is one way to win praise and favors from the "old man.") In short, the novice finds plenty of social support to neutralize any misgivings or doubts about selling it rather than *giving it away.*

In some cases the motives may be altruistic. James H. Bryan found among call girls an ideology that prostitution serves as a positive force for good:

> We girls see, like I guess you call them perverts of some sort, you know, little freaky people and if they didn't have girls to come to like us that are able to handle them and make it a nice thing, there would be so many rapes and nutty people really. I could say that a prostitute has held more marriages together as part of their profession than any divorce counselor.[44]

Thus the women become convinced that prostitution is not only adventurous but also considerably less shameful than the rest of society cares to believe.

Males who prostitute themselves must deal with motives regarding *two* deviant identities: being both a prostitute and a homosexual. Adjustments are made in nearly all possible combinations. Some hustlers, particularly older ones, see themselves as neither, and still others see themselves as hustlers but not homosexuals. How can people sell homosexual favors while denying a homosexual identity?

The answer to this question can be found in Albert J. Reiss, Jr.'s study of lower-class delinquent boys.[45] He found that, just as with females who become prostitutes, some boys learn from their close associates the advantages of selling sex; as with females it is simply a matter of easy money. However, they also learn that "getting a queer"—being paid by a homosexual for services—need not be a sign of being either a hustler or a queer as long as certain rules in the relationship are maintained. First, money must be the only goal; seeking sexual satisfaction from the relationship is forbidden. Second, the relationship must be limited to the adult orally stimulating the boy; no other sexual contacts are permitted. Third, no affection between participants may be displayed during the relationship; the service is to be dispensed and accepted in an indifferent, businesslike manner. Fourth, no violence is to be used if the customer conforms to the norms of the situation. (It is possible that violence will occur if the customer does anything that threatens the boy's self-concept as a person who neither hustles nor is a homosexual. For example, calling the boy "sweetheart" in front of his buddies is an invitation to disaster.)

3. Recognition of high financial return and restricted alternatives. Any single explanation of why people enter prostitution would have to concentrate on the economics of the situation. Money alone is not a sufficient explanation, unless one considers that for most prostitutes, other avenues to comparable incomes are unavailable. For the young, uneducated, lower-class female, prostitution promises rewards that she could not dream of otherwise. In a matter of hours she can earn hundreds of dollars; she could find no other employment so lucrative for so short a period. Add to the money the promise of independence and excitement, and prostitution can become an exceedingly attractive choice for the unskilled or poorly skilled woman.

At the other extreme a similar situation holds true even for the older, educated woman. If she possesses both beauty and an attractive personality, prostitution can provide her a greater financial return than can most other available work. One prostitute explains the economics of the matter this way:

> Even a call girl could never make as much in a straight job as she could at prostitution. All prostitutes are in it for the money. With most uptown girls, the choice is not between starvation and life, but it is a choice between $5,000 and $25,000 or between $10,000 and $50,000. That's a pretty big choice; a pretty big difference. You can say that they're in this business because of the difference of $40,000 a year. A businessman would say so. Businessmen do things because of the difference of $40,000 a year. Call girls do go into capitalism and think like capitalists.[46]

The same woman goes on to explain that women generally, and black women in particular, are restricted in their economic choices; for the poor black woman there may be virtually no choice at all.[47]

One specific economic factor frequently mentioned as a contributor to prostitution is *dependence on illegal drugs*.[48] Paul J. Goldstein investigated the hypothesis that since, these drugs are priced well beyond the earning capacity of most lower-class women, addicted women often may turn to prostitution as a means of maintaining their habits. Among lower-class prostitutes—streetwalkers—he found the expected relationship between heroin use and subsequent entry into the profession. In short, for these prostitutes drug dependence created an economic necessity.

In some places it has also created an economic hardship for other prostitutes. Street walkers accustomed to getting $20 per trick have complained that addicts sometimes provided the same services for $5 to $10.[49] However, among higher-class prostitutes—call girls—he found that drug dependence *followed* their entry into the profession. For these women the most common dependence was on stimulants, which helped them meet the pace and pressures of their work. Two call girls told the following stories:

> "I really needed them . . . because I was in the business and had to work and I was crashing. Like . . . in the morning and I had a whole day to get through. I would need them because I had a regulation and a schedule in my life I had to meet. . . . But as far as being into the head of speeding all the time and wanting them for that reason . . . no."
>
> "On a convention, when you're working seventy-two hours straight through . . . you take ups. In fact, that's where I first tried "black beauties" [biphetamine capsules]."[50]

It is evident that while many prostitutes share common experiences, we cannot say that entering prostitution depends upon a single personality trait or background characteristic. An understanding of careers in prostitution can come only by considering a variety of influences involving both childhood and adult experiences. Cathy Spatz Widom proposes that a multidimensional approach is necessary to explain why a person enters and continues a life of prostitution.[51] She suggests that *physiological and genetic predispositions* are part of the process; for example, they may contribute to the desire for excitement and independence that many prostitutes exhibit. In addition, there are *early environment and socialization experiences* that might include early sexual experiences and abuse. *Socioeconomic and demographic characteristics* and *situational factors* are also involved; for example, limited economic opportunities because of one's social class and specific personal crises stemming from underemployment or unemployment, drug use, and so on may influence one to at least experiment with prostitution as a solution. In addition, another factor—*society's response to behavior*—serves either to reinforce or to undermine the continuation of the behavior. Thus according to Widom, a variety of factors may promote a career in prostitution. This variety may be reflected in the heterogeneity of prostitute types: transvestites, streetwalkers, part-timers, and so on.

Once a person accepts prostitution as a career, he or she will find it filled with risks: In addition to the possibility of drug dependence, there are dangers of arrest, disease (including the AIDS virus), overwork, violent customers, and feelings of self-abasement that conventional society freely encourages. Yet for those who can deal with these problems and remain independent, prostitution emerges as a rational and perhaps adventuresome occupational choice. For many—and probably most—who enter the profession, however, the fortune and glamour are illusory goals. We have no idea what proportion of prostitutes emerge from the occupation financially secure, but it seems to be a small minority, and the wear and tear of the work appears to take a tremendous toll on youth and health. Prostitutes may earn hundreds of dollars a day yet have little to show for their efforts. The reason? Many prostitutes simply do not plan for the future, a fact that hardly distinguishes them from many other people, regardless of their occupations. As one incarcerated prostitute told her social worker, "Look lady, I make lots more than you do. I don't need lectures or job counseling. I need help with this financial planning thing!"

Women prostitutes, in their search for excitement and for financial and individual independence, are often beguiled into a servitude that deprives them of those very goals. Nothing better personifies that servitude than the *pimp*.

The Pimp

Those who profit from prostitution are far more numerous than one might first imagine. The prostitutes do, of course, but so do hotel operators, lawyers, bail bondsmen, taxi drivers, police, physicians, bartenders, bellhops, and the owners and operators of various outlets for prostitution such as massage parlors, nightclubs, and brothels. (Recently, a candidate for president of Thailand was a man who had made his fortune as owner of several brothels.) But the one individual who profits the most for the least amount of effort is the pimp. Even though prostitution today involves a wide variety of independent, entrepreneurial efforts, the pimp is still an important part of the industry.[52]

There are few livelihoods about which there are such divergent opinions. To some the pimp represents perfect success, for he has totally conned the system; to others he is simply a base exploiter of women; and to the prostitutes in his *stable,* he is an essential part of their lives—he is what they live and work for. In short, a balanced opinion of pimping is difficult to find.

What does the pimp do? He buys the prostitute's clothes and furniture (with her money, of course); pays her rent and doctor bills; arranges for bail and a lawyer when she is arrested; and provides her with affection, attention, and moral support. In return, the prostitute turns over all her earnings to him. Whether this is a fair exchange obviously depends upon your perspective.

The world of the pimp is clearly one in which success breeds success. The more material goods the pimp displays, the greater advantage he has in convincing women that they ought to join his stable. The more women in his stable, the more goods he can purchase and the greater discretion he can use in recruiting. Stables vary in size from 1 to 20 (usually streetwalkers), but size is not the true measure of a pimp's success. Productivity is.[53] And high productivity is clearly visible: It can buy a suede-upholstered Lincoln Continental with telephone, chauffeur, and color television; custom-made clothing; a butler; a house in the country; a penthouse in the city; and pedigreed dogs—the bigger or the smaller the better. These are the indicators of the pimp who has made it.

Whether prostitutes "need" a pimp is a question beyond the scope of this discussion. There is no doubt that many women are convinced that they do for several reasons, including business guidance, protection, status among other prostitutes, and emotional stability. The philosophy of the pimp does nothing to discourage this conviction.

Relationships between prostitutes and their pimps vary greatly, so it is impossible to state categorically the real costs and benefits to the women. But there is no question that some relationships are maintained in an atmosphere of terror.[54] Some pimps set a quota that their women must earn each night; if they fall short of that quota the consequences range from being locked out of their apartments to being beaten.[55] (The "official" pimp weapon is a wire coat hanger wrapped in cotton to minimize bruising.) Police vice squads frequently must protect prostitutes who are threatened with mutilation, or worse, from their pimps.[56]

Other, and probably most, pimp-prostitute relationships are not so terrifying. The woman accepts the pimp as a boyfriend, business agent, and protector. He persuades her that she "needs" a man to shelter her and care for money details. She, in turn, feels that she needs someone "to come home to." Jennifer James regards the relationship between pimps and prostitutes as similar to many relationships between men and women in conventional society:[57]

Prostitution and Conflict

Traditionally there have been moral crusades to eliminate prostitution as an institution. Throughout the nineteenth century in the United States, however, prostitution was widespread but tolerated. Streetwalkers ran the risk of being arrested, but brothels were seldom bothered. Officials were generally content with the situation because localized brothels simplified control and regulation.

But the first decades of the twentieth century found the larger U.S. cities caught in the fervor of vice crusades that were inspired by "revelations" about prostitutes were sometimes contradictory but always negative. Prostitutes were variously portrayed as moronic and immoral producers of numerous moronic and immoral offspring, as weak-willed women enticed by the lure of easy money, as good but gullible innocents forced into white slavery, as corrupting influences on middle- and upper-class youths, and as the primary sources of syphilis.

To counter this evil, several educational and lobbying organizations were formed. Three years of pressure from such reform groups as well as religious leaders and newspapers forced the Chicago City Council in 1910 to establish a commission to study the vice situation.[58] The commission's report conceded that the ultimate ideal could not be achieved until "lust in the hearts of men" was eradicated. The commission also found little evidence that white slavery was a major factor in prostitution; instead, it was a lack of education and the promise of high economic rewards that led girls into the occupation. Despite these findings, the report set forth a series of suggestions for legal repression that were to influence states and municipalities across the country.

Among the commission's recommendations were that "segregated vice" (i.e., the red-light districts) be abolished; that imprisonment or probation replace fines for prostitution; and that police departments add special morals squads. By October 1912, the Chicago brothels were closed. By 1918 approximately 200 more cities had closed theirs. The visibility of the brothels had contributed to their undoing, and the era of the red-light district had ended.[59]

Legal repression was only one step in a wider social reform movement that encompassed education, labor, government, and the general rights of all individuals—a reform movement couched in the ideals of the rural, Protestant, native, white middle class.

However, the reform movement did not eliminate, or perhaps even diminish, prostitution. But it did alter prostitution's context: The women went underground, they dispersed, and they migrated to areas where law enforcement was more accommodating. Since 1918 the status of prostitution has fluctuated in some areas from openness to stricter laws and back again. Honolulu, for example, legalized brothels from 1920 until 1944, then closed them following World War II.[60]

From a historical perspective the interest groups arrayed against prostitution usually include citizens who seek its complete repression and criminal justice officials who simply want to keep it under control. Rarely has anyone openly favored prostitution. Recently, however, two groups have entered the struggle on the side of the prostitutes: *feminists* and *prostitutes* themselves.

Feminists face a dilemma: They side with prostitutes but detest prostitution. They regard prostitution as a blatant symbol of the sexism that feminists are attempting to destroy:

> The presence of prostitution is a crime against all people. It legitimates people treating others as objects to be bought and sold without respect to human dignity, it supports an illegal market place (police payoffs, pimps, drug pushers, etc.) which results in crime and violence; it enforces a one-sided monogamy and it perpetuates racist and sexist attitudes, dehumanizing women and Third World people.[61]

While feminists condemn prostitution, it is a feminist tenet that a woman has the right to do what she pleases with her body—even selling it. Most prostitutes are women who have more or less voluntarily chosen to be what they are, and the more vocal prostitutes claim that aside from discriminatory law enforcement practices, they are not degraded, underprivileged, or male-victimized.

Contemporary feminists still regard the prostitute as a symbol of both sexual liberation and sexual bondage, but the dilemma is resolved by viewing the situation as both a short- and a long-term problem.[62] In the long term the feminist goal is to eliminate prostitution by eliminating the sexism that creates the demand. In the short term the feminist goal is to reduce the prostitute's victimization by the law in particular and by society in general.[63]

In recent decades prostitutes have become more outspoken on their own behalf. In 1973 Margo St. James, an ex-prostitute, formed a streetwalkers' organization in San Francisco called COYOTE, an acronym for "Call Off Your Old Tired Ethics." Other prostitutes' unions followed: (PENET, Prostitutes Education Network), PONY (Prostitutes of New York), and ASP (Association of Seattle Prostitutes). Also we now have the United States Prostitutes Collective (U.S. Pros), part of the International Prostitutes Collective (IPC); the North American Task Force on Prostitution; the International Committee for Prostitute Rights (ICPR), also founded by St. James; World Whores' Congresses; and finally, Women Hurt in Systems of Prostitution Engaged in Revolt (WHISPER).[64] The unions attempted to alleviate many of the oppressive conditions facing streetwalkers by

> providing adequate counsel, arranging for bail when prostitutes are arrested, and helping prostitutes learn how to fill out arrest forms; educating prostitutes to their rights—including their rights to plead not guilty and demand jury trials; developing a bail fund for prostitutes who so plea, and working for their release on their own recognizance . . . ; challenging requirements that arrested prostitutes be subject to V.D. [venereal disease] "quarantines" in jail before trial; providing emergency housing for women immediately out of jail; providing child care for women while they are in jail; helping develop job opportunities for women who wish to leave the profession.[65]

A major goal of the feminists, as we have noted, is shared by all prostitutes' unions: *decriminalization of prostitution.*[66] Societies can adopt one of three legal strategies on prostitution: prohibition, regulation, or decriminalization. Through our history, however, the strategy in the United States has been *prohibition.*[67]

Prohibition of prostitution has not been especially successful. But the effort *is* especially expensive. A study of New York City arrest patterns revealed that one out of nine arrests is for prostitution; it is the third most frequent arrest charge after larceny and drugs.[68] These statistics indicate that a great deal of law enforcement time *may* be spent picking up hookers, particularly in major cities. Other attempts to decrease the incidence or at least the visibility of prostitution have been tried, such as impounding the john's vehicle, using female police officers posing as streetwalkers, and publishing the names of those arrested (prostitutes and johns) in the local newspaper. One report by a female police decoy proves interesting: "You'd be surprised at the people that get arrested.[69]

One often recommended solution is *regulation* or *legalization.* Control takes a variety of forms such as licensing or registration requirements for prostitutes and laws concerning when, where, and how the business of prostitution may be conducted. The regulation of prostitution occurs in only one of the United States: Nevada. It is common in Europe, however. In Germany, for example, local governments define the geographic areas and the context in which prostitutes may operate.

Is regulation or legalization the answer? Prostitutes and feminists say no. Regulation certainly makes things convenient for the state because it facilitates the state's control of a revenue-making enterprise. But for the women the restrictions and stigmatization are a nightmare. In these brothels they are merely sex machines stamped "government approved." Rachel West calls legalized prostitution in Nevada and the Eros Center "the new sex assembly line" and suggests that women want to work as "independent business women, controlling . . . [their] working conditions."[70]

A common argument is that prostitution must be either prohibited or regulated to contain venereal disease and now the AIDS virus. Any licensing system has a requirement for periodic medical examinations so that prostitutes may be certified as "safe products." As has been mentioned, however, most venereal disease today—probably about 95 percent—is spread by nonprostitutes. (Can a similar argument be made for the AIDS virus?) One two-year study of Nevada prostitutes found not one case of AIDS.[71] (One reason may be the fact that prostitutes use condoms at a higher rate than nonprostitutes.)

Prostitutes want neither prohibition nor regulation of their trade; they want to be left alone and free of governmental harassment. They want *decriminalization.* The feminists agree. They see government regulation of prostitution as unnecessarily and permanently stigmatizing the women, making career changes difficult if not impossible.[72]

Whatever the reasons for the existence of commercial sex, it has not disappeared and will not disappear by imposing repression and hardship on those who are responding to a demand.

Homosexuality

I didn't play with Barbies as a child. The only thing I did with Barbie was to rip her hair out and run over her with my Tonkas, transformers, and stomper trucks. I didn't play dress-up as a child. I don't have track lighting, designer clothes or a limp wrist. I don't rape little boys. I don't wear makeup. I don't wish I were a woman. I don't say "gurl" all the time. I don't speak with a lisp or wear pink shirts. I don't walk with a swish. I don't fit the "gay stereotype," but I am gay. The best way I have found to describe myself . . . is that I'm a normal, masculine, laid back guy who happens to be gay. And that's it![73]

—Matt

Homosexuality: Condition or Behavior?

We do not yet fully understand the answer to the question, What causes homosexuality? (or What causes heterosexuality?) The answers are most likely to be found in a complex interaction of physical, psychological, and social variables. Research continues to accumulate indicating that to understand homosexuality, we must be able to think in three dimensions. First, since Kinsey, we have been aware that is not just one condition or behavior. Rather, individuals' sexual preferences range along a continuum from strongly homosexual to strongly heterosexual. Second, recent research indicates that the degree of that commitment can vary over one's lifespan. Third, recent research in the "hard sciences" indicates that it can be affected by genes, hormones, and differences in people's brains.

Alfred C. Kinsey and his colleagues note, however, that:

> A great deal of the thinking done by scientists and laymen alike stems from the assumption that there are persons who are "heterosexual" and persons who are "homosexual," that these two types represent antitheses in the sexual world, and that there is only an insignificant class of "bisexuals" who occupy an intermediate position between the other groups. It is implied that every individual is innately—inherently—either heterosexual or homosexual.[74]

Life would certainly be considerably simplified if we could divide the population so neatly. But Kinsey, in studying the sexual histories of white American males, discovered that the behavior of many is not an either-or proposition. There are those whose preferences have been exclusively homosexual or heterosexual throughout their lives. However, a considerable proportion have combined both preferences. Some are heterosexual during one part of their life and homosexual during another. Still others are involved with both sexes at the same time—the same year, month, week, day, or even moment.[75]

Consider these examples. Joe is married, has three children, and enjoys regular intercourse with his wife. But he occasionally stops in a public lavatory (known as a "tearoom" among homosexuals) to be fellated.[76] Fred has exclusively homosexual contacts between the ages of 15 and 23, then gets married and never has another homosexual contact. Pete has exclusively heterosexual contacts until he enters prison, where he engages in homosexual behavior; after his release from prison he returns to exclusively heterosexual behavior.

Kinsey found that only 4 percent of the American *white male* population are *exclusively homosexual* throughout their lives. Yet 37 percent of this population have had at least *one homosexual experience to the point of orgasm* between adolescence and old age. If one includes homosexual attraction that does not involve an orgasm, Kinsey found that half the white male population has had *some homosexual experience* during their adult lives. For *white females* the percentages are lower, but the same general pattern holds: Fewer than 2 percent are *exclusively homosexual* throughout their lives, 13 percent have had at least *one homosexual experience to the point of orgasm,* and 28 percent have had *some homosexual experience.*[77]

A word of warning is necessary here. The Kinsey data are often used to indicate the prevalence of homosexuality. However, the large number of prisoners in Kinsey's sample, the lack of black subjects, and other sampling biases make this a suspect practice. A survey conducted by the Playboy Foundation in the 1970s found roughly the same percentages.[78] However, the "Sex in America" study revealed that, although 9 percent of the men and 4 percent of the women had had some same-sex encounter since puberty, only 2.8 percent of men and about 1½ percent of the women said that they considered themselves homosexual or bisexual, and only 2 percent had had sex with a same-sex partner during the past year.[79] These findings were supported by additional research in the United States and abroad.[80] And a careful reading of Kinsey's work reveals that the great majority of males have no homosexual contacts after age 20. In addition, many individuals have varying degrees of commitment to both homosexuality and heterosexuality depending upon time, place, and other circumstances.

So elusive is the concept of homosexuality that at least one sociologist has suggested that the term "homosexual" is useless. According to Edward Sagarin,

> there is no such thing as a homosexual, for such a concept is a reification, an artificially cre-ated entity that has no basis in reality. What exists are people with erotic desires for their own sex, or who engage in sexual activities with same-sex others, or both. The desires constitute feeling, the acts constitute doing, but neither is being. Emotions and actions are fluid and dynamic, learnable and unlearnable, exist to a given extent for a limited or longer period of time, but are constantly in a state of change, flux, development, and becoming.[81]

Sagarin's point is well taken, especially considering that for most people sexual behavior is but a segment of their everyday activity. Why should one's sexual preference take precedence over all the other identities one has? Because this is one way society attempts to exercise social control over behavior it wishes to discourage. Labeling is part of a process to discourage behavior.

Anthropologic studies of preliterate societies indicate that many societies have no category of persons known as *homosexuals*—not because there is no homosexual behavior but because those societies have not labeled the actors as having a condition. In the major-ity of such societies, a certain amount of homosexual behavior is considered normal and acceptable. In a few societies limited participation in homosexual activities is not even a matter of preference but a duty.[82] Thus the "deviance" of homosexuality is a matter of social definition: sometimes it is permitted, other times it is not, depending upon time, circum-stances, and culture. Mary McIntosh traced the modern emergence of homosexuality as a condition to England at the end of the seventeenth century. Homosexual behavior had been condemned for centuries, but until that time, people who engaged in the behavior were not characterized or categorized as being different from others.[83]

Becoming "Homosexual"

Whether homosexuality is a condition (like measels or thinning hair) or simply a term broadly applied to various forms of behavior, research goes on to discover the origins of same-sex preference. The search for distinctions between those with a primarily same-sex orientation (whom, for the sake of convenience, we will continue to call "homosexuals") and those with a primarily opposite-sex orientation ("heterosexuals") has taken many forms.

But whether homosexuality is a condition or behavior, the question remains: What determines sexual preference? There is little point in listing the vast array of answers that have been proposed. Often such answers focus on another question that is frequently heard: Aren't homosexuals born that way? Some biological positivists have long thought that this was the case and that eventually some *genetic factor* would be linked with sexual orientation. Since the early 1990s, evidence has continued to accumulate that sexual preference is linked to some biological factor or factors. Research has focused differences in brain structure and function,[84] and on genetic factors.[85] With the discovery that some individuals possess statistically abnormal chromosome arrangements (e.g., XYY—see the discussion in Chapter 2), biologists became optimistic that certain genetic patterns might make persons more vulnerable to homosexuality.[86]

Other biologists have suspected that even if there is no specific genetic condition related to homosexuality, homosexuals might possess some other physiological characteristic unlike that found in heterosexuals. Initially, the most promising research along these lines involved levels of the male sex hormone *testosterone*. With some consistency research has indicated that low levels of the hormone were found in males who were predominantly or exclusively homosexual throughout their lives.[87]

This research appears promising, However, causation is difficult to prove and LeVay, for example, admits that, "his findings [currently] contain no direct evidence that the difference he observed actually causes homosexuality."[88] Even if biological factors can be positively identified, it is likely that biology explains only part of homosexuality and homosexual behavior.

Another widely accepted notion is that something in the *parent-child relationship* leads a child to develop a homosexual orientation. The precise nature of this predisposing parent-child relationship depends upon which theorist you read. Generally, however, it involves some combination of a mother who is domineering, seductive, overindulgent, and possessive and a father who is indifferent, distant, weak, and ineffectual. In reviewing studies conducted prior to 1968, Evelyn Hooker concluded that

> the evidence from these and many similar studies does not support the assumption that pathological parent-child relations are either necessary or sufficient antecedents or determinants of adult homosexuality. The evidence does indicate, however, that some forms of familial pathology appear to be associated with increased vulnerability of some individuals to homosexual development, and it suggests that psychopathology is more frequently associated with homosexuality in these individuals.[89]

A later study compared the parental backgrounds of over 300 males who were either exclusively or predominantly homosexual to those of males who were predominantly or exclusively heterosexual. Although the author, Marvin Siegelman, found that fathers of homosexuals tended to be more rejecting and distant, the presence of protective and demanding mothers was not indicated by the data. Siegelman also found that the more masculine types of homosexuals had experienced father-child relationships similar to those of heterosexuals. He concluded that his study showed no cause-and-effect relationship between parental behavior and sexual preference, and he doubted that any such relationship exists.[90]

The most ambitious study of sexual preference was conducted by researchers at the Alfred C. Kinsey Institute for Sex Research. Researchers interviewed 979 homosexual and 477 heterosexual men and women in the San Francisco Bay area. The data indicated that family characteristics have little influence on sexual orientation. In fact, the researchers found little of significance except that sexual preference appeared to be determined by the time of adolescence. They concluded that their "study [provided] no basis for rejecting biological explanations outright."[91]

In addition to asking whether homosexuals are born "that way," many people also wonder whether there is something mentally "wrong" with them. In his review of psychological and psychiatric research on homosexuals, John C. Gonsiorek arrives at a blunt conclusion:

> There is no empirical justification for the viewpoint that homosexuality, in and of itself, is a psychiatric illness or related to poor psychological adjustment. Research on psychological testing does not support an illness model. Further, since objective measures of psychological adjustment are probably the most powerful, reliable, and well-validated techniques for arriving at judgments about psychological adjustment, any theoretical position which postulates homosexuality as an illness is seriously shaken, if not refuted, by these results. If it is an illness, then homosexuals as a group should reliably score in a range which points to a pathological level of psychological functioning. They generally do not, and therefore such illness models are untenable on empirical grounds. In this light, researchers or practitioners who continue to advocate illness models are ignorant or irresponsible or both.[92]

Since sexual preference has not been satisfactorily explained by either biological or mental illness models, some scientists suggest that its origins lie in a learning process. According to Kinsey and his associates,

> the data indicate that the factors leading to homosexual behavior are (1) the basic physiologic capacity of every mammal to respond to any sufficient stimulus; (2) the accident which leads an individual into his or her first sexual experience with a person of the same sex; (3) the conditioning effects of such experience; and (4) the indirect but powerful conditioning which the opinions of other persons and the social codes may have on an individual's decision to accept or reject this type of sexual conduct.[93]

The import of the first factor is that all humans have the capacity to be sexually stimulated by someone of the same sex; this is certainly evident in those societies in which homosexual activities are normal occurrences. The "accident" mentioned in the second factor refers to any one or more of the enormous range of social situations to which one might be exposed at an early age: being seduced by an admired adult, being encouraged by friends to sell sex to "queers," developing strong emotional ties with a friend, finding family support for acting and playing like someone of the opposite sex, or being incarcerated in an institution where homosexual activity is rampant.

Regardless of the context in which initial homosexual desires or contacts occur, continued involvement and eventual commitment to homosexuality depend upon at least two other contingencies: the degree to which the behavior is *defined as pleasurable* and the degree to which socially imposed *inhibitions* against repeating the behavior can be overcome.

Kenneth Plummer categorizes four broad forms of homosexual experience, based on the social context of the sexual encounters and on the significance of these encounters to those involved:

1. **Casual homosexuality:** Fleeting sexual encounters and desires that are unstructured and of minimal significance to the participants' lifestyles or self-concepts. Examples are young boys who masturbate each other or men who have a brief sexual attraction for one another. Plummer estimates that there is a considerable amount of casual homosexuality, although we know little about either its extent or its characteristics.

2. **Personalized homosexuality:** Essentially chance encounters that are highly significant for the participants' self-concepts:

> The homosexual experience becomes a pivotal point of an individual's life, but he remains isolated from any well-developed group structures that could organize and support his experience. . . .
> One respondent . . . related how he had spent the previous sixteen years meeting homosexuals furtively, and infrequently, in public [restrooms], but had never been able to sustain a relationship for more than one night: he had never met another "homosexual" socially. . . . While he was constantly aware of his life, he knew nothing of the gay world, and had only the most meager experience of sociable homosexuality with other people.[94]

In short, this category refers to individuals who have a well-developed sexual preference for their own gender but remain socially isolated from like-minded people.

3. **Situated homosexuality:** More or less regular sexual encounters without significance for the participants' self-concepts. Such behaviors are relatively common in same-sex situations such as prisons. Homosexual behavior unaccompanied by a homosexual self-concept is illustrated in prisons by *wolves* or *jockers,* who avoid any hint of emotional attachment to their partners:

> The wolf or jocker plays the stereotyped "male" role in sexual activity. He views himself, and needs to be viewed by his fellow inmates, as "a man"; and within prison to be "a man" and still engage in homosexual acts, one must present an image of exaggerated toughness and unequivocal masculinity. The jocker, by consistently wielding force over or raping his sexual partners, maintains for himself and others a perception of his behavior as basically masculine under the circumstances. The more violence that surrounds his sexual acts, the closer the jocker comes to actually engaging in an emotionless act of rape, thereby escaping both homosexual anxiety and the imputation of "queerness" by his peers.[95]

Situated homosexuality is also exemplified by adolescent male hustlers and by some adult males who use tearooms (public restrooms) for sexual purposes. As we discussed earlier in this chapter, some boys regularly prostitute themselves to adult males but maintain a self-concept of being straight. A study reveals that many males frequent tearooms to be fellated because of perceived sexual needs but restricted outlets. They use the tearooms in search of service they either cannot find at home or cannot otherwise afford. This free, impersonal means of obtaining an orgasm does not threaten their masculine self-image.[96]

4. Homosexuality as a way of life: Many forms of homosexual behavior variously based on friendships, gay social activities, and political activism:

> Individuals experiencing this form of homosexuality have defined themselves as homosexuals; have made it a central part of their life style; have developed fairly stable patterns of interaction with other self-defined homosexuals; and have fostered their own series of beliefs, values, and perspectives on homosexuality. In many ways, this could be called a homosexual subculture.[97]

According to Plummer, individuals who enter the gay lifestyle go through four stages of socialization. The first, *sensitization,* is that point at which individuals perceive themselves as potentially homosexual. This perception may emerge from a variety of sources: a strong emotional attachment to someone of the same sex; a sense of "differentness" from others of the same sex (a boy who is sensitive, artistic, or frail; a girl who is active, masculine in appearance, or interested in sports); or labeling or encouragement from teachers and relatives to be "not like other children." The second stage, *signification,* is a process in which one's identity as a homosexual is affected by society's negative image of homosexuality. It is a period in which individuals feel anxious, guilty, isolated, and rejected because they are what they are. They feel alone in a hostile world. The following narration by a female college student illustrates signification:

> I would look at her in the dining room like I just wanted to eat her up and this went on for some time. And she was very tense and I was just kind of ecstatic and I felt loved. I really felt like I'd really blossomed and I just felt just beautiful and just wonderful. And then one day, I heard the word "lesbian" and it suddenly began to dawn on me what society thought of and labelled what I was feeling.
> . . . The one thing you want to scream to the world about has to be absolutely hidden because they can't see it that way. There's some rule that says that I was supposed to fall in love but not with a girl.[98]

For some individuals the process ends here; their experience becomes one of "personalized homosexuality." Accepting homosexuality as a way of life requires a third state: *coming out.* This term has several similar meanings in the gay community, but it refers essentially to the individual's abandoning secrecy and guilt by publicly acknowledging his or her sexual preference and entering into the social world of homosexuals.

A study by Barry M. Dank found that coming out occurred in several contexts, usually through association with self-admitted gays, but also through contacts with sympathetic straights and through reading. From these situations the individuals found the knowledge and support necessary to make their decision. The following are examples of comments by Dank's gay subjects:

"I met a lot of gay people that I liked and I figured it can't be all wrong. If so and so's a good Joe, and he's still gay, he can't be all that bad. . . . I figured it couldn't be all wrong, and that's one of the things I learned. I learned to accept myself for what I am—homosexual."

"I knew there were homosexuals, queers and what not; I had read some books and I was resigned to the fact that I was a foul, dirty person, but I wasn't actually calling myself a homosexual yet. . . . I went to this guy's house and there was nothing going on, and I asked him, Where is some action? and he said, There is a bar down the way. And the time I really caught myself coming out is the time I walked into this bar and saw a whole crowd of groovy, groovy guys. And I said to myself, there was this realization, that not all gay men are dirty old men or idiots, silly queens, but there are some just normal-looking and acting people, as far as I could see. I saw gay society and I said, 'Wow, I'm home.' "[99]

But coming out may be stressful.

"One evening gay friends invited me over for dinner and movies. I experimented with marijuana and got high as a kite. I was freaking out because I knew my mom was becoming suspicious and I knew the time was coming when I was going to have to come out to her. Emotions were at an all-time high, and all I knew to do to get through them and deal with them was to smoke my way through it. I ended up smoking so much that I blacked out, had a panic anxiety attack, and ended up just wanting to kill myself. The suicidal thoughts had been occurring for quite some time because, although I thought I was dealing with my sexuality OK, I really wasn't. Why I thought what I did, I have no clue, but I knew something was not right inside of me. I looked back now and think how stupid it was, but at the time, life was very stressful. Coming out is not easy."[100]

—Matt

If the previously learned connotations of homosexuality can be rejected, the meaning of the concept can be transformed from negative to positive. Individuals thus find new identities and satisfaction with their behavior. But coming out does not necessarily mean that gays have solved all their problems related to sexual orientation. Although they experience relief, release from tension, and feelings of belonging, among males the coming-out period can involve a *crisis of femininity*.[101] The range of possible male homosexual adaptations runs from being ultramasculine—complete with leather jackets, boots, and motorcycles—to dressing in *drag* or masquerading as females. Those adopting the latter roles may undertake careers as female impersonators or may become prostitutes for unwary straight males. The vast majority of gays fall between these extremes, but those just coming out may still be confronted by the issue of discovering their niche on the continuum.

Among females there are also different homosexual role adaptations, although more limited than for males, ranging from *butch* to *femme*. The butch projects a masculine image by wearing close-cropped hair and male clothing; the femme projects the ultrafeminine image in both demeanor and clothing. As in the case of males, the vast majority of gay women fall between these extremes. The extent to which some gay women undergo a "crisis of masculinity" is unclear from the literature.[102]

Regardless of the type of role gays eventually adopt, their coming out into the homosexual lifestyle means entering a social network that positively reinforces their self-concepts. This network—usually called the *gay community*—insulates gays from social stigma, provides verbalized motives for homosexual behavior, and eases anxieties and guilt feelings over such behavior. To straights the most visible indicator of the community is the gay bar, which serves as a meeting place for strangers with similar sexual interests and, of course, as a social center for acquaintances. Beyond the bar the community includes friendship groups, coffeehouses, residences, social and political organizations, and even pornography shops where gays are free from the constraints of conventional society and where they find acceptance.[103]

The fourth and final stage in the process of adopting homosexuality as a way of life is *stabilization.* This refers to a total acceptance of gay life and rejection of straight life. Plummer points out that while the decision to remain gay is voluntary, in many, if not most, cases, leaving the gay life is not easy. For example, someone who is used to making sexual contacts in the gay world will find it perplexing and difficult to do the same in the heterosexual world. Furthermore, just as there is pressure by straights against entering the gay world, gays also apply pressure against reentering the straight world.[104]

Homosexuality as Deviance

The Judeo-Christian tradition has severely condemned homosexual behavior. From the Middle Ages until the mid-eighteenth century, in Christian Europe, practicing homosexuals could be flogged, castrated, stoned, or burned alive.[105]

From a cross-cultural perspective, however, homosexuality has been more accepted than Judeo-Christian tradition indicates. It is estimated that among preliterate societies, 64 percent considered homosexual activities of one sort or another as normal and socially acceptable for certain members of the community.[106] To a certain degree, this was also true of the ancient Greeks. They openly approved of close relationships between adult males and pubescent boys in which the adult assumed the role of model, teacher, and lover to the boy.[107] True, we are not aware of any society that has approved of unrestricted homosexuality for most of its members. In ancient Greece, for example, homosexual relationships between *adults* were *disapproved.* But it is clear that many, if not most, societies have had relatively tolerant attitudes toward homosexual activities. Today, most nations place no restrictions on homosexual conduct between consenting adults in private, and the nations that have such restrictions generally impose lesser penalties than in the United States.

Do fewer sodomy laws and more laws protecting the rights of homosexuals mean that the legal control of homosexuality is disappearing? Yes and no. Even the existing sodomy statutes are rarely invoked, but police have relied and may continue to rely on other statutes. Thus the homosexual feared (and many still fear) police apprehension not because of the possibility of punishment—which would probably be either a fine or probation—but because of other potential effects: adverse publicity, loss of one's job, loss of a professional license, and embarrassment before family and acquaintances. Even if these consequences were of no concern, police harassment remained an inconvenience and an imposition on people who were doing nothing more than thousands of other males who were trying to find female sexual partners.

Blackmail. As the reader might suspect, the social stigma attached to homosexuals makes them particularly susceptible to blackmail. The most spectacular case involved a highly organized ring operated by an ex-policeman.[108] However, most homosexual black-mailing involves not elaborate rings but one-on-one situations. According to Joseph Harry, approximately 15 percent of all homosexuals have been threatened with extortion, and about 90 percent of such threats come from friends and acquaintances such as sexual part-ners or co-workers. One outstanding exception is the *shakedown,* which involves policemen or police impostors. These extortionists frequent public lavatories, gay bars, and lovers' lanes while on the lookout for people *in flagrante delicto.* They threaten the participants with public exposure, jail, fines, or whatever else it takes to obtain a bribe.[109]

Physical Danger. The following illustrates the point that homosexuals face more than threats of legal action and extortion: In late 1998, college student Matthew Shepard met two men in a bar. The men, posing as homosexuals, talked Shepard into admitting he was gay and leaving with them. Shepard was robbed, pistol-whipped, brutally beaten, and left tied to a fence dying. He hung there for eighteen hours. He was found unconscious and taken to the hospital, where he died. His attackers claimed they were just following Biblical teach-ings and attempted a "Gay Panic Defense," arguing that that Shepard's homosexuality had driven them temporarily insane. Both narrowly escaped the death penalty when Matthew's parents intervened in sentencing deliberations.[110] The viciousness of the incident drew pressure for stricter hate crime legislation from all parts of society.

Among some individuals, *queer-baiting* or *fag-bashing* is a pastime. Just as in the case of shakedown artists, fag-bashers deliberately seek victims in areas frequented by gays. Probably only the most serious cases of such beatings ever reach police records in any detail because of the victim's reluctance to elaborate on why he was the target. No doubt many cases either are not reported or are reported as "muggings."

It is impossible to estimate with accuracy the extent of fag-bashing. But in Harry's survey of homosexuals in the Chicago area, approximately 20 percent answered in the affir-mative to the question "Have you ever been beaten up or assaulted by straights because you were gay?"[111] Data gathered from other surveys show that lifetime victimization rates for homosexuals range from 11 percent in Utah to 20 percent in Massachusetts.[112]

Following passage of the Hate Crimes Statistics Act in April 1990, collection of data on crimes defined by Congress to be motivated by hatred (including hatred, bias, or preju-dice for sexual orientation) began in January 1991. The tally for 1996 was 10,702 hate crimes, of which 12 percent were based on sexual orientation.[113] Most of these were com-mitted by males who believed that the victims were homosexuals.

Discrimination. In the early 1950s Senator Joseph R. McCarthy accused the State Department of harboring communists and homosexuals—a double-barreled accusation implying that spies and perverts were similarly repugnant. In comparison with straights, gays were regarded as less trustworthy, less religious, less efficient, and less morally responsible. People believed that homosexuals could make good beauticians, florists, and musicians but not good ministers, teachers, and judges.[114] Such attitudes have real conse-quences for homosexuals.

Until the early 1970s, homosexuals were automatically barred or dismissed from fed-eral or state employment purely on the basis of their sexual orientation. Security clearances were denied to individuals if their sexual preference became known, and the "outing" of a military member would mean the automatic termination of a career.

More recently, however, laws and regulations have been put in place that prohibit discrimination on the basis of sexual orientation. These protections extend from the government employment to military service and private business. Private employers may not fire persons for no other reason than objection to their sexual preference, and the Americans with Disabilities Act of 1990 does forbid discrimination against persons who have the AIDS virus or who may be perceived to have the virus, and this is applicable to virtually every organization.[115] Wisconsin, in 1982, became the first state to pass a law prohibiting discrimination based on sexual orientation in public and private employment, housing, and public accommodations. Other states have laws much like New York's, which prohibit discrimination in state employment. And more states may be changing their positions on this issue.

The momentum of the antihomosexual rights drive ended in late 1978, but gays are still discriminated against in many contexts, and sexual preference remains a criterion by which Americans distinguish the deviant from the normal. However, as we will discuss, the AIDS virus, which struck the United States beginning in 1981, changed the focus of antihomosexual groups and even the homosexual rights activists. Both groups fought heated battles over such issues as the right of an AIDS victim to attend public school and funding for AIDS treatment and research. But as the AIDS fight became institutionalized, homosexual groups, which expanded to combat the AIDS crisis, found that they were stronger than ever.[116]

Homosexuality and Conflict

Until 1948 "homosexuality" was a word rarely heard or seen in print. Few, if any, U.S. universities would have permitted a lecturer to stand before undergraduates and discuss the subject. In dormitories, fraternities, and sororities discussions might have centered on sex, but it was *sex*—none of this *hetero* and *homo* stuff. Today, campus newspapers carry classified advertisements for roommates that specify gay or straight. Beyond the campus there are newspapers and magazines for gay readers, and there are dances, parades, clubs, fairs, churches, and therapy groups—all involving people who barely seemed to exist less than forty years ago. What happened?

Although it may be too early to place the so-called gay liberation movement into accurate historical perspective, it is quite remarkable that a deviant group has radically altered its position in society after being so persecuted for so long. A student of the gay liberation movement, Edward Sagarin, suggests three contributing factors:

1. Changing social climate. Following World War II, attitudes toward all forms of sexual behavior became more permissive. It was easier to discuss pregnancy, illegitimacy, venereal disease, and nearly anything about sex than it had been earlier. This change heralded a toleration of a wider variety of sexual activities and interests.

2. Growing personal anonymity. Increasing geographic mobility and urbanization separated more and more persons from the social control exercised by family, neighborhood, and community. The United States was becoming a nation of strangers, thus providing homosexuals with an atmosphere both more convenient and more safe for sexual pursuits.

3. The Kinsey Reports. We have already mentioned the work of Kinsey and his associates in conjunction with prostitution and homosexuality. The impact of Kinsey's first publication in 1948, which surveyed the sexual histories of U.S. males, is difficult to overestimate. The report showed that millions of males were exclusively homosexual and that millions more were predominantly homosexual during a significant portion of their lives. For the first time many homosexuals recognized that they were not alone—indeed, they began to see themselves as one of the largest minority groups in the United States.[117]

Circumstances were ripe for the formation of homosexual interest groups. The first were unpretentious local discussion groups, but 1950 saw the beginnings of a national organization, the Mattachine Society, named after medieval court jesters who told the truth while hiding behind masks. There followed a proliferation of homophile organizations for both males and females. It was soon discovered, however, that common sexual preference does not necessarily equate with unity of organizational goals. The organizations became highly diverse: Some were primarily social, others were educational, religious, or research oriented, and still others were active in agitating for legal changes to give gays increased civil rights.

The late 1960s were characterized by radical fervor and activity by militant blacks, feminists, and anti–Vietnam War groups. The gay movement assumed some of the same militancy, insisting that gays' passivity and meek resignation to insults and injustices must end. The end came dramatically in New York City on June 27, 1969, when police attempted to close the Stonewall Inn, a gay bar in Greenwich Village. Gay bystanders watching the proceedings became agitated and attacked the police with beer bottles, rocks, trash cans, and a parking meter.[118]

Shortly after the Stonewall Riot, the Gay Liberation Front (GLF) was founded. Its members felt a close alliance with militancy and revolutionary rhetoric and with any minority group that appeared to be oppressed. But the death of radicalism among the youth and some gay leaders' concern over the organization's direction undermined the GLF philosophy. The slogans "Gay Power" and "Gay Pride" remained as rallying calls, but another organization, the Gay Activist Alliance (GAA), became more influential. The GAA's activities ranged from confronting political candidates about their stand toward gay rights to staging sit-ins at firms that discriminated against gays.[119]

It is impossible to judge precisely how important a role gay organizations have played in overcoming discriminatory practices against homosexuals. But in the five years after the Stonewall Riot, from 1969 through 1974, gays fought against discrimination on several fronts and won important victories:

1. Over 200 college campuses officially recognized homosexual student groups, conferring on them all the rights and privileges of such groups as the Pershing Rifles and the Accounting Club. In many cases, if not most, recognition came after court actions were brought by gays against the schools.

2. Gays successfully pressured broadcasting stations to cancel television programs that gays found offensive.

3. Several cities enacted legislation to protect gays from discrimination in employment, housing, and public accommodations.

4. The American Psychiatric Association (APA) voted to drop homosexuality from its list of mental disorders—a position it had maintained for nearly a hundred years. The GAA and the newly formed National Gay Task Force were especially active in pressuring the association.[120] After a bitter debate in 1973 the APA's Board of Trustees deleted "homosexuality" as a diagnostic category. A referendum of APA members just months later indicated that 58 percent favored the trustees' decision.

But changing laws and diagnostic categories does not always mean changing attitudes. For example, gays faced a backlash in 1977 when Anita Bryant, a popular singer and Southern Baptist, successfully spearheaded drives to repeal gay rights legislation in several cities. That same year a poll of 2,500 psychiatrists revealed that 69 percent regarded homosexuality as a "pathological adaptation"; 60 percent thought homosexual men and 55 percent thought lesbians were "less capable of mature, loving relationships" than heterosexuals.[121] Things continued to change though, and by 1982 the APA's *Diagnostic and Statistical Manual of Mental Disorders* (third edition, revised) contained no reference to homosexuality.[122]

Beginning in 1981 gays had to confront the new danger that threatened their civil rights movement and their lives as well: acquired immune deficiency syndrome, or AIDS, which breaks down the body's defenses against infection. AIDS infects a changing population: For example, in 1983, 71 percent were urban male homosexuals between the ages of 25 and 45 with histories of habitual sexual promiscuity. The next highest risk group—about 25 percent—was intravenous drug users.[123] By the close of the 1990s fewer than 50 percent of new AIDS infections were in homosexual males, but the link between homosexuals and AIDS has remained in the public consciousness.

Apart from its medical consequences, AIDS has had far-reaching social consequences for gays because it has supplied antigays with a new adjective: "sexual deviants" have now become "disease-carrying sexual deviants."[124] For some in the straight world AIDS is simply a sign of God's divine wrath. For others it justifies the laws forbidding certain sexual activities and the continued discrimination against all gays. The civil rights gulf between gays and straights began closing after the Stonewall Riot.

Homosexuality was "demedicalized" by the American Psychiatric Association, and some legislation recognized that gays were more than simply people with a "deviant" sexual orientation. AIDS, however, threatened to reopen the gulf by focusing public attention on the sexual excesses of a few. The AIDS epidemic is now "institutionalized," and the gay community by and large has gone back to civil rights activism, lobbying for more favorable laws and supporting specific candidates. Currently, a major focus of its attention is the issue of gay marriage.

The Debate over Gay Marriage

In 1989, Denmark became the first country in the world to legalize same-sex "registered partnerships" or civil marriages. Denmark, Sweden, and other European nations followed suit. In 2000, in the United States, Vermont recognized a similar form of "civil union."[125] In 2004, Massachusetts became the first state to legalize gay marriage, thus breaking an age-old tradition that marriage is a covenant between a man and a woman. A heated debate continues in the United States over the legalization of same-sex marriage. Ironically, in Denmark, same-sex couples are specifically prohibited from adopting children into the relationship, while in the United States, gays, generally, may not marry, but are generally not specifically prohibited from adopting children.[126]

At issue is not only the status of marriage but also a wide range of social, philosophical, theological, civil rights, privacy, and economic concerns. The topic has also become a political and legal battle. Although a few states have ventured toward legalization of gay unions, about 80 percent have prohibitions against gay marriage, about 75 percent have some sort of legislation in place in defense of traditional marriage, and about 40 percent have urged passage of a federal ban on gay marriage. In this section we will look at some of the issues and arguments and some suggested methods of resolving the debate.[127]

The advocacy for gay marriage is spearheaded by the Lambda Legal Defense and Education Fund, a national organization "dedicated to fighting for the civil rights of lesbian, gay, bisexual, and transgendered people." They argue that marriage is not only a deeply personal choice made by people in love, but also "the vocabulary in which non-gay people talk of love, family, dedication, self-sacrifice, and stages of life, . . . love, equality, and inclusion." It defines relationships and confers a place in society, social acceptance, and inclusion.[128] Marriage also confers other social and legal rights and benefits such as access to custody of nonbiological children, hospital visitation rights, eligibility to serve as court-appointed guardian of a mentally incompetent partner, authorization to terminate life support of a terminally ill partner, and the right to make burial arrangements. It also has more concrete economic benefits including tax breaks, inheritance rights, social security and pension plan benefits, family leave and public assistance benefits, and access to partner's healthcare coverage and medical leave.[129] Advocates of gay marriage see laws prohibiting it as violations of their Constitutional right of equal protection. They view it as a form of discrimination similar to that which at one time prohibited the marriage of interracial couples. They contend that, "No gay person in the United States is a full-fledged citizen because unlike other folks, gay people cannot choose to marry the person they love."[130] In addition, they feel, "The issue of gay marriage (is) about more than marriage. . . . It (is) about how far a secular democracy would expand its arena of freedom."[131] Writing in defense of gay marriage, Rauch states, "Like it or not, homosexuality exists and is not going away. The question is how to ensure that it is pro-social rather than antisocial. I believe that marriage, the greatest civilizing institution ever devised, is the answer."[132]

Those who oppose gay marriage do not agree. They emphasize that marriage is one of our oldest and most important social institutions and a cornerstone of our civilization. Broom notes that, "In all societies throughout human history, families have been the main vehicles of (kinship and) group identity . . . , a dominant fact of life, the chief determinant of social status and economic well-being.[133] They see the special considerations provided families and family members as appropriate because of the important role families play in procreation and socialization of future generations. Central to the traditional concept of family is the marriage of a man and a woman each making unique contributions to the functioning of the institution.[134] They see gay marriage as a major threat to this institution. Some also argue that legalizing gay marriage would force redefinition of a cherished religious sacrament.

Anti-gay marriage legal rulings have found that, "History, common law, and the uniform laws of the United States all reach the conclusion that marriage does not extend to same sex couples. . . ."[135] Those opposing gay marriage also note that some supporters of the notion include radical feminists and gays previously highly critical of marriage per se.

Some question if the movement is being powered primarily by a search for love and social acceptance or by a quest for spousal benefits and health insurance. They note studies indicating a lesser degree of commitment to monogamy among homosexuals and fear that gay marriage could further erode values of monogamy and fidelity in traditional marriage. They find in the writings of family law activists such as Ettlebrick, Pollikoff, Stacey, and Ertman a "movement whose larger goal is to use legal gay marriage to push for state-sanctioned polyamory (or multiple partner arrangements) . . . and the replacement of marriage with a contract system that accommodates polyamory."[136]

Opponents also submit several "slippery slope" arguments against gay marriage. Gay marriage is being pursued under civil rights law. If marriage is opened to same-sex homosexual couples, for example, what is to keep same-sex heterosexual couples (two heterosexual single mothers, perhaps) from demanding the right to marry for tax breaks, employer-provided health insurance, social security benefits? If marriage is redefined, what is to keep polygamists from demanding their right to multiple partners? There is a longer and broader tradition of polygamy in the United States than of gay unions. What is to keep practioners of polyamory from demanding their right to group marriages reminiscent of the hippy communes of the 1960s?[137] Courts have already ruled for parental rights of sperm donors of lesbian partners' children.[138]

Possible methods of resolving the debate include, of course, continuing the ban on gay marriage or legalizing gay marriage. Other possibilities have been suggested as well. Booth advises that court cases could be pursued to gain for gay unions each of the rights held by married partners.[139] Eskridge suggests that gays might be granted "domestic partners" status similar to European "registered partnerships," which would confer all the rights of married couples without actually being a "marriage."[140] Baxandall suggests that the state could "get out of the marriage business altogether." He notes the precedent of "motherhood." The state decides custody in the case of divorce and when babies get switched at hospitals. However, it leaves allocation of such labels as "birth mother," "biological mother," and "real mother" to others. He suggests that, "The most sensible solution would grant legal equality by getting the state out of the business of distinguishing which civil unions should be called marriage."[141] The state should allow for the establishment of civil unions between any two adults and help enforce the rights and obligations of these partners. That is all. Whether to call it marriage should be left to major stakeholders such as religious institutions, communities, families, and the individuals involved.

Sexual Harassment

Sexual harassment is actually not a form of sexual deviance at all, but rather an abuse of power in which sex or sexually charged actions or communications are used as weapons. Sexual harassment is defined as (1) influencing or threatening to influence the career, pay, or job of another person in exchange for sexual favors; or (2) teasing, jokes, remarks, gestures, or physical contact of a sexual nature that interfere with a person's performance or create an intimidating, hostile, or offensive environment. An obvious form of sexual harassment includes the famous "casting couch" scenario in which the starlet was expected to provide sexual favors in exchange for a movie role. More subtle forms include sexually oriented jokes or remarks that have the effect of embarrassing, isolating, and excluding fellow workers.

Sexual harassment is sometimes confused with two other gender-related behaviors, sexism and sexual politics. Sexual politics is any attempt to use sex, sexuality, or sexual attractiveness to influence or obtain favors or such things as job-related rewards. Sexism is defined as any discriminatory behavior or practice based on sex, that is, treating people differently solely on the basis of their sex. Sexism is a direct parallel with racism.

The target of sexual harassment is most likely to be a woman. The target of sexual politics is most likely to be a man. Sexism targets both men and women, and both sexual harassment and sexual politics are more likely to occur in a sexist atmosphere.

There is a key difference in the nature of the power balance inherent in sexual harassment and sexual politics. The "victim" of sexual politics is, by definition, the more powerful person. He or she can, therefore, control the situation—at least to a point. The victim of sexual harassment is a lower status person in some respect and therefore at a much greater disadvantage in trying to control or extinguish the misconduct.[142]

Sexual harassment is not a new phenomenon. The Bible contains stories of behavior that would qualify. But it was not until the late 1970s and early 1980s that it became an important management issue. One of the first papers on the issue indicated that approximately 90 percent of women working in the private sector had experienced some form of sexual harassment during their careers.[143] Shortly thereafter, a major study conducted by an agency of the federal government found a similarly high proportion of sexual harassment in the federal workplace. Congressional hearings followed as well as additional studies, more public charges of sexual harassment, law suits, and six-figure settlements.[144] High-visibility charges such as Professor Anita Hill's accusations against Supreme Court nominee Clarence Thomas, Paula Jones's accusations against presidential candidate Bill Clinton, and more recently, the resignation of a governor accused of homosexual harassment of an aide have kept the issue in the spotlight.[145]

The Merit Systems Protection Board (MSPB) conducted major surveys of the federal workforce in 1980, 1987, and 1994. This research provides one of the best sources of data on sexual harassment. In the latest study, 44 percent of women and 19 percent of men reported having been sexually harassed during the previous two years.[146] Most victims report having experienced "less serious" forms of sexual harassment. While more than a third of the women and nearly 15 percent of the men in the latest MSPB study reported experiencing such things as teasing, jokes, and remarks, only 4 percent of the women and 2 percent of the men reported actual or attempted rape or assault.[147]

Since more time is spent with peers and co-workers than with superiors and supervisors, it is not surprising that most harassment is inflicted by peers. The sexual harasser is most likely to be a married man of the same racial/ethnic group as the victim. He is usually older than the victim, commits the harassment when alone with the victim, and has a history of sexually harassing others. Female harassers are very likely to have been victims of sexual harassment themselves and see the interaction as a game of some sort.[148] Harassers who commit the more serious forms of harassment are likely to be motivated by hostility, aggression, poor self-concepts, and a tendency to abuse power.[149] In this respect, sexual harassment is similar to the crime of rape. Rapists overpower their victims by brute strength and threat of loss of life. Sexual harassers bully their victims with career threats and possible loss of livelihood.

The most likely victim of sexual harassment is an inexperienced young woman working in the lower salary range, working because she needs the job, and working in a primarily male work group with a male supervisor.[150] She is most vulnerable if she has few alternatives, needs something the harasser can control, and has few allies.[151] The harassment she is subjected to is most likely to be verbal, but when she tries to cope with it by ignoring it, it frequently escalates to physical abuse. She considers the harassment a serious problem, but is unlikely to report it.[152]

Victims' most common reaction to being harassed are feelings of surprise, disgust, anger, fear, intimidation, degradation, and even guilt (What did I do—or wear or say—that caused this?). The most common response is to try to ignore it. Almost half of victims do nothing. Some choose to do nothing because they feel the harassment is not as serious as the possible consequences of a confrontation. Traditionally, others have ignored it because they feared that no one would believe them or that they would be labeled trouble makers.[153] The next most likely course of action is to ask or tell the harasser to stop. (About a fourth of the men and about 40 percent of the women choose this alternative.) Some just attempt to avoid the harasser or to make a joke of the situation. About 13 percent of men and about a fourth of women either report or threaten to report the behavior, but fewer than 10 percent take formal action. Most research indicates that, "The most effective responses to sexual harassment are informal, assertive ones such as confronting harassers and telling them to stop."[154]

A major concern in the area of sexual harassment is false charges.[155] Sexual harassment can include rape, and we have compared sexual harassment to the crime of rape. The analogy holds here as well. Both are "he said/she said," types of offenses. In both cases there are frequently no witnesses. In both, even allegations of impropriety can have very serious consequences. It is not unusual to go into a troubled organization and find that the women feel that if they report sexual harassment, no one will believe them, while the men believe that all a woman has to do is make a charge and they will automatically be found guilty. Often both sides have horror stories of reputed incidents of injustice. Fortunately, the number of such cases is small. Also, more and more organizations are not only holding harassers responsible for their behavior, but are also encouraging potential victims to speak up against sexual harassment and to do so before they file complaints. Many organizations are conducting training to let everyone know what is and is not acceptable and what is and is not sexual harassment.

CRITICAL THINKING EXERCISES

1. What is "white slavery"? How might the Internet be used to further the white slave trade?

2. What are the reasons why people become prostitutes? Are they logical reasons? Can people always avoid becoming prostitutes? Can people be prevented from becoming prostitutes? How?

3. Should gay marriage be legalized? Discuss.

4. Are people born homosexual and heterosexual? How would someone be socialized into homosexuality? Can people be socialized *out* of homosexuality?

5. Is sexual harassment a problem where you have worked or gone to school? What do you see as the greater problem, sexual harassment or false charges of sexual harassment?

CHECK IT OUT ON THE WEB

The Internet addresses listed below are intended to provide the reader with understanding of a wide range of perspectives on the subject matter discussed in this chapter. Some sites may contain objectionable material. The list is not intended to reflect the viewpoints or opinions of the authors or the publisher.

http://www.spectacle.org
> political opinion chat room on prostitution

http://www.feminista.com
> political support for prostitution

http://www.apostolic.net/biblicalstudies/homosexual.htm
> religious perspective

http://www.familyresearchinst.org
> brain research/homosexuality

http://www.actwin.com/eatonohio/gay/world.htm
> homosexual male prostitution

http://library.uncg.edu/depts/docs/us/harass.html
> sexual harassment resources

ENDNOTES

1. For a contextual approach to sexual deviance, see Clifton Bryant, *Sexual Deviancy and Social Proscription: The Social Context of Carnal Behavior* (New York: Human Sciences Press, 1982).

2. Alfred C. Kinsey, Wardell B. Pomeroy, and Clyde E. Martin, *Sexual Experience in the Human Female* (Philadelphia: W. B. Saunders, 1953).

3. Ibid.

4. Samuel S. Janus and Cynthia L. Janus, *The Janus Report on Sexual Behavior* (New York: John Wiley & Sons, 1993).

5. Edward O. Laumann, John H. Gagnon, Robert T. Michael, and Stuart Michaels, *The Social Organization of Sexuality: Sexual Practices in the United States* (Chicago: University of Chicago Press, 1994).

6. Staff Writer, "Prostitution: It's A Foreigner's Game," *The Economist* (September 4, 2004), pp. 53–54.

7. Alfred Kinsey et al., *Sexual Experience in the Human Female.*

8. James, "Prostitutes and Prostitution," p. 408; Martin A. Monto, "Why Men Seek out Prostitutes," in *Sex for Sale,* ed. Ronald Weitzer, p. 70–80; Martin A. Monto, "Female Prostitution, Customers, and Violence," *Violence Against Women, 10* (February 2004), pp. 160–189; Sandra Harley Carey, "Roosters at the Chicken Ranch: Characteristics of Clients at a Little House on the Prairie" (with J. Ronald Carey). Research paper presented at the Western Social Science Association Meetings, Denver, Colorado, May, 1975.

9. This typology is paraphrased from Jennifer James, "Prostitutes and Prostitution," in *Deviants: Voluntary Actors in a Hostile World,* ed. Edward Sagarin and Fred Montanino (Morristown, NJ: General Learning Press, 1977), pp. 403–409.

10. Harold R. Holzman and Sharon Pines, "Buying Sex: The Phenomenology of Being a John," *Deviant Behavior, 4* (October–December 1982), p. 111. See also Charles Winick, "The Customer and the Prostitute," in *Prostitution: Is It a Victimless Crime?* ed. Dorothy Bracey and Matthew Neary (New York: American Academy for Professional Law Enforcement, 1979), pp. 83–84.

11. Holzman and Pines, "Buying Sex," p. 112.

12. Martin A. Monto, "Female Prostitution, Customers, and Violence," pp. 160–189.

13. Staff Writer, "Prostitution: It's A Foreigner's Game," *The Economist,* p. 54.

14. Charles Winick and Paul M. Kinsie, *The Lively Commerce: Prostitution in the United States* (Chicago: Quadrangle Press, 1971), p. 3; in *Sex for Sale: Prostitution, Pornography, and the Sex Industry,* ed. Ronald Weitzer (New York: Routledge, 2000).

15. United Nations Children's Fund (UNICF), information available online at: http://www.horeb.pcusa.org/oga/diversity.advocom.html.

16. Representative Christopher Smith, press release in support of pending legislation, dated September 14 1999.

17. For a review of the current dangers of prostitution, see James A. Inciardi, Anne E. Pottieger, Mary Ann

Forney, Dale D. Chitwood, and Duane C. McBride, "Prostitution, IV Drug Use, and Sex-for-Crack Exchanges Among Serious Delinquents: Risks for HIV Infection," *Criminology, 29* (May 1991), pp. 221–235.

18. For a recent study on young males as well as females engaged in prostitution, see ibid.

19. In *Girls, Delinquency, and Juvenile Justice* (Pacific Grove, CA: Brooks/Cole Publishing Co., 1992), pp. 16–17, 37–38; Meda Chesney-Lind and Randall G. Shelden cite a 1979 study by S. Cernkovich and P. Giordano that reports that the percentage of self-reported delinquency for engaging in "sex for money" was 5.3 for males and 1.1 for females; they also report statistics on the number of female prostitutes, all of which vary widely.

20. For an account of a high-class New Orleans brothel, see Stephen Longstreet, *Sportin' House* (Los Angeles: Sherbourne Press, 1965).

21. Winick and Kinsie, *The Lively Commerce*, p. 132.

22. Ibid., pp. 131–184; Donald J. Black, "Forms and Reforms of Whoredom: Notes on the Sociology of Prostitution and Moral Enterprise," Center for Research on Social Organization, University of Michigan, Ann Arbor, 1966 (mimeographed).

23. For a sociological description of the operation of a contemporary brothel in a medium-sized city, see Barbara Sherman Heyl, *The Madam as Entrepreneur: Career Management in House Prostitution* (New Brunswick, NJ: Transaction Books, 1979).

24. Barbara G. Brents and Kathryn Haasbeck, "Prostitution—Nevada," in *Encyclopedia of Criminology and Deviant Behavior* (New York: Taylor and Francis, 2001), p. 277–279.

25. Penny Spar, "Coach and School Administrator Wife Get Probation for Running Sex Parlor," *Daily Sentinel-Tribune* (Bowling Green, OH), May 24, 1983, p. 15.

26. David J. Pittman, "The Male House of Prostitution," *Transaction, 8* (March/April 1971), pp. 21–27.

27. "Busting a State-of-the-Art Call-Girl Ring (Cloud Nine Escort Service of Berkeley, CA)," *Newsweek*, September 5, 1988, p. 52.

28. "Police Break up Prostitution Ring That Employed 200 Housewives, Career Women," *Daily Sentinel-Tribune* (Bowling Green, OH), August 23, 1983, p. 7.

29. Bryant, *Sexual Deviancy*, pp. 229–230; see also Paul K. Rasmussen, "Massage Parlors as a Sex-for-Money Game," in *The Sociology of Deviance*, ed. Jack D. Douglas (Boston: Allyn and Bacon, 1984), pp. 199–212; Ronald Weitzer, ed., *Sex for Sale*, p. 5.

30. Patricia A. Adler and Peter Adler, *Constructions of Deviance: Social Power, Context, and Interaction,* 4th ed. (Belmont, CA: Wadsworth/Thompson Learning, 2003), pp. 408–415.

31. James P. Sterba, "Prostitution Is Flourishing in Rich Exurban Market," *The New York Times*, June 9, 1974, sec. 1, p. 55.

32. Rochelle L. Dalla, "Exposing the 'Pretty Woman' Myth: A Qualitative Examination of the Lives of Female Streetwalking Prostitutes," *Journal of Sex Research, 37* (November 2000), pp. 344–354; Based on Gail Sheehy, *Hustling: Prostitution in Our Wide-Open Society* (New York: Delacorte Press, 1973), pp. 30–32.

33. Sagarin and Jolly, "Prostitution," p. 24. The discussion is based on this work. For another perspective, see Alan M. Klein, "Managing Deviance: Hustling, Homophobia, and the Bodybuilding Subculture," *Deviant Behavior, 10* (January/February 1989), pp. 11–27.

34. Sarah Shannon, "The Global Sex Trade: Humans as the Ultimate Commodity," *Crime and Justice International, 15: 22* (May 1999), pp. 5–7, 22.

35. Ibid., p. 6.

36. Ibid., p. 7; Helen Johnson, "Modern Babylon?: Prostituting Children in Thailand," *Canadian Review of Sociology & Anthropology, 40* (August 2003), p. 364.

37. Kevin Bales, in eds. Barbra Ehrenreich and Arlie Russell Hochschild, *Global Woman: Nannies, Maids, and Sex Workers in the New Economy,* (New York: Henry Holt and Company, 2002), pp. 207–229.

38. Denise Brennan, eds., in Barbara Ehrenreich and Arlie Russell Hochschild, *Global Women*, pp. 154–168.

39. Quoted in "White Slavery, 1972," *Time,* June 5, 1972, p. 24. Victor Minichiello, Rodrigo Marino, Jan Browne, Maggie Jamieson, Kirk Peterson, Brad Reuter, and Kenn Robinson, "Commercial Sex Between Men: A Prospective Diary-Based Study," *Journal of Sex Research, 37* (May 2000), pp. 151–161; Michael R. Stevenson, Manuel Fernandez-Alemany, and Janet Shibley Hyde, "Comparative Studies on Male Sex Work in the Era of HIV/AIDS," *Journal of Sex Research, 37* (May 2000), pp. 187–192.

40. Howard Blum, "The Gay Underground: Boy for Sale," *Village Voice,* February 8, 1973, p. 83.

41. For Stanford's autobiography, see Sally Stanford, *The Lady of the House* (New York: G. P. Putnam, 1966).

42. C. West, M. Williams, and J. Siegel, "Adult Sexual Revictimization," *Child Maltreatment, 5(1)* (February 2000), pp. 49–57.

43. Jody Raphael and Deborah L. Shapiro, "Violence Against Women," *Violence Against Women, 10* (February 2004), pp. 126–140. For a review of this literature, see Chesney-Lind and Shelden, *Girls, Delinquency, and Juvenile Justice,* pp. 37–42; for other explanations, see Thereza Penna-Firme, Robert E. Grinder, and Marcia S. Linhares-Barreto, "Adolescent Female Prostitutes on the Streets of Brazil: An Exploratory Investigation of Ontological Issues," *Journal of Adolescent Research, 6* (October 1991), pp. 493–504; and Ronald L. Simons and Les B. Whitbeck, "Sexual Abuse as a Precursor to Prostitution and Victimization Among Adolescent and Adult Homeless Women," *Journal of Family Issues, 12* (September 1991), pp. 361–379.

44. Quoted in James H. Bryan, "Occupational Ideologies and Individual Attitudes of Call Girls," *Social Problems, 13* (Spring 1966), p. 443.

45. Albert J. Reiss, Jr., "The Social Integration of Queers and Peers," *Social Problems, 9* (Fall 1961), pp. 102–120. See also Martin Hoffman, "The Male Prostitute," *Sexual Behavior, 2* (August 1972), pp. 16–21; and Klein, "Managing Deviance," pp. 11–27.

46. Quoted in Kate Millet, *The Prostitution Papers: A Candid Dialogue* (New York: Avon Books, 1973), p. 55. For more recent perspectives, see Jane Anthony, *Ms.* (January/February 1992), pp. 86–87; and Elizabeth Bibb, "Meet the Real Working Girls," *Mademoiselle* (March 1990), pp. 214–215.

47. The discussion of the three factors leading to a career in prostitution is an amalgamation of the following studies (alphabetically by author): Dorothy Heid Bracey, *"Baby-Pros": Preliminary Profiles of Juvenile Prostitutes* (New York: John Jay Press, 1979); James H. Bryan, "Apprenticeships in Prostitution," *Social Problems, 12* (Winter 1965), pp. 287–297; Nanette J. Davis, "The Prostitute: Developing a Deviant Identity," in *Studies in the Sociology of Sex,* ed. James M. Henslin (New York: Appleton-Century-Crofts, 1971), pp. 297–322; Diana Gray, "Turning-Out: A Study of Teenage Prostitution," *Urban Life and Culture, 1* (January 1973), pp. 401–425; Heyl, *Madam as Entrepreneur,* pp. 25–31, 197–234; Jennifer James, "Motivations for Entrance into Prostitution," in *The Female Offender,* ed. Laura Crites (Lexington, MA: Lexington Books, 1976), pp. 177–205; Robert E. Kuttner, "Poverty and Sex: Relationships in a 'Skid Row' Slum," *Sexual Behavior, 1* (October 1971), pp. 55–63; Winick and Kinsie, *Lively Commerce,* pp. 38–57; and "Bay Area Prostitutes: Middle Class, 'Good Background,' Sexually Abused," *Behavior Today, 11* (August 25, 1980), pp. 1–3. For a discussion of a similar career path among strippers, see James K. Skipper, Jr., and Charles H. McCaghy, "Stripteasers: The Anatomy and Career Contingencies of a Deviant Occupation," *Social Problems, 17* (Winter 1970), pp. 391–405.

48. A. Young, C. Boyd, and A. Hubbell, "Prostitution, Drug Use, and Coping with Psychological Distress," *Journal of Drug Issues, 30*(4) (Fall 2000), pp. 789–801.

49. Lawrence J. Oellet, W. Wayne Wiebel, Antonio D. Jimenez, and Wendell A. Johnson, "Crack Cocaine and the Transformation of Prostitution in Three Chicago Neighborhoods," in *Crack Pipe as Pimp: An Ethnographic Investigation of Sex-for-Drugs Exchanges,* ed. Mitchell S. Ratner (New York: Lexington, 1993), pp. 69–96; Jennifer L. Lauby, "Fast Lives/Tricking and Tripping," *Social Science and Medicine, 52* (June 2001), pp. 622–626.

50. Quoted in Paul J. Goldstein, *Prostitution and Drugs* (Lexington, MA: Lexington Books, 1979), pp. 129–130; see also Inciardi et al., "Prostitution."

51. Cathy Spatz Widom, "A Multidimensional Model of Prostitution." Paper presented to the annual meeting of the American Society of Criminology, Denver, Colorado, November 9–13, 1983.

52. Celia Williamson and Terry Cluse-Tolar, "Pimp-Controlled Prostitution: Still an Integral Part of Street Life," *Violence Against Women, 8* (September 2002), pp. 1079–1098; Maureen Norton-Hawk, "A Comparison of Pimp- and Non-Pimp-Controlled Women," *Violence Against Women, 10* (February 2004), pp. 189–195.

53. Fiona E. Kelly, "Runaway Kids and Teenage Prostitution," *Violence Against Women, 9* (February 2003), pp. 266–271; Christina Milner and Richard Milner, *Black Players: The Secret World of Black Pimps* (Boston: Little, Brown, 1972), pp. 178–271. For other discussions of the pimp, see Susan Hill and Bob Adelman, *Gentlemen of Leisure* (New York: New American Library, 1972); Gray, "Turning-Out," pp. 416–418; and Winick and Kinsie, *Lively Commerce,* pp. 109–120. The "bible" of pimps is said to be Iceberg Slim, *Pimp: The Story of My Life* (Los Angeles: Holloway House, 1969).

54. Ibid., pp. 243–244.

55. Lesley Oelsner, "World of the City Prostitute Is a Tough and Lonely Place," *The New York Times,* August 9, 1971, pp. 31, 33; and Tom Buckley, "Where Prostitutes Solicit Determines Arrest Chances," *The New York Times,* December 14, 1974, p. 44; see also Gerald M. Caplan, "The Facts of Life about Teenage Prostitution," *Crime and Delinquency, 30* (January 1984), pp. 69–74.

56. Howard Blum, "The Bed Patrol," *Village Voice,* April 4, 1974, pp. 1, 28–31.

57. James, "Motivations for Entrance into Prostitution," p. 183.

58. The Vice Commission of Chicago, *The Social Evil in Chicago* (1911), cited in Eric Anderson, "Prostitution and Social Justice; Chicago, 1910–15," *Social Service Review, 48* (June 1974), p. 211.

59. This discussion was based on Anderson, "Prostitution and Social Justice," pp. 203–228; Black, "Forms and Reforms of Whoredom"; and Kay Ann Holmes, "Reflections by Gaslight: Prostitution in Another Age," *Issues in Criminology, 7* (Winter 1972), pp. 83–101.

60. Winick and Kinsie, *Lively Commerce,* p. 223; for discussions of legal changes, see two articles by Pamela A. Roby: "Politics and Criminal Law: Revision of the New York State Penal Law on Prostitution," *Social Problems, 17* (Summer 1969), pp. 83–109; and "Politics and Prostitution: A Case Study of the Revision, Enforcement, and Administration of the New York State Penal Laws on Prostitution," *Criminology, 9* (February 1972), pp. 425–447.

61. Women Endorsing Decriminalization, "Prostitution: A Nonvictim Crime?" *Issues in Criminology, 8* (Fall 1973), p. 160; for a discussion of the feminist theory, see Sally S. Simpson, "Feminist Theory, Crime, and Justice,"

Criminology, 27 (November 1989), pp. 605–631. Sheehy, *Hustling,* pp. 197–200; Millet, *The Prostitution Papers,* pp. 18–26.

62. This terminology is drawn from Wendy Kaminer, "Laying Down the Law on Sex," *Village Voice,* March 30, 1983, p. 39.

63. Edwin M. Schur, *Labeling Women Deviant: Gender, Stigma, and Social Control* (New York: Random House, 1984), pp. 171–172.

64. Sarah Wynter, "WHISPER: Women Hurt in Systems of Prostitution Engaged in Revolt," in *Sex Work: Writings by Women in the Sex Industry,* ed. Frederique Delacoste and Priscilla Alexander (Pittsburgh: Cleis Press, 1987), pp. 266–270; for information on the other organizations, see ibid., pp. 290–296.

65. "Organizing the Oldest Profession," in *The Woman's Survival Sourcebook* (New York: Alfred A. Knopf, 1975), p. 20; for other goals of some of the unions, see Delacoste and Alexander, eds., *Sex Work,* pp. 290–296, 305–321; the discussion is based on "Organizing the Oldest Profession," pp. 20–23; Maurica Anderson, "Hookers, Arise!" *Human Behavior* (January 1975), pp. 40–42; "Call Me Madam," *Newsweek* (July 8, 1974), p. 65; and Marilyn G. Haft, "Hustling for Rights," in *The Female Offender,* ed. Laura Crites (Lexington, MA: Lexington Books, 1976), pp. 207–210. See also Mari Maggu, " 'Scapegoat' and the Prostitute," in *Prostitution,* ed. Bracey and Neary, pp. 58–61.

66. For views on this, see Rachel West, "U.S. PROStitutes Collective," in *Sex Work,* ed. Delacoste and Alexander, pp. 279–289; for the view of ICPR, see ibid., p. 305; and for a discussion of decriminalization, see Samuel Walker, *Sense and Nonsense About Crime: A Policy Guide,* 2nd ed. (Pacific Grove, CA: Brooks/Cole Publishing Company, 1989), pp. 235–240; Jo Doezema, "Ouch! Western Feminists' Wounded Attachment to the 'Third World Prostitute,' " *Feminist Review, 67* (Spring 2001), pp. 16–39.

67. Haft, "Hustling for Rights;" see also John F. Decker, *Prostitution: Regulation and Control* (Littleton, CO: Fred B. Rothman, 1979), pp. 81–92; for another view of regulating prostitution, one of "tolerance," see Charles H. McCaghy and Stephen A. Cernkovich, "Research Note: Polling the Public on Prostitution," *Justice Quarterly, 8* (March 1991), pp. 107–108.

68. Barbara Basler, "Computer Traces Crime Patterns in New York City," *The New York Times,* September 19, 1982, p. 36.

69. Patricia Gabbett Snow, "Albuquerque Vice," *Albuquerque Journal,* August 27, 1992, p. E1.

70. Decker, *Prostitution,* p. 138. The discussion is based on this work, pp. 74–76; David A. J. Richards, "Commercial Sex and the Rights of the Person: A Moral Argument for the Decriminalization of Prostitution," *University of Pennsylvania Law Review, 127* (May 1979),

pp. 1279–1285; and Mary Gibson, "The State and Prostitution: Prohibition, Regulation, or Decriminalization?" in *History and Crime: Implications for Criminal Justice Policy,* ed. James A. Inciardi and Charles E. Faupel (Beverly Hills, CA: Sage, 1980), pp. 193–200; Niki Adams, "Anti-trafficking Legislation: Protection or Deportation?" *Feminist Review 73* (Summer 2003), p. 135; Claude Jaget, *Prostitutes: Our Life* (New York: Falling Wall Press, 1982); West, "U.S. PROStitutes Collective," p. 279.

71. Carole A. Campbell, "Prostitution, AIDS, and Preventive Health Behavior," *Social Science and Medicine, 32* (Winter 1991), pp. 1367–1378; Richards, "Commercial Sex," pp. 1217–1218; and Gibson, "The State and Prostitution," p. 200; see also Priscilla Alexander, "Prostitutes Are Being Scapegoated for Heterosexual AIDS," in *Sex Work,* ed. Delacoste and Alexander, pp. 248–263; and Inciardi et al., "Prostitution," pp. 221–235.

72. See Women Endorsing Decriminalization, "Prostitution," p. 161. For conflicting views of two males on removing legal barriers to prostitution, see Robert Veit Sherwin and Charles Winick, "Debate: Should Prostitution Be Legalized?" *Sexual Behavior, 1* (January 1972), pp. 66–73. For nonfeminist arguments favoring decriminalization, see Decker, *Prostitution,* pp. 449–468; and Richards, "Commercial Sex," pp. 1195–1287.

73. Excerpt from a student paper by Matt.

74. Kinsey, Pomeroy, and Martin, *Sexual Behavior in the Human Male,* pp. 636–637.

75. Ibid., pp. 636–657; Nigel Dickson, Charlotte Paul, and Peter Herbison, "Same-sex Attraction in a Birth Cohort: Prevalence and Persistence in Early Adulthood," *Social Science and Medicine, 56* (April 2003), pp. 1607–1635.

76. For discussions of homosexuality in public rest rooms, see Laud Humphreys, *Tearoom Trade: Impersonal Sex in Public Places* (Chicago: Aldine, 1970); and Laud Humphreys, "Impersonal Sex and Perceived Satisfaction," in *Studies in the Sociology of Sex,* ed. James M. Henslin (New York: Appleton-Century-Crofts, 1971), pp. 351–374. For examples of other public homosexual contacts, see Edward William Delph, *The Silent Community: Public Homosexual Encounters* (Beverly Hills, CA: Sage, 1978).

77. Ibid.

78. Morton Hunt, *Sexual Behavior in the 1970s* (Chicago: Playboy Press, 1974), pp. 303–317. Also see Paul H. Gebhard, "Incidence of Overt Homosexuality in the United States and Western Europe," in *Homosexuality: Final Report and Background Papers,* ed. John M. Livingood (Rockville, MD: U.S. Department of Health, Education, and Welfare, National Institute of Mental Health, 1972), pp. 22–29.

79. Edward O. Llaumann, *The Social Organization of Sexuality,* p. 279.

80. Anne Johnson et al., *Sexual Attitudes and Lifestyles* (Oxford, UK: Blackwell Scientific Publications);

Robert T. Michael, *Sex in America,* pp. 174–176; Nigel Dickson, "Same-sex Attraction in a Birth Cohort"; Margot Canaday, "Who is a Homosexual? The Consolidation of Sexual Identity's in Mid Twentieth-Century American Immigration Law," *Law and Social Inquiry, 28* (Spring 2003), pp. 352–397.

81. Edward Sagarin, "Survey Essay: The Good Guys, the Bad Guys, and the Gay Guys," *Contemporary Sociology, 2* (January 1973), p. 10; Melissa Hines, Charles Brook, and Gerard S. Conway, "Androgen and Psychosexual Development," *The Journal of Sex Research, 41* (February 2004), pp. 75–82.

82. West, *Homosexuality,* pp. 17–21.

83. Mary McIntosh, "The Homosexual Role," *Social Problems, 16* (Fall 1968), pp. 182–192.

84. Traci Watson and Joseph P. Shapiro. "Is There a 'Gay Gene'?" *U.S. News and World Report* (November 13, 1995), pp. 93–95; Simon LeVay, *The Sexual Brain* (Cambridge, MA: MIT Press/Bradford, 1995).

85. Dean Hamer and Peter Copeland, *The Science of Desire: The Search for the Gay Gene and the Biology of Behavior* (New York: Simon & Schuster, 1995); Robert Pool, "Evidence for Homosexuality Gene," *Science, 261* (July 16, 1993), pp. 291–292.

86. John Money, "Sexual Dimorphism and Homosexual Gender Identification," *Psychological Bulletin, 74*(6) (1970), pp. 425–440; and John Money, "Agenda and Credenda of the Kinsey Scale," in *The Kinsey Institute Series,* vol. 2, ed. David P. McWhirter, Stephanie A. Sanders, and June Machover Reinisch (New York: Oxford University Press, 1990), pp. 41–60.

87. Quoted in Marcia Barinaga, "Is Homosexuality Biological?" *Science* (August 1991), pp. 956–960.

88. Ibid.

89. Evelyn Hooker, "Homosexuality," in *International Encyclopedia of the Social Sciences,* vol. 14, ed. David L. Sills (New York: Collier and Macmillan, 1968), p. 224; Therese Harrison, "Adolescent Homosexuality and Concerns Regarding Disclosure," *Journal of School Health, 73* (March 2003), pp. 107–113.

90. Marvin Siegelman, "Parental Background of Male Homosexuals and Heterosexuals," *Archives of Sexual Behavior, 3* (January 1974), pp. 3–18.

91. Alan P. Bell, Martin S. Weinberg, and Sue Kiefer Hammersmith, *Sexual Preference: Its Development in Men and Women* (Bloomington: Indiana University Press, 1981), p. 216.

92. John C. Gonsiorek, "Summary and Conclusions," in *Homosexuality,* ed. Weinrich et al., pp. 159–160.

93. Kinsey et al., *Sexual Behavior in the Human Female,* p. 447.

94. Kenneth Plummer, *Sexual Stigma: An Interactionist Account* (Boston: Routledge & Kegan Paul, 1975), p. 99.

95. George L. Kirkham, "Homosexuality in Prison," in *Studies in the Sociology of Sex,* ed. Henslin, p. 345.

96. Humphreys, "Impersonal Sex," pp. 362–372.

97. Plummer, *Sexual Stigma,* p. 100.

98. G. A. Vanderbelt-Barber, "A Lesbian Comes Out," in *Their Own Behalf: Voices from the Margin,* 2nd ed., ed. Charles H. McCaghy, James K. Skipper, Jr., and Mark Lefton (Englewood Cliffs, NJ: Prentice-Hall, 1974), p. 176.

99. Quoted in Barry M. Dank, "Coming Out in the Gay World," *Psychiatry, 34* (May 1971), pp. 185, 187.

100. Excerpt from student paper by Matt.

101. John H. Gagnon and William Simon, "Homosexuality: The Formulation of a Sociological Perspective," *Journal of Health and Social Behavior, 8* (September 1967), p. 182; and Weinberg and Williams, *Male Homosexuals,* pp. 158–159.

102. Sasha Gregory Lewis, *Sunday's Women: A Report on Lesbian Life Today* (Boston: Beacon, 1979), pp. 20–42; and Barbara Ponse, *Identities in the Lesbian World: The Social Construction of Self* (Westport, CT: Greenwood, 1978), pp. 114–121, 179–181.

103. For a description of the pornography shop's role in the gay community, see Kenneth B. Perkins and James K. Skipper, Jr., "Gay Pornographic and Sex Paraphernalia Shops: An Ethnography of Expressive Work Settings," *Deviant Behavior, 2* (January–March 1981), pp. 187–199. For discussions of other aspects of the gay community, see Maurice Leznoff and William A. Westley, "The Homosexual Community," *Social Problems, 3* (April 1956), pp. 257–263; Evelyn Hooker, "Homosexuality," p. 224.

104. Stephen M. Horowitz, David L. Weis, and Molly T. Laflin, "Differences Between Sexual Orientation Behavior Groups and Social Background, Quality of Life, and Health Behaviors," *The Journal of Sex Research, 38* (August 2001), pp. 205–209; the discussion is derived from Plummer, *Sexual Stigma,* pp. 96–101, 135–153. For a discussion similar to Plummer's, see John Alan Lee, "Going Public: A Study in the Sociology of Homosexual Liberation," *Journal of Homosexuality, 3* (Fall 1977), pp. 49–78.

105. This discussion is based on Edward Sagarin, *Odd Man In: Societies of Deviants in America* (Chicago: Quadrangle Books, 1969), pp. 81–84.

106. For analyses of Christian interpretations of homosexuality, see Peter Conrad and Joseph W. Schneider, *Deviance and Medicalization: From Badness to Sickness* (St. Louis: C. V. Mosby, 1980), pp. 172–180; and David F. Greenberg and Marcia H. Bystryn, "Christian Intolerance of Homosexuality," *American Journal of Sociology, 88* (November 1983), pp. 515–548.

107. Clellan S. Ford and Frank A. Beach, *Patterns of Sexual Behavior* (New York: Harper & Row, 1951), p. 130.

108. K. J. Dover, *Greek Homosexuality* (Cambridge, MA: Harvard University Press, 1978).

109. Council, *Challenge and Progress,* pp. 28–29; and Gilbert Geis, *Not the Law's Business? An Examination of*

Homosexuality, Abortion, Prostitution, Narcotics, and Gambling in the United States (Washington, DC: National Institute of Health, 1972), pp. 31–32.

110. Joseph Harry, "Derivative Deviance: The Cases of Extortion, Fag-Bashing, and Shakedown of Gay Men," *Criminology, 19* (February 1982), pp. 556–558.

111. Online at Wikipedia at http://wikipedia.org. matthewshephard

112. Harry, "Derivative Deviance," p. 555.

113. 1990–91 Violence Survey Results, prepared by the National Gay and Lesbian Task Force Policy Institute, Washington, DC, and included in a press release from the National Gay and Lesbian Task Force, Washington, DC, dated March 19, 1992. Data were collected on both lesbians and gay men who were assaulted because of their sexual orientation. The Massachusetts study was conducted by the Fenway Community Health Center, Boston; the Minneapolis–St. Paul study was conducted by the Gay and Lesbian Community Action Council, Minneapolis–St. Paul; the Utah study was conducted by the Gay and Lesbian Community Council of Utah, Salt Lake City; and the Seattle study was conducted by the Seattle Commission for Lesbians and Gays.

114. Frank Schmalleger, *Criminal Justice Today,* 5th ed. (Upper Saddle River, NJ: Prentice-Hall, 1999), p. 54.

115. Eugene E. Levitt and Albert D. Klassen, Jr., "Public Attitudes Toward Homosexuality: Part of the 1970 Survey by the Institute for Sex Research," *Journal of Homosexuality, 1* (Fall 1974), p. 32; and "Homosexuals Move Toward Open Life as Tolerance Rises," *The New York Times* (July 17, 1977), pp. 1, 34.

116. Title 42, United States Code Annotated, sec. 2101.

117. Marcus, *Making History,* pp. 405–406.

118. Toby Marotta, *The Politics of Homosexuality* (Boston: Houghton Mifflin, 1981), pp. 71–77.

119. This discussion is based on Sagarin, *Odd Man In,* pp. 84–110; Edward Sagarin, "Sex Raises Its Revolutionary Head," *The Realist, 87* (May/June 1970), pp. 1, 17–23; Laud Humphreys, *Out of the Closets: The Sociology of Homosexual Liberation* (Englewood Cliffs, NJ: Prentice-Hall, 1972), pp. 50–126; and Marotta, *The Politics of Homosexuality,* pp. 78–226.

120. These examples are drawn from Iver Peterson, "Homosexuals Gain Support on Campus," *The New York Times* (June 5, 1974), pp. 1, 32; Les Brown, "NBC Yields to Homosexuals over Episode of 'Policewoman,'" *The New York Times* (November 30, 1974), p. 51; and John J. O'Connor, "Pressure Groups Are Increasingly Putting the Heat on TV," *The New York Times* (October 6, 1974), sec. 2, p. 19.

121 Harold Lief, "Sexual Survey #4: Current Thinking on Homosexuality," *Medical Aspects of Human Sexuality, 11* (November 1977), pp. 110–111.

122. James L. Mathis, "Psychiatric Diagnoses: A Continuing Controversy," *The Journal of Medicine and Philosophy, 17* (April 1992), p. 255.

123. A. Beck, I. McNally, and J. Petrak, "Psychosocial Predictors of HIV/STI Risk Behaviors in a Sample of Homosexual Men," *Sexually Transmitted Infections, 79* (April 2003) pp. 142–147; Eliot Fremont-Smith, "AIDS: Latest Lit," *Village Voice* (August 16, 1983), pp. 43–44; "New Theory Given on AIDS Genesis," *The New York Times* (November 20, 1983), p. 15; and "28 AIDS Victims Died Last Month," *Daily Sentinel-Tribune* (Bowling Green, OH), September 7, 1984, p. 3.

124. This discussion is based on Fremont-Smith, "AIDS: Latest Lit"; William Beauchamp, "A 2d AIDS Epidemic," *The New York Times* (August 7, 1983), sec. 4, p. 21; and Tom Morganthau et al., "Gay America in Transition," *Newsweek* (August 8, 1983), pp. 30–40.

125. William N. Eskridge, Jr., "Equality Practice: Liberal Reflections on the Jurisprudence of Civil Unions," *Albany Law Review, 64* (Spring 2001), pp. 853–856.

126. Lawrence Ingrassia, "Danes Don't Debate Same-Sex Marriages, They Celebrate Them," in *Deviant Behavior: Annual Editions 96/97* (Guilford, CT: Dushkin Publishing Group, 1997), pp. 183–184.

127. Stateline.org, "50-State Rundown on Gay Marriage Laws" provided by the Human Rights Campaign and the National Conference of State Legislatures. Accessed October 6, 2004.

128. Evan Wolfson, "Homosexuals Should Be Allowed to Marry," in *Homosexuality: Opposing Viewpoints,* ed. Aurianna Ojeda (New York: Greenhaven Press, 2004), pp. 170–171.

129. Elliot H. Gourvitz, and Ari H. Gourvitz, "Why New Jersey Is a Friendly Forum for Gay Marriage." *New Jersey Law Journal, 169* (August 2002), pp. 1–3; William N. Eskridge, Jr., "Equality Practice: Liberal Reflections on the Jurisprudence of Civil Unions," p. 853.

130. Charles Toutant, "Gay Marriage Bar May Pave Way for Civil Union Law," *New Jersey Law Journal* (November 2003), n.p.

131. David Moats, "Civil Wars: A Battle for Gay Marriage," *Kirkus Reviews, 71* (December 2003), p. 1395.

132. Jonathan Rauch, "A Federal Marriage Amendment Would Undermine States' Rights," in *Homosexuality: Opposing Viewpoints,* ed. Aurianna Ojeda (New York: Greenhaven Press, 2004), p. 204

133. Leonard Broom and Philip Selznick, *Sociology: A Text with Adapted Readings,* 5th ed. (New York: Harper & Row, 1973), p. 315.

134. Stanley N. Kuntz, "Homosexuals Should Not Be Allowed to Marry," in *Homosexuality: Opposing Viewpoints,* ed. Aurianna Ojeda (New York: Greenhaven Press, 2004), p. 189.

135. Charles Toutant, "Gay Marriage Bar May Pave Way for Civil Union Law," n.p.

136. Stanley N. Kuntz, "Homosexuals Should Not Be Allowed to Marry," p. 185; Stanley Kurtz, "Beyond Gay Marriage: The Road to Polyamory," *The Weekly Standard* (August 4, 2003), p. D-1;

137. Stanley N. Kuntz, "Homosexuals Should Not Be Allowed to Marry," pp. 181–192, 185; Stanley Kurtz, "Beyond Gay Marriage: The Road to Polyamory," p. D-1.

138. Elliot H. Gourvitz, and Ari H. Gourvitz, "Why New Jersey Is a Friendly Forum for Gay Marriage," pp. 1–3.

139. Michael Booth, "State Says Gay-Marriage Issue Is for the Legislature, Not the Courts," *New Jersey Law Journal, 171* (March 2003), p. 5.

140. William N. Eskridge, Jr., "Equality Practice: Liberal Reflections on the Jurisprudence of Civil Unions," pp. 853–856.

141. Robert Phineas Blaxandall, "Altar-cation," *The American Prospect* (April 2004), pp. 4–6.

142. Lee A. Graf, and Masoud Hemmasi, "Risqué Humor: How It Really Affects the Workplace," *HR Magazine* (November 1995), pp. 64–69; Sandra Harley Carey, *Sourcebook on Sexual Harassment* (Washington, DC: Department of the Navy, 1982), p. 4; Sandra Harley Carey, *Navy Women in Operation Desert Shield and Desert Storm* (Washington, DC: Department of the Navy, 1991), p. IV-17.

143. Sandra Harley Carey, "Sexual Politics in Business," Paper presented at the Southwestern Social Science Association, Dallas, Texas, 1977.

144. Merit Systems Protection Board, *Sexual Harassment in the Federal Workplace,* (Washington, DC: U.S. Government Printing Office, 1995), pp. vii–ix; Sandra Harley Carey, "Sexual Harassment," *Reflections* (October–December 1980), pp. 20–22.

145. Aysan Sev'er, "Sexual Harassment: Where We Were, Where We Are, and Prospects for the New Millennium," *The Canadian Review of Sociology and Anthropology, 36* (November 1999), pp. 469–473; Alicia C. Shepard, "A No-win Situation: Media Coverage of Paula Jones' Accusation of President Bill Clinton," *American Journalism Review, 16* (July–August 1994), pp. 26–34.

146. Ibid.

147. Merit Systems Protection Board, *Sexual Harassment in the Federal Workplace,* p. 59.

148. Sandra Harley Carey, *Sourcebook on Sexual Harassment,* pp. 15–16; Brenda L. Russell and Debra L. Oswald, "Strategies and Dispositional Correlates of Sexual Coercion Perpetrated by Women: An Exploratory Investigation," *Sex Roles: A Journal of Research, 31* (July 2001), pp. 103–116.

149. J. B. Pryor, "Sexual Harassment Proclivities in Men," *Sex Roles: A Journal of Research, 17* (July 1987), pp. 269–290; Anne M. O'Leary-Kelly, Ramona L. Paetzold, and Ricky W. Griffin, "Sexual Harassment as Aggressive Behavior: An Actor-based Perspective" *Academy of Management Review, 25* (April 2000), p. 372.

150. James E. Gruber, "The Impact of Male Work Environments and Organizational Policies on Women's Experiences of Sexual Harassment," *Gender and Society, 12* (June 1998), pp. 301–321; Bodil Bergman and Lillemor Hallberg, "Women in a Male-dominated Industry: Factor Analysis of a Women Workplace Culture Questionnaire Based on a Grounded Theory Model," *Sex Roles: A Journal of Research, 32* (May 2002), pp. 311–323.

151. Caren B. Goldberg, "The Impact of the Proportion of Women in One's Workgroup, Profession, and Friendship Circle on Males' and Females' Responses to Sexual Harassment," *Sex Roles: A Journal of Research, 31* (September 2001), p. 359; Sandra Harley Carey, *Sourcebook on Sexual Harassment,* p. 19.

152. J. N. Cleveland and M. E. Kerst, "Sexual Harassment and Perceptions of Power: An Under-articulated Relationship," *Journal of Vocational Behavior, 42* (Summer 1993), pp. 49–67; Caren B. Goldberg, "The Impact of the Proportion of Women in One's Workgroup, Profession, and Friendship Circle on Males' and Females' Responses to Sexual Harassment," p. 359; Aysan Sev'er, "Sexual Harassment: Where We Were, Where We Are, and Prospects for the New Millennium," pp. 469–473.

153. Merit Systems Protection Board, *Sexual Harassment in the Federal Workplace,* pp. viiii–ix; Sandra Harley Carey, *Sourcebook on Sexual Harassment,* p. 19.

154. Ibid.

155. Sandra D. Nicks, "Fear in Academia: Concern Over Unmerited Accusations of Sexual Harassment," *The Journal of Psychology, 130* (January 1996), p. 79.

NAME INDEX

SUBJECT INDEX